The Anthropology of Spa

Blackwell Readers in Anthropology

As anthropology moves beyond the limits of so-called area studies, there is an increasing need for texts that attempt to do the work of both synthesizing the literature and of challenging more traditional or subdisciplinary approaches to anthropology. This is the object of the exciting new series, *Blackwell Readers in Anthropology*.

Each volume in the series offers what have emerged as seminal readings on a chosen theme, and provides the finest, most thought-provoking recent works in the given thematic area. A number of these volumes bring together for the first time a body of literature on a certain topic. Inasmuch, these books are intended to become more than definitive collections, they demonstrate the very ways in which anthropological inquiry has evolved and is evolving.

The Anthropology of Space and Place

Locating Culture

Edited by

Setha M. Low
and
Denise Lawrence-Zúñiga

Blackwell
Publishing

Editorial material and organization © 2003 by Blackwell Publishers Ltd
a Blackwell Publishing company

350 Main Street, Malden, MA 02148-5018, USA
108 Cowley Road, Oxford OX4 1JF, UK
550 Swanston Street, Carlton, Victoria 3053, Australia
Kurfürstendamm 57, 10707 Berlin, Germany

First published 2003 by Blackwell Publishers Ltd

Library of Congress Cataloging-in-Publication Data

The anthropology of space and place: locating culture/edited by Setha M. Low and Denise Lawrence-Zúñiga.
      p. cm. – (Blackwell readers in anthropology; 4)
   Includes bibliographical references and index.
   ISBN 0-631-22877-2 (alk. paper) – ISBN 0-631-22878-0 (pbk.: alk. paper)
    1. Human geography. 2. Human territoriality. 3. Spatial behavior. 4. Personal space.
   5. Open spaces. 6. Public spaces. I. Low, Setha M. II. Lawrence-Zúñiga, Denise. III.
   Series.

GF50 .A55 2003
304.2–dc21

                                                                               2002071219

A catalogue record for this title is available from the British Library.

Typeset in 10/12pt Sabon
by Kolam Information Services Pvt. Ltd, Pondicherry, India
Printed and bound in the United Kingdom
by MPG Books Ltd, Bodmin, Cornwall

For further information on
Blackwell Publishing, visit our website:
http://www.blackwellpublishing.com

Contents

Acknowledgments

Any book, especially a reader, depends on the contributions and cooperation of others. We are particularly indebted to those authors whose stimulating work is included in this volume. We owe a special thanks to our colleagues of the Anthropology of Space and Place Network who have sustained us through the past sixteen years. We especially would like to thank Deborah Pellow, Gary McDonogh, Cindy Wong, Robert Rotenberg, Theodore Bestor, Alan Smart, Josie Smart, Margaret Rodman, and Matthew Cooper. A special thanks also goes to Juris Milestone who has been running the Anthropology of Space and Place list serve helping all of us to stay in touch. And even though we cannot thank each by name, all of the participants in the many symposia and sessions organized through the Anthropology of Space and Place Network have added to our collective store of knowledge and case material. We appreciate all these contributions and hope this book will be an additional resource for those of us who teach, research, and theorize in this emerging subfield of anthropology.

As for our families, they have supported this endeavor from the beginning. Setha wishes to thank her husband, Joel Lefkowitz, who was always there, as companion in travel, photographer, editor, ideal reader and friend *par excellence*. Denise would like to express her appreciation to husband Richard Zúñiga for his unflagging support and encouragement.

We could not have completed this work without the contributions of our graduate students – Elena Danaila, Mike Lamb, Andrew Kirby, Suzanne Scheld, and Dana Taplin were graduate students at the time in the Ph.D. Program in Environmental Psychology or Anthropology at The Graduate Center of the City University of New York who helped find materials and articles. Cindi Katz, and the members of the Social Theory seminar at The Graduate Center also contributed insightful comments on the ideas presented in the introductory chapter. At Cal Poly Pomona, special thanks go to Landscape Architecture graduate students, especially Todd Jennings, for stimulating critical discussions of the literature on place.

Intellectually we would also like to thank Miles Richardson and James Fernandez for their groundbreaking work, and their support of our endeavor to create a more established field of the Anthropology of Space and Place.

The final book could not have been finished without the dedication of a great editor. Jane Huber provided just the right amount of support and editing, asking the right questions, at the right time.

The author and publishers gratefully acknowledge the following for permission to reproduce copyright material:

Appadurai, Arjun, "Sovereignty without territoriality: Notes for a postnational geography" (1996). From *The Geography of Identity*, Patricia Yeager, ed. Ann Arbor: University of Michigan, pp. 40–58.

Bestor, Theodore, "Supply-side sushi: Commodity, market, and the global city" (2001). Reproduced by permission of the American Anthropological Association from *American Anthropologist* 103(1). Not for sale or further reproduction.

Bourdieu, Pierre, "The Berber house of the world reversed" (1971). From *Echanges et communications: Mélanges offerts à Claude Lévi-Strauss à l'occasion de son 60e anniversaire*. Hague: Mouton, pp. 151–61, and 165–9. Reprinted previously in Mary Douglas, ed., 1973. *Rules and Meanings*. Harmondsworth: Penguin, pp. 98–110.

Duranti, Alessandro, "Indexical speech across Samoan communities" (1997). Reproduced by permission of the American Anthropological Association from *American Anthropologist* 99(2), pp 342–54. Not for sale or further reproduction.

Fernandez, James, "Emergence and convergence in some African sacred places" (1984). Reprinted with permission by Geoscience Publications, Department of Geography and Anthropology, Louisiana State University, Baton Rouge, Louisiana 70803 USA. This article originally appeared in Miles Richardson, ed., *Place: Experience and Symbol*, Geoscience and Man 24. Baton Rouge, LA: Geoscience Publications, Department of Geography and Anthropology, Louisiana State University, 1984, pp. 31–42.

Gable, Eric and Handler, Richard, "After authenticity at an American heritage site" (1996). Reproduced by permission of the American Anthropological Association from *American Anthropologist* 98(3), pp. 568–78. Not for sale or further reproduction.

Gray, John, "Open spaces and dwelling places: Being at home on hill farms in the Scottish borders" (1999). Reproduced by permission of the American Anthropological Association from *American Ethnologist* 26(2), pp. 440–60. Not for sale or further reproduction.

Gregory, Steven, from *Black Corona: Race and the Politics of Place in an Urban Community* (1998). Copyright © 1998 by Princeton University Press. Reprinted by permission of Princeton University Press.

Gupta, Akhil, "The song of the nonaligned world: Transnational identities and the reinscription of space in late capitalism" (1992). Reproduced by permission of the American Anthropological Association from *Cultural Anthropology* 7(1), pp. 63–79. Not for sale or further reproduction.

Hall, Edward T., "Proxemics" (1968). From *Current Anthropology* 9(2), pp. 83–95. Used with permission of the author.

Herzfeld, Michael, from *A Place in History: Social and Monumental Time in a Cretan Town* (1991). Copyright © 1991 by Princeton University Press. Reprinted by permission of Princeton University Press.

Kuper, Hilda, "The language of sites in the politics of space" (1972). Reproduced by permission of the American Anthropological Association from *American Anthropologist* 74(3), pp. 411–25. Not for sale or further reproduction.

Lofgren, Orvar, "The sweetness of home: Class, culture and family life in Sweden" (1984). From *Ethnologica Europea* XIV, pp. 44–64. Used with permission of the author.

Low, Setha M., "The edge and the center: Gated communities and the discourse of urban fear" (2001). Reproduced by permission of the American Anthropological Association from *American Anthropologist* 103(1). Not for sale or further reproduction.

McDonogh, Gary Wray, "Bars, genders, and virtue: myth and practice in Barcelona's *Barrio Chino*" (1992). From *Anthropological Quarterly*, January, pp. 19–33.

Munn, Nancy D., "Excluded spaces: The figure in the Australian aboriginal landscape" (1996). From *Critical Inquiry* 22, pp. 446–65. Reproduced by permission of The University of Chicago Press.

Rabinow, Paul, "*Ordonnance*, discipline, regulation: some reflections on urbanism" (1982). From *Humanities in Society* 5(3–4), pp. 267–78. Used with permission of the author.

Richardson, Miles, "Being-in-the-plaza: Material culture and the construction of social reality in Spanish America" (1982). Reproduced by permission of the American Anthropological Association from *American Ethnologist* 2, pp. 421–36. Not for sale or further reproduction.

Rodman, Margaret C., "Empowering place: Multilocality and Multivocality" (1992). Reproduced by permission of the American Anthropological Association from *American Ethnologist* 94(3), pp. 640–56. Not for sale or further reproduction.

The publishers apologize for any errors or omissions in the above list and would be grateful to be notified of any corrections that should be incorporated in the next edition or reprint of this book.

To our colleagues and friends
who have helped to make possible
the anthropology of space and place.

Locating Culture

Setha M. Low and Denise Lawrence-Zúñiga

The 1990s demonstrated renewed interest in issues of space and place across the social sciences (Soja 1989), not least of which has been in our own discipline – anthropology. As we described in our review of "The Built Environment and Spatial Form" (1990), spatial dimensions of cultural beliefs and practices have always held an interest for anthropologists. Studies of tribal and village societies customarily included descriptions of the natural landscape and material conditions of everyday life, and quite often contained analyses of these in support of other theoretical arguments. Increasingly, however, anthropologists have begun to shift their perspective to foregrounding spatial dimensions of culture rather than treating them as background, so that the notion that all behavior is located in and constructed of space has taken on new meaning.

This shift is consistent with and draws on an abundance of research and theory generated in disciplines outside anthropology, including geography, history, philosophy, and sociology. The most significant change for anthropology is found not in the attention researchers increasingly pay to the material and spatial aspects of culture, but in the acknowledgment that space is an essential component of sociocultural theory. That is, anthropologists are rethinking and reconceptualizing their understandings of culture in spatialized ways.

In putting together this volume, we have focused on anthropological studies of space and place and major changes in theory and method in the subfield. We have brought together classics in cultural anthropology with new theoretical approaches under six thematic categories: Embodied Spaces, Gendered Spaces, Inscribed Spaces, Contested Spaces, Transnational Spaces, and Spatial Tactics. These categories are not definitive or mutually exclusive, as there is considerable overlap in the ways that sociospatial problems are defined and theorized. Familiar spatial themes such as house form and sacred space have receded or been reconceptualized while new ideas about transnational spaces and spatial tactics have increased in importance. This classification then represents our sense of what are the most exciting and promising directions currently being explored. We provide context for each of these thematic groups by introducing each section with a theoretical and conceptual overview included in this introduction.

The direction of this research transforms the notion of a conventional anthropology. In many ways, the focus on spatial issues has liberated and challenged anthropologists to examine cultural phenomena that are not fixed in a faraway, isolated location, but surround us in the cities and countries in which we live. Studies of border issues and migration, nation and identity, multisited and global phenomena, tourism and authenticity, and race/class/gender segregation through architecture, planning, and design are drawing the attention of anthropologists equipped with new conceptual frameworks that account for spatial dimensions. This interest in space and place is not accidental; it is necessary for understanding the world we are producing and inserting our discipline into the heat of social and political debate.

Embodied Spaces

Spatial analyses often neglect the body because of difficulties in resolving the dualism of the subjective and objective body, and distinctions between the material and representational aspects of body space. The concept of "embodied space," however, draws these disparate notions together, underscoring the importance of the body as a physical and biological entity, as lived experience, and as a center of agency, a location for speaking and acting on the world.

We use the term "body" to refer to its biological and social characteristics, and "embodiment" as an "indeterminate methodological field defined by perceptual experience and mode of presence and engagement in the world" (Csordas 1994:12). Embodied space is the location where human experience and consciousness take on material and spatial form. After identifying the inherent difficulties in defining the body, body space, and cultural explanations of body experience, we trace the evolution of approaches to embodied space including proxemics (Hall 1968, this volume), phenomenological understandings (Richardson 1984, this volume), spatial orientation (Munn 1996, this volume) and linguistic dimensions (Duranti 1997, this volume). Embodied space is presented as a model for understanding the creation of place through spatial orientation, movement, and language. This idea is developed further in the sections on Gendered Spaces and Inscribed Spaces that follow.

The body

The space occupied by the body, and the perception and experience of that space, contracts and expands in relationship to a person's emotions and state of mind, sense of self, social relations, and cultural predispositions. In Western culture we perceive the self as "naturally" placed in the body, as a kind of precultural given (Scheper-Hughes and Lock 1987). We imagine ourselves experiencing the world through our "social skin," the surface of the body representing "a kind of common frontier of society which becomes the symbolic stage upon which the drama of socialization is enacted" (T. Turner 1980:112).

Bryan Turner (1984) points out that it is an obvious fact that human beings "have bodies," and "are bodies." Human beings are embodied and everyday life dominated by the details of corporeal existence. But he cautions that biological reductionism keeps us from focusing on the ways in which the body is also inherently social and cultural. Terence Turner (1995) argues that while the body is an individual organism that biologically depends for its reproduction, nurturance, and existence on other individuals and the environment, even this biological individuality is relative and dependent on other social beings. Thus the body is best conceived as a multiplicity: the "two bodies" of the social and physical (Douglas 1970), the "three bodies" of the individual body, social body, and body politic (Scheper-Hughes and Lock 1987), or the "five bodies," which adds the consumer body and the medical body to the other three (O'Neil 1985).

Body space

An early theory of the psychological relationship of the body to space is Eric Erikson's (1950) attribution of genital modes with spatial modalities. In his research on child development, young boys build tall block structures to heights that topple over, while young girls create places with static interiors and enclosed spaces. He concludes that in young children representational space is structured by an inter-penetration of the biological, cultural, and psychological aspects of gender, ex-pressed externally in architectural form.

Erikson's spatial analyses have been criticized by anthropologists who offer other psychoanalytic interpretations of bodily spaces (Pandolfo 1989). For instance, Robert Paul (1976) agrees with Erikson's contention that there is a relationship between the psyche and built spaces revealed in the Sherpa temple as an objectifica-tion of the subjective, internal experience of the Sherpa experiencing his religion. He modifies this understanding, however, to read temple architecture as a guide to the Sherpa's secret psychic life. Mariella Pandolfi (1990), however, suggests that while there is a "minimal" identity that finds in the experience of the body a way of describing and expressing the self, that identity is defined by historical social structures that inscribe the body, and naturalize a person's existence in the world. It is the inscription of sociopolitical and cultural relations on the body, not biology/psychology, that produces gendered body spaces and their representations.

Feminists take this critique even further by exploring the epistemological implica-tions of knowledge as embodied, engendered, and embedded in place (Duncan 1996). By disrupting the binary mind/body by positionality (Boys 1998), and focus-ing on the situated and colonized body (Scott 1996), states of mind become loosened from the location of social and spatial relationships (Munt 1998). Donna Haraway (1991) argues that personal and social bodies cannot be seen as natural, but only as part of a self-creating process of human labor. Her emphasis on *location*, a position in a web of social connections, eliminates passivity of the female (and human) body and replaces it with a site of action and of agency (Haraway 1991).

The majority of anthropologists emphasize the intrinsically social and cultural character of the human body. Marcel Mauss (1950) argues that acquired habits and somatic tactics, what he calls the "techniques of the body," incorporate all the "cultural arts" of using and being in the body and the world. Pierre Bourdieu (1977) explains how body habits generate cultural features and social structure by employing the term *habitus* to characterize the way body, mind, and emotions are simultaneously trained. He uses this concept to understand how social status, moral values, and class position become embodied in everyday life (Bourdieu 1984;

Mahmood 2001) (also see the section on Gendered Spaces). Mary Douglas (1971, 1978) theorizes the body as a medium of communication positing a direct relationship of spatial arrangements and social structure with the symbolism of the body and body boundaries. In later work, Mauss (1979) analyzes the importance of the human body as a metaphor, noting that architecture draws its imagery from human experience.

Cultural groups often draw upon the human body as a template for spatial and social relations. The Dogon describe village spatial structure in anthropomorphic terms spiraling down in scale to the plan of the house representing a man lying on his side, procreating (Griaule 1954); and the Batammalibans endow their social structure and architecture with body symbolism (Blier 1987). Many anthropologists use metaphor analysis to interpret the ways the human body is linked to myths and cosmology and describe how spatial and temporal processes are encoded with body symbolism (Hugh-Jones 1979; Johnson 1988). Other studies explore the body as isomorphic with the landscape, where the landscape provides a metaphor that is an expressive, evocative device transmitting memory, morality, and emotion (Bastien 1985, Fernandez 1988). A recent study of "closet space" uncovers how the "performativity" of space, through its metaphorical properties, constrain and define the body and personal identity (Brown 2000).

Proxemics

As early as 1955, Irving Hallowell identified cultural factors in spatial orientation, affirming that spatial schema are basic to human orientation, a position from which to view the world, and a symbolic means of becoming oriented in a spatial world that transcends personal experience. It would take a number of intervening years, research projects, and a shift in epistemological perspective, though, before anthropologists would bring this idea to fruition.

Edward Hall (1966, 1973) is best known for studying the influence of culture on spatial perception and behavior, establishing the field of proxemics, the study of people's use of space as an aspect of culture (1966). He postulates that humans have an innate distancing mechanism, modified by culture, that helps to regulate contact in social situations. Conceptualized as a bubble surrounding each individual, personal space varies in size according to the type of social relationships and situation. Hall proposes four general kinds of personal space ranging from intimate to public. Because these spatial aspects of behavior are tacit, actors usually become aware of the boundaries only when they are violated, often in culture contact situations. Appropriate spatial variations in social relations are learned as a feature of culture, and patterns vary by culture.

In his article, "Proxemics," Hall lays out the linguistic underpinnings of his work arguing that "the principles laid down by Whorf and his followers in relation to language apply to all culturally patterned behavior, but particularly to those aspects of culture which are most often taken for granted..." (Hall 1968:84; this volume, p. 52). His research casts doubt on the assumption of universally shared phenomenological experience: according to Hall, people not only structure spaces differently, but experience them differently and inhabit distinct sensory worlds. Individuals selectively screen out some types of data by "tuning out" one or more of the senses or by architecture. Thus, in proxemics, the body is a site of spatial orientation with multiple screens for interacting with others and the environment.

Embodied space

Miles Richardson (1982, 1984) addresses how body experience and perception become material by considering how we transform experience to symbol and then remake experience into an object, such as an artifact, a gesture, or a word. We use objects to evoke experience thus, molding experience into symbols and then melding symbols back into experience. In his work, embodied space is being-in-the-world – that is, the existential and phenomenological reality of place: its smell, feel, color, and other sensory dimensions.

In "Being-in-the-Market Versus Being-in-the-Plaza: Material Culture and the Construction of Social Reality in Spanish America" (Richardson 1982, this volume), Richardson uses ethnographic descriptions of Cartago, Costa Rica to conclude that the experience of being-in-the-plaza is about the concept of *cultura* – appropriate and socially correct behavior – which contrasts with *listo* – smart, ready, and clever behavior encoded in the experience of being-in-the-market. For him, the way these spatial realities are experienced communicates the basic dynamics of culture. Although he does not specifically discuss embodied space, he lays the methodological groundwork for this concept by focusing on how "being there" becomes cultural. He concludes by asserting that it is through actions that Spanish American culture forms, or better, *becomes*. This "becoming" takes place, literally and socially, in the construction of the two realities and through the dialectical tension between the two.

This phenomenological approach to embodied space is modified and elaborated by other scholars interested in how individuals make place as well as social structure (also see the sections on Inscribed Spaces and Gendered Spaces.) Geographer Allan Pred (1986) traces the history of microgeographies of daily life in Southern Sweden to determine how everyday behavior and movements generate spatial transformations in land tenure and local social structure. He concludes that place always involves "appropriation and transformation of space and nature that is inseparable from the reproduction and transformation of society in time and space" (Pred 1986:6).

Anthropologists also have noted the importance of body movement in the creation of place, conceptualizing space as movement rather than as a container (Pandya 1990). Melanesian ethnographers work in a cultural context that accentuates the importance of spatial orientation: in greetings, the passage of time, the definition of events, and the identification of people with land and/or the landscape (Rodman 1985; Kahn 1990).

Nancy Munn (1996, this volume) brings this work together by considering space-time "as a symbolic nexus of relations produced out of interactions between bodily actors and terrestrial spaces" (Munn 1996:449; this volume, p. 93). Drawing in part upon Lefebvre's concepts of "field of action" and "basis of action," she constructs the notion of a "mobile spatial field" that can be understood as a culturally defined, corporeal-sensual field stretching out from the body at a given locale or moving through locales.

In "Excluded Spaces: The Figure in the Australian Aboriginal Landscape" Munn's ethnographic illustrations are spatial interdictions. She is interested in the specific kind of spatial form being produced, "a space of deletions or of delimitations constraining one's presence at particular locales" (Munn 1996:448; this volume, p. 93). For instance, in following their moral-religious law, Aborigines make detours to keep far enough away to avoid seeing an ancient place or hearing ritual singing. She argues that by detouring, actors carve out a "negative space" which extends beyond their spatial field of vision. "This act projects a signifier of limitation upon the land or place by forming *transient but repeatable boundaries out of the moving body*" (Munn 1996:452; this volume, p. 95). Munn applies this idea to contemporary Aborigines' encounters with powerful topographic centers and "dangerous" ancestral places.

Munn demonstrates how the Ancestral Law's power of spatial limitation becomes "embodied" in an actor-centered, mobile body, separate from any fixed center or place. "Excluded spaces" become spatiotemporal formations produced out of the interaction of actors' moving spatial fields and the terrestrial spaces of body action. Her theory goes beyond Hall's concept of proxemics with culturally constituted spatial orientations and interpersonal distances and Richardson's phenomenological understanding of being-in-the-world by constructing the person (actor) as a truly embodied space, in which the body, conceived as a moving spatial field makes its own place in the world.

Stuart Rockefeller (2002) radicalizes this notion of actors' mobile spatial fields into a theory of public places formed by individual movements, trips, and digressions of migrants crossing national boundaries. Starting with Munn's idea that the person makes space by moving through it, he traces how movement patterns collectively make up locality and reproduce locality. Places, he argues, are not in the landscape, but simultaneously in the land, people's minds, customs, and bodily practices.

Language and embodied space

In a letter that accompanied the publication of "Proxemics" (Hall 1968, this volume) Dell Hymes (1968) criticizes the use of linguistic theory to understand body space. He comments that if current linguistic theory was taken as model, it would not place primary emphasis on phonological units, but on grammatical relationships, and chides linguists for not undertaking transcultural proxemic ethnography as well as transcultural descriptive linguistics. More recent critiques of the use of language models dispute whether experience can be studied at all, because experience is mediated by language, and language itself is a representation. This tension between "language" and "experience" and the subsequent dominance of semiotics over phenomenology is resolved by Paul Ricoeur (1991) in his argument that language is a modality of being-in-the-world, such that language not only represents or refers, but "discloses" our being-in-the-world (Csordas 1994:11).

Alessandro Duranti (1992) corrects these omissions through his empirical investigation of the interpenetration of words, body movements, and lived space in Western Samoa. He examines the sequence of acts used in ceremonial greeting, explicating that the words used cannot be fully understood without reference to bodily movements. The performance of ceremonial greetings and the interpretation of words are understood as located in and at the same time constitutive of the sociocultural organization of space inside the house. His theory of "sighting" embodies language and space through "an interactional step whereby participants not only gather information about each other and about the setting but also engage in a negotiated process at the end of which they find themselves physically located in the relevant social hierarchies and ready to assume particular institutional roles" (Duranti 1992:657). Duranti reinterprets proxemics within a linguistic model that includes language, spatial orientation, and body movement.

In "Indexical Speech across Samoan Communities," Duranti focuses his analysis on transnational communities where "speaking about space can be a way of bridging physically distant but emotionally and ethically close worlds" (1997:342; this volume, p. 110). He asks whether a relationship can be contained, represented, and enacted in the act of sitting and whether there is a particular mode of coexistence between one's body and an inhabited surface – between embodied space and inhabited space across translocalities (see the section on Transnational Spaces.) Duranti answers this question through a detailed examination of the Samoan expression *nofo i lalo*, sit down, comparing its use in a Western Samoan village and a suburban neighborhood in southern California. In the Californian setting, this indexical expression is used to establish a resting-place for children's bodies, but also as an attempt to recreate a distant kind of space, one without furniture and walls, and with different rules of cultural behavior. This establishment of a social and cultural space through language and body movement "binds the participants by constituting an emotional and a moral commitment to a culturally specific way of being and moving in a house inhabited by other human beings (parents and visitors) who deserve respect" (Duranti 1997:352; this volume, p. 122).

Duranti's integration of language, body movement, spatial orientation, inhabited space, and distant homelands as expressions of cultural connectedness and socialization, synthesizes many aspects of embodied space. His ideas when combined with the spatial orientation insights of Munn (1996, this volume) provide a productive and fleshed-out theory of embodied space for anthropologists to build upon.

Gendered Spaces

Gender is defined as the cultural interpretation of perceived physical, anatomical, or developmental differences between males and females; although gender elaborates on biological attributes, it is culturally constructed. The anthropological study of gender focuses on how behavior patterns and symbolic representations distinguish the sexes, and considers how differences in power, authority, and value are attributed to these sexual asymmetries. We define gendered spaces to include particular locales that cultures invest with gendered meanings, sites in which sex-differentiated practices occur, or settings that are used strategically to inform identity and produce and reproduce asymmetrical gender relations of power and authority.

The examination of gendered spaces as a subset of gender and feminist studies has received uneven attention in anthropology. While a number of initial gender studies emphasized, or at least attended to, spatial issues, anthropological interest in gendered space has not been focused and is fragmented. We have chosen to identify gendered spaces in this collection as a way to include some classic work in which gender and space intersect, to discuss theorizing gender, and to encourage further research.

The house is the most frequently recognized gendered space because of its pervasiveness, its centrality as a cultural object, and its role in the productive and reproductive activities of society. Concern with the house has generally implied greater interest in the spatial articulation of women's roles because they are portrayed as more frequent occupants, or confined by its boundaries, while men are "free" to move beyond (see Massey 1994:10). We include two articles in this section that describe gender issues as key aspects in the analysis of the sociospatial organization of home. Pierre Bourdieu's well-known study of the Kabyle house (1973; this volume) is a structuralist account of gender relations expressed in the metaphor of house form and an exposition of his theory of practice. Orvar Löfgren's (1984, this volume) study of 19th and 20th century Swedish bourgeois and working-class domesticity reveals not only the historic differences in gender conceptions between classes, but also identifies some western European characteristics that continue to underlie concepts of gender used by many anthropologists. Finally, Deborah Pellow (this volume) describes the historical and social construction of space and gender relations in Hausa compounds in Accra, Ghana.

Gender and space

Ethnographic description of the association of males and females with different spatial domains has been a staple of anthropological research. Much of it is characterized as symbolic and behavioral dualities linked to cosmology and everyday life. Anthropologists have found houses physically or conceptually divided into two parts, male and female (Bourdieu 1973, this volume; Humphrey 1974); arranged to combine male and female features (Hugh-Jones 1979); or associated with females while males are relegated to a separate "men's house" or public structure (Lea 1995). Although gender is often portrayed as a part of larger dualistic symbolic structures, differences do not always imply gender hierarchies. In considering asymmetries in power and authority relations, gender researchers have used spatial dimensions to theorize about the differences between males and females, and the asymmetries associated with men's greater power, authority, prestige, and status in society.

Michelle Rosaldo (1974) argues that women's subordination to men can be found in their primary association with the "domestic" sphere, a function of their reproductive roles, that contrasts with the social and political relationships formed by men in the "public" sphere. Rosaldo defines the domestic sphere in terms of "minimal institutions and modes of activity that are organized immediately around one or more mothers and their children" (1974:23). The public sphere includes extradomestic relationships linking mother – child groups in which males are "free" to develop. According to her model, the *firmer the differentiation* between the two spheres in any society, the lower women's status will be, largely because women are isolated or cut off from participating in larger social networks (Rosaldo 1974:36).

The clear separation of gender-differentiated spheres occurs most often in statelevel societies and in colonial and postcolonial settings. In the application of the domestic/public sphere as an analytical framework, the domestic sphere has been used to denote physical settings, as well as domestic work activities, relationships, and production and exchange (Mukhopadhyay and Higgins 1988:480). Although Rosaldo's theory did not explicitly state a spatial dimension, the organization, meaning, and use of space could be inferred, and is often employed to demonstrate women's subordination (Lugo and Maurer 2000).

In *Women and Space* (1993), Shirley Ardener and others argue that the organization, meanings, and uses of space express the hierarchy of social structural relationships and ideologies encoded in it. Although gender may be one of several characteristics, including class and ethnicity, expressed in space, it is most often revealed in relations of power where men dominate and women are a "muted" group. Ardener notes that spaces may be exclusively identified with males or females, and be separated or bounded, but they operate as part of larger ideological schemes used to confine or restrict women's behavior. While women may not directly control physical or social space, Ardener argues they are far from powerless and often occupy roles which allow them to influence male exercise of power and authority (1993:9). For instance, Wright (1993) indicates that Iranian women who are relegated to the domestic sphere and barred from "officially" participating in politics, gather information and slyly advise their husbands at home, while also maintaining the fiction of being structurally "muted" (see also Friedl 1967).

Structuralist and poststructuralist interpretations of gendered space

Some of the most productive approaches to understanding gendered spaces have employed a structuralist approach that discloses the underlying organization of a culture's distinctive features. These features include, among others, sexual asymmetries, organized in a system of interrelated homologous binary oppositions. Claude Lévi-Strauss (1963) postulates that unconscious mental structures are capable of generating cultural patterns; these structures account for consistencies that social and symbolic forms exhibit in relation to spatial organization. Structuralist interpretations of gender relations link women with categories of symbolic meaning such as "nature" in opposition to linkages between men, "culture," and other symbolic categories (Ortner 1974). To explain a gendered spatial order, structuralist accounts argue that the opposition of sexually associated features expresses an unconscious dualistic mental structure (Callaway 1993; Cunningham 1964; Hirschon 1989, 1993; Hugh-Jones 1979; Humphrey 1974; Sciama 1993; Tambiah 1985).

For Pierre Bourdieu, the Algerian Berber house is a metaphor for the organization of the universe structured on gender and other social-symbolic principles (1973, this volume). Bourdieu's analysis of architecture and cosmological principles symbolically link women to the lower, dark, and hidden parts of the house, associated with childbirth and death, where animals are kept, in opposition to the upper, light, warm spaces, associated with men, where cooking and weaving are done and family life occurs. Although women are associated with the domestic sphere and men with the public sphere outside the house, the interior of the house is a microcosm of all symbolic relations. Bourdieu argues the oppositions between female and male, nature and culture, lower and upper spaces conceptually divide the Kabyle house into two parts, but that these symbolic oppositions are resolved in the transformations of metaphoric and metonymic relations in which any part of the conceptual scheme implies the whole. In this fashion Berber social and spatial organizations derive from the same conceptual foundation.

Bourdieu, however, moves beyond the constraints of structuralist analysis by focusing on how meaning and action, or "practice," interact in interdependent ways to inculcate and reinforce cultural knowledge and behavior. He argues that postulating unconscious structures or identifying rules that actors follow does little to explain how people use these conceptual schemes practically and discursively to produce and reproduce their culture. Space can have no meaning apart from practice; the system of generative and structuring dispositions, or *habitus*, constitutes and is constituted by actors' movement through space (1977:214). Space is gendered in Bourdieu's scheme as it is invested with conceptual and symbolic notions of sexual asymmetry that are themselves tied to social and cosmological structures. Because social practice activates spatial meanings, they are not fixed in space, but are invoked by actors, men and women, who bring their own discursive knowledge and strategic intentions to the interpretation of spatial meanings.

Bourdieu's theory of practice provides the point of departure for Henrietta Moore (1986) in understanding how space takes on gendered meanings among the Endo of Marakwet in Kenya. Moore concurs that space only acquires meaning when actors invoke it in practice, but she asks why meanings that are advantageous to men dominate these interpretations. For instance, Endo women are identified with the house, but the meanings invoked in using the domestic sphere privilege men's economic and social position. Moore adopts Fernandez's notion of metaphor's capacity for creativity (see the section on Inscribed Spaces) and, from Geertz and Ricoeur, reading behavior and space as a text to inform her understanding of how spaces are subject to multiple interpretations. She rejects the idea that dominant and muted groups, men and women respectively, have different cultural models which produce distinct interpretations of space. Rather, men and women share the same conceptual structure but enter into it in different positions and therefore subject it to different interpretations (Moore 1986:163). The notion that spatial symbols are polysemic enables these creative interpretations. While women counter the dominant view by deception, asserting rights to resources, and overcoming isolation by joining with other women in ritual and practical activities centered on reproductive roles, men construct a "discourse of power" that subsumes and diminishes women and regulates social relations within the group, among men, and with the natural world.

Victorian spaces

The application of domestic/public spheres to explain gender relations in non-Western cultures raises questions about whether these schemes are bound to western European categories of thought and culture. Questioning her own gender theorizing, Michelle Rosaldo (1980) began tracing her ideas of gender asymmetries to ethnological legacies that informed early anthropological theories. She argued that in detailing the "origins" of women's subordination, many anthropologists' accounts seem to be little more than projections of Victorian assumptions about women's reproductive roles and attendant elaborations (Rosaldo 1980:392). Rosaldo saw the Victorian focus on women's roles that separated public and domestic spheres as their way to compensate for the insecurity of capitalist investment and employment in underwriting male authority, and the need to fully separate the self-interested world of work from the selfless love of home (Collier 2000).

Orvar Löfgren (1984, this volume) considers how Victorian gender relations were conceived in the 19th and 20th century Swedish family and home. His account demonstrates the power of physical surroundings in the production and reproduction of culture, and reveals how middle- and working-class women read home environments in contrasting and conflicting ways. His historical account traces the emergence of bourgeois domesticity as a dominant ideology and value system that found expression in the practice of homemaking, the materiality of which served to naturalize its worldview. For the Oscarians (Sweden's Victorians), home was a moral project that combined material, social, and spiritual ideals of home and family, and men's and women's places. The construction of the 19th century bourgeois family, was based on the fragile bond of love between husband and wife, parents and children, requiring intimacy for its nourishment and growth, but the house itself also served as a showcase with separate spaces for public display and private seclusion (Löfgren 1984:45; this volume, p. 142). The construction of the ideal housewife, *femina domestica*, exempt from heavy work but responsible for creating an emotionally supportive and spiritually uplifting domestic atmosphere, contrasted with *homo economicus*, the rational, efficient husband who worked in public settings (Löfgren 1984:49; this volume, p. 145). Löfgren argues that these values invested in the organization of space and materiality of the bourgeois home acted to "silently socialize" family members to its ideals.

Löfgren contrasts the Swedish bourgeois family with the rapidly growing urban working classes where a different kind of home and family life predominated (see Young and Willmott 1957; Bott 1957). Unlike bourgeois families, working-class families were far less home-centered, anchoring identity in the neighborhood, exhibiting sex-segregated roles, and, in spite of material limitations, setting aside parlor space to assert their own respectability. Throughout the first half of the 20th century, European and North American middle classes sought to transform working-class families by strategically promoting the reform of domestic spaces to make them into their own image (Lawrence-Zúñiga, in press). The middle class redefined family, gender, and home around progressive modern concepts of scientific rationality, elevating housework to an occupation and promoting egalitarian gender relations. Löfgren observes that the Swedish home became a cultural battlefield in which middle-class progressives sought to reform the working-class family, but they were met by working-class women who resented and resisted embourgeoisement.

Gendering houses

The focus on houses as gendered spaces continues to occupy the attentions of many anthropologists working in European cultures where the material changes to housing and other documentation yield insights into historical transformations of gender and family relations (Birdwell-Pheasant and Lawrence-Zúñiga 1999; Bestard-Camps 1991; Zonabend 1984). Increasingly, however, the migration and relocation of peoples creates new relationships. Drawing on Halbwachs (1980) and Bachelard (1969), Joelle Bahloul (1996) describes how Jewish women living in Paris use the house in pre-independence Algeria as a mnemonic for recalling their experiences where their families and Muslim families lived together. "Memory's discourse feminizes the house," in name associated with men, by reminding its female residents that it was designed to enclose and contain them (1996:30). Men's memories were of the street and their identities were of the town. Domestic life centered on the courtyard, a central space shared by the families, but Jewish women constructed their own identities around their ability to leave the house to work or go to school unlike the Muslim women they knew.

Using the physicality of the house to understand how gender plays a significant role is found in "house societies" in Southeast Asia and South America (Atkinson and Errington 1990; Carsten and Hugh-Jones 1995). Janet Carsten and Stephen Hugh-Jones take as their point of departure Lévi-Strauss's notion of house societies, by which he defined a hybrid or transitional society between egalitarian, kin-based and hierarchical, class-based, to describe societies in which neither kinship, property, nor residence alone plays a clear role in defining social groups (1995:10). Roxanna Waterson (1990, 1995) and Carsten and S. Hugh-Jones (1995) extend Lévi-Strauss's notion of the house to include its material dimensions as well as its domestic, economic, political, and religious functions. The house operates through its physicality as a complex idiom for defining social groupings, naturalizing social positions, and as a source of symbolic power (Carsten and Hugh-Jones 1995:21). In much of Southeast Asia gendered uses and meanings of space may be derived from and combined with or muted by other principles of social organization such as descent and marriage or social rank (Waterson 1990:170). Carsten and Hugh-Jones use the idea of "spatial text" to suggest that residents' practices reveal the variable polysemic qualities of domestic space, that can be associated with women, with men and women, or with men at different times and occasions, depending on who is involved (1995:41). Gendered meanings can also be subsumed or obliterated by other considerations of kinship and rank, and they can change in relation to cyclical and historical conditions.

Constructing gender identity and space

The construction of gender and space are mutually constituting processes that find expression over time. Deborah Pellow (this volume) describes the evolution of the compound in Sabon Zongo, a Hausa-based community, in Accra, Ghana, over the last 80 years. Based on a model of traditional housing derived from the northern Nigerian countryside, Pellow traces out the ideals of social relations realized in spatial forms. Central to the Zongo's original spatial order is the accommodation of *auren kulle* (marriage of seclusion) sanctioned by Hausa custom and Muslim law, that employs seclusion to separate men and women in everyday life. Pellow describes the organization of living spaces around central courtyards that provide a gradation of public spaces for men to increasingly private ones reserved for women and their children. In adapting to the rapidly changing postcolonial economy of Accra, Pellow describes how the Zongo has also changed over time to incorporate non-Hausa and a weakening of seclusion observances.

Although less fully explored, extra domestic spaces are also constructed as gendered, tacitly and explicitly. A number of researchers have drawn inspiration from feminist geographers (Massey 1994; Blunt and Rose 1994), and anthropological theories employing multivocal, or translocal and transnational approaches, much of it investigating the intersection of gender, class, ethnicity, and race in complex and often subtle ways. Research on factory settings that employ large numbers of women but are managed and operated by companies dominated by men has produced fruitful insights into how non-domestic space is gendered and gendered identities are produced and reproduced (Kondo 1990; Ong 1990). Begoña Aretxaga (1997) describes how the quiet intimacy of home has been shaken and shattered by violence for Catholic women in West Belfast, while their involvement in "the troubles" forces them into dangerous public spaces. Their relationships with one another produce and reproduce an emotional space in which to shelter wanted men and differentiate the men from themselves (Aretxaga 1997:53). Low (2000) also describes the gendering of plazas in San Jose, Costa Rica, noting that the traditional Parque Central is not only dominated by men, but women who use the space come with children or male escorts at culturally acceptable times. However, the new Plaza de la Cultura attracts young people, tourists, and single women who can realize modern concepts of gender in a public setting.

The study of gendered space has moved away from earlier conceptions of fixed symbolic and territorial associations to consider more complex understandings. Historical studies of gender constructions over space and time reveal variability within cultures and the complex interlinkages of gender with social, economic, and political influences. An examination of the physical dimensions of the house and kinship relations in "house societies" suggests promising future directions for further gender study. In rapidly changing postcolonial societies the spatial dimensions of gender construction appear the most challenging to understand as traditional and new sociospatial forms interact with shifting dimensions of class, ethnicity, and race. All of these provide ample room for further explorations of gendered spaces.

Inscribed Spaces

"Inscribed spaces" focus on how various scholars define the fundamental relationship between humans and the environments they occupy. Inscribed space implies that humans "write" in an enduring way their presence on their surroundings, yet we do not wish to imply that this is solely a metaphor for describing the relationship. Rather, we acknowledge the role anthropologists play in making written records of these relationships and that, in creating texts, anthropologists not only document the narratives of those with whom they work, but increasingly consider their own positions in that work. In this section we are interested in how people form meaningful relationships with the locales they occupy, how they attach meaning to space, and transform "space" into "place." We are interested in how experience is embedded in place and how space holds memories that implicate people and events.

Furthermore, the relationship between people and their surroundings encompasses more than attaching meaning to space. It involves the recognition and cultural elaboration of perceived properties of environments in mutually constituting ways through narratives and praxis.

Architectonic space

James Fernandez (1974, 1977, 1984, this volume) conceives of the relationship between people and their environment as reciprocal and mutually constituting, one in which identity is negotiated through interactions with the environment and especially in the ritual enactment of metaphor. In his work among the Fang, Fernandez is interested in what makes spaces sacred and how they become places. People are influenced by the environment that surrounds them, and take qualities of that environment into themselves, "predicating upon themselves objects from other (non literal) domains of experience" (1984:32; this volume, p. 187), they create metaphors in constituting their identity (1974:120). In taking in these qualities, people also project them into space, creating buildings and settlement plans as part of larger "architectonic" space.

The architectonics of Fang culture, however, are not limited to physical settings but also include personal, social, domestic, cosmological, and mythical spaces produced by their mythology and cosmology, migration, forest and village relations, and social relations (Fernandez 1977:38). Instead, the architectonics create "quality space" that holds within it emergent qualities of experience activated during ritual events. Quality space is metaphoric space that includes architectural settings, but also contains "an extension of personal body images and an intension of mythical and cosmic images" (1977:39; see also the section on Embodied Spaces). During ritual performances, the metaphors of quality space are activated and participants experience complex feeling states, and a sense of revitalization.

Using this theoretical framework to explore the evocative power of sacred spaces, Fernandez compares the different architectonics of the Fang, Zulu, and Mina peoples (1984, this volume). He characterizes Fang culture as having centrifugal tendencies, Zulu culture as centripetal, while the Mina appear to be more centered. Fernandez points to the contrasting natural and human-made environments in which these groups live – the Fang in the forest made claustrophobic with its limited vistas, the Zulu in their ingathering spaces in the big open savannah, and the Mina with the constant motion brought by winds at the shore. Sentiments evoked by these environments comprise the material for the architectonic development of quality space that differentiates each culture. In contrasting the Fang and Zulu, Fernandez points to differences in settlement plan and architectural forms – the Fang rectilinear and the Zulu circular – and different social experiences with their natural and built surroundings. Woven into Fang architectonics, for instance, are the social oppositions between the men's council house and women's combined sleeping-cooking spaces, and the village relation to the forest, but also extensions of microcosmic body imagery with macrocosmic features of mythology. Fernandez also argues that while both cultures aim to experience vitality in ritual performances, Fang rituals tend toward the centrifugal, emphasizing oppositions, while the Zulu concentrate and centralize their ritual practices (1984:40; this volume, p. 198).

Place and voice

Although Fernandez casts much of his discussion of Fang architectonics in terms of conventional notions about environmental forms, sacred space, and the creation of place, he is also one of the first anthropologists to question the assumptions underlying key spatial categories used in ethnological analysis. In a 1988 special issue of *Cultural Anthropology*, Appadurai, Fernandez, and others argue that anthropologists have often used specific locales to identify the particular groups that inhabit them, and associated these with specific research topics that profoundly limit and narrow our understandings. "Ethnography thus reflects the circumstantial encounter of the voluntarily displaced anthropologist and the involuntarily localized 'other'" (Appadurai 1988:16). Equally problematic is the issue of voice by which Appadurai suggests that it is often unclear who is speaking in ethnography. In organizing fieldwork conversations into ethnography, does the ethnographer speak for the native, the native for the ethnographer, or does only the selected native speak? This reflexive concern with representations of anthropological knowledge, then, focuses attention on assumptions underlying core concepts and methods.

Arguing that far more attention has been given to the problem of voice in anthropology, Margaret Rodman (1992, this volume) focuses attention on the definition and use of place as an analytical construct. She criticizes anthropological conceptions of place that provide taken-for-granted settings to situate ethnographic descriptions, are used analytically as metaphors, or are reduced to a locale that imprisons natives. Rather, places are socially constructed by the people who live in them and know them; they are "politicized, culturally relative, historically specific, local and multiple constructions" (1992:641; this volume, p. 203) . Place can have a unique reality for each inhabitant, and while the meanings may be shared with others, the views of place are often likely to be competing, and contested in practice. Rodman suggests that anthropologists "empower" place by returning control over meanings of place to the rightful producers, and empower their own analysis of place by attending to the multiplicity of inhabitants' voices found in places about place (1992:644; this volume, p. 207).

Rodman outlines how understanding place as social construction can inform an anthropology that cannot be practiced in a "traditional" world where the natives stay put. Rodman proposes the concept of "multilocality" to describe considerations of place(s) affected by influences of modernity, imperial history, and contemporary contexts. In addition to accommodating polysemic meanings of place, "multilocality" seeks to understand multiple, non-Western, and Eurocentric viewpoints in the construction of place, effecting a more decentered anthropological analysis that acknowledges that there are no "others." Multilocality is also useful for understanding the network of connections among places that link micro and macro levels, as well as the reflexive qualities of identity formation and the construction of place as people increasingly move around the globe (Rodman 1992:646–647; this volume, p. 210). Rodman's multivocal approach urges us to listen to the voices infrequently heard such as native people who claim power by employing the autochthonous imagery of "rootedness" to suggest they are inseparable from place, or by asserting primordial connections of oneness with the land. She proposes the concept of social landscape as a broad perspective that rests on the notion of lived space of an individual's experience in the world and attention to "How different actors construct, contest and ground experience in place" (1992:652; this volume, p. 216).

Landscape as place

The concept of landscape, like place, is frequently used by anthropologists to casually describe settings pertinent to ethnography, but it is rarely defined or problematized. Eric Hirsch (1995) corrects this problem by identifying two meanings of landscape in anthropology, one as a framing device used "objectively" to bring a people into view, the other, similar to Rodman's socially constructed place, to refer to the meaning people impute to their surroundings (1995:1). Drawing on its etymological roots in Western art history, Hirsch defines landscape as developing from and involving a tension between idealized or imagined settings which he calls "background" against which the "foreground" of everyday, real, ordinary life is cast. In Hirsch's scheme, landscape's foreground actuality is to background potentiality, as place is to space, inside is to outside, and image is to representation (1995:4). In western European culture these notions can be traced to Renaissance rationality that separated people from nature, abstracted both, and created a separate ideal, a background, of objective reality. Using this framework he explores comparable foreground-background elements of landscape in other cultures and finds, in some, attempts to activate a relationship with background potentiality to overcome everyday struggles.

The concept of landscape is productive in accounting for the social construction of place by imbuing the physical environment with social meaning. Suggesting that landscape meaning is formed from densely mediated relationships with places through kinship, Gow (1995) argues that the Piro know the landscape through action in it with others and narrative; landscape implicates kin relations by acting as a mnemonic for recalling prior social events. The concept of landscape is also productive in examining notions of foreground-inside in relation to background-outside. Tom Selwyn (1995) describes how Israeli conceptions of national identity based on defending and conserving the natural landscape invert the original insider position of Arab inhabitants to outsider. Caroline Humphrey (1995) defines the Mongolian landscape by the different ways in which chiefly and shamanist energies are envisaged and, as social agencies, constitute the material world in complementary and dynamic ways.

Narrating place

The use of narrative to inform the anthropological understanding of place focuses on details of how local populations construct perceptions and experience place. Much of this ethnography attempts to describe "local theories of dwelling" (Feld and Basso 1996) and draws implicitly or explicitly on phenomenological approaches, a direction already much in use among cultural geographers who study place. Narrative and its interpretation is at the center of methods because, as Keith Basso indicates, cultural constructions of the environment can only be understood by talking to natives about landscapes (1996:68). But there are important assumptions and understandings derived from phenomenological approaches that find their way into and orient the use of narrative and the dependence on ethnographic description and its interpretation to serve as explanation.

An ethnographic exemplar employing narrative in describing place is found in Keith Basso's writings about his long-term work among the western Apache. Basso considers "what humans take their environments to mean," by focusing on the reciprocal influence of conceptions of the land and the self through which people produce a moral relationship with the land. His research on stories about places and place names, the vehicles of ancestral authority, reveals their roles as "symbolic reference points for the moral imagination and its practical bearings on the actualities of lives" (1988:102). The figurative language found in the stories that describe how the crossing got named "Coyote Pisses in the Water" or the place became known as "Grasshoppers Piled Up Across" suggests the western Apache use the landscape as a mnemonic for self-reflexive activity, a necessary action for acquiring wisdom. Wisdom, or the capacity for prescient thinking, can be learned, but only conscientiously, from Apache elders whose knowledge is enacted by visiting places, naming their names, and recounting traditional stories that demonstrate how insightfully "smooth" minds triumph over selfish, stupid, or foolish ones (Basso 1996:76). Basso tells us that by thinking of narratives set in place and the ancestors who originated them, Apaches inhabit their landscape and are inhabited by it in an enduring reciprocal relationship (1988:102).

Although Australian Aboriginal cultures also tell stories about their ancestors situated in place like the Apache, their narratives have a different character and function (Myers 1991; Morphy 1995). Fred Myers argues that among the Pintupi the relationship between place and family is linked to the concept of "The Dreaming", narratives about the mythological past in which "totemic ancestors" traveled from place to place and finally became part of the land (1991:48). The Dreaming is the means by which Pintupi selves are formed and identity is known, by which an individual "owns" a place, and the rights to live in an area and sacra associated with it. The Dreaming contrasts with the immediate and visible world, constituting an invisible but primary reality that is as unchanging and timeless as the cosmos. Myers says the Pintupi transform the landscape into narrative by invoking The Dreaming in their interactions with it and using each place as a mnemonic for telling and reenacting the story of their whole "country" (1991:66).

The inscription of place with meaning is not limited, however, to telling stories, but can include poetry, music, and songs (Feld 1990, 1996; Roseman 1998; Weiner 1991). Marina Roseman describes the Temiar use of songs to map their historical relationship with rain forest, claim rights to its resources, and translate the forest into culture by releasing forest spirits in song to sing in dreams and rituals (1998:111). A significant contribution to the literature on narrating place can be found in *Senses of Place* (Feld and Basso 1996). There, philosopher Edward Casey examines anthropological suggestions that the people we study transform a pre-existing, empty, and absolute space into meaningful place. Casey suggests the contrary – that place is general, and includes space, and that space is particular and derived from it (1996:15). He identifies the emergence of the idea of "space" as a modern concept preceded by the premodern notion of place, or perhaps followed by one that is postmodern – place, then, is primary, universal, and general (1996:20).

While not eschewing the narrative approach to understanding the social construction of place, Gray (1999, this volume) argues that praxis be included. Gray's
description of the political economy of sheep farming emphasizes how UK and EU
economic development policies favoring rational use of flat, open land for commodity production tend to ignore and marginalize hill areas which become fertile sites
for the production of cultural identities steeped in sheep herding and border history.
The *hirsel*, a unified place that includes both a shepherd's sheep and their grazing
area, is constituted by the shepherd's walking and biking in the hills to care for his
sheep (Gray 1999:449; this volume, p. 229). The act of shepherding, or "going
around the hill," is place-making requiring a shepherd's detailed knowledge of the
terrain, but also how his sheep bond to parts of the terrain, and how these parts are
linked together by paths to form his hirsel. Shepherds feel a deep connection to the
land by caring for their sheep, by understanding their grazing habits, and by being
able to see them to keep them out of trouble. The emphasis on walking the hills
demonstrates the critical ways in which places that may be separately named and
recalled are connected to one another and form a unified whole. Gray's reliance on
narrative as well as documented practices, gleaned largely by walking the terrain
with the shepherds, suggests a promising avenue to capture a deeper understanding
of place as lived space.

Anthropological study of inscribed spaces increasingly acknowledges the depth
and complexity with which people construct meaningful relationships with their
surroundings. In describing and recording these relationships, however, anthropologists have also struggled to incorporate reflexive considerations of place, voice, and
authority in their own work. Many scholars continue to describe the intricacies of
mutually constituting social relations with place through ritual and metaphor, but
the concern for discovering and representing the multiple views of places and their
meanings within a culture is yielding an increasingly rich understanding of the role
of place in constructing identity and holding memory. These avenues of research
promise a rich avenue for further explorations of the knowledge and meanings of
particular local places which are threatened by pressures from an increasingly
globally interconnected world.

Contested Spaces

Our consideration of "contested spaces" addresses social conflicts that are focused
on particular sites. We define "contested spaces" as geographic locations where
conflicts in the form of opposition, confrontation, subversion, and/or resistance
engage actors whose social positions are defined by differential control of resources
and access to power. While these conflicts principally center on the meanings
invested in sites, or derive from their interpretation, they reveal broader social
struggles over deeply held collective myths (McDonogh, 1992, this volume) In this
way, contested spaces give material expression to and act as loci for creating and
promulgating, countering, and negotiating dominant cultural themes that find expression in myriad aspects of social life. Spaces are contested precisely because they
concretize the fundamental and recurring, but otherwise unexamined, ideological,
and social frameworks that structure practice.

Theoretical approaches to understanding contested spaces vary by the type of site, and/or the social context in which the site is contested. Many studies of contested spaces could be considered equally under our other categories of embodied, gendered, inscribed, transnational, or tactical spaces because many sociospatial relations often include contestation. To create a foundation for considering contested spaces, we have included an article by Hilda Kuper (1972, this volume) on Swazi sites that have political importance in their struggles with colonial administrators. Gary McDonogh (1992, this volume) describes the history of how bourgeois elites and residents diverge in their characterization of the *barrio chino* in Barcelona as part of his larger work on the urban development of that city. We have also included an excerpt from Steven Gregory's *Black Corona: Race and the Politics of Place in an Urban Community* (1998) to highlight how an urban American discourse conflating race, poverty and place is countered and subverted through activism in an urban community.

The language of sites

In a seminal article on the Swazi, Hilda Kuper (1972, this volume) sets out the main parameters for the study of contested sites. Drawing on the classificatory and ideational characteristics of space rather than its physical or "empirical" aspects, Kuper defines "social space" experientially, whereby individuals attach values to space through social and personal experiences, and culturally as a conceptual model. Kuper suggests that the power of sites lies in their capacity as symbols to communicate through condensed meanings, especially as they are activated during the drama of political events. The symbolic meanings of sites are articulated through a complex system of social and ideational associations, which have manifest and latent qualities. Swazi narratives of political events reveal a "verbal imagery" of sites that express issues of identity in their struggles for power with colonial administrators. Kuper argues that some sites have more power and significance than others; "these qualities need have no *fixed* relationship to a physical, empirical dimension," although "political influence may manifest itself in bestowing these qualities through the manipulating of forms" (1972:421; this volume, p. 257). Thus, for Kuper, sites are social spaces that function in politicized dramas as condensed symbols operating within complex social and ideational structures. Kuper notes that the maximum effect of the politics of space is probably evident in colonial countries where white settlers have assumed control over strategic resources. The contestation of space among the Swazi is not unique in the way it opposes parties of unequal power and resources, and serves to articulate identities that attach to social space.

Producing urban sites of contestation

Urban environments provide frequent opportunities for spatial contests because of their complex structures and differentiated social entities that collude and compete for control over material and symbolic resources. Macro-level analyses of contested spaces have focused on struggles to control the outcomes of urban redevelopment schemes related to housing and neighborhood (Castells 1983) and urban sacred space (Harvey 1985) where local inhabitants organize to oppose the dominant classes and political elite (see also the section on Transnational Spaces). These analyses of class-based struggles in response to state-imposed spatial regimes emphasize how space is constitutive of power, and how resistance takes the form of social movements and local activism. While absolute command over physical space is the focus of these contests, because it ensures "invisible" control over the social reproduction of power relations, that control cannot be understood apart from conceptualizations of space which legitimize and naturalize sociospatial relations and which are manipulated in conflict situations (Lefebvre 1991).

Setha Low distinguishes between the physical and symbolic aspects of urban space by defining *social production* as the processes responsible for the material creation of space as they combine social, economic, ideological, and technological factors, while the *social construction* of space defines the experience of space through which "peoples' social exchanges, memories, images and daily use of the material setting" transform it and give it meaning (2000:128). The planning, design, and construction of the city are processes of social production responsible for shaping the urban environment, encoding it with intentions and aspirations, uses and meanings that are often themselves contentiously produced. For instance, professional designers and political elites together negotiate competing future images of the city, but these are rarely consistent with the daily spatial experiences of urban residents and workers. Interventions that physically shape the urban landscape attract opposition because they reproduce key symbolic forms that reference deep and still unresolved or unresolvable conflicts among social actors and collectivities.

Robert Rotenberg (1995) addresses this issue of design by tracing the historical production of successive urban gardens in Vienna as they represented changing relations of power and ideology. He shows how each new garden design contested social truths and power relations embedded in the previous one. During the 19th century, the Viennese city government created several major public parks as part of the Ringstrasse urban redevelopment scheme. "The city council built these parks, like the public buildings on the Ringstrasse, to represent the battle between the ideologies of absolutism and liberalism" (Rotenberg 1995:135). The English style of garden design that allowed plants to grow freely as in a picturesque landscape was favored by liberals who sought to portray their commitment to unfettered economic and political freedoms. Absolutists found the formal, manicured French style garden to be a more faithful representation of the imperial capital. While ordinary citizens had been banned from absolutist parks, their use of the new parks was encouraged; some French design elements were incorporated to control their potentially destructive behavior, however. Despite the inclusive gestures towards the public, Rotenberg suggests the Ringstrasse redevelopment was more important as camouflage that hid benefits given to private capitalist investors who acquired land to develop for middle-class housing (1995:140). Rotenberg argues that the effectiveness of these and subsequent gardens, even today, is found in their capacity to teach residents of Vienna about their own history as successive and competing forms of metropolitan knowledge.

Urban planning proposals and development schemes for transforming urban landscapes typically serve the interests of political elites and monied interests – indeed, the city is often envisioned as a site for the production of value – symbolic and monetary (see also the section on Tactical Spaces). Parts of the city long ignored and neglected often become attractive targets of these projects; their depressed land values make them ripe for exploitation and development in the realization of the urban vision. Gary McDonogh (1991) argues that as hegemonic discourse these visions of the future often ignore the values of urban life in marginal areas of the city. In describing the *barrio chino* of Barcelona, McDonogh (1992, this volume) focuses on the role of bars in the characterization of the neighborhood by their association with prostitution, drugs, and criminal activity. McDonogh argues bars not only act as signifiers linking notions of vice, gender, and doubtful morality to an entire lower-class neighborhood and the people who live there, but are made to "appear to be the causes rather than attributes of marginality" (1992:29). Much of this imagery is constructed from outside the barrio by the urban bourgeoisie who generalize from the reputations of certain specialty bars rather than common neighborhood bars which serve as social centers for local residents. While barrio residents contest this negative image by portraying themselves as virtuous and orderly, they still recognize the stereotype of the neighborhood. Indeed, McDonogh reports that residents used to tolerate illegal activities in the past as part of a culture of resistance. The imagery of bars and the barrio operate in a mutually constitutive and repressive system that serves the elite classes of Barcelona who claim the right to condemn an entire segment of the city, thus making it subject without recourse to planning schemes that ostensibly seek to ameliorate conditions.

Setha Low (2000) describes the conflict surrounding the renovation of the Parque Central, one of the oldest and most emblematic of public spaces in San Jose, Costa Rica. Professional and middle-class Josefinos, reacting to the apparent decline of the Parque due to an increased presence of lower-class users, promoted the idea of returning the site to their image of an elite, turn-of-the-century public space. City planners and officials, incorporating citizen input, adopted a compromise design that aimed to improve safety and cleanliness, reducing the amount of seating, eliminating roving venders and adding police – design strategies meant to displace the previous users and reclaim the Parque as a symbol for those who rarely used it. The newly designed Plaza de la Cultura, by contrast, was intended to express the aspirations of the dominant political party to represent Costa Rica as a modern country with European sensibilities while also recognizing its indigenous pre-Columbian heritage. Its big empty open spaces and North American businesses attract teenagers, tourists, speakers and performers, and gay cruisers, but it is viewed ambivalently by Josefinos who think of it as unattractive and unsafe. Successful in representing the interests of the politicians and the professional elite, Low concludes that these public spaces do little to serve the needs of everyday Costa Ricans (2000:202).

When the appropriation of land for urban redevelopment threatens to limit access to or exclude certain groups from using public spaces, these plans may be contested by local segments of the population whose identity is variously bound to the site. Matthew Cooper (1993) describes how the city of Toronto initially planned to create an urban "meeting place" on its waterfront where the culturally diverse vitality of the city could be realized, but was threatened by occupants of the development's office buildings, luxury condominiums, and upscale shopping who quickly organized to exclude access to others. Timothy Sieber (1993) also argues that as working waterfronts have waned in the United States, bourgeois and professional classes have sought these spaces by the water as a recreational or leisure resource, to be consumed by viewing. Using design guidelines that promote visual consumption, the

Boston waterfront can be experienced by taking walks, bicycling, and dining with a view of the water, but excludes facilities favored by the working classes.

Although liberal democracies ideally guarantee their citizens access to and unimpeded use of public spaces, elites may challenge and limit use through permits and police activity if it threatens their interests. Street vending from New York City (Stoller 1996) to Dar es Salaam (Lewinson 1998) is heavily regulated making streets contested spaces that disadvantage the poor. City streets and squares may be temporarily appropriated by social groups who compete to express social and political positions in the form of ritualized protests and demonstrations (Davis 1986). Public festivities, parades, performances, and spontaneous demonstrations are often used to temporarily invert dominant power relations to contest political and social issues (Lawrence 1992), or they may be used to give public voice to "invisible" or lesser known segments of the urban social order (Kugelmass 1994; Kasinitz 1992).

State hegemony and the memory of sites

The specific location in which local conflicts play out is increasingly seen as the stage upon which social memory is constructed (Sawalha 1998). The production and reproduction of hegemonic schemes require the monopolization of public spaces in order to dominate memories. "History is a central focus of social contest because the meanings of the past define the stakes of the present" (Alonso 1988:49). Popular and official memories codefine each other, often in shifting relations, but the state controls public spaces critical to the reproduction of a dominant memory while marginalizing the counter-histories of peasants, women, working classes, and others.

Some of these processes are seen most dramatically in cities located in the former Soviet Union which are just now reconstructing their urban landscapes and collective memories. In Poland and Germany attempts by citizens and governments to rename streets in honor of local heroes or to eliminate references to socialists may encounter resistance (E. Tucker 1998; DeSoto 1996). In Krakow, redevelopment plans for the Jewish Kazimierz district which sought to "restore" the past by erasing the Nazi occupation and 40 years of communism were contested (Kugelmass and Orla-Bukowska 1998). In Moscow, the construction of great public works projects and monuments has been historically linked to the production of mythologies to legitimize political visions of particular leaders (Khazanov 1998). The patronage of Moscow's mayor for the creation of "infantile" public sculptures by the artist Tseretseli has made these contested sites. Bruce Grant (2001) suggests that monuments are vehicles by which politicians project their own images as a mythical practice onto the empty receptacle of the state (also see McDonogh 1993). The fanciful imagery of the sculptures draws on children's fairytales, but according to Grant, the monuments and their mythical properties form a political practice which anesthetizes and tranquilizes the public and diverts Moscovites from asking serious questions about political and economic accountability.

Tourist sites

The quality of the physical setting is critical to tourism – it must provide some attractive, often "visual" features (Urry 1990) to motivate visits – but tourist sites are likely to be contested spaces because, like urban spaces, they lie at the intersection of diverse and competing social, economic, and political influences. Tourist landscapes are often developed and marketed under the aegis of national and international economic and political institutions which lie outside the control of local residents who work in and inhabit these spaces. A major threat to local cultures is the commercial success of mass tourism, much of it increasingly organized through networks of international cooperation (Greenwood 1989, Boissevain 1996). Development is aimed at creating landscapes for consumption by a leisured class of tourists rather than accommodating the needs and desires of local residents (Odermatt 1996). The recent growth of "cultural tourism" which seeks to bring hosts and guests into direct contact (Boissevain 1996), and the "heritage industry" which ostensibly markets traditional culture are intended to satisfy the tourist's growing desire to consume "authentic" landscapes as a means to experience imagined communities full of appealing, heroic, or colorful people (Selwyn 1996; H. Tucker 1997).

Even when the local population is actively involved in the tourism economy, however, changes to the physical environment and way of life, or the actual presence of tourists, can provoke opposition and sometimes overt conflict (Black 1996; Pedregal 1996). Local residents may develop strategies of resistance to mitigate the effects of the tourist presence, even as they participate in the tourist enterprise, by creating physical or temporal boundaries to protect a "backstage" area for private use (MacCannell 1976; Boissevain 1996; Black 1996; Crain 1996).

The meaning of the physical settings transformed to promote tourism may become the focus of conflict between tourists and residents. Edward Bruner (1996) describes the vastly different significance a coastal slave fort in Ghana has for visiting African Americans searching for identity and diasporic meaning in contrast with local Ghanaian's perceptions of the site as a source of economic development and a representation of a long history of colonial contacts. The effects of global mass tourism on particular sites and relations between tourists and the host country can have dangerous implications. Policing the pyramids in Giza, Egypt, has become necessary as they have been targeted by militant Islamic groups who identify the monument with the unacceptable penetration of Western control and conspicuous consumption (Kuppinger 1998).

Some tourist sites play critical roles in the ideological hegemony of states which use them to construct and legitimize the nation, and in the construction of national identity (Selwyn 1995). In England, the prehistoric site of Stonehenge has long attracted Druids and other alternative-culture groups whose interpretations and uses are contested by the official vision of the national icon owned and managed by the National Trust and English Heritage. Between 1985 and 1999 these groups, who use the site in unconventional ways, had been prohibited by force from using the site because they did not constitute "bona fide tourists" who paid fees (Bender 1993: 271). Archaeologist Barbara Bender contemplates archaeologists' participation in the production of the official, scientific interpretation of the monument at the behest of the state, one that strategically silences and excludes the voices and uses of others (1998:121).

Place identities and the politics of representation

The strategic construction of social identities articulated in terms of place or a specific site may play an important role in disputes over territory or development of the land (Forbes 1999; Whittaker 1994). Michele Dominy (1995) describes white settler (Pakeha) claims to Crown pastoral lease properties in New Zealand contested by Maori by describing their spiritual attachment through intimate knowledge and stewardship of the landscape. Pakeha discourse resists their inclusion with other white settlers and struggles for authenticity and legitimacy in a "dynamic discursive field of contested meanings" (Dominy 1995:369). Donald Moore (1998) argues that individual agency operates in constructing place identity and entitlement claims in a Zimbabwe land resettlement scheme where memories of struggle and resistance to colonial evictions carry more weight than birthright. Governments, however, may find ways to reject or ignore the legitimacy of land claims by asserting the superiority of the state's notion of a legal space that trumps local residents' claim to a lived-in moral, spiritual, community place (Gaffin 1997).

Because the arena in which the discourse of spatial identities and the politics of representation can be quite broad, stigmatized and marginalized groups can and do contest the legitimacy of these stereotypes. Steven Gregory (1998, this volume) describes how the dominant discourse about black identity in the United States links an ideology of welfare dependency, family pathology, and criminal activity to place in ways that disadvantage local residents. The residents of Lefrak City housing development in New York City were particularly targeted by this discourse in the 1970s as the racial composition of the complex began a court-ordered change. The rhetoric conflating race, pathology, and space encoded in media coverage of the community seemed to express a kind of "enclave consciousness" among whites who felt squeezed between the power of corporate and political elites on the one side and the poor and undesirables on the other.

Gregory argues that the rhetoric especially targets teenagers and young adult males with disorderly images of drug use and criminal activity which makes them objects of police surveillance. The social construction of a negative identity among Lefrak residents inhibits their participation in neighborhood planning processes. Rather than giving in to repressive hegemonic practices of the state, Lefrak City residents organized youth to participate in a clean-up campaign as a means to counter negative stereotypes, and formed networks and alliances to promote a collective identity and construct an alternative political space in which to find avenues for participation. The construction of new identities and social relations in Lefrak City aimed to rework the American cultural myth of race and poverty through place-based practices.

These studies of contested spaces make clear the inextricable and reinforcing connection between the meaning of place and identity. Revelations that the "power of sites" rests on their capacity to make manifest tacit understandings and unquestioned frameworks – the mythologies – that structure everyday practices represents a long-established anthropological tradition. Our understandings, however, have been expanded to include a wide array of contexts, from urban development schemes to sites of global tourism, as well as the often-contested social conditions under which spaces are produced and constructed.

Transnational Spaces

We use the term "transnational spaces" to encompass global, transnational, and translocal spatial transformations produced by the economy of late capitalism, focusing on people on the move. We identify three approaches to defining how space has been transformed:

1. Global spaces – The global economy and flows of capital transform local places, creating homogenized, deterritorialized spaces. These analyses of how capital and political economy produce space and place focus on the importance of the global and informational city, uneven development, and flexibility of capital and labor in the social production of space (Sassen 1991, 1996a; Castells 1996; Harvey 1990).
2. Transnational spaces – With the globalizing economy, people move across borders creating new transnational spaces and territorial relationships (Schiller et al. 1992; Ong 1999).
3. Translocal spaces – Globalization also radically changes social relations and local places due to interventions of electronic media and migration, and the consequent breakdown in the isomorphism of space, place, and culture. This process of cultural globalization creates new translocal spaces and forms of public culture embedded in the imaginings of people that dissolves notions of state-based territoriality (Gupta and Ferguson 1992; Appadurai 1996a).

In discussing each of these perspectives, and their usefulness in formulating an anthropological approach to transnational space, we emphasize the movement of peoples rather than the flow of capital and commodities.

Global space and deterritorialization

The critical spatial issue in global debates is the deterritorialization of places of work and community as a byproduct of post-Fordist forces and economic restructuring (Sassen 1991, 1996b; Low 1996a; Susser 2002). Manuel Castells (1989) captures this transformation in his analysis of a dual city, one in which the "space of flows" supersedes the local meaning of places. Ulf Hannerz (1992) also imagines a society based on cultural flows organized by nations, markets, and movements and criticizes world-systems analyses as being too simplified to reflect the complexity and fluidity of the "creolisation" of postcolonial culture (Hannerz 1987, 1996). Thus, global space is conceived of as the flow of goods, people, and services – as well as capital, technology, and ideas – across national borders and geographic regions – resulting in the deterritorialization of space, that is, space detached from local places.

The notion of global deterritorialization, however, has come under considerable criticism in that the "role of capital in changing place notions of a borderless world misses much of the reality of capitalism" (Smart 1999:380). Although capital has

become more mobile and thus placeless to some extent, it has become more territorial in other places as a result of uneven development. Global flows bypass some poor
residents without access to capital, entrapping them in disintegrating communities
while entangling others.

Anthropologists have challenged a view of globalization as all-encompassing and
pervading every sector of society, by studying "the local" and examining the articu-
lations of the global and the local (Low 1999; Ong 1999). For instance, Fran
Rothstein and Michael Blim (1991) and others explore how global industrialization
restructures the everyday lives and localities of factory workers, and how new
workers recreate meaning and community in the context of their transformed
lives. Other examples of localizing or indigenizing the global include Theodore
Bestor's (1999) ethnography of the Tsukiji wholesale fish market in Tokyo and
Alan Smart's (2000) study of local capitalisms created by foreign investment in
China. Ethnographic studies of the displacing effects of global forces also reveal
the power of individuals to reterritorialize the landscapes; studies of "queer" pilgrimage to San Francisco as a homeland and sanctuary from oppression (Howe
2001) and *moreno* Mexicans' territorial claims based on memory (Lewis 2001)
provide evidence of the richness of this approach.

Global flows of commodities and people also can create places and spatial
networks while at the same time deterritorializing them. Theodore Bestor (2001,
this volume) discusses multisited ethnography's potential for linking globalization to
the establishment of new spaces, institutions, and structures in "Markets and Places:
Tokyo and the Global Tuna Trade." In a seemingly "dis-placed" world of the global
circulation of capital, commerce, and culture, he examines the reconfigurations of
spatially and temporally dispersed relationships within the international seafood
trade. By focusing on sushi-quality tuna, Bestor is able to trace the commodity
chains, trade centers, and markets that make up this global space. He argues that
market and place are not disconnected through the globalization of economic
activity, but reconnected generating spatially discontinuous urban hierarchies.

The various dimensions of the tuna commodity chain, the social relationships of
fishermen, traders, and buyers as well as the economic relationships of markets,
marketplaces, and distribution circuits create global space. Responding to critiques
of the (fieldwork) "sites" of anthropology (Olwig and Hastrup 1997; Metcalf 2001),
Bestor crafts an ethnography that captures the complexities of capital flows and
globalization in material spaces and real time.

Transnational spaces, territory, and identity

The globalization/deterritorialization model, however, does not focus on the *horizontal* and *relational* nature of contemporary processes that stream across spaces
and does not express their "*embeddedness* in differently configured regimes of
power" (Ong 1999:4). Aihwa Ong (1999) prefers "transnational" to "global" to
denote movement across spaces and formations of new relationships between
nation-states and capital. She defines transnational spatial processes as situated
cultural practices of mobility that produce new modes of constructing identity and
result in zones of graduated sovereignty based on the accelerated flows of capital,
people, cultures, and knowledge.

Within anthropology, the term *transnational* was first used to describe the way that immigrants "live their lives across borders and maintain their ties to home, even when their countries of origin and settlement are geographically distant" (Schiller et al. 1992: ix). Part of this effort was to understand the implications of a multiplicity of social relations and involvements that span borders. Eric Wolf (1982) laid the theoretical groundwork in his landmark history of how the movement of capital and labor has transformed global relations since the 1400s, dispelling the myth that globalization is a recent phenomenon. However, while Wolf's approach to the issue of global connections is seminal, it deals primarily with issues of power and its allocation, and only indirectly with the spaces of daily life. It is much later, through the detailed ethnographies of the rhythms of daily life in transnational migrant communities, that a sense of transnational **spaces** emerges (Mountz and Wright 1996; McHugh 2000).

There is a tendency to conceive of transnational spaces as sites of resistance, and to depict cultural hybridity, multipositional identities, border crossings and transnational business practices by migrant entrepreneurs as conscious efforts to escape control by capital and the state (Guarnizo and Smith 1998). Some migrant studies describe new forms of resistance, so-called "counter-narratives of the nation" (Guarnizo and Smith 1998:5), which disrupt the ideological strategy of the nation-state by challenging its "imagined community" (Anderson 1983). For instance, Michael Kearney (1991) traces the counter-hegemonic creation of autonomous political spaces by Mixtec migrant farm workers in California and Oregon. Roger Rouse (1991) describes a new kind of social space created by the experiences of working-class groups affected by capitalist exploitation. By breaking down "community" to encompass more than a single, bounded space, he imagines a social terrain that reflects the cultural bifocality of migrants and describes a fragmented reality made up of circuits and border zones (Rouse 1991). And while some people regard borders as increasingly permeable sites of crossing, others encounter them as militarized sites of immobility and surveillance, controlling and restricting movements of individuals identified by race, gender, and class (Elder 1998).

These migration studies dissolve conventional notions of borders, boundaries, nations, and community redefining the relationship of the global, transnational, and the local. In doing so they reformulate social and political space, supplanting static concepts of center and periphery, as well as cultural core and difference at the margins, to create fluid, transnational space produced by "ordinary" people (Marston 1990; Rouse 1991). Cultural differences found at the margins (and across borders), initially interpreted solely as signs of exclusion from the center, now also refer to limitations of the nation-state to represent the whole (Tsing 1993).

This reformulation of transnational space as fluid and fragmented, produced by people on the move, complements studies of the sovereignty and citizenship and the reconsideration of the nation-state as a spatial entity or territory (Sassen 1996a). Diaspora and refugee studies of the "displaced," "uprooted," and "homeless" have brought attention to the analytical consequences of territorializing concepts of identity (Malkki 1992; Lovell 1997). The territorialization expressed in maps and ordinary language such as "the land," "the country," or "the soil," connects territory with producing national identities in the form of roots, trees, ancestries, and racial lines as essentializing images, spatially incarcerating the native (Appadurai 1988; Malkki 1992).

Akhil Gupta (1992, this volume) in his article "The Song of the Nonaligned World: Transnational Identities and the Reinscription of Space in Late Capitalism" problematizes the limitations of this territorialized notion of nationalism by juxta-posing it with other forms of spatial commitment and identity. He begins by exploring the "structures of feeling" (Williams 1961) that produce the nation, and argues that First and Third World nationalisms are inherently dissimilar in their relationship to late capitalism and postcolonialism.

His analysis of the comparative success of the Third World Nonaligned Move-ment (NAM) and the European Community (EC) illustrates the problems that arise when trying to create identities based on transnational imagined communities. The NAM has no binding structures of feeling attached to a distinct geographical unit, thus attempts to create a new kind of transnational, or "Third World," identity, failed. In contrast, the EC, also a transnational imagined community, but one with contiguous national borders and a common history, evokes feelings embedded in its territoriality, and thus is able to muster greater member support and political identification. Based on this analysis Gupta concludes that citizenship "ought to be theorized as one of the multiple subject positions occupied by people as members of diversely spatialized, partially overlapping or non-overlapping collectivities" (1992:73; this volume, p. 309).

Translocal spaces and mobile sovereignty

Arjun Appadurai's (1988) critique of the lack of multivocality and multilocality in ethnography also questions the way anthropologists write about their subjects as located in one "place" and speaking with one "voice." For a discipline based on fieldwork, "there has been surprising little self-consciousness about the issue of space in anthropological theory" (Gupta and Ferguson 1992:6). An often assumed isomorphism of space, place, and culture results in a number of problems: an inability to deal with peoples who inhabit the borderlands and account for cultural difference within a locality; an assumption that countries embody their own dis-tinctive culture and society; and a lack of understanding of hybridity and disjuncture in postcoloniality (Appadurai 1988; Gupta and Ferguson 1992).

In response, Appadurai (1992) proposes the study of "ethnoscapes," landscapes of group identity, focusing on how deterritorialization affects loyalties of groups in diaspora, manipulation of currencies and other forms of wealth, and strategies that alter the basis of cultural reproduction. He theorizes a rupture in modern subjectiv-ity produced by electronic mediation and mass migration in cultural processes, since it is only "in the past two decades or so that media and migration have become so massively globalized" (Appadurai 1996a:9). Cultural globalization and "public culture" cut across conventional political and social boundaries, while cultural reproduction is occurring outside of the nation-state and stable cultural landscapes (Appadurai 1996a; Ong 1999).

Appadurai (1996b, this volume) in his article "Soveignty without Territoriality: Notes for a Postnational Geography" describes a world where minorities and migrants are flowing into nation-states, threatening the stability of ethnic coherence and traditional rights. There is increasing pressure to maintain the nation-state in territorial terms, while at the same time it is increasingly apparent that territory, in the sense of states, nations, territories, and ideas of ethnic singularity, are disintegrating into translocality. This mix of translocalities, migrant citizenries, and diasporic communities challenges the dominance of the nation-state, resulting in "mobile sovereignties." Appadurai (1996b, this volume) resolves the split between territoriality and governance through the emergence of what he calls a "postnational geography," proposing a reformulation of citizenship based on a concept of sovereignty that is limited and translocal (Appadurai 1996a).

Translocal spaces are also produced by other forms of cultural deterritorialization such as travel, tourism, and religious diaspora. Marc Augé (1995) considers the airport a non-place, a space of supermodernity, where customers, passengers, and other users are identified by names, occupation, place of birth, and address, but only upon entering and leaving. Airports along with superstores and railway stations are non-places that "do not contain any organic society" (1995:112); social relations are suspended and this non-place becomes a site of coming and going.

Travelers as well as anthropologists are creating new forms of spatiality. For instance, James Clifford (1992) employs the metaphor of the traveler to propose a more mobile theorization of anthropology based on routes and itineraries. The anthropologist, traveler, and the tourist generate their own kind of translocality as they move from one setting to another in search of authenticity and place (MacCannell 1992; Cresswell 1997; Löfgren 1999) (see also sections on Contested Spaces and Spatial Tactics).

Tourism also unhinges the stability of people and place through the rapid circulation of mass media, tourists, money, and commodities, detaching the locale from the rise of global interdependency. Based on an ethnography of Kathmandu, Mark Liechty (1996) identifies how shared histories of translocalities differentiate groups as much as they connect them. Reterritorialization occurs only when tourists and locals imagine places and long for meaning, creating place as a destination and a site of collective imagination.

Religious diasporic centers, linked by ties of personal loyalty and marked by religious rituals, are also expanding spaces of Islamic knowledge and spiritual power (Werbner 1996). Centers of Sufiism, whether in Africa, Asia, or England, create new translocal spaces, recentering the sacred topography of global Islam. This case of reverse colonization and spatial appropriation, Werbner argues, decenters Western dominance and reinscribes space in alternative – moral, cognitive, aesthetic, and spatial – ways.

Each of these perspectives – the global, the transnational, and the translocal – offers a critical approach to spatiality and the production of space. Anthropologists who focus primarily on the circulation of people and ideas, however, take the position that what global capital means in different parts of the world is less clear and still remains exploratory. However, there are a number of anthropologists who are attempting to wed the insights of Marxist geographers concerned with the circulation of goods and capital with the anthropological position of framing this discussion in its cultural and intercultural context. The anthropological contribution to an understanding of these new forms of spatiality will continue to center on the individual and his/her movement throughout the world, focusing on how vernacularization resists global forces while at the same time acknowledging the underlying importance of political economy and global capital in social production and reproduction. The challenge is to look at space outside, across, and beyond the nation-state, while at the same time retaining an ethnographic perspective that situates these transnational spaces in the bodies of people with feelings and desires.

Spatial Tactics

By "spatial tactics" we mean the use of space as a strategy and/or technique of power and social control. Power relations have been considered in other sections, but here we want to highlight the way space is used to obscure these relationships. The assumed neutrality of space conceals its role in maintaining the social system, inculcating particular ideologies and scripted narratives (Yeager 1996).

Henri Lefebvre (1991) views space as a social product that masks the contradictions of its production. This "illusion of transparency" is such that "within the spatial realm the known and the transparent are one and the same thing" (Lefebvre 1991:28). For instance, in the Latin American plaza, colonial space disguises underlying indigenous place-making and religious meanings. This obfuscation is remedied by historical, ethnographic, and archaeological research on underlying spatial relations that encode indigenous peoples' political resistance and cultural continuity in the face of Spanish hegemonic practices (Low 2000).

We draw heavily on the work of Michel Foucault and Jean Baudrillard as well as Michel de Certeau and Gilles Deleuze for our departure point, exploring some of the spaces of late capitalism and mass communication – heterotopias and hyperspaces – where the relationship of material space to representational space becomes ephemeral and in some cases completely detached. A number of ethnographies have been able to tease out this divergence of sign and object – often embedded in the architecture and spatial arrangement of the place – located in a particular setting. We consider planned new towns (Rabinow 1982, this volume), historically preserved sites (Herzfeld 1993, this volume), tourist villages (Gable and Handler, this volume), and residential gated communities (Low 2001, this volume) as relevant exemplars.

Space, power, and knowledge

Michel Foucault (1975, 1984) approaches the spatial tactics of social control through analysis of the human body, spatial arrangements, and architecture. He examines the relationship of power and space by positing architecture as a political "technology" for working out the concerns of government – that is, control and power over individuals – through the spatial "canalization" of everyday life. The aim of such a technology is to create a "docile body" (Foucault 1975:198) through enclosure and the organization of individuals in space.

Foucault (1975) uses Jeremy Bentham's 1787 plan for the Panopticon to represent an architectural mechanism of control in its ideal form. The Panopticon was designed as an arrangement of cell-like spaces, each of which could be seen only by the supervisor and without the knowledge of the individual being observed. The inmate must behave as if under surveillance at all times, thus becoming his/her own guardian. In his synthesis of space, power, and knowledge, Foucault gives other examples of what he calls a "structural" organization of space serving disciplinary ends, such as the military hospital at Rochefort, and factories, hospitals, and planned new towns.

Paul Rabinow (1989) links the growth of spatial forms of political power with the evolution of aesthetic theories, concentrating on the ordering of space as a way to understand "the historically variable links between spatial relations, aesthetics, social science, economics, and politics" (Rabinow 1982:267; this volume, p. 352). His larger concern, however, is with the "emergence of modern urbanism" (Rabinow 1989:267) as a turning point in the development of modern forms of political power and techniques for governance. Rabinow's (1989) analysis of colonial planning in Morocco uncovers how French colonists sought to use architecture and city planning to demonstrate their cultural superiority through the building of *villes nouvelles*, modern French settlements, next to but separate from Morocco's existing cities.

His article, "*Ordonnance*, Discipline, Regulations: Some Reflections on Urbanism" (Rabinow 1982, this volume), reiterates the importance of space as a tool to locate and identify relations of knowledge and power, and the centrality of space, both analytically and politically. He depicts Foucault's three regimes of space and power: the *sovereign* in which the basic unit is territory, the *disciplinary* where the problem is the control of bodies by spatial ordering, and *bio-power* in which power is exercised on a population existing in a particular milieu, and the "relative simultaneity of these different spatial-political concerns" (Rabinow 1982:271–272; this volume, p. 355).

For example, Rabinow describes Richelieu, a planned city built in France during the Classic Age, as an example of the disciplinary ordering of space. Urban planning in Nantes, however, is an example of the role of space within the framework of bio-power in which there is no longer a direct relationship between the operation of political power and its spatial representation. In fact, in Nantes individual capitalists are responsible for planning spaces based on commercial flow, rather than the state setting guidelines based on governmental power and spatial practices. Rabinow (1982; this volume) draws upon these examples to argue that it is only towards the end of the 19th century that a new discipline, urbanism, which combines the planning of space with political control based on a scientific understanding, comes into being.

Rabinow and Foucault address how architecture and planning function as spatial tactics contributing to the maintenance of power of one group over another at a level that includes the control of the movement and the surveillance of the body in space as well as the transformation of spatial ideologies. They do not focus, however, on individuals' everyday resistance to spatial forms of social control.

Spatial tactics

Michel de Certeau (1984) takes this omission as his starting point, setting out to show how people's "ways of operating" constitute the means by which users reappropriate space (1984:xiv). These practices are articulated in the details of everyday life and bring to light the clandestine "tactics" used by groups or individuals "already caught in the nets of 'discipline'" (de Certeau 1984:xiv–xv). By tracing out the operations of walking, naming, narrating, and remembering the city, he develops a theory of lived space in which spatial practices elude the discipline of urban planning. The pedestrian's walking is the spatial acting-out of place, creating and representing public space rather than subject to it.

For de Certeau, power is about territory and boundaries in which the weapons of the strong are classification, delineation, and division – what he calls *strategies* – while the weak use furtive movement, short cuts and routes – so-called *tactics* – to contest this spatial domination (Cresswell 1997). Tactics never rely on the existence of a place for power or identity; instead they are a form of consumption, "never producing 'proper places' but always using and manipulating these places" (Cresswell 1997:363). Thus, the spatial tactics of the weak are mobility and detachment from the rationalized spaces of power. In this sense, the spatial tactics of the weak and the pedestrian are not the same as those of the migrant or traveler who, upon arrival at his/her destination, takes on its identity and comes under the state's control.

Gilles Deleuze and Felix Guattari (1986) are also concerned with how people resist the spatial discipline of the state. They distinguish between the ordered and hierarchical machinations of the state, and the "war machine" of the nomad, who moves by "lines of flight" or by "points and nodes" instead of by place to place (Deleuze and Guattari 1986; Cresswell 1997). The nomad escapes the state by never becoming reterritorialized, slipping through the "striated spaces" of power, and remains undisciplined, a metaphor for all the forces that resist state control.

This spatial mobility based on "a horizontal vista of mobile meanings, shifting connections, temporary encounters" (Chambers 1986:213) is characteristic of the propinquity of encounters in the city (Copjec and Sorkin 1999). It is also found in the world of the international airport with its "shopping malls, restaurants, banks, post-offices, phones, bars, video games, television chairs and security guards" (Chambers 1990:57–58), a simulated metropolis inhabited by a community of modern nomads. Within the miniaturized world of the airport, the metaphor of the nomad becomes emblematic of postmodern life.

Hyperreality and hyperspace: The postmodern crisis of representation

The production of a simulated metropolis is only one aspect of late capitalism's crisis of representation referred to as "postmodernity." Jean Baudrillard argues that the moment signs become separated from their referents and the distinction between object and representation is no longer valid, a new world emerges constructed out of models or "simulacra" which have no referent or reality except their own (Poster in Baudrillard 1988:6). "Simulation is no longer that of a territory, a referential being or a substance. It is the generation of models of a real without origin or reality: a hyperreal" (Baudrillard 1988:166). Baudrillard suggests culture is dominated by simulations that have no relationship to reality, and that this "hyperreality" is spread by the media. He traces the steps by which this "radical negation" occurs: (1) the representation is a reflection of basic reality; (2) it masks and perverts a basic reality (as in the case of the Latin American plaza); (3) it masks the absence of a basic reality (as in the case of the airport); and finally, (4) "it bears no relation to any reality whatever; it is its own pure simulacrum" (Baudrillard 1988:170).

Edward Soja (1989, 1997) applies the notion of simulacra and hyperreality to describe the landscape of downtown Los Angeles where the space of Westin Bonaventure Hotel is totally disconnected from the streetscape – a perfect example of "depthlessness and spectacle" – becoming a new kind of "hyperspace" altogether. Frederic Jameson (1991) also contends that late capitalism has a distinctive cultural logic which is reshaping the form and functioning of the city – creating "postmodern" urban space. Christine Boyer (1994) calls it the "city of illusion," Sharon Zukin (1995) the "city of cultural consumption," and Charles Ruthesier (1996) a "nonplace urban realm" where the packaging of cities as commodities produces a city as a set of scenographic sites.

Walt Disney World in Orlando, Florida and Disneyland in Anaheim, California are perfect models of simulation and the city of illusion. They have become a major middle-class pilgrimage center in the United States, "partly because of the brilliance of its cross-referential marketing and partly because its utopian aspects appeal strongly to real people's real needs in late capitalist society" (Fjellman 1992:10). Cinema and the scenographic presentations structure one's experience there, with activities organized as movie scenes. According to Baudrillard, Disneyland is presented as imaginary in order to make us believe that the rest is real, when in fact all of Orange County and the America surrounding it is no longer real, but of the order of the hyperreal and of simulation. "It is no longer a question of a false representation of reality (ideology), but of concealing the fact that the real is no longer real, and thus of saving the reality principle" (1988:172).

John Dorst's (1989) analysis of the preservation of Chadd's Ford, Pennsylvania as a representative display of a place that exists only in Andrew Wyeth's paintings, demonstrates the theoretical power of ethnography when applied to such a postmodern site. Dorst uses the concept of hyperspace and its depthless surfaces to explain the visual impact of the mirror-glass surface of the Brandywine Museum and its enframed scenes (1989:108). More recently he has focused on the hegemonic discourse of "visuality" in his excursions into preserved landscapes of the American West (Dorst 1999).

Michael Herzfeld (1993, this volume), in "Histories in Their Places," also employs ethnography to understand conflicting visions of the past and their realization through historic preservation practice and regulation in Rethemnos, Greece. He is concerned with who decides what constitutes the history of the place, and how the materiality of this history is negotiated. Residents are distressed about the dirt which "crumbling, damp-ridden walls impose on them," and the historic designation of their homes, while at the same time agreeing with the preservation of monumental architecture (Herzfeld 1993:227; this volume, p. 362). He explains how the poor deploy official ideology in support of their own goals, by analyzing how "each new disposition of space embodies the consequences of a particular negotiation of relevant facts" (1993:228; this volume, p. 363) using rhetoric and violence as well as spatial tactics to pursue their interests against the law.

Herzfeld's (1993) discussion of the contestation of surfaces combines the arbitrariness of historic preservation designation and practice with the everyday tactics of poor people defending their homes and town against the power of the state. Architectural facades become detached from their original meanings, taking on new roles in the ongoing conflict. In this ethnographic example, the spatial tactics and subversions of de Certeau (1986) are used by town residents, and the hyperreality of Baudrillard (1988), in which architectural facades reconstitute and reinscribe history, is integrated into the practice of everyday life.

Heterotopias: Authenticity and tourism

Museums, historic villages, cemeteries, gardens as well as theme parks are identified by Michel Foucault as "heterotopias," places where "all the other real sites that can be found within the culture are simultaneously represented, contested, and inverted" (1986:24). He argues that the museum and the library are both heterotopias of time, characteristics of 19th century Western culture's passion for accumulations.

Tony Bennett (1995) elaborates how, in fashioning this new space of representation for the modern public, the museum was constructed and defended as rational by differentiating it from competing institutions such as fairs and circuses where scientific practices of collecting and ordering were not used. The same nexus of science, aesthetics, politics, and economics identified by Rabinow (1989) as constituting modern urbanism, are at work in the social production of the museum.

This refashioning of space combined with the reordering of reality is also the objective of historic preservation projects where the political ideology of these practices is hidden in the details of material culture and the organization and flow of space (Boyer 1994). Gable and Handler (1996, this volume) argue that heritage museums are perfect places for working out modern anxieties about what has been "lost" and what must be preserved, and as such become arbiters of authenticity. Yet all historic preservation strategies as well as museum exhibitions entail some amount of "artful fakery." They explore what happens to a heritage site "after authenticity," "where the pursuit of an elusive authenticity remains a goal even as it generates public statements intended to call into the question the epistemology of authenticity" (Gable and Handler 1996:568; this volume, p. 369). They point out the many ways staff and management attempt to make the Williamsburg experience authentic, describing "impression management" aimed at upholding the universal ideals and values Williamsburg is thought to represent (Gable and Handler 1996:573; this volume, p. 376). In this sense, the heritage site is similar to other spatial tactics, in that it creates illusion in order to further ideological goals and defend a particular reality, in this case of the nation and its colonial past.

The fortress city and the gated community

The fortress city is a spatial tactic described by Mike Davis (1990) in his history of Los Angeles, in which he traces the control of media, seizure of land, busting of unions, rigging of water rights, and exclusion of minorities from political participation. Davis (1992) explains that the resulting "militarization" of the landscape into enclaves and citadels took a long time to develop, with many periods of working-class and minority resistance producing minor successes. But ultimately Bunker Hill and the surrounding downtown area became emblematic of the fortress city with the physical separation of:

the new [financial] core and its land values behind a rampart of regraded palisades, concrete pillars, and freeway walls. Traditional pedestrian connections between Bunker Hill and the old core were removed, and foot traffic was elevated above the street on "pedways"... access to which was controlled by the security systems of individual skyscrapers. (Davis 1998:365)

The social production of the fortress city is found in the underlying logic of large urban redevelopment projects where the built environment forms contours which structure social relations, causing commonalities of gender, sexual orientation, race, ethnicity, and class to assume spatial identities. At the same time people "imprint themselves physically on the urban structure through the formation of communities, competition for territory, and segregation – in other words, through clustering, the erection of boundaries, and establishing distance" (Fainstein 1994:1). Large mixed commercial and residential development projects reinforce social segregation, further cutting off communities by visual boundaries, growing distances, and ultimately walls.

In the fortress city, youth gangs and homeless youth are part of the new social imaginaries (Ruddick 1996). Space takes on the ability to confirm identity as institutional and private forces increasingly constrain and structure the lives of street addicts and other marginalized groups within the public arena (Waterson 1993). Within this context, acts of violence and crime are increasingly feared. Eli Anderson (1990) describes the "streetwise" behavior of Philadelphians in which residents cross the street when faced with oncoming young black males. Löic Wacquant (1994) portrays the isolation of families in Chicago's Black Belt, where the streets are deserted and no longer patrolled by police. Philippe Bourgois (1995) portrays the fear and sense of vulnerability experienced by El Barrio residents with the violence of those who sell crack in East Harlem, New York City.

Sally Merry (1990) suggests that in middle-class and upper-middle-class urban neighborhoods, residents seek privacy and segregation simply because they desire peace and can afford it. Such neighborhoods are marked by patterns of avoidance of social contact: building fences, cutting off relationships, and moving out in response to problems and conflicts. This "moral minimalism" is characterized by spatial separation, privacy, and insulation from strangers (Baumgartner 1988). At the same time the government expands its regulatory role: "Zoning laws, local police departments, ordinances about dogs, quiet laws, laws against domestic and inter-personal violence, all provide new forms of regulation of family and neighborhood life" (Merry 1993:87).

Most studies of the fortress city have focused on Los Angeles, Chicago, and New York, even though the United States does not have a monopoly on this type of social and physical development. Teresa Caldeira (2001) describes the increasing fear of street crime and building of fortified enclaves in Sao Paulo justified by residents' fear of violence. She sees the walls as both a response to fear and part of the modernist planning scheme, the coalescing of two spatial tactics. Emanuela Guano (2002) critiques the increased segregation by fortified enclaves characteristic of "modern" Buenos Aires, and Ivelisse Rivera-Bonilla (1999) examines class and community in a gated community in Puerto Rico.

Moral minimalism, governmental regulations, and modes of enforcement in the United States translate into gated communities when the spatiality of social control becomes concrete (Flusty 2001; Blakely and Synder 1997). Neighborhood watch schemes, closed-circuit television and surveillance technology are not perceived as sufficient and architecture is reclaimed as the material system of representation (Ainley 1998). It would seem that Foucault's panopticism found in the patterns of our visible life-paths would be adequate for "reasonably successful enforcement of normality in today's society" (Hannah 1997:353), but for some families, walls and gates are used to separate themselves to create a sense of security.

In "The Edge and the Center: Gated Communities and the Discourse of Urban Fear," Setha Low (2001, this volume) explores how the search for security by middle-class families is changing the design of suburban residential development. As part of the fortress city scenario, New York residents are fleeing deteriorating urban neighborhoods with increased ethnic diversity, while in San Antonio, Texas they are concerned about "Mexicans" who might kidnap their children. Residents say that they are moving to gated communities to protect their family and property from dangers perceived as overwhelming, yet even the spatial tactic of gating – the so-called "forting up" of the suburbs – offers only incomplete boundedness from feared groups who enter to work for residents.

In her study, Low addresses how this discourse of fear of violence and crime legitimates residents' residential segregation. Similar to the residents of Rethemnos, gated-community residents are using spatial and rhetorical tactics to disguise their class-based strategies of exclusion, while "workers," "Mexicans," and "others," practice subversive spatial tactics through movement, escaping these controls by their presence within these guarded, gated, and walled communities. In the gated community all of the spatial tactics discussed are practiced alternatively: by the residents – through the discourse of fear, spatial control, and legitimating ideology, by the workers – through their daily, erratic movement and place of work, by the architects – through their plans and enclave designs that create gated environments, and by the developers who produce this landscape for popular consumption.

Conclusion

When we first reviewed the literature on the built environment and spatial form, the theorizing of transnational spaces and spatial tactics was just appearing on the anthropological horizon. Glimmerings of these ideas were evident in the discussion of the political economy of space: the ways race, class, and gender relations are spatially reproduced, the emergence of a global system of production, and the impact of capital accumulation on built form (Lawrence and Low 1990:486). We identified the role of design and planning in capitalist transformations of the landscape (Harvey 1985), and local resistance through social movements to spatial changes produced by uneven development (Castells 1983; Smith 1984).

Yet the changes in the representational aspects of space that we trace to the cultural disjuncture produced by late capitalism – the separation of material reality and symbol, of mass communication and local knowledge, and of migrants and stable populations – are equally important to understand. It was in writing about the global city (King 1995; Low 1996a), connecting the social construction and production of space (Low 1996b, 2000), and rereading the work of Arjun Appadurai (1988, 1991, 1996) and Akhil Gupta and James Ferguson (1992), as well as David Harvey (1990) and Manuel Castells (1989, 1996) that the significance of reconceptualizing cultural spaces based on flows of people, locales, and capital became apparent. This volume is the result of this rethinking of the global and local, body and space, of territory and deterritorialization.

The terrorist attacks on the World Trade Center and the Pentagon on September 11, 2001 irrevocably altered the spaces and consciousness of New York City and Washington, D.C., disrupting the everyday lives, place attachment, and place identity for thousands. In the ensuing analysis of the impact of the disaster and decisions about rebuilding or other alternatives, our anthropological perspectives can prove insightful. The anthropology of space and place offers diverse theories and methods for spatializing and locating culture as well as identifying the contradictions of territory, cultural and economic globalization, and modernity that lie at heart of this contemporary tragedy. We hope that this volume will help address the problems that we currently face in our shattered world.

October 2001
New York City
Los Angeles

REFERENCES

Ainley, Rosa (1998) Watching the Detectors: Control and the Panopticon. In R. Ainley (ed.) *New Frontiers in Space, Bodies and Gender* (pp. 88–100). London: Routledge.

Alonso, Ana Maria (1988) The Effects of Truth: Re-Presentations of the Past and the Imagining of Community. *Journal of Historical Sociology* 1(1), 33–57.

Anderson, Benedict (1983) *Imagined Communities: Reflections on the Origin and Spread of Nationalism.* London: Verso.

Anderson, Eli (1990) *Streetwise: Race, Class, and Change in an Urban Community.* Chicago: University of Chicago.

Appadurai, Arjun (1988) Introduction: Place and Voice in Anthropological Theory. *Cultural Anthropology,* 3(1), 16–20.

Appadurai, Arjun (1991) Global Ethnoscapes: Notes and Queries for a Transnational Anthropology. In R. Fox (ed.) *Recapturing Anthropology* (pp. 191–210). Santa Fe: School of American Research.

Appadurai, Arjun (1996a) *Modernity at Large: Cultural Dimensions of Globalizations.* Minneapolis: University of Minnesota Press.

Appadurai, Arjun (1996b) Sovereignty without Territoriality: Notes for a Postnational Geography. In P. Yeager (ed.) *The Geography of Identity* (pp. 40–58). Ann Arbor: University of Michigan Press.

Ardener, Shirley (1993) Ground Rules and Social Maps for Women: An Introduction. In S. Ardener (ed.) *Women and Space: Ground Rules and Social Maps* (pp. 1–30). Originally published 1981. Oxford: Berg.

Aretxaga, Begoña (1997) *Shattering Silence: Women, Nationalism, and Political Subjectivity in Northern Ireland.* Princeton: Princeton University Press.

Atkinson, Jane M. and Shelly Errington (eds.) (1990) *Power and Difference: Gender in Island Southeast Asia.* Stanford: Stanford University Press.

Augé, Marc (1995) *Non-Places: Introduction to an Anthropology of Supermodernity.* London: Verso.

Bachelard, Gaston (1969) *The Poetics of Space.* Translated by M. Jolas. Boston: Beacon Press. (First published in French in 1957).

Bahloul, Joelle (1996) *The Architecture of Memory.* Cambridge: Cambridge University Press.

Basso, Keith (1988) "Speaking with Names": Language and Landscape among the Western Apache. *Cultural Anthropology,* 3(2), 99–130.

Basso, Keith (1996) Wisdom Sits in Places: Notes on a Western Apache Landscape. In S. Feld and K. Basso (eds.) *Senses of Place* (pp. 53–90). Santa Fe: School of American Research Press.

Bastien, Joseph W. (1985) *The Mountain of the Condor: Metaphor and Ritual in an Andean Ayllu.* Prospect Heights: Waveland Press.

Baudrillard, Jean (1988) *Selected Writings.* M. Poster (ed.). Palo Alto: Stanford University Press.

Baumgartner, M. P. (1988) *The Moral Order of a Suburb.* Oxford: Oxford University Press.

Bender, Barbara (1993) Stonehenge – Contested Landscapes (Medieval to Present Day). In B. Bender (ed.) *Landscape: Politics and Perspectives* (pp. 245–280). Providence: Berg.

Bender, Barbara (1998) *Stonehenge: Making Space.* Oxford: Berg.

Bennett, Tony (1995) *The Birth of the Museum: History, Theory, Politics.* London: Routledge.

Bestard-Camps, Joan (1991) *What's in a Relative? Household and Family in Formentera.* Oxford: Berg.

Bestor, Theodore (1999) Wholesale Sushi: Culture and commodity in Tokyo's Tsukiji Market. In S. M. Low (ed.) *Theorizing the City: The New Urban Anthropology Reader* (pp. 201–244). New Brunswick: Rutgers University Press.

Bestor, Theodore (2001) Supply-side Sushi: Commodity, Market, and the Global City. *American Anthropologist,* 103(1): 76–95.

Birdwell-Pheasant, Donna and Denise Lawrence-Zúñiga (eds.) (1999) *House Life: Space, Place and Family in Europe.* Oxford: Berg.

Blier, Susan Preston (1987) *The Anatomy of Architecture: Ontology and Metaphor in Batammaliba Architectural Expression.* New York: Cambridge University Press.

Black, Annabel (1996) Negotiating the Tourist Gaze: The Example of Malta. In *Coping with Tourists: European Reactions to Mass Tourism,* J. Boissevain (ed.) (pp. 112–142). Providence: Berghahn Books.

Blakeley, Edward and Mary Gail Synder (1997) *Fortress America.* Washington, D. C.: Brookings Institute.

Blunt, Alison and Gillian Rose (1994) Women's Colonial and Postcolonial Geographers. In A. Blunt and G. Rose (eds.) *Writing Women and Space* (pp. 1–14). New York: Guilford Press.

Boissevain, Jeremy (ed.) (1996) *Coping with Tourists: European Reactions to Mass Tourism.* Providence: Berghahn Books.

Bott, Elizabeth (1957) *Family and Social Network: Roles, Norms, and External Relationships in Ordinary Urban Families.* London: Tavistock Publications.

Bourdieu, Pierre (1973) The Kabyle House. In M. Douglas (ed.) *Rules and Meanings* (pp. 98–110). Harmondsworth: Penguin Books.

Bourdieu, Pierre (1977) *Outline of a Theory of Practice.* Cambridge: Cambridge University Press.

Bourdieu, Pierre (1984) *Distinction.* Cambridge: Harvard University Press.

Bourgois, Philippe (1995) *In Search of Respect: Selling Crack in El Barrio.* Cambridge: Cambridge University Press.

Boyer, M. Christine (1994) *The City of Collective Memory.* Cambridge: MIT Press.

Boys, Jos (1998) Beyond Maps and Metaphors. In R. Ainley (ed.) *New Frontiers of Space, Bodies, and Gender* (pp. 203–217). London: Routledge.

Brown, Michael P. (2000) *Closet Space: Geographies of Metaphor from the Body to the Globe*. London: Routledge.

Bruner, Edward (1996) Tourism in Ghana: The Representation of Slavery and the Return of the Black Diaspora. *American Anthropologist*, 98(2), 290–304.

Caldeira, Teresa P. R. (2001) *City of Walls*. Berkeley: University of California Press.

Callaway, Helen (1993) Spatial Domains and Women's Mobility in Yorubaland, Nigeria. In S. Ardener (ed.) *Women and Space: Ground Rules and Social Maps* (pp. 165–182). Originally published 1981. Oxford: Berg.

Carsten, Janet and Stephen Hugh-Jones (1995) Introduction. In J. Carsten and S. Hugh-Jones (eds.) *About the House: Lévi-Strauss and Beyond* (pp. 1–46). Cambridge: Cambridge University Press.

Casey, Edward (1996) How to Get from Space to Place in a Fairly Short Stretch of Time: Phenomenological Prolegomena. In S. Feld and K. Basso (eds.) *Senses of Place* (pp. 13–52). Santa Fe: School of American Research Press.

Castells, Manuel (1983) *The City and the Grassroots*. Berkeley: University of California Press.

Castells, Manuel (1989) *The Informational City: Information, Technology, Economic Restructuring and the Urban-Regional Process*. Oxford: Blackwell.

Castells, Manuel (1996) The Net and the Self: Working Notes for a Critical Theory of the Informational Society. *Critique of Anthropology*, 16(1), 9–38.

Chambers, Iain (1986) *Popular Culture: The Metropolitan Experience*. London: Methuen.

Chambers, Iain (1990) *Border Dialogues: Journeys in Postmodernity*. London: Routledge.

Clifford, James (1992) Travelling Cultures. In L. Grossberg et al. (eds.) *Cultural Studies* (pp. 96–112). London: Routledge.

Collier, Jane F. (2000) Victorian Visions. In A. Lugo and B. Maurer (eds.) *Gender Matters: Rereading Michelle Z. Rosaldo* (pp. 145–159). Ann Arbor: University of Michigan Press.

Cooper, Matthew (1993) Access to the Waterfront: Transformations of Meaning on the Toronto Lakeshore. In R. Rotenberg and G. McDonogh (eds.) *The Cultural Meaning of Urban Space* (pp. 157–171). Westport, CT: Bergin & Garvey.

Copjec, Joan and Michael Sorkin (1999) *Giving Ground: The Politics of Propinquity*. New York: Verso.

Crain, Mary (1996) Contested Territories: The Politics of Touristic Development at the Shrine of El Rocio in Southwestern Andalusia. In J. Boissevain (ed.) *Coping with Tourists: European Reactions to Mass Tourism* (pp. 27–55). Providence: Berghahn Books.

Cresswell, Tim (1997) Imagining the Nomad: Mobility and the Postmodern Primitive. In G. Benko and U. Strohmayer (eds.) *Space and Social Theory* (pp. 360–382). Oxford: Blackwell.

Csordas, Thomas (1994) *Embodiment and Experience*. Cambridge: Cambridge University Press.

Cunningham, Clark E. (1964) Order in the Atoni House. *Bijdragen tot de Taal-, Land-en Volkenkunde* 120, 34–68.

Davis, Mike (1990) *City of Quartz: Excavating the Future in Los Angeles*. London: Verso.

Davis, Mike (1992) Fortress Los Angeles: The Militarization of Urban Space. In M. Sorkin (ed.) *Variation on a Theme Park* (pp. 154–180). New York: Noonday Press.

Davis, Mike (1998) *Ecology of Fear: Los Angeles and the Imagination of Disaster*. New York: Metropolitan Books.

Davis, Susan (1986) *Parades and Power: Street Theatre in Nineteenth Century Philadelphia*. Philadelphia: Temple University Press.

de Certeau, Michel (1984) *The Practices of Everyday Life*. Berkeley: University of California.

DeSoto, Hermine (1996) (Re)Inventing Berlin: Dialectics of Power, Symbols and Pasts, 1990–1995. *City & Society Annual Review* 1996, 29–49.

Deleuze, Gilles and Felix Guattari (1986) *Nomadology: The War Machine.* New York: Semiotext(e).

Dominy, Michele (1995) White Settler Assertions of Native Status. *American Ethnologist,* 22 (2), 358–374.

Dorst, John D. (1989) *The Written Suburb: An American Site, An Ethnographic Dilemma.* Philadelphia: University of Pennsylvania Press.

Dorst, John D. (1999) *Looking West.* Philadelphia: University of Pennsylvania Press.

Douglas, Mary (1970) *Natural Symbols.* Harmondsworth: Penguin.

Douglas, Mary (1971) Do Dogs Laugh? A Cross-cultural Approach to Body Symbolism. *Journal of Psychosomatic Research,* 15, 387–90.

Douglas, Mary (1978) *Cultural Bias.* Occasional Paper No. 34 of the Royal Anthropological Institute of Great Britain and Ireland. London: Royal Anthropological Institute.

Duncan, Nancy (1996) (Re)placings. In N. Duncan (ed.) *BodySpace: Destabilizing Geographies of Gender and Sexuality* (pp. 1–10). London: Routledge.

Duranti, Alessandro (1992) Language and Bodies in Social Space: Samoan Ceremonial Greetings. *American Anthropologist,* 94, 657–691.

Duranti, Alessandro (1997) Indexical Speech Across Samoan Communities. *American Anthropologist,* 99(2), 342–354.

Elder, Glen S. (1998) The South African Body: Space, Race and Heterosexuality. In Herdi Nast and Steve Pile (eds.) *Places Through the Body* pp. 153–164. London: Routledge.

Erikson, Erik H. (1950) *Childhood and Society.* New York: W. W. Norton.

Fainstein, Susan (1994) *City Builders: Property, Politics and Planning in London and New York.* Oxford: Blackwell.

Feld, Steven (1990) *Sound and Sentiment: Birds, Weeping, Poetics and Song in Kaluli Expression.* 2d edn. Philadelphia: University of Pennsylvania Press.

Feld, Steven (1996) Waterfall of Song: An Acoustemology of Place Resounding in Bosavi, Papua New Guinea. In S. Feld and K. Basso (eds.) *Senses of Place* (pp. 91–136). Santa Fe: School of American Research Press.

Feld, Steven and Keith Basso (1996) Introduction. In S. Feld and K. Basso (eds.) *Senses of Place* (pp. 3–12). Santa Fe: School of American Research Press.

Fernandez, James W. (1974) The Mission of Metaphor in Expressive Culture. *Current Anthropology,* 15(2), 119–133.

Fernandez, James W. (1977) *Fang Architectonics.* Working Papers in the Traditional Arts, No. 1. Philadelphia: Institute for the Study of Human Issues.

Fernandez, James W. (1984) Emergence and Convergence in Some African Sacred Places. *Geoscience & Man,* 24, 31–42.

Fernandez, James W. (1988) Andalusia on Our Minds. *Cultural Anthropology,* 3(1), 21–34.

Fjellman, Stephen M. (1992) *Vinyl Leaves: Walt Disney World and America.* Boulder: Westview.

Flusty, Steven (2001) The Banality of Interdiction: Surveillance, Control, and the Displacement of Diversity. *Journal of Urban and Regional Research,* 25(3).

Forbes, Ann (1999) Mapping Power: Disputing Claims to Kipat Lands in Northeastern in Nepal. *American Ethnologist* 26 (1), 114–138.

Foucault, Michel (1975) *Discipline and Punish: The Birth of the Prison.* New York: Vintage.

Foucault, Michel (1984) *Des Espaces Autres. Architecture, Mouvement, Continuité,* October, 46–9.

Foucault, Michel (1986) Of Other Space. *Diacritics,* Spring, 22–27.

Friedl, Ernestine (1967) The Position of Women: Appearance and Reality. *Anthropological Quarterly* 40 (3), 97–108.

Gable, Eric and Richard Handler (1996) After Authenticity at an American Heritage Site. *American Anthropologist*, 98(3), 568–578.

Gaffin, Dennis (1997) Offending and Defending US Rural Place: The Mega-Dump Battle in Western New York. *Human Organization* 56 (3), 275–284.

Gow, Peter (1995) Land, People and Paper in Western Amazonia. In E. Hirsch and M. O'Hanlon (eds.) *The Anthropology of Landscape: Perspectives on Place and Space*, (pp. 31–42). Oxford: Clarendon Press.

Grant, Bruce (2001) New Moscow Monuments, or, States of Innocence. *American Ethnologist*, 28(2), 332–362.

Gray, John (1999) Open Spaces and Dwelling Places: Being at Home on Hill Farms in the Scottish Borders. *American Ethnologist*, 26(2), 440–460.

Greenwood, Davydd (1989) Culture by the Pound: An Anthropological Perspective on Tourism as Cultural Commoditization. In V. Smith (ed.) *Hosts and Guests* (pp. 171–186). Philadelphia: University of Pennsylvania Press.

Gregory, Stephen (1998) *Black Corona: Race and the Politics of Place in an Urban Community*. Princeton: Princeton University Press.

Griaule, Maruel (1954) The Dogon. In Daryll Forde (ed.) *African Worlds* (pp. 83–110). London: Oxford University Press.

Guano, Emauela (2002) Spectacles of Modernity: Transnational Imagination and Local Hegemonies in Neoliberal Buenos Aires. *Cultural Anthropology*, 17(2), 181–209.

Guarnizo, Luis Eduardo and Michael Peter Smith (1998) The Locations of Transnationalism. In L. E. Guarnizo and M. P. Smith (eds.) *Transnationalism From Below. Volume 6, Comparative Urban and Community Research* (pp. 3–34). New Brunswick: Transaction.

Gupta, Akhil (1992) The Song of the Nonaligned World: Transnational Identities and the Reinscription of Space in Late Capitalism. *Cultural Anthropology*, 13(3), 63–79.

Gupta, Akhil and James Ferguson (1992) Beyond "Culture": Space, Identity and the Politics of Difference. *Cultural Anthropology*, 7(1), 6–23.

Halbwachs, Maurice (1980) *The Collective Memory*, trans. F. Ditter and V. Y. Ditter. New York: Harper and Row. (First published in French in 1950.)

Hall, Edward T. (1966) *The Hidden Dimension*. New York: Doubleday.

Hall, Edward T. (1968) Proxemics. *Current Anthropology*, 9(2), 83–95.

Hall, Edward T. (1973) Mental Health Research and Out-of-Awareness Cultural Systems. In L. Nader and T. W. Maretzki (eds.) *Cultural Illness and Health* (pp. 97–103). Washington, D.C.: American Anthropological Association.

Hallowell, A. Irving (1955) *Culture and Experience*. New York: Schocken Books.

Hannah, Matt (1997) Imperfect Panopticism: Envisioning the Construction of Normal Lives. In G. Benko and U. Strohmayer (eds.) *Space and Social Theory* (pp. 344–360). Oxford: Blackwell.

Hannerz, Ulf (1987) The World in Creolisation. *Africa*, 57(4), 546–559.

Hannerz, Ulf (1992) *Cultural Complexity: Studies in the Social Organization of Meaning*. New York: Columbia University Press.

Hannerz, Ulf (1996) *Transnational Connections: Culture, People, Places*. London: Routledge.

Haraway, Donna (1991) *Simians, Cyborgs, and Women: The Reinvention of Nature*. New York: Routledge.

Harvey, David (1985) *Studies in the History and Theory of Capitalist Urbanization, Consciousness and the Urban Experience, Volume I*. Oxford: Basil Blackwell.

Harvey, David (1990) *The Condition of Postmodernity: An Enquiry into the Origins of Cultural Change*. Oxford: Basil Blackwell.

Herzfeld, Michael (1993) *A Place in History: Social and Monumental Time in a Cretan Town*. Princeton: Princeton University Press.

Hirsch, Eric (1995) Introduction. In E. Hirsch and M. O'Hanlon (eds.) *The Anthropology of Landscape: Perspectives on Place and Space*, (pp. 1–30). Oxford: Clarendon Press.

Hirschon, Renee (1989) *Heirs of the Greek Catastrophe: The Social Life of Asia Minor Refugees in Piraeus*. New York: Oxford University Press.

Hirschon, Renee (1993) Essential Objects and the Sacred: Interior and Exterior Space in an Urban Greek Locality. In S. Ardener (ed.) *Women and Space: Ground Rules and Social Maps* (pp. 70–85). Originally published 1981. Oxford: Berg.

Howe, Alyssa Cymene (2001) Queer Pilgrimage: The San Francisco Homeland and Identity Tourism. *Cultural Anthropology*, 16(1), 35–61.

Hugh-Jones, Christine (1979) *From the Milk River: Spatial and Temporal Processes in Northwest Amazon*. Cambridge: Cambridge University Press.

Humphrey, Caroline (1974) Inside a Mongolian Tent. *New Society*, 31, 273–275.

Humphrey, Caroline (1995) Chiefly and Shamanist Landscapes in Mongolia. In E. Hirsch and M. O'Hanlon (eds.) *The Anthropology of Landscape: Perspectives on Place and Space*, (pp. 135–162). Oxford: Clarendon Press.

Hymes, Dell (1968) Letter. *Current Anthropology*, 9(2–3), 100.

Jameson, Frederic (1984) Postmodernism, or the Cultural Logic of Late Capitalism. *New Left Review*, 146, 53–92.

Jameson, Frederic (1991) *Postmodernism, or the Cultural Logic of Late Capitalism*. New York: Verso.

Johnson, Norris Brock (1988) Temple Architecture as Construction of consciousness: A Japanese Temple and Garden. *Architecture and Behavior*, 4(3), 229–250.

Kahn, Miriam (1990) Stone Faced Ancestors: The Spatial Anchoring of Myth in Waimira, Papua New Guinea. *Ethnology*, 29, 51–66.

Kasinitz, Philip (1991) *Caribbean New York*. Ithaca: Cornell University Press.

Kearney, Michael (1991) Borders and Boundaries of State and Self at the End of Empire. *Journal of Historical Sociology*, 4(1), 52–74.

Khazanov, Anatoly (1998) Post-Communist Moscow: Re-Building the "Third Rome" in the Country of Missed Opportunities? *City & Society Annual Review*, 269–314.

King, Anthony (1990) *Urbanism, Colonialism and the World Economy: Culture and Spatial Foundations of the Urban World System*. New York: Routledge.

King, Anthony (1995) Re-presenting World Cities: Cultural Cities in a World System. In P. L. Knox and P. J. Taylor (eds.) *World Cities in a World System* (pp. 215–231). Cambridge: Cambridge University Press.

Kondo, Dorinne (1990) *Crafting Selves: Power, Gender, and Discourses of Identity in a Japanese Workplace*. Chicago: University of Chicago Press.

Kugelmass, Jack (1994) *The Greenwich Village Halloween Parade*. New York: Columbia University Press.

Kugelmass, Jack and Anna Maria Orla-Bukowska (1998) If You Build it They Will Come: Recreating a Jewish District in Post-Communist Krakow. *City & Society Annual Review*, 315–353.

Kuper, Hilda (1972) The Language of Sites in the Politics of Space. *American Anthropologist*, 74, 411–425.

Kuppinger, Petra (1998) The Giza Pyramids: Accommodating Tourism, Leisure and Consumption. *City & Society Annual Review*, 105–120.

Lawrence, Denise (1992) Transcendence of Place: The Role of *La Placeta* In Valencia's *Las Fallas*. In I. Altman and S. Low (eds.) *Place Attachment* (pp. 211–230). New York: Plenum.

Lawrence, Denise and Setha M. Low (1990) The Built Environment and Spatial Form. *Annual Review of Anthropology*, 19, 453–505.

Lawrence-Zúñiga, Denise (In Press) Material Conditions of Family Life, 20th Century. In M. Barbagli and D. Kertzer (eds.) *The History of the European Family*, Volume 3. Yale University Press.

Lea, Vanessa (1995) The Houses of the Megengokre (Kayapo) of Central Brazil – A New Door to their Social Organization. In J. Carsten and S. Hugh-Jones (eds.) *About the House: Lévi-Strauss and Beyond* (pp. 206–225). Cambridge: Cambridge University Press.

Lefebvre, Henri (1991) *The Production of Space*. Oxford: Blackwell.

Lévi-Strauss, Claude (1963) *Structural Anthropology*. New York: Basic Books.

Lewinson, Anne (1998) Reading Modernity in Urban Space: Politics, Geography and the Informal Sector of Dar es Salaam, Tanzania. *City & Society Annual Review*, 205–222.

Lewis, Laura A. (2001) Of Ships and Saints: History, Memory, and Place in the Making of *Moreno* Mexican Identity. *Cultural Anthropology*, 16(1), 62–82.

Liechty, Mark (1996) Kathmandu as Translocality: Multiple Places in a Nepali Space. In P. Yaeger (ed.) *The Geography of Identity* (pp. 98–130). Ann Arbor: University of Michigan.

Löfgren, Orvar (1984) The Sweetness of Home: Class, Culture and Family Life in Sweden. *Ethnologia Europaea* XIV, 44–64.

Löfgren, Orvar (1999) *On Holiday: A History of Vacationing*. Berkeley: University of California Press.

Lovell, Anne M. (1997) "The City is my Mother." Narratives of Schizophrenia and Homelessness. *American Anthropologist*, 99(2), 355–68.

Low, Setha M. (1996a) The Anthropology of Cities: Imaging and Theorizing the City. *Annual Review of Anthropology*, 25, 385–409.

Low, Setha M. (1996b) The Social Production and Social Construction of Public Space. *American Ethnologist*, 23(4), 861–879.

Low, Setha M. (1999) *Theorizing the City: The New Urban Anthropology Reader*. New Brunswick: Rutgers University Press.

Low, Setha M. (2000) *On the Plaza: The Politics of Public Space and Culture*. Austin: University of Texas Press.

Low, Setha M. (2001) The Edge and the Center: Gated Communities and the Discourse of Urban Fear. *American Anthropologist*, 103(1): 45–58.

Lugo, Alejandro and Bill Maurer (2000) The Legacy of Michelle Rosaldo: Politics and Gender in Modern Societies. In A. Lugo and B. Maurer (eds.) *Gender Matters: Rereading Michelle Z. Rosaldo* (pp. 16–34). Ann Arbor: University of Michigan Press.

MacCannell, Dean (1976) *The Tourist: A New Theory of the Leisure Class*. New York: Schocken.

MacCannell, Dean (1992) *Empty Meeting Grounds: The Tourist Papers*. New York: Routledge.

MacCannell, Dean (1999) Neo-Urbanism and its Discontents. In J. Copjec and M. Sorkin (eds.) *Giving Ground* (pp. 106–128). New York: Verso.

Mahmood, Saba (2001) Feminist Theory, Embodiment, and the Docile Agent. *Cultural Anthropology*, 16(2), 202–236.

Malkki, Lisa (1992) National Geographic: The Rooting of Peoples and the Territorialization of National Identity Among Scholars and Refugees. *Cultural Anthropology*, 7(1), 24–44.

Marston, S. A. (1990) Who are "the People"? Gender, Citizenship, and the Making of the American Nation. *Environment and Planning D: Society and Space*, 8, 449–458.

Massey, Doreen (1994) *Space, Place, and Gender*. Minneapolis: University of Minnesota Press.

Mauss, Marcel (1950) *Les Techniques du Corps. Sociologies et Anthropologie*. Paris: Presses Universitaires de France.

Mauss, Marcel (1979) *Sociology and Psychology*. London: Routledge and Kegan Paul.

McDonogh, Gary (1991) Discourses of the City: Policy and Response in Post-Transitional Barcelona. *City Society*, 5(1), 40–63.

McDonogh, Gary (1992) Gender, Bars, and Virtue in Barcelona. *Anthropological Quarterly*, 65, 19–33.

McDonogh, Gary (1993) The Geography of Emptiness. In R. Rotenberg and G. McDonogh (eds.) *The Cultural Meaning of Urban Space* (pp. 3–16). Westport, CT: Bergin & Garvey.

McHugh, Kevin (2000) Inside, Outside, Upside Down, Backward, Forward, Round and Round: A Case for Ethnographic Studies in Migration. *Progress in Human Geography*, 24(1), 71–89.

Merry, Sally (1990) *Getting Justice and Getting Even*. Chicago: University of Chicago Press.

Merry, Sally (1993) Mending Walls and Building Fences: Constructing the Private Neighborhood. *Journal of Legal Pluralism*, 33, 71–90.

Metcalf, Peter (2001) Global "Disjuncture" and the "Sites" of Anthropology. *Cultural Anthropology*, 16(2), 165–185.

Moore, Donald (1998) Subaltern Struggles and the Politics of Place: Remapping Resistance in Zimbabwe's Eastern Highlands. *Cultural Anthropology*, 13(3), 344–381.

Moore, Henrietta (1986) *Space, Text and Gender: An Anthropological Study of the Marakwet of Kenya*. Cambridge: Cambridge University Press.

Morphy, Howard (1995) Landscape and the Reproduction of the Ancestral Past. In E. Hirsch and M.O'Hanlon, (eds.) *The Anthropology of Landscape: Perspectives on Place and Space*, (pp. 184–209). Oxford: Clarendon Press.

Mountz, Alison and Richard A. Wright (1996) Daily Life in the Transnational Migrant Community of San Augustín, Oaxaca, and Poughkeepsie, New York. *Diaspora*, 5(3), 403–428.

Munn, Nancy (1996) Excluded Spaces: The Figure in the Australian Aboriginal Landscape. *Critical Inquiry*, 22, 446–465.

Mukhopadhyay, Carol and Patricia Higgins (1988) Anthropological Studies of Women's Status Revisited: 1977–1987. *Annual Review of Anthropology*, Volume 17. Palo Alto: Annual Reviews.

Munt, Sally R. (1998) Sisters in Exile: The Lesbian Nation. In R. Ainley (ed.) *New Frontiers in Space, Bodies and Gender* (pp. 3–19). London: Routledge.

Myers, Fred (1991) *Pintupi Country, Pintupi Self: Sentiment, Place and Politics among Western Desert Aborigines*. Berkeley: University of California Press.

Odermatt, Peter (1996) A Case of Neglect? The Politics of (Re)presentation: A Sardinian Case. In *Coping with Tourists: European Reactions to Mass Tourism*, J. Boissevain (ed.) (pp. 84–111). Providence: Berghahn Books.

Olwig, Karen Fog and Kirsten Hastrup (1997) *Siting Culture: The Shifting Anthropological Object*. London: Routledge.

O'Neil, John (1985) *Five Bodies: The Shape of Modern Society*. Ithaca: Cornell University Press.

Ong, Aihwa (1990) State Versus Islam: Malay Families, Women's Bodies, and the Body Politic in Malaysia. *American Ethnologist*, 17(2): 258–276.

Ong, Aihwa (1999) *Flexible Citizenship. The Cultural Logics of Transnationality*. Durham: Duke University Press.

Ortner, Sherry (1974) Is Female to Male as Nature Is to Culture? In M. Rosaldo and L. Lamphere (eds.) *Woman, Culture, and Society* (pp. 1–16). Stanford: Stanford University Press.

Pandolfi, Mariella (1990) Boundaries Inside the Body: Women's Sufferings in Southern Peasant Italy. *Culture, Medicine, and Psychiatry*, 14(2), 255–274.

Pandolfo, Stefania (1989) Detours of Life: Space and Bodies in a Moroccan Village. *American Ethnologist*, 16(1), 3–23.

Pandya, Vishvajit (1990) Movement and Space: Andamanese Cartography. *American Ethnologist*, 17(4), 775–97.

Paul, Robert A. (1976) The Sherpa Temple as a Model of the Psyche. *American Ethnologist*, 3(1), 131–46.

Pedregal, Antonio Miguel Nogues (1996) Tourism and Self-Consciousness in a South Spanish Coastal Community. In *Coping with Tourists: European Reactions to Mass Tourism*, J. Boissevain (ed.) (pp. 56–83). Providence: Berghahn Books.

Pred, Allan (1986) *Place, Practice, and Structure: Social and Spatial Transformation in Southern Sweden – 1750–1850*. Totowa, New Jersey: Barnes and Noble.

Rabinow, Paul (1982) *Ordonnance*, Discipline, Regulation: Some Reflections on Urbanism. *Humanities in Society*, 5(3–4), 267–278.

Rabinow, Paul (1989) *French Modern: Norms and Forms of Missionary and Didactic Pathos*. Cambridge: MIT Press.

Richardson, Miles (1982) Being-in-the-Plaza versus Being-in-the-Market: Material Culture and the Construction of Social Reality. *American Ethnologist*, 9, 421–436.

Richardson, Miles (1984) Material Culture and Being-in-Christ in Spanish America and the American South. *Built Form and Culture Conference Proceedings*, October 18–20. Lawrence: University of Kansas.

Rockefeller, Stuart (2002) *Where are you Going? Work, Power and Movement in the Bolivian Andes*. Ph.D. Dissertation. Department of Anthropology, University of Chicago.

Ricoeur, Paul (1991) *From Text to Action: Essays in Hermeneutics II*. Evanston: Northwestern University Press.

Rivera-Bonilla, Ivelisse (1999) Building Community Through Gating: The Case of Gated Communities in San Juan, Puerto Rico. Paper presented at the American Anthropological Association Annual Meeting, Chicago, November.

Rodman, Margaret (1985) Moving Houses: Residential Mobility of Residents in Longana, Vanuatu. *American Anthropologist*, 87, 56–72.

Rodman, Margaret (1992) Empowering Place: Multilocality and Multivocality. *American Anthropologist*, 94(3), 640–656.

Rosaldo, Michelle (1974) Woman, Culture, and Society: A Theoretical Overview. In M. Rosaldo and L. Lamphere (eds.) *Woman, Culture, and Society* (pp. 1–16). Stanford: Stanford University Press.

Rosaldo, Michelle (1980) The Use and Abuse of Anthropology: Reflections on Feminist and Cross-Cultural Understanding. *Signs* 5 (3), 389–416.

Roseman, Marina (1998) Singers of the Landscape: Song, History, and Property Rights in the Malaysian Rain Forest. *American Anthropologist* 100(1), 106–121.

Rotenberg, Robert (1995) *Landscape and Power in Vienna*. Baltimore: Johns Hopkins Press.

Rothstein, Frances Abrahamer and Michael L. Blim (1991) *Anthropology and the Global Factory: Studies of the New Industrialization in the late Twentieth Century*. New York: Bergin and Garvey.

Rouse, Roger (1991) Mexican Migration and the Social Space of Postmodernism. *Diaspora*, 1(1), 8–23.

Ruddick, Susan (1996) *Young and Homeless in Hollywood: Mapping Social Identity*. New York: Routledge.

Rutheiser, Charles (1996) *Imagineering Atlanta: Making Place in the Non-Place Urban Realm*. New York: Verso.

Sassen, Saskia (1991) *The Global City*. Princeton: Princeton University Press.

Sassen, Saskia (1996a) *Losing Control? Sovereignty in an Age of Globalization*. New York: Columbia University Press.

Sassen, Saskia (1996b) Whose City is it? Globalization and the Formation of New Claims. *Public Culture*, 8(2), 205–224.

Sawalha, Aseel (1998) The Reconstruction of Beirut: Local Responses to Globalization. *City & Society Annual Review*, 133–148.

Scheper-Hughes, Nancy and Margaret Lock (1987) The Mindful Body. *Medical Anthropology Quarterly*, 1(1), 6–41.

Schiller, Nina Glick, Linda Basch, and Cristina Blanc-Szanton (1992) *Towards a Transnational Perspective on Migration: Race, Class, Ethnicity and Nationalism Reconsidered.* New York: New York Academy of Sciences.

Sciama, Lidia (1993) The Problem of Privacy in Mediterranean Anthropology. In S. Ardener (ed.) *Women and Space: Ground Rules and Social Maps* (pp. 87–110). Originally published 1981. Oxford: Berg.

Scott, Joan (1996) *Feminism and History.* Oxford: Oxford University Press.

Selwyn, Tom (1995) Landscapes of Liberation and Imprisonment: Towards an Anthropology of the Israeli Landscape. In *The Anthropology of Landscape: Perspectives on Place and Space*, E. Hirsch and M. O'Hanlon (eds.) (pp. 114–134). Oxford: Clarendon Press.

Selwyn, Tom (1996) Introduction. In *The Tourist Image: Myths and Myth Making in Tourism*, T. Selwyn (ed.), (pp. 1–32). Chichester: John Wiley.

Sieber, R. Timothy (1993) Public Access on the Urban Waterfront: A Question of Vision. In R. Rotenberg and G. McDonogh (eds.) *The Cultural Meaning of Urban Space* (pp. 173–193). Westport, CT: Bergin & Garvey.

Smart, Alan (1999) Flexible Accumulation: Across the Hong Kong Border. Petty Capitalists as Pioneers of Globalized Accumulation. *Urban Anthropology*, 28(3–4), 373–406.

Smart, Alan (2000) The Emergence of Local Capitalism in China: Overseas Chinese Investment and Patterns of Development. In S. Li and W. Tang (eds.) *China's Regions, Polity and Economy* (pp. 65–95). Hong Kong: Chinese University Press.

Smith, Neil (1984) *Uneven Development.* Oxford: Blackwell.

Soja, Edward W. (1989) *Postmodern Geographies: The Reassertation of Space in Critical Social Theory.* New York: Verso.

Soja, Edward (1997) Planning in/for Postmodernity. In G. Benko and and U. Strohmayer (eds.) *Space and Social Theory* (pp. 235–249). Oxford: Blackwell.

Stoller, Paul (1996) Spaces, Places, and Fields: The Politics of West African Trading in New York City's Informal Economy. *American Anthropologist*, 98(4), 776–788.

Susser, Ida (2002) *The Castell's Reader on Cities and Social Theory.* Oxford: Blackwell Publishers.

Tambiah, Stanley (1985) *Culture, Thought and Social Action: An Anthropological Perspective.* Cambridge, MA: Harvard University Press.

Tsing, Anna Lowenhaupt (1993) *In the Realm of the Diamond Queen.* Princeton: Princeton University Press.

Tucker, Erica (1998) Renaming Capital Street: Competing Visions of the Past in Post-Communist Warsaw. *City & Society Annual Review*, 223–244.

Tucker, Hazel (1997) The Ideal Village; Interactions through Tourism in Central Anatolia. In *Tourists and Tourism: Identifying with People and Places*, S. Abram, J. Waldern and D. Macleod (eds.) (pp. 91–106). Oxford: Berg.

Turner, Bryan S. (1984) *The Body and Society.* Oxford: Basil Blackwell.

Turner, Terence (1980) The Social Skin. In J. Cherfas and R. Lewin (eds.) *Not Work Alone* (pp. 112–40). London: Temple Smith.

Turner, Terence (1995) Social Body and Embodied Subject: Bodiliness, Subjectivity, and Sociality Among the Kayapo. *Cultural Anthropology*, 10(2), 143–170.

Urry, John (1990) *The Tourist Gaze: Leisure and Travel in Contemporary Societies.* London: Sage Publications.

Wacquant, Löic J. D. (1994) The New Urban Color Line: The State and Fate of the Ghetto in Postfordist America. In C. Calhoun (ed.) *Social Theory and the Politics of Identity* (pp. 231–276). Oxford: Blackwell.

Waterson, Alisse (1993) *Street Addicts in the Political Economy.* Philadelphia: Temple University Press.

Waterson, Roxanna (1990) *The Living House: An Anthropology of Architecture in South-East Asia.* New York: Whitney Library of Design.

Waterson, Roxanna (1995) Houses and Hierarchies in Island Southeast Asia. In J. Carsten and S. Hugh-Jones (eds.) *About the House: Lévi-Strauss and Beyond* (pp. 47–68). Cambridge: Cambridge University Press.

Weiner, James (1991) *The Empty Place: Poetry, Space and Being among the Foi of Papua New Guinea.* Bloomington: University of Indiana Press.

Werbner, Pnina (1996) Stamping the Earth with the Name of Allah. *Cultural Anthropology*, 11(3), 309–338.

Whittaker, Elvi (1994) Public Discourse on Sacredness: The Transfer of Ayers Rock to Aboriginal Ownership. *American Ethnologist*, 21(2), 310–334.

Williams, Raymond (1961) *The Long Revolution.* New York: Columbia University Press.

Wright, Susan (1993) Place and Face: Of Women in Doshman Ziari, Iran. In S. Ardener (ed.) *Women and Space: Ground Rules and Social Maps* (pp. 135–155). Originally published 1981. Oxford: Berg.

Wolf, Eric (1982) *Europe and the People Without History.* Berkeley: University of California Press.

Yeager, Patricia (1996) Narrating Space. In P. Yeager (ed.) *The Geography of Identity* (pp. 1–39). Ann Arbor: University of Michigan Press.

Young, Michael and Peter Willmott (1957) *Family and Kinship in East London.* London: Routledge and Kegan Paul.

Zonabend, Francoise (1984) *The Enduring Memory: Time and History in a French Village.* Manchester: Manchester University Press.

Zukin, Sharon (1995) *The Cultures of Cities.* Oxford: Blackwell.

Part I

Embodied Spaces

Our first section addresses the fundamental role of the human body in the definition and creation of space, and the development of spatial experience and consciousness. Embodied space is presented as a model for understanding the creation of place through the body's spatial orientation and movement, and its action in language. *Proxemics*, Edward T. Hall's study of people's use of space as an aspect of culture, proposes that individuals are surrounded by a bubble of personal space the size of which varies according to social relationship and setting. People use this distancing mechanism to regulate interaction and engage in nonverbal communication. Miles Richardson employs the body as the ground for understanding perceptual processes of "being-in-the-world" in his phenomenological analysis of distinct public spaces of market and plaza in Costa Rica. Combining elements of both to understand the individualized experience of space, Nancy Munn proposes the "mobile spatial field" to account for a culturally defined, corporeal-sensual field extending from the body at each locale, but also moving across locales. She uses this concept to explain how Australian Aborigines individually make detours to avoid encounters with dangerous topographic centers of ancestral power. Finding linguistic analysis no less spatial, Alessandro Duranti investigates the interpenetration of language, body movement, lived space, and distant homelands among Western Samoans living in southern California. His analysis suggests that their use of language and body movement establishes a particular Samoan social and cultural space in a transnational setting.

Further References

Duranti, Alessandro (1992) Language and Bodies in Social Space: Samoan Ceremonial Greetings. *American Anthropologist*, 94, 657–691.
Pandolfi, Mariella (1990) Boundaries Inside the Body: Women's Sufferings in Southern Peasant Italy. *Culture, Medicine, and Psychiatry*, 14(2), 255–274.

Pandolfo, Stefania (1989) Detours of Life: Space and Bodies in a Moroccan Village. *American Ethnologist*, 16(1), 3–23.
Paul, Robert A. (1976) The Sherpa Temple as a Model of the Psyche. *American Ethnologist*, 3(1), 131–46.

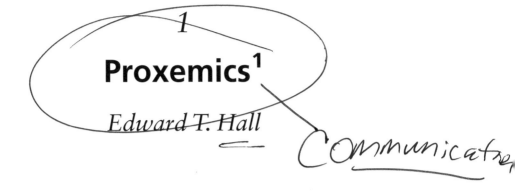

1

Proxemics[1]

Edward T. Hall

Western man has conceptualized space in many ways, ranging from Bogardus' (1933, 1959) social space and Sorokin's (1943) sociocultural space to Lewin's (1948) topologies. Chapple and Coon (1942) and Hallowell (1955) treated distance technically when they described how it is measured in different cultures.[2] Jammer (1960) has dealt with the concepts of space (including their historical underpinnings) in physics. Proxemics,[3] the study of man's perception and use of space, pertains to none of these directly. It is much closer, instead, to the behavioral complex of activities and their derivatives known to the ethologists as territoriality. It deals primarily with out-of-awareness distance-setting,[4] and owes much to the work of Sapir (1927) and Whorf (1956).

Because of my communications bias, the subjects of proxemic research have generally been members of my own culture. Like Bateson (1948), I have learned to depend more on what people do than on what they say in response to a direct question, to pay close attention to that which cannot be consciously manipulated, and to look for patterns rather than content (Hall 1966). However, except in a few exceptional instances, I have never been able to be really certain of the correctness of my own interpretations of observed behavior in other cultures. In interpreting the actions of people in other cultures, the only thing about which I am reasonably certain is my own fleeting responses. Working in a detailed way on the micro-cultural level (Hall 1966:96) and only where it was possible to detect responses on the affective, as well as the behavioral, level has motivated me to concentrate on my own culture as it has been revealed against the contrasting backdrop of other cultures. In this sense, I am in agreement with Lévi-Strauss (1966b) when he speaks of the anthropology of the future as a science in which people study themselves. My approach has been to use myself and others as measuring devices (or "controls," if you like) at those times when we have been subjected to contrasting cultural environments. This last is important, for one can be no more than vaguely aware of one's own culture in the absence of face-to-face encounters with people of other cultures.[5]

I first became aware of my own interest in man's use of space when I was training Americans for service overseas and discovered that the way in which both time and space were handled constituted a form of communication which was responded to as if it were built into people and, therefore, universally valid. In 1963a, I wrote:

> ... Americans overseas were confronted with a variety of difficulties because of cultural differences in the handling of space. People stood "too close" during conversations, and when the Americans backed away to a comfortable conversational distance, this was taken to mean that Americans were cold, aloof, withdrawn, and disinterested in the people of the country.[6] U.S.A. housewives muttered about "waste-space" in houses in the Middle East. In England, Americans who were used to neighborliness were hurt when they discovered that their neighbors were no more accessible or friendly than other people, and in Latin America, exsuburbanites, accustomed to unfenced yards, found that the high walls there made them feel "shut out." Even in Germany, where so many of my countrymen felt at home, radically different patterns in the use of space led to unexpected tensions.

It was quite obvious that these apparently inconsequential differences in spatial behavior resulted in significant misunderstanding and intensified culture shock, often to the point of illness, for some members of the American overseas colonies. Examination of the very strong and deep responses to spatial cues on the part of overseas Americans highlighted many of the patterns implicit in the United States. These observations directed my thinking to Whorf. As I have stated elsewhere (1966):

> ... only to a handful of people have the implications of Whorf's thinking become apparent. Difficult to grasp, they become somewhat frightening when given careful thought. They strike at the root of the doctrine of "free will," because they indicate that all men are captives of the language they speak.[7]

It is my thesis that the principles laid down by Whorf and his followers in relation to language apply to all culturally patterned behavior, but particularly to those aspects of culture which are most often taken for granted and operate as Sapir (1927) so aptly put it "... in accordance with an elaborate and secret code that is written nowhere, known by none, and understood by all."[8] It is this elaborate and secret code that becomes confused with what is popularly conceived of as phenomenological experience. It has long been believed that experience is what men share and that it is possible to bypass language by referring back to experience in order to reach another human being. This implicit (and often explicit) belief concerning man's relation to experience is based on the assumption that when two human beings are subjected to the same "experience," virtually the same data are being fed to the two nervous systems and the two brains respond similarly. *Proxemic research casts serious doubts on the validity of this assumption, particularly when the cultures are different.* People from different cultures inhabit different sensory worlds (see Hall 1966: chaps. 10, 11). They not only structure spaces differently, but experience it differently, because the sensorium is differently "programmed."[9] There is a selective screening or filtering that admits some types of data while rejecting others. Sometimes this is accomplished by individuals "tuning out" one or more of the senses or a portion of perception. Otherwise, it is accomplished by screening, which is one of the many important functions performed by architecture.

If the spatial experience is different by virtue of different patterning of the senses and selective attention and inattention to specific aspects of the environment, it would follow that *what crowds one people does not necessarily crowd another.* Therefore, there can be no universal index of crowding, no known way of measuring crowding for all cultures. Instead, what one must ask is, "Are the people involved being stressed, and, if so, to what degree, and what senses are involved?" To answer questions such as these requires specialists from many disciplines, including pathology, biochemistry, experimental psychology, and kinesics.[10] The work of Gibson (1950) on perception and of Kilpatrick and others (1961) in transactional psychology have provided useful leads.

In 1953, Trager and I postulated a theory of culture based on a linguistic model.[11] We maintained that with the model we were using, it must be possible ultimately to link major cultural systems (of which there were several) to the physiology of the organism; i.e., that there should be not only a prelinguistic base (Trager 1949) but a precultural base as well. In 1959, I suggested the term "infra-culture" be used to designate those behavioral manifestations "that preceded culture but later became elaborated into culture." It followed from this that it might be helpful in the analysis of a primary cultural system, such as proxemics, to examine its infra-cultural base. A look at the various manifestations of territoriality (and these are many) should help provide both a foundation and a perspective to be used in considering more complex human elaborations of space.

Much can be learned in this regard from the ethologists.[12] It is difficult to consider man with other animals, yet, in the light of what is known of ethology, it may be appropriate to consider man as an organism that has elaborated and specialized his *extensions*[13] to the point where they are rapidly replacing nature. In other words, man has created a new dimension, the cultural dimension, in relations to which he maintains a state of dynamic equilibrium. This process is one in which both man and his environment participate in molding each other. Man is now in the position of creating his own biotope. He is, therefore, in the position of determining *what kind of organism* he will be. This is a frightening thought in view of how little we know about man and his needs. It also means that in a very deep sense, man is creating different types of people in his slums, his mental hospitals, his cities, and his suburbs. What is more, the problems man is facing in trying to create one world are much more complex than was formerly assumed. Within the United States we have discovered that one group's slum is another's sensorily enriched environment (Fried and Gleicher 1961, Gans 1960, Abrams 1965).

Hediger's unique work in zoology and animal behavior is particularly important to proxemics. He has devoted himself to the study of what occurs when men and animals interact in the wild, in zoos, and in circuses as well as in experimental situations. Hediger has demonstrated the very point that anthropologists would hope to make for man, namely that if one is to interact realistically with any organism, it is essential to gain a basic mastery of that organism's communications systems. Hediger is deeply committed to the position that the most common error in interpreting animal behavior is anthropomorphizing or interpreting the animals' communications as though they were human. His studies of the domestication process not only underline the necessity of thoroughly understanding the sensory symbolic world of a species (how it marks its territory, for example, or the components that go to make up its biotope), but also stress the importance of knowing the specific way in which the species handles distance beyond strictly territorial considerations (Hediger 1950, 1955, 1961). For example, the reduction or elimination of the flight reaction is essential for the survival of an organism in captivity. In addition, it provides us with an operational definition of domestication. Hediger distinguished between contract and non-contract species,[14] and he was the first to describe in operational terms personal and social distances. He has also demonstrated that critical distance is so precise that it can be measured in centimeters.[15]

Schäfer (1956) has written about both "critical space" and "critical situations." While he has stressed the danger of drawing analogies from non-human forms, his descriptions of social and group responses to crowding and his formulation of the concepts of the "critical densities" and "crises" are not only highly suggestive for man but appear to involve processes that embrace an extraordinarily broad spectrum of living substance.

Recent studies of spacing among animals reveal that one of the primary functions of proper spacing is to permit the completion of what Tinbergen (1952, 1958) terms "action chains." Tinbergen has demonstrated that the life of the stickleback and other species is made up of predictable behavioral sequences according to set paradigms. If a sequence is broken or interrupted, it is necessary to start over again from the beginning.[16] Both animals and man, according to Spitz (1964), require, at critical stages in life, specific amounts of space in order to act out the dialogues that lead to the consummation of most of the important acts in life.

The findings of ethologists and animal psychologists suggest that: (*a*) each organism inhabits its own subjective world,[17] which is a function of its perceptual apparatus, and the *arbitrary separation of the organism from that world alters context and in so doing distorts meaning;*[18] and (*b*) the dividing line between the organism's internal and external environment cannot be pinpointed precisely.[19] The organism-biotope relationship can only be understood if it is seen as a delicately balanced series of cybernetic mechanisms in which positive and negative feedback exert subtle but continuous control over life. *That is, the organism and its biotope constitute a single, cohesive system* (within a series of larger systems). To consider one without reference to the other is meaningless.

Two further ethological studies draw attention to the connection between territoriality and population control.[20] Christian's (1960) classic study of the James Island Sika deer advances the thesis that populations are controlled by physiological mechanisms that respond to density. In a summary made at a symposium on crowding, stress, and natural selection (Christian, Flyger, and Davis 1961), it was stated that:

> Mortality evidently resulted from shock following severe metabolic disturbance, probably as a result of prolonged adrenocortical hyperactivity, judging from the histological material. There was no evidence of infection, starvation, or other obvious cause to explain the mass mortality.

Christian's study is only one of a number of similar studies of population collapse[21] due to stress from sensory overload (crowding).[22]

Calhoun's experiments and observations are also noteworthy for their behavioral data.[23] He allowed wild Norways rats, which were amply fed, to breed freely in a quarter-acre pen. Their number stabilized at 150 and never exceeded 200 (Calhoun 1950). With a population of 150, fighting became so disruptive to normal maternal care that only a few of the young survived. The rats did not distribute themselves evenly throughout the pen, but organized into a dozen colonies averaging 12 rats each (apparently the maximum number of rats that can live harmoniously in a natural group).

The disorders of Calhoun's overcrowded rats bear a striking resemblance to those of some contemporary Americans who live in densely packed urban conditions. Although comparative studies of humans are rare, Chombart de Lauwe (1959a, b) has gathered data on French workers' families and has demonstrated a statistical relationship between crowded living conditions and physical and social pathology. In the United States a health survey of Manhattan (Srole et al. 1962) showed that only 18% of a representative sample were free of emotional disorders while 23% were seriously disturbed or incapacitated.

Research Methods and Strategies

In the Foreword to Jammer's book *Concepts of Space*, Einstein has summarized many of the methodological problems in proxemics:

> The eyes of the scientist are directed upon those phenomena which are accessible to observation, upon their appreciation and conceptual formulation. In the attempt to achieve a conceptual formulation of the confusingly immense body of observational data, the scientist makes use of a whole arsenal of concepts which he imbibed practically with his mother's milk; and seldom if ever is he aware of the eternally problematic character of his concepts. He uses this conceptual material, or, speaking more exactly, these conceptual tools of thought, as something obviously, immutably given; something having an objective value of truth which is hardly ever, and in any case not seriously, to be doubted.

In my study of proxemics, one of my objectives has been to examine a small slice of life in the United States – the experience of space – and to learn about some of the things Americans take for granted. My emphasis has not been on either the manifest or even the latent *content* but rather on the structural details, the implicit perceptual elements.

Most individuals, try as they will, can specify few if any of the elements that enter into perception.[24] They can only describe the end product. Thus, the student of proxemics is faced with the problem of developing techniques to isolate and identify the elements of space perception. What he aims to achieve is a sense-data equivalent of the morphophonemic structure of language or the chemist's periodic table of the elements. His data should be verifiable and the elements capable of being combined with predictable results. Where does one look for procedural models when exploring a new field? Descriptive linguistics, faced with similar problems, has provided methods applicable to proxemics.

sounds Diff for diff language

Since the days of the Sanskrit grammarians, linguists have recognized that *Language is a system* with structure and regularity. All writing systems are abstracted from the building blocks or sounds of the language represented. These are identifiable and finite in number. The way to isolate them is to obtain spoken texts as raw data and then to record the details of speech as precisely as possible, using a notation system that is based on identifiable physiological processes so that any trained observer can make the same transcriptions. In linguistics, the physiological structure points of the system have been worked out. These structure points were *not* known for proxemics when I began may research. It was clear, however, that in the perception of space, something more than the visual system was involved. The questions then became: What other systems? and, How do we know that they have been correctly indentified?

Collection methods

During the early stages of my research, I used a wide range of methods and techniques for identifying the elements of space perception – not just because proxemics appeared to involve many different types of variables, but on the theory that what I learned in one way could be used to check what I learned in other ways. Some of the research techniques, briefly described below, are: observation, experiment, interviews (structured and unstructured), analysis of the English lexicon, and the study of space as it is recreated in literature and in art.

Observation

By observing people over a long period of time as they use and react to space, one can begin to discern definite patterns of proxemics behavior. While photography is only a supplement to other forms of observation – an extension of the visual memory, as it were – it is an absolutely indispensable aid in recording proxemic behavior. It freezes actions and allows the investigator to examine sequences over and over again. The difficulty is to photograph people without intruding or altering their behavior. Practice in using a very small camera (Minox), which I carry with me at all times, has taught me how to photograph unobtrusively, and this has made it possible to use larger cameras as well.[25] Several thousand photographs have thus far been taken of people interacting under natural conditions in the United States, France, England, Italy, Greece, and Switzerland. These photographs have provided data against which visual observations can be checked.

The camera and the photographs it produces are extraordinarily subtle and complex tools (see Collier 1967, Byers 1966, Worth 1966). For proxemics, the camera has served as a record and reminder system and a training aid for students. It has also been very useful in investigating how subjects structure their particular perceptual worlds. One of my assistants, a German, illustrated this point when asked to take an "intimate" photograph followed by a "public" photograph of a female subject. I had expected distortion in the intimate shot and great detail in the public shot. Not at all. The intimate portrait was crisp and clear and the public shot deliberately out of focus "... because you aren't really supposed to look at people in public" (or photograph them, either).

In our recent investigations of proxemic behavior of various ethnic groups in the United States, my students and I have discovered that it is essential to use a member of the group we are studying as the photographer. Not only does the photographer constantly interact with his subjects (Byers 1966), but what he selects to photograph represents culture-bound choice. Photographer subjects have provided valuable insights on a number of points at which the groups involved were at odds. They also have noted serious omissions from photographic texts taken by others (not of their own group). For example, in photographing lower-class Negro, Puerto Rican, and Spanish-American subjects, our goal was to discover the specific ways in which these ethnic groups code and organize their senses in face-to-face encounters. (My experience in intercultural relations had taught me that differences in the proxemic behavior lead to what Goffman [1961] calls "alienation in encounters.") In the beginning, one of my assistants (a German photographer) photographed lower-class American Negro subjects interacting with each other. Later these sub-jects were shown slides and 8 × 10 inch prints of themselves and were asked what was happening in the photographs. They were rarely able to tell us. However, when one of the Negro subjects was given the control of a motorized drive camera and told to push the button whenever *he* saw something happening, he took frame after frame of what I, as a white, middle-class American, considered identical pictures. Interviews with the Negro photographer and the subjects demonstrated that they were acting out and recording a highly structured dialogue in which the cues were more subtle than, and quite different from, those used by the white, middle class population. It would appear that in this particular lower-class Negro group, a great deal of information is communicated by very small movements of the hands and fingers. These movements were almost imperceptible to my students and me.[26]

In addition to direct observation and photographs, another source of data is the unself-conscious comment people make as a result of some breach of spatial eti-quette. Such comments often help identify the structure points in the proxemic system under study. Examples that occur frequently are statements like these:

> I wish he would stop breathing down my neck. I can't stand that!
> Have you noticed how she is always *touching* you? She can't seem to keep her hands to herself.
> He was so close his face was all distorted.

Physical contact between people, breathing on people or directing one's breath away from people, direct eye contact or averting one's gaze, placing one's face so close to another that visual accommodation is not possible, are all examples of the kind of proxemic behavior that may be perfectly correct in one culture and absolutely taboo in another.

Experimental abstract situations

It is possible to learn a good deal about how members of a given culture structure space at various levels of abstraction by setting up simple situations in which they manipulate objects.[27] I used coins and pencils and asked my subjects to arrange them so that they were "close" and "far apart" and "side by side" and "next to each other" and then to tell me whether two objects were "together" or not. Arab subjects were unable or unwilling to make a judgment as to whether two objects were close together or not *if the surrounding area was not specified*. In other words, Arabs saw the objects *in a context*; Americans saw the objects only *in relation to each other*.

Structured interviews

My wife and I interviewed both American and foreign subjects in depth, following a detailed interview schedule. The shortest interviews took six hours; the longest lasted six months and was still producing data when that phase of the work was terminated. In the course of these studies, it became apparent that, although the answers of different subjects to any particular question might vary, the interview schedule as a whole could teach us much about how the subjects structured and experienced space. Conclusions could be drawn from the way in which the questions were answered and from the difficulties encountered in understanding particular questions.

The protocol for the interviews began with a general question concerning the home and household, and the activities and named areas contained in the house. The home was chosen as a starting point not only because everyone has one, but also because it had been our experience that subjects can usually talk about the concrete features of the home even when they find it difficult or inappropriate to talk about other topics. Once the home picture had been recorded along with drawings and diagrams, the same material was covered in a different way by exploring such topics as privacy, boundaries, the rights of propinquity, and the place of the particular home in its social and geographic setting. Furniture arrangements in home and office provided added data on social relationships, and so did linguistic features such as words or concepts that were difficult to translate. Altogether, some 90 topics were covered.

One of the most valuable features of our protocol was that it was sufficiently culture-bound to cause foreign subjects to raise questions that revealed not only the structures of their own proxemic systems but the taken-for-granted aspects of our system as well. "Where do you go to be alone?" – a normal question for Americans – puzzled and sometimes angered Arabs. Some representative Arab replies are, "Who wants to be alone?" "Where do you go to be crazy?" "Paradise without people is Hell." Trespassing is thought of in the United States as a universally recognizable violation of the mores, yet our interviews failed to turn up anything even approaching this concept among urban Arabs. The actual structure of the interview proved to be a valuable research instrument. The point is both subtle and important. By following a standard protocol, then, we were conducting research simultaneously on two different levels: level A was the manifest content, Answers to Questions; and level B (the more important and basic) was the contrast in structure of two cultural systems, one being used in context to elicit the other. The most valuable sessions turned out to be those in which foreign subjects took issue with our spatial categories.

One section of our questionnaire dealt with listening behavior[28] and was designed to elicit information on where subjects looked at the person being addressed for feedback. This proved to be one of the most productive sections of our questionnaire. What emerged from interviews with foreign subjects was not a direct answer to the questions but a series of complaints that Americans never listen or complaints about what Americans communicate by the *way* in which they listen. Arabs said we are ashamed all the time. What made them think so? The fact that we withhold our breath and direct it away from the other person. Latin American subjects complained that Americans never listened or were always breaking off, a conclusion they drew from the fact that our eyes wander. The information that we sought by this line of inquiry concerned the type of perceptual involvement of the two subjects.

Analysis of the lexicon

I have long maintained (Hall and Trager 1953, Hall 1959) that *culture* is basically a communicative process. This process occurs simultaneously on many levels, some of them more explicit than others. Language is one of the explicit levels. Boas (1911) was the first anthropologist to emphasize the relationship between language and culture. He made his point in the simplest, most obvious way by analyzing lexicons of languages. Whorf (1956) went beyond Boas and suggested that language plays a prominent role in molding the perceptual world of a culture. He states,

> We dissect nature along lines laid down by our natural languages. The categories and types that we isolate from the world of phenomena we do not find there....

Whorf observed that in Hopi, time and space are inextricably bound up in each other; to alter one is to change the other. He says,

> The Hopi thought world has no imaginary space....In other words, the Hopi cannot, as speakers of Indo-European languages do, "imagine" such a place as Heaven or Hell. Furthermore "hollow" spaces like room, chamber, hall are not really *named* objects but are rather located....

[handwritten marginal note: Hopi connection time & space]

Sapir's and Whorf's influence, extended far beyond the confines of descriptive linguistics, caused me to review the lexicon of the pocket Oxford Dictionary and to extract from it all the terms having spatial connotations such as: "over," "under," "away from," "together," "next to," "beside," "adjacent," "congruent," "level," "upright." Altogether, some 20% of this dictionary, or approximately 5,000 lexical items, were recorded.[29]

Interpretation of art

Paralleling Whorf's thinking about language, the transactional psychologists have demonstrated that perception is not passive but is learned and in fact highly patterned. It is a true transaction in which the world and the perceiver both participate. A painting or print must therefore conform to the Weltanschauung of the culture to which it is directed and to the perceptual patterns of the artist at the time he is creating. Artists know that perception is a transaction; in fact, they take it for granted.

The artist is both a sensitive observer and a communicator. How well he succeeds depends in part on the degree to which he has been able to analyze and organize perceptual data in ways that are meaningful to his audience. The manner in which sense impressions are employed by the artist reveals data about both the artist *and* his audience.

Gideon (1962), Dorner (1958), and Grosser (1951) have contributed to the specific understanding of the way European man has developed his perceptual organization through the ages.[30] For example, Grosser comments that the portrait is distinguished from any other kind of painting by a psychological nearness which "... depends directly on the actual interval – the distance in feet and inches between the model and painter." He sets this distance at four to eight feet and notes that it creates the characteristic "quality" of a portrait, "the peculiar sort of communication, almost a conversation, that the person who looks at the picture is able to hold with the person painted there." Grosser's discussion of the difficulties of foreshortening and of the distortions that occur when the painter or perceiver gets too close to his subject closely parallels my subjects' descriptions of their perception of others when they are "too close."

The distinction made by Gibson (1950) between the *visual field* (the image cast on the retina) and the *visual world* (the stable image created in the mind) is essential to the comprehension of the differences in the work of two artists like Hobbema and Rembrandt. Hobbema depicted the visual world perceived in the same way a scene outside a window is perceived, as a summary of hundreds, if not thousands, of visual fields. Rembrandt, in contrast, painted visual fields.[31] In effect, he made static the scene which is generally perceived in an instant.

The principal difficulty in using art as cultural data is to distinguish between the artist's technique (which alone reveals the building blocks of his creation) and his subject matter, which may be designed to be persuasive and is often controversial[32] because tastes in art differ. Despite such complexities, the data are sufficiently rich to warrant any effort that is required.

Analysis of literature

An examination of the writer's sense impressions reveals much about his perceptual world. If a writer refers to vision to build his images it is possible to examine these images to determine what kind of vision he uses. Is it foveal, macular, or peripheral vision? Which of Gibson's numerous ways of seeing perspective does he employ? What is the role of olfaction and touch?

Writers express what readers already know and would have expressed if they had possessed the requisite analytic capability, training and skills. When the writer succeeds, there is a close register between his descriptions and his reader's own sensory pattern, since writers evoke spatial images in the reader. The question I asked myself was: "What clues does the writer provide the reader that enable him to construct a spatial image?" It seemed to me that an analysis of passages that are spatially evocative would be revealing. I asked subjects to mark such passages in a sample of over a hundred representative novels. The first texts used were those which contained spatial images that subjects vividly recalled from past reading. This group of passages, elicited from those who had spontaneously commented on them, ultimately proved to be of the most value.

As in painting, the representation of space in literature changes over time, and appears to reflect rather accurately growing awareness of the nature as well as the proxemic patterns of the culture. McLuhan (1963) notes, for example, that the first reference to three-dimensional visual perspective in literature occurs in *King Lear*, when Edgar seeks to persuade the blinded Duke of Gloucester that they indeed stand atop the cliffs of Dover. Thoreau's *Walden* is replete with spatial images. Referring to his small cabin and its influence on his conversation, he writes:

> ...our sentences wanted *room* to unfold and form their columns in the interval. *Individuals*, like nations, *must have* suitable broad and natural *boundaries, even a neutral ground* between them...If we are merely loquacious and loud talkers, then we can afford to stand very near together, *cheek to jowl, and feel each other's breath*; but if we speak reservedly and thoughtfully we want to be farther apart, *that all animal heat and moisture* may have a chance to evaporate (italics mine).

Mark Twain was fascinated with spatial imagery and its distortion. He set out to create impossible spatial paradoxes in which the reader "sees" intimate details at incredible distances, or experiences spaces so vast that the mind boggles at comprehending them. Most of Mark Twain's distances are visual and auditory. Kafka, in *The Trial*, emphasizes the body and the role of kinesthetic distance perception. The vitality of St. Exupery's images is in his use of kinesthetic, tactile, olfactory, and auditory perceptions.

Concepts and Measures

Three categories of space

It has proved helpful in proxemic research to be able to refer to the degree to which cultures treat proxemic features as fixed, semi-fixed, or dynamic (Hall 1963a, 1966). In general, walls and territorial boundaries are treated as fixed features. However, territory may be a seasonal affair, as it is with the migrating Bedouin of Syria, and therefore, territory is sometimes classified as semi-fixed or dynamic. Furniture can be either fixed or semi-fixed. Interpersonal distance is usually treated informally[33] and is dynamic for most peoples of North European origin. These distinctions are important in intercultural encounters. If one person treats as moveable that which is considered fixed by someone else, it causes real anxiety. For example, a German subject (an immigrant to the United States), who treated furniture as fixed, had bolted to the floor the chair on which visitors sat in his office. This caused great consternation among American visitors. One of my Chinese subjects informed me that in China a visitor would not dream of adjusting the furniture to conform to his unwritten definition of an interaction distance unless specifically instructed to do so by his host. American students in my classes, who cover a wide spectrum of ethnic, class, and regional cultures within the United States, have been evenly divided between those who adjust the furniture to conform to an informal norm and those who do not.

Sociopetal and sociofugal space

Another type of observation to be made by proxemic fieldworkers is whether the space is organized so that it is conducive to communication between people (socio-petal) or whether it is organized to produce solitarity (socio*fugal*) (Osmond 1957). What is sociofugal to one culture or subculture may be sociopetal to another. An Arab colleague has noted, for instance, that his small, paneled recreation room was "sehr-gemüttlich" or "cozy" to German friends but had just the opposite effect on Arabs, who found it oppressive.

The relationship of the spoken language to proxemics

The content of conversation is linked to distance and situation as well as to the relationship of the participants, their emotions, and their activity. Joos (1962) relates linguistic analysis to distance and situation in a manner applicable to a proxemic frame of reference. His five styles – intimate, casual, consultative, formal, and frozen – can be equated roughly with the intimate, personal, social-consultative, and public zones of United States proxemic patterns. The fact that Joos treats language as a *transaction* (introducing feedback) rather than as a one-way process makes his conceptual model especially applicable to proxemics. His work is also relevant in that it introduces the situational dialect (Hall 1960b).[34]

Hockett (1958) has defined communication as any event that triggers another organism. (This definition would include the environment, although it is not clear that Hockett intended this.) Originally, he listed seven design features for language:

1. duality (units or *cenemes* that build up)
2. interchangeability ("A" can play "B's" part, and vice-versa)
3. displacement (in time or space)
4. specialization (the attachment of specific meanings to specific things)
5. arbitrariness (there is no necessary connection between the event and the symbol)
6. productivity (novel forms can be created)
7. cultural transmission (as contrasted with genetic transmission)

Later, Hockett (1960) expanded the list to 13 in an effort to sharpen or clarify his definition of language. In the process he cleared up some problems while creating others. Hockett's concept of the design features represents a breakthrough in our understanding of communication. As a culturally elaborated form of communication, proxemics satisfies all of Hockett's seven original design features, even productivity (the architect or designer striving to create new forms). In general, the evolutionary studies of language as outlined by Hockett and the infra-cultural basis for proxemics seem to parallel each other. There are some points of departure. Displacement in time and space of an incipient but recognizable form occurs with territorial marking at the level of mammals. When ungulates are frightened by a panther they release an olfactory sign from the gland in their hoofs that warns others of their kind traveling the same trail later that there is danger in the bush. By presenting us with a well-laid-out scheme that compares communication systems across species and genera lines, Hockett not only has provided a series of specific points held up to the mirror of life but also has related them in a particular way. His points should be taken not as absolutes but as positions on a continuum. As an *absolute*, for instance, total feedback does not exist, because the speaker only hears and is aware of *part* of what he is saying. Duality of patterning, the "small arrangements of a relatively very small stock of distinguishable sounds which are in themselves wholly meaningless," would, by the substitution of a single word ("information" for "sounds"), prove to be a characteristic of all life beginning with RNA and DNA and ending with communicative forms that are present but have yet to be technically analyzed. It is with language, then, that we complete the circle, beginning and ending with species other than man.

No known universal distance-setting mechanism

Observations, interviews, analysis of art and literature, all point to the fact that there is *no* fixed distance-sensing mechanism (or mechanisms) in man that is universal for all cultures. One of the complexities of proxemic research is the fact that not only are people unable to describe how they set distances, but each ethnic group sets distances in its own way. In fact, their measuring rods are different. Some of the perceived distances expand and shrink according to circumstances. *Interpersonal distance is a constellation of sensory inputs that is coded in a particular way.* For instance, middle-class American subjects of North European extraction set many of their interpersonal distances visually (Hall 1964a, b, 1966).[35] This is accomplished to some extent by signals received from muscular feedback in the eyes, gauged by the point at which the subject begins to feel cross-eyed or has difficulty focusing, etc. Additional visual references used are the size of the retinal image, perceived detail, and peripheral movement. The visual interaction of Arabs is intense; they are directly and totally involved. The Arab stares; the American does not. The Arab's olfactory sense is actively involved in establishing and maintaining contact. Arabs tend to stay inside the olfactory bubble of their interlocutor, whereas Americans try to stay outside of it.

All the senses are ultimately involved in setting distance and bear the same relation to proxemics as the vocal apparatus (teeth, tongue, hard and soft palate, and vocal cords) does to phonetics. If man is thought of as being in a constant transaction with his environment, sometimes actively, sometimes passively, it can be seen that *selective screening* is as necessary as *patterned stimulation* of the senses. It is no wonder then that one of our subjects, a German professor, found even the solid architecture of early 20th century America unsatisfactory to him because it failed to screen out enough sound when he was working in his study. As a contrast in sensory needs, Fried and Gleicher (1961) and Fried (1963) found that West End Bostonians of Italian descent required great auditory involvement, and it is my interpretation that part of their shock at being relocated away from the Boston West Side to more modern buildings was due to an unfamiliar and uncongenial sensory mix. They felt shut off from people. American middle-class subjects working in Latin America miss *visual* involvement with their neighbors and feel shut out by the adobe walls that make every Latin-American home a private affair. Frenchmen, accustomed to a wide assortment of pungent odors as they move along city streets, may suffer a form of sensory deprivation in the American urban setting with its uniform acrid smell.

Elsewhere (1963b), I have described a notation system based on eight different dimensions or scales for the senses (1) postural-sex; (2) sociofugal-sociopetal; (3) kinesthetic; (4) touch; (5) retinal; (6) thermal; (7) olfactory; (8) voice loudness. This system enables the fieldworker to focus his attention on specific behavioral segments that will ultimately enable him to distinguish between the behavior of one group and that of another.

> ... in spite of their *apparent* complexity, cultural systems are so organized that their context can be learned and controlled by all normal members of the group... The anthropologist knows that what he is looking for are patterned distinctions that transcend individual differences and are closely integrated into the social matrix in which they occur.

[...]   *Social matrix*

Areas to be Investigated

comparative relative

Research in proxemics underscores what anthropologists know, that what is taken for granted in one culture may not even exist in another. It is therefore impossible to make up a universal list of questions for revealing the structure of proxemic systems. Our experience with the extensive protocol referred to earlier was that it was at best only a culturally biased sounding board. Although great pains had been taken to make the protocol as culture-free as possible, this turned out to be impossible. The following list of problems for proxemic research will also reflect the biases of its originator's culture, not only in its organization but also in its content.

1. How many kinds of distance do people maintain? (It would be useful to know the total range of human behavior in this respect.)
2. How are these distances differentiated?
3. What relationships, activities, and emotions are associated with each distance?
4. In general, what can be classified as fixed feature, semi-fixed feature, and dynamic space?
5. What is sociofugal and what is sociopetal?
6. Boundaries:
    a. How are boundaries conceived?
    b. How permanent are they?
    c. What constitutes a violation of a boundary?
    d. How are boundaries marked?
    e. When and how do you know you are inside a boundary?
7. Is there a hierarchy of spaces from, for example, most intimate and most sacred to most public?
8. Related to both (1) and (7), is there a hierarchy of distances between people? Who is permitted in each, and under what circumstances?
9. Who is permitted to touch, and under what circumstances?

10. Are there taboos against touching, looking, listening, and smelling? To whom do they apply?

11. What screening needs are there? For what senses and which relationships?

12. What is the nature of the sensory involvement for the different relationships in the normal course of everyday life?

13. What specific spatial needs are there?

14. What are the spatial references in the lexicon?

15. Is there a special handling of space between superordinates and subordinates?

NOTES

1   The research reported on in this paper was supported by the National Institute of Mental Health and the Wenner-Gren Foundation for Anthropological Research.

2   Hallowell's introduction to his chapter 9 (Cultural Factors in Spatial Orientation) is particularly relevant to space perception.

3   In the course of the development of proxemics, the work was spoken of as "social space as bio-communication," and "micro-space in interpersonal encounters." These were actually abbreviated technical descriptions in which the proper meanings of the terms of reference were known only to a few specialists. Further, the widespread interest in activities connected with outer space provided an incentive to distinguish between my work and that of the outer-space scientists. I decided to invent a new term that would indicate, in general, what the field was about. Among the terms I considered were human topology, chaology, the study of empty space, oriology, the study of boundaries, chorology, the study of organized space. I finally chose "proxemics" as the most suitable for that audience most likely to encounter the topic in the near future.

4   The following quote (Hall 1963) speaks to the matter of levels of awareness: "Any culture characteristically produces a simultaneous array of patterned behavior on several different levels of awareness. It is therefore important to specify which levels of awareness one is describing . . . .

"Unlike much of the traditional subject matter of anthropological observation, proxemic patterns, once learned, are maintained largely out of conscious awareness and thus have to be investigated without resort to probing the conscious minds of one's subjects. Direct questioning will yield few if any significant variables, as it will with such topics as kinship and house type. In proxemics one is dealing with phenomena akin to tone of voice, or even stress and pitch in the English language. Since these are built into the language, they are hard for the speaker to consciously manipulate."

Also see Hall (1959: chap. 4) for a more complete statement concerning levels of awareness relating to change.

5   The problem of self-awareness has been a stumbling-block for psychologists for years. We really do not know by what means the brain interprets the data fed to it by the senses. Recently there has been some progress in solving this problem. The solution appears to hinge on *contrasts* built into the receptors rather than simple stimulation leading to a specific response (McCulloch 1964).

6   One can never be sure initially of the true significance of this sort of behavior. One learns with time to pay attention to casual remarks engendered by the original response. Instead of saying that a particular American was cool, aloof, or distant, an Arab subject remarked: "What's the matter? Does he think I *smell* bad?" In this instance, the reference to olfaction provided an important clue to Arab distance-setting mechanisms.

7   By stressing the importance of Whorf's observations, I do not mean to imply that there is
     no external reality to be discovered, nor do I think that Whorf believed this. The reality
     can remain constant, but what different organisms perceive is determined largely by
     "what they intend to do about it," in the words of a colleague.
8   By "all" one assumes that Sapir meant the members of a given ethnic community.
9   The precise methods can only be surmised by which the young are taught to selectively
     attend to some things while disregarding others and to favor one sense channel while
     suppressing another. It is reasonable to assume, however, that culture provides a pattern,
     among other things, for a rather elaborate and extraordinarily detailed, but less con-
     trived, Skinnerian (1953) reinforcement schedule in which individual reinforcements are
     of such short duration that they are not ordinarily isolated out of the context in which
     they occur. The work of Condon (1967) and others has demonstrated the extraordinary
     degree to which people are capable of responding to each other and coordinating their
     behavior during conversations. Frame-by-frame examination of movies taken at 24 and
     48 frames per second and study of simultaneous electroencephalograms reveals organ-
     ized, coherent, synchronous behavior that is not normally observable without the aid of
     high-speed cameras. One can put forth the suggestion, in these terms, that positive and
     negative reinforcement can and does occur subliminally.
10   The relationship of proxemics to kinesics (Birdwhistell 1952, Hayes 1964, and Condon
     1967) has been treated elsewhere (Hall 1963b). Basically, and in the simplest possible
     terms, proxemics is not primarily concerned with the observation and recording of the
     details of gestures and body movements. Proxemics deals with architecture, furniture,
     and the use of space, whereas kinesics, at present, is only indirectly concerned with the
     setting. Proxemic notation is simpler than that employed in kinesics. Proxemics seeks to
     determine the how of distance-setting (a question of epistemology). It is important for the
     proxemicist to know as much as possible about the physiology of the eye, and the many
     other ways in which man perceives distance.
11   A version of this original series of postulates was published in 1959.
12   Margaret Mead (1961) has also suggested that anthropologists have much to gain from
     the study of the works of ethologists.
13   The term "extension" summarizes a process in which evolution accelerates when it occurs
     outside the body (see Hall 1959, 1966).
14   McBride does not entirely agree with Hediger's basic distinction and, instead, holds that
     there are times when animals may be contact and other times when they may not. A three-
     way friendly polemic by mail between McBride, Hediger, and me has resolved many of
     McBride's objections. It now appears that, like dominance in genetics, contact/non-
     contact behavior is a matter of degree and situation.
15   For a description of these distances, see Hall (1966).
16   The territorial concept is complex, representing a wide variety of behavior patterns.
     Carpenter (1958), for example, lists 32 functions associated with territoriality. In the
     context in which I am using the term at present, what is important is that *the sensory
     paradigms are not broken or interfered with.*
17   Lissman (1963) has the following to say on this subject: "Study of the ingenious adapta-
     tions displayed in the anatomy, physiology, and behavior of animals leads to the familiar
     conclusion that each has evolved to suit life in its particular corner of the world. Each
     animal also inhabits a private subjective world that is not accessible to direct observation.
     This world is made up of information communicated to the creature from the outside in
     the form of messages picked up by its sense organs."
18   Social scientists trained in the North European tradition are familiar with the trap laid by
     a dichotomizing of language and culture. Some of the time we make our observations in
     context, but often we do not. Most, if not all, of Berelson and Steiner's (1964) "findings"

separate the organism, including man, from the matrix of life both conceptually and operationally. Their interpretation of Lewin's (1935) adopted version of Zeigarnik's (1927) study is seen in terms of *drive* rather than of *social* acts. It remained for Spitz (1964) to place Zeigarnik's work in context again. Berelson and Steiner's chapter on culture is particularly fragmented. The work of the transactional psychologists is most conspicuous for its absence from their work. One is left with the impression that for many Americans one does not really "know" something *except when it is out of context*. At the risk of stating the obvious, I wish to underscore what appears to be a growing consensus among ethologists and ecologists that the organism and its environment are so inextricably intertwined that to consider either as separate is an artifact of our own particular way of looking at things.

19 See "The Biochemistry of Crowding and Exocrinology," in Hall (1966).
20 Other studies that have contributed to the formation of my thinking are: Allee (1958); Bonner (1963); Calhoun (1962a; b); Christian (1963); Christian and Davis (1964); Christian, Flyger, and Davis (1961); Deevey (1960); Eibl-Eibesfeldt (1961); Errington (1956, 1957, 1961); Frake (1960); Gilliard (1960, 1963); Goffman (1959); Hediger (1950, 1955); Hinde and Tinbergen (1958); Howard (1920); Lévi-Strauss (1966a); Lissman (1963); Lorenz (1964); McBride (1964); McCulloch (1948); McCulloch and Pitts (1947); Parks and Bruce (1961); Portmann (1959); Rosenblith (1961); Schäfer (1956); Selye (1956); Snyder (1961); Sullivan (1947); Tinbergen (1952, 1958); and Wynne-Edwards (1962).
21 Notable among these is the work of Paul Errington (1956, 1957, 1961). His studies of muskrats and their behavioral responses to the stress from crowding are most revealing. He states that *muskrats share with men* the propensity for growing savage under stress from crowding (italics mine).
22 See my 1966 summary of Christian's work.
23 It is impossible to do justice to Calhoun in any summary. The full implication of this thinking is comprehended only when virtually everything he has written has been mastered. To understand properly his experiments conducted under laboratory conditions, for example, one must be conversant with his earlier studies conducted in the open in a natural setting.
24 Subjects included English, French, German, Swiss, Dutch, Spanish, Arab, Armenian, Greek, South Asian, Indian, Japanese, and West Africans.
25 For the past three years, a motorized drive, 250-exposure bulk film 35 mm Nikon has been used. The 35 mm negative enlarges well and provides excellent detail at low cost, and the camera is somewhat less bulky than a high-quality 16 mm movie camera. The half-frame 35 mm camera has also proved to be a very convenient, compact instrument. So far, the 8 mm and super-8 movie cameras have not provided either the quality or the slow speeds essential for this work.
26 The research referred to is currently under way and will appear in a handbook of procedures and methods in proxemic research.
27 Little (1965, 1967) has established that the correlation between the way a subject perceives two other people, two silhouettes, two dolls, or two cylinders of wood is such that for all practical purposes they are interchangeable. One must observe, however, that in all these contexts, the subject is judging spatial relations *as an outsider* and not *as a participant*.
28 It long has been taken for granted that the signal, sign, or message is what the social scientist concentrates on when doing communications research. I observed some years ago that much of the slippage in intercultural communication occurs because the speaker cannot tell whether the person he is addressing is listening or not (Hall 1964b).

29   It goes without saying that unless the anthropologist is thoroughly conversant with the language as it relates to the rest of the culture, the use of the lexicon as an analytic tool is not possible. In this regard, I have received invaluable aid from my colleague Moukhtar Ani, who has devoted years to the preparation of an Arab-English dictionary. Ani's immersion in the lexicons of the two languages has made it possible for him to deal explicitly with contrasts that would not otherwise be so obvious.

30   Western art is analyzable according to the perspective categories identified by Gibson (1950). Linear perspective is only one of a great many different ways in which objects are seen in depth.

31   Like all great artists, Rembrandt painted in depth, communicating on many different levels. In some of his pictures, there are two or more visual fields, so that the eye jumps from one to the other. He undoubtedly was ahead of his time, and he certainly violated the art mores. His recording of the *instant* of perception appears to be extraordinarily accurate (for those of us who learned to see in the European tradition). It is only recently that popular culture has begun to catch up with him.

32   It is important to emphasize that the procedures used in this series of studies were not concerned with that level of analysis that deals with art styles or subject matter or content in the conventional sense. Both stylistic and content analyses represent valid points of entry into an analysis of art, but they are more suitable to intrasystemic analysis than to the comparison of *two or more different systems*.

33   The term informal, as used here, refers to one of three levels of culture. The other two levels are formal and technical. The formal level of culture is that which is integrated into the entire culture; everyone knows it and takes it for granted. The informal level is made up of those imprecise attitudes that are situational; the technical level is the fully explicated and analyzed activity (see Hall 1959).

34   The term "situational dialect" refers to the different forms of language that are used in and are characteristic of specific *situations*, such as officialese, the language of the marketplace, and the specialized dialects of different occupational, professional, and subclass groups. Mastery of the situational dialect marks the individual as a member of the group. The term situational dialect was originally suggested to me by Edmund S. Glenn in a conversation in 1960. To my knowledge no adequate inventory of the situational dialects of any language exists. Such an inventory would provide an easy measure of relative social complexity of a given culture. Leach (1966) refers to the different "brands" of English embodying "social categories" in such a way as to indicate that he is referring to situational dialects. Lantis' (1960) article also pertains to the situational dialect.

35   They are not exclusively visual, but they do have a visual bias.

REFERENCES

Abrams, Charles. 1965. *The city is the frontier*. New York: Harper & Row.

Allee, Warder C. 1958. *The social life of animals*. Boston: Beacon Press.

Argyle, M. and J. Dean. 1965. Eye-contact, distance, and affiliation. *Sociometry* 28: 289–304.

Auden, W. H. 1965. *About the house*. New York: Random House.

Bain, A. D. 1949. Dominance in the Great Tit, Parus Major. *Scottish Naturalist* 61: 369–472.

Barry, Herbert, III. 1957. Relationships between child training and the pictorial arts. *Journal of Abnormal and Social Psychology* 54:380–83.

Bateson, Gregory. 1948. "Sex and culture," in *Personal character and cultural milieu*, pp. 94–107. Ann Arbor: Edwards Brothers.

Berelson, Bernard, and Gary A. Steiner. 1964. *Human behavior*. New York: Harcourt, Brace & World.

Birdwhistell, Raymond L. 1952. *Introduction to kinesics*. Louisville: University of Louisville Press.

Black, Max. 1962. *Models and metaphors: Studies in language and philosophy*. Ithaca: Cornell University Press.

Bloomfield, Leonard. 1933. *Language*. New York: H. Holt.

Boas, Franz. 1911. "Introduction," in *Handbook of American Indian Languages*. Bureau of American Ethnology Bulletin 40.

Bolinger, Dwight L. 1961. *Generality, gradience, and the all-or-none*. The Hague: Mouton.

Bonner, John T. 1963. How slime molds communicate. *Scientific American* 209(2): 84–86.

Burke, Kenneth. 1966. "The thinking of the body," in *Language as symbolic action*, pp. 308–43. Berkeley and Los Angeles: University of California Press.

Byers, Paul. 1966. Cameras don't take pictures. *Columbia University Forum* 9.

Calhoun, John B. 1950. The study of wild animals under controlled conditions. *Annals of the New York Academy of Sciences* 51:113–22.

——.1962a. "A behavioral sink," in *Roots of behavior*. Edited by Eugene L. Bliss, pp. 295–316. New York: Harper & Brothers.

——.1962b. Population density and social pathology. *Scientific American* 206: 139–46.

Carpenter, C. R. 1958. "Territoriality: A review of concepts and problems," in *Behavior and evolution*. Edited by A. Roe and G. G. Simpson, pp. 224–50. New Haven: Yale University Press.

Carpenter, Edmund, Frederick Varley, and Robert Flaherty. 1959. *Eskimo*. Toronto: University of Toronto Press.

Chombart de Lauwe, Paul. 1959a. *Famille et habitation*. Paris: Editions du Centre National de la Recherche Scientifique.

——.1959b. Le milieu et l'étude sociologique de cas individuels. *Informations Sociales* 2:41–54.

Chomsky, Noam. 1957. *Syntactic Structures*. The Hague: Mouton & Co.

——.1959. Review of: *Verbal behavior*, by B. F. Skinner. *Language* 35:26–56.

——.1965. *Aspects of the theory of syntax*. Cambridge: M.I.T. Press.

Christian, John J. 1960. Factors in mass mortality of a herd of Sika deer (*Cervus nippon*). *Chesapeake Science* 1:79–95.

——.1963. The pathology of overpopulation. *Military Medicine* 128:571–603.

Christian, John J., Vagh Flyger, and David E. Davis. 1961. Phenomena associated with population density. *Proceedings of the National Academy of Science* 47:428–49.

Christian, John J., and David E. Davis. 1964. Social and endocrine factors are integrated in the regulation of growth of mammalian populations. *Science* 146:1550–60.

Collier, John, Jr. 1967. Holt, Rinehart, & Winston. In press.

Condon, W. S., 1967. A segmentation of behavior. MS.

Condon, W. S., and W. D. Ogston. 1966. Sound film analysis of normal and pathological behavior patterns. *The Journal of Nervous and Mental Disease* 143(4):338–47.

Deevey, Edward S. 1960. The hare and the haruspex: A cautionary tale. *Yale Review*, Winter.

Diebold, A. R., Jr. 1967. "Anthropology and the comparative psychology of communicative behavior," in *Animal communication: Techniques of study and results of research*. Edited by T. A. Sebeok. Bloomington: Indiana University Press. In press.

Dorner, Alexander. 1958. *The way beyond art*. New York: New York University Press.

Eibl-Eibesfeldt, I. 1961. The fighting behavior of animals. *Scientific American* 205(6):112–22.

Errington, Paul. 1956. Factors limiting higher vertebrate populations. *Science* 124:304–7.

——.1957. *Of men and marshes*. New York: The Macmillan Company.

——.1961. *Muskrats and marsh management*. Harrisburg: Stackpole Company.

Fischer, J. L. 1961. Art styles as cultural cognitive maps. *American Anthropologist* 63:79–93.

Frake, Charles O. 1960. "Family and kinship in Eastern Subanun," in *Social structure in Southeast Asia*. Edited by G. P. Murdock, pp. 51–64. Viking Fund Publications in Anthropology no. 29.

Fried, Marc. 1963. "Grieving for a lost home," in *The urban condition*. Edited by Leonard J. Duhl. New York: Basic Books.

Fried, Marc, and Peggy Gleicher. 1961. Some sources of residential satisfaction in an urban slum. *Journal of the American Institute of Planners* 27:305–15.

Gans, Herbert. 1960. *The urban villagers*, Cambridge: The M.I.T. Press and Harvard University Press.

Gerbner, George. 1966. On defining communication: still another view. *The Journal of Communication* 16:99–103.

Gibson, James J. 1950. *The perception of the visual world*. Boston: Houghton Mifflin.

Gibson, J. J. and A. D. Pick. 1963. Perception of another person's looking behavior. *American Journal of Psychology* 76:386–94.

Gidion, Sigfried. 1962. *The eternal present: The beginnings of architecture*, Vol. II. New York: Bollingen Foundation, Pantheon Books.

Gilliard, E. Thomas. 1962. On the breeding behavior of the Cock-of-the-Rock (Aves. *Rupicola rupicola*). *Bulletin of the American Museum of Natural History* 124:31–68.

——.1963. Evolution of bowerbirds. *Scientific American* 209(2):38–46.

Gleason, H. A., Jr. 1965. *Linguistics and English grammar*. New York: Holt, Rinehart, and Winston.

Goffman, Erving. 1959. *The presentation of self in everyday life*. New York: Doubleday.

——.1961. *Encounters*. Indianapolis: Bobbs-Merrill.

Goodenough, Ward H. 1963. *Cooperation in change*. New York: Russell Sage Foundation.

Grosser, Maurice. 1951. *The painter's eye*. New York: Rinehart.

Hall, Edward T. 1955. The anthropology of manners. *Scientific American* 192:85–89.

——.1956. "A microcultural analysis of time." *Proceedings of the Fifth International Congress of Anthropological and Ethnological Sciences, Philadelphia, Sept. 1-9, 1956*, pp. 118–22.

——.1959. *The silent language*. Garden City: Doubleday.

——.1960a. The madding crowd. *Landscape*, Autumn, pp. 26–29.

——.1960b. *ICA participant English language requirement guide, part 1*. Washington, D.C.

——.1963a. "Proxemics – The study of man's spatial relations and boundaries," in *Man's image in medicine and anthropology*, pp. 422–45. New York: International Universities Press.

——.1963b. A system for the notation of proxemic behavior. *American Anthropologist* 65:1003–26.

——.1964a. "Adumbration in intercultural communication," in *The ethnography of communication*. Edited by American Anthropologist 66(6), part 2:154–63.

——.1964b. "Silent assumptions in social communication," in *Disorders of communication* XLII. Edited by Rioch and Weinstein, pp. 41–55. Baltimore. Research Publications Association for Research in Nervous and Mental Disease.

——.1966. *The hidden dimension*. New York: Doubleday.

Hall, Edward T., and George L. Trager. 1953. *The analysis of culture*. Washington, D.C.: American Council of Learned Societies.

Hall, Edward T., and William F. Whyte. 1960. Inter-cultural communication. *Human Organization* 19(1):5–12.

Halliday, M. A. K., Angus Mcintosh and Peter Strevens. 1964. *The linguistic sciences and language teaching*. London: Longmans.

Hallowell, A. Irving. 1955. "Cultural factors in spatial orientation," in *Culture and experience*, pp. 184–202. Philadelphia: University of Pennsylvania Press.

Harris, Zellig. 1951. *Structural linguistics*. Chicago: University of Chicago Press.

Hayes, Alfred S. 1964. "Paralinguistics and kinesics: Pedagogical perspectives," in *Approaches to semiotics*. Edited by T. H. Sebeok and A. S. Hayes. The Hague: Mouton.

Hediger, H. 1950. *Wild animals in captivity*. London: Butterworth.

——.1955. *Studies of the psychology and behavior of captive animals in zoos and circuses*. London: Butterworth.

——.1961. "The evolution of territorial behavior," in *Social life of Early Man*. Edited by S. L. Washburn, pp. 34–57. Viking Fund Publications in Anthropology no. 31.

Hellersberg, Elizabeth F. 1950. *Adaptation to reality of our culture*. Springfield: C. C. Thomas.

——.1966. Spatial structures and images in Japan, a key to culture understanding. MS.

Hinde, R. A., and Niko Tinbergen. 1958. "The comparative study of species-specific behavior," in *Behavior and evolution*. Edited by A. Roe and G. G. Simpson, pp. 251–68. New Haven: Yale University Press.

Hockett, Charles F. 1958. *A course in modern linguistics*. New York: Macmillan.

——.1960. The origin of speech. *Scientific American* 203:338–96.

Howard, H. E. 1920. *Territory in bird life*. London: Murray.

Hymes, Dell. 1964. "Introduction: Toward ethnographies of communication," in *The ethnography of communication*. Edited by John Gumperz and Dell Hymes, pp. 1–34. Washington, D.C.: American Anthropological Association.

——.1966. "Two types of linguistic relativity," in *Sociolinguistics*. Edited by William Bright, pp. 114–58. The Hague: Mouton.

——.1967a. "The anthropology of communication," in *Human communication theory*. Edited by Frank X. W. Dance, pp. 139. New York: Holt, Rinehart, and Winston.

——.1967b. "On communicative competence," in *Research planning conference on language development in disadvantaged children*, pp. 1–16. New York: Yeshiva University.

Jammer, Max. 1960. *Concepts of space*. New York: Harper.

Joos, Martin. 1962. The five clocks. *International Journal of American Linguistics* 28(2): Part V.

Keesing, Felix M., and Marie M. Keesing. 1956. *Elite communication in Samoa: A study of leadership*. Stanford Anthropological Series no. 3.

Keiter, Friedrich. 1966. *Verhaltensbiologie des Menschen auf kulturanthropologischer Grundlage*. München-Basel.

Kilpatrick, Franklin P. Editor. 1961. *Explorations in transactional psychology*. New York: New York University Press.

La Barre, W. 1964. "Paralinguistics, kinesics, and cultural anthropology," in *Approaches to semiotics*. Edited by T. A. Sebeok, A. S. Hayes, and M. C. Bateson, pp. 191–220. The Hague: Mouton.

Lantis, Margaret. 1960. Vernacular culture. *American Anthropologist* 62:202–16.

Leach, Edmund R. 1965. Cultural and social cohesion: An anthropologist's view. *Daedalus*, Winter, pp. 24–38.

Lévi-Strauss, Claude. 1966a. The scope of anthropology. *Current Anthropology* 7:112–23.

——.1966b. Anthropology: Its achievements and future. *Current Anthropology* 7:124–27.

Lissman, H. W. 1963. Electric location by fishes. *Scientific American* 208(3):50–59.

Little, Kenneth B. 1965. Personal space. *Journal of Experimental Social Psychology* 1:237–47.

——.1967. Value congruence and interaction distances. *Journal of Social Psychology*. In press.

Lorenz, Konrad. 1963. *On Aggression*. New York: Harcourt, Brace & World.

——.1964. *Das sogenannte Bose; zur naturgeschichte der Agression* (the biology of aggression). Vienna: Dr. G. Borotha Schoeler.

Lynd, Robert S. 1948. *Knowledge for what?* Princeton: Princeton University Press.

McBride, Glen. 1964. *A general theory of social organization and behavior.* St. Lucia, Australia: University of Queensland Press.

McClellan, James E. 1966. Skinner's philosophy of human nature. *Studies in Philosophy and Education* 4:307–32.

McCulloch, Warren S. 1948. Teleological mechanisms. *Annals of the New York Academy of Sciences* 50:259–77.

——.1964. "Reliable systems using unreliable units," in *Disorders of Communication* XLII. Edited by Rioch and Weinstein, Baltimore: Research Publications Association for Research in Nervous and Mental Disease.

McCulloch, Warren S., and Walter Pitts. 1947. How we know universals; the perception of auditory and visual forms. *Bulletin of Mathematical Biophysics* 9:127–47.

McHarg, Ian. 1963 "Man and his environment," in *The urban condition.* Edited by Leonard J. Duhl. New York: Basic Books.

McLuhan, Marshall. 1963. *The Gutenburg galaxy.* Toronto: University of Toronto. Press.

——.1964. *Understanding Media.* New York: McGraw-Hill.

Mead, Margaret. 1961. Anthropology among the sciences. *American Anthropologist* 63:475–82.

Murdock, G. P. 1957. World ethnographic sample. *American Anthropologist* 59:664–87.

Osmond, Humphrey. 1957. Function as the basis of psychiatric ward design. *Mental Hospitals* (Architectural Supplement) April, pp. 23–29.

Parkes, A. S., and H. M. Bruce. 1961. Olfactory stimuli in mammalian reproduction. *Science* 134:1049–54.

Portmann, Adolf. 1959. *Animal camouflage.* Ann Arbor: University of Michigan Press.

Reusch, Jurgen. 1961. *Therapeutic communication.* New York: Mouton.

Roe, Anne, and George G. Simpson. Editors. 1958. *Behavior and evolution.* New Haven: Yale University Press.

Rosenblith, Walter A. 1961. *Sensory communication.* New York: The M.I.T. Press and John Wiley & Sons.

Sapir, Edward. 1929. The status of linguistics as a science. *Language* 5:207–214.

——.1931. Conceptual categories in primitive languages. *Science* 74(578).

——.1938. Why cultural anthropology needs the psychiatrist. *Psychiatry* 1:7–12.

——.1949. Selected writings of Edward Sapir in *Language, culture, and personality.* Edited by David Mandelbaum. Berkeley: University of California Press.

Schäfer, Wilhelm. 1956. *Der kritische raum und die kritische situation in der tierischen sozietät.* Frankfurt: Krämer.

Schlesinger, Arthur M., Jr. 1965. *A thousand days.* Boston: Houghton Mifflin.

Sebeok, T. A. 1963. Review of: *Porpoises and sonar,* by Winthrop N. Kellogg (Chicago: University of Chicago Press, 1961) and *Communication among social bees,* by Martin Lindauer (Cambridge: Harvard University Press, 1961). *Language* 39:448–66.

Selye, Hans. 1956. *The stress of life.* New York: McGraw-Hill.

Snyder, Robert. 1961. Evolution and integration of mechanisms that regulate population growth. *National Academy of Sciences* 47:449–55.

Spitz, René A. 1964. The derailment of dialogue. Stimulus overload, action cycles, and the completion gradient. *Journal of the American Psychoanalytic Association* 12:752–75.

Srole, Leo, et al. 1962. *Mental health in the metropolis: The Midtown Manhattan Study.* Thomas A. C. Rennie Series in Social Psychiatry. New York: McGraw-Hill.

Sullivan, Harry Stack. 1947. *Conceptions of modern psychiatry.* Washington: William Alanson White Psychiatric Foundation.

Thiel, Philip. 1961. A sequence-experience notation for architectural and urban space. *Town Planning Review,* April, pp. 33–52.

Tinbergen, Niko. 1952. The curious behavior of the Stickleback. *Scientific American* 187(6):22–26.

——.1958. *Curious naturalists*. New York: Basic Books.

Trager, G. L. 1963. *Linguistics is linguistics*. Studies in Linguistics: Occasional Papers, no. 10.

Uexküll, J. von. 1926. *Theoretical biology*. New York: Harcourt, Brace.

Wallace, Anthony F. C. 1961. *Culture and personality*. New York: Random House.

Watson, Michael, and Theodore Graves. 1966. An analysis of proxemic behavior. *American Anthropologist* 68:971–85.

Whorf, Benjamin Lee. 1956. *Language, thought, and reality*. New York: The Technology Press and John Wiley & Sons.

Wynne-Edwards, V. C. 1962. *Animal dispersion in relation to social behavior*. New York: Hafner.

2

Being-in-the-Market Versus Being-in-the-Plaza: Material Culture and the Construction of Social Reality in Spanish America

Miles Richardson

Being human, as every anthropologist surely knows, is to be an extraordinarily complicated, and even contradictory, creature. In one mode of being, we appear to be focused directly on the business at hand and to be unconsciously absorbed in responding to the actions of others; we seem to experience the world around us as a thing given, as a matter of fact. In another mode of being human, we appear to be detached from the tasks at hand and to be self-conscious in our responses to others; we seem to experience the world as a thing fashioned, as a matter of fiction.

This ability to shift modes of being poses critical questions about the relationship between our existence and the world in which we exist. The very fact that we are capable of such dramatic shifts suggests that there is a symbiotic interdependence between the two modes, an interdependence aptly described by Heidegger (1962) as being-in-the-world

As a single, unitary phenomenon, being-in-the-world means that for us to be we must have a *world* to be in. We cannot otherwise exist. Yet "world" is not an external thing, existing apart from our actions and awaiting our entrance; but it is dependent upon our *being in*. Through our actions, our *inter*actions, we bring about the world in which we then are; we create so that we may be, in our creations.

In this article I examine the phenomenon of being-in-the-world in the ethnographic context of Spanish America. Spanish America, however, is far too abstract a thing for a flesh-and-blood human to be in; thus, to examine being-in-the-world of Spanish America we have to look at concrete places where Spanish Americans are in process of being.

Two such places ideally suited for this purpose are the market and the plaza. They are common throughout the region, they lend themselves to ethnographic investigation, and, most importantly, they exhibit the two modes of being-in-the-world alluded to earlier: in the market, a factlike world is constructed; in the plaza, a more aesthetic one emerges. How is this accomplished? How do people transform simply being there physically to being in two distinct worlds? The answers would seem to lie in what differentiates the two places, that is, their material culture. That being the case, we need to consider the nature of material culture and its relationship to the process of world building.[1]

We may begin by noting that several social scientists, writing from an interpretive, interactionist perspective, argue that the world-building, or culture-building, process is one of ongoing public discourse. Herbert Blumer (1969), the sociologist who coined the term *symbolic interactionism*, and who draws heavily on George Herbert Mead's social/functional theory of mind (see Troyer 1978; Strauss 1964: 66–67), argues that people respond to objects on the basis of what those objects mean and that the meaning of those objects arises out of the negotiated experience of social interaction. Clifford Geertz (1973), the anthropologist known for his interpretive theory of culture and who draws upon Mead and also upon Gilbert Ryle, insists that culture, "this acted document . . . is public" (1973:10), because meaning is – that is, the meaning of a wink, real or burlesqued (to use Geertz's example from Ryle), lies not in knowing the rules governing how to wink, but in the winking; or, perhaps more precisely, in the interpretive *response* to the winking.

From this view, the human world, because it is brought about by a trafficking in symbols, is not mainly in our individual heads, as a scholar with a strict cognitive view of human affairs might argue; nor is it largely external to our subjectivities, as a dedicated positivist might insist. It is an intersubjective world, lying out there, between the "you-ness" of you and the "me-ness" of me.

Material culture epitomizes this attribute of human life. The material being of house, park, and community lies out there, between us, an intersubjective world fixed for the moment in brick, plants, and street patterns. Viewed thus, material culture becomes, in Mead's phrase, a series of "collapsed acts, the signs of what would happen if the acts were carried to completion" (cited in Troyer 1978:251). The experience of others, as the geographer Yi-Fu Tuan (1980) notes, is fleeting. A glance, a touch, and then they are gone. But with the ability to make artifacts, we can fix our experience – much in the manner that a text fixes discourse (Ricoeur 1979) – and in so doing employ the material items to recall, reconstitute, and communicate our experience. As the objectification of our subjective experience of social interaction (Berger and Luckmann 1967), material culture, then, is not simply there, like an object of nature, structuring our movements by its mere physicality. Instead, it assumes the dramatistic qualities that Kenneth Burke (1962:7–19; 1966:3–57) attributes to words and so becomes a "scene," or better, an opened text, whose narrative we read even as we interact.

If it is granted that material culture is our intersubjective world expressed in physical substance, then how do we respond to material culture in such a way as to move ourselves from simply being there in our own physicality to being-in-the-world? If material culture is like an opened text, how do we bring ourselves and the text together to establish a unity of being-in-the-text? A path to answering that question lies in a familiar, but still incisive, concept in social science: the definition of situation.

Customarily, W. I. Thomas's (Thomas and Thomas 1938:572) famous statement, "If men define situations as real, they are real in their consequences," has meant the portrayal of subjective and often irrational reactions to a given objective situation. Both Ball (1972) and Perinbanayagam (1974) have effectively argued, however, that if the concept is taken seriously, *existentially*, as a description of the human condition, then the so-called objective reality to which people subjectively respond is itself not an external given but the very result of their actions. In this light, defining the situation becomes synonymous with being-in-the-world and shares that concept's investigatory thrust. The matter may be stated thus: If material culture is the physical expression of the world in which we are, then defining the situation means how people incorporate material culture into the situation they are creating so that they bring about unity between the situation and the material setting. When this is accomplished, one may say that the situation has been placed; it has achieved material existence. People are no longer simply there physically; they are also in-the-world.

The process of incorporating material culture into the definition of situation, although probably not a strictly linear progression, can best be presented as three analytically distinct steps or components: the preliminary definition supplied by the material culture of a setting; the interaction occurring within that setting; and the image emerging out of the interaction and completing the definition by restating that situation's sense of place. The ethnographic data will be organized accordingly, but first it is necessary to report how those ethnographic data were collected.

The Ethnographic Experience

In the summer of 1975, I took up residence in a corner of the market and on a bench in the plaza of Cartago, Costa Rica. In Cartago, the plaza – as it does in every Spanish-American community founded as part of Spain's policy to conquer, civilize, and Christianize the New World (Foster 1960; Stanislawski 1947) – forms the aesthetic focal point of a grid of streets stamped in perfect rectangularity upon curvilinear nature. A block north of the plaza and occupying one of the rectangles is the market. It fronts the main thoroughfare that links Cartago to the Atlantic port of Limón to the east and to the nation's capital, San José, some 25 km to the west. Behind the market, railroad tracks parallel the highway's route from the coast to the capital, and a local complex of roads ties Cartago and its hinterland of farms and small communities to these national links. The transportation network and the historical status of Cartago as the colonial capital of Costa Rica ensure that it, a pleasant community of 35,000 in a friendly country of 1,871,000, occupies a significant niche in the national hierarchy of urban places (Dirección General 1974).

During two previous summers, 1972 and 1973, I had made several efforts to relate place to behavior and behavior to place. Although I had accumulated considerable data, I was dissatisfied with what I was doing and even wondered why I was there. During that summer of 1975, however, for reasons that I still do not understand, things came together.

It began when, listening to the market's harsh noises or admiring the plaza's gentle order, I became fascinated with the act of watching. Of course, I did more than watch. Through the medium of colonial documents, travelers' accounts, local histories, and old photographs, I followed the evolution of the plaza from being a colonial parade ground to being, in the 19th century, an open-air market, and to being converted, in the early 20th century, to a garden park with the market moved to its present location (Richardson 1978). Back in the present, I interviewed various city officials and the administrator of the market. For the most part, however, I listened to people who wanted to talk to me – men, women, and children whom I had met the two previous summers and new acquaintances, some with a rounded view of Cartago and others with a knowledge limited to specifics. There was one individual whose words still stir within me: "Man possesses memory, intelligence, and particularly, imagination. Of all the animals only man can imagine, and with imagination man can know God." Of all the animals only man can fictionalize, and through fiction man can know reality.

The conviction came to me that if I watched the people around me with sufficient skill and passionate concern, the simple acts of buying lettuce and of gentle strolling might expand and transform to reveal a glimpse of the peculiar reality in which we humans operate. But what to watch? What to note down? What to ignore? Recording the material manifestation of the market and plaza was easy enough. I took photographs, paced distances for maps, and wrote descriptions to myself. Recording interaction was much more difficult I visited both places at different times during the day and on various days during the week. In the plaza I tried to make maps of people's actions and scribbled rapidly as they leisurely moved from bench to bench: The swirl of people around the market made even this modest effort impossible. The familiar works of Edward Hall and Ray Birdwhistell came frequently to mind, but I found their notational systems too finely grained for a single observer equipped with a pencil, paper, and a still camera. Nonetheless, I kept reminding myself to be sensitive to the proxemic distance between individuals and between clusters of people and to note occasions of territoriality.

Although I tried to keep count of categories, such as age, sex, and wealth, more and more I caught myself watching particular individuals, those whom the scene revealed as heroic – the old, the poor, and the very young – and with a jerk, I had to remind myself to watch the man in the suit and the woman with carefully coiffured hair. As I watched, I began to notice exchanges among these individuals and compiled incidents that seemed "situational" (Goffman 1963:22): micro-dramas that were not merely *in* the market or the plaza but were *of* each place, interactions that either incorporated or challenged the definition of the situation being proposed. Thus, from my reading, from my listening, but again mostly from my watching, I tried to comprehend the process of being-in-the-world of the Spanish American market and plaza.

The brief report of the ethnographic experience now finished, the data collected are presented in the three components mentioned earlier: the preliminary definition of the material setting, the interaction taking place in the setting, and the image that completes the definition. In the presentation of the data, the last thing I want to do is to draw an overly sharp division between market and plaza; at the same time, I do not want to retreat into phrases that purport to describe the market's or plaza's ideal patterns – either cognitive or behavioral. To do one or the other would seem to obscure the realities of the two places and do violence to the interpretive, interactionist emphasis on the public, ongoing manner in which we construct social reality. The stylistic aim, then, is to convey something of the immediacy of being there and something of the understanding that being there calls forth.[2]

Being-in-the-Market and Being-in-the-Plaza

The material component

To use the material culture of a setting as a preliminary definition of the situation means that people respond to the setting in part through "reading" its textlike characters (Richardson 1980b), but perhaps primarily through experiencing its phenomenological presence. What people respond to in a setting are the overt messages that objects present through their appearance and arrangement and the more implicit theme that the setting in its totality conveys. In all probability, what constitutes a setting and defines its limits lies not so much in the isolated setting but in the manner in which the physical and thematic features distinguish, in a quasi-phonemic fashion, that setting from others in the community. In this, material settings resemble a series of semantic domains, domains which, as people literally enter them, provide a preliminary understanding of the interaction going on around them and, consequently, of the situation developing before them. Thus, the preliminary definitions of the settings of the market and of the plaza are revealed through contrasting the context, the arrangement, and the theme of each.

The market structure in Cartago is physically situated in a context of business concerns. Lining the main street that fronts the market are small stores owned by local enterprises and larger ones headquartered in San José. Lining the railroad tracks in back of the market are numerous cantinas and a "hotel" or two where a peasant, celebrating a moment's release from weekly toil, can wake up with a heavy head and an empty pocket.

Bracketed by the square block in which it sits, the market building itself is a large, square, metal "box" made of corrugated tin welded to a steel frame. No curlicues or bric-a-brac adorn the walls, and only a coat of blue-green paint relieves their metallic monotony. Inside the structure, a statue of the Sacred Heart of Jesus provides the only relief from utilitarian starkness. The barnlike interior space is checkerboarded with wooden compartments called *tramos* (literally, contiguous pieces of terrain separated from each other by whatever means at hand). Individual *tramos* may vary from a tiny cubicle, barely large enough for the vendor to sit behind a display of lurid paintings of the saints, to ones over thirty feet long. Each has an open space extending from waist to head level, through which the vendor and the customer exchange brief words about the customer's needs and the vendor's price. The top of the *tramo* is only a foot or so from the vendor's head and from it hang objects he is selling: sausage, if he is a sausage, cheese, and egg man; boots if he is selling footwear; and harnesses, belts, and rope if he sells leather goods. Smaller merchants who do not have the wherewithall to gain access to a *tramo* ring the outside of the building with makeshift benches rented from the market administration. On Saturday, the principal market day, every inch of this space is occupied by the vendors and their products: coarse sacks bulging with brown potatoes;

twisted strings of white onions; red tomatoes arranged in perfect pyramids, or topical fruits piled in brilliant, multicolored clusters.

Thematically, the market is a place where nature is present as a precipitate of human action. With the exception of fish caught wild in the ocean, nature here is in the form of domesticates (potatoes, onions, or fruit) or as fabricated items (clothes, shoes, or pictures of the Virgin). Managed by man, bagged, strung, and stacked, nature is now an object for purchase; it has been converted into a commodity.

The surroundings of the plaza are considerably more sedate than those of the market. One side is entirely occupied by the *palacio municipal*, which houses both local and provincial offices within modernistic concrete-and-glass confines. On the adjacent side are the remains of a church, unfinished and abandoned since the devastating earthquake of 1910. The parish church had been located here since the founding of Cartago in the 1560s, but after the earthquake another church nearby became the parish church, and the remains, known locally as the "ruins," have become a kind of picturesque park. On the other two sides of the plaza are small business, homes, and a movie theater.

In 1890, after the market was moved to its present location, the plaza was made into a garden-park (in Costa Rican Spanish, it changed from a *plaza* to a *parque*). A fence of iron, given to the city by the country's president in appreciation for political support, bounded the plaza, and a large bandstand formed the center. Later, the fence was removed, the bandstand was reduced to a small shelter in a corner, and a large fountain became the centerpiece. Today, the plaza is a series of rough circles enclosed within a square border and dotted with commemorative objects. The center circle is the fountain, rarely flowing, the base of which is sunk slightly below street level. At the base is another circle of water cluttered with candy wrappers and cigarette butts. These mix with aquatic plants to form a scum through which, miraculously, tiny fish swim. Circling the fountain is a paved walkway, then a strip of grass and bushes, another curved walkway, a larger area of shrubs and trees, the square border, and, finally, the street. A series of cast concrete benches spaced at regular intervals circle the fountain. Other benches spaced with equal precision line the three entranceways that lead from the street to the fountain; still other benches line the square border and face the streets. On the side that borders the *palacio municipal*, a triangular arrangement of flagpoles encloses a triangular-shaped pillar commemorating Costa Rican independence. Nearby is a large bust of the founder of the Red Cross. On the far side are small busts of a local clergyman and a physician. Along the side that faces the "ruins," embedded in the grass, is the wheel of the International Rotarian movement. Opposite this side and squeezed between an entranceway and a street is the small bandstand.

As with the case of the market, the theme of the plaza is the management of nature: tall, needle-leafed trees tower above shorter, broad-leafed trunks; smaller bushes and pink flowering shrubs form alternate assemblages on green lawns; and lush water herbs around the fountain contrast with a cluster of spinous shrubs and palms planted near a walkway. Even dirt, the primeval pollutant, is discreetly covered with grass. Although managed, nature in the plaza is not meant to be exchanged as a commodity; rather, it is intended to be an ornament, a substance that lends grace, a quality that adorns.

In sum, the material features of the market and plaza contrast in context, arrangement, and theme. A busy street, stores, and railroad tracks surround the market; quieter streets, government buildings, and the church "ruins" circle the plaza. The market, like most places in this highly carpentered environment, is principally indoors and square, while the plaza is uniquely outdoors and circular. The market concentrates individuals into narrow streams flowing past stationary vendors, and the plaza distributes people into clusters focused primarily on the fountain. Only the enigmatic Sacred Heart of Jesus is on display in the market, while the plaza displays busts, flagpoles, an independence marker, and the Rotarians' wheel. Finally, the thematic feature that distinguishes the material environment of the two places is that nature in the market is a commodity and in the plaza it is an ornament.

The interaction component

As people approach the market and the plaza, they begin constructing situations preliminarily defined by their interpretive responses to the semantic contrasts in the material culture of the two places. During the course of their interaction with the material settings and with each other, their behavior becomes meaningful, one might suggest, to the extent that it incorporates or challenges their initial understanding of what is happening around them. In actuality, from a purely ethological, neutral-observer point of view, the behavior occurring in the settings varies over a wide range and the recording of that variation, as mentioned, is extremely difficult. A portion of what people do and say may not be critical to either incorporating or challenging the emerging definition. The behavior is *in*, but not *of*, the setting. The matter is further complicated not only by having to decide what behavior is merely *in* and what behavior is critically *of* but also by the fact that the apparently incidental "in" behavior may form the context for interpreting the "of" behavior.

To set aside the "in" and "of" problem for the moment, interaction that people interpret as incorporating the preliminary definition transforms a purely "crude," ethological "conversation of gestures" (Strauss 1964:154–162) to meaningful, symbolic interaction. The movement is from simply being there to being-in-the-world. Conversely, interaction that people interpret as challenging the preliminary definition also achieves meaning but the meaning it achieves is that of being out of place, of being-out-of-the-world now taking shape. Out-of-place and in-place behaviors exist in a sort of dialectic, reinforcing one another in their very antagonism. Yet, at the same time, what is in-place and what is out-of-place is situational, and what is situational depends, preliminarily at least, on people's interpretive responses to the material setting.

Since the ethnographer obviously wants to avoid the imposition of categories that do violence to the process he is trying to understand, the best way to handle both the "in" and "of" problem and the in-place and out-of-place distinctions is to contrast a broad sample of market behavior with that of the plaza and extract from that contrast critical interactions that illustrate the incorporation of the material settings into the emerging situations. This is attempted by first giving a running account of representative activity in the two places and then by making a more systematic comparison to underscore the contrast between market and plaza behavior.

In a slow, subdued manner, the market is open all week; but the tempo quickens as the weekend nears, and on Saturday it peaks. In the fresh light of early morning, heavily loaded trucks, battered old American Chevrolets, and bright new Japanese Datsuns maneuver through the small space and finally stop. Pulling and pushing carts of all sizes, workers quickly move the produce from truck to stall. By 7:00 the now-empty trucks pull away, and as if he were the official starter of the day's activities, the man selling tickets for the weekly lottery first calls to the crowd, "Tomorrow it plays. What is your number? Your number? Your number?"

Within the market building and in his *tramo* the vendor moves about his domain, his head automatically ducking under straw bags hanging from the roof, his hand reaching above the rice bin for a can of peaches. Before he has finished with one customer, he is calling out, "Señor, what pleases you? Señora, what offers itself to you?" Arrogantly, his voice implies why should the customer be so stupid as to buy from anyone other than him.

At an entrance, a boy stands with a box full of wet lettuce He calls out, "Lettuce! Lettuce! Two for a peso." He makes a quick sale, but before he can make another, one of the market officials hurries up and tells him he is blocking the passage. The boy moves away, and a pale, thin man with a small box of white thread takes his place. With his mind in strange and distant places, he gently offers the box to the people pouring through the entrance. He does not make a single sale and quietly drifts off. The lettuce boy reappears with his partner, a man in his twenties. "Sell them three for one," he advises. The boy makes several sales, but again the official comes and drives him away.

At a *tramo* selling staples, a young mother is buying her weekly supply. The vendor is attentive and courteous. Little of the vigorous bargaining supposedly characteristic of Latin American markets marks their exchange. As the lady makes a purchase, the vendor wraps each item in newspaper and places it carefully in a bag made of shiny *cabuya*, a fiber spun from a local plant. She finishes her purchases and buys one cigarette. After lighting the cigarette she motions to her son, who, without a word, backs up to the counter. The vendor lowers the sack on the boy's back and carefully adjusts it as the boy, still without expression, staggers under the weight. Bent nearly double by the load, the boy turns to follow his mother as she and an even younger child pass into the crowd, the smoke of her cigarette lingering delicately in the air.

At noontime, at one of the market's small restaurants – which is only a counter, five stools, and a name, "The Gardenia" – a comfortable-looking man is eating a dish of rice and beans topped with a fried egg. He rises halfway from his stool and says something to the waitress. She laughs and tosses her head. Nearby, another man, drawn out and crumpled, peeks out of a face that barely emerges from a tattered, brown sweater. He spots the customer, blinks, and touches him on the arm. The customer, fresh from his exchange with the young waitress, scrapes a portion of his dish onto his bread plate. Immediately the small man grabs a dirty spoon and starts eating. A dog hurries by but pauses to piss on a crate of tomatoes.

Outside, one of the two regular shoeshine boys works on the ethnographer's boots. A few spaces down, a boy is perched on the edge of a crate selling fruits – guavas, mangoes, and oranges. A larger boy, horsing around, gives him a shove. The boy falls backward and hits the ground hard. Hurt and full of anger, he jumps up swinging. Instantly, a circle of eager men forms. They prod the two boys on with shouts and gestures. Someone bombards them with hard palm fruit. The shoeshiner, winking at the ethnographer with a knowing thrust of his head, joins in the shouting but continues slapping on polish. From the circle come more eager shouts and prodding gestures. Finally, the two are separated, and the circle disappears as quickly as it formed.

The market day grinds on through the afternoon, the morning freshness lost, forever, it seems, in the mounting piles of garbage. Over the roar of the street noise the bored calls of the vendors punctuate the shouts of the lottery man, who continues to call with an almost frenzied optimism, "Tomorrow it plays! (Potato, potato, potato.) What is your number, your number, your number? (Banana, banana, banana.) Your number, your number, your number? (Potato, potato; banana, banana.)"

On weekdays, Cartago stirs early, and by 6:30 A.M., as the bells of the church chime their first call, people are cutting through the plaza on their way to work. Some are taking their places at the retail stores along the city's main street, but many are traveling to San José, where perhaps more than a third of Cartago's work force is employed. While these people are leaving Cartago, others from the smaller neighboring communities are arriving at the city and are trying to squeeze out of packed buses stopping at the plaza. The man in charge of keeping the plaza clean gets his broom out from a storage area underneath the fountain and starts sweeping. The plaza guard, in freshly pressed khakis, arrives, and the sweeper stops to talk to him.

An old man, barefooted and gray, with a sack over his shoulders, slowly picks his path through a swarm of schoolchildren, on his way to gather in the last days of living. The children, their white and blue uniforms flashing against the plaza's green, shout and call to each other. One tiny girl, barely larger than her book satchel, pulls an even tinier brother by the hand, the two rushing to learn what the old man never knew.

The morning moves on, and women on their way to the retail stores or to the market cut through the plaza. Young mothers, having finished their housework or having left it to the maid, push their strollers around walkways, stopping to sit and admire each other's babies. As the noon hour approaches, the shoppers return carrying straw bags filled with purchases. They lean the bags against the benches and sit: a woman with two children talking to an older woman, two women together, or occasionally an older man by himself.

At noon the church bells chime the hour and the plaza fills with kids, running in packs, whirling about, pausing, and then taking off again. One older boy jumps about Kung Fu style, making the appropriate noises and impressing his younger playmate. The guard orders them off the grass. A nattily dressed man in suit and tie sits down on a bench not far from the ethnographer. He takes typewritten pages out of his attache case and looks at them with a serious expression on his face. Other men, singly and in small groups, are scattered about the plaza. An older man, driven by the heat of the sun, sits down on the edge of a shady bench occupied by two teenage boys. He crosses his legs and orients his body away from them. They leave, and he recrosses his legs and orients his body toward the middle of the bench, unconsciously establishing a territorial claim to his domain. A man, about the same age as the ethnographer, walks slowly and carefully by. The thick soles of his bare feet are dark with mud. His ragged pants are too big for him, and he holds them to his waist with an unsteady hand. His eyes, innocent and childlike, peer out of a face black with sun, dirt, and hair. He lies down on a bench, but immediately the guard comes over and nudges him. Without protest the man gets up, smiles weakly at the guard, and walks away, tugging at his sagging pants.

In the empty plaza in the slow afternoon the ethnographer sits reading Goffman's (1963) *Behavior in Public Places*. The day's movement begins to reverse itself, but without the energy of the morning's expectations. Even the children, tired from numbers, history, and verbs, are subdued as they cross the plaza. The guard has little trouble keeping them off the grass and out of the fountain. The return flow from San José starts and goes on until after supper. The guard leaves and the church bells chime for the last time. At 7:30 P.M. a small crowd of young men gather in front of the Teatro Apolo, located on the corner across from the *palacio municipal*. The feature is *La Ultima Pelicula*. It is here for only one night, and no Cartagoan is attracted to a movie about the last picture show in a small Texas town. The show is preceded by slides advertising local merchants, and then the movie begins. The audience soon gets restless; to them the images on the screen are too culturally specific, the fiction is too factual. But the ethnographer sits in a trance as the seamed character of Ben Johnson and the voice of Hank Williams, heartsick and lonely, take him back to the 1950s and home.

On Sundays or on holidays, such as the one on July 25 commemorating the annexation of Guanacaste (a Pacific province formerly part of Nicaragua), people fill the plaza. After mass or after the soccer game, families stroll about in their best casual dress. One father picks up his small daughter and places her on the edge of the fountain. He carefully holds her hand as she solemnly walks around the edge: she, the little princess in starched dress and laced pants; he, the proud father, enchanted with the magic of his daughter's being. Wandering through the plaza are occasional clusters of adolescent girls, at times attached to someone's older brother. This is all that remains of the *paseo*, the formal promenade of separate circles of unmarried girls and young men, and even now the girls leave the plaza for a nearby ice cream counter.

A raucous roar of motorcycles rips the peace of the plaza. Three young men charge their machines across one edge of the park. The guard blows his whistle at them again and again. The trio glance at him and without even a shrug they drive away. A tourist bus from San José arrives at the "ruins," and as the North American passengers get out, the fountain bursts forth. Its spray describes the human trajectory: defying nature the individual drops go up toward the sky to catch the sunlight briefly and then, inevitably, fall back, their momentary individuality disappearing into the pool below.

The afternoon grows cool as coastal clouds ascend the mountains to hide the sun. The rain splatters down and drives people from the plaza. Evening comes and the rain turns to mist. The crowds gather at the movie to watch Charlton Heston save the passengers in *Airport 1975*. The 747, which few have seen, becomes more real to them than the Texas town depicted so realistically the other night. Scattered about the plaza, one pair to a bench, couples in tight embrace warm themselves against the growing chill of the darkening night.

A more systematic contrast between market and plaza behavior is now ventured. Of necessity, the contrast will be between large, generalized categories, several steps

removed from the actual behavior. The first distinction is between engaged participation and disengaged observation.

Basic market activity requires that people engage each other's presence. Because
their livelihood depends on it, the vendors *must* intrude themselves into the customer's sphere and disrupt the customer's reflection. They must engage the customer in
a rapid, sequential fashion, for the greater the number of different individuals they
intrude themselves upon, the greater the chance of a sale. At the same time a
merchant must keep the attention of the customer before him, lest he seek another
vendor. Those who cannot manage the balance between many, ephemeral customers
and fewer, loyal ones may find themselves on the economic and physical peripheries,
like the pale, thin man and his box of thread. The physical organization of the
market – the *tramos* lined up one after another and the checkerboard arrangement of
the aisles – facilitates the close, two-party, face-to-face exchanges between vendor
and customer. Similarly, the austere setting and the near absence of monumental
displays means that the market setting remains inconspicuous and does not detract
from the important business of doing business.

Contrary to the focused participation of the market, plaza interaction necessitates
that people self-consciously become observers even as they respond to the actions of
others. The organization of plaza space distributes clusters of men, women, and
children so that as they sit or stroll together, they become the audience for other
small groups. Likewise, the very uniqueness of the plaza, its circularity in a squared
world, its outdoor setting, its cultivated greenness, and its monumental displays,
means that it conspicuously intrudes itself into people's awareness and encourages
them to distance themselves from their absorption into the actions of others.

Another contrast, closely related to the first is between intense and serene action.
In the market, space is a scarce commodity and competition for it is high – the
vendors, in fact, must pay a fee for it. Proxemically, then, the space between
individuals is small and engagement in the market world demands that a person
navigate the physical body and the social self past constant aggressive intrusions into
personal space. The sudden explosion of behavior that the fight between the two
boys triggered may well be a product of the tension generated by the crush of too
many bodies, too many hands, and too many eyes. In the plaza, competition for
space – with the exception of a shady bench on a hot day – is low, and therefore the
zone of personal space is relatively large. Intrusion into that space – hand-holding
and embracing – is by mutual invitation. Thus, in the plaza world, where boys only
pretend to fight, disengagement means to be "away," to stroll in solitude, even as
others walk alongside, and to disappear into the interior of the body, thereby
releasing the self from its task of "face work" and allowing it to flitter across the
dream sky (Goffman 1963:69–75).

Yet, "being away" may be more characteristic of Anglo-American park behavior
than Spanish-American plaza performance. In the plaza, people are quite conscious
of being in the presence of others, and they act accordingly. In other words, they
present themselves as "being onstage" (Goffman 1959:108–140). Earlier in Cartago's history, the stone pillar and iron railing that surrounded the plaza strengthened
the impression of it being a stage; an older informant remarked that in those days the
plaza was an enchantment. Coincidentally, those were also the days of the formal
paseo when people were even more conspicuous about their onstage performance.

Today, the plaza, as a decorative ornament, continues "to enchant" behavior and bestow upon it a theatrical quality. Those whose presence spoils the effect, such as the man with innocent eyes and filthy dress, are out of place and are not permitted to be.

If people are onstage in the plaza, they are offstage in the market. Here in the back region of the urban center, away from the front regions, people can appear to be more natural and show themselves as having less concern with the demonstration that they are maintaining certain standards. As they switch into a less careful mode of behavior, they become more tolerant of those who are down-and-out and no longer consider them out-of-place and defiling. They may even, as did the man in "The Gardenia," share their table scraps with the more lucky of the unfortunate ones.

In sum, the contrast between market and plaza behavior reveals that the critical interactions – those that are *of* the two places, that are characteristically *in place* and thus interactions preliminarily defined and then facilitated by the material setting – are, for the market, engaged participation, intense action, and offstage performance; and for the plaza, disengaged observation, serene action, and onstage performance.

The image component

During the course of their interaction with the material setting and with each other, people respond to the material setting by incorporating its preliminary definition into their behavior. In so doing, they transform their ethological "conversation of gestures" into symbolic interaction. Behavioral challenges to the definition are responded to as being out-of-place, and their out-of-placeness heightens the definition of the situation being proposed. Thus, out of the ongoing process of interaction emerges a sense of the situation that is being defined. The final step in the process of incorporating the setting into the ongoing situation is the objectification of the sense of the situation upon the setting so that the setting becomes a material image of emerging situation.

The objectification of the emerging sense upon the material setting is essentially the transfer of the *what* of the ongoing social experience onto the *where* of the material setting. The "what" is the sense, or the understanding, of the situation that is emerging out of people's interpretive responses to one another's actions. The objectification of that sense onto the "where" of the setting means that the social situation becomes physically *placed*. This, in turn, means that the setting, which earlier (prior to the situation being formed) was a preliminary definition, now becomes a full exposition of what is occurring. The material image, in brief, is the implicit, preliminary definition made explicit and complete; with its formation the participants have moved from simply being there to being-in-the-world.[3]

From the ethnographer's view, the material image is what he sees upon the completion of his analysis. Having considered the setting and the interaction separately, he now brings them together for a statement on the overall meaning of the two places. For the market, the commercial context and the arrangement of largely indoor, squared space into rows of adjacent booths with the near absence of monumental displays combine to define in a preliminary way interaction that is engaged, intense, and offstage. Out of that interaction, the implicit theme of nature as a commodity is restated, the ethnographer suggests, in the image of the market as a place for being *listo*. In the case of the plaza, the governmental context and the arrangement of outdoor space in circles around a fountain, dotted at measured intervals with benches and monumental displays, preliminarily defines interaction that is disengaged, serene, and onstage. From this interaction the implicit theme of nature as an ornament is restated, in the ethnographer's view, in the image of the plaza as a place for having *cultura*. Being *listo* and having *cultura* are now contrasted.

Cartago merchants often describe their peasant customers as being *listo*, and similar depictions are found in the stories of the Costa Rican *costumbrista* writer Manuel González Zeledón (1968). In these cases *listo* is frequently coupled with the verb *ser* and means "to be smart or clever." If this meaning is tied to the meaning of *listo* when it is coupled with the verb *estar* (to be ready or predisposed to act), then being *listo* conveys, in an especially vivid manner, the image of the market: a place where one is ready to act and to act opportunistically.

In the market, where nature is a commodity, everything from tomatoes to love has a price. Participating in the market means negotiating that price to one's advantage, to act smart. To act smart also means to act quickly, as did the boy selling his lettuce by the entrance, as well as the down-and-out seeking his daily bread. If one does not act, then he risks failure, for as the lottery vendor cries out prophetically, "Tomorrow, it plays," and by then the opportunity will be lost. The market is a tough place where a person can succeed and be a winner or fail and be a loser; and in the market, the two sit at the same table.

Although being *listo* is a quality that most people exhibit in varying degree, having *cultura* in Spanish America is limited to certain humans. These people live within the rectangular confines of the urban grid and traditionally near the plaza. They possess, and exhibit in their manner of life, a rationality that separates them from those, such as outlaws and Indians, who live out of the city and away from its *cultura* and next to nature and its rudeness. In literature, the genre *la novela de la selva* (the novel of the wilderness; the bush; the jungle) portrays the conflict between the rational, urban life and the barbaric way of nature. Frequently, the conflict ends, as in the case of the classic example *La Vorágine*, by José Eustasio Rivera, with nature devouring humanity (León Hazera 1971; Franco 1970:140–141).

The plaza is a near-perfect construction of the reverse image of rationality subduing nature. Located in the central nexus of urbanity and surrounded by institutions that represent order and authority, the plaza describes a nature that has been tamed and arranged according to a reasoned plan; as such, it depicts the triumph of rationality over barbarism. Within the plaza's greenery, no boas loop down from an overhead limb and no piranhas rip apart an unwary prey in the fountain. For here, surrounded by ornamental nature, people are in the plaza to applaud each other's performances. Kids, notorious for their uncouth attacks on decorum, are watched carefully; and couples, who warm themselves in modern embrace, do so only in the darkness of the fallen night. Finally, those who would tarnish the play with raucous machines earn the guard's shrill whistle, and those who would defile the image with the animalistic filth of the down-and-out are told to move on, for the plaza is not a place for failures to be.[4]

Being-in-the-World of Being Human

With the incorporation of the material setting into the situation, and with the movement from simply being there to being-in-the-world, the people of Cartago have created two distinct realities in which to be: that of the market, with its image of being *listo*, and that of the plaza, with its image of having *cultura*. These two social realities, in turn, constitute segments of the larger universe of Spanish America. Indeed, I want to suggest that through the dialectical interplay of these two complementary but antagonistic realities, Spanish-American culture takes shape. First, however, I need to review a particular point to make certain it is clear.

As anyone who has been in Spanish America knows, there are exceptions to the contrasts that I have drawn between the market and the plaza. In smaller communities, the market may still compete with the plaza for central space. Even in Cartago, a vendor wheels his ice cart into the plaza to catch the noonday school trade. So the question will surely arise: Are the contrasts mine or are they those of the participants?

This perennial problem ultimately concerns the locus of culture and the role of the ethnographer in the ethnographic process. If it is not solvable here, it is at least discussable. According to the interpretive, interactionist view, the human world or culture is not secluded in inaccessible areas of our individual subjectivities, but is "out there," located in public discourse, and thus available for study and comment.

Part of that public discourse is the ethnographic experience that parallels, I believe, the incorporation of the material setting into the definition of "situation." Just as it does for the participants, so the material setting provides the ethnographer with his first clues to what is happening around him. This preliminary insight is either substantiated or challenged by subsequent observational responses to people's behavior – including the ethnographer's own action. Out of the ethnographic experiencing of both setting and interaction, then, comes the ethnographic text, which, rather than the material image, is the objectified result of the ethnographic experience. "What does an ethnographer do?" Geertz (1973:19) asks; and the answer is, here as elsewhere, "He writes."

Should you ask in reply, and no doubt you should, "How do we, the readers, know if what is written in the text corresponds to what is inscribed in the material culture of the market and plaza?" the truthful response has to be that you do not know. I hasten to add, however, that I am not claiming that what I have written and what you see here correspond in a one-to-one fashion with what is in Cartago. "*A Skeleton Key to Finnegan's Wake* is not *Finnegan's Wake*," Geertz (1973:15) reminds us. I am claiming that what I have written here explicates what has happened in the market and plaza in Cartago and in Spanish America, by which I mean that I have sought to bring out the social significance of the material setting of the two places. To do this, I have tried to convey the experiential sense of the market and plaza and to extract from that experiential sense what, in the context of public action, the two places mean. My explication is, I argue, insightful, but its validity does not lie in any claim to be a faithful reproduction of what is in Spanish America, and certainly not what is in Spanish-American heads.

With that point at least clarified if not solved, I conclude with an observation on the composition of culture and its real realness. The basic thrust of this article is that in the process of incorporating the material setting into the situation and thereby moving from simply being there to being-in-the-market or plaza, people in Cartago are constructing a Spanish-American world so that they may *be*. Further, it is through their actions that Spanish-American culture forms, or better, *becomes*. This "becoming" takes place, literally and socially, in the construction of the two realities, but it is especially realized through the dialectical tension between the two. On the one hand, being *listo* is Spanish-American culture in an engaged, opportunistic, factual mode; on the other hand, having *cultura* is Spanish America in a disengaged, proper, aesthetic mode. The two modes appear to be mutually exclusive and antagonistic: people cannot be-in-the-market and be-in-the-plaza at the same time, physically or socially. The incorporating of the material setting into the modes anchors this division in physical space, and by this further separation enhances their distinctiveness and counterposes them more clearly, one against the other.

The dialectical interplay between these two modes does not, of course, exhaust the ways in which Spanish-American culture becomes. Being-in-the-church and in the world of the sacred, for example, has an intriguing relationship with being-in-the-market and in the world of commerce. Markets in small communities may front a church; and even in larger towns and cities, religious statuary, as in the case of Cartago's Sacred Heart of Jesus, occupy a visible position in the market place (see Buechler 1978; Swetnam 1978). By contrast, the plaza, while organized around the disengaged and aesthetic, rarely has, to my knowledge, religious objects in its greenery. It is the organization of secular *cultura*, not religious faith; yet *cultura* and *fe* are linked in Spanish America, and the common location of the plaza in front of the parish church may express a dialectic between the sunlight life of the plaza and the dark suffering and death inside the church.

This line of thought suggests that cultures are composed of multiple realities, counterposed against one another like semantic domains and, through this juxtaposition, defining each other. The pattern that results from these juxtapositions, the culture, would appear to be in no sense a fixed entity – certainly not something you could capture in a butterfly net – but a pattern whose very existence shifts with each new arrangement among the social realities that compose it. Only when we, as participants or as ethnographers, counterpose it against some other tenuous pattern, such as Anglo-American culture, does it achieve an existence that resembles a fixed thing. In that instance, as in the case of its component realities, we bring it about through our public discourse and endow it with a worldliness so that we may be.

Creating specific cultures so that we may be particular persons is a distinctly peculiar human trait, a point that, although not always taken seriously, is not new. My contribution here lies in the attention given to the ongoing creative effort that the human condition necessitates. The struggle to construct a world so that we may be is a continual one, and one from which, for the human creature, there is no escape. To paraphrase Sartre, we are condemned to create. Thus, we are constantly at the job of building cultures; shaping, molding, fitting together materials produced not only by the experience of social interaction but also from materials produced by nature. Transformed by the magic of symbols, these objects shape our lives even as we shape them; and in this manner, caged but free, driven but heroic, we *are*.

NOTES

Acknowledgments. I gratefully appreciate the kind assistance of Don Javier Montoya and Servor Francisco Rodriguez, citizens of Cartago, and Dra Maria Bozzoli de Wille and Lic. Marta Eugenia Pardo de Jarquin, anthropologists at the University of Costa Rica. I am also grateful to Drs. Arden King, Fred Kniffen, and Forrest La Violette, three distinct spokesmen from three different fields, for their continual encouragement. I thank Dr. Norman Whitten, editor of this journal, for his patient counsel. The Graduate School of Louisiana State University provided partial support for fieldwork carried out during the summers of 1972, 1973, and 1975. The ideas expressed here represent a continuing effort to relate place to behavior and behavior to place in the context of symbolic communication (Richardson 1974a, 1974b, 1978, 1980a, 1980b) Other versions of the article were read at the 1979 meeting of the American Anthropological Association and at the 1980 meeting of the Association of American Geographers.

1   Other than Edward Hall, the individual most familiar to anthropologists for his work on behavior and objects is probably Amos Rapoport His *Human Aspects of Urban Forms* (1977) provides a comprehensive survey of the various approaches to the subject. Mention also must be made of the exciting efforts of some archaeologists to break free of the constraints of prehistory and to redefine their discipline as the study of material culture, ancient, historic, and contemporary (Rathje 1979; Gould and Schiffer 1981) In addition, anthropologists can greatly benefit from the rich literature in geography on place (e.g. Meinig 1979; Buttimer and Seamon 1980; Gade 1976; Robertson 1978, and especially Tuan 1976, 1977).

2   The overall process of incorporating material culture into the definition of situation includes the longer-term cycle of constructing, modifying, and replacing the material expression of a community and the shorter cycle of responding to the existing material landscape. The two cycles are closely linked The physical creation of a setting impinges directly upon the social responses to that setting. Likewise, the day-to-day social use of a setting may lead to physical modification, either on a small scale (a new arrangement of goods in a vendor's booth) or on a large one (the construction of a new market building). The analysis here focuses on the shorter cycle of responses to the existing setting.

3   It is important to note that the implicit thematic message is not so much a fixed cognitive map with instructions on how to behave as it is a series of collapsed acts to which people experientially respond. Out of that response meaning arises, and that meaning is objectified upon the setting so that the setting becomes a full statement, a *read* text, and therefore the material image of the situation. With allowance for the fact that Moore (1981) is dealing with changes from one architectural form to another, his explication of the "sign-image" of Cuna architecture seems similar to my attempts to decipher how established settings achieve meaning.

4   Although mine differs from his, I am indebted to Morris Freilich's (1972, 1980) provocative formulation of being smart and being proper.

REFERENCES

Ball, Donald W.
    1972   The Definition of Situation: Some Theoretical and Methodological Consequences of Taking W. I. Thomas Seriously. *Journal of the Theory of Social Behavior* 2:61–82.

Berger, Peter L., and Thomas Luckmann
    1967   *The Social Construction of Reality*. Garden City, NY: Anchor Books.
Blumer, Herbert
    1969   *Symbolic Interactionism*: Englewood Cliffs, NJ: Prentice-Hall.
Buechler, Judith-Maria
    1978   The Dynamics of the Market in La Paz, Bolivia. *Urban Anthropology* 7:343–359.
Burke, Kenneth
    1962   *A Grammar of Motives*. New York: World Publishing.
    1966   *Language as Symbolic Action*. Berkeley: University of California Press.
Buttimer, Anne, and David Seamon, eds.
    1980   *The Human Experience of Space and Place*. London: Croom Helm.
Dirección General de Estadistica y Censos.
    1974   *Censo de Población*, 1973. San José: Ministerio de Economia, Industria, y Comercio.
Foster, George
    1960   *Culture and Conquest: America's Spanish Heritage*. Chicago: Quadrangle Books.
Franco, Jean
    1970   *The Modern Culture of Latin America: Society and the Artist*. Middlesex, UK:
            Penguin
Freilich, Morris
    1972   Manufacturing Culture. Man the Scientist. In *The Meaning of Culture*, Morris
            Freilich, ed., pp. 267–325 Lexington, MA: Xerox College Publishing.
    1980   "Culture" Is "Proper," Not "Smart": A Conceptualization Which Makes a Differ-
            ence. Paper presented at the 1980 Annual Meeting of the American Anthropological
            Association, Washington, DC.
Gade, Daniel
    1976   The Latin American Central Plaza as Functional Space. *Proceedings of the Confer-
            ence of Latin American Geographers* 5:1–23.
Geertz, Clifford
    1973   *The Interpretation of Cultures* New York: Basic Books.
Goffman, Erving
    1959   *The Presentation of Self in Everyday Life*. Garden City, NY: Anchor Books.
    1963   *Behavior in Public Places*. New York: The Free Press.
Gould Richard A., and Michael B. Schiffer, eds.
    1981   *Modern Material Culture*. New York: Academic Press
González Zeledón, Manuel
    1968   *Cuentos de Magón*. San José: Antonio Lehmann.
Heidegger, Martin
    1962   *Being and Time*. John Macquarrie and Edward Robinson, transls. New York.
            Harper & Row.
León Hazera, Lydia de
    1971   *La Novela de la Selva Hispanoamérica*. Bogotá: Instituto Caro y Cuervo.
Meinig, Donald W., ed.
    1979   *The Interpretation of Ordinary Landscapes*. New York. Oxford University Press.
Moore, Alexander
    1981   Basilicas and King Posts. A Proxemic and Symbolic Event Analysis of Competing
            Public Architecture among the San Blas Cuna. *American Ethnologist* 8:259–277.
Perinbanayagam, R. S.
    1974   The Definition of the Situation: An Analysis of the Ethnomethodological and
            Dramaturgical View. *The Sociological Quarterly* 15:521–541.
Rapoport, Amos
    1977   *Human Aspects of Urban Form*. Oxford: Pergamon.

Rathje, William L.
   1979   Modern Material Culture Studies. In *Advances in Archaeological Method and Theory*. M. Schiffer, ed., pp. 1–37 New York: Academic Press.
Richardson, Miles
   1974a   Images, Objects, and the Human Story. In *The Human Mirror. Material and Spatial Images of Man*. Miles Richardson, ed., pp 3–14. Baton Rouge: Louisiana State University Press.
   1974b   The Spanish American (Colombian) Settlement Pattern as a Societal Expression and as a Behavioral Cause. In *Man and Cultural Heritage*: Papers in Honor of Fred B. Kniffen. H. J. Walker, and W. G. Haag, eds., pp. 35–51. Geoscience and Man, Vol. 5. Bob F. Perkins, gen. ed., Baton Rouge: Louisiana State University, School of Geoscience.
   1978   *La Plaza Como Lugar Social*: EI Papel del Lugar en el Encuentro Human. Vinculos, Revista de Antropologia del Museo Nacional del Costa Rica 4:1–20.
   1980a   Culture and the Urban Stage. The Nexus of Setting. Behavior, and Image in Urban Places. In *Human Behavior and Environment: Advances in Theory and Research*. Vol. 4: Environment and Culture. I. Altman, A. Rapoport, and J. Wohfwill, eds., pp. 209–241. New York: Plenum Press.
   1980b   The Spanish American *Iglesia* and the Southern Baptist Church as Texts about Christianity. Paper presented at the 1980 Annual Meeting of the American Anthropological Association, Washington, DC.
Ricoeur, Paul
   1979   The Model of the Text: Meaningful Action Considered as a Text. In *Interpretive Social Science*. P. Rabinow and W. Sullivan, eds., pp. 73–102. Berkeley, University of California Press.
Robertson, Douglas
   1978   A Behavioral Portrait of the Mexican *Plaza Principal*. Ph.D. dissertation. Geography Department, Syracuse University.
Stanislawski, Douglas
   1947   Early Spanish Town-Planning in the New World. *Geographical Review* 37:94–105.
Strauss, Anselm, ed.
   1964   *George Herbert Mead on Social Psychology*. Chicago: University of Chicago Press.
Swetnam, John J.
   1978   Class-based and Community-based Ritual Organization in Latin America. *Ethnology* 17 425–438.
Thomas, William I., and Dorothy Swaine Thomas
   1938   *The Child in America*. New York: Knopf.
Troyer, William L.
   1978   Mead's Social and Functional Theory of Mind. In *Symbolic Interaction*, Jerome G. Manis and Bernard N. Meltzer, eds, pp. 247–251. Boston: Allyn and Bacon.
Tuan, Yi-Fu
   1976   Humanistic Geography. *Annals of the Association of American Geographers* 66:266–276
   1977   *Space and Place. The Perspective of Experience*. Minneapolis: University of Minnesota Press.
   1980   The Significance of the Artifact. *Geographical Review* 70:462–472.

3

Excluded Spaces: The Figure in the Australian Aboriginal Landscape

Nancy D. Munn

Commenting on Pausanias's description of his travels through Greece, James Frazer wrote: "without [Pausanias] the ruins of Greece would...be a labyrinth without a clue, a riddle without an answer."[1] Perhaps Frazer imagined the sanctuary at Nemi as a picturesque landscape riddle and he himself as the travelling Pausanias in the guise of anthropological detective – purveying both clues and answers as he unrolled that ever-expanding labyrinth *The Golden Bough*. Needless to say, I offer here nothing so mysterious or endless as this quest of Frazer's to explain the King of the Wood – the key "figure in his landscape" (to adapt John Dixon Hunt's book title),[2] and the dangerous and endangered, excluding agent of Frazer's "place." Nevertheless, my aim is to explore some ancient places of power and certain interactions between persons and space entailed in modern Australian Aboriginal spatial taboos. In doing so I examine the question of spatial prohibition less as an issue in itself than as a way of posing certain more general problems in the analysis of social space and time.

Frazer's own interest in places and in the spatiality of actors and events was mostly stylistic and mood setting rather than theoretical.[3] Unlike his friend Robertson Smith or Arnold Van Gennep, a social theorist whose concept of spatial separations and passages across them drew in part on a geopolitical discourse of frontiers and boundaries, Frazer's ideas about taboo are not focussed on the exclusionary powers of "sacred places" (although they take account of them). Indeed, given his theoretical and methodological biases, it is not surprising that, as Jonathan Smith has noted, Frazer finally sheds the King of the Wood as "merely a puppet" of his own rationalist search for the "evolution of human thought."[4]

The present essay goes in another direction: it assumes that, in comparative anthropological studies, the spatiotemporal dimensions of a theoretical problem not only are intrinsic to it but require analytic foregrounding. In this respect, I intend to speak to some current preoccupations in the humanities and social theory with space, time, and bodily action; with "places" and their "powers"; and with what David Parkin has recently described as a discourse "of positions, stances, moves...close and distant gazes...of spatial orientation and separation."[5]

My topic is certain Australian Aboriginal spatial interdictions that are pervasive wherever Aborigines still treat the land in everyday life as the ancestrally derived locus of Aboriginal law.[6] For heuristic reasons, I focus (with one exception) on central and western desert and some desert fringe, riverine peoples of the Australian interior.[7] When I use the term *Aborigines* without further qualification, I mean essentially peoples of these regions, although the interdictions involved may have wider applicability. These interdictions create a partially shifting range of excluded or restricted regions for each person throughout his or her life. A specific kind of spatial form is being produced: a space of deletions or of delimitations constraining one's presence at particular locales.

This negative space is well conveyed by the widely used Aboriginal English expression "no room," meaning a person's lack of sociomoral or legal space at a given locale.[8] At any given moment, a person's space is a patchwork of regions where he or she has "no room": these regions overlap only in part with those of others in the community. A familiar example is the barring of adult women and men from each other's secret power places, although children may be barred, in some cases, from both. Particular excluded regions thus vary for different people and shift through a person's lifetime.

The time span of a locale's participation in this kind of excluded space also varies. Many of the ancient, named, and owned places are permanently barred to *someone* – certainly to anyone defined as an outsider or a stranger. Other regions may be closed contingent on transient events such as deaths, ritual performances and travel, or the presence there of a person's tabooed in-law.[9] We have here a complex kind of relative spacetime, not simply a set of determinate locales or "places." Mervyn Meggitt once implied something like this when he suggested that the Walpiri construction of "their socio-geographical environment into regions of greater or less space or personal mobility... [resembles] the Lewinian notion of the life-space."[10]

Although my own approach bears no similarity to Kurt Lewin's, I share his interest in relational models. Thus I address the "synoptic" anthropological notions of taboo and sacred places in two related ways: by dissolving them into a more general spatiotemporal analytics of (culturally significant) location, distancing, movement, relative duration, and boundaries; and by considering spacetime as a symbolic nexus of relations produced out of interactions between bodily actors and terrestrial spaces. We shall see that once we make these theoretical moves, questions involving the locus of powers of exclusion, or how boundaries emerge and are signified in cultural practices, can be articulated in the same paradigm.

My focus will be on spatial prohibitions as a mode of boundary making. In Aboriginal societies, the existence of topographical boundaries demarcating owned places is highly problematic. This feature has recently been highlighted by political contention over boundaries in the process of establishing another kind of "excluded" space, namely, the Aboriginal ancient place protected from Western industry and trespass by "sacred site" legislation and sometimes marked as a transcultural enclave by surrounding fences and written signs. These markers fix the visible signs of the power of what the Aborigines call "whitefella's law" on the demarcated limit of an ancient place that now conjoins the "two laws" (a stereotypic Aboriginal expression referring to the different Aboriginal and Euro-Australian laws). I cannot discuss this mode of excluded space here, but it remains as an implicit contrast in the back-ground of the present argument.[11]

Since spatial prohibitions limit a person's presence at a particular place, we can initially view these practices as a problem in *location* in its dual sense of "a locale" and "locatedness"; for our purposes, *locatedness* refers primarily to mobile actors rather than things. Lefebvre calls this "the basic duality" of social space as a "*field of action*" and a "*basis of action*." By the latter he means "places whence energies derive and whither energies are directed."[12] I take up this dualism as a dynamic interrelation between two modalities of space that are operative in constructing an exclusionary spacetime.

Lefebvre's "field of action" can also be viewed as the "mobile *spatial* field" of the actor in contrast to a determinate region or locale;[13] the latter is the concrete "basis of action," which lends itself at any given moment to the actor's moving field. Linguists and other scholars frequently describe what I call the spatial field by labels such as *indexical* or *ego-centered*. It is space defined by reference to an actor, its organizing center. Since a spatial field extends from the actor, it can also be under-stood as a culturally defined, corporeal-sensual field of significant distances stretch-ing out from the body in a particular stance or action at a given locale or as it moves through locales. This field can be plotted along a hypothetical trajectory centered in the situated body with its expansive movements and immediate tactile reach, and extendable beyond this center in vision, vocal reach, and hearing (and further where relevant). The body is thus understood as a spatial field (and the spatial field as a bodily field).[14]

The particular locale that a spatial field embraces changes with the mobile actor from one "moment" to the next. The field is literally a "shifter" that, as Erwin Straus puts it, "constantly goes with us" as we move around.[15] Of course, in going with us as an aspect of ourselves, it leaves particular locales behind and reaches others up ahead; equally, its deterrence from some spaces is part of its interaction with them, in a negative mode.

A simple but important example of this negative interaction is the detour, a pervasive type of Aboriginal act, generally made either to avoid the temporary location of certain persons or certain *contemporary* events, or the enduring agentive powers left in the country's named places by ancestors during *ancient* events.[16] For instance, at a 1980s gathering of mourners on the Yuendumu–Alice Springs road, Aborigines approaching in their cars "would stop and turn around to find another track to their destination."[17] In this example, detours are made only for the duration of the event. But Aborigines make detours of other locales for reasons inhering in the land itself. For example, a Warlpiri woman from Lajamanu, speaking to Barbara Glowczewski, remembered: "'When I was small, my mother required me to always make a large detour to look for water on the other side of this hill [where certain ancestors had travelled]. All the women repeatedly told the children not to go there because it was dangerous: there were spirits . . . who kidnapped children. We didn't go there because we were very frightened.'"[18]

In detouring, vision and, secondarily, hearing (for instance, of ritual singing temporarily going on at a given place) are the key measures Aborigines use to delimit a person's spatial field. On the whole, a detour of an ancient place must be far enough away to avoid seeing it.[19] But a finer calibration of vision operates in ritual performances of ancestral events (not necessarily held at a power place). For in-stance, Warlpiri women with special rights in certain men's rituals may be allowed to stand closer to some performances than other women; and some senior Warlpiri men may be permitted to briefly enter women's ceremonial grounds, while others may observe these rituals at a distance.[20] A person's sensual-spatial field is controlled here by distancing, but we will see other means later.

In the act of detouring, actors also carve out a negative space – a locale – where they do not go, part of which extends beyond their own spatial field of vision. This act projects a signifier of limitation upon the land or place by forming *transient but repeatable boundaries out of the moving body*. Excluding acts thus give concrete if transient (and, spatially, somewhat shifting) form to boundaries of a quasi-perimetric kind: people "go around" a place, as expressed in a basic Warlpiri term for *detour*.[21] Boundaries are here "given their practical senses as movements of the body."[22] People-in-action not only produce boundaries and boundary experiences but, to paraphrase an idea of Simmel's, are themselves boundaries.[23]

In the instance noted above, the agentive power of the Law enforcing the detour is embedded in the detoured area as "child kidnappers"; in other places it might be other personae or forces springing from the enduring presence of ancestors. Places "take notice of who is there."[24] For the moment, we must turn then from the moving spatial field of the excluded actor to the spatiotemporal organization and potencies of this kind of place.

I have noted that Aboriginal law is said to be in the ground, especially the rocks. "You see that hill over there? Blackfellow Law like that hill. It never changes...[It] is in the ground," said a Yarralin man to Deborah Rose.[25] The "Law" is the hill, or is in the hill. The Law's *visible signs* are topographic "markings" – rocks, rock crevices and stains, soaks, trees, creek beds, clay pans, and so forth – remnants of the multiple, so-called totemic ancestors who made the land into distinguishable shapes. Indigenous terms for *Law*, like the Warlpiri *jukurrpa* (popularly glossed nowadays by Aborigines and others as "Dreaming"), are the same as for these ancestors.

However, these features, which are concentrated loci of a place's authoritative power, do not define its spatial boundaries. Rather, they are the identifying *centers* from which a space with uncertain or ambiguously defined limits stretches out. For instance, Warlpiri places have been compared to "a gravitational field weakening out from the [topographic] center."[26] There may be some qualifications to this sort of spatialization, but Aboriginal-owned places are typically "not clearly bounded, discrete locations but...foci whose influence extends outward."[27]

In the case of certain major places, the Law's power may extend well beyond its center, spanning a region of other named places (or sub-places). This radius of power is also not clearly delimitable. Within this extended sphere, a place responds to violations (to forbidden presences or incorrect comportments) by causing physical danger such as potential illness or death to the violator. In short, the Aboriginal ancient place can be characterized as "center-oriented" – S. J. Tambiah's term for a spatio-political domain that is formed "as a variable sphere of influence that dimin-ishes as...power radiates from a [spatial] center."[28]

It now seems evident that ancient places are organized like the mobile, centered fields of actors, as spaces stretching out from a reference point to vague peripheries. Indeed, these places are the topographic remnants of the centered fields of ancient actors. The transformations of ancestors' bodies so extensively discussed in the Australian literature are not simply their bodies in some generalized sense but situated bodies in particular stances or states, such as lying down, sitting, dancing, standing and looking at something, or scattered into fragments from a fight – all forms conveying some momentary action or participation in events at a given location. The center, William Hanks says in a Mayan context, "is not merely the body, but the body as it normally engages in movement and action."[29]

The center may also reflect the body's tactile reach just beyond the bodily core of the actor's spatial field. The standard notion of imprints (prototypically, the ordinary footprints or body prints of daily life) involves transformations on the edge of the body. Two ancestral sisters crawling along – pressing against the unmarked land – imprint a winding creek just beyond their own body surfaces.[30] At one place on Ayers Rock, where poisonous snakes threw spears at pythons, the rock is scarred by potholes marking the endpoints of the spears' trajectories.[31] The snakes' remnants reflect a more extended tactile reach of their spatiocorporeal fields. Multiple transformations turn centered mobile fields into the fixed topographic centers of locales, objectified as identifiable places to or towards which others can then travel (or from which they can be excluded). They become locales to which "Aboriginal people can point . . . saying [for example], here is the mark of the Carpet Snake, coming over the sand hills; . . . here is the spear wound in her body."[32] Thus the ancestors' spatiocorporeal or action fields turn into enduring "bases" for the future transient action fields of others.

This perspective on topographic transformation helps to explain how it is that travelling ancestors can be transfixed in more than one place. What they leave behind in each instance is not simply their bodily selves in some general sense but the fixed, momentary *forms* taken by their action fields at that location. It is these located particulars that are, as Aborigines say, "still" or (in an alternative translation) "always" there.[33] Nor do they become "timeless," as the Westernized glossing of such Aboriginal notions often asserts; rather, the time index shifts from the relative transiency of actions to a duration indefinitely extended into the future beyond that of the original ancestral occurrence. That this shift has a mundane temporal (more specifically, spatiotemporal) sense is well shown by the scope of the Warlpiri notion *jukurrarnu* (a term for "long lasting"). As one Warlpiri's explanation goes, "*Jukurrarnu* is what we call a Dreaming [ancestor *jukurrpa*] . . . [who] is always there and a lover . . . still in love with the same person for a long time. Or a person who stays in one place all the time without going anywhere else."[34] The term *jukurrarnu* thus seems to connote "being still there" – a kind of intensification of one position through its temporal extension. In the context of ancient places, "being still there" asserts a legal claim. In this respect, it contrasts with "went right through" – an action leaving no known visible traces (which Aborigines often use in the land claims cases to indicate that no rights can currently be read out of the land from these travels).

The property significance of enduring visibility is not, of course, entirely foreign to Western understandings of property. The legal philosopher Carol Rose points out that in certain "common understandings . . . the very claim of property is that it is something lasting"; and this claim in turn may be meshed with ideas about the unchanging character of visible features like boundary markers.[35] If Aboriginal fixed markers of dominion are visible centers rather than place boundaries, we shall see nevertheless how they create certain kinds of boundaries by moving out from these centers and how at the immobile center they can also become boundaries.

Returning to the dynamics of exclusion, we now find that mobile spatial fields and the terrestrial space of locales are becoming transposable; in certain culturally specified ways, they seem to be shifting back and forth into each other. Here I want to explore this process as manifested in "dangerous encounters" between visitors and the Law of ancient places rather than in detours that avoid such dangers. Beginning with an ancestral encounter, I then take up some modern ones. My aim is to exemplify some permutations of these modes of Aboriginal boundary construction.

One of the key dangerous places in the Alice Springs region is a rocky gorge called Anthwerrke (Emily Gap).[36] Although the gorge is the center of this Aranda place, its influence extends well beyond it at least to the town's edge. According to Spencer and Gillen's classic study, a powerful Aranda witchetty grub ancestor guarded the gap's northern entrance, sometimes sending his instructions beyond the gap in singing that controlled the passage of new witchetty grub immigrants and halted their passage on their way towards the gorge.[37] For instance, one immigrant party was first halted within about two miles of the autochthon, whose singing they heard at a distance. Leaving one man there (apparently at the song's behest), they travelled on, stopping occasionally "to listen for the singing." Approaching the gap "they could [now] plainly hear...[the owner] singing of...[their] coming" and thus permitting them to go to the entrance; but on their arrival, he refused them passage through the gap. So entering the ground, they came up just beyond it, leaving no marks within the gorge. Although they wanted to travel on from the place of their emergence, the owner told them to stay there. Groups of trees arose marking the last spot where they stood before entering the ground and where they remained ("sat down") afterwards.[38]

Although the gap is the owner's bodily location, the center of his control, his voice is part of his sensual reach – an extending movement of his spatiocorporeal field that impacts directly on the fields of others, affecting both their directional passage and its limits.[39] The owner's combined excluding and permissive action typifies Aboriginal notions about the entry of outsiders into these places and, in some respects, into residential communities as well. As one Victoria River man said:

> In our law we are frightened to go...outside our own country because we don't want to give cheek to that other man who owns the country [that is not ours]...If [someone] wants to see any important dreaming place he must ask the owner of that place to allow him to go in...If the owner says no,...you can't do anything about it, you'll have to keep away.[40]

Within the sphere of the owner's sensual reach, the visitors leave persons and terrestrial markers with his permission or when they "halt" to listen for his song;[41] individuals left at a place proceed no further but are allowed to take up residence at a certain distance from the gap, while, finally, at the gap and beyond, trees mark the imposed limits and residential instructions defined for the remaining group. Zones of closeness to the major center are thus mapped on terrestrial space, but obviously they are not simply differentiated regions of space. Rather, they objectify controls and limits on the visitors' spatial fields, which have been defined by the owner's vocal extension (that is, the extent of his own activated spatiosensual field). His power projects these limits directly on the body's mobility; only then can the body and its positional limits be topographically fixed.

The trees at the gap define points after which the group must travel underground until they emerge beyond where other trees visibly embody them. Underground passage signifies that travellers have no visible presence in a region (although their covert passage may leave open the possibility of some future discovery of such signs in the area). It is as if, warned by the owner that they had "no room" inside the gorge, the would-be visitors detoured underground, carving out an excluded locale in their spatial field. But unlike the detours discussed earlier, in which the boundary marker was the transient body itself in the act of detouring, this one transposes the corporeal boundary onto the land (at the points of the beginning and end of the detour) giving it fixed, relatively enduring markers.

I turn now to some modern encounters, beginning with a case from the northern coastal region.[42] The force of the autochthonous power extending from the center appears even more clearly in the recent account of a Belyuen woman: "A boatload of [non-Aboriginal] land claim researchers and...Aborigines from Belyuen and Darwin," out on a mapping trip, were attacked by a manifestation of the place's ancient owner, a Blanket Lizard; the Lizard's "'finger emerged that Dreaming's, she moved...toward...them...[wanting] to down then, they were frightened. [But] that old [Belyuen] lady...talked to the Dreaming now, and it submerged.'"[43]

Since the Lizard recognizes the woman's speech, it "knows" her from previous casual visits; and she in turn knows how to behave towards the Lizard.[44] Otherwise it would "block" the visitors' passage. Belyuen people may say, "No room there, 'im blocked." The blockage must "shift," to "open up the road."[45] Two kinds of spatiotemporal priority and claim are shown to the land claim investigators: that of the autochthon "still there" in the place – who can effectively bar everybody's presence – and that of the Aboriginal visitor whose claim is based on her own past presence, resulting in the *place* recognizing her.

Whether the Aborigines felt that they were within the Lizard's ancestral place when attacked remains vague, but they were clearly within its power ambience. Indeed, the event is reminiscent of widespread Aboriginal notions about rainbow snakes who, ordinarily coiled unseen inside their water holes, angrily rise up to attack trespassers: "When we take strangers or children to a water hole...for the first time," goes a story from Balgo,

> "we tell them to throw in a rock so the snake can 'know' them. If the snake doesn't know someone, he might...make them ill. Or he might come up...and make a whirlpool to pull the stranger under...When he's angry...a Dreamtime snake leaves his water hole [followed by a thunderstorm as he travels]. All this is still here today."[46]

Power is conveyed by an upward emergence from the center much as the power of the Emily Gap owner was conveyed by his verbal control of an extended distance.[47] Unlike a written sign carrying information about later fines for trespass, or a spatially fixed barrier such as a fence, the Belyuen Lizard or the ubiquitous rainbow snake is simultaneously a moving barrier, the dangerous force of the Law, and the place's autochthonous power manifesting itself as it moves out from the center.

This kind of boundary making suggests de Certeau's notion of "the mouthpiece of the limit," which emerges as a region's embodiment in an aggressive narrative agent: "'Stop,' says the forest the wolf comes out of. 'Stop!' says the river, revealing its crocodile." But the Aboriginal autochthon does not emerge beyond the "frontier" of its domain (the river or trees) and thus "establish a border... by saying what crosses it" (as does de Certeau's "mouthpiece");[48] rather, he or she comes up or out from a center without topographic frontiers.[49] Only a transient interaction momentarily gives visible experiential form to the place's enduring character as a bounded, inhabited property *irrespective of any spatially fixed boundaries*. The property's boundedness can thus be apprehended wherever the particular location of the interaction occurs.

Some encounters also involve infringement on the topographic centers where power is *always* manifest. For instance, a Warlpiri man told Glowczewski that his son had once mistakenly touched the "petrified vertebrae" of an ancestor. The boy was unharmed only because his body contained the ancestor's markings and essence (that is, he belonged to the same patrilineal line).[50] In this encounter, antecedent bodily identifications between the place and the child abrogated the boundary just as the Belyuen woman's interiorized knowledge gained from her prior presence at the Blanket Lizard's place saved the land claim group.

"To face danger" – Franz Steiner said in his study of taboo – "is to face another power."[51] The lizard's emergence is a sign of this otherness affecting the group. In Charles S. Peirce's terms, it "addresses somebody," creating an "interpretant" – a responding sign in the minds of the visitors.[52] But it is also a medium of force having what Peirce calls the property of "secondness" – a striking event felt to be occurring out there in the Aborigines' surrounding world; as such, it creates the experience of "compulsion, [an] absolute constraint" requiring participants to modify their action to take account of this external agency.[53] This combination of communication and force characterizes the Aboriginal sense of country.

It is not very far from the Belyuen encounter with a mobile manifestation of place to encounters in which the excluded locale changes because the endangering local center of the Law is temporarily defined by reference to a *mobile* rather than a fixed topographic center. In the context I discuss here, the spaces where some people have "no room" are themselves *in transit*.

Consider Aboriginal regulations of motor travel along Northern Territory roads in Aboriginally held land west of Alice Springs. During journeys for men's or women's ceremonies – called "Business" in Aboriginal English – some of these roads may be restricted because of possible encounters with Business travellers.[54]

The truck carrying the key people in a ritual performance may be called the "'Law' truck."[55] It is, so to speak, the "Law-on-wheels," carrying the power center of authority between places. This truck must always go ahead of any other travellers to the ceremony. Other people have "no room" when it is on the road – the truck must "go first";[56] its entourage must travel behind or come later. The truck thus becomes the organizing center for the road space "up ahead" of and behind it. Travellers unconnected with the entourage are excluded from these selected roads and sometimes avoid them for many days in fear of encounters.[57]

    In this way, the ancestral Law's power of spatial limitation on movement becomes directly embodied in a centered mobile field apart from any fixed, enduring center. As it travels along, the truck defines different excluded regions in its immediate vicinity at any given moment. These exclusions in turn enjoin spatial detours and temporal delays for people's own journeys that keep them off any roads in the entire trajectory during the expected time of the truck's travel. In this respect, the power ambience of the truck extends beyond its immediate moving field at a given moment, affecting the whole projected route, its wider ambience of power. Since travelling for varied reasons is a major part of contemporary Aboriginal life, and the availability of vehicles has increased the ability to journey long distances, major, collectively organized "Business journeys" can markedly affect widely separated Aboriginal communities.

    In organizing routes of Business travel, the Aboriginal towns and settlements involved implicitly define the excluded spaces to which they all become temporarily subject. Although roads are relatively enduring, fixed, and bounded spaces with marked terrestrial limits, the route is a temporary mobile field organized by reference to this travelling power center. Since the truck's route puts common delimitations on travel for the period of its activation, it would seem that people in the affected regions, no matter how distant – where trips are delayed or detoured by these prohibitions – are temporarily brought into an "imagined community" (to use Benedict Anderson's phrase) of common, excluded travel space, a unitary spacetime.[58]

    Despite the regulations, wrongful encounters may occur. If you encounter groups of Aboriginal men travelling to initiations you must get off the road, and "all women [in the vehicle must] hit the floor"; failure to conform can invoke quite severe penalties for men and women.[59] In such an encounter, the Law truck both delimits the space that the other vehicle and its travellers can occupy and constrains the body's verticality and extended sensual fields (specifically, the vision) of the women. Carrying the power of boundary making with it, the Law projects temporary mobile signifiers of its delimiting powers onto the spatiocorporeal fields of others. Instead of creating a distance, as in a detour, bodily comportment cuts off vision. The body becomes its own barrier, shaped into an icon of limitation, that is, of the limits of its own spatial field.

    This form of boundary can operate in conjunction with zoned distancing when, for example, Warlpiri women are legitimately present on men's ritual grounds during performances of ancestral events. In one instance in my experience from the 1950s, women sat behind a low brush windbreak on the other side of which men sat singing. The brush shade marked differential zones of distancing from the power center of the performance. (This zoning is comparable to that created by the visitors' differential access to and exclusions from the power center of Emily Gap, which we saw earlier.) At certain moments, men told women to lie or crouch down under blankets so as to see nothing at all. The women's spatiocorporeal field was thus cut off at different zones of extension. Initially barred in part by the brush shade a little in front of them, it was wholly blocked at the immediate limits of their bodies when they were covered with blankets. In this moment, their constrained, covered, and terrestrially bounded spatial fields appear as definitive icons of "no room."

    To summarize, Aboriginal "excluded spaces" can be understood as particular spatiotemporal formations produced out of the interaction of actors' moving spatial fields and the terrestrial spaces or bases of bodily action. From this perspective, the analytic problem of spatial boundaries cannot automatically refer to limits marked out on pieces of land (or in architectural forms); nor can bodily boundaries be dealt with as body surfaces apart from the body's spatiality, actions, and locatedness.

We have seen that within these interactions, different kinds of what might be called "transposabilities" emerge between Aboriginal locales of power and the mobile, spatial fields of actors.[60] In different ways, and for variable time spans, Aboriginal power places and the immobilized powers in the topography switch over or are transposed into actors and their mobile spatial fields. So, for instance, the Belyuen Lizard is roused into motion; or the power of Law fixed in the country becomes a moving space – a Law truck with its travellers. Conversely, actors are transposed into fixed locales and terrestrial forms (as when the spatial fields of ancient actors become named topographies).

Furthermore, although I have been unable to discuss it here, a well-known aspect of Aboriginal practices allows ancient topographic features to be detached from fixed locations and reproduced in iconographic designs, which can then be mobilized for varying time spans as aspects of persons, objects, or other spaces. Thus topographies (in their inconographic form) can be transposed onto actors' bodies (through painting) and onto different terrestrial spaces (as in ground paintings or drawings). Similarly, some people may be prohibited from seeing these painted forms; they must turn away from them or keep a distance from the locations of their temporary embodiments.[61] In other words, transposability opens up various spatiotemporal channels between persons and terrestrial space, and along these channels the power of the Aboriginal Law circulates, creating multiple spaces and time spans of exclusion.

Of course, transposabilities have very different bases and purposes and take multiple, varied forms in different societies and social contexts. Before concluding, I want to point beyond this essay to its implicit, comparative concerns by drawing attention to a familiar Western context where transposabilities of another kind are crucial. My example is Olmsted and Vaux's 1850s design for New York's Central Park, a mid-nineteenth-century American variant of those much-written-about "landscape" practices to which John Dixon Hunt's "figure in the landscape" refers.[62]

In Olmsted and Vaux's construction of the park one can find transpositional "switch points" between persons and terrestrial space. For instance, working from the basic cultural assumptions of these landscape practices, the architects plotted "scenes" (which they also called views or pictures) into the land. Their scenes or views had variable (sometimes crosscutting, sometimes more or less coincident) relations to the park's more overt topographic organization into named places, but the scenes constituted a different kind and level of spatial organization. Unlike the named places, they were formulated in terms of the mobile spatiosensual fields of actors. The architects designed such views by considering how the topography looked (and how they wanted it to look) from the vantage point of a situated observer, that is, by assuming a viewer, a park visitor, from whom the scene stretched out as his or her spatiosensual field. For instance, land near one of the major gates was designed and materially constructed in a way that was to draw the "visitor's eye" to "an unbroken meadow...[so that] the observer, resting for a moment to enjoy the scene...cannot but hope for still greater space than is obvious before him."[63] In fact, the architects themselves are the prototypic creator-viewers – the first observers – who are embedding their own "views" or spatiosensual fields in the landscape. By this design practice of viewing and materially reconstructing the land in accord with the desired views, they project themselves into the land in the form of objectifications of their own spatial fields.

Thus, through scenic construction, the parkland was invested with a category of actor (a visitor-viewer) to be repetitively actualized by future visitors. In this sense, the land itself was being transposed into present and future subject-centered fields. Moreover, visitors were to be drawn into the park and affected by the "poetic" influence of certain qualities of the scenes; these qualities had the power to act on people's inner states of being or mind, and so make life "healthier and happier" in the city.[64] Spatial qualities, such as openness, or diffuse expressive qualities, such as tranquility (both standard components of the topographic aesthetics of the land-scape tradition), were to be built into the scenic topography; for instance, open space is made available to experience in the "unbroken meadow" noted above. Tranquility can most easily illustrate the sorts of transpositions between persons and locales these qualities engendered. For if the parkland was to "present an aspect of . . . tran-quility," tranquility was also taken as a desired subjective state that could infuse persons present in these locales.[65] The potency of the landscape was thus concen-trated in transposable qualities that could shift from its visible surfaces into the inner beings of actors.

It should then be evident that park scenes and their qualities are spatial fulcra of transposabilities between the bodily persons of actors (or mobile spatiosensual fields) and terrestrial space. In this respect, they can be compared with the ancestral, centered places of Aborigines, although they obviously operate in fundamentally different ways. Indeed, the differences between them are instructive in understand-ing the distinctive spatiotemporal forms involved; but these issues lie outside my argument here.

The present essay has argued against certain commonplace assumptions about space, boundaries, and time. That space is static and to be contrasted with the dynamism of time; that spatial boundaries are always fixed, relatively enduring forms marked off on the ground may seem self-evident to some, but, as Jameson has put it, "the self-evident draws its force from hosts of buried presuppositions."[66] Thus, if we understand space simply as referring to culturally meaningful terrestrial places or regions, we disarticulate the dynamic relations between spatial regions and moving spatial fields. This sort of reification in turn dissolves the integrity of space and time, for it extracts from the analytic model the centering subject – the spatially and temporally situated actor – through whom and in whose experience the integrity of space and time emerges. What we need, then, is a paradigm that works against abstracting the problem of space from that of the body and action, and against the oppositional separation of space and time. To counteract these objectivist distinc-tions, I have considered Aboriginal practices of spatial exclusion in terms that coordinate elements of space, time, and bodily action within a single paradigm of changing relations. In short, I have attempted to keep intact what Bakhtin calls the "concrete architectonic" of the lived world.[67]

NOTES

This essay is a slightly revised form of the Frazer Lecture presented at Oxford University in May 1995. The analysis is part of a larger work in progress on the cultural anthropology of space and time. Grateful acknowledgement is made to the Guggenheim Foundation for a fellowship supporting part of the basic research for this work and the present essay.

1   James G. Frazer, *Pausanias and Other Greek Sketches* (London, 1900), p. 159.
2   The phrase is Thomas Hardy's. See J. Hillis Miller, *Topographies* (Stanford, Calif., 1995), p. 4. See also John Dixon Hunt, *The Figure in the Landscape: Poetry, Painting, and Gardening during the Eighteenth Century* (1976; Baltimore, 1989).
3   For a commentary on Frazer's aesthetic interest in setting scenes, see Stanley Edgar Hyman, *The Tangled Bank: Darwin, Marx, Frazer, and Freud as Imaginative Writers* (New York, 1966), pp. 254–55. One possible exception to Frazer's primarily mood-setting approach to space is his theory of the "origins" of totemism in Aboriginal notions of a person's conception at particular totemic places; see Frazer, "The Beginnings of Religion and Totemism among the Australian Aborigines (II)," *Fortnightly Review* 78 (Sept. 1905): 452–66. But the local aspect of this totemism is secondary to Frazer, who argues that totemic localities enter into Aboriginal conception notions only through accidents of association with some feature of the place "where [one's]...mother happened to be" (p. 457). In any case, the significance of place as such is never drawn into theoretical focus.
4   Frazer, *The Golden Bough: A Study in Magic and Religion*, 3d ed., 10 vols. (London, 1911–13), 10:vi; quoted in Jonathan Smith, "When the Bough Breaks," *Map Is Not Territory: Studies in the History of Religions* (Chicago, 1978), p. 211.
5   David Parkin, *Sacred Void: Spatial Images of Work and Ritual among the Giriama of Kenya* (Cambridge, 1991), p. 1.
6   Numerous studies draw attention to these interdictions. Mention should be made of Kenneth Maddock, "Dangerous Proximities and Their Analogues," *Mankind* 9 (June 1974): 206–17, and David Biernoff, "Safe and Dangerous Places," in *Australian Aboriginal Concepts*, ed. Leslie Hiatt (Atlantic Highlands, N.J., 1978). I discuss only a small portion of the range of interdictions here.
7   The names and locations of key peoples and places discussed in the essay are as follows: the Aranda (now also written Arrernte) of central Australia (the Northern Territory) who own Emily Gap (Anthwerrke) and its environs southeast of the desert town of Alice Springs; the Warlpiri (also Walbiri) who have towns and communities north and northwest of Alice Springs (I mention Yuendumu, some 175 miles northwest, and Lajamanu across the Tanami desert northwest of Yuendumu); western desert Kukatja peoples living around Balgo, near the Western Australian border; and the peoples of Yarralin, in Victoria River country of the northwest Northern Territory. I also refer to the huge monolith, Ayers Rock (Uluru), of the southwest Northern Territory, which belongs to speakers of several western desert dialects, including Pitjantjatjara. The only coastal community discussed is Belyuen (home of speakers of a number of languages), which is near the north central coast of the Northern Territory, west of the northern coastal center of Darwin.
8   There appears to be no indigenous equivalent for this expression (according to Francesca Merlan, written communication with author, Feb. 1995), although there are, of course, terms for avoidance. The full extent of its use among Aborigines is not documented, but it appears to be widespread in the desert region and at least to some extent beyond. See Diane Bell, *Daughters of the Dreaming* (North Sydney, 1983), p. 15 and personal communication with author, 1995; Michael Jackson, *At Home in the World* (Durham, N.C., 1995), p. 53; David Nash, written communication with author, Jan. 1995; and Elizabeth

Povinelli, conversation with author, Sept. 1994. In my own experience it was operative among Yuendumu Walpiri in the mid-1950s. However, according to Merlan (telephonic and written communication with author, Feb. 1995), Aborigines in Katherine township (north-central Northern Territory) do not employ this usage, but may use *room* in the expected English sense of a spatial unit or of insufficient physical space irrespective of moral-legal constraints. See also Cliff Goddard, *I.A.D. Basic Pitjantjatjara/Yankuntjat-jara–English Dictionary* (Alice Springs, 1987), p. 122; reference courtesy of Janet Simpson. In some cases, the expression may be used in both ways; see Nash, written communication with author, Jan. 1995. Bell gives an excellent illustration of the difference between the expected English usage and "no room" in the more complex moral-legal sense discussed here. When attempting to drive Aboriginal women along a road that looked clear to her ahead, Bell was stopped by one of the women who said she couldn't "go down there, too much...son-in-law, no room" (Bell, *Daughters of the Dreaming*, p. 15). Although this road offered physically clear travel space, they would have been moving too close to the camp of the woman's tabooed son-in-law. In this sense, there was not enough physical space because of the distances required by the moral law.

9   Still other exclusions depend on the presence in a given region of gender-related camps or residences, which are avoided by people of the opposite sex; for example, men avoid the women's group residence and gathering place. In this essay, I do not discuss in-law avoidances and only briefly note avoidances connected with deaths. However, I take all these exclusions to entail, at any given moment, avoidance of a specific region, even though, as in the case of in-law avoidances, the particular region involved may be entirely dependent on the presence of certain persons, changing with their location. We shall see that the framework I propose precludes treating persons apart from their spatial situatedness and space apart from persons. Thus, among other things, one cannot abstract "social space" from "concrete space."

10 Mervyn J. Meggitt, *Desert People: A Study of the Walbiri Aborigines of Central Australia* (Sydney, 1963), p. 54. In making this analogy, Meggitt remarks that regions can be "distinguished" by varying intensities of emotions such as fear or shame "attendant on entering them" (ibid.). In the present essay, I concentrate on contexts where fear or apprehension is a prominent attitude, and danger of varying degrees is involved. Meggitt also speaks of the Walbiri sense that they might "lack space" in a given region, apparently using the term *space* for the Walbiri English *room*.

11 The *Northern Territory Aboriginal Sacred Sites Act* (1978; emended 1989) was established as a complement to the general *Aboriginal Land Rights (Northern Territory) Act* (1976). Since the 1970s, anthropological discussions of Aboriginal place-boundaries (or their absence) have to be understood as occurring in a litigious milieu of contestations involving Aborigines, the government, and other parties interested in the spatial definitions of areas to be protected and the location of their limits. Apart from conflicting politico-economic and cultural concerns, these issues are fuelled by the fundamentally different means of constructing space characteristic of Aboriginal and Western industrial/postindustrial cultures. For analytic purposes, one should not, therefore, conflate Aboriginal-named place constructs with these new sorts of Aboriginal places ("sacred sites" in the legal sense). Different kinds of enclaves are created in this process and the definitional practices themselves have changed. If signs are erected they may state the area is a "Registered Sacred Site" thus indicating Euro-Australian legal status; information about penalties of violations and the site's Aboriginal significance may also be given. The pervasive use of the label *sacred site* for Aboriginal ancient places (a label now used popularly by Aborigines as well as others to denote Aboriginal ancestral places in general) arose in connection with the Aboriginal land claims. For a brief history of this

usage see Maddock, "Metamorphosing the Sacred in Australia," *Australian Journal of Anthropology* 2, no. 2 (1991): 213–33.

12 Henri Lefebvre, *The Production of Space*, trans. D. N. Smith (Oxford, 1991), p. 191. Lefebvre's formulation articulates the dualities of an old problem entailing the relations between relative, or subject-centered, and nonrelative, "absolute" or "objective," human space, which others have articulated in different terms and from variable perspectives. See, for example, Edward S. Casey, *Getting Back into Place: Toward a Renewed Understanding of the Place-World* (Bloomington, Ind., 1993); Michel de Certeau, "Spatial Stories," *The Practice of Everyday Life*, trans. Steven Rendall (Berkeley, 1984), pp. 91–130; Gareth Evans, *The Varieties of Reference*, ed. John McDowell (Oxford, 1982), chap. 6; Alfred Gell, "How to Read a Map: Remarks on the Practical Logic of Navigation," *Man* 20 (June 1985): 271–86; William Hanks, *Referential Practice: Language and Lived Space among the Maya* (Chicago, 1990); and Erwin Straus, *The Primary World of the Senses: A Vindication of Sensory Experience*, trans. Jacob Needleman (New York, 1963).

13 In this essay I use the labels *locale* or *region* as general cover terms for any kind of location or space. When discussing Aboriginal space, I use *place* in a narrower sense, confining it to contexts where Aborigines would make use of the relevant indigenous term it can gloss (for instance, Warlpiri *ngurra*, camp habitation, ancestral site place). In practice, I apply *place* primarily to ancestral locales (which I call "ancient named places"). Terms with a similar semantic range to the Warlpiri *ngurra* are pan-Aboriginal and crucial to Aboriginal spatial practices.

14 This framing resonates with a variety of approaches to the spatiality of the body, such as those of Casey, *Getting Back into Place*; Pierre Bourdieu, *Outline of a Theory of Practice*, trans. Richard Nice (1972; Cambridge, 1977); Hanks, *Referential Practice*; Maurice Merleau-Ponty, *Phenomenology of Perception*, trans. Colin Smith (London, 1962); and Abraham A. Moles and Elisabeth Rohmer, *Psychologie de l'espace* (Paris, 1978).

15 Straus, *The Primary World of the Senses*, p. 319.

16 An illustrative term for this type of act is the Warlpiri *warri-ngirntiri*, bypass, the long way around, which explicitly carries the sense of circling around. See Mary Laughren and Kenneth Hale, *Warlpiri-English Encyclopaedic Dictionary*, electronic files, at Department of English, University of Queensland, Brisbane. I am indebted to the authors for their generosity in making this dictionary available to me.

17 Susan Kesteven, "A Sketch of Yuendumu and Its Outstations" (master's thesis, Australian National University, 1978), p. 21. Locales linked with the remembered or recent dead are detoured or avoided.

18 Barbara Glowczewski, *Les Rêveurs du désert: Aborigènes d'Australie, les Warlpiri* (Paris, 1989), p. 188; my translation.

19 As the ethnomusicologist Richard Moyle puts it, "'if you can see it, then you're too close'" (Richard Moyle, "Songs, Ceremonies, and Sites: The Agharringa Case," in *Aborigines, Land, and Land Rights*, ed. Nicolas Peterson and Marcia Langton [Canberra, 1983], p. 72). In Warlpiri, the term *seeing-without* may be used in connection with detouring. See Laurie Reece, *Dictionary of the Wailbri (Walpiri) Language of Central Australia*, 2 vols. (Sydney, 1975/1979), 2:44.

20 See Françoise Dussart, "Warlpiri Women's Yawalyu Ceremonies: A Forum for Socialization and Innovation" (Ph.D. diss., Australian National University, 1988), p. 52, and Nancy D. Munn, *Walbiri Iconography: Graphic Representation and Cultural Symbolism in a Central Australian Society* (1973; Chicago, 1986), pp. 49, 52.

21 See above, n. 16.

22 Bourdieu, *Outline of a Theory of Practice*, p. 117; emphasis removed. We tend to conceive of boundaries as relatively permanent, fixed aspects of space detached from

human movement. But all such boundary markers are the result of some boundary-making acts of definition and production, including verbal acts of *"spatial legislation,"* as de Certeau has stressed (de Certeau, *The Practice of Everyday Life*, p. 122). It is helpful to think of boundary-making practices as ranging from the use or creation of a spatially fixed, detached marker (whether "natural" or "artificial") with long-term durability to boundary-making acts that do not construct any relatively enduring, fixed, concrete spatial marker detached from actors. Within this range one finds, for instance, people making boundaries by repetitive acts of renewal that set out detachable but temporary material markers (see, for example, Robert J. Thornton, *Space, Time, and Culture among the Iraqw of Tanzania* [New York, 1980], chap. 4), or boundary making by repeated acts of walking off and "looking" to define and redefine topographical bounds by travelling across or looking beyond previous limits. See Joanne Rappaport, "History, Myth, and the Dynamics of Territorial Maintenance in Tierradentro, Colombia," *American Ethnologist* 12 (Feb. 1985): 27–45.

23 See Georg Simmel, "The Transcendent Character of Social Life," *On Individuality and Social Forms: Selected Writings*, ed. Donald Levine (Chicago, 1971), p. 353; however, Simmel is talking about persons as boundaries in a sense quite different from my discussion here.

24 Deborah Bird Rose, *Dingo Makes Us Human: Life and Land in an Aboriginal Australian Culture* (Cambridge, 1992), p. 109. Rose is referring to the peoples of Yarralin, but this is a characteristic feature of the Aboriginal sense of space throughout Australia; nor should it be read as simply metaphorical (see also below, on Belyuen).

25 Quoted in ibid., p. 56.

26 Peterson, Stephen Wild, and Patrick McConvell, *Claim to Areas of Traditional Land by the Warlpiri and Kartangarurru-Kurintji* (1976), p. 5.

27 Ian Keen and F. Merlan, "The Significance of the Conservation Zone to Aboriginal People," Resource Assessment Commission: Kakadu Conservation Zone Inquiry, consultancy no. 8 (Dec. 1990), p. 45. Concern with the question of Aboriginal delimitations of ancient places has long been a preoccupation in the anthropological literature; the complex details of the arguments are necessarily beyond my purview here. See, among many others, Bell, "Sacred Sites: The Politics of Protection," in *Aborigines, Land, and Land Rights*, pp. 278–93; Ronald M. Berndt, "The Concept of 'the Tribe' in the Western Desert of Australia," *Oceania* 30 (Dec. 1959): 81–107 and "Territoriality and the Problem of Demarcating Sociocultural Space," in *Tribes and Boundaries in Australia*, ed. Peterson (Canberra, 1976), pp. 133–61; Erich Kolig, *Dreamtime Politics: Religion, World View, and Utopian Thought in Australian Aboriginal Society* (Berlin, 1989), chap. 2; Maddock, "Australia a Sacred Site?" *Your Land Is Our Land: Aboriginal Land Rights* (Ringwood, Victoria, 1983), pp. 131–51, and Nancy Williams, "A Boundary Is to Cross: Observations on Yolngu Boundaries and Permission," in *Resource Managers: North American and Australian Hunter-Gatherers*, ed. Williams and Eugene S. Hunn (Boulder, Colo., 1982), pp. 131–53.

28 S. J. Tambiah, *World Conqueror and World Renouncer: A Study of Buddhism and Polity in Thailand against a Historical Background* (Cambridge, 1976), p. 112. See also Benedict R. O'G. Anderson, "The Idea of Power in Javanese Culture," in *Culture and Politics in Indonesia*, ed. Claire Holt, Anderson, and James Siegel (Ithaca, N.Y., 1972), pp. 1–69. Anderson also points to the fundamental spatial distinction between a "frontier"-oriented polity and one "defined by its center, not by its perimeter" (p. 29).

29 Hanks, *Referential Practice*, p. 90.

30 The example comes from Berndt, "Territoriality and the Problem of Demarcating Sociocultural Space," p. 137, but the principle of imprinting is basic. See Munn, "The Transformation of Subjects into Objects in Walbiri and Pitjantjatjara Myth," in *Austra-*

lian Aboriginal Anthropology: Modern Studies in the Social Anthropology of the Australian Aborigines, ed. Berndt (Nedlands, 1970), pp. 141–63. Imprinting of this kind is in some respects an epitomizing instance of some aspects of Casey's philosophy of place and body. Casey takes the view that because everything, and most notably all human bodies, has a "place" (where they are "at"), place itself cannot be separated from the body that is its "inner boundary" (Casey, *Getting Back into Place*, p. 29). However, in the present context, bodies are also defining/creating the distinctive "places" where they are, for although the women go along on a pregiven ground, it is not a locale in Aboriginal terms until particularized by markings.

31 See Robert Layton, *Uluru: An Aboriginal History of Ayers Rock* (Canberra, 1986), pp. 7–8, and Charles P. Mountford, *Ayers Rock: Its People, Their Beliefs, and Their Art* (Sydney, 1965), p. 40 and plates 14a and b (p. 44).

32 Layton, *Uluru*, p. 15.

33 The Warlpiri and Pitjantjatjara terms, *tarngna* and *titu*, respectively, may be glossed in either way.

34 Laughren and Hale, *Warlpiri-English Encyclopaedic Dictionary*. In this passage, *always* translates the Warlpiri *tarnnga; a long time* and *all the time* both translate *jukurrarnu*.

35 Carol M. Rose, *Property and Persuasion: Essays on the History, Theory, and Rhetoric of Ownership* (Boulder, Colo., 1994), p. 272.

36 See Bell, "Sacred Sites," for a recent relevant discussion.

37 Witchetty grubs are edible larval forms of various tree-boring insects. The contemporary literature refers to the ancestral totemic beings dominating the Emily Gap–Alice Springs region as caterpillars; see, for example, Bell "Sacred Sites," p. 286. But Baldwin Spencer and Francis James Gillen, *The Native Tribes of Central Australia* (1899; London, 1938), call them witchetty grubs (glossing a specific indigenous term). For convenience, I follow their gloss here.

38 Spencer and Gillen, *The Native Tribes of Central Australia*, pp. 431–32. The estimate of the gap's distance from their first halt is mine, based on information in ibid., p. 425. For other Aboriginal notions connecting singing and control over distance, see especially John von Sturmer, "Aboriginal Singing and Notions of Power," in *Songs of Aboriginal Australia*, ed. M. Clunies Ross, T. Donaldson, and S. Wild (Sydney, 1987).

39 This kind of boundary-making power through sensual reach outward from a fixed position can be found, for instance, in parts of South Asia in connection with the images of deities fixed in temples or shrine houses whose eyesight can wield extended boundary-making force. David Scott discusses the narrative of one such Sinhala deity. Standing high in its shrine house, its vision "stretching out over the ocean, [it] formed a steadfast, transparent wall, a sort of beam of eye energy, preventing the trespass of the colonial invaders" who could not cross its line of sight (David Scott, *Formations of Ritual: Colonial and Anthropological Discourses on the Sinhala "Yaktovil"* [Minneapolis, 1994], p. 42).

40 Quoted in Darrell Lewis and Deborah Bird Rose, *The Shape of the Dreaming: The Cultural Significance of Victoria River Rock Art* (Canberra, 1988), p. 66. See also Spencer and Gillen, *The Native Tribes of Central Australia*, p. 431 n. 1.

41 Spencer and Gillen's account in *The Native Tribes of Central Australia* does not make explicit the principle that leaving people behind implies leaving terrestrial marks, which are themselves the reembodiments of actors and their activities.

42 See above, n. 7.

43 Povinelli, *Labor's Lot: The Power, History, and Culture of Aboriginal Action* (Chicago, 1993), pp. 44, 45.

44 See ibid., p. 46.

45 Povinelli, conversation with author, 1994.

46   Gracie Greene, Joe Tramachi, and Lucille Gill, *Tjarany Roughtail: The Dreaming of the Roughtail Lizard and Other Stories Told by the Kukatja* (Broome, 1993), pp. 26, 29. Warlpiri accounts of the rainbow snake rising up in the storm, which were given to me in verbal and visual form in the 1950s, were both descriptions of the way rain emerges from the ground and storms across the country, and narratives of particular ancestral events.

47   "Coming out/up – going in/underneath" is a general pattern of movement entailing change into a visible form (emergence) and conversely into invisibility (submergence); compare the Aranda case above.

48   De Certeau, *The Practice of Everyday Life*, p. 127.

49   The autochthon does move, however, from the domain of inside/underneath to the outside/above; this is the "crossing" that makes the difference in Aboriginal terms, since through it the autochthon becomes visible.

50   Glowczewski, *Les Rêveurs du désert*, p. 43.

51   Franz Steiner, *Taboo* (London, 1956), p. 146.

52   Charles S. Peirce, *Philosophical Writings of Peirce*, ed. Justus Buchler (New York, 1955), pp. 99, 100.

53   Ibid., p. 89.

54   See Elspeth Young, "Continuité et changement dans la mobilité des Aborigènes: Les Warlpiri du désert central australien," *L'Espace géographique* 12 (Jan.–Mar. 1983): 42, and Young and Kim Doohan, *Mobility for Survival: A process Analysis of Aboriginal Population Movement in Central Australia* (Darwin, 1989), pp. 92–95. See also Christopher Anderson, conversation with author, 1992.

55   Young and Doohan, *Mobility for Survival*, p. 99.

56   Laughren, conversation with author, 1992.

57   See Young and Doohan, *Mobility for Survival*, p. 94.

58   According to Young and Doohan, communities carry out "lengthy negotiations over the tracks which can be used . . . [taking into account] the dreaming tracks of the [relevant] ancestral beings, as well as . . . existing roads and . . . [road] usage" (Young and Doohan, *Mobility for Survival*, p. 93). The authors also give a specific case of the coordination of a number of desert Aboriginal communities involved in a long-distance Business trip of 1982–83.

59   Langton, conversation with author, 1992.

60   Technical use of this term is made by linguists. My own usage is somewhat different but not unrelated. See John Haviland, "Projections, Transpositions, and Relativity," Cognitive Anthropology Research Group, working paper no. 3 (Nijmegen, Oct. 1991), and also Hanks, *Referential Practice*, for a discussion of transpositional processes in Mayan ritual.

61   For additional characteristic types of Aboriginal transpositions, see relevant commentaries on conception, birthmarks, and related notions in Munn, "The Transformation of Subjects into Objects in Walbiri and Pitjantjatjara Myth."

62   For Olmsted and Vaux's plan, see especially Frederick Law Olmsted, *Creating Central Park: 1857–1861*, vol. 3 of *The Papers of Frederick Law Olmsted*, ed. Charles E. Beveridge and David Schuyler (Baltimore, 1983). The comments are adapted from my own analysis in a working paper, part of a larger work in progress. See Munn, "Creating a Heterotopia: An Analysis of the Spacetime of Olmsted's and Vaux's Central Park," unpublished working paper prepared for a conference on "Place, Expression, and Experience," School of American Research, Mar. 1993.

63   Quoted in Olmsted, *Creating Central Park*, pp. 183–84 n. 19, from Olmsted and Vaux's comments about the Central Park design in their report on Prospect Park, 1866.

64   Olmsted, "Superintendant of Central Park to Gardeners," *Frederick Law Olmsted: Landscape Architect, 1822–1903*, ed. Frederick Law Olmsted, Jr., and Theodora Kim-

ball, 2 vols. in 1 (1922: New York, 1970), 2:356. In this 1870s directive to park gardeners, Olmsted states: "The character of...[the park landscape's] influence [on visitors] is a poetic one and it is to be produced by means of scenes" (ibid.).

65   Olmsted, "Description of the Central Park," *Creating Central Park*, p. 212. See also Olmsted and Vaux's remarks on the "tranquilizing" effects of pastoral landscapes from their report on Prospect Park cited in Beveridge, "Frederick Law Olmsted's Theory on Landscape Design," *Nineteenth Century* 3 (Summer 1977): 38.

66   Fredric Jameson, *Marxism and Form: Twentieth-Century Dialectical Theories of Literature* (Princeton, N.J., 1971), p. 308.

67   See Mikhail M. Bakhtin, *Toward a Philosophy of the Act*, trans. Vadim Liapunov, ed. Michael Holquist and Liapunov (Austin, Tex., 1993).

4

Indexical Speech across Samoan Communities

Alessandro Duranti

In transnational communities, speaking about space can be a way of bridging physic-ally distant but emotionally and ethically close worlds. A comparison of the use and context of one particular Samoan expression, *nofo i lalo!* ("sit down!"), as used in a Western Samoan village and a suburban neighborhood in southern California, sug-gests that the indexical grounding of this expression within a horizon of specific body orientations and material artifacts not only opens it to a variety of interpretations but also makes it "ready-to-use" in establishing connections with a distant world that might be unknown to the recipient of the message. In the United States, a Samoan mother might issue an instruction in Samoan regarding proper spatial orientation to children who have never been to a Samoan island and have not experienced the world of material possessions and ethical stances that is presupposed by such an instruction. In this context, such a command is more than an instruction uttered by a frustrated mother who is trying to control restless children jumping around in the living room. It is also an attempt to evoke an interpretive horizon where vertical and horizontal positioning of one's body in the living space has socioethical implications that, once recognized, can establish a cultural continuity that is otherwise defined by the built environment in which the interaction takes place. "Talking space" in this way then becomes another contested ground where the battle between continuity and change can be fought. It is another way of drawing the boundaries of the community, this time not on paper but in the interactional fabric of live discourse.

Before engaging in the analysis of living space in two distant Samoan commu-nities, I must first deal with a problem in the language of anthropologists. Although an expression used by earlier researchers as a general label for a range of local notions and practices might help us make sense of what we are experiencing, it might also stop us from seeing other, equally important practices.

Old and New Anthropological Key Expressions

Each ethnographer has a stock of anthropological *key expressions*, representing misleadingly simple concepts with the unique power to evoke endless streams of associated meanings and provide countless occasions for anecdotes, descriptions, and hypotheses, reaching all the way into local or even universal theories of the human mind, the social nature of things, the thingness of human action. For many cultural anthropologists key expressions are either a single word or a pair of words, usually an oppositional set. A classic example is Clifford Geertz's (1983) use of the Arabic term *nisba*, which he elucidates with a long list of associated meanings and etymologically related terms. According to Geertz, to understand *nisba* means to get a hold of the main instrument through which Moroccans "sort people out from one another and form an idea of what it is to be a person" (1983:65). *Nisba*, then, becomes a key expression for understanding the Moroccan sense of person, a central focus of Geertz's brand of interpretive anthropology.

Another example is the pair *liget/beya*, roughly "knowledge/anger, passion," in Michelle Rosaldo's (1980) ethnography of the Ilongots. For Rosaldo, understanding how the semantic domains associated with these two terms are organized, and how they are made sense of in everyday practices, means coming to terms with the Ilongot worldview and way of life, including head-hunting practices. As Daniel Rosenberg has rightly pointed out, in this kind of lexically organized representation of culture, we risk essentializing a vast range of complex cultural practices in terms of one or two words (Rosenberg 1990:166). We also use language in a very limited sense, distilling a few drops of lexical material out of the multifarious and rich usages that characterize any real-life situation.

Yet key expressions have been shown to be powerful tools for the researcher/ observer. These words and (more rarely) phrases, smuggled through the invisible and yet quite real customs of anthropological inspection, have the power to connect first us and later our audience to a group of strangers, a place, a time, an unfolding of events that otherwise seem either too ordinary to be worth attention or too extraordinary to be described at all. Key expressions make the experience of "being there" not only real but almost scientific (Geertz 1988). Despite my training in linguistics and discourse analysis, I too was attracted to the possibility of representing what were obviously complex social interactions through the use of such expressions – although I chose a phrase describing an action rather than a noun describing a concept.

As a fourth-generation linguistic anthropologist, I have had a peculiar relationship with the key expressions I used in the field. For one thing, I was not the one who made them up or "discovered" them. The first time I went to Western Samoa, in 1978–79, I worked as part of a research team. We could count on a number of already existing ethnographies from which to extract key words to enlighten our experience. Our professional heritage was partly shared by our subjects. Many adult Samoans in 1978 knew about Margaret Mead, although only a few had ever read her *Coming of Age in Samoa*. Our entrance in the village where we ended up living was facilitated through a chain of contacts that started with a conversation with fellow cultural anthropologist Bradd Shore a few months earlier. It was from Shore's unpublished 1977 dissertation, or perhaps his stories and recommendations at the 1978 annual meeting of the Association for Social Anthropology in Oceania, that I took one of his favorite key expressions: *teu le vā* (take care of the relationship). Here is his revised published version:

> Not only are there in Samoan no terms corresponding to the English "personality,"
> "self" or "character," but there is also an absence of the corresponding assumptions
> about the relations of person to social action. A clue to the Samoan notion of person is
> found in the popular Samoan saying *teu le vā* (take care of the relationship). Contrasted
> with the Greek dicta "Know thyself" or "To thine own self be true," this saying suggests
> something of the difference between Occidental and Samoan orientation. [Shore
> 1982:136]

After a few months of fieldwork, I started to focus on the discourse produced by
chiefs and orators during the meetings of the village council (*fono*). It is a discourse
full of fancy metaphors and respectful terms that try to cover or transform
(depending on the point of view) the tension that all participants can feel through
their bones and hear through their ears. After examining the transcripts of several
meetings with long and heated debates about hurt relationships and attempts to
mend them, I decided that *teu le vā* was quite appropriate for what the *matai*
(titleholders) are up to in the fono. (The expression actually found in the fono
speeches was *teuteu le vā*, which means something like "make the relationship
beautiful," used as an encouragement to mend the relationship with a nearby
village.) The fono enterprise as a whole could be adequately characterized as an
attempt to take care (*teu*) of the relationships (*vā*) among the participants and not
only between the village and other political entities. As an *event*, the fono is a classic
conflict-negotiation setting, a crucial step in an unfolding "social drama" (Turner
1974) where talk is used to "disentangle" (Watson-Gegeo and White 1990) the
interpersonal disharmony created by past or forthcoming events. Relationships
must be restored to their ideal if not original condition, to what participants refer
to as *featofani* (mutual love, harmony).

Teu le vā also became an expression that Elinor Ochs, Martha Platt, and I used in
the field to explain our own or other people's behavior. We used it when we tried to
convince ourselves that we should or should not do something, trying to come to
terms with the tension between our latent beliefs and ideologies and the ethics of a
profession that values empathy (or at least neutrality) over confrontation. In other
words, we found that we were also engaged in taking care of the relationship, the
one between us and our hosts, the people we had gone to study.

Many years later, when I started to pay more attention to the discourse of
household interactions, among women and children in particular, I realized that,
had I decided to concentrate on those settings, I might have chosen a different key
expression.

Directives in the Discourse of Caregivers

I remember that during our first field trip I had been shocked by how many orders in
the grammatical form of imperatives – "do this," "go there," "bring that," and so on
– could be found in the transcripts of the household interactions recorded by Elinor
and Martha. As I recount in my 1994 book, this realization was frustrating for a
grammarian and discourse analyst looking for "canonical transitive clauses," that is,
utterances with fully expressed agents, such as "the boy dropped the cup," "the

woman fed the baby," or "the man built a boat." The women's style was also in contrast with the men's interaction that I had been recording, especially the oratorical styles of the fono and the ceremonies attended by titleholders.

Fifteen years later, as I read through newly collected transcripts of interaction between Samoan children and their caregivers, I find myself dealing with similar situations and a similar discourse, full of orders and elliptical clauses. This time, however, I have not been an analyst of data collected by someone else.

In 1993, Elinor Ochs and I started a three-year project in a Samoan community in southern California, focusing on children's activities, collective problem solving, and literacy tasks (Duranti and Ochs 1996, in press). This time I found Samoans only 30 miles from our house, across several socioeconomic boundaries and close to a freeway exit that I had not explored before this project started. The Samoan families I visited live at walking distance from one another and, more importantly, at walking distance from the Samoan church they all attend (Duranti et al. 1995).

While examining the transcripts of interactions that I had videotaped during one of the visits to a family in our study, I discovered that many of the imperatives in the mother's directives were about locations in space. It was then that I was reminded of the frequent commands in the adult–child interaction recorded in Western Samoa. I realized that, had I started from the interactions among children, their older siblings, and adult relatives, I might have been tempted to pick something quite different from *teu le vā* as my key expression, perhaps something more ordinary, less abstract, and yet equally enlightening.

By looking through the 18,000 pages of handwritten transcripts collected in Western Samoa, I could have seen that one of the most common instructions uttered by adults to children, especially but not exclusively when adult visitors are around, is *nofo i lalo!*[1] This expression is composed of a verb (*nofo*) that describes the body posture of sitting, a preposition (*i*) roughly translatable in English as "to, in the direction of," and *lalo* (down, bottom). The three words together are best translated in English with the phrase "sit down." Here is an example of its actual use from an interaction where a mother is imploring her oldest son, Niulala, who is 3½, to act more maturely:

> *Niulala! Niulala! Niulala!*
> Niulala! Niulala! Niulala!
> *'oe si kama makua?*
> you Aff boy old
> (are) you a dear old boy?
> *ngofo lelei i lalo 'ā?*
> sit good Dir down Tag
> sit down properly, okay?
> [Transcript, "Niulala," April 4, 1979, book 59][2]

Were I feeling the need for a semantic continuity between the fono and the household situations, I could have used an expression I recently found in a dinner conversation recorded in Western Samoa in 1988, when a mother said to her son during a dinner, "Teu lau nofo" (Take care of your sitting).[3] Can a relationship *(vā)* be contained, represented, enacted in the act of sitting, in a particular mode of coexistence between one's body and an inhabited surface? In the rest of this article, I argue that it can.

To Hold One's Body, to Know One's Place

Control over the relationship with a lived space seems the paramount preoccupation of adult Samoans trying to control their children's unruly or at least potentially inappropriate behavior. Of course, once we look more closely at the situations in which such instructions are uttered, we realize that ultimately they *are* about relationships with people and not just with space. For instance, these commands are concerned with the relationship between a child's body's position and the positions of others, especially adults, around him. But adults do not need to be around for the child to be expected to assume a particular posture and position in space. The child is instructed on how to hold his body vis-à-vis other real or potential viewers or bystanders along a vertical axis and a horizontal one. (See Firth 1970 for similar observations about Tikopia postures of respect.) The child's body should be lower or no higher than any other older person's body (vertical axis) and with his legs crossed rather than stretched out (horizontal axis). This posture seems to occupy the least room and yet maintains an upward position of the upper body, which must face outward. Figures 4.1 and 4.2 illustrate this posture, called *fātai* or *fa'atai*, as held by a group *('aukengi)* of young caretakers who are attending young babies and making a broom with the midribs of pandanus leaves.

Children who are not supervised and are engaged in relatively stationary activities might take on different positions, such as squatting, where a group of young boys are playing a fantasy game with make-believe trucks and cement.

It should be no surprise that children's behavior is controlled in terms of the relationship between their bodies and the space they inhabit, and that they are expected to show "respect" *(fa'aaloalo)* in this fashion, especially when around adults. Anthropologists have known for a long time that space is often a metaphor for society and that knowing one's place might mean knowing where one stands in society. This is true in English as well as in Samoan, where even high-status individuals might be reminded of their proper "place." The term *tūlanga* means "position, place" in both the physical and metaphorical sense. It is used in the fono by speakers who want to scold the behavior of their distinguished colleagues by reminding them of their proper place and, hence, demeanor.

Even Shore's metaphor *teu le vā*, as he points out (1982:311 n.8), contains a spatial reference. The word *vā*, translated as "relationship" in *teu le vā*, also means "space" or "between" when followed by the preposition *i*, as in *vā-i-taimi* ("interval," literally "between times") or *vā-i-niu* (interval between coconut trees) (Milner 1966:310). It is easy, then, to hypothesize that the social connotation of "relationship" in the word *vā* is derived from, or at least related to, the meaning of a physical space between people or things.

Choosing a key expression that deals with location in space entails entering a rich domain of discourse, one that has been subjected to several lines of analysis (Lawrence and Low 1990; Lynch 1993). In particular, distinctions made within linguistic anthropology help clarify how control over who is sitting where and in what posture

Figure 4.1   Young caregivers sitting cross-legged (*fa'tai*) on mats. (Western) Samoa, 1981

Figure 4.2   Same group from another point of view

relies upon and evokes a complex sociohistorical world. This world may not be shared by the participants in the interaction, especially when they are people of different ages and therefore with different ties to and experiences of the "home" country.

The Study of Deixis

Traditionally, linguistics have been interested in space as part of a larger set of phenomena called *deixis*. This is the name given to those aspects of language whose interpretation is relative to the occasion of utterance; to the time of utterance, and to times before and after the time of utterance; to the location of the speaker at the time of utterance; and to the identity of the speaker and the intended audience. [Fillmore 1966:220]

Personal pronouns *(I, you)*, demonstratives *(this, that)*, temporal adverbs and prepositions *(now, then, before)*, and spatial markers and expressions *(here, there, up, down)* are classic examples of deictics (Lyons 1977). Since their meaning shifts from one context to the next, these expressions have also been called shifters by Jespersen (1922; see also Jakobson 1971 [1957]).

A Samoan term such as *i lalo* (at the bottom, down) can only be interpreted relative to a particular person's or object's position in a situation. The request to sit down needs reference to a number of coordinates, including the addressee's starting position, or *origo* (see Hanks 1990), at the time of the utterance, a position the addressee is asked to abandon, and a target position the addressee is asked to assume.

Deixis, together with the more general phenomenon called indexicality, has received a considerable amount of attention in recent years among linguistic anthropologists, especially thanks to the work of Michael Silverstein and some of his students. Starting with his 1976 paper "Shifters, Linguistic Categories, and Cultural Description," Silverstein extended Charles Peirce's work on types of signs and Roman Jakobson's work on deixis into a theory of indexicality that goes beyond spatiotemporal coordinates to include social reference in both its *presupposing* and *creating* force. For example, in the English expression *this table*, the referent of the token of *table* must be identifiable, must exist cognitively, for the deictic *this* to be interpretable. This is an example of indexical presupposition. In the case of second-person pronouns such as *you* in English, Silverstein argues that language is the main or even the only medium through which the social category of addressee/recipient is made to exist. Languages that have socially differentiated second-person pronouns, such as the classic T/V type of distinction of many European languages (French *tu/vous*, Spanish *tu/Usted*, German *du/Sie*, and Italian *tu/Voi* or *tu/Lei*) are more extreme examples of systems in which words (in this case pronouns) are used to activate or establish the relevant social coordinates of equality/inequality, solidarity/power (Brown and Gilman 1960). These are indexes that Silverstein sees as "maximally creative or performative." As we shall see shortly, the creative function of indexes can also be at work in spatial deixis.

William Hanks's (1990) detailed study of deixis in Maya develops some of these insights by integrating a number of theoretical approaches, including Merleau-Ponty's phenomenological appreciation of the role of the corporeal field in perception and Erving Goffman's work on frames and participation frameworks. Hanks underscores that "to engage in referential practice is to locate oneself in the world, to occupy a position, however fleetingly, in one or more sociocultural fields" (1990:514). In order to understand spatial expressions, we make hypotheses about the perceptual and cultural horizon against which spatial expressions are used. This horizon, Hanks reminds us, is constituted by the human body, the socially lived space, and the dynamic relationship between individual space and community spaces.

Within a different and yet related tradition of research, the work of Charles and Marjorie Goodwin on language, bodies, and material tools highlights different aspects of the lived space, focusing on the ways in which it becomes a resource used by participants in an interaction to test their understanding of each other's actions, words included (see C. Goodwin 1994; Goodwin and Goodwin 1996).

These contributions suggest that any expression that makes reference to movement in space must be understood against perceptually available surfaces, whether material or conceptual. Thus "sit down" has a different meaning in English depending on which target hard surfaces are available. In a room with chairs, the action of sitting down would be usually understood not only as meaning "sit down on a chair" but also as implying some horizontal adjustment to make sure that the relevant surface of one's body would match the surface of a "seat" or any other "seat-able" artifact. In some cases the question of which chair one might or should sit on might be obvious or indifferent, but in other cases it might be highly contested. It is not unusual to find oneself in a situation in which one does not know *where* to sit and ends up sitting in the "wrong" place. I did this recently in a doctor's office, where I responded to "have a seat" by sitting in what turned out to be the doctor's chair. The unavailability of artifacts or mediums that (in Gibson's [1986] ecological terms) "afford" sitting might be interpreted as implying the floor as the target. The criteria by which availability is evaluated are, to various degrees and in various combinations, subjective and context- and culture-specific. For instance, is a chair occupied by another or by objects a possible target? When a floor and a chair are both available, should one always select the chair? It depends.

In the case of Samoan children growing up in a village, the instruction to *nofo i lalo*, for instance, is understood differently according to whether they are at school or at home. In a classroom, to "sit down" typically means to sit down on one's seat at one's desk.

At home, to "sit down" means instead to sit on the floor or on a mat that is covering the floor (see Figures 4.1 and 4.2). This is consistent with a general expectation that most interactions inside a house will take place among people who are sitting on the floor, or to be more precise, among people who sit on mats that are lying on the floor. Such expectations cover formal and informal gatherings. Everyone, even young children, sits cross-legged on a mat on the floor. Furthermore, as is common in many houses in Western Samoa, there are no chairs or other visible pieces of furniture.

Figure 4.3 shows a group of chiefs and their wives sitting in a Samoan-style house *(fale Sāmoa)* during a formal Sunday meal *(to'ona'i)*. In this case, sitting down also implies sitting at the periphery of the house floor according to a logic of spatial orientation that pays homage to status and rank distinctions (Duranti 1992, 1994; Shore 1982).

Sitting on a mat on the floor is the unmarked position for a person who is talking with someone else inside a house. This is confirmed by a number of cultural practices, including the loud cry *'aumai fala!* (bring in the mats!), which announces that one or more adult visitors are entering the family compound. Furthermore, visitors who come inside the house are expected to sit on the floor before introducing the reason for their visit. A visit properly begins after the newcomer has sat down, as demonstrated by the fact that the exchange of ceremonial greetings between the hosts and the guests begins only after the guests have located themselves in a

Figure 4.3 Chiefs (right and center) and wives (left) during a formal Sunday lunch with an invited preacher (*to'ona'i*). *(Western) Samoa, 1988*

particular spot on the floor, usually a "front" section already covered by a seating mat (Duranti 1992).

In my experience, the preference for sitting on the floor continues in the villages in Western Samoa even today, when many houses have chairs or benches. Adults who are under the same roof typically sit down on mats on the floor to engage in protracted conversation, consume food, or engage in certain types of work that mostly need the hands, including weaving and the making of strings or brooms.

Sitting Down in Southern California, or "How Far Down?"

Samoan children living in southern California share some of the activities of their peers on the islands, but they inhabit a very different environment from the one I described above. They too go to school five days a week and to the pastor's school on Sunday and sometimes during the week, but they are surrounded by an environment in which the relationship between furniture and movement is different from what is experienced in an island community. In Los Angeles, houses are not large open spaces with no furniture or with a few pieces kept at the periphery, but typical suburban houses filled with beds, tables, desks, closets, cabinets, chairs, couches, fridges, stoves, ovens, televisions, and even video games. Samoan children in southern California routinely go out to shopping malls, grocery stores, fast-food restaurants, movie theaters, video-game arcades, and toy stores. They also visit friends who are from different ethnic groups, and they are surrounded by a peer culture that is

Samoan in their homes and in their church but is otherwise working-class or lower-middle-class American.

When we look through data collected in southern California, we find that the instruction to "sit down" is not as pervasive as in Western Samoa. This is in itself an important index of the changing cultural ecology of everyday interaction. I did, however, find that in one of the four families we visited the parents often insisted that their younger children "sit down" and "sit properly." In one videotape (recorded June 7, 1993), over a period of one hour and 20 minutes, I found 14 cases of *nofo i lalo* and three cases of its polite counterpart, *saofaʻi i lalo* (see below). In contrast with other families in the study, "sitting down" for this family means that children sit on the floor, even though there is furniture present and the instruction could be reasonably understood by children as meaning to sit on a chair or a couch.

Figure 4.4– 4.7 show a set of body orientations, by a four-year-old girl, Tina, and her five-year-old brother, taken from a videotape segment of about five minutes, which contains several instructions to "sit down."[4] The sequence starts around

Figure 4.4   Girl dances following rhythm of music on TV show. (13:22)

Figure 4.5   Brother playfully "attacks" with a karate move. (13:53)

13:25 (min:sec), with disco music being played on television. At this point Tina starts dancing across the floor (see Figure 4.4). A few seconds later (at 13:53) her brother enters the dance floor with a fake karate move that is not reciprocated (Figure 4.5). She continues, lifting up her T-shirt to make it in the shape of a bikini top, presumably imitating the televised dancers (not visible on camera). This attracts the attention of her older sister, seven-year-old Fala, who reports on her to an older male cousin. The mother hears this report and tells Tina to straighten up her shirt *(faʻalelei lou ofu!)* (14:04). But Tina does not follow the instruction; she continues to dance with her shirt lifted while her siblings are busy carrying out other activities and largely ignoring her. Tina attempts a few new moves, doing acrobatics on the floor (14:52) (Figure 4.6), and then, after her brother has tried again to engage her physically by pulling her by the shirt, the mother directs her to sit down. This is phrased as an indirect request, with the special word *saofaʼi*, a respectful verb (RV) usually used in talking about chiefs in their presence. Here it is used, as it is by mothers in Western Samoa, to invoke respectful behavior in a child. This is another case of a creative use of a deictic term, this time a social deictic.

Figure 4.6 Acrobatics on the floor. (14:52)

15:18 *e le'i iloa saofa'i lelei i lalo?*
       TA Neg know sit [R] good Dir down
       don't you know (yet) to sit down properly?

When Tina does not respond, the mother becomes more direct:

15:20 *Tina, alu e nofo i lalo.*[5]
       go to sit Dir down
       Tina, go to sit down.

But Tina continues not to comply, taking advantage of the fact that her mother is busy monitoring the activities of the older children, one of whom wants to leave the house to go swimming. Two minutes later, their 12-year-old sister, Vae, intervenes. She threatens to turn off the television or else change channels, and finally the mother manages to get some attention.

17:18 *nofo i lalo!*
       sit down!

This time the boy sits down, but it will take a lot longer to get Tina to sit down. Although her sister Fala pulls her shirt and tells her "Down!" (in English), Tina sits only when the music ends and the show goes back to dialogue. But even though Tina

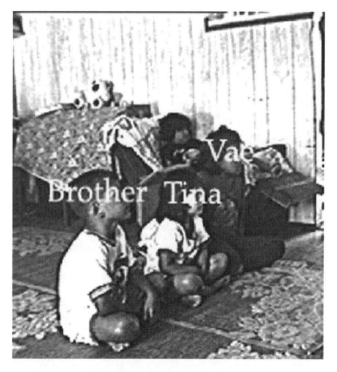

Figure 4.7   Children sit down with their legs crossed (*faʻatai*). (18:09)

and her brother have finally sat down, they are not yet in the "right" position. The boy is first asked to move back (*sosō i kua*) (17:23) and then instructed to fold his leg properly *(nofo faʻalelei lā ia ma faʻatai ʻou vae)*.[6] Figure 4.7 shows the final seating arrangement and postures that satisfy the mother's request.

Although the series of *nofo i lalo* produced during this recording does not end at this point, I will end the ethnographic description here. There are sufficient data to make some general observations.

Interpreting the Directive "Sit Down"

There are many questions raised by these data, even when presented in a cursory fashion. Let me start by answering the most obvious and perhaps least interesting question: Is this all happening because I am present? This question is partly answered by the fact that (as I discussed earlier) sitting down cross-legged is a posture that is quite widespread in Samoan communities. My presence, which is explicitly referred to a couple of times, seems occasionally to work more like *another* excuse or reason to get the children to do something they would be asked to do anyhow. It seems much more reasonable to assume that the instruction to sit down is a common strategy in this household, probably used to control the younger children especially, but not exclusively, when other adults are around. Given the limited space in the house and the high number of children – a total of 11, ranging in age from six months to 18 years – it is understandable that the mother would want the physically more active ones to calm down a bit.

Is the protracted resistance to follow their mother's request a sign of resistance to maternal authority? Do the children understand the directive when it is said in Samoan? What does it mean to understand it? What is implied by it? The expression *i lalo* is certainly working as a deictic, as defined above. It is an index that points to a particular relationship between the living body and a perceptually available and yet culturally organized space. As predicted by Hanks's theoretical framework, the indexical expression in this case mediates between different sociocultural spaces. As suggested by Goodwin and Goodwin (1996), the interpretation of an indexical expression, "down" in this case, is a socially negotiated process that relies on existing artifacts, hand gestures, eye gaze, and previous experiences, which are differently known, stored, and reproduced by different participants in the interaction. But what is most striking to me is that the kind of space that is being pointed to is only partly *there*, and we are left to wonder how in fact such a space could become part of the "context" at all. Yes, the children know how to satisfy their mother's request, and eventually, however reluctantly, they do give in and sit on the carpet with their legs crossed *(fa'atai)*. This, they are told, is the proper (or "good") way of sitting, of showing respect *(fa'aaloalo)*, when a visitor is around and even more so when the visitor is a man with a movie camera who might show the tape to others. But there is more that is being said; there is more that is expected, more to see, hear, and feel.

The mother's instruction "Sit down!" has a power and carries a set of implications that go beyond the usual struggle between adults and children coming together at the end of a long day of work, whether in the workplace, at home, or at school. Using Silverstein's classification of indexes, I suggest that *nofo i lalo!* must be understood as a highly *creative* indexical expression, one that does more than mediate between generations and conflicting goals that include watching television, dancing, doing homework, and making decisions. *Nofo i lalo!* mediates an encounter between an immediately perceivable space and a distant domain of action that is, for the children, invisible and unknown or little known.

In the Los Angeles house, the Samoan mother uses the command *nofo* (sit) with the indexical expression *i lalo* (down) to bring order in the middle of the chaotic behavior of restless young children who, after a long day at school, want to watch television, have a snack, dance, roll on the floor, pretend to be karate masters, and engage in other activities that we call "being kids." But the spatial domain of such a command is a world made out of houses with no walls, almost no furniture, and floors covered with movable seating mats that have been woven in the same space by women, that is, children's mothers, aunts, and older sisters. In Los Angeles, the built environment is different. There is plenty of furniture, which is routinely used by both children and adults. And yet the mother's directive must be satisfied by sitting on the carpet on the floor. Despite the fact that the children have not directly experienced the cultural space where the command would have a unique interpretation, they know what is meant by it and eventually comply with it.

This is a highly creative use of an indexical expression because it does more than establishing a resting-place goal for the children's bodies. It is an attempt to transfer into the present, and re-create in a very different context, a distant kind of space. Such a transfer is not only a cognitive one, in which a mental image, held in the mother's memory, needs to be interpreted by the children. It is also the establishment of a social and cultural space, which blinds the participants by constituting an emotional and a moral commitment to a culturally specific way of being and moving in a house inhabited by other human beings (parents and visitors) who deserve respect. This is the paramount goal of Samoan socialization, implying a series of expectations about what it means to be a child and, ultimately, a social being (Ochs 1988).

In conclusion, talking about indexical speech within the framework provided in this article means to pull together a number of implications that constitute the core of a theory of spatial indexicality that must bridge places, identities, and communities. What I have shown here supports the following generalizations:

1. Deictic tokens (shifters, indexes) alone cannot provide the key to their own interpretation.
2. The anchoring of deictic tokens to a specific time and place relies on cultural expectations that organize their salience.
3. Different participants might connect linguistic tokens and physical space in ways that show a mutual understanding of the immediate spatiotemporal coordinates of the interaction.
4. And yet, participants might have a different reading of what kind of space is being evoked, how far back in time and how far away in physical distance it might be.

What might be simply a here-and-now space for one person might simultaneously be a there-and-then space for another – a space of memory, affect, and duty to invisible and yet quite present beings.

The study of such minute and misleadingly innocuous details of everyday speech becomes, for linguistic anthropologists, not only a chronicle of how different members of the same family understand the language that is being used in their home but also an index of change. It shows us (and the participants) the extent to which a family is oriented toward the here-and-now as opposed to the then-and-there. It is no accident that the family where we found the highest number of sitting instructions is also the family that espouses one of the strongest commitments to the *fa'a-Sāmoa* (Samoan way of life) as opposed to the *fa'apālangi* (Western way). Talking space is a creative act whereby family members can try to infer their identity, while at the same time negotiating their place in history.

NOTES

Acknowledgments. Special thanks to James Soli'ai and Elia K. Ta'ase for transcribing some of the segments discussed in this article, and to Benjamin Bailey, Jennifer Reynolds, and three anonymous reviewers for feedback on an earlier draft. Fieldwork on which this article is based was done in collaboration with Elinor Ochs in Western Samoa (in 1978–79, 1981, and 1988) and in Los Angeles (in 1993–95). Research in Western Samoa was supported by the National Science Foundation (Linguistics Section) and the work in Los Angeles by the U.S. Department of Education through a grant to the National Center for Research on Cultural Diversity and Second Language Learning, University of California, Santa Cruz. An earlier version of this article was delivered at the 94th Annual Meeting of the American Anthropological Association in Washington, DC, November 1995, in the invited session "Theorizing Space: Dialogues across Anthropology," organized by Setha Low; I wish to thank Gary Wray McDonogh for his insightful and encouraging discussion of my paper.

1   In this article, I will use traditional Samoan orthography, including the inverted comma for the glottal stop, [2]. The only two exceptions will be the adoption of the letters *ng* in place of the letter *g* for the velar nasal ŋ (I will write *tūlanga* instead of *tūlaga*, *faʻapālangi* instead of *faʻapalagi*) and the phonetic symbol ŋ for the transcription of actual speech (see below), which will be quoted between obliques. The choice of *ng* over *g* might upset some Samoan purists but should help reduce the mispronunciation of Samoan words by the many readers who are not familiar with Samoan orthography.

The most frequent pronunciation of the phrase *nofo i lalo* is /ŋofo i lalo/, due to the fact that in most cases the Samoan spoken in the village is the variety called "bad speech" (*tautala leanga*), where the alveolar segments /n/ and /t/, found in the written form (hence in the citation forms used here) and in the speech of most school and church activities, are replaced by their velar counterparts, namely, /ŋ/ and /k/ (Duranti and Ochs 1986). I will also follow Mosel and Hovdhaugen (1992:144) and will not distinguish between the locative *i* and the directional *ʻi*, which are historically the reflexes of the proto-Polynesian **i* and **ki* respectively. This decision is based on a number of factors, including the difficulty that many native speakers currently have making the distinction between the two prepositions and the general tendency not to really articulate the glottal stop in fast speech.

2   Abbreviations for interlinear glosses: Aff = affective particle, Dir = locative-directional preposition, Neg = negation, [R] = word expressing respect, TA = tense/aspect marker, and Tag = confirmation particle used in Tag questions.

3   This was actually pronounced /keu lau ŋofo/. See note 1 for transcription conventions.

4   All names are pseudonyms. The total number of children in this household was 11 at the time of the study. During recording sessions, which took place after the children had come back from school, the three oldest brothers were not usually around. In this family, as is typical of families living in urban and suburban communities, teenage boys were more occupied with after-school sports activities and in general left to be more independent than their female siblings.

5   Pronounced /alu e ŋofo i lalo/.

6   Pronounced /ŋofo faʻalelei lā ia ma faʻakai ʻou vae/.

REFERENCES

Brown, Roger, and Albert Gilman
    1960   The Pronouns of Power and Solidarity. In *Style in Language*. T. A. Sebeok, ed. Pp. 253–276. Cambridge, MA: MIT Press.
Duranti, Alessandro
    1992   Language and Bodies in Social Space: Samoan Ceremonial Greetings. *American Anthropologist* 94:657–691.
    1994   *From Grammar to Politics: Linguistic Anthropology in a Western Samoan Village*. Berkeley: University of California Press.

Duranti, Alessandro, and Elinor Ochs
    1986   Literacy Instruction in a Samoan Village. In *Acquisition of Literacy: Ethnographic Perspectives.* B. B. Schieffelin and P. Gilmore, eds. Pp. 213–232. Norwood, NJ: Ablex.
    1996   *Syncretic Literacy: Multiculturalism in Samoan American Families.* National Center for Research on Cultural Diversity and Second Language Learning Research Report, 16. Washington, DC: Center for Applied Linguistics.
    In press Syncretic Literacy in a Samoan American Family. *In Discourse, Tools, and Reasoning.* L. Resnick, R. Saljo, and C. Pontecorvo, eds. Berlin: Springer-Verlag.
Duranti, Alessandro, Elinor Ochs, and Elia K. Ta'ase
    1995   Change and Tradition in Literacy Instruction in a Samoan American Community. *Educational Foundations* 94:57–74.
Fillmore, Charles J.
    1966   Deictic Categories in the Semantics of Come. *Foundations of Language* 2:219–227.
Firth, Raymond
    1970   Postures and Gestures of Respect. *In Échanges et communications: Mélanges offerts à Claude Lévi-Strauss à l'occasion de son 60ème anniversaire.* J. Pouillon and P. Maranda, eds. Pp. 188–209. The Hague: Mouton.
Geertz, Clifford
    1983   *Local Knowledge: Further Essays in Interpretive Anthropology.* New York: Basic Books.
    1988   *Works and Lives: The Anthropologist as Author.* Stanford, CA: Stanford University Press.
Gibson, James J.
    1986   *The Ecological Approach to Visual Perception.* Hillsdale, NJ: Erlbaum.
Goodwin, Charles
    1994   Professional Vision. *American Anthropologist* 96:606–633.
Goodwin, Charles, and Marjorie Harness Goodwin
    1996   Formulating Planes: Seeing as a Situated Activity. *In Distributed Cognition in the Workplace.* D. Middleton and Y. Engestrom, eds. Pp. 61–95. Amsterdam: Benjamins.
Hanks, William F.
    1990   *Referential Practice: Language and Lived Space among the Maya.* Chicago: University of Chicago Press.
Jakobson, Roman
    1971[1957]   Shifters, Verbal Categories, and the Russian Verb. *In Selected Writings of Roman Jakobson.* Vol. 2, Word and Language. Pp. 130–147. The Hague: Mouton.
Jespersen, Otto
    1922   *Language: Its Nature, Development, and Origin.* London: George Allen and Unwin.
Lawrence, Denise, and Setha Low
    1990   The Built Environment and Spatial Form. *Annual Review of Anthropology* 19:453–505.
Lynch, Michael
    1993   *Scientific Practice and Ordinary Action: Ethnomethodology and Social Science Studies of Science.* Cambridge: Cambridge University Press.
Lyons, John
    1977   *Semantics.* Cambridge: Cambridge University Press.
Milner, G. B.
    1966   *Samoan Dictionary: Samoan-English English-Samoan.* London: Oxford University Press.
Mosel, Ulrike, and Even Hovdhaugen
    1992   *Samoan Reference Grammar.* Oslo: Scandinavian University Press, Institute for Comparative Research in Human Culture (distributed by Oxford University Press).

Ochs, Elinor
    1988   *Culture and Language Development: Language Acquisition and Language Social-
    ization in a Samoan Village.* Cambridge: Cambridge University Press.
Rosaldo, Michelle Z.
    1980   *Knowledge and Passion: Ilongot Notions of Self and Social Life.* Cambridge:
    Cambridge University Press.
Rosenberg, Daniel V.
    1990   Language in the Discourse of the Emotions. *In Language and the Politics of
    Emotion.* C. A. Lutz and L. Abu-Lughod, eds. Pp. 162–185. Cambridge: Cambridge
    University Press.
Shore, Bradd
    1977   A Samoan Theory of Action: Social Control and Social Order in a Polynesian
    Paradox. Ph.D. dissertation, University of Chicago.
    1982   *Sala'ilua: A Samoan Mystery.* New York: Columbia University Press.
Silverstein, Michael
    1976   Shifters, Linguistic Categories, and Cultural Description. In *Meaning in Anthropol-
    ogy.* K. H. Basso and H. A. Selby, eds. Pp. 11–56. Albuquerque: University of New
    Mexico Press.
Turner, Victor
    1974   *Dramas, Fields and Metaphors: Symbolic Action in Human Society.* Ithaca, NY:
    Cornell University Press.
Watson-Gegeo, Karen, and Geoffrey White, eds.
    1990   *Disentangling: Conflict Discourse in Pacific Societies.* Stanford, CA: Stanford
    University Press.

Part II

Gendered Spaces

This section of our reader focuses on sites invested with gendered meanings based on cultural interpretations of perceived physical, anatomical, or developmental differences between males and females. The cultural construction of gender incorporates behavior patterns and symbolic representations that distinguish the sexes, and includes differences in power, authority, and value attributed to sexual asymmetries. Domestic settings are the most frequently discussed gendered sites, but the concern with the house has generally implied a greater interest in the spatial articulation of women's roles rather than men's. We include a well-known study by Pierre Bourdieu of the Kabyle house in which he provides a structuralist account of gender relations as expressed in the cosmological microcosm of house form. Bourdieu argues that the complementary symbolic oppositions of gender as a part of cosmology are expressed in the physicality of domestic space, and enculturate those who live and move through home spaces. As we noted in our introduction, the tendency to dichotomize gendered spaces in terms of contrasting public and private spheres has been a concern of some theorists who fear the projection of Western gender notions on non-Western cultures. Orvar Löfgren explores this issue by examining the social construction of 19th and 20th century Swedish bourgeois and working-class domesticity to reveal not only the historic differences in gender conceptions between classes, but how those conceptions were realized in the materiality of the home and homemaking. Finally, we include a new work by Deborah Pellow on the historical and social construction of space and gender relations in Hausa compounds and how they have evolved in an urban Hausa community in Accra, Ghana. Pellow investigates how the custom of secluding women is expressed in traditional house form, but traces how these ideals are challenged in practice with increasing urbanization and social heterogeneity.

Further Reading

Ardener, Shirley (1993) *Women and Space: Ground Rules and Social Maps* (pp. 1–30). Originally published 1981. Oxford: Berg.

Birdwell-Pheasant, Donna and Denise Lawrence-Zuniga (eds.) (1999) *House Life: Space, Place and Family in Europe*. Oxford: Berg.

del Valle, Teresa (ed.) (1993) *Gendered Anthropology*. London: Routledge.

Hirschon, Renee (1993) Essential Objects and the Sacred: Interior and exterior Space in an Urban Greek Locality. In S. Ardener (ed.) *Women and Space: Ground Rules and Social Maps* (pp. 70–85). Originally published 1981. Oxford: Berg.

Moore, Henrietta (1986) *Space, Text and Gender: An Anthropological Study of the Marakwet of Kenya*. Cambridge: Cambridge University Press.

5

The Berber House

Pierre Bourdieu

The interior of the Kabyle house is rectangular in shape and is divided into two parts at a point one third of the way along its length by a small lattice-work wall half as high as the house. Of these two parts, the larger is approximately 50 centimeters higher than the other and is covered over by a layer of black clay and cow dung which the women polish with a stone; this part is reserved for human use. The smaller part is paved with flagstones and is occupied by the animals. A door with two wings provides entrance to both rooms. Upon the dividing wall are kept, at one end, the small clay jars or esparto-grass baskets in which provisions awaiting immediate consumption, such as figs, flour and leguminous plants, are conserved; at the other end, near the door, the water-jars. Above the stable there is a loft where, next to all kinds of tools and implements, quantities of straw and hay to be used as animal-fodder are piled up; it is here that the women and children usually sleep, particularly in winter. Against the gable wall, known as the wall (or, more exactly, the 'side') of the upper part or of the *kanun*, there is set a brick-work construction in the recesses and holes of which are kept the kitchen utensils (ladle, cooking-pot, dish used to cook the bannock, and other earthenware objects blackened by the fire) and at each end of which are placed large jars filled with grain. In front of this construction is to be found the fireplace; this consists of a circular hollow, two or three centimeters deep at its centre, around which are arranged in a triangle three large stones upon which the cooking is done.[1]

In front of the wall opposite the door stands the weaving-loom. This wall is usually called by the same name as the outside front wall giving onto the courtyard (*tasga*), or else wall of the weaving-loom or opposite wall, since one is opposite it when one enters. The wall opposite to this, where the door is, is called wall of darkness, or of sleep, or of the maiden, or of the tomb; a bench wide enough for a mat to be spread out over it is set against this wall; the bench is used to shelter the young calf or the sheep for feast-days and sometimes the wood or the water-pitcher. Clothes, mats and blankets are hung, during the day, on a peg or on a wooden cross-bar against the wall of darkness or else they are put under the dividing bench. Clearly, therefore, the wall of the *kanun* is opposed to the stable as the top is to the bottom (*adaynin*, stable, comes from the root *ada*, meaning the bottom) and the wall of the weaving-loom is opposed to the wall of the door as the light is to the darkness. One might be tempted to give a strictly technical explanation to these oppositions since the wall of the weaving-loom, placed opposite the door, which is itself turned towards the east, receives the most light and the stable is, in fact, situated at a lower level than the rest; the reason for this latter is that the house is most often built perpendicularly with contour lines in order to facilitate the flow of liquid manure and dirty water. A number of signs suggest, however, that these oppositions are the centre of a whole cluster of parallel oppositions, the necessity of which is never completely due to technical imperatives or functional require-ments.

The dark and nocturnal, lower part of the house, place of objects that are moist, green or raw – jars of water placed on benches in various parts of the entrance to the stable or against the wall of darkness, wood and green fodder – natural place also of beings – oxen and cows, donkeys and mules – and place of natural activities – sleep, the sexual act, giving birth – and the place also of death, is opposed, as nature is to culture, to the light-filled, noble, upper part of the house: this is the place of human beings and, in particular, of the guest; it is the place of fire and of objects created by fire – lamp, kitchen utensils, rifle – the symbol of the male point of honour (*ennif*) and the protector of female honour (*horma*) – and it is the place of the weaving-loom – the symbol of all protection; and it is also the place of the two specifically cultural activities that are carried out in the space of the house: cooking and weaving. These relationships of opposition are expressed through a whole set of convergent signs which establish the relationships at the same time as receiving their meaning from them. Whenever there is a guest to be honoured (the verb, *qabel*, 'to honour' also means to face and to face the east), he is made to sit in front of the weaving-loom. When a person has been badly received, it is customary for him to say: 'He made me sit before his wall of darkness as in a grave,' or: 'His wall of darkness is as dark as a grave.' The wall of darkness is also called wall of the invalid and the expression 'to keep to the wall' means to be ill and, by extension, to be idle: the bed of the sick person is, in fact, placed next to this wall, particularly in winter. The link between the dark part of the house and death is also shown in the fact that the washing of the dead takes place at the entrance to the stable. It is customary to say that the loft, which is entirely made of wood, is carried by the stable as the corpse is by the bearers, and the word *tha'richth* refers to both the loft and to the stretcher which is used to transport the dead. It is therefore obvious that one cannot, without causing offence, invite a guest to sleep in the loft which is opposed to the wall of the weaving-loom like the wall of the tomb.

In front of the wall of the weaving-loom, opposite the door, in the light, is also seated or rather, shown off, like the decorated plates which are hung there, the young bride on her wedding-day. When one knows that the umbilical cord of the girl is buried behind the weaving-loom and that, in order to protect the virginity of the maiden, she is made to pass through the warp, going from the door towards the weaving-loom, then the magic protection attributed to the weaving-loom becomes evident. In fact, from the point of view of the male members of her family, all of the girl's life is, as it were, summed up in the successive positions that she symbolically occupies in relation to the weaving-loom, which is the symbol of male protection: before marriage she is placed behind the weaving-loom, in its shadow, under its protection, as she is placed under the protection of her father and her brothers; on her wedding-day she is seated in front of the weaving-loom with her back to it, with the light upon her, and finally she will sit weaving with her back to the wall of light, behind the loom. 'Shame,' it is said, 'is the maiden,' and the son-in-law is called 'the veil of shames' since man's point of honour is the protective 'barrier' of female honour.

The low and dark part of the house is also opposed to the high part as the feminine is to the masculine: besides the fact that the division of work between the sexes, which is based upon the same principle of division as the organization of space, entrusts to the woman the responsibility of most objects which belong to the dark part of the house – water-transport, and the carrying of wood and manure, for instance – the opposition between the upper part and the lower part reproduces within the space of the house the opposition set up between the inside and the outside. This is the opposition between female space and male space, between the house and its garden, the place *par excellence* of the *haram*, i.e. of all which is sacred and forbidden, and a closed and secret space, well protected and sheltered from intrusions and the gaze of others, and the place of assembly (*thajma'th*), the mosque, the café, the fields or the market: on the one hand, the privacy of all that is intimate, on the other, the open space of social relations; on the one hand, the life of the senses and of the feelings, on the other, the life of relations between man and man, the life of dialogue and exchange. The lower part of the house is the place of the most intimate privacy within the very world of intimacy, that is to say, it is the place of all that pertains to sexuality and procreation. More or less empty during the day, when all activity – which is, of course, exclusively feminine – is based around the fireplace, the dark part is full at night, full of human beings but also full of animals since, unlike the mules and the donkeys, the oxen and the cows never spend the night out of doors; and it is never quite so full as it is during the damp season when the men sleep inside and the oxen and the cows are fed in the stable. It is possible here to establish more directly the relationship which links the fertility of men and of the field to the dark part of the house and which is a particular instance of the relationship of equivalence between fertility and that which is dark, full (or swollen) or damp, vouched for by the whole mythico-ritual system: whilst the grain meant for consumption is, as we have seen, stored in large earthenware jars next to the wall of the upper part, on either side of the fireplace, the grain which is intended for sowing is placed in the dark part of the house, either in sheep-skins or in chests placed at the foot of the wall of darkness; or sometimes under the conjugal bed, or in wooden chests placed under the bench which is set against the dividing wall where the wife, who normally sleeps at a lower level, beside the entrance to the stable, rejoins her husband. Once we are aware that birth is always rebirth of the ancestor, since the life circle (which should be called the *cycle of generation*) turns upon itself every third generation (a proposition which cannot be demonstrated here), it becomes obvious that the dark part of the house may be at the same time and without any contradiction the place of death and of procreation, or of birth as resurrection.

In addition to all this, at the centre of the dividing wall, between 'the house of the human beings' and 'the house of the animals' stands the main pillar, supporting the governing beam and all the framework of the house. Now this governing beam which connects the gables and spreads the protection of the male part of the house to the female part (*asalas alemmas*, a masculine term) is identified explicitly with the master of the house, whilst the main pillar upon which it rests, which is the trunk of a forked tree (*thigejdith*, a feminine term), is identified with the wife (the Beni Khellili call it 'Mas'uda', a feminine first name which means 'the happy woman'), and their interlocking represents the act of physical union (shown in mural paintings in the form of the union of the beam and the pillar by two superimposed forked trees). The main beam, which supports the roof, is identified with the protector of family honour; sacrifices are often made to it, and it is around this beam that, on a level with the fireplace, is coiled the snake who is the 'guardian' of the house. As the symbol of the fertilizing power of man and the symbol also of death followed by resurrection, the snake is sometimes shown (in the Collo region for example) upon earthen jars made by the women and which contain the seed for sowing. The snake is also said to descend sometimes into the house, into the lap of the sterile woman, calling her mother, or to coil itself around the central pillar, growing longer by the length of one coil of its body after each time that it takes suck. In Darna, according to René Maunier, the sterile woman ties her belt to the central beam which is where the foreskin is hung and the reed which has been used for circumcision; when the beam is heard to crack the Berbers hastily say 'may it turn out well', because this presages the death of the chief of the family. At the birth of a boy, the wish is made that 'he be the governing beam of the house', and when he carries out his ritual fast for the first time, he takes his first meal on the roof, that is to say, on the central beam (in order, so it is said, that he may be able to transport beams).

A number of riddles and sayings explicitly identify the woman with the central pillar: 'My father's father's wife carries my father's father who carries his daughters'; 'The slave strangles his master'; 'The woman supports the man'; 'The woman is the central pillar.' To the young bride one says: 'May God make of you the pillar firmly planted in the middle of the house.' Another riddle says: 'She stands but she has no feet'; a forked tree open at the top and not set upon her feet, she is female nature and, as such, she is fertile or, rather, able to be fertilized. Against the central pillar are piled the leather bottles full of *hij* seeds, and it is here that the marriage is consummated. Thus, as a symbolic summing up of the house, the union of *asalas* and *thigejdith*, which spreads its fertilizing protection over all human marriage, is in a certain way primordial marriage, the marriage of the ancestors which is also, like tillage, the marriage of heaven and earth. 'Woman is the foundations, man is the governing beam,' says another proverb. *Asalas*, which a riddle defines as 'born in the earth and buried in the sky', fertilizes *thigejdith*, which is planted in the earth, the place of the ancestors who are the masters of all fecundity, and open towards the sky.

Thus, the house is organized according to a set of homologous oppositions: fire: water; cooked: raw; high: low; light: shadow; day: night; male: female; *nif*: *horma*; fertilizing: able to be fertilized; culture: nature. But in fact the same oppositions exist between the house as a whole and the rest of the universe. Considered in its relationship with the external world, which is a specifically masculine world of public life and agricultural work, the house, which is the universe of women and the world of intimacy and privacy, is *haram*, that is to say, at once sacred and illicit for every man who does not form part of it (hence the expression used when taking an oath: 'May my wife – or my house – become illicit – *haram* – to me if . . .'). As the place of the sacred or the left-hand side, appertaining to the *horma* to which are linked all those properties which are associated with the dark part of the house, the house is placed under the safeguard of the masculine point of honour (*nif*) as the dark part of the house is placed under the protection of the main beam. Any violation of the sacred space takes on therefore the social significance of a sacrilege: thus, theft in an inhabited house is treated in everyday usage as a very serious fault inasmuch as it is offence to the *nif* of the head of the family and an outrage upon the *horma* of the house and consequently of all the community. Moreover, when a guest who is not a member of the family is introduced to the women, he gives the mistress of the house a sum of money which is called 'the view'.

One is not justified in saying that the woman is locked up in the house unless one also observes that the man is kept out of it, at least during the day.[2] As soon as the sun has risen he must, during the summer, be in the fields or at the assembly house; in the winter, if he is not in the field, he has to be at the place of assembly or upon the benches set in the shelter of the pent-roof over the entrance door to the courtyard. Even at night, at least during the dry season, the men and the boys, as soon as they have been circumcised, sleep outside the house, either near the haystacks upon the threshing-floor, beside the donkey and the shackled mule, or upon the fig-dryer, or in the open field, or else, more rarely, in the *thajma'th*. The man who stays too long in the house during the day is either suspect or ridiculous: he is 'the man of the home', as one says of the importunate man who stays amongst the women and who 'broods at home like a hen in the henhouse'. A man who has respect for himself should let himself be seen, should continuously place himself under the gaze of others and face them (*qabel*). He is a man amongst men (*argaz yer irgazen*). Hence the importance accorded to the games of honour which are a kind of dramatic action, performed in front of others who are knowing spectators, familiar with the text and all the stage business and capable of appreciating the slightest variations. It is not difficult to understand why all biological activities such as eating, sleeping and procreating are excluded from the specifically cultural universe and relegated to the sanctuary of intimacy and the refuge for the secrets of nature which is the house, the woman's world. In opposition to man's work which is performed outside, it is the nature of woman's work to remain hidden ('God conceals it'): 'Inside the house, woman is always on the move, she flounders like a fly in whey; outside the house, nothing of her work is seen.' Two very similar sayings define woman's condition as being that of one who cannot know of any other sojourn than that tomb above the earth which is the house and that subterranean house which is the tomb: 'Your house is your tomb'; 'Woman has only two dwellings, the house and the tomb.'

Thus, the opposition between the house and the assembly of men, between the fields and the market, between private life and public life, or, if one prefers, between the full light of the day and the secrecy of the night, overlaps very exactly with the opposition between the dark and nocturnal, lower part of the house and the noble and brightly-lit, upper part. The opposition which is set up between the external world and the house only takes on its full meaning therefore if one of the terms of this relation, that is to say, the house, is itself seen as being divided according to the same principles which oppose it to the other term. It is therefore both true and false to say that the external world is opposed to the house as male is to female, or day to night, or fire to water, etc., since the second term of these oppositions divides up each time into itself and its opposite.[3]

In short, the most apparent opposition: male (or day, fire, etc.)/female (or night, water, etc.) may well mask the opposition: male/female–male/female–female, and in the same way, the homology male/female; female–male/female–female. It is obvious from this that the first opposition is but a transformation of the second, which presupposes a change in the field of reference at the end of which the female–female is no longer opposed to the female–male and instead, the group which they form is opposed to a third term: female–male/female–female → female (= female–male + female–female)/male.

As a microcosm organized according to the same oppositions which govern all the universe, the house maintains a relation with the rest of the universe which is that of a homology: but from another point of view, the world of the house taken as a whole is in a relation with the rest of the world which is one of opposition, and the principles of which are none other than those which govern the organization of the internal space of the house as much as they do the rest of the world and, more generally, all the areas of existence. Thus, the opposition between the world of female life and the world of the city of men is based upon the same principles as the two systems of oppositions that it opposes. It follows from this that the application to opposed areas of the same *principium divisionis*, which in fact forms their very opposition, provides, at the least cost, a surplus of consistency and does not, in return, result in any confusion between these areas. The structure of the type a: b; b_1: b_2 is doubtless one of the simplest and most powerful that may be employed by a mythico-ritual system since it cannot oppose without simultaneously uniting (and inversely), while all the time being capable of integrating in a set order an infinite number of data, by the simple application of the same principle of division indefinitely repeated.

It also follows from this that each of the two parts of the house (and, by the same token, all of the objects which are put there and all of the activities which take place there) is in a certain way qualified to two degrees, namely, firstly as female (nocturnal, dark, etc.) inasmuch as it participates in the universe of the house, and secondly as male or female inasmuch as it participates in one or the other of the divisions of this universe. Thus, for example, when the proverb says: 'Man is the lamp of the outside and woman the lamp of the inside,' it is to be understood that man is the true light, that of the day, and woman the light of the darkness, the dark light; moreover, she is, of course, to the moon what man is to the sun. In the same way, when she works with wool, woman produces the beneficent protection of weaving, the whiteness of which symbolizes happiness; the weaving-loom, which is the instrument *par excellence* of female activity and which faces the east like the plough, its homologue, is at the same time the east of the internal space of the house with the result that, within the system of the house, it has a male value as a symbol of protection. Likewise, the fireplace, which is the navel of the house (itself identified with the womb of the mother), where smoulder the embers, which is a secret, hidden and female fire, is the domain of woman who is invested with total authority in all matters concerning the kitchen and the management of the food-stores; she takes her meals at the fireside whilst man, turned towards the outside, eats in the middle of the room or in the courtyard. Nevertheless, in all the rites where they play a part, the fireplace and the stones which surround it derive their potent magic from their participation in the order of fire, of that which is dry and of the solar heat, whether it is a question of providing protection against the evil eye or against illness or to summon up fine weather. The house is also endowed with a double significance: if it is true that it is opposed to the public world as nature is to culture, it is also, in another respect, culture; is it not said of the jackal, the incarnation of all that is savage in nature, that it does not have a home?

But one or the other of the two systems of oppositions which define the house, either in its internal organization or in its relationship with the outside world, will take prime importance according to whether the house is considered from the male point of view or the female point of view: whereas, for the man, the house is less a place one goes into than a place from which one goes out, the woman can only confer upon these two movements and the different definitions of the house which form an integral part with them an inverse importance and meaning, since movement towards the outside consists above all for her of acts of expulsion and it is her specific role to be responsible for all movement towards the inside, that is to say, from the threshold towards the fireplace. The significance of the movement towards the outside is never quite so apparent as in the rite performed by the mother, on the seventh day after a birth, 'in order that her son be courageous': striding across the threshold, she sets her right foot upon the carding comb and simulates a fight with the first boy she meets. The sallying forth is a specifically male movement which leads towards other men and also towards dangers and trials which it is important to *confront* like a man, a man as spiky, when it is a question of honour, as the points of the comb. Going out, or more exactly, opening (*fatah*), is the equivalent of 'being in the morning' (*sebah*). A man who has respect for himself should leave the house at daybreak, morning being the day of the daytime, and the sallying forth from the house, in the morning, being a birth: whence the importance of things encountered which are a portent for the whole day, with the result that, in the case of bad encounters (blacksmith, woman carrying an empty leather bottle, shouts or a quarrel, a deformed being), it is best to 'remake one's morning' or 'one's going out'.

Bearing this in mind, it is not difficult to understand the importance accorded to the direction which the house faces: the front of the main house, the one which shelters the head of the family and which contains a stable, is almost always turned towards the east, and the main door – in opposition to the low and narrow door, reserved for the women, which opens in the direction of the garden, at the back of the house – is commonly called the door of the east (*thabburth thacherqith*) or else the door of the sheet, the door of the upper part or the great door. Considering the way in which the villages present themselves and the lower position of the stable, the upper part of the house, with the fireplace, is situated in the north, the stable is in the south and the wall of the weaving-loom is in the west. It follows from this that the movement one makes when going towards the house in order to enter it is directed from the east to the west, in opposition to the movement made to come out which, in accordance with the supreme direction, is towards the east, that is to say, towards the height, the light and the good: the ploughman turns his oxen towards the east when he harnesses them and also when he unharnesses them, and he starts ploughing from west to east; likewise, the harvesters arrange themselves opposite the *qibla* and they cut the throat of the sacrificial ox facing the east. Limitless are the acts which are performed in accordance with this principal direction, for these are all the acts of importance involving the fertility and the prosperity of the group. It will suffice to

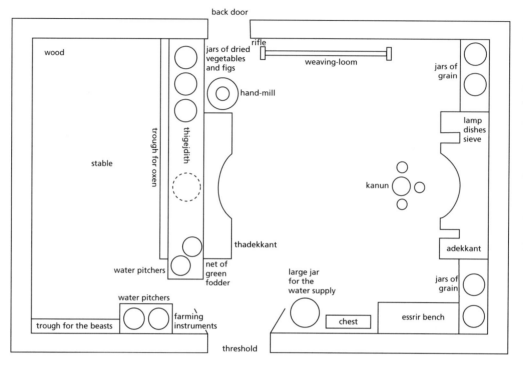

Figure 5.1 Plan of the house

note that the verb *qabel* means not only to face, to affront with honour and to receive in a worthy manner, but also to face the east (*lqibla*) and the future (*qabel*).

If we refer back now to the internal organization of the house we will see that its orientation is exactly the inverse of that of the external space, as if it had been obtained by a semi-rotation around the front wall or the threshold taken as an axis. The wall of the weaving-loom, which one faces as soon as one crosses the threshold, and which is lit up directly by the morning sun, is the light of the inside (as woman is the lamp of the inside), that is to say, the east of the inside symmetrical to the external east, whence it derives its borrowed light. The interior and dark side of the front wall represents the west of the house and is the place of sleep which is left behind when one goes from the door towards the *kanun*; the door corresponds symbolically to the 'door of the year', which is the beginning of the wet season and the agrarian year. Likewise, the two gable walls, the wall of the stable and the wall of the fireplace, take on two opposed meanings depending on which of their sides is being considered: to the external north corresponds the south (and the summer) of the inside, that is to say, the side of the house which is in front of one and on one's right when one goes in facing the weaving-loom; to the external south corresponds the inside north (and the winter), that is to say, the stable, which is situated behind and on the left when one goes from the door towards the fireplace. The division of the house into a dark part (the west and north sides) and a light part (the east and

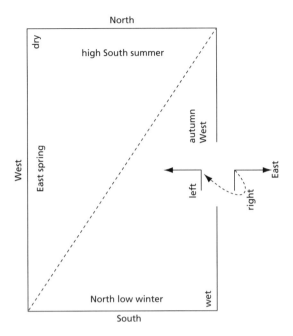

Figure 5.2 The double space orientation of the house (the right-angle arrows indicate the person's position)

south sides) corresponds to the division of the year into a wet season and a dry season. In short, to each exterior side of the wall (*essur*) there corresponds a region of interior space (which the Kabyles refer to as *tharkunt*, which means, roughly, the side) which has a symmetrical and inverse sense signification in the system of internal oppositions; each of the two spaces can therefore be defined as the set of movements made to effect the same change of position, that is to say a semi-rotation, in relation to the other, the threshold acting as the axis of rotation.

It is not possible completely to understand the importance and symbolic value attached to the threshold in the system, unless one is aware that it owes its function as a magic frontier to the fact that it is the place of a logical inversion and that, as the obligatory place of passage and of meeting between the two spaces, which are defined in relation to socially qualified movements of the body and crossings from one place to another, it is logically the place where the world is reversed.

Thus, each of the universes has its own east and the two movements that are most pregnant with meaning and magical consequences, the movement from the threshold to the fireplace, which should bring plenitude and whose performance or ritual control is the responsibility of woman, and the movement from the threshold towards the exterior world which, by its inaugural value, contains all that the future holds and especially the future of agrarian work, may be carried out in accordance with the beneficent direction, that is to say from west to east. The twofold orientation in the space of the house means that it is possible both to go in and to go out starting from the right foot, both in the literal and the figurative sense, with all the magical benefit attached to this observance, without there ever being a break in the relation which unites the right to the upper part, to the light and to the good. The semi-rotation of the space around the threshold ensures then, if one may use the expression, the maximization of the magical benefit since both centripetal and centrifugal movement are performed in a space which is organized in such a way that one comes into it facing the light and one goes out of it facing the light.

The two symmetrical and inverse spaces are not interchangeable but hierarchized, the internal space being nothing but the inverted image or the mirror-reflection of the male space. It is not by chance that only the direction which the door faces is explicitly prescribed whereas the interior organization of space is never consciously perceived and is even less desired to be so organized by the inhabitants. The orientation of the house is fundamentally defined from the outside, from the point of view of men and, if one may say so, by men and for men, as the place from which men come out. The house is an empire within an empire, but one which always remains subordinate because, even though it presents all the properties and all the relations which define the archetypal world, it remains a reversed world, an inverted reflection. 'Man is the lamp of the outside and woman the lamp of the inside.'

NOTES

1 All the descriptions of the Berber house, even the most exact and methodical ones (such as R. Maunier, 1930a and b), or those that are most rich in detail concerning the interior organization of space (such as those made by E. Laoust, 1912, 1920, or by H. Genevois 1955) contain, in their extreme meticulousness, regular omissions, particularly when it is a question of precisely situating things and activities. The reason for this is that these descriptions never consider objects and actions as part of a symbolic system. The postulate that each of the observed phenomena derives its necessity and its meaning from its relation with all the others was the only way of proceeding to a systematic observation and examination capable of bringing out facts which escape any nonsystematic observation and which the observers are incapable of yielding since they appear self-evident to them. This postulate is rendered valid by the very results of the research-programme which it establishes: the particular position of the house within the system of magical representations and ritual practices justifies the initial abstraction by means of which the house is taken out of the context of this larger system in order to treat it as a system itself.

2 In order to hint at how much the men are ignorant of what happens in the house, the women say: 'O man, poor unfortunate, all day in the field like a mule at pasture.'

3 This structure is also to be found in other areas of the mythico-ritual system: thus, the day is divided into night and day, but the day itself is divided into a diurnal–diurnal part (the morning) and a diurnal–nocturnal part (the evening); the year is divided into a dry season and a wet season, and the dry season is comprised of a dry–dry part and a dry–wet part. There should also be an examination of the relation between this structure and the structure which governs the political order and which is expressed in the saying: 'My brother is my enemy, my brother's enemy is my enemy.'

REFERENCES

Genevois, H. (1955), *L'Habitation Kabyle*, Fort-National.

Laoust, E. (1912), *Étude sur la Dialecte Berbère du Cherona*, Levoux.

Laoust, E. (1920), *Mots et Choses Berbères*, Maisonneuve Larose.

Maunier, R. (1930a), 'Le culte domestique en Kabylie', in *Mélanges de sociologie Nord-Africaine*, Alcan.

Maunier, R. (1930b), 'Les rites de la construction en Kabylie', in *Mélanges de sociologie Nord-Africaine*, Alcan.

6

The Sweetness of Home: Class, Culture and Family Life in Sweden

Orvar Löfgren

Introduction

The road back home:

> New winds are blowing in Sweden. Winds which are carrying us back home again. *Home, to a house of our own.*
>
> In a society with growing insecurity the family ties are strengthened and we feel it important to safeguard the integrity of the family.
>
> We have discovered leisure. More and more of us have a growing ambition to use our leisure time in a meaningful way.
>
> Quality of life has become a popular concept and this is something which really concerns the home-maker.
>
> We need a fixed point in our lives. A firm ground to stand on, where the members of the family can come together and develop.
>
> We need a feeling af hominess.
>
> At Scandinavian Housing we have thought a lot about hominess. It is hardly something we can include in our building contracts. But we can supply the prerequisites...

Most things can be marketed today, even feelings like homeliness, as in the advertisement above, published by a Swedish firm selling prefabricated houses. It is hardly a coincidence that commercial messages like that have become more common during the 1980s. They echo a longing for a stable and secure family, a haven of privacy, warmth and togetherness in times of growing social and economic insecurity.

There is, however, nothing new in the message. The concepts of home and family are powerful symbolic images and metaphors in Western culture, but the way they have been used differs widely between classes, periods and social settings.

There exists a large literature on the development of a familistic life style in modern European history. Much of the research has focused on the formation of a domestic ideology and the new constructions of gender among the rising bourgeoisie from the 18th century to the present.[1]

This paper explores the gap between ideals and realities in home and family among Swedes during the last hundred years. My perspective is anthropological and I am mainly interested in the cultural processes which relate ideology and value systems to praxis. How are ideas about domesticity anchored in everyday rituals and routines, how are they communicated and internalized in social life?

Such a cultural analysis calls for a historical perspective in order to demonstrate how notions of home, gender and family life are produced and reproduced in society, how different classes develop their cultural constructs of domestic life in a dialectical dependence on, and in opposition to, other classes.

My starting point is the emergence of a familistic ideal in 19th century Swedish bourgeois culture. I will discuss how this ideal was expressed in the material setting of the home, in the socialization of children, in the new sexual division of labour and the rituals of family life. My examples are mainly drawn from what is called the late "Oscarian" period of Swedish history circa 1880–1910.[2] This is the period when a bourgeois lifestyle emerged as a distinct and elaborated dominant culture in Swedish society.

My material has been presented elsewhere and consists of autobiographies, oral histories, manuals of etiquette, handbooks of home making and children's education etc. from this period.[3]

The second part of the paper deals with the ways in which this ideal of domesticity became part of a dominant culture and worldview: the natural order of things. The children of the Oscarian bourgeoisie redefined themselves as representatives of a middle-class normality and tried as cultural missionaries to spread their ideals to the working class. The turn of the century debate is compared to the campaigns for better homes and 'modern living' during the 1930s and 40s, when the foundations of the Swedish Welfare State were laid. In this period the home became an arena of cultural warfare, where conflicting values and interests clashed.[4]

Public and Private – the Victorian Home as Stage and Shelter

The family ideal of the rising 19th century bourgeoisie was based upon a new definition of love. Sentiment and love between the married couple and between parents and their children should bind the family together, but the new ideal was also built upon ideas of intimacy and privacy: the sacredness and sweetness of home. Neither the peasants nor the old aristocracy shared these notions.

In early 19th century bourgeois culture the concept of intimacy in personal relations became very important. It was often used as a cultural weapon against the traditional elite, the aristocracy. The bourgeoisie asserted the sincerity, involvement, and sentiment of their own family life against 'the amoralistic and shallow life style' of the old nobility. By the end of the century the good home had become a key symbol and a powerful metaphor in the worldview of the Oscarian bourgeoisie.

But what is a home? If we look in a manual of etiquette from 1930 we get this definition:

> Fine furniture and expensive interiors do not create a home, but we may talk of both a good and a superior home, where the inhabitants of the house have tact and good manners...

In bourgeois culture home was not only a practical but a moral project, and words like home-sick, home-loving, home-made and homeliness were loaded with important values.

When discussing the role of home in bourgeois culture, we don't have to limit our discussion to ideals and norms about what a home ought to be. The actual lay-out of houses and apartments, their interior decoration and all the material objects which make up a home display for us the ways in which ideals were realized in everyday life. The study of home-making thus becomes a key to the understanding of how family life changed during the last century and how ideology was put into practice.

During the latter half of the 19th century middle-class living in Sweden changed radically. Up to the middle of the century dwellings were characterized by simplicity and austerity. The pieces of furniture were few and placed along the walls. The same room could be used for different functions: eating, working, entertaining and sleeping. This traditional pattern started to change in the mid-century period. A totally new world was created inside the walls of the home. Austerity was replaced by opulence and almost a *horror vacui*. The floors were filled with bulging sofas and curved chairs, doors and windows were draped in heavy silk and smooth velvet. The walls were bestrewed with pictures and ornaments. Empty spaces were filled with plants, bric-à-brac and souvenirs. Tassels and lace decorated everything.

During the period of around 1860–1910 different styles were mixed with a bold heart, but the basic themes remained the same: romance, sentimentality and fantasy characterized interior decoration.

When one looks at pictures of these overloaded interiors, their theatrical features are striking. As never before, families invested time, money and a burning interest in designing their domestic tableau, creating impressive landscapes and special atmospheres in room after room.

There was, of course, a material foundation for these displays and interests. The growing wealth of the rising bourgeoisie made investments in better housing and more extravagant interior decoration possible, while new technological innovations made housing arrangements more comfortable and mass-production of furniture and ornaments feasible. The social transformation of Swedish society also produced another important resource for Oscarian home-making: a growing rural proletariat from which cheap domestic labour could be recruited. The sweetness of home depended upon the drudgery of numerous servants.

For the bourgeoisie the home was both a show-case to the world and a shelter against it. The family home became the stage on which the family paraded its wealth and displayed its social standing. In this period of rapidly changing class boundaries the communication of status and social ambitions was of great importance, which increased the representative function of the home.

At the same time there was a development which stressed the significance of the home as a private domain and haven. The same economic class which administrated the new production system under capitalism also created a compensatory world of intimacy, cosiness and warmth. The Oscarian home became an antipole to the growing anonymity, rationality and effectivity of the outside world. This cultural contradiction is important to remember.

The actual layout of the typical Oscarian home was a testimony to this dual function of the home as stage and shelter. A number of spatial boundaries were drawn with the use of entrances, passages, doors and files of rooms to separate public from private, servants from family and children from their parents.

The history of the bedroom is a good example of this rearrangement of social space. The notion of a private and secluded room for sleeping was generally unknown in early 19th century Sweden. Even in upper-class settings the bedchamber was used for social entertaining. With the growing emphasis on the privacy and intimacy of the married couple the bedchamber was transformed into the *sleeping* room. During the Victorian era it was moved as far away from the entrance of the house as possible, and it became the most private domain of the home, open only to the married couple. Its back-stage atmosphere was underlined by the fact that it often was furnished with older, less fashionable furniture. The eyes of a visitor would never fall on it. Towards the end of the century the new ideology of "hygien-ism" underlined the special atmosphere of this room. The whiteness of the walls, the polished brass or shining mahogany of the large double bed stress that here lies the sanctum for the most intimate of all social relations, that between man and wife. It was the arena in which the only form of legitimate sexuality could be performed in total seclusion and privacy, and a room to which the married couple could withdraw at night in order to discuss the happenings of the day.

It is hardly surprising that it was the bedroom of the parents which was relocated and reconfigured in this way. The adults did not worry all that much about the sleeping arrangements of the other members of the household. In bigger apartments the maid could have a room of her own; however, the servant girls usually slept in the kitchen or with the children.

In new apartment buildings and villas a separate room for the maid was included towards the end of the century. It was usually located next to the kitchen with room for a single window, a bed and a dresser. Maids were denied any great amount of privacy in middle-class homes.

Children were also given a low priority in Oscarian housing arrangements. As late as the 1870s separate nurseries were rare. Children usually slept with the servants in a small dark room furnished with "left-overs". For most children the parent's bedroom was forbidden territory: "Behind the dining room was a world I never entered, but where I guessed my parents had their rooms," recollects one Oscarian. He remembers his father, a judge, visiting the nursery only once during his child-hood. Another Oscarian states that he shared rooms with the servants above his parents' apartment and that he had "rather shady ideas about what went on downstairs". In these upper-middle-class settings the sweet sound of tiny feet should only be heard at suitable occasions.

When the campaign for light and roomy nurseries with their own style in furniture started toward the end of the century, it was initiated by changing perceptions of both the meaning of childhood and the role of children in family life. It is also at this stage that parents started worrying about the unsuitable closeness between children and servants. (This had never been much of a problem for the aristocracy.) New boundaries, both cultural and physical, were drawn between these two social categories in many middle-class homes.

The changing significance of the bedroom and the nursery illustrates the growing stress on intimacy and privacy in family relations. A private sphere emerged, a territory to which outsiders were denied access. At the same time as this back stage of the home developed, the public part or the open stage of the home was elaborated and differentiated. Visitors were sorted out according to rank. Some had to go through the tradesman's entrance or the kitchen door, others were only allowed to enter the hall or were told to remain on the doorstep. In larger apartments and houses we find an intricate system of social sluices: entrance, hall, drawing-room and sitting-room were stations leading toward the heart of the home. The actual rituals of entering these stations became more complex. An analysis of Swedish etiquette books shows that the chapters on the art of visiting considerably expanded towards the end of the 19th century.

The drawing-room becomes the main stage for greeting visitors (of the right social standing) and it is a room which had to be decorated with great care. In a contemporary handbook of interior decoration this rule was laid down as follows:

> The drawing room is the place for entertaining visitors, the place for social contacts between the family and the outside world. From this follows that this is the room in which the house must present itself in a most spectacular fashion...

> ...Empty tables, naked walls, bare surfaces can in no way be tolerated in the drawing-room. The chilly atmosphere would counteract the warmth of the welcoming, during which the conversation should cover thousands of topics, all the time drawing its inspiration from the surroundings.

This conscious or unconscious theatrical aspect of home-making fits well into one of the main themes in 19th century bourgeois worldview: the view of 'Civilized Man' as a polished and sophisticated actor, who maintains self-control and a pleasant but restrained facade towards others. Another home-making manual states that the master's study should be decorated in a way which underlines the sincere and masculine, dark colours and strict patterns are to be preferred. Different roles could be acted out against different domestic stage settings.

The interior of the home was also given a form which stressed its function as a place of retreat and rest. A cosy and comfortable world was created in drawing-rooms and sitting-rooms with the help of bulging padding and a multitude of cushions. The half-lit rooms had a quiet and restful atmosphere, and there was a radiance of sensuality coming from the warm colours, the rounded edges, the soft materials. Home was like a snug and sheltered theater box, from which the family looked at the stage of the busy outside world. The feeling of homeliness was growing...

The Heart of the Home

> A real home-loving person is a kind of sun. Whether she sits in her own corner, smiling genially, or walks from house to house, spreading warmth, she is always at home, radiating cosiness. Such a person is invincible... (Wahlman 1902:68).

In this way a leading Swedish architect defined the home-loving person in 1902, or rather the home-loving woman – it is quite obvious that the production of homeliness was woman's work. During the Oscarian era the qualities of home became the qualities of women. Notions of home and womanhood, privacy and sentiment were strongly interwoven.

Other economic and moral rules were applied more in the domestic than in the public sphere. 'Home' stood for emotions and warmth, for security, harmony and cosiness. While the Victorian middle-class male was defined through qualities like rationality and efficiency which were demanded in the sphere of production, his wife should have her life filled by love and care, being passive rather than active. In this new construction of gender differences the career-oriented *homo economicus* is contrasted to the tender *femina domestica* (Cominos 1973).

The woman stands as the guardian of home and its many virtues. If we examine Victorian childhood memories, home and mother appear to have been an inseparable entity: "What was the lifework of my mother?", asks the daughter of a civil servant and continues, "it was the home she built for us. In this task she invested all her most painstaking cares and her warmest love. This was her calling..." Another author summarized the same feeling in the words "Home was, above all, Mother..."

The ideal existence of *femina domestica* was defined by men. Middle-class women, were supposed to be spared heavy and dirty chores at home. Real productive work was not for them, they were expected to express their womanhood through other activities. It was up to the housewife to provide an atmosphere of homeliness. Inside her own home a woman was free to build her own fantasy world, she was able to paint and embroider, as well as plan and decorate. Her delicate piano playing and her warm smile ideally should have filled the house. The lovingly arranged bric-à-brac on shelves and mantelpieces symbolized the new womanhood. There were always a thousand ways to elaborate and ritualize the day, while daydreaming and waiting for the man of the house to return home from the outside world.

Female ambitions were expected to focus on making home a pleasant domain. However, for whose benefit? The new manuals for good house-keeping state it quite clearly, as in this example from 1888:

> A man, who spends most of his day away from the family, who has to work outside, counts on finding a restful and refreshing atmosphere when he returns home. Maybe sometimes even a little merriment or a surprise. The man who not only provides for his family but even brings it some of the delights of life, if his financial situation admits it, has the right to demand a warm welcome and it is his wife's duty to provide it. She must do her utmost to make his stay at home as pleasant as possible; this way she can continue to influence him and keep his affection undiminished...

In order to understand the new images of domesticity we have to relate them to the bourgeois reorganization of gender. Contrary to notions of gender in, for example, traditional Swedish peasant culture, the new conceptions were based upon a notion of complementary emotional structures. The ideal of the rational and disciplined male operating in the public sphere was constructed with the help of a new femininity. A loving wife and a supportive home became an important asset for the man who wanted to conquer the world. But home was not only a female domain, it was also a cultural breathing space where men could act out the more emotional or even feminine parts of their cultural personality.

Every evening the Oscarian child was able to witness the transformation of Father, the capable, disciplined and rational professional or business man, into Daddy, the family man. The ritual transformation from the dark coat and the polished leather boots into soft slippers and a velvet smoking jacket also signalled a change in roles and expectations. In the secluded privacy and intimacy of the home, surrounded by his nearest and dearest, he was able to behave in a more relaxed and often boyish fashion, showing emotions which were taboo in the public sphere.

The new construction of gender polarities was not a fixed set of male and female roles, but rather polarities of masculinity and feminity which had a more dialectic relationship. The *femina domestica* helped to underline the maleness of the man in the public sphere but also created a private antidote to the outside world, a cultural space where men would be under the spell of female domesticity and intimacy.

However, when looking at this Oscarian era it is important to distinguish between male dreams and ideals about femininity and the actual everyday activities of women. The majority of middle-class housewives spent most of their time doing other things than playing the piano or producing needle-work. They became home-makers in a more practical sense. Running a household in this period was a complex task, especially if the suitable level of respectability, orderliness and ritual complexity were to be kept up. Even in urban households there remained quite an amount of self-sufficiency, with the time-consuming preparation and preservation of food. The wives of civil servants, factory owners and clerks had few opportunities for idle day-dreaming, and this was even less the case in the vicarage or the small manor house in the countryside. The discrepancy between the ideal and the real was as greatly marked in this area as it was in many other fields of Oscarian culture.

The Hidden Heritage

It is evident that most middle-class children who grew up around the turn of the century left home with strong notions about what family life should be like.

An analysis of childhood reminiscences from this period shows how much children learned about social relationships and cultural rules from the actual physical arrangements in their home, which became part of a silent and unconscious socialization. The walls kept talking to the children.

The strict musty colours of Father's study with its impressive and disciplined array of books and polished desk communicated ideas about "serious work" and male responsibilities, just as the choice of colours and furniture for the boys' and girls' rooms provided pervasive comments on gender.

The many mirrors scattered around the house gave them a chance of observing their own behaviour and countenance, and also reminded them how important it was to know how 'to carry yourself'.

Above all the silent socialization of the home kept bombarding them with one of the essential ground rules of bourgeois culture. *There is a time and place for everything.* The need to learn how to separate people, activities and functions was taught with the help of the many spatial and temporal rituals which structured everyday life at home. Children learned to respect the boundaries separating various arenas of the home, never to enter their parents' bedroom without permission and to be aware that you had to behave differently in the drawing-room than in the nursery. They observed the difference between the atmosphere and language of the kitchen (where the servants reigned), and the restrained behavior in the dining-room.

They were reminded of the importance of time and time-keeping by the multitude of clocks and the constant reminders of the need for keeping time. Time was everywhere. Even as the child moved around in the stillness of his or her home, the sound of ticking and chiming clocks was ubiquitous.

Each family meal became a lesson in the necessity for functional differentiation and self-discipline: Be on time for dinner, wash your hands before sitting down at the table, keep your elbows in and your mouth shut, only answer when you are spoken to!

In their memories of these Oscarian childhood days, people also reorganize and reinterpret the past. The process of idyllic idealization suggests that actual experiences are repressed or reinterpreted. It is interesting to compare what people want to remember with the way the cultural stereotypes of family togetherness and parental love were constructed. Although parents were, in reality, often distant and formal figures, it is the memories of the family gathered around the evening table or Mother as a warm, radiant sun one seeks to remember. These memories are more of a symbolic statement on the way family life ought to be.

The fact that there were so many cultural contradictions in bourgeois world view and such a gap between ideals and realities of domestic life meant that we find a great deal of compartmentalization of conflicting messages and experiences. Most children of that era grew up with very clear ideas about what life at home ought to look like and these ideals became part of their ambitions to reform and educate the lower classes.

Towards the end of the 19th century the old social structure of Swedish society was crumbling. Traditional rules of hierarchy, loyalty and social control no longer seemed to be functional. The rapidly growing working class was seen as a menace to the old social stability. There was an atmosphere of tension, of clashing values, which made those at the top frightened. If the old order could not be rebuilt, certainly a new moral cement was needed in order to keep society from disintegrating. For some, one of the answers to this problem was found in the importance of a good home life. If only the working classes could be domesticated, if only their unrest and ambitions could be turned inwards, towards the home and family, many problems would be solved. The change should be moral rather than economic.

A government committee stressed the importance of state loans for working-class home-makers who wanted a small house of their own. In their report from 1899 they state:

> There is all reason to believe that a home-owning worker will feel stronger for both his community and his fatherland... (Egnahemskommittén 1899:14).

A home-owner's journal was started and it carried the motto: "Goal: A home of your own on freehold land. Means: Industry, thrift and godliness." A number of organizations worked to protect the values of home or to increase the love of home in society. One of the most ardent missionaries of this perspective wrote in 1910:

> If all good thoughts were united into a mighty wave to save our homes and protect our nation. *To make our homes sweet and loveable and make our nation strong and healthy.* This would carry us forward, it would protect us from much evil and avert dangers. This would be a new year's promise we ought to give in every home, our hands united in a closed circle as a symbol of our unity, our strength... (Tenow 1910:28).

The virtues of a stable home life were echoed in parliamentary debates, in newspaper articles and pamphlets. The ideals were spread through many channels, such as housing and educational reform programs, welfare agencies, and campaigns for good housekeeping among working-class women.

It would be wrong, however, to talk in terms of a well-planned attack with the explicit goal of pacifying the unruly working class. Many of the social reformers saw themselves as missionaries of 'the good life', of modernization and development. They wanted to improve housing conditions, food habits and child care. Many of them were not aware of the fact that their reforming activities exhibited heavy moral overtones. Many of these reformers complained of the suspicion and ungrateful attitudes directed towards them by the workers, who resented these moral connotations.

Working-Class Homes

What about the actualities of working-class life at the beginning of the 20th century? The most striking feature was overcrowded homes. As late as in the 1930s the majority of Swedish working-class families lived in a single room and kitchen or just one room with a small stove in the corner. Both in rural and urban areas living conditions were poor and housing shortages made rents relatively high.

In these conditions family life took on a rather different character than evidenced in middle-class settings. A young middle-class boy, whose family moved into a working-class neighborhood during the 1920s, was surprised to find out that the local children insisted on adding a bachelor to the list of characters when playing mummy-daddy-kids. He gradually realized that lodgers were a normal part of working-class households. Single people had to attach themselves to existing families who needed the extra cash.

We can contrast middle-class ideals about family life by looking more closely at life in a rather typical working-class urban setting during the period 1910–1940, in the town of Landskrona.[5]

Life in a single-room apartment meant that beds and various other sleeping arrangements took up most of the interior space. "Home" was not a place where you longed to spend your spare time. Socializing had to be carried out elsewhere.

A striking feature of working-class life up to the Second World War was the relative unimportance of family togetherness. The men spent their time with their mates, women visited each other and children often looked after themselves, playing in backyards or roaming about the neighborhood. There were neither material conditions nor cultural traditions for a more familistic lifestyle, village life had also been based on a rather sex-segregated pattern of socializing.

This meant that the social landscape of working-class children who grew up during this period had a far less home-centered focus than in middle-class settings.

The childhood memories of Landskrona workers are organized around many more *we*'s than just the family: "we on our street, in our neighbourhood, in our apartment house..."

One's social identity was to a great extent anchored in these territorial units. The boundaries between "us" and "them" were manifested in many ways, from neighborhood nicknames to gang fights. Local solidarity was also maintained through systems of reciprocity and sharing. Across hallways, backyards and alleys there was a steady flow of cups of sugar, flour and other necessities. This borrowing between households had both economic and symbolic aspects. Unlike middle-class families, working-class households lacked both resources and space for independent domestic budgeting. The constant borrowing was a part of the working-class economy just as the weekly visits to the pawnbroker; however, by entering a network of reciprocity you also manifested a social belonging.

There is, however, a note of ambivalence in memories of these neighborhood networks in Landskrona as in many other working-class settings. People will talk about the steady borrowing among housewifes and then add: "but in our family we always kept ourselves to ourselves" or "we always managed on our own". To fend for yourself, to be dependent upon neither neighbors nor welfare was an important mark of working-class respectability. This cultural contradiction was usually resolved by the discrepancy between normative statements and actual behaviour; however, beneath the notion of fending for yourself was an important working-class fight for self-esteem and pride in a society where you constantly were reminded by representatives of the dominant culture that your home and family life rarely reached desirable standards.

There were always examples of families in the neighborhood, who "had given up" or "no longer cared". They were families living at the mercy of social welfare and thus in the hands of the municipal authorities.

It is therefore quite misleading to equate notions about respectability with a process of *embourgeoisement,* of imitating middle-class values of domesticity and propriety. Working-class families did not simply reproduce patterns of the dominant culture. Although they often appropriated cultural forms from it, these elements were charged with new meaning as part of a different cultural system.

A number of detailed surveys threw public light on the poor housing conditions of the working class during the 1920s and 30s. Both conservative and progressive commentators could agree on the graveness of this problem but both their analysis and solutions tended to disagree.

Was the overcrowded home an economic or cultural problem? An official survey from 1933 in the city of Gothenburg argued that overcrowding "is not a result of economic necessity but must be related to habits of home and family life which seem unsatisfactory from a social perspective". The problem, the authors said, is not lack of money in the first place but a tendency for working-class family members to squander their money on other things than a decent standard of housing (SOU 1933:25). This moralizing attitude has a long tradition in middle-class discourse on working-class life: no long-term planning, wrong priorities, insufficient love of home. They demonstrate a lack of understanding of both working-class culture and material realities.

Another argument found in the housing debate of the period is that working-class families used their living space incorrectly. The most blatant example of such bad habits was found in the use of the parlour.

Let us return to Landskrona and a typical description of the domestic scene from the son of a cooper, who grew up in the 1920s:

> We mainly lived in the kitchen. The room my parents used as parlour should be on parade and you had to be very ill to get to lie down in there. When the doctor came to visit you couldn't of course be bedded down in the kitchen. Apart from that all the five of us lived in the kitchen. And the kitchen wasn't big, something like 2,5 × 3,5 meters. It was kept warm by an iron stove, but when times were real hard we had a miniature burner on top of it. It was warm enough and we had a good home . . . Nearly all of us shared beds in those days. When I got a little bit older Mum and Dad made me an extra bed on top of a couple of boxes. We all slept in the kitchen and the other room was kept neat.

". . . and the other room was kept neat". This phrase is echoed in most other childhood memories from the period:

> We had a parlour too, it was so neat that you barely was allowed to touch the door-knob . . . It was always like that. No matter how little space you had, there had to be a parlour . . .

> I had a mate at work, his family had a room and kitchen. Well, they took in a lodger, a bachelor, who got the parlour, but he always thought it nicer out in the kitchen, so that room stood empty most of the time . . .

For middle-class intellectuals this seemed a strange and wasteful way to live. They found it hard to understand that working-class wives fought hard for their parlours. To have one silent and well-kept room, where no one was allowed to sleep, was well worth the nuisance of an overcrowded kitchen or second room. The parlour with its plants, its mantelpiece clock and lace-decorated sofa was not a simple attempt to imitate bourgeois life styles, instead, the room had its own symbolic meaning in working-class culture.

It was a cultural space separated from the drudgeries of everyday life, and when you entered it you were ritually transformed. It had an atmosphere all of its own.

Does Mother Really Know Best?

The puzzle of the parlour also bothered many left-wing intellectuals. When the Social democrats gained power in 1932, improved working-class housing was a top priority. Although depression meant that implementation of the development programs was slowed down, progressive architects, planners and social scientists were busy drawing up blueprints for the new welfare society, which also included the concept of a new modern family.

Functional living! was the rallying call for these intellectuals. With great optimism they argued that science and technology would defeat poverty and traditionalism. Change was not only a question of giving the working class a better standard of living, but, it was also a question of reorganizing everyday life on a more scientific and rational basis. To change society and the family one had to start at home.

At the great Stockholm exhibition in 1930 this plea for rational and modern living was forcefully presented with the help of model homes. The author Ivar-Lo Johansson has captured the atmosphere of the exhibition summer:

> I drifted out along the main street to the big Stockholm exhibition in 1930. It was summer and piercing hot. The sun of the new decade was shining on my forehead. A whole new city of steel, glass and concrete had been created on the plain, until then just an empty space. Houses, restaurants and music grand stands looked like birds rising with stiff wings. In the crowd people spoke about the new architecture which would give birth to a new spirit of life. A door handle, a picture window, a matter-of-fact piece of furniture would in short time influence the family living in the house so that their feelings and thoughts became open and transparent... (Lo-Johansson 1957)

In the radical manifesto of the exhibition, aptly named *Acceptera!* (Accept!), it was argued that there was a problematic cultural lag in Swedish society. While industrialization totally had changed technology and production, home life was still hopelessly old-fashioned. However, a modern family was emerging and this new family would have needs and goals in life that differed from the needs and goals of the traditional family.

The arguments for modern living and modern homes were expressed in the image of the home as "a machine for living". Great energy was taken not only to redesign housing and home interiors but also to develop a domestic science that would make it possible to modernize home life. The key concept was *rationality*. "Modern living" involved a strict division of functions: such as working, cooking, eating, entertaining, resting, sleeping, cleaning. Play and leisure activities as well should preferably be separated in the home. During the 1930s there was a rapidly expanding literature on the scientific reorganization of domestic life. A good example of this genre is the work of a committee for the standardization of kitchens, which produced its detailed report in 1935. It starts out with a general motto:

> A pleasant, practical and hygienic work place for those who handle the daily care of the house is the primary condition for an orderly home. (Kommittén... 1935:23).

This new domestic order was firmly founded in scientific notions. With great care every thinkable function of the home and the kitchen is listed in this report. No task was too trivial to be analyzed. The source of inspiration was modern industry, the authors state. It was the art of scientific management and the time-budgeting of Taylorism which began to enter the home.

The suggestions for improvement in the report were not limited to the planning of the kitchen but also included advice about the rationalization of housework. Here one could, step by step, learn the proper method of washing up after dinner or the correct way to organize kitchen utensils in the cupboards.

Establishing a field of home economics also embraced a redefinition of the role of *femina domestica*. Because more working-class women returned to the home during the depression and many middle-class women no longer could afford the same amount of domestic help previously available, this interest in the role of the house-wife is hardly suprising.

During the interwar period there was a marked tendency to talk of housework as an occupation and housewifery as an occupational role. This notion was also related to the discussions of equality between the sexes. By raising the domestic tasks to the level of *work*, an ideological symmetry was created between the wage-labour of men and the housekeeping of women. For example, the committee on the standardization of kitchens stressed that work in the kitchen should be regarded like any other job. A symbolic expression of this was the advice that one should create a small office corner for the wife at home, where records and recipes could be kept as well as being a place where budgeting and planning could be carried out.

The authors also tried to define the minimum requirements society should demand of those engaging in housekeeping:

1. Effective and economic care of all the tasks necessary for the livelihood of the family (housing, clothes, food, heating etc.)
2. A mentality directed towards the creation of a "homely atmosphere," of sym-pathy, stimulation, renewal, education which in turn calls for:
3. An organization and cultivation of both material and spiritual resources, from which also follows
4. The Possibilities to partake in the welfare work of the greater home – the society and nation ... (Kommittén 1935:37).

In retrospect it is easy to satirize this flood of normative statements and well-meaning advice with which housewives were swamped. It is, however, important to remember that the propagandists for modern housekeeping were a heter-ogenous group with diverse ideological motivations. The intensive discussions about the role of the housewife during the 30s and 40s mirror several distinct interests.

One of them was anchored in the emergence of a new welfare state in which the link between the little home and the "greater home" of the state and nation became important. It is hardly a coincidence that the Social Democrats named their vision of a future, more egalitarian society the *"people's home"*. In this integrative process the mother and housewife was given a key role. She was seen as a very important mediating link between the new welfare reform programs and the everyday life of individuals (cf. the discussion in Frykman 1984). Social change had to start at home, where new ideas about child upbringing, health, hygiene and rational behavior had to be implemented.

Ideas about scientific housekeeping and a symmetrical family thus cannot be reduced to an attempt to domesticate working-class family life. For the radical planners it was seen as a way of constructing a modern family, a more democratic family, and in this process they fought both against "the old bourgeois family life" and against the lack of knowledge among "the common people". In this utopian ideal the family was no longer the sheltered haven or refuge but it was seen as the foundation of an open, democratic society.

For conservative commentators their interest in the role of the housewife and the home was more of a worry that the true values of home and its guardian angel *femina domestica* was threatened, and the rapid changes in society had to be counteracted by a fight for domesticity in a campaign for "women back to the home".

A third influence is found in the growth of a consumer goods market during this period. We find a commerical concern for the housewife and the home as an expanding market for household appliances. Here modern living was equated with investing in new technology, from vacuum-cleaners to germ killers.[6]

Many of the ideas about modern home-keeping were never more than ideals. The progressive reformers who wanted to change the situation of over-worked housewives, making the drudgeries of household work easier, were often surprised at the resistance they met in spreading their ideas.

It turned out that middle-class housewives readily embraced the ideology of modern living. This is hardly surprising as the ideals to a great extent reflected middle-class values and worldview, especially among the expanding groups that saw themselves as champions of a progressive lifestyle – the *modern* middle class (cf. the discussion in Frykman & Löfgren 1984).

Resistance was more marked in working-class settings. The reformers often did not realize that their preachings had an element of class moralizing and a paternalistic tone which did not go unnoticed among working-class women. Furthermore, all the well-meaning advice which was meant to strengthen the self-respect of the women often had a contrary effect. They felt threatened by the new specialists.[7]

In these campaigns traditional forms of cultural competence were lifted from the common individual into the waiting arms of specialists and experts. Social knowledge was redistributed and fragmented. A cultural insecurity often resulted from this process: Am I a good mother and a modern housewife, is our home organized in a rational manner? Mother no longer knows best.

The working-class resistance to the arguments for modern living posed a problem for progressive intellectuals who saw themselves as champions of the welfare society. While workers in the Oscarian era were accused of a *lack* of culture, middle-class commentators in the 1930s accused workers of being too traditional, too conservative in their home life.

One reason for this "working-class conservatism" was again the lack of resources. Even during the 1930s and 1940s few families could afford bigger flats, in which the grand schemes of scientific and functional living could be carried out. Who could separate family activities in a one-room apartment? Even in cases where families acquired more space there was a reluctance to follow the advice of the functionalists. The primacy of the parlour continued to be an important symbol of working-class respectability. The home became a cultural battlefield during this period, an arena where different value systems and different cultural priorities clashed. One more example may help illuminate this process. Let us return to the kitchen.

According to functionalist dogma, this room, should be used for productive work only: cooking and cleaning. In working-class homes, however, families stuck to the rural tradition of using the kitchen as the heart and centre of the home. The kitchen was a place where unannounced visitors dropped in for a cup of coffee, the place where one had one's meals, where mother mended clothes, the children played and Dad took a nap on the kitchen bench.

This crowding of people and activities was judged as both unsound and unhygienic. In many of the new housing estates planned in the 30s kitchens were made very small, in order to force alternative activities into other rooms. To their disappointment architects found that people persisted in crowding into the kitchen, leaving the parlour which architects had renamed "the everyday room" empty and on parade for special visitors and ritual occasions.

These battles about the correct ways to organize your home life illustrate several points. First of all, it is obvious that much of the obsession with *functional differentiation* in fact had less to do with the demands of "hygiene" or "objective science" than with one of the basic foundations of Oscarian worldview viz: the bourgeois fear of mixing categories, of not drawing sharp boundaries, of sleeping and eating in the same room, of mixing meat and potatoes on the dinner plate. The Oscarian motto 'there's a time and place for everything' was still imprinted on the mind of the intellectuals who thought that they were busy creating a totally new society in the 1930s. Just as the Oscarians complained about the sloppy and unorganized life of the peasants, the new middle-class intellectuals could not see that the life of working-class families had its own cultural order, its own rules and norms.

The Dying Family

The class bias is easier to detect in the conservative debate on the future of home and family that occured in the '30s and '40s. While the radical intellectuals complained about the fetters of tradition and suggested the need for a new type of family with new sex roles and new methods of child-rearing in the modern welfare state, conservative commentators viewed this utopia with less enthusiasm. Conservatives saw the Social Democratic visions and the working-class demands for a better material life as a threat to the established order, and as an attempt to cut everybody down to the same size. Their lament was that the traditional values of family and home were eroded and their utopia was not to be found in the future but in the past. They extolled the happy and sound family life of the Victorians:

> ...We need a revival of the family. Modern Man who has lost so many of his illusions and so much of the support found in traditions must not be bereaved of the values we still own. The family can provide the security and the happiness which our hunted mankind needs, today more than ever. The family must not only be defended; it must be made to render more support than it has done for the last generations...(Hem och familj 1941:5).

A detailed program was presented to further this aim. Children were to be given a more positive view of the home and the family. They should receive more instruction in home economics and home-making, they should be prepared for marriage and their parental duties.

[...]

In the interest in education and enlightenment both conservative and progressive intellectuals sometimes joined hands. The need for more stable and healthier homes also called for a domestication of husbands. In accordance with the new marriage ideal of spouses as comrades or equal partners in the joint family business, men had to change. Boys should be encouraged to take a greater interest in their future roles of good husbands, men ought to spend more time with their families etc. No longer should the domestic sphere simply be a female domain or a male resting-place. Building a happy home called for two interested and well-educated spouses.

But why all this worry and concern? Looking back on the 1940s one can argue that during no other period of Swedish history has the family had such a strong and clearly delineated position in the social landscape. At this time the old collectivity of working-class neighborhoods had started to disintegrate and we find a much more familistic lifestyle emerging also among workers.

The Threatened Home

[...]

We have to ask "Why is the family portrayed as a threatened institution, who is supposed to threaten it and who feels threatened?" In order to understand the debate on the future of the family in 1900 or 1930 we must see concepts like home and family as powerful images, symbols and metaphors. We may argue that the family seemed to have been a rather stable social institution in the 1940s at least compared with the situation a hundred years earlier. The image of a disintegrating family system should rather be seen as a metaphor for other social anxieties. It mirrors the self-conception and the worries of the middle class, which felt itself threatened during this period. It is not necessarily the family which is changing but society. We find the same tendencies in the Victorian debate on the family.

Different social groups and classes will, for different interests, use the image of the home or the family as a cultural weapon. In this process the past will often be reorganized for the present. The Victorian middle class extolled the virtues of family life in the "traditional peasant culture". The picture they painted of a stable, home-centered life, of obedient children and loving parents tells us more of their own aspirations and ideals than about historical realities. Their homage to the mythical "Grand Family" mirrored the longing for a more stable and patriarchal structure in a rapidly changing society.

In the same way critics of the welfare state in the 1940s created their picture of the sound and happy family life of the Victorian bourgeoisie and used that to prove their point that the family was going under fast. Contemporary radicals turned history the other way round and talked about the unhealthy and false family life of the Victorians.

But *who* was threatening the family? All kinds of dark forces are called forth depending on who is formulating the argument, but there is a strong tendency to put the blame on the working class, which rarely seems to have managed a tolerable family life at all. There is at least a strong element of class moralizing in the debates of both the 1880s and the 1930s, a moralizing which is hiding behind the dominant culture's definition of normality.

[...]

What even radical observers often failed to see was that working-class resistance to change could be part of a fight for identity and self-respect. If one grows up in a society where one is constantly being bombarded by messages from the official, dominant culture, messages which tell you that there is something wrong with the way you live your life, then you will most probably develop cultural defences. One of them is turning a deaf ear to the flood of good advice and admonitions, another is turning home into a private shelter. You may be ordered around at work, at school or at the welfare agency, but here, at home, nobody has the right to meddle, to tell you what to do.

[...]

In my paper I have argued for a cultural analysis in which ideas about the home and the family are studied in a wider social and historical context. I have stressed the dialectics between the private world and the outside world. The sweetness of home tends to increase as the world outside becomes more complex and problematic, but terms like home, privacy and respectability must never be used as transhistorical concepts. They need to be anchored in time, space and class, they mean different thing for different people.

The class dimension is important here. We cannot talk of a simple process of *embourgeoisement* during the 20th century. It is important to distinguish between form and content when discussing working-class appropriation of middle-class life styles. Elements may be borrowed but they are charged with new cultural meanings.

The same class perspective is necessary if we want to understand the heated debate on home life in Swedish society during the last hundred years. In a society where open references to class interests or class differences become more and more of a taboo, class conflicts tend to be acted out on other cultural stages. The home becomes one of these battlegrounds and in order to analyze processes of cultural confrontation we have to constantly change perspective and contrast middle-class visions of home life with working-class ones. The same cultural phenomena will take on different meanings when viewed from different positions in a social hierarchy.

NOTES

1 I will make no attempt to present this rapidly expanding literature but only acknowledge the inspiration I got from the pioneering works of Leonore Davidoff (1976) and Davidoff et al. 1976) and the studies edited by Martha Vicinus (1973 and 1977) as well as from the anthropological discussion in MacCormack & Strathern (1980).
2 "Oscarian" refers to the reign of king Oscar II of Sweden 1872–1907.
3 See Löfgren 1979. Unless otherwise stated the Swedish quotations translated by me into English come from this work.
4 See the discussion in Löfgren 1981 and the empirical analysis of the family in the period 1920–1950 in Frykman and Löfgren 1984. The translated Swedish empirical examples in this later part of the paper have been fetched from this study, unless otherwise stated.
5 The following discussion is based upon interviews which are presented in Frykman & Löfgren 1984.
6 Cf. the American discussion of domestic ideology and scientific housekeeping in Hayden (1982), Wright (1980), Ewen (1976) and Ehrenreich & English (1979).
7 This cultural confrontation in Sweden of the 1930s has been discussed by Aström (1984). See also Martin (1981:53ff).

REFERENCES

Aström, Lissie 1984: Husmodern möter folkhemmet. In: Frykman & Löfgren (ed): *Moderna tider. Vision och vardag i folkhemmet*. Malmö.

Asplund, Gunnar et al. 1931: *Acceptera!* Stockholm.

Cominos, Peter 1973: Innocent Femina Sensualis in Unconscious Conflict. In: M. Vicinus (ed.): *Suffer and Be Still. Women in the Victorian Age*. Bloomington.

Davidoff, Leonore 1976: The Rationalization of Housework. In: Allen & Bates (eds): *Dependance and Exploitation in Work and Marriage*. London.

Davidoff, Leonore et al. 1976: Landscape with Figures: Home and Community in English Society. In: J. Mitchell & A. Oakley (eds): *The Rights and Wrongs of Women*. Harmondsworth.

Egnahemskommittén 1899: 1899 års Egnahemskommittés betänkande, I. Stockholm.

Ehrenreich, Barbara & English, Deidre 1979: *For Her Own Good. 150 Years of Experts' Advice to Women*. London.

Ewen, Stuart 1976: *Captains of Consciousness. Advertising and the Social Roots of Consumer Culture*. New York.

Frykman, Jonas 1984: Ur medelklassens familjeliv. In: B.-E. Andersson (ed): *Familjebilder. Myster, verklighet, visioner*. Stockholm.

Frykman, Jonas & Löfgren, Orvar 1979: *Den kultiverade människan*. Lund.

Frykman, Jonas & Löfgren, Orvar 1984: Klassbilder. I: Frykman & Löfgren (eds): *Moderna tider. Vision och vardag i folkhemmet*. Lund.

Hayden, Dolores 1982: *The Grand Domestic Revolution: A History of Feminist Designs for American Homes, Neighborhoods and Cities*. Cambridge, Mass.

Hem och familji i skolans undervisning 1941: Utredning. Stockholm.

Kommittén för standarisering av byggnadsmaterial 1935: Köket och ekonomiavdelningen i mindre bostadslägenheter. Förslag till systematisering. Stockholm.

Lo-Johansson, Ivar 1957: *Författaren*. Stockholm.

Löfgren, Orvar 1979: Familjemänniskan. In: Frykman & Löfgren: *Den kultiverade människan*. Lund.

Löfgren, Orvar 1981: *On the Anatomy of Culture*. Ethnologia Europaea XII: 24–26.

MacCormack, Carol & Strathern, Marlyin (eds) 1980: *Nature, Culture and Gender*. London.

Martin, Bernice 1981: *A Sociology of Contemporary Cultural Change*. Oxford.

Matovic, Margareta 1984: *Stockholmsäktenskap. Familjebildning och partnerval i Stockholm 1850–1890*. Stockholm.

SOU 1933: Utredning rörande behovet av... bostadsstatistik. *Statens offentliga utredningar 1933: 14*. Stockholm.

Tenow, Elsa 1910: *Kärlek och lycka*. Stockholm.

Wahlman, L. J. 1902: En gård och dess trefnad. *Ord och bild*.

Vicinius, Martha (ed) 1973: *Suffer and Be Still. Women in the Victorian Age*. Bloomington.

Vicinius, Marta (ed) 1977: *A Widening Sphere. Changing Roles of Victorian Women*. Bloomington.

Wright, Gwendolyn 1980: *Moralism and the Model Home. Domestic Architecture and Cultural Conflict in Chicago 1873–1913*. Chicago.

7

The Architecture of Female Seclusion in West Africa[1]

Deborah Pellow

Introduction

A people's culture includes norms, values, attitudes, and symbolic representations. Culture is manifest in the social connections and structures that that culture regulates – the organization of individuals into groups, their statuses, their relationship to one another. Both culture and social system are grounded in space. That is to say, people interact within physically defined areas that carry meaning and they do so in particular ways. Social and physical space are two dimensions of the same system; the third is temporality. All three are bounded and mutually constitutive. Physical, social, and temporal organization encode information, which is to say, they communicate. Lifestyle, which varies with culture, is evident in social organization. This in turn harmonizes with spatial organization, as people behave in accordance with spatial cues. And there is both continuity and change in these dimensions over time.

It is not just that people are anchored in space. They also claim that space, develop it, build on it, divide it up into varying shapes and sizes, mark it as their own. They design and build dwellings, that is, they produce spaces to live in the space they have claimed. How a group designs its housing relates to its cultural habits. As spatial cues encode social information (Rapoport 1982), studies of domestic architecture provide data on basic issues of ethnography such as social organization, religion, and economic activities (Schwerdtfeger 1982).

Until recently, anthropologists have largely neglected the role of the house, even as this building is a basic representation of spatial organization and is an integral part of culture. Like language, space is socially constructed; people everywhere produce houses whose spatial organization suits the inhabitants' social life. Presumably then, people sharing a cultural tradition may well also share sociospatial traits. Thus, like all material culture, the house has embedded cultural values that are expressed through social relationships. "[A]nd like the syntax of language, the spatial arrangements of our buildings and communities reflect and reinforce the nature of gender, race, and class relations in society" (Weisman 1992:2).

The widespread gendering of space is significant at both symbolic and behavioral levels. In nonindustrial societies, men and women are often segregated within the home, and architecture can play a role in maintaining this through territorial barriers and symbolic differentiation. In this chapter, my theoretical focus is the co-evolution of house form and gender roles over the past 80-plus years in the Accra (Ghana) community of Sabon Zongo. The community was founded by migrant Muslim Hausa from Northern Nigeria, where the seclusion of adult Hausa women was and is normative. When the first of these Hausa migrated to Accra in the late 1800s, they lived at Zongo Lane in downtown Accra, among an ethnically mixed Muslim community, that included Yoruba, Nupe, and Wangara. These other groups were less "orthodox" in their Islam, which included nonobservance of wife seclusion. The differences in religious practice provided an important impetus for some of the Hausa to move to Sabon Zongo, where residents could avoid "any contradiction in our religion which is Islam."[2]

The original houses built in Sabon Zongo follow the Kano (Northern Nigeria) archetype designed to enable *kulle*, wife seclusion. Sabon Zongo's landlords, overwhelmingly Hausa, did not and do not practice *kulle*. Those interviewed in the contemporary period say that *kulle* is too difficult, too costly. Yet, other practices, like the month-long fast of Ramadan, while difficult, are observed. The community's Hausa residents today follow Hausa sartorial fashion, eat Hausa foods, maintain 30 mosques in the community and pray regularly in them, and they aspire to make *hajj*, pilgrimage to Mecca.

So why not wife seclusion? What I hypothesize is that social change (including the initial dislocation to Christian southern Ghana), economic change, and the attachment of Sabon Zongo residents to their community, have culminated in adaptive social and spatial behaviors that make "doing *kulle*" impossible. While the Northern Nigerian city Kano, for example, is about 98 percent Muslim Hausa, Accra has pockets of Hausa Muslims but is far more Westernized and is basically a Christian city.

Muhammad-Oumar, a scholar of Hausa architecture, set out to examine what might happen to domestic space when ethnic and occupational specifications demand different or various functional requirements and/or solutions from the built forms. He proposed that "different ethnic and/or occupational groups may well adapt an achetype...in order to accommodate specific work functions and/or ethnic idiosyncracies" (Muhammad-Oumar 1997:34). Such "ethnic idiosyncrasies" express cultural values and include status distinctions between males and females and, in northern Nigeria, the consequent sequestering of women. In Sabon Zongo, sexual separation is diluted. The cultural norm of the separation between the sexes has been trumped by the pull of community, when spatial and economic needs come to the fore.

Practicing Space

As anthropologists have come to appreciate the cultural codes and meanings implicated in the organization of space in society, they have been influenced by theorists such as Henri Lefebvre. Lefebvre (1991) emphasizes the symbolic meaning and significance of particular spaces, in effect how spaces are culturized, but also how culture is spatialized, how practices are lived in space. Indeed, through her ethnography of the Marakwet of Kenya, anthropologist Henrietta Moore (1986:116) pushes us to see the organization of space as a *context*, which is developed through *practice*, that is through the interaction of individuals. In other words, the organization of space defines relationships in the *specific context* of a set of interactions and activities. Like geographer Doreen Massey (1993), she posits the inseparability of the social and the spatial, with social practice as inherently spatial.

The social constructions of place and gender are intimately connected. Indeed, men and women may each be associated with different spaces or differently valued in space. The social realities that produce and are produced by ordering domestic space explains the meaning of spatial organization (Moore 1986:107). Cross-culturally, the house is women's spatial domain; it is here that they are most strongly connected. Looking at the world this way, "the identities of 'woman' and of the 'home-place' are intimately tied up with each other" (Massey 1994:180). Woman's social and biological roles, and the human attributes and emotions associated with them, "merge in the strong and cherished image of the dwelling" (Weisman 1992:17). Ethnographers support this characterization among the Navajo (Witherspoon 1975), urban African-Americans (Stack 1974), working-class East Londoners (Young 1962), Iranians (Wright 1981), the imperial Chinese (Pollock 1981), ancient Greeks (Jameson 1990), the Swahili (Donley-Reid 1990), to name a sampling. That their spatial identification is overwhelmingly domestic explains their differentiation from men.

There is nothing ethereal about female role imperatives when they are viewed as grounded in physical space and built into physical structures, whether kitchens or courtyards. Simultaneously, women's placement in space provides support for the ideology and energizes the cultural definition of female roles. We see the realization of women's relationships to one another, to men, to children, to society at large, in their spatial placement. The division of space according to sex role differentiation reinforces sexual stereotypes, carries certain understandings of what the permissible roles and behaviors of each sex are, and may limit or enhance learning a variety of skills (Weisman 1981).

If there are rules separating women from men, there are devices or regulations to maintain that separation (Ardener 1981). Social understandings are generally manifest in spatial delineations, although not always. A variety of nonphysical mechanisms such as rules (hierarchies, avoidance, etiquette) and psychological bearing (internal withdrawal) work to prevent interaction (Rapoport 1980:31). If the ideology decrees that women are not only to be separate from men but also subordinate to them, then social and spatial structures will also define this *hierarchy*. By delimiting the areas of women's mobility, in a spatial sense, one is also bounding their social and economic options.

A New Community

A *zongo* (Hausa: stranger quarter) is a community in both the social and the spatial sense. Peil (1979:126) characterizes Ghana's zongos as "northern" in their religious preference (Islam), education (enthusiasm for Quranic, resistance to Western) and cultural orientation. The zongos have been strongly influenced by the Northern Nigerian Hausa, whose presence in Accra dates back to the late 19th century. The first Nigerians who migrated to Accra lived in the old downtown area among the other Muslims (primarily Nigerian) as guests of the indigenous Ga. Interethnic Muslim squabbling became so intense that the British closed the main mosque for seven years (see Pellow 1985).

Sabon Zongo (new *zongo*) is located on the periphery of Accra. The community was founded in 1910 by Malam Bako, a Hausa leader, when his followers outgrew their space in the old downtown area. He welcomed the opportunity to remove his people from the problematic situation by creating a distinct Hausa quarter; here they would have their own place, under their own control, where they could observe Islamic orthodoxy (Pellow 1985, 1999).

Their orthodoxy, an outgrowth of generations of intertwined Hausa and Muslim custom, included rules and regulations circumscribing heterosexual contact. Both social and spatial, they are based upon a code of modesty derived from the Quran. As stated in the Quran, Sura IV:34, "Men are the protectors and maintainers of women, Because God has given the one more [strength] than the other..." (Quran 1975:190). And furthermore, their modesty must be guarded, as in Sura XXIV:31 Yet the Quran is ambiguous on how wifely modesty is to be enforced, and this has generated a range of modes of "symbolic shelter" to protect the honor of men and the family. Variability in modes of such shelter conveys the differences implicit in the female experience, say spatial confinements as opposed to veiling, and the attendant freedoms and constraints (see for example Vatuk (1982) for India; Odeh (1993) for Iran; Bourdieu (1979) for Algeria). The twin customs of veiling and secluding women, overseen by men and imposed upon women, are two types of "symbolic shelter" that protect the honor of the family.

Throughout the world, the position of women and their mobility varies according to the extensiveness of sexual segregation. Its most extreme form is represented among Muslims through the Hausa institution of *kulle*, which clearly spells out cultural attitudes toward women through a sociospatial hierarchy. Among the Hausa, marriages are classified socially according to the mode of arrangement and degree of wife seclusion (Smith 1965).

Seclusion itself varies greatly according to time, place, class, and so on, but its origins stem from the model established in the Kano (Northern Nigeria) palace. In the 15th century, the Emir Rumfa firmly established Islam in Kano at the state level and also instituted royal wife seclusion (Nast 1996). Palace life introduced bodily and sociospatial innovations; thus, the palace represented the ideal for wealthy rulers. Later, it was copied by lower chiefs and titled men. Before the 19th century, wife seclusion was limited to urban areas, although in fact few urban women, and then only the wealthy, were kept in seclusion as it was not economically sustainable without child labor. The jihad of Usman dan Fodio in 1803 instated seclusion as the ideal in urban Hausaland (see Pittin 1996; Robson 2000). Today, in Northern Nigeria it has spread across classes (Robson 2000).

Auren kulle, the Hausa marriage of seclusion, is sanctioned by religious teachings and values. *Kulle* "refers to the practice of married women keeping to their domestic compound" (Robson 2000:183). It is a way of controlling sexuality and procreative capacity; it is a sign of socioreligious status/identity and respectability: even post-menopausal women in Northern Nigeria are expected to observe limited mobility, "deemed as decorous and appropriately 'good' behaviour. Some older women, notably wives of malams, continue to observe seclusion beyond the menopause as part of their particular high socio-religious status" (Robson 2000:f.n.7, p. 196).

But *kulle* is most understandable in economic terms – the expendability of the wife's labor, the ability of the husband to provide entirely for the wife, indeed the social prestige that accrues to the husband whose wife/ves are secluded, and by extension secluded women. In Northern Nigeria, the norm of seclusion is so well established that today "it is primarily its absence which attracts attention, bringing shame upon the offending wife and her husband" (Pittin 1984:474).[3]

Among the Hausa in Northern Nigeria, seclusion is a means of enforcing the division between men and women and the ranking of them relative to one another. Certainly "adulthood means separation, even avoidance, between male and female" (Pittin 1996:34). In effect, men and women occupy two different worlds. They celebrate rites of passage and festivals separately. They observe a strict sexually defined division of labor. Seclusion has enabled gendered spatial divisions of labor: womanhood is associated with "heavily guarded 'private' domains; manhood in contrast...taking place in 'public' areas outside the female domain" (Nast 1996:45). Hausa custom and Muslim law not only conceptualize women as a group apart, but classify them as legal, political, and religious minors and the economic wards of men (Callaway 1987; Schildkrout 1986; Smith 1978; Yeld 1960).

When Malam Bako established Sabon Zongo, he set out to reinstill spatial expressions of Muslim orthodoxy, including *kulle*. His son Malam Gambo remembered that if his father Malam Bako "saw a woman out like this," that is, selling on the street, he would call her husband and talk to the husband and wife with his elders. If they did not accept his judgment, Gambo says, Malam Bako would send them to the British, that is for counsel or punishment (5/4/1982). His sense when I interviewed him was that during his childhood wives and mothers did not just go out; they sent maidservants on errands. He remembered men and their male visitors sitting in the *zaure* (entryway), while the only non-family members who could enter the house were girls. Rejecting a straight economic explanation he observed, "Even if you didn't have money, you could do *kulle*. You can do *kulle* if you know you can look after the girl" (5/4/1982).

But in fact, among Sabon Zongo's early Hausa residents, seclusion was not so much a norm as an ideal. One might say that the first generation of Zongolese practiced a kind of temporary confinement of their women. In those early days, according to another Bako son, Hamisu (4/9/1982), Sabon Zongo's women worked from the house, like the secluded Hausa women in seclusion in Kano today. Using their children to sell their products outside, they made *k'afa* and *gari* (maize flour) and *tawada* (Hausa ink). When asked, all of the Hausa elders in Sabon Zongo today were unsure when *kulle* began and when it ended; what they were sure about was that Malam Bako and Ali Ango were the only two men who really practiced it (M. Barko 9/25/2001). Gambo and Hamisu's recollection were probably colored by the fact that their father Malam Bako, whose house they grew up in, was trying to keep his wives in seclusion and the knowledge that their father was trying to make *kulle* the norm in Sabon Zongo. And yet, one of Malam Bako's grandsons, Alhaji Baba Mai Doki, claims that only Malam Bako's senior wife, Amina, was in *kulle* (M. Barko 9/25/01).

Thus Sabon Zongo's Hausa women were not entirely immobilized. With their husbands' permission (as among the secluded in Northern Nigeria today), they could attend events, such as marriages, where the others in attendance were all women; and on other occasions, after dark, they visited family members in other compounds. Travelling in the company of other women or children and wearing a prayer shawl over the head, they were provided with a moving shield of protection which communicated to men that they should keep their distance.

Models to Follow: Gendered Space

Malam Bako demarcated living space and allocated lots at Sabon Zongo to his people. When first surveyed, the 75 acres were sub-divided into 32 parcels, varying somewhat in size and greatly in the number and dimensions of compounds. By 1912 the residents had built about 165 compounds.

The structures they built express the African archetype of rooms within/around a courtyard. Ghanaian vernacular architecture is constituted by a variety of characteristics that vary in different parts of the country. For example, rectilinear layout is found in the south and circular in the northeast. In addition, outside influences on building design, materials and techniques introduced by Europeans in the south and the Muslims in the north also affect form (Architecture 1978). Whatever the building types, however, they express the archetype: "The indigenous concept of a family dwelling, commonly described as the courtyard – or compound house" (Architecture 1976:451). This cuts across ethnicity, although it assumes a diversity of forms. Accra's Ga people, for example, recognize the difference in male and female needs and lifestyles. They traditionally house men and women in sex-specific compounds, but there is no ideological barrier to traffic between them.

In Hausa domestic architecture, in addition to the courtyard, the compound wall is a particularly important feature – currently, it "demarcates an area within which members of the family may withdraw from society and remain in privacy. It also serves the same defensive function for the family as does the city wall for the community as a whole" (Moughtin 1985:54). This fortress-like and inward-facing structure creates an immediate physical presence (Pittin 1996:18). And as Muhammad-Oumar substantiates in his research, the spatial articulation of the "ordinary" houses of Hausa living in Kano is an expression of ideological and spatial control, both transmission and product of Hausa culture (Muhammad-Oumar 1997).

The "typical" Hausa urban house (called *gida*) is divided into a forecourt (*k'ofar gida*, the public area) and the central courtyard (*cikin gida*, the private area, literally the interior of the house)[4] (see Figure 7.1). The public and the private areas of the house are clearly defined in form and layout and are respected by the public (Moughtin 1985; Schwerdtfeger 1982). The door openings become visual foci, and all interaction is concentrated around these.

The *zaure* is the only entryway into the house. It is here that the gradations of privacy, deriving quite specifically from Hausa/Muslim practice, grow more pronounced as they mediate between public and private space (Prussin 1986:212). The *zaure* is the domain of the male compound head. In the *zaure* "he entertains his visitors and friends, takes his meals and, if possible, pursues his occupation such as weaving, tailoring, embroidery, or teaching the Koran" (Schwerdtfeger 1982:28). Male visitors may also sleep here.[5]

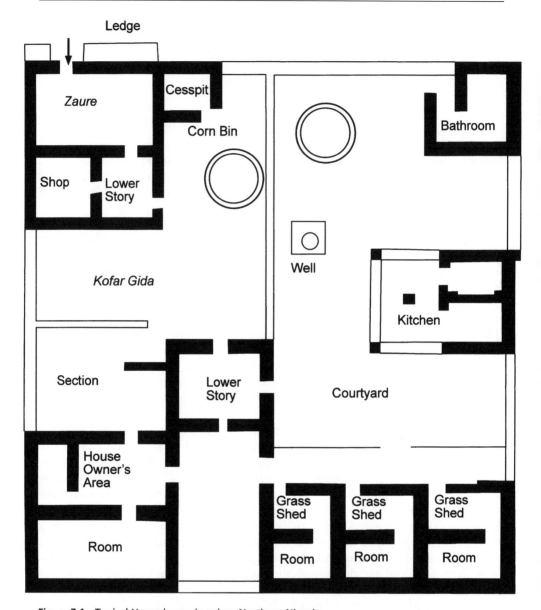

Figure 7.1 Typical Hausa house in urban Northern Nigeria

The *zaure* leads into a forecourt (*k'ofar gida*), an intermediate zone between the outside world and the compound center, where male youths from the household or male guests sleep in huts. It leads to the *shigifa*, a transitional entryway with staggered doorways designed to prevent a direct view into the *cikin gida*, the inside section of the home. This is the arena for family life where women play a central role. Little girls learn that the women's quarter is off-limits to men and boys.

These spatial divisions are essential to the Hausa emphasis on sexual differences and stratification. Their world is clearly divided into male and female domains, and, as Bourdieu has described for the North African Berbers (Bourdieu 1979), the house is a microcosm of the world at large organized by the same divisions (Bourdieu theorizes them as oppositions and homologies). There are contrivances employed to advertise this ordering to those outside the household and to socialize those within.

Seclusion bespeaks a restrictive range of social contacts and activities, as expressed in physical space – the confinement of women in an exclusive and private domain. Men try to exert social control, and thus spatial control, over the adult women of their compounds by defining the house as the container of women and restricting women to it (Callaway 1987; Pittin 1984). Yet as Pittin observes, while spatial boundaries may reflect social boundaries, they "undergo revision, resistance, and renegotiation" (Pittin 1996:184). Men in fact have little control over the women's interaction within the compound, as they are so rarely there; by the same token, if the husbands travel, women may take advantage of their absence to leave the house (Pittin 1996:184; Schildkrout 1983).

In addition to being an enculturating space for females (see Pellow 1991), the interior compound is also an entertaining space – for other women, both family and friends. And it is here that the newly married woman displays her dowry, known as *kayan d'aki* (things for the room), that she brings into the marriage. Some of the *kayan d'aki* are goods essential to running the household, practical utensils, but of greater importance to the woman's status are the decorative objects. They enhance the women's symbolic capital. The *kayan d'aki* represent a purely female type of capital; while a woman's seclusion reflects her husband's solvency, the display items are hers, not the household's, and do not necessarily reflect the household's well-being.

Not only do Hausa husbands and wives not share the same space, they do not socialize with one another. Polygyny is the ideal, the maximum number of wives allowed by Islam, four. The sleeping rooms for the various family members – householder, young men, wives – are huts grouped within the compound yard according to sex, generation, relationship, allowing for such domestic activities as cooking.

An important Hausa rule holds that each wife has her own room, where she keeps her possessions and her young children sleep (Smith 1981:23; cf. Moughtin 1964; Schwerdtfeger 1982). In average urban households, each wife has one or two rooms. Most compounds include a separate room, or set of rooms, or indeed a whole section of the house, for the compound head (Pittin 1996:182).

The original housing structures built in Sabon Zongo are vestiges of northern Nigerian Hausa style, cultural templates carried by the early settlers. The courtyards or compounds represent a gradation of space from the public exterior to the private interior living area of the family. The front vestibule is the point of transition (Prussin 1986).

Some scholars have theorized the palace of the Emir of Kano (Northern Nigeria) as the social and spatial prototype of the "normal" Hausa compound house "because it is the most traditional and conservative" (Mack 1992:79; Moughtin 1985:74).[6] I support their position and suggest that Malam Bako, as Sabon Zongo's creator and first headman, had his compound built as a model of the ideal layout to be followed by the early settlers in Sabon Zongo (Figure 7.2). His compound is a rectangular enclosure, as is true for indigenous design in urban Northern Nigeria, as well as southern Ghana (Moughtin 1985).[7] Like the Northern Nigerian Hausa compounds, Malam Bako's is walled on the outside. The perimeter is rectangular and the *cikin gida*, the interior courtyard where the women lived, could only be entered through a series of entrance halls. To maintain the (ideal of) segregation, there is *a zaure* (entrance hall) at the front of the compound, where Malam Bako met with elders, judged disputes, and entertained male visitors.

True to form, none of his wives' rooms, nor the rooms of his sons' wives, are directly visible from the forecourt. There are two inner courts. That to the right leads into the rooms of some of Malam Bako's adult sons and their wives. There was also a stable here, where the Malam kept horses. The court to the left could be entered only through a second entrance hall (*shigifa*), which also has a *zaure* and where only close associates or especially important persons would be entertained. The second

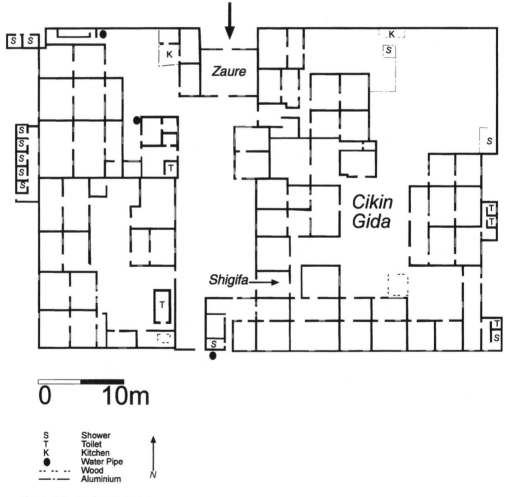

Figure 7.2   Malam Bako's house

entrance room opens into the *cikin gida*, where the household head had his own room.

In Malam Bako's day, the Sabon Zongo woman's social and spatial relationships were formalized. The potential for disharmony among co-wives, always high, necessitated careful regulation of their social and spatial behavior in the house: each was allocated her own quarters, for her and her young children, and equal time to cook for and spend the night with her husband. The women's most important or regular spatial relationships there were with their co-wives and children (cf. Pittin 1979). Women ate with one another and/or their children; men ate alone or with their male friends in the *zaure*. Just as the women's occupation of the space provided social definition to it, so the space reminded them of their social roles (cf. Callaway 1987; Pittin 1979; Weisman 1981; Wright, 1981). Even though they were not in seclusion, their movement was carefully monitored, at least during daylight hours. The only space accorded them by the culture was in the compound; accordingly, their social roles centered on family or female-oriented activities within compound walls. Like Hausa women in Northern Nigeria and elsewhere in the Hausa diaspora, these women amassed *kayan daki*. And as I have written about Accra's housing in general, it was and is particularly women for whom the compound has been an enculturating space (Pellow 1991:199; see also Mack 1991; Mack 1992; Pittin 1979, 1996).

Male–female lines of division were thus well-reinforced, based upon cultural and spatial norms. The only people who freely entered and exited the compound were the resident males and children. But, in looking today at representative compounds from the early days,[8] the *zaure* served more like a hanging-out point for the menfolk than a checking point to entry into the heart of the compound. And indeed, none of those houses practiced *kulle*.

Continuity and Change

Socially and spatially, today's Sabon Zongo is considerably different from its early days. Its residents are far more connected with Accra's other Muslim communities, especially that of Central Accra, than in Malam Bako's day. The Hausa continue to have an overarching influence, but many non-Hausa (Muslim and even Christian) have swelled the ranks of the community's residents. The interethnic mix, while not part of the original idea, occurred gradually. Compounds are still overwhelmingly owned by descendants of the original Hausa families, even as more and more rent out rooms to non-family, and some family-owned compounds are rented in their entirety. As in the Hausa compound in Northern Nigeria, there is constant adaptation to changing family circumstances (Moughtin 1985).

While Islam and Hausa-ness color the worldview and behavior of the northerners in Accra's zongo and male–female distinctions are ideologically marked, the restrictions on male–female social mixing in Sabon Zongo are less stringent than in Northern Nigeria and the separateness of men and women is vestigial at best.

The spotty seclusion remembered from past years, when unrelated boys did not enter the house and the men sat in the *zaure*, has not existed anywhere in

Sabon Zongo for years. "All of this has changed," Malam Hamisu mused, "because people come together from areas. Some are Zabrama, Hausa, Mossi, Buzanga, and others. They marry each other. Buzanga and Zabrama don't do *kulle*, so if your tribe doesn't do *kulle* and I come and marry you, I'll never put you in *kulle*" (4/9/1982).

According to Chief Sha'aibu:

> Here in Ghana, it's very hard to have *kulle*, because we were not brought up with *kulle* ... It was our great grandfathers who wanted to make the *kulle*. But gradually ... The up and coming generations weren't brought up in *kulle*. And at the same time some of them cannot do the *kulle*, because it is difficult to live in *kulle* in Ghana. [Then], when you had even a penny you could buy, you would be satisfied with that one penny. Now, because of money, men want their wives to go and sell and get money. (5/11/1982)

Like Malam Bako's house, all of the residents in the Badamase house (Figure 7.3) are Hausa, all are related and are members of the Bako extended family. One of the oldest houses, originally it consisted of just three front rooms and the *zaure*, with an outside wall. It has clearly been renovated: it no longer has a proper wall, except in the front; the entire structure is concrete block; there are 17 rooms. It is painted bright pink, with a paved compound yard, and the verandahs are framed by block walls, the blockwork Asante decorative design. The compound has one central yard, in effect the *cikin gida*, and there is a proper *zaure*, about 2 × 4.5 meters; one room (one of the original) opens directly into the *zaure*.

What is intriguing about this house is that all of the women seem to spend a lot of time in the *zaure* – relaxing, talking, selling groundnuts. At the same time, the two senior men are always in the *cikin gida*, the tailor working on a sewing machine in the vicinity of his room, his retired elder brother sitting in a shaded corner of the compound on a mat on the ground.

The compound of Sha'aibu Bako (Figure 7.4), chief from 1981 until his death in March 2001, is down the road from the Badamase house and Malam Bako's palace. He lived there with his third wife Saratu and various grown offspring. Sha'aibu moved to this house the day of his marriage to his first wife Rakiya in 1935 and never left. When he moved in, there were two rooms only: the *cikin gida*. Sha'aibu enlarged the *cikin gida* and put a rafia wall (*zana*) around the property. Visitors had to go through the side *zaure*. After Sha'aibu became chief on August 15, 1981, he renovated and gave the *zaure* its present shape, where he meets with members of his *fadawa* and individuals come by to greet or consult with him. The wall of the *zaure* is the property wall.

Given its layout, Sha'aibu's house could fulfill all of the functions of traditional housing. It has a *cikin gida*, which one can get to only by crossing through at least two entryways, one of which is now his formal audience room. There is a large semi-private forecourt and a simple doorway to the *cikin gida*; the chief's room and his wife's room ring a rectangular courtyard. The shower room and KVIP[9] (which is kept locked) are for the family only.

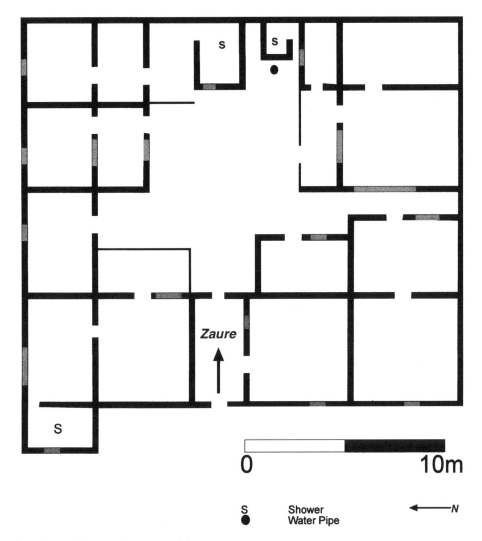

Figure 7.3 Mohammed Badamase's house

Sha'aibu's compound also represents a modification of his grandfather Malam Bako's space: in addition to housing his immediate family, 12 rooms are rented to 22 adult tenants (in June 2000, 14 Akan, seven Yoruba, and one Ewe) and there is a spare for visitors. Their rooms are accessed through the original *zaure*, as can be the *cikin gida*. The *zaure*, the traditional transit point, becomes a corridor. Thus, principles of Hausa spatial organization take on an altered form.

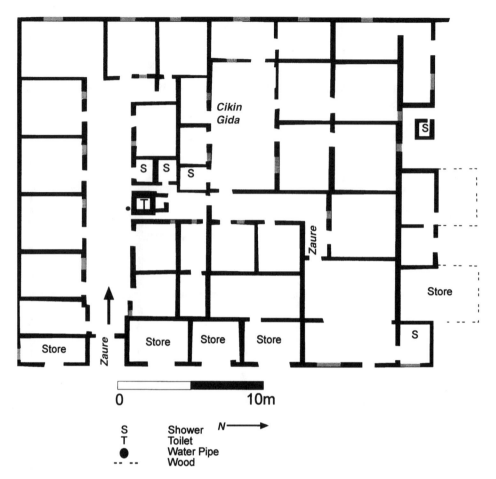

Figure 7.4   Chief Sha'aibu Bako's house

The chief's wife is responsible for domestic tasks, but she has considerable mobility – certainly more than Malam Bako's wives did. She attends celebrations of life-cycle events but in the company of other women. When out, she wears her head veil over her shoulders. While she no longer has primary relationships in the house with co-wives (she has been Sha'aibu's only wife for years), she spends much of each day with her married daughter, who comes over, often with a child in tow. They engage in all sorts of grooming activities, and also cook, eat, and gossip. The tenant women at the other end of the house cook and wash dishware in the old *zaure*. When at home, the chief divided his time between the inner house, his *zaure*, and a room beyond where he prayed, read, and napped out of sight of family and subjects.

Compound Space – Variations on a Theme

The layout of the houses has evolved from a Hausa template to a synthetic one, in part reflective of urban Accra, in part a dilution of traditional norms. The compound house is still significant because of the activities and relationships it anchors, because of its flexibility in accommodating activities. The compound's heterogeneity – its variation on a theme of the Hausa model as well as that of southern Ghana – encourages new forms of interaction, new roles, new identities. The compounds have boundaries that define the interactions.

Alhaji Yaro's property (Figure 7.5) is enormous, both in space and inhabitants. Like the classic form, it retains the courtyard. Unlike the classic form, however, it has four separate courtyards, each representing a section. The left rear section was the first quadrant built, which is where Alhaji Yaro and his father lived till their deaths (Yaro died in 1997). The one *zaure* in the compound leads into that section. Over time, and with need, Yaro built the second, third, and fourth quadrants for his children, each with its own central yard. The lane into the property is basically a pathway. The lane at Alhaji Yaro's has four termini, one at each of three compounds and at the *zaure* that leads into the first. The *zaure* is dark and dank and as at Sha'aibu's, it is nothing more than a passageway.

A total of 140 adults live in this property, 76 inside, 64 in the outside rooms. The degree of genealogical relationship, as in most houses, dictates who lives where: the most interior would be House 1. This is where the elder, wives and children, have always lived. The furthest from the family core are the outside rooms, all occupied by tenants.

Especially pertinent to my concern here is the case of Ali Ango and his three wives. Ali Ango was Alhaji Yaro's cousin; their fathers were brothers. Ali Ango, who died about five years ago, had married two women, whom he kept in *kulle* in the family house kitty-cornered to Alhaji Yaro's. In 1967, he married a third woman, Hajiya Kubra, a member of the Bako family, and ensconced her in House 2 at Yaro's. She refused to live in *kulle*. "So the other two women also 'liberated' themselves the day the third wife was brought to her matrimonial home and since that time, they were 'free' women. And that was in 1967" (M. Barko 9/25/01).

Contrary to both southern Ghanaian and Northern Nigerian plans, Sabon Zongo's houses do not all reproduce the atrium form. Many have lost the integrity of the central all-purpose yard as owners have built in rather than up or out to create more rooms. This has resulted in what I call the involuted compound: as free-standing rooms are built in the middle of the courtyard, an intricate pattern of interior lanes or corridors results and one must snake around through them to get to the other end of the property. Gidan Bak'i (Figure 7.6) is a superb example of this outcome: here as in many of Sabon Zongo's compounds, over time the space has been adapted and elaborated upon to meet the needs of an expanding family and the desire to rent to tenants.

Gidan Bak'i was founded by Salisu Abubakar, no longer alive, who was a son of Malam Garuba, first Chief Imam of Ghana. While there are tenants in this compound, it is thought of as a family house – 20 lineal kinsmen live there. All of Salisu's children (including the eight sons and their sons living here now) were born in this

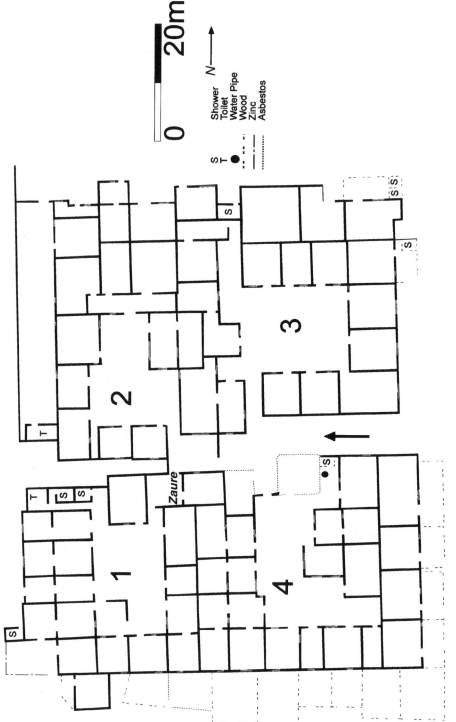

Figure 7.5 Alhaji Yaro's house

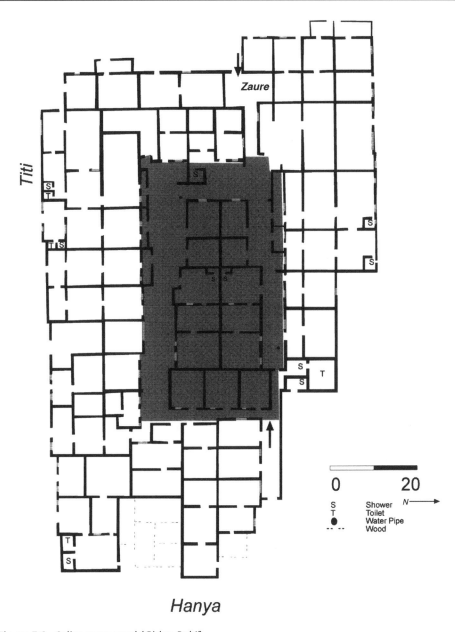

Figure 7.6 Salisu compound (*Gidan Bak'i*)

house. Only the son Ilyashu lives elsewhere in Sabon Zongo and that is because he succeeded in acquiring land and building his own house. The living quarters of the sons tend to be more elaborate than those of the other residents.

Gidan Bak'i has 87 rooms and a complex structure resembling a maze. It has two entrances, only one with a *zaure*, and the *zaure* is nothing more than a corridor into the compound. The 47 tenants include southerners (Fanti, Kwahu, Asante, Akwa-pim, Ewe) and northern Frafra, all of whom are Christians; the Zabrama, like the tenant and kin Hausa, are Muslims. Four of the seven Hausa women who trade do so in the doorway or in front of the house; two others engage in what the Yoruba call *jojoma* (always, i.e. everyday) giving something to the market women to sell for them; and the last trades at one of Accra's main markets.

While the original layout of Gidan Bak'i would be easy to reconstruct, the current structure, its residents' social characteristics, and the work habits of the women, make it very different than its Hausa archetype, where wives could be secluded.

Tenanted Homes: Extremes of Change

Since the early days of Sabon Zongo, with changes in society at large that included independence, economic development, and migration to Accra, organization of compound space and the social life that goes on within has changed as well. For women, life is still primarily organized around the domestic space; however, their roles and mobility are greater. Moreover, that space looks different and is less exclusively defined. Its embedded cultural values are modified as is the particular significance of the space. Indeed, the compound itself has been redefined to extend beyond the compound walls. Its residents are far more varied, coming not only from different families but even from different ethnic groups and religions as well. These changes become particularly evident in the tenanted/rental housing, where there is no illusion about all-encompassing sexual segregation or women's visibility in daily life. "How can you 'make *kulle*' with tenants?" asks Malam Gambo, one of the last-surviving sons of Malam Bako and who died in 1998.

This is clearly expressed on the ground at one of Baba Mai Doki's properties. Baba Mai Doki (aka Alhaji Sulieman Bako), one of Sabon Zongo's highly respected elders, is the son of Idrissu Bako (first gazetted chief of the community). He lives opposite Gidan Baki in a compound which he co-owns with his sister. He also owns a fair amount of rental property in Sabon Zongo, including the housing that envelops the mosque named after his father. That property (Figure 7.7) also includes another small compound on the other side, and wraps round the back, with rooms opening out onto the empty space. Next to the mosque is a pen with sheep and usually a horse or two. The house was originally a stable, which may explain why little of it is mud or cement – almost all is built out of wood.

All 58 adult residents are tenants, 29 of them women. They represent a breath-taking melange of ethnicities: there are 33 southerners, primarily Ewe, and all but one Ga man are Christian; the "northerners," who are all Muslims, include Hausa, Yoruba, Wanagara, Adar, and Fulani. Along with countless children, they live in 71 rooms in this sprawling property, of varying shapes and sizes. The rooms range from the mosque side, around to the back, and to the other side of the mosque. Each room or set of rooms is entered from outside. None of the classic features of the Hausa, or for that matter, southern Ghanaian compound is present. Most of the rooms on the east side (behind the stables) have an enclosed open roofless area, where the women can cook. All of the other rooms on the south and west sides open directly to the public area, and each woman cooks in front of her

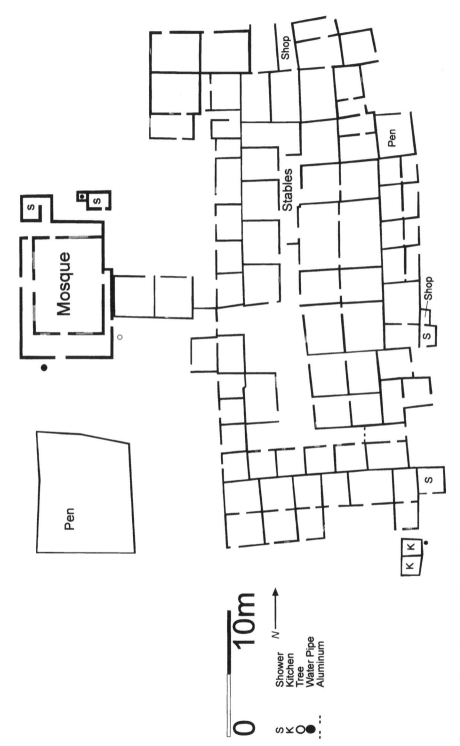

Figure 7.7 Alhaji Baba Mai Doki's rental property

dwelling. On the north side of the mosque, however, a small compound has emerged. It is bordered by the mosque's wall. At the front, alongside the road, there is no outside wall. In years past, there was a tall pile of blocks; now a kiosk partially obstructs compound life from passers-by. The women living there all cook in the compound yard.

Idrissu built the housing currently behind the mosque for family. There were four rooms and a wall made from zinc. When everyone died, he began to rent out rooms to tenants. All around were fields. Baba Mai Doki was a fine horseman (hence his name, Baba, the master of a horse), and he became a professional jockey. He built a stable in the middle of the fields. Inside the stable house there are seven stable rooms, with rooms for the horses and a horse boy. There are also rooms for the men (and their families) who work with the horses. As the number of horses waxes and wanes, the stables outside near the mosque are enlarged or reduced.

Marking Social Change

Cultural codes articulate with space through cultural practices. What I have examined in this chapter is how these artifacts, the compounds, are both physical expressions of peoples' lifestyles and the forces that enable them. They not only embody social life; they themselves exemplify social life. Each compound has a history, and each in itself or in combination represents the progressive nature of the community's culture and its change.

Because the behavioral or conceptual segregation has never been the reality in this Accra community, it is hard to say when the architectural changes have occurred and whether the changes in use have caused changes in conception. Those who might be able to clarify the direction of cause and effect are no longer alive. I would observe that house ownership is important in Hausa culture, and the early houseowners would build models that were culturally salient. They carried the spatial template as part of their cultural baggage, in the sense of a useful or familiar idea, since from the start, the practice of seclusion was already long gone – remember, the early settlers at Sabon Zongo had moved up from the old Ga core neighborhood where such practices were nonexistent.

The social attributes of ethnicity, religion, hometown provenance, customs, are differentially incorporated in the compound as in the community; even in the Hausa family house, the value of *kunya* (modesty) for women is maintained, albeit in an altered form. For example, the tradition of seclusion, the norm in urban Northern Nigeria, has not been practiced in Sabon Zongo for 35 years (and even then by perhaps only two men). Formerly in each house, there was a husband and a wife; now there are also tenants. Remember the *post-hoc* explanation of Malam Bako's sons about the impossibility of doing *kulle* when there are tenants present.

Moreover, over the years the Hausa have intermarried with members of other ethnic groups – mainly Muslim "northerners" such as Zabrama, Fulani, and Wangara, but also northern and southern Ghanaians who converted to Islam. While religion may have been held constant, cultural institutions and practices varied among the different ethnicities. Such variation would impact on the articulation of religion and culture, including house design and spatial usage.

But the fact that seclusion does not operate in the community, that compounds include unrelated persons (tenants) does not mean that, as one proud Hausa husband declared, "women can just go roaming about." Among the Hausa there is a tradition of female reserve, which plays out on a continuum. At one end there is a vestigial separateness of women from men and the public domain, at the other end is seclusion in the compound. Thus many who work – preparing and/or selling cooked food, selling provisions, sewing – or spend time with friends and family, now situate themselves in front of the outside wall of the compound, or just under the eaves or in the doorway. Hausa men and men of other ethnicities as well who live in Sabon Zongo do not hang around the inside of the house. Men have a variety of hanging-out spots. The *zaure*, by custom the men's space, is only used in the traditional manner at Malam Bako's palace – for meetings with the chief or as a place to camp for long-distance visitors (most frequently Tuareg and other traders from Niger). At other houses, female residents use the *zaure* as a workspace to cook, engage in trade, watch happenings on the street, sit through the ritual of wakekeeping at death.

I observed at the beginning that Sabon Zongo's Hausa, while only one ethnic group among many in their community today, have tenaciously held on to many of the practices from Northern Nigeria and these mark their daily life. Seclusion never really took hold in the beginning – it was an ideal not a reality – and while Northern Nigerian urban communities have evidenced a return to *kulle*, Accra's Hausa have not. The zongolese Hausa when asked to explain its lapse do so in terms of custom (it was only their fathers who practiced it)[10] and finances (the need to rent to tenants).

Nobody talks about *kulle* and when asked, the elders get a far-off look on their faces. It is clearly a non-issue, something no one has thought about for years. In 1982, I attended a wedding at Sha'aibu Bako's palace. Alhaji Abas, the Chief Imam in Accra, was presiding. In his blessing he reminded the new couple to follow the teachings of Islam. And then he preached to those congregated: "no men should go and talk to some woman on the road when she is not his wife; women shouldn't wear lavender, because when a man is passing, the smell will attract him." Clearly, seclusion was not part of the formula, but modesty was.

Is an unintended consequence of the reworked compound spaces a change in gender roles? Certainly seclusion becomes more difficult. But is that cause or effect? Throughout the postcolonial world, changes have occurred in roles, relationships, and material culture, due in part to the historical transformations, rural–urban connections, and global flow of people and ideas. Ferguson's (1999) theory of "localist" and "cosmopolitan" as two contrasting cultural modes in contemporary Zambia holds for Accra as well. As he observed:

> localistic stylistic markers seemed to distinguish those who had a strong sense of continuing allegiance to a rural "home" community...cosmopolitan style, on the other hand...signified a shrugging off of localist cultural traits...along with an embracing of Western-dominated transnational mass culture. (1999:92)

As he found for urban Zambians, Accra dwellers whose work and attachments fall within the "modern" mode might adopt the "localist" image of the home, and those adopting the "cosmopolitan style" need not correspond to high social status or education. People "perform" their identity, for example through the housing they erect, and through the roles they play, such as the enactment of gender. These become strategies of survival, depending upon the larger social, political, and context.

The first two generations of Sabon Zongo dwellers are very attached to the community and do not want to move out; this is their social strategy. Even those who have succeeded in building outside of the community use such properties as investments. If they stay, tenanting aside, their families grow and their offspring need rooms. As in the adaptability of the Northern Nigerian Hausa compounds, so too here: new rooms are constructed, thereby destroying the courtyard form. People die, the rooms become empty and they are (perhaps temporarily) rented out. Strangers join the compound.

In Accra, the absence of *kulle* is intertwined with various elements of culture change: socialization and familiarity, finances, gendered customs and practices, and rental versus ownership. These have produced and been reinforced by changes in house form.

NOTES

1   I presented an earlier version of this paper for the Women's Studies Program, Syracuse University, November 2000, and at the interdisciplinary colloquium on Hausa society, Identity and Marginality in West Africa, Tulane University, September 2001. I want to thank Denise Lawrence-Zúñiga for her incisive theoretical space and place critique. The participants in the Hausa colloquium (Adeline Masquelier, Steven Peirce, Rudi Gaudio, Sue O'Brien, and Heidi Nast) made me think and re-think seclusion in Accra and why change may have occurred the way it did. Heidi in particular directed me to work on the geography of seclusion that I would not have otherwise consulted. Muhsin Barko was ever helpful at the Accra end, in chasing down necessary materials and introducing me to crucial landlords. I am grateful to the landlords I interviewed in Sabon Zongo for enabling my work and assisting me whenever necessary. Joe Stoll, the cartographer with the Department of Geography at Syracuse University, and Dr Mark Hauser used their Computer Assisted Drawing (CAD) abilities to make the house drawings and maps clear and reproduceable. Mark came to my aid more times in more crunches than I care to remember, and I am ever grateful. I alone am responsible for any errors.
2   Letter from Malam Bako to Y. Ex., 10/24/1907, ADM 11/1502, NAG.
3   In fact, wife seclusion has been increasing in Hausaland in Northern Nigeria over the past 20 years, undergirded in the late 1990s by the enforcement of shari'a law throughout the region.
4   Muhammad-Oumar (1997:57) breaks down the *cikin gida* into *tsakar gida* (central courtyard) and *kuya* (inner section).
5   Poor compounds may lack a *zaure*, instead having a *k'ofa*, a doorway or recessed entrance (Smith 1965).
6   Barbara Cooper has seen few compounds in Maradi, Niger, that emulate the element of the *cikin gida* and, disagreeing with Mack, suggests that one could argue that if the chief keeps to the model, no one else need do so.
7   Hausa town architecture is striking in its distinctiveness: unlike that of the countryside, "house and boundary walls and roofs in the towns were built of mud...the basic house walls were often made of mud" (Denyer 1978:35).

8   These include the compounds of Danmaley (Malam Bako's chief barber and a competitor for the community headmanship), of Salisu (the offspring of Accra's Chief Imam Garuba, known as Gidan Bak'i), of Kariki (the first and second chief linguist), Tahiru Bako (a son of Malam Bako's daughter), and of Abokin Ango and his kinsman Alhaji Yaro (both early settlers).

9   The Kumase Ventilated Improved Pit Latrine is simply a pit latrine provided with a vent (flue) that channels the odors out of the space. It is usually built with two pits. One is used and when it fills up, the seat is changed to the other pit.

10 Even though they did not – it was an ideal that never took hold.

REFERENCES

Architecture, Faculty of
  1978   Traditional Forms of Architecture in Ghana. *International Social Science Journal* XXX(3):449–476.
Ardener, Shirley, ed.
  1981   *Women and Space: Ground Rules and Social Maps.* NYC: St. Martin's Press.
Bourdieu, Pierre
  1979   *Algeria 1960: The Disenchantment of the World: The Sense of Honour: the Kabyle House or the World Reversed.* Cambridge: Cambridge University Press.
Callaway, Barbara
  1987   *Muslim Hausa Women in Nigeria.* Syracuse: Syracuse University Press.
Denyer, Susan
  1978   *African Traditional Architecture.* NYC: African Publishing Co.
Donley-Reid, Linda
  1990   A Structuring Structure: The Swahili House. In *Domestic Architecture and the Use of Space: An Interdisciplinary Cross-Cultural Study.* S. Kent, ed. pp. 114–126. Cambridge: Cambridge University Press.
Ferguson, James
  1999   *Expectations of Modernity: Myths and Meanings of Urban Life on the Zambian Copperbelt.* Berkeley: University of California Press.
Jameson, Michael H.
  1990   Domestic Space in the Greek City-State. In *Domestic Architecture and the Use of Space: An Interdisciplinary Cross-Cultural Study.* S. Kent, ed. pp. 92–113. Cambridge: Cambridge University Press.
Lefebvre, Henri
  1991   *The Production of Space.* Oxford: Blackwell Publishers.
Mack, Beverly
  1991   Royal Wives in Kano. In *Hausa Women in the Twentieth Century.* C. Coles and B. Mack, eds. pp. 109–129. Madison: University of Wisconsin Press.
Mack, Beverly
  1992   Harem Domesticity in Kano, Nigeria. In *African Encouters with Domesticity.* K. Tranberg-Hansen, ed. pp. 75–97. New Brunswick: Rutgers University Press.
Massey, Doreen
  1993   Politics and Space/Time. In *Identity and the Politics of Space.* M. Keith and S. Pile, eds. pp. 141–161. London: Routledge.
Massey, Doreen
  1994   *Space, Place and Gender.* Minneapolis: University of Minnesota Press.

Moore, Henrietta
    1986   *Space, Text and Gender: An Anthropological Study of the Marakwet of Kenya.*
    Cambridge: Cambridge University Press.
Moughtin, J. C.
    1964   The Traditional Settlement of the Hausa People. *The Town Planning Review*
    XXXV:21–34.
Moughtin, J. C.
    1985   *Hausa Architecture.* London: Ethnographica.
Muhammad-Oumar, Abdulrazzaq Ahmad
    1997   *Gidaje: The Socio-Cultural Morphology of Hausa Living Spaces.* PhD, University
    College London.
Nast, Heidi J.
    1996   Islam, Gender, and Slavery in West Africa Circa 1500: A Spatial Archaeology of the
    Kano Palace, Northern Nigeria. *Annals of the Association of American Geographers*
    86(1):44–77.
Odeh, Lama Abu
    1993   Post-Colonial Feminism and the Veil: Thinking the Difference. *Feminist Review*
    43:26–37.
Peil, Margaret
    1979   Host Reactions: Aliens in Ghana. In *Strangers in African Societies.* W. Shack and
    Elliot Skinner, eds. pp. 123–140. Berkeley: University of California Press.
Pellow, Deborah
    1985   Muslim Segmentation: Cohesion and Divisiveness in Accra. *Journal of Modern
    African Studies* 23: 419–444.
Pellow, Deborah
    1991   Spaces That Teach. In *Attachment to the African Compound Place Attachment.* I.
    Altman and S. Low, eds. pp. 187–210. NY: Plenum Press.
Pellow, Deborah
    1999   The Power of Space in the Evolution of an Accra Zongo. In *Theorizing the City: The
    New Urban Anthropology Reader.* S. Low, ed. pp. 277–314. Highland Park, NJ: Rutgers
    University Press.
Pittin, Renee
    1979   *Marriage and Alternative Strategies: Career Patterns of Hausa Women in Katsina
    City.* PhD dissertation, University of London.
Pittin, Renee
    1984   Documentation and Analysis of the Invisible Work of Invisible Women: A Nigerian
    Case Study. *International Labour Review* 123(4):473–490.
Pittin, Renee
    1996   Negotiating Boundaries: A Perspective From Nigeria. In *Setting Boundaries: The
    Anthropology of Spatial and Social Organization.* D. Pellow, ed. pp. 179–194. Westport
    CT: Bergin & Garvey.
Pollock, N. L.
    1981   Women on the Inside: Divisions of Space in Imperial China. *Heresies* 3(3):34–38.
Prussin, Labelle
    1986   *Hatumere: Islamic Design in West Africa.* Berkeley: University of California Press.
Quran
    1975   *The Holy Quran.* Text translation and Commentary Abdullah Yusuf Ali, trans.
    London: Islamic Foundation.

Rapoport, Amos
  1980   Cross-Cultural Aspects of Environmental Design. In *Human Behavior and Environment: Advances in Theory and Research*. I. Altman, A. Rapoport, J. F. Wohlwill, eds. pp. 7–46, Vol. 4. Environment and Culture. NYC: Plenum Press.
Rapoport, Amos
  1982   *The Meaning of the Built Environment: A Nonverbal Communication Approach*. Beverley Hills: Sage.
Robson, Elsbeth
  2000   Wife Seclusion and the Spatial Praxis of Gender Ideology in Nigerian Hausaland. *Gender, Place and Culture* 7(2):179–199.
Schildkrout, Enid
  1983   Dependence and Autonomy: the Economic Activities of Secluded Hausa Women in Kano. In *Female and Male in West Africa*. C. Oppong, ed. pp. 107–126. Boston: Allen & Unwin.
Schildkrout, Enid
  1986   Widows in Hausa Society: Ritual Phase or Social Status? In *Widows in African Societies: Choices and Constraints*. B. Potash, ed. pp. 131–152. Stanford: Stanford University Press.
Schwerdtfeger, Friedrich W.
  1982   *Traditional Housing in African Cities: A Comparative Study of Houses in Zaria, Ibadan and Marrakech*. New York: John Wiley & Sons.
Smith, M. G.
  1965   The Hausa of Northern Nigeria. In *Peoples of Africa*. J. Gibbs, ed. pp. 21–155. NYC: Holt, Rinehart, Winston.
Smith, M. G.
  1978   *The Affairs of Daura*. Berkeley: University of California Press.
Smith, Mary
  1981   *Baba of Karo: A Woman of the Muslim Hausa*. New Haven: Yale University Press.
Stack, Carol
  1974   Sex Roles and Survival Strategies in an Urban Black Community. In *Woman, Culture and Society*. M. Z. Rosaldo and L. Lamphere, eds. pp. 113–128. Stanford: Stanford University Press.
Vatuk, Sylvia
  1982   Purdah Revisited: A Comparison of Hindu and Muslim Interpretations of the Cultural Meaning of Purdah in South Asia. In *Separate Worlds: Studies of Purdah in South Asia*. H. Papanek and G. Minault, eds. pp. 54–78. Columbia MO: South Asia Books.
Weisman, Leslie Kanes
  1981   Women's Environmental *Rights: a Manifesto*. Heresies 3:6–8.
Weisman, Leslie Kanes
  1992   *Discrimination by Design: A Feminist Critique of the Man-Made Environment*. Urbana: University of Illinois Press.
Witherspoon, G.
  1975   *Navajo Kinship and Marriage*. Chicago: University of Chicago Press.
Wright, S.
  1981   Place and Face: of Women in Doshman Ziari, Iran. In *Women and Space: Ground Rules and Social Maps*. S. Ardener, ed. pp. 136–157. NY: St. Martin's Press.
Yeld, E. R.
  1960   Islam and Social Stratification in Northern Nigeria. *British Journal of Sociology* 11(2):112–128.
Young, Michael and Wilmott, Peter
  1962   *Family and Kinship in East London*. NY: Penguin.

Part III

Inscribed Spaces

In this section we are interested in how people collectively form a meaningful relationship with the locales they occupy, how they attach meaning to space, or transform "space" into "place." We are equally interested in how experience is embedded in place and how space holds memories that implicate people and events. The relationship between people and their surroundings entails more than attaching meaning to space, but involves the recognition and cultural elaboration of perceived properties of environments in mutually constituting ways through narratives and praxis. Anthropologists' considerations of inscribed spaces focus on the fundamental ways in which humans "write" or impute in an enduring way their presence on their surroundings. We begin with the work of James Fernandez, whose analysis of Fang "architectonics" in a comparative study focuses on the mutually constituting relationship between humans and their natural and built environments. The architectonics of a culture which extends beyond physical settings to include personal, social, and cosmological space holds emergent qualities that are activated during ritual events. We trace the development of interest in space and place issues to Margaret Rodman's consideration of the role of voice(s) in defining multiple perspectives of place. Finally, the chapter by John Gray whose use of narrative in describing relations of Scottish shepherds to their hilly borderland surroundings demonstrates the critical importance of praxis in constructing place-based identities.

Further Reading

Basso, Keith (1988) "Speaking with Names": Language and Landscape among the Western Apache. *Cultural Anthropology* 3(2), 99–130.

Feld, Steve and Keith Basso (eds.) *Senses of Place* (pp. 53–90). Santa Fe: School of American Research Press.

Kahn, Miriam (1990) Stone-Faced Ancestors: The Spatial Anchoring of Myth in Waimira, Papua New Guinea. *Ethnology*, 29, 51–66.

Myers, Fred (1991) *Pintupi Country, Pintupi Self: Sentiment, Place and Politics among Western Desert Aborigines*. Berkeley: University of California Press.

Roseman, Marina (1998) Singers of the Landscape: Song, History, and Property Rights in the Malaysian Rain Forest. *American Anthropologist* 100(1), 106–121.

8

Emergence and Convergence in some African Sacred Places

James Fernandez

A Comparison of Architectonics

One way to understand the anthropological emphasis on participant observation in our studies is to see in this method an effort to turn the spaces we go out to inhabit into places with whose feeling tones we are familiar. Participation enables us to feel something of what our informants feel in the spaces they occupy and in which they act. It is essentially a method aimed at the experience of place. For me the term "architectonic" raises the question of the feeling tones that activity in various constructed spaces evokes and that makes them places. Sacred places have an additional quality – an additional evocativeness that is symbolic in nature. This is because there is a contrast between the normal processing and the symbolic processing of experiences. On the one hand, the normal processing of experience is that of the work-a-day, subject–object world in which we operate and interact by accustomed signal-cued routines and reasonable and reasoned out procedures; on the other hand, symbolic processing is that in which everyday routines are some-how challenged or frustrated and unusual associations are evoked. The symbolic question is: what is it about sacred places that provokes these evocations? The problem of symbol is the problem of evocative structures of experience – their aptness or appropriateness. We will address this question and problem by examining and comparing the constructed evocativeness of three African sacred places. What is their architectonic? That is, how are they evocative? What qualities converge and emerge in them that make them appropriate places for human interaction for certain times and cultures. The predominant comparison will be between Fang and Zulu architectonics. Comment upon the feeling tone of Mina constructed space will serve as a point of reference to this main comparison. Consideration of the Mina material also expands our notion of the diversities of architectonics, while it provides a necessary complication to the elemental contrast we will draw out between Fang centrifugation and Zulu centripetalism. We might also point out that much architectonic meaning lies condensed in key symbols (Ortner 1973) found in these sacred places. We will focus on the interpretation of these symbols.

We must first grasp the striking differences in the life milieus of three African peoples: the Fang of equatorial Africa, the Mina of seaside West Africa, and the Zulu of arid southeast Africa. Fang live within the dense equatorial forests, where they chop out their village sites every ten to fifteen years. In these arduously achieved arenas they build a rectangular and carpentered world for themselves (Segal et al. 1966). The Zulu, in contrast, live in the virtually treeless subtropical savannah of Natal. The landscape is heavily rolling, in part, and otherwise accented with steep escarpments, kopjes, table mountains, and other striking relief features that rise in the distance. Men looking around can orient themselves by such distant features. In respect to their kraals and villages the Zulu world is a round world – noncarpentered.[1] The Mina (or Mina-Ewe) are fisher folk clustered in compound villages of raffia and palm fonds along the West African coast (Ghana and Togo). Living between the ocean and the inland lagoons, which they exploit, theirs is a linear environment with clan villages – indistinguishable from each other by any feature of environment – strung out intermittently east and west beneath the palms, beside the sea, in front of the lagoon.

In general terms I should like to demonstrate that in the Fang sacred spaces there is a characteristic emphasis on controlled centrifugation in ritual arenas and the vitality of the ritual experience is achieved by opposition of ritual areas. In Zulu sacred spaces there tends to be an ingathering or concentration of forces toward a vital center. There is a predominant centripetalism to their ritual arenas. I say predominant because I am talking about central tendencies. Any ritual is a complex of formalized movement through time and space that cannot be simply summarized as "centrifugal" or "centripetal" without great loss of detail. Nevertheless, there is predominance. Both Fang and Zulu rituals of these sacred spaces produce in the participants a sense of an imminent appelative presence – a "calling." In response to that "calling" Zulu seem to say, as in American English, "I'm coming." Fang seem to say, as in Spanish (voy), "I am going."[2] The Mina seem to say "I am here." A central ritual of theirs emphasizes tranquil disposition with minimal activity at a central place.

These emphases have something to do, in some part, with both the natural and hand-made environments within which these people habitually live and move. My own experience in the equatorial forest, it is true, was one of claustrophobia, even though it is an interesting milieu in its own way. Sooner or later, the limited vistas, the leaning over upon one and the pressure of the forest, evoke centrifugal sentiments. Of course, I must be cautious about my feelings here. Nevertheless I have ample evidence that the Fang share them. They are not like the pygmies: long-time residents of the forests. They have taken up their residence in the forests in the past two hundred years in all likelihood.

In Zululand I have a different feeling. Where is one to go in that vast expanse of grass, thornbush, and sky? It is true that there are pilgrimage spots on the horizon, but the predominant sentiment is one of sheltering up and gathering together so as to create one familiar arena in such a windblown, sunstruck milieu. One is anxious to find a place. Indeed, the importance of making reference to place is grammatically enforced in the Zulu locative (Amakheleni, "at the old man's place"). It verbalizes substantives, so to speak, tying them down and making them fixed objects of action. There is no locative in Fang – a neo-Bantu language. Nor is there one in Mina.

In the beachside life of the Mina one is surrounded by motion – the constant crash of the surf to the south, the constant ocean winds above, the constant shifting sands below. One seems always to be squinting, raising the voice above the wind, desiring some surcease of the constant motion, despairing of asserting any effective human action against it, hoping for some more harmonious relation to it. This environment puts constant pressure upon the Mina.

The pressure that their vast environment puts upon the Zulu (they are subject to awesome displays of thunder, lightning, wind, and storm) is seen in the institution of the "heaven herd." The purpose of one of the most important diviners was to prevent the roiling herds of heaven from overwhelming the Zulu village – its crops, its cattle, its men. The Fang have no such institution. They feel well ensconced and, in this respect, protected by the overarching and oppressive forest. This is so even though the arrival of the intertropical front and the rainy season puts on as powerful a display of wind, lightning, and water as in Zululand or on the Mina coast. They feel no need to hunker down like the Zulu, to create a heaven herd to medicine every hut against lightning and to rush out when storm clouds gather and shake a spear against the sky!

The theory

This discussion arises from and seeks to expand upon a theory of emotional move-ment in social life referred to by some as "pronominalism" (Fernandez 1974). The argument is that social subjects, the Is, yous, hes, theys, of social life, are essentially inchoate and must recurrently obtain identity – a set of satisfactory feelings of quality – by predicating upon themselves objects from other (non-literal) domains of experience. However, not only do men predicate identities upon themselves from other domains of experience, they also create domains, ritual arenas as it were, in which they can transform, or go through a series of transformations in, their iden-tities. In these ritual arenas, or sacred quality places,[3] there is both a convergence and an emergence of qualities. Here one can fall back upon an old distinction found in John Locke between primary, secondary, and emergent qualities. Primary qualities are those – apparently external – qualities that inhere in the object world in our perception of it, say, color, sound, configuration, bulk, number, situation, and state, whether in motion or at rest. Secondary qualities are those – apparently internal – qualities or feeling states that are produced by our interaction with the object world, say, taste, weight, warmth, and other qualities induced in us by some intercourse with the object, and which do not coincide with our perception of it as it is out there. Emergent qualities are always complex feeling states in the pronoun brought about by various kinds of synesthesia, the systematic bringing together, in ritual experience for example, of various qualities. In a sense, secondary qualities are emergent. They emerge from the intentional interaction of the subject with the object. But they do not have the complexity of emergent qualities. Emergent qualities are feelings created by the taking place of expressive events as complex systems of synesthesia.

Our particular focus here – we cannot detail all the primary and secondary qualities of these ritual arenas – are the emergent qualities that participants realize by ritual action in these sacred places. More particularly, we are interested in the constraints laid upon these emergent qualities by the culture itself and its spatial orientations. One can, perhaps, overestimate these constraints, as did Kenneth Burke, for example, in his analysis of dramatic scenes:

> From the motivational point of view there is implicit in the quality of a scene, the quality of the action that is to take place within...thus when the curtain rises to disclose a given stage-set, this stage-set contains simultaneously, implicitly, all that the narrative is to draw out, as a sequence, explicitly. (Kuper 1972)

Nevertheless, the scene does make its important contribution to the emergent qualities of the scenario. And we have taken pains to set the scene of Fang and Zulu and Mina culture. But just as surely, all the images or dramatic metaphors performed, and whose performance brings qualitative changes in participants and spectators, are not contained implicitly in the scene but are brought to it by costume, gait, gesture, and dialogue of the actors. In the same way the qualities that emerge in sacred places are not all contained implicitly in the place but are brought to it by performance, the acting out of images. Emergent qualities arise in the interaction of the images men bring to scenes or sites with the sites themselves. As I have elsewhere (Fernandez 1974, 1970, 1977) examined the sequence of images that are brought to ritual scenarios, I will here concentrate upon the contribution of the scene or sacred space both in itself and insofar as it reflects spatial notions in the culture itself.

Fang village (adzal) and Zulu kraal (umuzi)

Visual inspection of the Fang village and the Zulu kraal shows striking contrasts in rectangularity and circularity. How much cosmological, legendary, religious, and socioeconomic experience reverberates in the Fang village! There is first of all the contrast between the forest and the village. The forest is cold, yet the prime arena of male activity. The village is hot, yet the arena of women's work, for women's valence is otherwise cool. When one passes from the village to the forest, one passes through various life zones, each redolent with its particular set of associations according to the activities carried out there. One begins in the central court of the village (*nsun*) passing along the wall of houses on either side and out the back door (*mbi e fala*), which opens upon the zone of small gardens and banana groves (*fala*). The terrain of each family stretches out in a rectangle behind their dwellings. Crops that must be closely watched are planted here, as are those crops that are predominantly the concern of men: tobacco, oil palm, and the cash crops currently of importance, coffee and cocoa. At its fringes we find isolated stands of forest (*okan*) where the latrines are located and where ceremonial activities of the ancestor cult and the secret societies take place. Wild fruit trees are maintained here, *asas, mvut*, and *tom*, and during their season the okan is the scene of much pleasurable activity. Beyond this zone is the zone of the large gardens or "plantations" (*efakh*).

Beyond the plantations is the forest on the frontiers of which men do their battle, slashing and burning new fields, laying traps for its fauna, and entering into it for hunts. Deep within the forest a stream or a ridge marks the frontier with another clan-segment, a zone of potential hostility. But the forest itself, regardless of the societal frontier, quickens the thought, for therein men engage in the chase, while families camp out (*ke mvan*) on fishing expeditions of hilarity and solidarity, and therein shades of the troubled dead and other malevolent spirits wander. Thus is the forest contrasted with the village in Fang thought.

As for the village itself, with its two long rows of houses facing each other across the barren courtyard, and its two men's council houses (*aba*) facing each other lengthwise down the courtyard, the feeling of opposition is provoked in the observer. It is an opposition that corresponds, in some respects, to social structure, for men of a common *ndebot* (the minimal segment) build side by side, while those of the *mvogabot* (medial segment), already subject to fissionary pressures, build opposite. The village can be palisaded and unified in times of external threat. But day in and day out the predominant fact is the opposition between parts. The village expresses in its construction the vitality of segmentary and other oppositions in Fang life. But it could become a self-contained enclave and, thus, the village contains in itself the ever-present possibility of unity and solidarity along with its central statement of opposition and imminent fission.

There are oppositions in the Zulu kraal as well. For example, there is the opposition between the *inGqadi* (right-hand wife) and her people, on the one hand, and the *iKholwa* (left-hand wife) and her people, on the other. But the dominant fact is the orientation towards the *indlunkulu* (chief's hut) at the top end of the kraal opposite the main entrance. Moreover, the entire kraal is orientated around the *isibaya* (cattle byre), which is an arena of powerful attraction to Zulu and other Nguni peoples. Krige (1965:42) says that the cattle byre *is* the Zulu temple.

> Here are kept the treasured cattle of the village and here the grain is stored in underground pits . . . (here) the spirits of the ancestors are thought to linger, the place where sacrifices take place when the spirits are asked to protect the inmates or thanked for blessings received.

Kuper (1972) discusses the *umphakatsi* (traditional capitol) of the Swazi and points out how central the isibaya is: "the site of important national gatherings and royal rituals" (1927:416). "The whole village is laid out in the form of a crescent moon or as 'horns of cattle' curving around the *sibaya*. People and things of greatest national value are protected by an outer semicircle of huts occupied by ordinary citizens and by the regiments whose barracks are built at the entrance to the village. The *sibaya* is always the first structure . . . an *axis mundi*, or sacred center of the Swazi cosmos" (1972:412).

The Zulu, like the Swazi, not only have a clear central place in village life, but also in the life of the nation, for the Zulu kings maintained their great kraals as well (Shaka's *kwaBulawayo*, Dingane's *umGungundlovu*, Cetshwayo's *Ulundi*), upon whom the life of the nation was focused. These kraals of more than a thousand huts and many thousand inhabitants were mainly military or regimental in character. Nevertheless, they reproduced the essential features of the domestic kraal, including orientation and slope.[4] The king and his women lived at the head opposite the entrance.

There was no central place or royal place for the Fang. In the nineteenth century during periods of unrest and internecine strife, the Fang, like the Zulu, might gather together in large villages of many hundreds of huts. But unlike the Zulu and typically of the Fang, these huts were not built around a central focus. The plaza was simply lengthened, sometimes to more than a kilometer, with council houses interspersed from time to time. Not only did Fang have no national focus, these exceptional villages in themselves had no centrality.

The Fang huts (nda-kisin and aba) and the Zulu hut (indlu)

There are two different buildings in the Fang village, each with different meanings to the Fang: *aba*, the men's council house, and *nda-kisin*, the sleeping and cooking hut. The Zulu hut, however, has no other structure, with the exception of the cattle byre itself, standing in strong functional contrast to it in the way that the Fang council house as the center of the men's life stands in contrast to the sleeping and cooking huts.[5] Of course there are important distinctions between the chief's or kraal owner's hut and the huts of the various wives, his married huts, and the bachelor huts. But such distinctions are still not as striking as between the aba and the nda-kisin.

The character of Fang village space, in fact, is revealed in the relationship between the men's council house and the combination women's sleeping quarters and cook hut. The men's legends and customs support the fact that the council house is almost exclusively a male arena, and the cook hut is a female arena.[6] The qualities that emerge in these two structures can be grasped by considering a ritual that occurs in relation to these buildings and that gives us insight into what they represent. We find, in fact, that these qualities have very much to do with elementary experiences – bodily experiences are extended into the dwellings.

In the case of difficult delivery when labor is exhausting the mother, the expectant father is encouraged to climb upon the roof of the nda-kisin and, carefully poking about, discover the spot in the roof precisely above the stomach of his wife. Thrusting a hollow banana stem through the thatch, he then pours medicinal water through the stem onto his wife's belly. This medicine is the same as is already employed liberally by the midwives within the hut.

The ritual is called simply *biang ndu* (roof medicine). It appears to assimilate the house to the womb as well. The father having penetrated the womb to create the child must "penetrate" it again in symbolic form to release the child. The ritual that I observed was witnessed by perhaps a dozen villagers. Their quiet amusement at the father's poking around on the roof – the sense of the ribald – would seem to confirm the interpretation we have put upon the act.

There are many other customs that show us the way that village structures are linked with bodily experiences. When the witch doctor exorcises evil spirits within the house of a sick person he heats the machete in the fire and strikes it against the walls and supports of the house. For just as the witchcraft is said to lodge itself upon the integuments, the interstitial structures of the body, so it is sympathetically dislodged by attacking the structure of the house within which the patient suffers and which is assimilated to his body.

If the nda-kisin is the scene of the Fang's most vital primary experiences (men are born there, and in the final stages of their illness they may return there to die), it is not surprising that the structure is assimilated to the corporeal arena of these experiences. Men's experiences, and most particularly primary experiences within bounded and unbounded spaces of their cultures, are sure to influence their feelings about these spaces and even their thinking about space itself.

Let us look briefly at the aba, which contrasts so sharply with the nda-kisin. The aba was a male house par excellence. During unsettled times in former days when the villages were palisaded, the aba was the most heavily armed structure and the center of defense. Throughout the day and night men were on guard within it. It was the structure from which the whole village was surveyed. Since the suppression of warfare, it has functioned as a center of judicial dispute. And though it is no longer so centrally placed as to survey the entire village, it still maintains its importance in social and cultural affairs. As a center of major ceremonies it provides a place of concealment for the changing of costumes or for the examination of neophytes. The main supporting post of the entrance, the *akon aba*, upon which a gorilla skull is often hung, is at the center of these ceremonies. The post accumulates over time a certain power from the habit of men of laying a hand on it as they enter and leave. Its primary association is with the power of the male world.

If the village is to be ritually cleansed, the aba is the last and most important place to undergo purification. It is a lounging place during the day and most masculine activities such as netmaking and repairing, basketry, iron and brass founding, carving, and the weaving of raffia roofing sheets take place within. At night it is the center of story telling or of entertainment by traveling troubadours who recount *mvett*, the great legends and wonder tales of the Fang past. It becomes an arena for the imagination and for the recreation of that past. If the nda-kisin is the arena of the primordial experiences of men's lives, the aba is the arena of the creative imagination.

Both the nda-kisin and the aba contain oppositions within themselves: one house, two beds, the Fang say (*nda mbo binong biban*). The council house has two rows of benches that face each other across the fire. The nda-kisin has a bed and a cooking area in each corner. Sometimes there are four wives, although the more usual case is for two wives to share the hut with their children. Unlike the Zulu hut, the nda-kisin has neither center poles nor center fire pit. There are at least two fire pits, often four. In the men's council house there is a symbolically important pole at either entrance (the akon aba: Fernandez 1977; Swiderski 1969), one of which functions virtually as a central pillar.

Of course, there are important distinctions in areas within the Zulu hut. Directly in the center is the stone cooking hearth, and directly behind it against the farther wall is the *umsamo*, where the spirits are thought to dwell if they are not in the cattle kraal.[7] No one is allowed there except the kraal head or the woman who is head of the hut. Pots and utensils and the owner's most valuable offerings are kept there as well as beer offerings to the ancestors. A newborn child is ritually bathed there – after all, he was shaped by the spirits – and his umbilical cord buried there. In contrast to the floor of a Fang hut, which has permanent "bamboo" beds, with hearths, cooking utensils, and storage containers always about, the Zulu hut floor tends to be clear. During the day mats and bedding and baskets are hung from the walls (Krige 1965:46). The interior of the Zulu hut may seem to have several clear focuses of attention: a domestic hearth, two center poles, and the umsamo. But the umsamo is the focus of attention much beyond these other arenas.

Where the Fang maintain sex distinctions in the buildings themselves as between the nda-kisin and the aba, the Zulu, to whom sex distinctions are also marked and important in all spheres of their social activity, maintain these distinctions by assigning the right side of the hut as the men's side (*isililo samadoda*) and the left side (*isililo sesifazana*) as the women's side. Men and women keep to their respective sides (Krige 1965:46), a practice that is reiterated in the ceremonial structures we consider below. There is not an interchange of ritual arenas.

The Zulu chief's hut, indlunkulu, was thus the focus of attention of domestic life. The man might maintain that hut, if he were not living there with the first wife, as the hut to which all his wives came in revolving fashion to fulfill their connubial responsibilities. And every day, every wife sent food to that hut to feed him and his guests. Or he might move from one to another of his wifes' huts and he might be fed in each hut accordingly. In either case the indlunkulu maintained its centrality, for in evenings of folklore and amusement all the wives and children might gather there. It was there that the chief offerings were made to the ancestors if they were not made in the cattle kraal. It was there that the chief went first on returning from a long journey. The indlunkulu provided as far as the huts were concerned a necessary centrality. For otherwise, the house-property complex, the rights (virtual ownership) over hut, goods, and cattle enjoyed by each wife in the interest of her sons, could create a competitive and divisive situation (Fernandez 1971).

The birth customs, which we have referred to for the Fang and which give us some sense of the association between the hut and the primary events that take place within it, are not found among Zulu. It is true that both Fang and Zulu isolate the newborn and his mother in the birth hut. But whereas among the Fang the baby is finally brought out of the hut and presented to the men's council house, among the Zulu after the isolation period it is the baby who receives visitors, including his father and other men.

We note similar differences in the moving back and forth between poles and quadrants in ritual space among the Fang and the essential concentration of forces upon a central place in the Zulu when we compare marriage ceremonies. Among the Fang, the ceremonies go back and forth between the kitchen of the bridegroom's mother, where the girl is ritually incorporated, and the men's council house, where the bride's mother presents a ritual meal to the men of the two clans. After this presentation the men go to the kitchen to complement the women. Fang marriage ceremonies begin with mocking dances between the women of the two families and the men. Early on the bride is pushed out into the center area to be admired by her new family and to sit in the courtyard with her husband under general scrutiny. After this public display the bride joins the women in the nda-kisin and her husband joins the men in the aba. This contrasts with the Zulu, where the bride is brought to her new kraal encircled by members of her family so that she cannot be seen. She goes to a hut of seclusion where her husband's people only gradually obtain entrance and eventually bring the bride by a series of aggregation rites (Krige 1965:148) to her husband's hut. Like the Fang, the Zulu have mocking dances belittling each other's wedding presents. Still, statements of opposition are not dominant. The Zulu bride is brought surrounded by her own people and gradually she becomes surrounded by her husband's people, incorporated into the new kraal. The Fang bride is brought at the forefront of her father's people, joined in public display to her husband, and then separated from him as men and women of both parties separate into their separate but interacting arenas.

There are many other indications in Zulu life of their attraction to central places, their tending to concentrate and converge on vital centers. The ancient graves of former kings are preserved as the object of important national rites such as first fruit ceremonies or the formation of new regiments. The Fang, in their relatively rapid migration, remember the *elik* (former living sites), where their ancestors are buried. There is nostalgia in visiting them. But they are not centers of ritual, for the Fang carry their ancestors with them – or the power to summon their ancestors from the realm of the dead – in their reliquaries. There are no vital centers to national life. This is seen cosmologically as well. The Fang conceive of their origin as lying variously in a distant and abandoned savannah or seaside, on the other side of the forest from where they now live. The Zulu conceive of their people as having emerged from underground at one place (although where this place may be is uncertain and is not a ritual center in Zulu land). There is a groundedness to Zulu life, moreover, that is not found among the Fang. The ancestors live in the ground of the kraal, whereas the Fang ancestors live under the waters of rivers or wander deep in the forest. Thereby "their hearts were brought together." Medicines of various kinds were characteristically buried by the Zulu in the ground of kraals. The Fang are not grounded in this way, nor do they have a Great Place.

Finally we note a difference in the sense of the architecture of the cosmos! The Zulu are said to believe that the sky is a solid "blue rock" that completely encircles the earth, and in the center of which the Zulu find themselves (Krige 1965:410). The Fang have no such sense of cosmic centrality. Their cardinal directions are northeast-southwest or upstream-downstream, and their predominant sense is of moving along that vector from sea to sea (Fernandez 1977:3–8).

Fang, Zulu, and Mina orientations in some contemporary sacred places

It is illuminating to examine the expression of these dominant traditional old-culture vectors in some contemporary sacred places. In doing this we get an idea of the persistence of these orientations in a situation of very rapid culture change as well as an idea of the changes in these vectors brought about through the pressures of that change.

We have already indicated that in Zulu ancestor cult the prime tendency was to concentrate ritual at the head of the hut or the head of the kraal (hut and kraal structurally replicate each other), which was the abode of the ancestors. This concentration contrasts with the Fang distribution into various arenas. These Fang ancestral ceremonies begin in the village where the initiates, sitting on banana tree stems and surrounded by singing, dancing, and drumming, ingest large amounts of an alkaloid, malan (*alchornea florubundia*), until they fall back unconscious. They are rushed out to the forest precincts of the cult to be quickened. There, in the foyer of the *elik bieri*, beyond two raffia arches and a barrier of banana leaves, they are laid out upon the ground and revived by a medicinal swathing. Once revived, and although still groggy, they will be shown the sacra of the cult, the ancestral skulls. They are shown the skulls in a mirror as the curtain to the "sanctum sanctorum" is lifted behind them, or the curtain is lifted and the initiates are wheeled around abruptly to face the skulls. The gradual depressing of the initiates' faculties that took place in the village is countered by the arousal that they experience at suddenly being confronted by the sacra of the cult. The initiates are washed down either in the precincts or at a nearby stream. Then the entire cult group prepares to return to the village. First, however, the uninitiated in the village may be invited out to the first barrier of the elik to watch the dancing of the *eyima bieri* or *mwan biang* (the ancestor figures). After this the cult group, with its new members, dances back into the village and reincorporates itself.

What we see in the Fang *bieri* ceremonies is a toing and froing between various arenas rather than a Zulu concentration of forces. The sacred space of the Fang ancestral cult has polarities – corners – to it. There is ceremonial interplay – an important tension – between these various arenas. This sense of a sacred space distributed in several arenas appears in various transitional ceremonies of Fang. Two movements that appeared among Fang in the late 1940s are of interest here: the *ngol* dance or movement (named after Charles De Gaulle) that flourished among the southern Fang, and the Alar Ayong (Knitting Together of the Clans) movement that was widespread among the northern Fang. If we look at the ritual arenas, the sacred spaces, employed by these cults, we find again the polyvalence of space, the interplay of arenas.

We see in the *ngol* dance pavilion separate lodges for the various bureaucratic officials. We see an opposition between the side of the pavilion where the various officials in charge of the dance are lodged and that side for women and children and spectators. The dance proceeds round and round from one side to another, from arena to arena. Early in the evening before ngol himself appears (he is the leader of the dance team in white face with kepi and uniform), mostly the women dance and the male leaders sit in their various lodges. When ngol comes and by his presence establishes order in the pavilion – he rewards harmonious dancers and fines the disorderly – the men begin to dance alone and with the women. Although it would appear that there is centrality to this pavilion – the "band box" so to speak – in fact it is the interaction between parts of the pavilion and the coming and going between the various lodges that provide for the truly satisfactory experience of the dance.

The forest precincts of the Alar Ayong movement are in many ways similar to the ngol pavilion. Additionally, it also preserves from ancestor cult ceremonies the "sanctum sanctorum" of the ancestors. As in ngol we find the various lodges of the bureaucratic leaders of the local chapter. And there is a great deal of circulation between these various lodges. The women sit on one side of the arena and the men sit in their lodges on the other side. It is true that there is a platform in the center of the arena upon which the various male leaders stand to harangue the assemblage into order. But as with ngol the orderliness that is achieved in other than rhetorical terms is achieved by moving people about between the various arenas. The women and nonmembers are recurrently presented to the various lodges and the male members from the main arena move finally to a visitation of the "sanctum sanctorum" of the ancestors.

The most interesting of the modern Fang rituals for the making of our point are found in the modern religious movement of *Bwiti*. One could discuss at length both the architectonics of this religion (Fernandez 1970) – the careful laying out of the various areas of the chapel into male side–female side, sun side–moon side, red side–white side, birth side–death side, this world side–other world side – and the complexity of the rituals. The distribution of valences into various areas of the cult house and the ritual requirement that the membership, in order to achieve fully effective polyvalent performance, must move back and forth between these areas, conforms with the emphasis upon the spatial distribution of sacred experiences in the traditional Fang ceremonies previously noted.

There is, however, plenty of centripetalism of movement in Bwiti dance patterns. Most particularly, this is found in the midnight and first-light dances of *nlem mvore* (one-heartedness). At midnight the entire membership, preceded by the cult harp, go out into the forest in a single line, holding candles, in search of any of the ancestors who may be still lost and wandering in the deep forest. They proceed along narrow paths cut in the bush. After half an hour of filing through the forest they return to the cult house where they wind into a very tight circle, candles held above their heads, so as to form virtually one flame. This centripetal concentration is an important ritual event and the "one-heartedness" it obtains is an important quality in the membership to emerge from these rituals.

Nevertheless, the overall quality of Bwiti worship I would regard as being "controlled centrifugation" obtained by moving the membership back and forth between various arenas: chapel and village court, and village and forest, male side and female side, birth side and death side, this world and other world. Moreover, there is an overall directionality in Bwiti worship, a desire to pass over the crossroads of life and death that makes of the centripetal concentration only a passing moment in worship.

Moving to some recent Zulu rituals, we note an evident contrast to the Fang centrifugal tendencies. Perhaps the strongest contrast is provided by the urban Zionists who meet weekly and dance their religion in the circles trodden in the grass of many an unused or abandoned urban lot. The object of this religion is to obtain the power of the Holy Spirit by running around in the outer circle until one is drawn to the inner circle where the final laying on of hands or some other form of engagement with the spirit may take place. If we compare the Zionists' circles with the Zulu hut or with the kraal itself, the resemblance is immediate and there is no doubt that the concentrated circularity of the traditional life is being reiterated in these circles. The addiction to the more traditional pattern – and the circle-hut association – is confirmed in the Zionists' need to periodically return to the reserves and to worship, in all-night ceremonies, in the chief's hut in the kraal of a friend or relative.

There are centrifugal elements in Zionist circle worship. Should a member not be sufficiently pure, he will be thrown out of the circle in a state of "bad spirit" possession. When this occurs (it is reminiscent of the flights out into the bush at puberty rites by Zulu boys and girls), other members immediately go to protect the member from the onslaughts of the spirit and to retrieve him to the circle. Another centrifugal element occurs periodically during the year in the large Zionist congregations that go to the ocean for baptism. Individuals are baptized as the group lines up out into the ocean. Ocean baptism combines a purification function with a direct confrontation with the Holy Spirit felt to be embodied in the power and movement of the ocean. But this centrifugation returns to centripetalism as the members immediately after baptism form an *impi* (a regimental group) upon the water's edge. Now in power, they dance up towards the dunes. Soon they form a circle around a particularly afflicted member of the congregation. The leader steps into the circle while the members sing, concentrating all their power upon the member to purify him and make efficacious the laying on of hands.

Not all Zionists worship in grass circles. Large congregations often worship in rectangular sheds. Yet the high point of the evening is the invariable laying on of hands. The members form a vital circle in which the head of the cult may step in and empower the purified member (Fernandez 1966). The tendency in Zulu contemporary cults to reshape rectangular architectural frameworks to conform with concentrated circularity may be seen in the Amakhehleni, a non-Zionist divine healing cult on the outskirts of Durban. The healing kraal shows us an almost random redistribution of the old kraal elements. Yet the cattle byre is still present, and sacrifices still take place there, the umsamo is still present, although in a separate small building, and the chief's hut and the various wives' huts are also present. What interests us most, however, is the large rectangular shed in which divination takes place. This shed would seem to be providing a number of arenas within which action can be distributed. In point of fact, when we examine the building closely, we find it to be a reinterpretation of the cattle byre. There is an entrance in which sacrifices take place, and there is a head of the "byre" where the sacrifices are presented. There is a man's side and a woman's side, but dancing takes place not between or across these arenas but in place and directed toward the "spirit kraal." Action and attention are very much concentrated and not distributed. The presence of cowhide rugs on the earthen floor, the commotion of the animals present and about to be sacrificed, the summoning of the spirits for divination, and, eventually, the traditional regimental dances that erupt as men come into power, are all reminiscent of old kraal (cattle byre) activity with its centripetal concentrations. And all this takes place in a rectangular hut.

For several decades now among the Mina, Christianism Celeste, a religious movement whose origin lies in Porto Novo, Benin, among the Nago-Yoruba, has been important. Its main concern is with the healing of spiritual and physical affliction. On first approach this new religion seems decidedly Christian, availing itself very little if at all of the Pantheon-of-Gods complex of this part of the Guinea Coast. But the Christianity of the members of this cult is in many ways superficial, and periodically during the year various rites are performed that show the continued hold of traditional beliefs and the need to come to terms with them. The rite that interests us here is a beachside one in which the membership chooses a lone signal palm and digs a deep hole in the sand until inside it the moisture of the water table wells up. Candles are then lit inside this hole, biblical verses are recited or read, various healthful fruits – citrus, lemon, coconut – are distributed to the members, holy seawater is bottled and blessed, and then the members dispose themselves around the hole, preferably with the hole at their heads and their bodies radiating out. Under white cloth sheets they lie sleeping for an hour or more. The tranquility of this rite contrasts with the dynamic centrifugation or centripetalism of the Fang and Zulu rituals. These Mina "new believers" regard the hole and its discovery as a kind of central spot that needs no toing and froing, but requires simply quiet and peaceful disposition. Most believe it to be a hole in which they can communicate with the coastal water deity, the goddess of the near ocean and lagoon, called Mameh Wateh in this part of Africa. But it is also a hole by which they can communicate with the great gods of the pantheons and with God Himself.

There are a number of things we have to know to interpret this tranquil and highly centered ritual, such things as the peripheral place of these Mina fisher folk in the turbulence of West African-Guinea Coast history, the undistributed quality of compound life, and the conflicting claims of the various supernaturals, old and missionary-derived, in this, religiously speaking, most complex part of Africa. If these Mina seem passive, quiescent, in the presence of the supernaturals compared with the activity whether centrifugal or centripetal of the Fang and Zulu, this, in part, is compatible with the peripheral role, the submissive and quiet role, they have played in relation to the assertive and turbulent interior peoples, the imperial peoples of the interior Guinea Coast. If they are passive and expecting to be worked on in relation to the supernaturals, so have they been in relation to the powers of this world.

Like the Fang and the Zulu, Mina find impurities in themselves. In contrast to these other people, Mina do not take an active role in the eradication of these impurities. We have only to compare the dynamic of purification among the Zulu. Mina have more of an "impedence" notion of their role in relation to the flow of supernatural forces. Sickness for them and impurity – at least for the members of this religion – is somehow caused by their "impeding" the flow of supernatural forces. Too great ritual activity on their part would only add to that impedence. They must dig a hole to the forces of the below – the water spirit, specifically – so that the water spirit can communicate with the above. One of the consequences of being peripheral to the well-organized pantheons of the interior kingdoms has been some uncertainty about the relationships of the supernatural powers to each other. Missionary intervention has only complicated the matter. Essentially this rite attempts to bring the gods back into communication with each other so that men and women can be restored to their purity by being transparent to, and not impeding, that communication.

Some emergent qualities of spatial activity

It is not enough to watch activity in space and assess centrifugal and centripetal emphases. It is also important by means of direct inquiry with participants to determine qualitative changes in state, the emergent qualities, that result from activity in that space. Deriving from my own discussion with Fang and Zulu participants, I should like to put forth brief lexicons of the qualitative states achieved or counteracted in the various sacred spaces. Any ritual has a variety of objectives, but I believe it can be said that the general objective of both Zulu and Fang rituals is vitality: a lively control of one's circumstances. The Fang call this *ening*, which is usually translated "life" but is more appropriately translated "lively survival," and includes the capacity for controlled but lively activity – *elulua*. The objective generally in mind in these Zulu ritual cultivations of the spirit is *amandla*, often translated (power) but more appropriately translated as "strength to resist and to control." These vital states I believe are emergent qualities of the most general importance in these rituals.

At the same time these desirable states of vitality are only fully understood – and the rituals that produce them are only fully understood – over against undesirable states that they counteract. The Fang seek their ritual vitality in order to relieve or avoid tiredness, sluggishness (*atuk*), or bad body (*nyol abe*), which opens one up to a variety of misfortunes. The Zulu seek strength through ritual in order to escape the *umuyama* (dark gloomy and confused condition), the state of foreboding, the drifting toward disaster, the *isinyama* (calm before the storm), *amapkuta* (state of weakness), *usekoneni* (the feeling of uncleaness). These are the qualities that, willy nilly, men bring to their rituals and against which the rituals struggle.

For the Mina, though they will name any of a great variety of specific afflictions that have brought them to their seaside excavation, the fundamental and generic problem is heaviness or denseness of body, which makes for the "impedence" to which the particular rite we have examined is directed. The emergent quality of the drowsy rite they prefer to call *etat celestial*, which is to say a kind of transparent incorporation or identification with all the gods – indeed the entire cosmos – together. It is a word they have had to coin and whose meaning they do not feel is adequately represented in traditional lexicon.

Discussion with the Fang and Zulu informants readily yields these objectives of vitality. For Fang, it seems to me, the rituals are largely constrained for controlling centrifugation through balanced opposition of different valenced arenas. These rituals are aimed at achieving that quality of even-handedness, of tranquil balance of active and passive forces, which the Fang call *mvwaa*. It is this quality that first emerges from ritual and that is antecedent to true vitality. The Zulu rituals that we consider here are very much constrained toward an inner space, in which purifying, cleansing, and eventually fortifying contact with the ancestral or Holy Spirit can be made. There is at once an emphasis on corporeal purification of an inner space through purgation or through ingestion of Holy Water (or through cleansing medicines) and a ritual directedness toward a pure inner place as the essential part of the ritual arena. In any case the emergent quality of these Zulu rituals – a quality antecedent to the obtaining of vital strength – is *ukuhlanzeka* (internal cleanliness or purity). The Mina, too, are preoccupied with internal states, although rather than affecting these states directly by the laying on of hands or vertiginous centrifugal or centripetal activity, they try to affect these internal states directly in a modest little ceremony, by rearranging the communication of the cosmos and thus indirectly their own well-being as part-integral to the cosmos.

If Mina come to an identification of self with cosmos in this rite, it should be pointed out that the achievement of bodily vitality in the Fang and Zulu, ostensibly achieved by distribution or concentration of ritual actions in these sacred places, depends as well upon microscosm–macroscosm extensions. That is, in some respects the ritual arenas are understood metaphorically as bodies with inner and outer parts, with heads, feet, vital organs. We have discussed briefly this extension for Fang building. It is present as well in the inner space of Zulu ritual (see Kuper 1972:419). I have elsewhere discussed at length the body–chapel identification for Bwiti (Fernandez 1977). Thus ritual actions in ritual space imitate and are coercive upon bodily states and bodily activities. The point is that the ideas human beings have of place are always in some part a projection of their own body image, and, vice-versa, their own body image is an introjection of their experience in such places. The situation is paradoxical, but it is a fact of man–space negotiations. Men predicate space upon themselves and obtain qualities that they, in turn, project upon space. These predications and projections, in important measure, transform spaces into places.

Conclusion

In this paper we have been concerned with the architectonic interpretation of elementary symbols from three African religious movements. We have sought to interpret these spatial symbols by giving some indication of the antecedent experiences and beliefs of the people involved, which give to these symbols their affective and healing power. We have sought to show – all too briefly – how the architectonic in which these symbols are set is made relevant experientially by virtue of its association to these antecedent experiences and beliefs. It is only in and through this architectonic understanding, we argue – an understanding arduously obtained by long-term participant observation – that we can convert (as men and women within cultures constantly do) observed spaces into understood places.

We can't pretend that we have made the final sufficient and necessary interpretation of these symbols and their associated architectonic. However simple and elemental they may be, they have complex associations, all of which no stranger, however long his sojourn (and very few members of the culture itself), can fully divulge. Just in the matter of the vectors alone – to end here with some simplicities beyond the complexity – the problems of interpretation are substantial. Have we really said all that is to be said about Fang controlled centrifugation by relating it to their valued quality of even-handed tranquility; to their milieu of an encroaching and claustrophbic forest; to their highly egalitarian and fissionable society recently involved in rapid migration into and through the equatorial forest; to their puzzlement because of missionary evangelization in trying to relate God Above to Gods Below? How sufficient is the environmental explanation for the Zulu impulse to concentrate activity in space? Important differences in physiological philosophy – in body image – would seem to be at work with the Zulu focusing much greater attention on pure and impure inward states – objects of violent purgation. Compare this to the Fang, who are more oriented toward distal events and body surfaces, to surface lustrations in the matter of purity. And compare this to the Mina Celestial Christians who, feeling body-heavy, look outward to small rearrangements of the cosmos rather than inward. Of course the whole Zulu social-political order, in contrast to the Fang scattered egalitarianism and the Mina's political dispersion, favors powerful concentrated centrality in architectonics.[8]

We could go on adducing comparisons and plausible and relevant associations. That is always useful in anthropological discourse. But let us end with this summary statement. In the sacred places we have examined we find men and women achieving emergent qualitative states in which both inchoate men and women and inchoate space itself are given shape, character, and meaning. Among the Fang there is directionality – one vector of movement centrifugal in nature with periodic centripetal poses. Among the Zulu centripetalism is the dominant mode with occasional centrifugal excursions out into space. Among the Mina quiet distribution around a central place and without marked centripetalism or centrifugation guarantee the celestial flow of forces between the above and the below.

NOTES

1   Cf. Segal et al. (1966). The Fang protocols were administered by my wife and myself. In respect to the two cultures considered here there is no significant difference of response – in either adults or children – in the Perspective-Drawing Illusion. As the Zulu contemplate much longer vistas than Fang, they should be more susceptible to foreshortening... they might even find such judgments adaptive. In respect to the carpentered world hypothesis, although Fang have a strikingly more carpentered world than Zulu, there was no significant difference in response to either Muller-Lyer or the Sander parallelogram. Indeed Zulu have higher means on the Muller-Lyer than Fang, and Zulu children higher means than the Fang children on the Sander parallelogram. On the Horizontal–Vertical Illusion the Fang were significantly more susceptible than Zulu contrary to prediction. The Zulu data, otherwise described as disorderly by the authors, was in some part, as much as a third, taken from those who had moved from round to rectangular dwellings.

2   These deictic elements in language that show or point out directionality to actors would seem good indicators of a culture's spatial sense: he went out of his head, he came to his senses, down east, out west, etc. Fang and Zulu generally use exclamatives, *ya* or *yo*, of assenting whereabouts (the here I am response). When one was summoned to the Zulu king, the reply was, "We hear you high One," and as one approached one called out the royal praises so as not to arrive in silence (Krige 1965:238).

3   The notion of a sacred place held here is the following: any space in interaction with which individuals find produced in themselves exceptional qualities or feeling states of arousal or pacification – exceptional by reference to the everyday world of their literal or practical (profane) occupations and obligations. A sacred place is a special kind of quality space of special heightening or dampening of emotion or both together.

4   The Zulu village is usually built on sloping ground facing east. The main entrance is thus below the head of the kraal. The tendency in villages built by Fang was an east–west orientation or upriver–downriver direction – one entrance and council house to the east and the other to the west.

5   Zulu do have men's sleeping huts (*ilawu*), but these were not focuses of attention like the *aba*.

6   The legend goes that man and wife built one house to live in together. But life became unbearable so man left and built the *aba*. Man and women can only live together by living apart.

7   It is of interest to compare the Zulu notion of the continued indwelling and proximity of the spirits after death with the Fang notion that spirits properly go off into the forest to the village of the dead after death. Mortuary ceremonies a year after death are instituted, in fact, to facilitate that departure for any troubled spirit. Zulu, when moving their villages, take special pains to ensure that the spirits are agreeable to coming along. They are also very carefully guided from the old to the new village.

8   Although not explored here, of particular interest are questions of what occurs to the constancies of visual space at peak moments of ritual arousal. The Fang take an alkaloid, *tabernenthe eboga*, and in initiation experience lengthy, relatively stereotyped journeys through spiritual realms, journeys that in some respects are almost a reversal of their migration experiences (Fernandez 1972). Zulu with whom I have worked, when possessed by spirits in the hearts of their ritual arenas, have no sense of spatial excursion and feel rather a closing in of space, an overpowering concentration of space upon themselves in the form of spirit. The pressure becomes so great that they generally leap up and dance around or shoot out in a rush of efferent impulse. Thus when maximum arousal is

obtained there tends to be a reversal. Fang are stable and quiet under afferent impulses and Zulu suddenly mobile and energetic under efferent impulses. In part this is, no doubt, a response to the drug itself, in other part there would seem to be a cultural element.

REFERENCES

Armstrong, R. P. 1971. *The affecting presence*. Urbana: University of Illinois.

Becken, H. J. 1968. On the holy mountain. *Journal of Religion in Africa* 1 (2): 138–56.

Burke, K. 1962. *A grammar of rhetoric motives*. New York: Viking.

Douglas, Mary. 1972. Symbolic order and the use of domestic space in Ucko, Trinkham, and Dimbleby. In *Man, settlement and urbanism*, 7. Cambridge.

Fernandez, J. W. 1966. Revitalized words from the parrot's egg and the bull that crashes in kraal. *Proceedings of the American Ethnological Society*, 43–69.

Fernandez, J. W. 1970, 1977. *Tabernenthe eboga*: narcotic ecstasis and the work of the ancestors. In *The flesh of the gods*, ed. Peter Furst. New York: Praeger.

Fernandez, J. W. 1971. Bantu brotherhood: symmetry, socialization, and ultimate choice in two Bantu cultures. In *Kinship and Culture*, ed. F. L. K. Hsu, 339–66. Chicago: Aldine.

Fernandez, J. W. 1974. The mission of metaphor in expressive culture. *Current Anthropology* 15 (2): 119–46.

Fernandez, J. W. 1977. *Fang architectonics*. Philadelphia: Institute for the Study of Human Issues.

Krige, E. 1965. *The social system of the Zulu*. 3d ed. Capetown: Shuter and Shooter.

Kuper, E. 1972. The language of sites and the politics of space. *American Anthropologist* 74 (3):418–30.

Ortner, S. 1973. On key symbols. *American Anthropologist* 75:49–63.

Seagal M., D. Campbell, and M. J. Herskovitz. 1966. *The influence of culture on visual perception*. Indianapolis: Bobbs Merrill.

Swiderski, S. 1969. *Le symbolisme du poteau central au gabon*. Vienna: Mit. der Anthro. Gesellschaft.

Tessman, G. 1913. *Die Pangwe*. 2 vols. Munster: Ernst Wassmuth.

Vilakazi, A. 1962. *Zulu transformations*. Pietermaritzburg: Shooter and Shuter.

9

Empowering Place: Multilocality and Multivocality

Margaret C. Rodman

Place is a problem in contemporary anthropological theory. The problem of place arises, paradoxically, because the meaning of place too often seems to go without saying. As anthropologists and as ordinary people living in the world, we are as situated in place as we are in time or culture. The people we study in non-Western, less industrialized countries may have even more immediate and full relationships with place insofar as time–space relations are less fragmented and they retain more local control over their physical and social landscapes. Yet anthropologists who take pains to lead students through the minefields of conceptualizing culture often assume that place is unproblematic. It is simply location. It is where people do things. This article takes the kind of hard look at place that others have taken at culture. It suggests how anthropologists can learn from current thinking about place in geography. And it applies anthropological thoughts on voice and place, especially multivocality and multilocality, using examples from Melanesian ethnography and field research in Vanuatu (the ex-New Hebrides).

The article approaches the anthropological problem of place from two vantage points, exploring in the process some of the terrain between them. The first is that of places as anthropological constructions. Places in anthropological writing have been equated with ethnographic locales. As such, they could be taken for granted. They were just space, "the dead, the fixed, the undialectical, the immobile" in Foucault's lament. They became the settings, albeit often exotic ones, where things happened.[1] Anthropologists have critiqued places as localizing strategies (Fardon 1990) or ideas (Appadurai 1988a, 1988b); for example, India has exemplified the concept of hierarchy. Others have objected to the use of places as metonyms in which one locale stands, inappropriately, for a whole area (Fernandez 1988), as, for example, Andalusia has been made to stand for all of Spain. But insufficient attention has been paid to conceptualizing place in anthropology as something other than a physical setting or a passive target for primordial sentiments of attachment that flow from life's "assumed 'givens'" (Geertz 1973:259).[2]

Places are not inert containers. They are politicized, culturally relative, historically specific, local and multiple constructions. Anthropologists have accepted the polyphony of the voices they hear and represent ethnographically. What Appadurai (1988a:17) has called "the problem of voice ('speaking for' and 'speaking to')" may intersect with "the problem of place ('speaking from' and 'speaking to')," but the former has certainly received more critical attention. One goal of this article is to show that place as an anthropological concept is as complex as voice.

A further problem is that place and voice are not, or not just, academic creations. Places are not defined simply by researchers or by the topics that preoccupy them in particular settings. Places in the world of our research are not totalized, essentialized Western creations.

This leads to the second point of view in the article, namely, that of places as socially constructed. Here the emphasis is on places in the world, on the agency of individuals and of forces beyond individual control. Places have multiple meanings that are constructed spatially. The physical, emotional, and experiential realities places hold for their inhabitants at particular times need to be understood apart from their creation as the locales of ethnography. While anthropologists indeed create places in ethnography, they hold no patent on place-making.

I advocate a different approach to place than the traditional ethnographic focus on setting. I argue for a more critical usage of place than is common in contemporary anthropology and take seriously the attendant dimensions of power. I raise questions (and do not try to answer all of them) about how the anthropological study of place relates to experiences of living in places. In so doing, I explore the idea of multilocality as one way of "constructing regional worlds in experience," to borrow Nancy Munn's (1990) evocative phrase.

Organizationally, the article begins with a selected overview of the study of place in contemporary geography, emphasizing work that seems especially appropriate to anthropology. I go on to evaluate new approaches to place and the related concept of region in anthropology. The next section of the paper pays particular attention to place as lived experience. Using recent studies in Melanesia concerning power and social landscapes (esp. Lindstrom 1990), I point to some ways that the work of Foucault applies to understanding multivocality ethnographically. I suggest how Giddens's (1990) views on space–time distanciation also can be helpful for understanding multivocality and multilocality in non-Western places. Examples from my own fieldwork in Vanuatu illustrate a multivocal, multilocal approach to understanding the social construction of place anthropologically.

Geographers and Place

To some extent, the concept of place and, on a larger scale, that of region have languished even in geography. "Chorology," the study of region and place, was marginalized as a theoretical subject in the 1950s and 1960s as geographers, like anthropologists of the period, sought to make their discipline more scientific. This does not mean that regional studies disappeared. Even within Melanesia their continued contribution remained evident into the 1970s (see, e.g., Brookfield with Hart 1971). But regional studies became a largely descriptive field.

Geographers now are expressing renewed interest in the theoretical concepts of place and region.[3] Entrikin (1989:40) regards this interest as part of attempts to "redirect geographical research toward a concern for the richness of human experience and an understanding of human action.... [T]hey are taking seriously the cultural significance of everyday life."

In his recent introduction to systemic regional geography, Dov Nir (1990:59–60) observes that there are two opposing views of "region" in contemporary geography. For some, "region" is just a concept, a mental construct or analytical tool. For others, regions are realities that exist in space. Anthropologists similarly hold these two seemingly opposing views with regard to place, as the two viewpoints from which this article is organized suggest – that is, place as (1) an anthropological construct for "setting" or the localization of concepts and as (2) socially constructed, spatialized experience.[4] Nir (1990:10) proposes that both views can be compatible insofar as regional studies are in fact studies of places, spatial relationships (Claval's [1984] "social space"), and values attached to places and relationships. Others would call this concatenation "lived space."

Berdoulay (1989:130) defines "lived space" (*l'espace vécu*) to include living space (territory, activity areas), social space, and the values attached to both. He notes that current interest in lived space, especially among French writers, grows out of the contribution of Vidal de la Blache's (1917) possibilism to the development of regional studies and analyses of place. One aspect of Vidalian geography focused on the tensions between the influence humans exert on their environments and, reciprocally, the impacts their environments have on them. Berdoulay suggests (1989:126) that "the Vidalian thrust in geography is compatible with the current interest in place. It was very attentive to the environment as experienced by people. The concern for people's plans, worries, initiatives, and efforts gave this geography the highly humanistic overtones which have frequently been noted by non-French commentators" (such as Buttimer [1971], and Ley and Samuels [1978]).

In this sense, places not only feature in inhabitants' (and geographers') narratives, they are narratives in their own right: "a place comes explicitly into being in the discourse of its inhabitants, and particularly in the rhetoric it promotes. Thus the geographer's discourse uses the same ways as the people who define their own place" (Berdoulay 1989:135; see also Tuan 1991). Entrikin (1991:3) suggests that such discourse productively blends distinctions between place as an analytical concept, on the one hand, and as "situatedness" in a real world, on the other: "We understand the specificity of place from a point of view, and for this reason the student of place relies upon forms of analysis that lie between the centered [subjective, experiential] and decentered [objective, transcendent] view; such forms may be described as narrative-like syntheses." Entrikin's book, *The Betweenness of Place*, goes on to advocate a position interstitial to the two viewpoints, one that could suggest a resolution of their apparent contradiction for anthropologists as well:

> This divide between the existential and naturalistic conceptions of place appears to be an unbridgeable one, and one that is only made wider in adopting a decentered [objective] view. The closest that we can come to addressing both sides of this divide is from a point in between, a point that leads us into the vast realm of narrative forms. From this position we gain a view from both sides of the divide. We gain a sense both of

being "in a place" and "at a location," of being at the center and being at a point in a centerless world. To ignore either aspect of this dualism is to misunderstand the modern experience of place. [1991:134]

One problem here is the tendency to privilege verbal communication. Ironically, while this has been common in anthropology, it has been rare in geography until recently. Lack of attention to speech now troubles geographers interested in narrative. Tuan (1991:684) points to the neglect of speech as a "curious gap in the extensive and growing literature on place." He advocates an expansion of human geography to include speech and writing as integral to both place-making and geographic inquiry. One approach he favors "is cultural – the varying ways by which different societies use speech and/or the written word to realize place" (1991:695).[5] But places come into being through praxis, not just through narratives. One should also be wary of the assumption that the geographers' and the inhabitants' discourses will be consistent and that all inhabitants (and all geographers) will share similar views. The briefest glance at recent anthropological writing on ethnography and on rethinking culture would cast doubt on those assumptions. Entrikin, but not Tuan, seems well aware of recent work in this area.

The Marxist urban geographer David Harvey (1989) notes that time–space relations are fundamental to social relations, yet time has tended to receive much more attention than space.[6]

> The priority given to time over space is not in itself misplaced. Indeed, it mirrors the evolution of social practices in important ways. What is missing, however, is an appreciation of the practices that underlie the priority. Only in such a light can we understand those situations in which location, place, and spatiality reassert themselves as seemingly powerful and autonomous forces in human affairs. And such situations are legion. [1989:175]

Harvey quips that "the question of space is too important to be left exclusively to geographers."

New Approaches to Place in Anthropology

Despite considerable reappraisal of "voice" in anthropology, "place" has received surprisingly little attention and virtually no critical reassessment. There is little recognition that place is more than locale, the setting for action, the stage on which things happen. Anthropologists would do well to follow geographers' renewed interest (Agnew and Duncan 1989b:2) in reunifying *location* (i.e., the spatial distribution of socioeconomic activity such as trade networks), *sense of place* (or attachment to place), and *locale* (the setting in which a particular social activity occurs, such as a church) to yield a more rounded understanding of places as culturally and socially constructed in practice.

The idea, well established in geography, that places produce meaning and that meaning can be grounded in place, has yet to attract much theoretical interest in anthropology. Denise Lawrence and Setha Low's (1990) article in *Annual Reviews in*

Anthropology begins to redress this neglect, although their concern is with studies of the built environment rather than place more broadly. They and others involved in the Place and Space group have made important contributions to the anthropological study of place and space. This work deserves more critical theoretical attention.[7]

Place too often is subsumed as part of the problem of voice, so that geography becomes purely metaphorical. For example, Rosaldo speaks of *Miami Vice* TV episodes as places that are the "site of the implosion of the Third World into the First" (1988:85).

Alternatively, places have come to stand for particular problems in anthropology. Thus, for example, Melanesianists as "areal specialists" are likely to study adoption or the invention of tradition. Appadurai (1988a:16) defines this "problem of place" as "the problem of the culturally defined locations to which ethnographies refer." In his view, ethnographic places become metonyms for certain anthropological images and ideas. As an example, he traces the attachment of the idea of hierarchy to India. In urging anthropologists to contest such "topological stereotypes," Appadurai is in effect advocating a regional approach. The ideas that seem to represent the essence of certain places would be recognized, in this approach, as merely momentary localizations or coalescences of ideas from all over (Appadurai 1988b:46). Further, he encourages "the production and appreciation of ethnographies that emphasize the *diversity* of themes that can fruitfully be pursued in *any* place" (1988b:46, emphasis in original).

The "problem of place," as Appadurai defines it, is well addressed in a theme issue of *Cultural Anthropology* (1988). My complaint is that the "problem," as defined, misses one larger point. It is time to recognize that places, like voices, are local and multiple. For each inhabitant, a place has a unique reality, one in which meaning is shared with other people and places. The links in these chains of experienced places are forged of culture and history.

Recent writing, as evident in the *Cultural Anthropology* theme issue on place and voice, suffers from a failure to be critical of place as an anthropological concept. Place is at best seen purely as locale, and the "problem" is defined as if place were entirely an anthropological creation, a metonymic prison that incarcerates natives, in Appadurai's terms (1988b:37). In his view, such a prison is produced when certain images come to stand for particular areas. To be sure, there are dangers in reifying place (A. Strathern 1990:376). The hegemony of particular research topics, such as exchange, is as evident in Melanesian ethnography as in the Indian example of hierarchy that interests Appadurai. But it would be arrogant and naive to assume that places exist only as localizations of totalized anthropological voices. Anthropologists need to become more aware of Western bias and not assume that "place" means those places foreign ethnographers or metropolitan theory define.

Returning control over the meanings of place to the rightful producers requires reconsideration of questions of power and agency that implicate both anthropology and the people we study. It requires coming to terms with Entrikin's (1991) "betweenness of place" in anthropological contexts, as both subject and object. "What has to be cancelled," argues Marilyn Strathern (1988:94), "is the basis of the comparison" so that we, as Westerners, no longer privilege our own vantage point and peripheralize all other places. Rather than places becoming exemplars of *our* concepts, they should be seen as, to varying degrees, socially constructed products of *others*' interests (material as well as ideational) and as mnemonics of *others*' experiences. The contests and tensions between different actors and interests in the construction of space should be explored. We should consider what Munn (1990) has called "constructing regional worlds in experience."

Ironically, Munn's real interest in her stimulating article on regional worlds is in time more than space. She traces the incorporation of an episode from a *kula* transaction into the construction of events elsewhere in the region some six years later. She wants to understand how people become aware of and use past, distant events as horizons that can inform present action:

> My intent is to stress that for the subject a regional world is not given but lived, as Williams (1977:129) has put it, "in singular and developing forms" and created in the "living." Instead of considering the formation of a regional order through the structure and functioning of given social forms such as types of social organization, exchange or communication (see for example Werbner 1977; Smith 1976), I am concerned with its ongoing formation in certain experiential syntheses that actors create in practices, and the events that transpire in their terms. [Munn 1990:2]

Space is only a frame for the action in Munn's article. But at least it is a frame that is locally made. Place could be taken more seriously by broadening her approach. What if we look at places as well as actors and at the ongoing formation of experience that occurs in a particular place or network of places? In other words, instead of confining the analysis to the *actor's* view of a wider *social* milieu, as Munn does, let us consider how specific *places* implicate each other in a wider *geographical* milieu as well. Landscapes, too, can be "listening posts" to somewhere else (cf. Munn 1990).

Her "event history" is similar enough to the geographer Berdoulay's idea of the narrativity of place to suggest a synthesis of their approaches. Both are phenomeno-logical, culturally shaped constructions. For Munn, "the relations between events are developed in the practice of everyday life through infusing the experience of a given event with pasts (or possible pasts) and futures" (1990:13). As well, one could argue that regional relations between *lived spaces* are developed through infusing experience in one place with the evocation of other events and other places.

Rabinow's defense of anthropology as nominalism elaborates on the idea of "horizons" in a way that would have been useful to Munn's argument, had she considered it. The task of anthropology, as passed down from Kant to Foucault to Rabinow (1988:356), is to elucidate the language of social relations through which people create the world as they know it:

> As these worlds appear only from the horizon of the present, whose frontiers they form, they function as limits to who we are and what we can know, hope, do. These worlds, along with the structures of our reason, constitute the limits of our experience. For that reason, anthropology taken pragmatically occupies that place where humans learn to recognize their own culture as "l'école du monde,"...in which universality and par-ticularity are joined in a single relationship. [Rabinow 1988:356]

But how do we decenter this approach so that the "school of the world" is not dominated by *our* (Western) schools of thought and *our* worlds? How do we deal

with the problem of multivocality and with the differential power relations implicit
in such cultural constructions of place? Munn conveys no sense of contested,
competing views in the social construction of regional, lived space. How were
various actors' interpretations of Gawa events smoothed into the single narrative
she presents? Depending on the placement of the observer, the horizons of the
regional world could be quite different. Munn does not deal with this phenomenological problem of constructing a shared narrative from individually unique experiences. Nor does she deal with associated doubts that could be raised concerning the
future of comparison and generalization.[8]

The "true defining horizon" of our concepts of "otherness" and "difference," in
Edward Said's (1989:217) view, is the fact of empire. We can only understand the
world from within our culture, he argues, if we understand the imperial contest that
shaped and continues to shape it. Thus an anthropology grounded in place would
have to be historically as well as geographically constituted. Then, like Berdoulay's
grounded narratives and Munn's regional worlds, cultures may:

> be represented as zones of control or of abandonment, of recollection and of forgetting,
> of force or of dependence, of exclusiveness or of sharing, all taking place in the global
> history that is our element. Exile, immigration, and the crossing of boundaries are
> experiences that can therefore provide us with new narrative forms or, in John Berger's
> phrase, with *other* ways of telling. [Said 1989:225]

How do we restore agency to the people we study while remaining keenly aware
of their imperial historical (and contemporary) contexts? "Multi-locale ethnography" is George Marcus's term for one way to solve this problem. "The idea is
that any cultural identity or activity is constructed by multiple agents in varying
contexts, or places, and that ethnography must be strategically conceived to represent this sort of multiplicity and to specify both intended and unintended consequences in the network of complex connections within a system of places" (Marcus
1989:25; see also Marcus and Fischer 1986:94). The goal is to reconceptualize
regional ethnography in a way that eliminates distinctions between macro and
microlevels. Marcus wants to preserve the ethnographic concern with place but
push it further. He seeks "an ethnography that while it encompasses local conditions,
is aimed at representing system or pieces of system" (1989:25). This decentered
discourse has ethnographic locale at its heart. It is constrained by the limited notion
of place as nothing more than locale. It is also constrained by the notion of system,
which needs further definition in his article. Presumably, Marcus does not mean to
suggest that such local systems are self-contained or homogenous. But it is not clear
how he means to apply the idea of "system" to contemporary cultural analysis.

As for "locale," Giddens (1979:206) has developed the concept to link the individual to what Marcus might call "the system" through human agency, but Marcus
does not cite Giddens, so this seems not to be the usage he has in mind. By locale,
Giddens means "the physical settings of social activity as situated geographically"
(1990:18; see also 1984: ch. 3). The emptying of time integral to modernity, Giddens
argues, leads to a concomitant "emptying of space" or separation of space from
place. Localized activities dominated the shaping of space into place in what Giddens calls "traditional" or "premodern" societies. But distanciated relations predom-

inate in the world today and provide the basis for new spatial as well as temporal zones and boundaries:

> The advent of modernity increasingly tears space away from place by fostering relations between "absent" others, locationally distant from any given situation of face-to-face interaction. In conditions of modernity, place becomes increasingly *phantasmagoric*: that is to say, locales are thoroughly penetrated by and shaped in terms of social influence quite distant from them. [1990:18–19, emphasis in original]

Like geographers Entrikin and Berdoulay, anthropologists Marcus and Munn, and other scholars (notably Said) discussed so far, Giddens sketches an analytic framework that dissolves macro–micro oppositions. Multilocality, like multivocality, becomes a theme to be explored. For Giddens, place is "phantasmagoric" in that we experience it as a constantly shifting, complex succession of images. The extent to which space–time distanciation prevails varies, ironically, in space and time. In places such as Melanesia today, local identity defined by and expressed through place remains stronger than in much of the West. But place is still fragmented and multilocal in its construction to some degree. This is evident in the commodification of land, its use for cash cropping that relies on foreign markets, the use of such media as radio and newspapers to talk about land and national identity, the construction of an urban identity in terms of a place one no longer lives in, and so on.

The fragmentation of place in Melanesia is not nearly so startling as the postmodern landscapes, epitomized by Los Angeles, that fascinate postmodern geographers. Edward Relph, best known to anthropologists for his *Place and Placelessness* (1976), considers such landscapes in his recent work. Postmodern landscapes confuse and juxtapose times and places. Relph asks (1991:104), "[W]hat happens when the imagineered logic of Disneyworld becomes the logic of the rest of the world?" The resulting landscapes he calls "heterotopias." The term originated with Foucault (1970:xviii), who contrasted the imagined places of utopias, which directly reflect or invert "real" societies, with heterotopias, which are "a kind of effectively enacted utopia in which the real sites, all the other real sites that can be found within the culture, are simultaneously represented, contested, and inverted" (1986:24). Foucault's examples of heterotopias include cemeteries, museums, libraries, brothels, carnivals, and gardens. For Relph, heterotopias are not so orderly:

> Heterotopia is the geography that bears the stamp of our age and our thought – that is to say it is pluralistic, chaotic, designed in detail yet lacking universal foundations of principles, continually changing, linked by centreless flows of information; it is artificial and marked by deep social inequalities. [Relph 1991:104–105]

Foucault's (1980:24) first principle of "heterotopology" is that "there is probably not a single culture in the world that fails to constitute heterotopias," but by far the greatest impact of this notion has been in geographers' study of Western, urban, postmodern landscapes. As we shall see, anthropologists working in other places could use the concept productively.

Heterotopias are sites. Multilocality is a way of experiencing those and other places. Building on Giddens and Marcus, I see multilocality as having a number of dimensions. First, it assumes a decentered analysis, not in Entrikin's sense of "object-ive" analysis but in seeking to understand the construction of places from multiple, non-Western as well as Eurocentric viewpoints. Multilocality in this sense means looking at places from the viewpoint of Others, while recognizing that there really are no "others" in a world in which everyone can potentially suffer from one agent's actions (as, for example, in oil spills or nuclear accidents). As Gupta and Ferguson (1992:16) argue, anthropologists should be willing to question "the apparent 'given' of a world in the first place divided into 'ourselves' and 'others'."

Second, multilocality can refer to comparative or contingent analyses of place. Marcus advocates paying attention to this dimension. Some activities (e.g., markets, social movements) arise from the actions of multiple agents in different places and can only be understood by identifying "both intended and unintended consequences in the network or complex connections within a system of places" (Marcus 1989:25).

Third, multilocality can refer to reflexive relationships with places. An anthro-pologist, traveler, or anyone whose place has been transformed, for example, by a natural disaster or suburban development – in other words, anyone dislocated from his or her familiar place, or from the possibility of local identity – is keenly aware of contrasts between the known and the unfamiliar. In such situations, people often see a new landscape in terms of familiar ones. This is a multilocal way of sorting out meaning. Alternatively, as Basso (1988) has observed, strange landscapes can baffle and silence observers just as strange languages can.

Finally, a single physical landscape can be multilocal in the sense that it shapes and expresses polysemic meanings of place for different users. This is more accurately a multivocal dimension of place, but multilocality conveys the idea that a single place may be experienced quite differently.

All these dimensions of multilocality are predicated on connections, on the inter-acting presence of different places and different voices in various geographical, anthropological (cultural), and historical contexts. I agree with Fabian (1990:771) that our goal should be "to transform ethnography into a praxis capable of making the Other present (rather than making representations predicated on the Other's absence)." The way that Fabian proposes to do this is through a concern with performance and the writing of ethnography. But there are other ways. For our purposes, let me sketch the outlines, or "horizons," of a view toward empowering place as a critical concept in anthropology. Application to Melanesia of recent anthropological and geographical theorizing about place illustrates how place recip-rocally shapes individuals and society through human agency.

The first step is to recognize that space is socially constructed, and contested, in practice. The sociocultural construction of space has received considerable attention from Marxist urban geographers (e.g., Castells 1977; Gottdiener 1985; Harvey 1973, 1989). For many scholars, urban space has been of primary interest. In North America and Europe, the development of capitalism and the "local state" have been crucial in structuring space (e.g., Logan and Molotch 1987). Confron-tation between enterpreneurs concerned with exchange values and residents con-cerned with use values, such as quality of life, must focus on "the complex articulation between symbolic universes of meaning, capital accumulation and space" and are crucial for the analysis of urban development (Gottdiener 1985:155).

In my research on Toronto housing cooperatives with Matthew Cooper (Cooper and Rodman 1990, 1992; Rodman and Cooper 1989), we have shown that when exchange-value considerations are removed, as in nonprofit housing cooperatives, other social processes involved in the creation and manipulation of the use values of urban space come into sharper focus. By use values I mean such noncommodified dimensions of place as quiet enjoyment or feeling at home. Hypothetically, the same may be true of the social construction of space in Melanesia. There capitalism has less impact and use values remain of central importance to most rural islanders, although exchange-value considerations enter the picture through mining, forestry, tourism, and even cash cropping. Very little research has been conducted on the social construction of space outside of the urban centers of the capitalist world. Studying the social construction of place in Melanesia enriches our understanding of people for whom, individually and collectively, places remain integral to social life.

Empowering Place: Examples from Contemporary Melanesia

Margaret Jolly has addressed this issue ethnographically, pointing to the inseparability of place and people in Vanuatu identity.[9] She and I have each written about the powerful condensation of person and place in the concept of *man ples* (Jolly 1990:17; Rodman 1987:35–36). As she aptly remarks, "such imagery was not only crucial in reclaiming the land as inalienably attached to the people of the place, but proclaiming the people as necessarily in control of the place" (Jolly 1990:17). Giddens (1990:88) might consider this a form of re-embedding, an attempt to counter the space–time distanciation initiated through the colonial process. In Vanuatu, this was accomplished less by face-to-face contact than by a rhetorical emphasis on the rootedness of people in place, or autochthony.

Jolly notes the primordialism, or evocation of an original state in which people and place were one, that runs through Vanuatu constructions of place. This expression of connectedness between people and places creates what Giddens (1990:102) refers to as an "environment of trust" in kin relations, local communities, cosmology, and tradition, which is place-based. The strong assertion of the inalienability of land in Vanuatu no doubt responds to the extensive alienation of land for plantations in the colonial period, which only ended in 1980. It also harkens back to the insecurity of pre-pacification life (prior to about 1930). Warrior leaders might seize their followers' land, as well as that of their enemies, and hold it for a lifetime or longer. The connection between place and voice was direct. Followers who lacked the power to voice their objections also lacked the power to regain their land.

Jolly contrasts the meaning of place in contemporary Fiji and Vanuatu. Fijian "custom" is less fused with concepts of place – although it is called *vakavanua*, "the way of the land." Jolly argues that the British valued Fijian traditional culture and tried to blend it with colonial administrative practice. In Vanuatu, however, the British and French pursued a policy, albeit haphazard, of land alienation in which respect for traditional culture played little part. For the people of Vanuatu, independence became associated with regaining their land as well as their cultural past. As Jolly puts it, "*kastom* was expressly the reclaiming of a place, against European occupation of the land and the reclaiming of a past which had been lost or expressly abandoned" (1990:17).

[…]

Power

As Foucault (1980:70) suggests, it is time to stop devaluing space and begin "to trace the forms of implantation, delimitation, and demarcation of objects, the modes of tabulation, the organisation of domains [which means] the throwing into relief of processes – historical ones, needless to say – of power." Lamont Lindstrom applies a discursive model of knowledge and power to the analysis of Tannese society in southern Vanuatu. This is Foucault in the bush, a fine illustration of how Foucault's ideas play out incisively in a non-European context. And he adds a new dimension to Foucault, for on Tanna, in Lindstrom's view, power *is* localized (1990:22). He regards "geography," or place, as one of three Tannese "disciplines" that organize people's know-how. (The others are medicine and magic.) Power is crucial in the uneven distribution of all disciplinary knowledge. Inequality is such that men, especially older ones, are the most qualified to "talk seriously" and exercise power (1990:59). The verbal power so evident among adult men is, as Lindstrom recognizes, muted in women and in the young, who tend to be silenced where serious talk occurs and power is expressed.

Lindstrom's explanation of the intricacies of discursive power is impressively systematic and smart. It comes at a time in the history of anthropological thought when systematicity needs the kind of conceptual rehabilitation he provides. By this I mean that Lindstrom recognizes the complexity of social patterns while never assuming that culture is a bounded whole. He traces the links between dreams, land disputes, kava drinking, and quashing dissent in national politics. He persuasively shows how, in all these domains, "knowledge is made to be ordinary or ridiculous, truth or lies" (1990:173). His analytic framework would work as well for Ambae, where I conducted fieldwork, as it does for Tanna. In this sense it provides a framework for regional analysis of discursive practice. But to understand nondiscursive power one would have to go further, taking place more seriously than Lindstrom does.

Practical rather than discursive knowledge organizes much of social life in Vanuatu. Lindstrom recognizes this but sets aside serious consideration of it in order to focus on his topic. Nondiscursive knowledge is harder for anthropologists to get at, even though it is expressed right before our eyes. Lindstrom acknowledges that "[s]ignificant bases of power stand outside conversation per se: the physical structures of village house and forest clearing mutely organize island talk" (1990:175). Nevertheless, he privileges the verbal, which in Vanuatu means privileging the powerful, those who "know how" (and are allowed) to talk.

Multivocality

To hear the voices of those silenced in island conversations requires listening with all of one's senses. Multivocality often involves multilocality. Polysemic places bespeak people's practices, their history, their conflicts, their accomplishments. Narratives of places are not just told with words; they can be told and heard with senses other than speech and hearing.[10] Such narratives can be expressed through the sight of a rock that grew, through certain smells, in the way the wind blows, or the taste of a mango. The house in which my family and I lived in Vanuatu looked out on a large rock that had been brought to the village as a small stone. The village itself was named for a wind shift that touched the cheek of a culture hero who was passing through. On his journey, like many an explorer, he named the places he "discovered" and, by discovering, created. He transformed the physical landscape into a multi-local, social one.

In *Masters of Tradition* (1987), I discussed the grounding of identity in place evident in both a child's and an old man's tour of the area surrounding the village where we lived. The rootedness of identity is similar to processes Salmond describes for the Maori, for whom "specific knowledge is 'bound into' specific landmarks" (1982:84).[11] The narrative landmarks of the influential old man included black palms that had once been little stakes to which tusked pigs were tied when he first took rank in the graded society. He pointed out palisades surrounding his natal village, now abandoned, that had taken root and grown into trees that towered above the forest floor. Warfare and pig killing were reciprocally related; pig killing signaled and required peace. Both rank-taking ceremonies and raids were multilocal phenomena. A rank-taker could not kill primarily his own pigs but was dependent on the gifts of others, often people from distant villages and even other islands. Warfare, too, was a multilocal pattern of shifting alliances.

The landscapes of the ten-year-old boy described in my book identified places with names and owners. In part, I think this reflected the emphasis on food in a boy's landscape. A boy needed to know who owned which mango tree, for example, to know if he could eat freely of the fruit. Unlike girls, who stayed close to home, boys on Ambae ran freely through plantations, gardens, and forest. Except for those who had an opportunity to travel by plane or boat, a boy's sense of place was of one continuous territory with clearly defined centers, paths, and boundaries. Place, while regionally zoned, was not locally fragmented, as in our own lives. But it was multi-local in that there were many connected, named places within that territory, places that linked living people and dead ones with the child through landmarks.

The landmarks of women also speak. As I mapped the village, a grandmother told me about the birth sites of her children. One birth house had been over here, another time she had given birth in a menstruation hut over there, realizing she would not make it to the hospital eight miles away in time. Although I put an X on my map in the locations she pointed out, they were marked by nothing I could see in the landscape. Yet for the old woman these memories were etched as clearly in the landscape as if they bore commemorative plaques. Other memories had visible landmarks with special meanings for her. She thought of her daughters every time she harvested nuts or mandarins from trees they had planted. One of the mandarin trees shaded the smoothed ground where the first house she and her husband had shared once stood.

In the woman's, child's, and man's narratives of place that I have described, use values predominate. The exchange value of the land that means so much to them is negligible, except for the portion of the old man's land planted in coconuts. The child and the woman have no claims of ownership in any case, but only rights of use. These use rights, nevertheless, are a modicum of power.

The most powerless people have no place at all. Here, as elsewhere, the discursive and practical worlds intersect. A widowed woman from Santo island remained on Ambae island for eight years after her husband's death. She lived in a house on land set aside for the Anglican church. She was allowed to use a garden belonging to her husband's kin, but she felt she lived on the sufferance of others. As Lindstrom (1990) might have predicted, she expressed her insecurity about having no place that was really her own by saying how afraid she was of talk: "If I weren't careful people would talk about me. They would say, 'Where's her place?'" (Rodman 1987:40). On my last visit to Ambae, she was dead and her bamboo home was gone. The house site had reverted to communal use. It had become the village volleyball court.

[...]

Social landscapes

A focus on place, like Marcus's multi-locale ethnographies, can eliminate the micro–macro distinction, for region and village are points on a sliding scale. Both are "social landscapes," albeit seen in different degrees of detail. The concept of a lived space is phenomenological, emphasizing individuals' experience in the world. But a "social landscape" takes a broader view of time and space. The concept is not new in Melanesian ethnography (cf. Leenhardt 1979[1947]). As developed by Pacific archaeologist Chris Gosden (1989), it links the archaeological record to the ways that social groups interact with landscapes that are partly structured by previous social groups. The social landscape is both context and content enacted and material. It is the lived world in physical form. It can be radically emic – the social landscape indigenous people (collectively or individually) define through particular experiences or interests. Or it can be an analyst's map, marking "differences that make a difference," in Bateson's (1972:453) sense, and depicting the archaeologist's classification or understanding of the local people's categories.

Miriam Kahn (1990) provides recent examples of the "spatial anchoring of myth" in what might well be viewed as social landscapes in Papua New Guinea.[12] She observes that places in the landscape, notably stones, are linked to mythical stories, often about traveling culture heroes or ancestors. "Melanesian ideas about the passage of time are conceived of in a spatial framework" (1990:61). Consequently, she argues, anthropologists should be careful not to give too much weight to verbal (discursive) communication; they should be more aware of the ways "myths are recorded and recalled by other devices, such as physical forms in the landscape. Stones, while not the only type of physical marker, provide pertinent and interesting examples of the Melanesian attachment to place and the recording of myth and history in terms of space" (Kahn 1990:53).

Through greater awareness of the social construction of meaning in the landscape, we can begin to understand the experience of places that live in ways different from our own. Kahn asserts that "each village uses local landscape to make the myth its own" (1990:59). Each village, in this sense, creates its own social landscape, as does each person. But each community, or each individual, is also part of a chain of attachment to places. "Geographic copyright" (Lindstrom 1990:78) is the authority to speak in public about names and places. It would seem to apply as well to the Papua New Guinean situation of which Kahn writes as to Tanna. Men can silence the less knowledgeable or those who might be said to be out of place in speaking about what is not theirs. So when Kahn comments that Melanesians discredited each others' versions of a myth or discovered kin connections to each other through the fact that they told her identical details of a myth, she is speaking implicitly of this kind of "copyright." Each teller and each mythically charged stone is part of a social landscape whose horizons overlap other social landscapes. Individuals are most strongly attached to particular named places, and can speak of those places (and their pasts) with the most authority. But the story and its larger landscape binds them to other experts and other places.

Conclusion

The themes of power, multivocality, multilocality, narrativity, and social landscape are interwined in a final example. The dynamic, socially constructed qualities of place in Ambae are especially evident at the boundaries expressed in funerary feasts. These feasts are heterotopias in Foucault's (1986) sense. They mark and contest boundaries between the living and the dead, between places, and between the conflicting interests of different people.

When a person dies, he or she does not go far from the land of the living for one hundred days. The dead person's spirit hovers near the tops of fruit trees or coconut palms, waiting and watching as kinsmen exchange gifts below. The dead person is still strongly attached to his or her place. Gift exchanges and feasting occur after every death, but the scale of the activity varies. The biggest and most contested ceremonies are those following the death of a major landholder. Landholders are almost always male.

Multilocality comes into play in understanding funerals at several levels. First, it is important to realize that the stakes have changed during the past half-century as plantation land has become commoditized. Elsewhere (Rodman 1987), I have described the multilocal "chain of copra" that linked the beaches of the colonial New Hebrides with oil-processing mills in Marseilles. Second, the use value of land for subsistence gardening and housing competed with the exchange value of the same land for growing coconuts that could be dried and sold as copra. If a person had access to multiple locales, he or she could earn some money from copra while still keeping a garden. Third, the funerary ceremonials dislocate dead individuals from the places that were integral to their identities as persons and, in establishing new ownership, shape new identities. In this sense, multilocality is the goal of the exchanges and feasts.

When a landholder dies, funerary feasts held every five days are competitive arenas in which each gift can help build a claim to the dead person's land. Knowledge about the history of the land's connection to people, living and dead, is displayed in competing men's verbal power plays and assertions of what Lindstrom calls "geographic copyright." The social landscape is in flux during the transition between one person's control of a large parcel of land and the new order that follows the feast on the hundredth day after a death. Multivocality is evident in the flow of competing gifts as some relatives use a rhetoric of "helping" to undercut each others' claims or give huge gifts to shame those who cannot reciprocate. It is evident, too, in the silences, in the women and less powerful men who would say they "cannot speak" to oppose an influential man who tries to take control of their dead relative's land through funerary gifts.

At the end of a hundred days, members of a dead person's matriline give a final gift that detaches the deceased from his or her place. With this gift, the dead person leaves the treetops and departs from the world of humans. (In the past, the spirit would have jumped off a cliff into the sea and ended up in the crater lake at the top of the island. Now, many feel, the spirit goes to heaven.) As this detachment of the person's identity from his or her place occurs, a new social landscape is affirmed, for these gifts also ensure that fertility will return to the dead person's trees. Death is turned to life in a living place as life moves on, away from the trees, to the place of death.

In this article, I have suggested that place should be taken more seriously. Although the problem of voice has received considerable attention, related problems of place have too often been reduced to questions of setting. We must acknowledge and try to understand the complex reality of the places in which we do fieldwork. But in empowering place conceptually, it must not be exoticized or miconstrued as the essence or totality of other cultures. Place must not become, for example, a metonym for Melanesia. The socially contested, dynamic construction of places represent the temporary grounding of ideas. These are often overlapping narratives of place, as the examples drawn from a man, woman, and child's landscapes illustrate. They can be competing narratives, as in the example of funerary feasts. We need to consider how different actors construct, contest, and ground experience in place.

Rather than being "incarcerated" (Appadurai 1988b) in ethnographic places anthropologists define, the people we study are constructing their own places. These places are not simply settings for social action, nor are they mere reflections of society. I have tried to show that Melanesian places can be as rich and polyphonous an expression as their voices. By joining multilocality to multivocality, we can look "through" these places, explore their links with others, consider why they are constructed as they are, see how places represent people, and begin to understand how people embody places.

NOTES

Acknowledgments. Portions of an earlier version of this paper were presented at a workshop called "Not in Isolation: Regional Studies in Melanesian Anthropology," organized by John Terrell and Rob Welsch. The workshop, held April 3–5, 1991, at Field Museum of Natural History, was sponsored by the museum and by the Wenner-Gren Foundation for Anthropological Research. I am grateful to the sponsoring institutions, as well as to the Social Sciences and Humanities Research Council of Canada, which supported my research in Vanuatu in 1978, 1982, and 1985. The ethnographic material on funerals was part of a paper I gave at the 1991 annual meeting of the American Anthropological Association in an American Ethnological Society invited session organized by Setha Low. I am especially grateful to her and to William Rodman for their detailed suggestions and sustained support. I also appreciate the helpful comments made by anonymous reviewers, by Matthew Cooper, James Fernandez, Michael Lambek, and Edward Relph, and by participants in the Wenner-Gren workshop.

1   Although place generally has played a passive role in ethnography, some have taken its interaction with social life seriously from the earliest days of anthropology. Durkheim, Mauss, and Morgan all addressed the interplay between the built environment and society. For a discussion of early theories of accommodation and adaptation of people and places to each other, see Lawrence and Low (1990:456–457).

2   A notable exception is Ferguson and Gupta's (1992) theme issue of *Cultural Anthropology*, entitled "Space, Identity, and the Politics of Difference," which appeared as this article was in preparation.

3   See, for example, the papers in Agnew and Duncan (1989a), and in Buttimer and Seamon (1980).

4   The problem social analysts face of being part of the phenomena they study is at issue here. See Giddens's (1990:45 and earlier publications) comments on the reflexivity of knowledge and the double hermeneutic of modern social life.

5   Harris (1991) also notes the increasing importance of cultural context as historical geography becomes more interdisciplinary. Relph (1991:102) makes a similar observation regarding postmodern geography.

6   This view is shared with Soja (1989:11), who calls for spatializing the narrative of historical explanations integral to Marxist geography.

7   The Place and Space group meets at each American Anthropological Association annual meeting and keeps members informed of planned place-related sessions and meetings via a newsletter.

8   Marilyn Strathern (1988, 1991) has contributed a great deal to rethinking comparison through her concern with polyphony; see also Holy (1987) for a defense of the comparative method.

9   This section in no way seeks to deal comprehensively with literature from Melanesia about place. Were I to do so, Malinowski's (1922) "mythic landscapes" and Leenhardt's (1979[1947]) observations about space, social landscape, and personhood would be cornerstones of such a review. Instead, this section deals with a few, selected recent examples, mostly from Vanuatu, to apply the theoretical points made so far.

Place has also figured prominently in the work of the French geographer Joel Bonnemaison (1986), in Vanuatu. Other anthropologists who have written about place in Vanuatu include Larcom (1982), Rubinstein (1978), and Tonkinson (1982).

10 For a recent example of anthropology that acknowledges the importance of senses other than the auditory and verbal see Howes (1991).

11 Salmond (1982) compares the Maori embeddedness of knowledge and place with Western "theoretical landscapes," in which knowledge is represented metaphorically as if it were a territory.

12 Myths of rootedness are common in Melanesia. For another recent example of the persisting power of such myths see Gewertz and Errington's (1991:33–38) discussion of the mythic charter for construction of a Chambri men's house as, literally, a tourist "attraction."

REFERENCES

Agnew, John A., and James S. Duncan, eds.
  1989a   The Power of Place. London: Unwin Hyman.
  1989b   Introduction. *In* The Power of Place. John A. Agnew and James S. Duncan, eds. Pp. 1–8. London: Unwin Hyman.

Appadurai, Arjun
    1988a   Introduction: Place and Voice in Anthropological Theory. Cultural Anthropology
        3:16–20.
    1988b   Putting Hierarchy in Its Place. Cultural Anthropology 3:36–49.
Basso, Keith
    1988   "Speaking with Names": Language and Landscape among the Western Apache.
        Cultural Anthropology 3:99–130.
Bateson, Gregory
    1972   Steps to an Ecology of Mind. New York: Ballantine.
Berdoulay, Vincent
    1989   Place, Meaning, and Discourse in French Language Geography. In The Power of
        Place. John A. Agnew and James S. Duncan, eds. Pp. 124–139. London: Unwin Hyman.
Bonnemaison, Joel
    1986   La Dernière Ile. Paris: Arlea-ORSTOM.
Brookfield, Harold C., with Doreen Hart
    1971   Melanesia: A Geographical Interpretation of an Island World. London: Methuen.
Buttimer, Anne
    1971   Society and Milieu in the French Geographic Tradition. AAG Monographs, Vol. 6.
        Chicago: Rand McNally.
Buttimer, Anne, and David Seamon, eds.
    1980   The Human Experience of Space and Place. London: Croom Helm.
Castells, M.
    1977   The Urban Question. London: Edward Arnold.
Claval, P.
    1984   The Concept of Social Space and the Nature of Social Geography. New Zealand
        Geographer 40:105–109.
Cooper, M., and M. Rodman
    1990   Conflict over Use Values in a Toronto Housing Cooperative. City and Society
        4:44–57.
    1992   New Neighbours: A Case Study of Cooperative Housing in Toronto: University of
        Toronto Press.
Cultural Anthropology
    1988   Theme Issue: Place and Voice in Anthropological Theory. 3(1).
Entrikin, J. Nicholas
    1989   Place, Region and Modernity. In The Power of Place. John A. Agnew and James S.
        Duncan, eds. Pp. 30–43. Winchester, MA: Unwin Hyman.
    1991   The Betweenness of Place: Toward a Geography of Modernity. Baltimore, MD:
        Johns Hopkins University Press.
Fabian, Johannes
    1990   Presence and Representation: The Other in Anthropological Writing. Critical
        Inquiry 16:753–772.
Fardon, Richard
    1990   General Introduction. In Localizing Strategies: Regional Traditions of Ethnographic
        Writing. R. Fardon, ed. Pp. 1–35. Washington, DC: Smithsonian Institution Press.
Ferguson, James, and Akhil Gupta, eds.
    1992   Theme Issue: Space, Identity, and the Politics of Difference. Cultural Anthropology
        7(1).
Fernandez, James W.
    1988   Andalusia on Our Minds. Cultural Anthropology 3:21–35.
Foucault, Michel
    1970   The Order of Things. New York: Random House.

1980　Power Knowledge. Brighton: Harvester.

1986　Of Other Spaces. Diacritics 16(1):22–27.

Geertz, Clifford

1973　The Interpretation of Cultures. New York: Basic Books.

Gewertz, Deborah, and Frederick Errington

1991　Twisted Histories: Representing the Chambri in a World System. Cambridge: Cambridge University Press.

Giddens, Anthony

1979　Central Problems in Social Theory: Action, Structure and Contradictions in Social Analysis. Berkeley: University of California Press.

1984　The Constitution of Society. Berkeley: University of California Press.

1990　The Consequences of Modernity. Stanford, CA: Stanford University Press.

Gosden, Chris

1989　Prehistoric Social Landscapes of the Arawe Islands, West New Britain Province, Papua New Guinea. Archaeology in Oceania 24:45–58.

Gottdiener, M.

1985　The Social Production of Urban Space. Austin: University of Texas Press.

Gupta, Akhil, and James Ferguson

1992　Beyond "Culture": Space, Identity, and the Politics of Difference. Cultural Anthropology 7:6–23.

Harris, Cole

1991　Power, Modernity and Historical Geography. Annals of the Association of American Geographers 81(4):671–683.

Harvey, David

1973　Social Justice and the City. London: Edward Arnold.

1989　The Urban Experience. Baltimore, MD: Johns Hopkins University Press.

Holy, Ladislav, ed.

1987　Comparative Anthropology. Oxford: Basil Blackwell.

Howes, David, ed.

1991　The Varieties of Sensory Experience. Toronto: University of Toronto Press.

Jolly, Margaret

1990　Custom and the Way of the Land: The Politics of Tradition in Vanuatu and Fiji. Paper presented at the annual meeting of the Association for Social Anthropology in Oceania, Kauai, Hawaii.

Kahn, Miriam

1990　Stone-Faced Ancestors: The Spatial Anchoring of Myth in Wamira, Papua New Guinea. Ethnology 29:51–66.

Larcom, Joan

1982　The Invention of Convention. Mankind 13(4):330–337.

Lawrence, Denise, and Setha Low

1990　The Built Environment and Spatial Form. Annual Reviews in Anthropology 19:453–505.

Leenhardt, Maurice

1979[1947]　Do Kamo: Person and Myth in the Melanesian World. B. M. Gulati, trans. Chicago: University of Chicago Press.

Ley, David, and M. Samuels, eds.

1978　Humanistic Geography. Chicago: Maaroufa Press.

Lindstrom, Lamont

1990　Knowledge and Power in a South Pacific Society. Washington, DC: Smithsonian Institution Press.

Logan, J., and H. Molotch
    1987   Urban Fortunes: The Political Economy of Place. Berkeley: University of California
       Press.
Malinowski, Bronislaw
    1922   Argonauts of the Western Pacific. London: Routledge and Kegan Paul.
Marcus, George
    1989   Imagining the Whole: Ethnography's Contemporary Efforts to Situate Itself. Cri-
       tique of Anthropology 9(3):7–30.
Marcus, George, and Michael Fischer
    1986   Anthropology as Cultural Critique. Chicago: University of Chicago Press.
Munn, Nancy
    1990   Constructing Regional Worlds in Experience: Kula Exchange, Witchcraft and
       Gawan Local Events. Man (N.S.) 25:1–17.
Nir, Dov
    1990   Region as a Socio-environmental System: An Introduction to a Systemic Regional
       Geography. Geojournal Library Series, Vol. 16. Wolf Tietze, ed. Boston: Kluwer Aca-
       demic Publishers.
Rabinow, Paul
    1988   Beyond Ethnography: Anthropology as Nominalism. Cultural Anthropology 3:255–
       364.
Relph, Edward
    1976   Place and Placelessness. London: Pion.
    1991   Post-Modern Geography. Canadian Geographer 35(1):98–105.
Rodman, Margaret C.
    1987   Masters of Tradition: Consequences of Customary Land Tenure in Longana, Vanu-
       atu. Vancouver: University of British Columbia Press.
Rodman, M., and M. Cooper
    1989   The Sociocultural Production of Urban Space: Building a Fully Accessible Toronto
       Housing Cooperative. City and Society 3:9–22.
Rosaldo, Renato
    1988   Ideology, Place and People without Culture. Cultural Anthropology 3:77–87.
Rubinstein, Robert
    1978   Placing the Self on Malo: An Account of the Culture of Malo Island, New Hebrides.
       Ph.D. dissertation, Department of Anthropology, Bryn Mawr.
Said, Edward W.
    1989   Representing the Colonized: Anthropology's Interlocutors. Critical Inquiry
       15:205–225.
Salmond, Anne
    1982   Theoretical Landscapes: On a Cross-Cultural Conception of Knowledge. In Seman-
       tic Anthropology. David Parkin, ed. Pp. 65–87. London: Academic Press.
Smith, Carol A., ed.
    1976   Regional Analysis, Vol. 2: Social Systems. New York: Academic Press.
Soja, Edward
    1989   Postmodern Geographies: The Reassertion of Space in Critical Social Theory.
       London: Verso Press.
Strathern, Andrew
    1990   Review of The Evolution of Papua New Guinea Societies, by D. K. Feil. American
       Ethnologist 17:376–383.
Strathern, Marilyn
    1988   Commentary: Concrete Typographies. Cultural Anthropology 3:88–96.

1991   Partial Connections. ASAO Special Publications, No. 3. Deborah Gewertz, ed. Lanham, MD: University Press of America.
Tonkinson, Robert
1982   National Identity and the Problem of *Kastom* in Vanuatu. Mankind 13(4):306–315.
Tuan, Yi-Fu
1991   Language and the Making of Place: A Narrative-Descriptive Approach. Annals of the Association of American Geographers 81(4):684–696.
Werbner, R. P., ed.
1977   Regional Cults. New York: Academic Press.
Williams, Raymond
1977   Marxism and Literature. Oxford: Oxford University Press.

10

Open Spaces and Dwelling Places: Being at Home on Hill Farms in the Scottish Borders

John Gray

In a previous article (Gray 1996a), I portrayed hill sheep farms in the Scottish Borders as interpositional "places," "nowhens" consisting of "an instantaneous configuration of positions" (de Certeau 1984:94, 117). I did so by looking at them from afar (by reading my field notes and interrogating my memory), by seeing the whole (European Community) of which they are a part, and by locating them in a simultaneous system of dual constraint. These constraints consist of the natural characteristics of hardy sheep, the marginal land on which they live, and those agricultural programs of the United Kingdom and the European Community Common Agricultural Policy that affect hill sheep farming. In that article, I tended toward voyeurism, taking pleasure in constructing a spectacle of institutions and relations impinging upon the lives of hill sheep farming people while bracketing the sensuous activities through which they transformed the farm spaces (spaces of my own analytical description) into farm places (places of their everyday lifeworlds).[1] In this article, I redress this by describing the work of hill shepherding *in* the Scottish Borders as one of the primary ways of "place-making" (Basso 1996:5–8; Gupta and Ferguson 1997:4, 6–12). I consider the ways in which shepherds encounter the hills, perceive them, and invest them with significance (Feld and Basso 1996:8–9). And, I consider identity making as a cultural process through which, in creating places in the hills and forming attachments to them, people also implicate a historicized image of themselves as people *of* the Scottish Borders (cf. Basso 1996:6–7).

In exploring the difference between "place" and "space,"[2] de Certeau descends from the 110th floor of New York's World Trade Center into the streets where he follows the footsteps of the wandering people who use the city. "Neither author nor spectator" (de Certeau 1984:93), a pedestrian appropriates the city kinesthetically through practices that resist the normative meanings of the anonymous subjects presumed by cartographers and city planners. In this sense, "space is a practiced place" (de Certeau 1984:117) where historically and culturally situated people create a locality of familiar *heres* and *theres* in the same way that speakers act out language systems in the creation of vernacular meanings. It was de Certeau's image of this constitutive *walking* in the city that captured my imagination and suggested a way of understanding hill shepherding and the lived spatiality of hill sheep farms in the Scottish Borders. For hill sheep farmers and shepherds, walking (and more recently motorbiking)[3] around the hills is the most important activity for ensuring the welfare of sheep and the successful breeding of lambs for sale on the European agricultural market. Yet raising sheep is more than merely an economically motivated activity. The hills are not just spaces for work. For most of the year, shepherds are in the hills every day for several hours on treks that cover ten to twelve miles. One shepherd, Jim, expressed what I came to understand as the special, sensual, and intimate attachment people feel toward the hills in which they spend so much time – a feeling of being in their proper place, a feeling I try to capture with the phrase "being at home in the hills":

> You know, while walking around these hills shepherding, you could die of a heart attack and no one would be able to find you very easily. . . . It tells you of the isolation of the hills and shepherding. . . . It's scary for certain folk [people from towns] but not to me. But in the same way, I'm uncomfortable in Hawick [one of the larger Border towns] with the traffic and people. If someone didn't look out for me, I could easily be hit by a car in the traffic. I wonder about city folk who decide to give up living in the city and move to the country because they are out of place.

Being at home in the desolate hills of Border sheep farms is the mark not only of those who live and work on them; it is also a dimension of the identity and distinctiveness of the Scottish borderlands. As I describe below, an important historical dimension of Borderers' identity is the 14th- to 16th-century border *reivers*. Reiving refers to acts of robbery, raiding, marauding, and plundering that became pervasive during the three centuries of intermittent warfare between England and Scotland. Local land-owning *lairds* on both sides of the Border recruited raiding parties of 12 to 50 (sometimes nearly 300) men from among their kin and feudal dependents for purposes of armed robbery, arson, kidnapping, blackmail, and occasionally murder against the enemy over the Border as well as against the lord's neighbors.[. . .]

The theme I develop in this article is that going around the hills and being at home in them has a triple significance for hill sheep farming people. It is a practice distinctive of hill farming in the Borders; its meanings permeate hill sheep farming and its way of life; and by associating their contemporary work places in the hills to the exploits of reivers, hill sheep farming people become part of a wider Borders regional identity.

Place Making

"The ethnography of locality," in Cohen's terms, is "an account of how people experience and express their difference from others" and "the ways in which people express their attachment to a locality" (1982:2–3). Yet in analyzing the relationships that contribute to this sense of belonging to a locality or community, Cohen focuses almost exclusively on the social relations between people and groups that make up the local population. Locality and place tend to be treated as passive settings for relational matrix among people (see Rodman 1992:640–641, 643). There is little attention paid to the "sense of place" of these social relations (see Mewett 1982). In recent years, a growing number of ethnographers and geographers interested in the processes of place making have addressed this oversight by examining how people create places, from attachments to them, and, simultaneously, define the self (see Basso 1996; Bender 1993; Duncan 1990; Feld and Basso 1996; Gupta and Ferguson 1997; Hirsch and O'Hanlon 1995; Myers 1986; Rodman 1992; Weiner 1991).

In drawing inspiration from de Certeau, I wish to emphasize his analogy between walking and language since this analogy provides the basis for my own critical position in analyzing place making in the Scottish borderlands. Walking is similar to speaking (*la parole*) not to the language system (*la langue*) in that pedestrians "reappropriate" the city of the cartographers and planners to their own interests and rules (de Certeau 1984:xiii–xiv). The ensemble of city "places" that are constituted by the improvised bodily movements of pedestrians using the streets are distinguished from the static and structured text of cartographic "spaces" that are inscribed and read from a distance with a totalizing eye.[4] Like a language system, a city has a systemic grid of named spaces that are prior to pedestrian use but "these names make themselves available to the diverse meanings given them by passers-by" (de Certeau 1984:104). The import of de Certeau's approach is that understanding the city of pedestrians involves interpreting the process of walking as building meaningful "places" rather than inscribing the paths of pedestrians onto a map and analyzing or reading the resulting cityscape or text of spaces where pedestrians have passed:

> It is true that the operations of walking on can be traced on city maps in such a way as to transcribe their paths (here well-trodden, there very faint) and their trajectories (going this way and not that). But these thick or thin curves only refer, like words, to the absence of what has passed by. Surveys of routes miss what was: the act itself of passing by. The operation of walking, wandering, or "window shopping," that is, the activity of passers-by, is transformed into points that draw a totalizing and reversible line on the map. They allow us to grasp only a relic set in the nowhen of a surface of projection. Itself visible, it has the effect of making invisible the operation that made it possible. . . . The trace left behind is substituted for the practice. It exhibits the (voracious) property that the geographical system has of being able to transform action into legibility, but in doing so it causes the way of being in the world to be forgotten. [de Certeau 1984:97]

I wish to raise two issues in relation to place making. The first concerns the way places are conceived. De Certeau points to two possibilities. The first is the distancing and totalizing perspective of the cartographer, urban planner, and, may I suggest, also a number of ethnographers (see Hirsch and O'Hanlon 1995) who use a landscape perspective to frame the issue of place, place making, and sense of place. For example, Cosgrove notes that "landscape is not merely the world we see, it is a construction, a composition of that world" (Cosgrove 1984:13), and Relph suggests that "landscapes cannot be embraced, nor touched, *nor walked around*. As we move so the landscape moves, always there, in sight but out of reach" (1985:23, emphasis added).[5] Like de Certeau's cartographer and urban planner looking down from the

World Trade Center, adopting a landscape perspective on place making distances both inhabitants and ethnographers from place(s) so that the totality can be seen and analyzed.[6]

Landscape perspectives tend to treat localities as "an ordered system of objects, a text" (Duncan 1990:17) whose positioning of places and their meanings has already been inscribed upon the landscape by people's actions. The ethnographer composes the landscape into a text or describes how the inhabitants compose it (Hirsch 1995:1). The ethnographer then reads the meanings embedded or concretized in the text. Basso uses this landscape perspective throughout his analyses of Cibecue Apache place making. His book is punctuated by composed photographs of named sites that attempt to replicate the landscapes portrayed by the place names he analyzes in his text (see also Bloch 1995; Layton 1995). Basso illustrates how descriptive Apache place names provide "crisp mental pictures" of geographical sites (Basso 1996:61) so that Apaches can imagine looking at the site from a particular spatial perspective. Place making among the Apache, furthermore, involves treating these places as texts as people read morally instructive stories into the sites. These stories relate events that occurred on the sites in the distant past. As a result, "the Apache landscape is full of named locations" that function as a "repository of distilled wisdom" (1996:62–63).

In a similar manner, Dominy studies the toponymic systems of high country pastoralists in New Zealand. She uses maps and structured tables of place names to give a distanced and composed view of the locality. In her analysis, these maps become composed texts of places, and she reads the pattern of place names for their inscription of the pastoralists' "perception of the physical and constructed features" and "a history of events and ownership into the landscape" (1995:26–27). The strength of analyses based upon a landscape perspective is the way they demonstrate how places viewed or imagined *at a distance* have "reflexive and contemplative qualities" (Feld 1996:114). These qualities provide the basis for the well-recognized way places act as means of shaping conceptions and producing experiences of self and identity (Basso 1966; Feld and Basso 1996; Gupta and Ferguson 1997:12–17).

De Certeau eschews this landscape perspective in preference for one that privileges the practices through which those who *use* spaces make them into meaningful places. This is the approach I adopt for the ensuing analysis. My narrative follows shepherds as they walk or bike through the hills, creating places imbued with their personal experiences, memories of shepherding, and thoughts of reivers' exploits. This is a close view of the hills, one that does not include the total area covered by shepherds in their treks. It is also a sensual view in which knowledge of the hills is gained through lived experience. In this respect, Jackson also recognizes this sensual dimension of place making, "meaning is not invariably given to activity by the conscious [reflexive] mind or in explicit verbal formulations. Meaning should not be reduced to that which can be thought or said, since meaning may exist simply in the doing and in what is manifestly accomplished by an action" (1996:32).

This brings up the second issue, which concerns the kind of activity that de Certeau identifies as crucial to place making. In contrast with Berdoulay, who suggests that "place comes explicitly into being in the discourse of its inhabitants" (1989:135), de Certeau focuses on nonverbal practices of walking.[7] Rodman criticizes the emphasis on verbal practices in landscape studies as resulting in a metonymic conflation in which one kind of practice stands for the totality of place making. As Rodman notes, "Places come into being through praxis, not just through narratives" (1992:642). I concur with Rodman, and, furthermore, found the situation in the hills similar to that described by de Certeau. Like his city, there are British Government Ordnance Survey maps of farms that textualize pre-existing topographic and toponymic systems so that the place-making activity of going around the hill does not involve the acts of place naming that others have highlighted (Basso 1996; Dominy 1995; Feld 1996). Instead, the place names on the maps of the hills are "opaque" (Stuart-Murray 1995:30–31) in the sense that the semantic meaning of a name does not determine the meaning of a locale. Meanings are open, established by shepherds in the act of going around the hill. My aim in this article, then, is to analyze how, in going around the hill, shepherds make a variety of places to which they become attached as a matter of their identity as hill sheep people and Borderers. I begin with the hills themselves as the situational contexts for this activity, and I adopt the spatial terminology prevalent among geographers and anthropologists concerned with place making (for example, Casey 1996; Pickles 1985; Relph 1985; Thomas 1993; Tilley 1994). In this terminology, space is a situational context constructed by and for human action, and places are "centers of...human significance and emotional attachment" (Tilley 1994:15). In the following section, I analyze the hills as spaces of human activity partially created by capitalist relations of European agricultural production – in which the hills are integral as the natural resource of hill sheep farms and as a locality of the Border region.

Open Spaces: A Political Economy of Meaning

Teviothead consists of between 150 and 200 residents living in 15 farms and nearly 30 cottages that straddle the 18 kilometer stretch of the River Teviot from its source to the mill town of Hawick. The farms in Teviothead range in size from 160 to over 2,000 hectares, with flocks from 450 to 2,000 breeding ewes. The principal farming activities are breeding sheep and selling lambs for food in the United Kingdom and the European Community.[8]

The agricultural space comprising these farms consists of hilly terrain reaching 600 meters at the river's watershed. The hills gradually decrease in height and density as the river valley widens in a northwesterly course toward the town of Hawick. Hill sheep farmers divide the land into two categories in terms of their physical characteristics: weather, topography, soils, and vegetation. Outbye (rough grazing or hill ground) lies at altitudes in excess of 300 meters, where temperature decreases and wind increases. Outbye has a complex topography of steep hills, valleys, streams, knolls, gorges, and ravines. Its vegetation is poor because the predominantly boggy soil retards the natural breakdown of organic matter into nutrients for plant growth. Outbye land is suitable for grazing only for the hardy, purebred hill sheep.[9] The purebred lambs are too small to be sold directly for slaughter. Preparing them for sale requires extended on-farm supplementary feeding or sale to lowland farms for fattening and eventual resale on the fat market. Inbye (park) is areas of lower altitude and flatter land that are ploughable. Inbye soils are fertilized to grow a high-quality grass. Inbye land is used for rearing less hardy but larger crossbred ewes whose lambs are generally sold directly on the fat market for slaughter. Inbye is also used to grow fodder such as barley, silage, and turnips. All farms in the valley contain both types of land. [...]

While farmers describe the land in terms of its physical characteristics, inbye and outbye ground are not neutral geometric spaces within and upon which the practices of shepherding occur. Rather they are distinct geographical spaces organized through the sale of lambs they nourish, by differential relations to the capitalist market for agricultural commodities, and according to the policies of the European Community that regulate that market.[10] Tilley suggests that the space created by capitalist-motivated action is above all governed by principles of utility and rationality (Tilley 1994:21). The control of such space is associated with the disciplinary aims of institutions. Similarly, Relph identifies "the paradox of modern [capitalist] landscapes" (1981:104) as dehumanized and, by implication, impoverished of meaning, precisely because humans have excessively shaped and planned them in terms of economic efficiency. While inbye and outbye lands are both integrated into the capitalist market, their integration differs by degree. They thus have different potentials as spaces in which to feel at home.

According to the categorization of agricultural land adopted by the United Kingdom Department of Agriculture and the European Community Common Agricultural Policy, Teviothead is considered a Less Favoured Area because of the region's high proportion of outbye land. [...] Farms in Less Favoured Areas are eligible for special subsidies and grants from the government of the United Kingdom and the European Community. [...]

In Tilley's and Relph's terms, inbye land, with its tendency to flat open space, is more amenable to rational and useful control than outbye land. Inbye land has greater capacity to be humanized in service of more efficient capitalist production. [...] Compared with outbye, inbye land has been subjected to more human intervention and control. This can be seen in the flatness of the fields, the monoculture of the grasses and crops planted, and the straight lines of drains and fencing. The other effect is on the sheep. Park lambs are bred on fenced, easily accessible inbye ground where they are subject to greater surveillance and control. Moreover, because of their crossbreeding and better grazing, they appear on the fat market as finished lambs ready for immediate slaughter and sale as an agricultural commodity. In comparison with the price of hill lambs sold on the store market, the price of finished lambs from crossbred park ewes is not subsidized and thus is less protected from the effects of the European and world agricultural market. In this sense, farmers view lambs sold on the fat market as more commoditized than hill lambs, and the significance of park lambs is restricted to their function as objects for sale.

The characteristics of outbye land that diminish its potential as a natural resource for capitalist production of commodities enhance its potential for the cultural production of meaning. In terms of agricultural production, outbye land is marginal. Harsh weather, poor soil and vegetation, and complex topography render it unsuitable for any form of cultivation and significant technological improvement such as grading, draining, and reseeding. Outbye land is used for purebred hill sheep that are genetically adapted to the harsh conditions but whose small lambs are less marketable, as noted above. As a result, while eligible for the same subsidies as those who raise park sheep under the European Community Sheep Meat Regime, farmers who raise hill sheep attract additional headage payments. The head payment distances their lambs, to a greater degree than park lambs, from the economic forces of the agricultural market. One consequence of distancing, suggested by Tilley and Relph, is that outbye land as well as the ewes and lambs living on it are less domesticated through technological intervention. Thus, their significance to sheep farming people is not confined to meanings derived from rational use and efficiency in terms of producing commodities for the capitalist market. Hill lambs are less commodities than they are symbols of hill sheep people and their way of life.

People in Teviothead distinguish between "farmers" and "shepherds." Farmers are either owner-occupiers or tenants of a farm and, most importantly, own the live-stock. Shepherds are workers hired by farmers to take care of sheep. In the early 1990s, there were 11 shepherds working on eight farms in Teviothead. On most farms, including those with hired shepherds, farmers do some or all of the shepherd-ing work. The following description of shepherds' association with sheep applies to both shepherds and farmers who do shepherding work.

Shepherds use the possessive pronoun to describe their sense of connection to their sheep on the hill. Such usage does not indicate ownership of sheep as capital but an association between shepherd and sheep that results from the particular way shep-herding is practiced. Shepherds spend most of their time alone walking the ground where their sheep graze. Their overall brief is to watch over the natural habits of sheep through the breeding cycle and intervene if necessary. Shepherds are respon-sible for several tasks that are done with the help of other farm personnel. These include dipping, weaning, castrating, and selecting lambs for replacement stock. They represent only a small proportion of a shepherd's yearly routine. Shepherds work what the Scottish Agricultural Wages Board describes as "customary hours." This means that shepherds should be available to work around the clock, seven days a week. Their workday varies from the daily dawn-to-dusk herding during the lambing season to the less frequent tours that combine maintenance with supervision of sheep during the shorter days of winter, when sheep in the early stages of pregnancy need less attention. Thus shepherds organize and experience their daily and annual lives around the requirements of their sheep; and conversely sheep come to embody a shepherd's knowledge and skills as a stockman. In this respect sheep express a significant dimension of a shepherd's identity.

[...]

Sheep farming people in Teviothead expressed a superabundance of meaning in their characterization of hill land and sheep as "wild" and more difficult to control. In comparison with park land, hill land is subject to more severe weather conditions, is much more geometrically complex, and has remained largely undifferentiated and uncontrolled by fencing. [...]

The wildness of hill land and sheep was under discussion at a local agricultural show that I attended. This show included sheep dog trials in which dogs (extensions of human control and surveillance) are judged on their ability to herd sheep into pens. Unlike other shows, sheep used in these trials were hill ewes from what was known as one of the "wild" hill farms in the valley. There, people said, the shepherding was neglectful, raising challenges for the dogs since normally sheep used for trials are the more docile inbye sheep. They added that these particular sheep would be "more wild" since they probably had not seen a human for several weeks. This incident illustrates the more general view of farmers and shepherds that hill sheep are wild not just genetically but also because they, like the ground on which they live, are less subject to everyday human contact and, by implication, to the market-oriented supervision and feeding applied to park sheep enclosed in fields. As I describe below, the outbye's wild terrain provides dense topographical formations that can be named and used as a system of spatial differentiation. Such differentiation is central to the construction of place, the meanings of which are derived from the way sheep live on the hills, the personal biographical experiences of shepherds, and Border history.

Circumspection: Going around the Hills

I now turn to the activities of shepherding whether these are carried out by farmers or shepherds. Shepherding transforms the hills into an enveloping world where farming people of Teviothead carry out a way of life, a place where they properly belong and feel at home. In local parlance, the principal type of place in the hills is called *hirsel*, a term referring simultaneously to one shepherd's sheep and the area of the hills they graze. I begin with a narrative of going around the hill in order to illustrate how sheep mediate the creation of and attachment to places. Shepherds structured their walks around the hirsel in relation to the topography and the movement of the flocks in a way that allows them to see all the sheep; they created places within their hirsels in relation to the movements of the sheep. One narrative is an edited version of my field notes from an evening walk around the hill with Danny, a hired shepherd on Bowanhill Farm.

Fieldnotes: Danny's walk around his hirsel. Danny's hirsel amalgamates two hirsels, Bowanhill and Colterscleuch Shiel, belonging to farms of the same names. There is an abandoned shepherd's cottage sitting at the bottom of the Colterscleuch Shiel near the march (or boundary) with Bowanhill. Here Danny has a small field for grazing weak sheep and small pens for keeping problem ewes and lambs at lambing. I quote from my field notes:

> As we left his cottage and went up the steep hill just behind it, Danny discussed some features of his hirsel and how this affected his walk around it. Danny's tasks at this time of year are to move the sheep to the tops of the hills for the night and to check for couped ewes.[11] He points out that the weather tonight is quite warm: "This affects the sheep…with them being heavy with wool and the warm weather, the sheep don't like to move under these conditions. Otherwise, they would move to the tops of the hill more by themselves."
>
> When we began the walk, Danny said that there were several different routes he could take around his hirsel at night. The basic pattern of all the routes was a clockwise circle around the bottoms of the hills starting from his cottage, heading to the Northhouse side of the hirsel near the road, walking up through the Bowan Hill part to Colterscleuch Shiel, leaving Bowan Hill for a while to walk around the Shiel, then re-entering the Bowanhill section on The Binks side of the farm and walking back down to the road and his cottage.

As we walked up the hill, we had a good view of a part of the hirsel that Rob Kyle of Northhouse herds. On the morning round, Danny had seen a couped sheep on North-house, and he said he expected that Rob would have spotted it on his morning rounds, but he hadn't. We saw it still there at 3:15 p.m. At first, Danny thought it was probably dead since it had been there since the morning, at least, and he did not see its legs moving in the air. So he sent the dog after it first; he hoped that, if it was still alive, the couped sheep would struggle as the dog approached. But he was not able to get the dog to go over the dyke and approach the sheep, so he decided to go over himself saying, "We help each other out." The sheep was alive, and he righted it. When he came back he said, "It's awkward (about couping); a sheep could coup right after you've seen her on your rounds, and she'd be dead by the time you went around the hill again."
[...]
Far Height cut – here Danny sent the dog wide to push the sheep up to the top of the Far Height. This is the last cut (an area of grazing for a group of ewes) on the Bowan Hill part of Danny's hirsel. He has done only part of this cut, but he will leave it at this point to do the Colterscleuch Shiel; then, after that, he re-enters Bowan Hill again on the Far Height cut and looks at the remaining part of it.
The Colterscleuch Shiel has two cuts on it, Long Meadow and Great Moor. The Long Meadow runs from the cottage along the hill side and is easy to see at night, but you have to take a long walk along it in the morning. As a whole, the Shiel is easy, and Danny said that originally when it was the responsibility of one herd, it would have been a very nice job to have.

The walk around Danny's hirsel is typical, covering six to ten miles over a period of several hours. There are three points of highlight about this narrative that I will use in the analysis below. First, the walk around the hirsel was punctuated by places whose meanings for Danny derive from his personal memories of events, such as couped sheep. Second, Danny was always concerned to ensure that he could see all the sheep, and he selected paths that enabled him to do so. Third, Danny's hirsel is divided into smaller named areas called cuts which I will describe in more detail below.
[...]

Dwelling Places

In the hirsel, sheep and space are unified by the way sheep use and live on the land. The hirsel illustrates the central dimensions of Heidegger's concept of dwelling (1971) – my theme in the remainder of this article. *Dwelling* refers to the creation of meaningful places that together form a surrounding world (*Um-welt*). It entails people's relationship to the world, motivated by concern and consequent involve-ment. "Dwelling" thus privileges the practical and the spatial in the constitution of knowledge and meaning. The formative acts of dwelling and knowing are doing things with objects, picking them up, manipulating them, and discarding them. Acts of dwelling have implications for the organization of space and definition of place in at least four ways. First, in doing things with objects people abolish the distance between themselves and the things they use, thereby bringing them into a spatial relationship. "Dwelling involves a *lack of distance* between people and things...an engagement which is neither conceptualized nor articulated, and which arises through *using* the world rather than through scrutiny" (Thomas 1993:28, emphasis added). Second, dwelling in everyday life has a referential function. The use of any one thing implicates the use of other things so that together these uses constitute a coherent totality, a world in which each thing has a proper – and thus meaningful and nameable – place in spatial and practical terms. Third, dwelling is therefore a way of seeing. Fourth, by using objects, people gather them together spatially to form a place whose meaning derives from both actions and objects. Going around the hill is an activity of creating places that entails a sentimental attachment to them.

Concern and Bringing Close

Going around the hill is motivated shepherds' abiding concern for the welfare of sheep as sources of farm income and personal identity. Because of the poor quality of land and harsh weather conditions, hill sheep farming is relatively small in scale with flocks ranging in size from 400 to 4000 breeding ewes. This scale magnifies the financial and cultural significance of each ewe and increases the importance of frequent walking or biking around the hills. Going around the hill removes the distance between shepherds, ewes, and land. Such closeness and distance to sheep have not just a physical dimension but also a knowledge dimension.

Hill herding is labor intensive. To ensure the health and survival of sheep, shepherds must be very attentive to their flocks. Each shepherd is responsible for the care of a relatively small number of sheep, between 600 and 1,000 ewes.[12] When going around the hill, shepherds see each ewe almost every day. During lambing and postlambing, when ewes are at greatest risk, they see each ewe twice every day. If there is a problem, shepherds can deal with it quickly and monitor the results. Such frequent seeing and handling results in shepherds' knowing some individual characteristics of each ewe. In this sense, they express their sense of being at home in the hills as detailed knowledge of sheep. In almost every discussion of shepherding in which I engaged, shepherds and farmers emphasized that one of the characteristics of a good shepherd is the ability to "ken the sheep" or be a good "kenner." By this, they meant the ability to recognize individual sheep by their unique physical attributes, as well as to remember their histories, bloodlines, and distinctive habits. [...]

Paths of Seeing and Gathering

Going around the hill consists of seeing and gathering the sheep, terrain, and people into the totality of the hirsel. It is significant that the round – and the practices of seeing and gathering places – begins and ends at the place where the shepherd and his family live. For hired shepherds, the provision of a cottage is a condition of employment, and in most cases the cottage is located in or near the shepherd's hirsel.[13] At their cottages, shepherds don boots and protective clothing; they collect the dogs to maneuver the sheep, and they gather other equipment – crook, medicines, and hoof clippers – they might need. In carrying out these preparations, shepherds extend the bounds of their homes to include the sheep of their hirsel as well as the topographical and climatic conditions that affect their flocks and their movements.[...]

From the cottage, shepherds follow an established path – in both a historical and practical sense – around their hirsel.[14] By following this path on foot or bike, shepherds not only gather the sheep, they also create places of meaning and gather them into a region they call a hirsel. When men come into a farm or are hired as shepherds, they spend the first weeks and months learning both the topography of the land and the habits of the sheep of the hill hirsel. Usually, a new shepherd starts out by following the path used by the previous shepherd. Over time he modifies this path to suit the knowledge he acquires in traversing the hill terrain, in observing the behavior of the sheep, and in handling individual ewes himself.

[...]

All shepherds stressed to me that there are two principles for constructing a path around hirsels: visibility and mobility. A path should be adapted to the terrain in order to allow a shepherd to see all the ground of the hirsel. If a sheep is in trouble anywhere on the hill, a shepherd should be able to observe it during his round and take remedial action. Shepherds thus connect sight lines directly to the life and well-being of the sheep. Because the topography of the land is complex with intersecting hills, ridges, ravines, knolls, streams, tall grasses, bracken, moss, and heather, shepherds realize they must go around the hirsel many times to become familiar with all the areas where a sheep might disappear from view. The paths shepherds establish meander over the terrain in relation to the sheep's mobility, visibility, and risk. While walking around the hills with me, each shepherd pointed out locations that were obscured and where sheep had died because they could not be seen from the path. They also described how they had modified the path so these places could be seen. In these practices, seeing is a form of constituting locations as meaningful places with respect to the activity of sheep and shepherds' memories of them. Paths are created in order to see these places, and seeing these places as part of following a path is a gathering of them into a hirsel. Spatially, then, a hirsel is a set of places that unfold as men and sheep live in direct association with each other.

[...]

The second principle of constructing a path around a hill hirsel is to adapt the shepherd's route to the sheep's grazing habits. While grazing, hill sheep tend to move from lower to higher ground during the late afternoon. Sheep spend the night at or near the tops of hills, returning to lower ground in the course of the day. As they range over the land, sheep, too, learn the topographical and pasturage areas on the hill of significance for eating, mating, lambing, and sheltering. These areas become the known and remembered places of a grazing domain where the ewes return to fulfil their needs. In so doing, sheep create a bond to a region in which they remain throughout their lives. Throughout the Borders, the process of creating this spatial bond between a group of sheep and a specific territory on the hills is called *hefting on*, and the area of the farm's hill land and the group of sheep that form an attachment to it are called a *heft* or *cut*. As with the concept of hirsel, a cut unifies sheep and space through the practice of using land.

As spaces defined by their adaptive significance for sheep, cuts are also the primary places for herding within a hirsel. In this way, cuts form building blocks for the organization of human labor on a farm. Shepherds use cuts to divide the flock into grazing and breeding units. In November, when ewes are mated, shepherds bring particular rams to each cut. One of the tasks for shepherds includes going around the hill at this time to ensure that the rams are impregnating only the ewes in their assigned cut. Ewes remain in the same cut over their breeding lives of five or six years. Every year, farmers replace the oldest cohort of ewes with ewe lambs who themselves were born within the cut. Thus, a cut consists of four to five generations of breeding ewes who comprise a matriline tied to a particular territory. One farmer described a cut as "daughters of daughters." Furthermore, the spatial relation between ewes and land is construed by shepherds as literally incorporated in the sheep themselves; the cut is manifest in their distinctive characteristics. For example, on one farm ewes of a particular cut have more twins; on another farm, ewes of one cut are particularly good mothers. When a farmer moves to a new farm, he does not bring the ewes from his previous farm because they are not adapted to the parasites living in the ground of the new farm.

Using their detailed knowledge of how sheep negotiate topographical features, shepherds construct paths so as to come up behind the sheep, pushing the sheep in the direction of their usual routes. Because sheep move in different directions in the morning and evening, the different paths for going around the hill depend upon the time of day. Shepherds tend to state that the pattern is for the path to "go around the tops [of the hills]" in the morning in order to drive the sheep down and "to go around the bottoms [of the hills]" in the evening in order to drive the sheep up. If a shepherd walks "against" the natural movement of sheep, shepherds say he will scatter them. As such, "maintaining the cuts" consists of keeping sheep in their proper place by gathering them together as a group in a specific territory, or cut, within a hirsel.[15]

Cuts form the largest unit of meaningful place within a hirsel. Thus when we went around the hill, when they described their routes to me, or when they talked to me about walking around the hill, shepherds organized their journeys and their narratives in terms of the cuts within their hirsels.

[...]

The relation between the two types of places on a hill – cuts and hirsels – is crucial to being at home in the hills. Cuts are spaces defined by the natural tendency of sheep to bond to a particular territory. Cuts become places for shepherds through the knowledge of locations of adaptive significance for particular groups of sheep, knowledge acquired by shepherds as they go around the hill to maintain the cuts. A hirsel is built by the paths the shepherd follows to gather the cuts (as meaningful places for a shepherd because they are significant for the sheep) into a region or world where sheep and shepherd feel at home.

Naming and Taming

Seeing and gathering places into cuts and cuts into hirsels are also referential acts. In going around the hill, the paths followed by shepherds link spatially and temporally the places where they know sheep are likely to be or to get into trouble. As a result, any one place refers to other places connected by the paths so that they form a coherent whole, the cut, in relation to a specific set of sheep. Likewise, these same paths connect several cuts into a coherent whole, the hirsel, in relation to a shepherd whose daily life and reputation are determined by the quality of the sheep in the cuts for which he is responsible. As a referential practice, going around the hill also includes acts of naming places. The geographer Porteous aptly describes the significance of naming in the creation of places where people feel at home:

> One familiar method of directing or controlling the external environment is the act of naming. Mapless travelers are often disturbed by their inability to discover the "correct" names of the landscape features they encounter. Naming is a powerful act. By naming landscape features, butterflies, persons, we in part possess them and simultaneously exorcise their chthonic magical powers. Nature, disturbing or fearsome, can be humanized by applying familiar terms to it. [Porteous 1990:72]

In naming places, shepherds tame (and thereby domesticate) the wild open space of the hills.

The complexity of outbye geography provides a source of topographical differences for a system of naming localities in the hills that are significant to sheep and to shepherds. The place names used by hill people are in most cases the same ones found on the Ordnance Survey maps. In this respect, the names are mostly "opaque" (Stuart-Murray 1995:31). Like the place names in de Certeau's city, place names on the Borders have "slowly [lost], like worn coins, the value engraved upon them, but their ability to signify outlives [their] first definitions" (1984:104).

The most prominent feature of place names in outbye land is their binomial structure. The first element derives from, or resembles, names of people (e.g., Allen, Gray, Carsey), other places (e.g., Skelfhill), and things or attributes (e.g., Doe, Cow, Millstone, Peat, Stobiecote [cottage made with nails], Staney [stony], Wester [west direction], Crummie [cow with crooked horns], White, Grey). While these words may have had some substantive meanings for identifying the locations when first created, these earlier meanings, usually hypothesized from their etymologies, have decayed over time to the point that they have become purely nominal. This is particularly so for the names of farms. For example, the name "Skelfhill" is derived from Scandinavian and "describes the shape of the hill which has a small peak at the end of a long, shelf-like plateau" (Macdonald 1991:38); [...] "Bowanhill," derived from Old English, means "rounded or bow-shaped hill" (Macdonald 1991:38); and "Caerlanrigg" means "the long rig with the fort" (Macdonald 1991:37). People in Teviothead are largely unaware of these etymologies; however, these place names are meaningful in identifying locations even if they have become meaningless as words (see Nicolaisen 1976:4). The binomial name of a place can become the first part of the name of another place. Thus, on Skelfhill farm, the whole place name "Crummie Cleuch" (etymologically, "the gorge or ravine of the cow with crooked horns" (Robinson 1985:123) becomes the first part of another spatially related place name "Crummiecleuch Rig" (for the ridge of high ground running above the Crummie Cleuch). This usage reveals an important feature of the words that make up the first part of place names. Because they can be used for a number of different locations, they do not by themselves name a place.

The second element of place names includes a term that is topographically descriptive but spatially undefined. These words can be used wherever they are appropriate to the topography of the location under consideration. Words in this category include *brae* (hillside), *burn* (stream, brook), *cleuch* (gorge, ravine), *fell* (steep, rocky hill), *foot* (lower end of a piece of ground or stream), *grain* (branch of a valley or stream), *hass* (neck of land). [...]

The combination of these two types of words forms a place name that identifies a unique spatial location. This is how place names are used on maps. In going around the hill, shepherds imbue these opaquely named spaces with meanings thereby transforming them into places where they feel at home. The following examples are extracts from field notes of my walks around the hills with shepherds. They illustrate how shepherds tame the hills by associating their personal experiences and memories of shepherding as well as their historical knowledge of Border reiving with named locations. In this way, shepherds make places into their own as both individuals and as people of the Scottish Border country:

> During our walk around the hill, Jimmy stopped and pointed out a particular location and described an experience he had had there one day: "It was a dull day and I was on the Tanlaw Naze [the name of a hill within his hirsel.] I had stopped to look at the sheep and to do so I had to look towards the hills of Lymiecleuch [the neighboring farm]. Just as I was looking over those hills, the sun broke through the clouds in one place, and a bright ray of sunlight fell upon the top of one of the hills. I thought to myself that by the sunlight falling on that patch of ground it was saying to me, 'This is the best place in the world.'" [...]
>
> Glen described part of his hirsel as follows: "Travelling along the Peat Rig, I look back into the lower parts of the Long Burn, but from here I can't see that blind spot in the Todhill Rig so I go down to the Peatrig Stell, and I can see into the blind spot from there." [...]
>
> When Watt and I came away from the Haggis Side, we made our way up to the top of the Wrang Way Burn. He then told me the story behind the name "Wrang Way Burn" which associates the place with Border history and the reiving of the 16th century. The story shows how Borderers' intimate knowledge of the hills allowed them to elude capture: "Some raiders – the Johnnie Armstrong kind – were being chased by the English. The English were getting close... so the raiders were going up the burn, but instead of continuing up the burn they slipped over to Eweslees [the neighboring farm], through Eweslees Doors, and lay down in the bracken. The English did not see them and continued up the Wrang Way Burn and missed them – they went the 'wrang way'!"[16]
>
> [...]

Conclusion: At Home in the Borders

In concluding this article, I move from considering how hill sheep people come to feel at home in the hills to how this sentiment becomes the basis for their identity as Borderers, that is, feeling at home in the Borders. First, I must explain why this is an issue for them.

In talking to me about his special attachment to the hills, Jim, the shepherd I quoted at the beginning of this article, also said that he did not feel at home in the town of Hawick. He assumed, conversely, that townspeople do not feel at home in the hills. I came to realize that this sentiment, and the opposition between city and country it entails, was pervasive among hill people. I spent a considerable amount of time traveling with farmers and shepherds to shows and sales around the Borders. During these trips, we could leisurely reflect upon life on hill sheep farms, and farmers often asked me how I liked living in Teviothead. Knowing that I had lived in cities all my life, they expressed surprise when I said that I enjoyed living in both types of locations. Invariably, their response was that they could not live in a town or city because it was a place that lacked the scenery and the open space of the country. "Just look out my cottage window," said one shepherd. "Here in the country you don't see another house the same as your own [referring to the dreary housing estates in Hawick] or near your own." This opposition between town or city and country, widespread throughout the United Kingdom (see Williams 1975), is given a particular spin in the Borders. It affects the way town and country people relate to each other in forming a Borders identity, and it contributes to the way analysts have portrayed the distinctiveness of Borders identity.

The study of the Borders region has been structured by this town and country opposition despite the economic interdependence of rural and urban areas.[17] Since the early work of Littlejohn (1963) on the sociology of a rural hill sheep farming valley near Teviotdale, most research on the Borders has focused on towns and, in particular, upon the well-known annual civic ceremonies known as "Common Ridings" (Neville 1979, 1989, 1994; Smith 1993, 1995, 1996). Common Ridings are celebrated in some form in most Border towns and portray a town and country opposition in the form of a struggle over land (Neville 1994:4–6). The festival's major event entails encircling a town's boundaries on horseback to protect the community's common lands from encroachment by rural landowners. In Selkirk, the Common Riding is also a ritual of remembrance of the town's men killed during the Battle of Flodden (1513) in which Borderers bravely fought, died, and lost their King (James IV) to the English armies in one of the innumerable battles of the 300 year war of independence between England and Scotland (Neville 1994). In the town of Hawick, riding the boundaries also recalls the Battle of Flodden. The town's common lands were granted by Sir James Douglas of Drumlanrig "in recognition of the faithful services of the men of Hawick at the Battle of Flodden, and in commisseration [sic] for the great loss they sustained" (Oliver 1887:108). In Hawick's Common Riding, the young Cornet leading the rides carries a banner that refers to the story of the brave youths of the town (*callants*) who surprised and captured the flag of an English raiding party that was exploiting the post-Flodden English dominance of the region by "burning and destroying all that came their way" (Oliver 1887:98). These references to the Battle of Flodden further implicate an opposition between England and Scotland. For both Neville and Smith, this latter opposition is crucial to constructing a separate regional identity for the Borders. Implicitly reiterating the opposition between town and country in their analyses of Common Ridings, Neville and Smith generalize to the whole Borders region an identity derived only from the perspective of its towns and their histories. Excluded are rural people and the history of their experience as Scottish Borderers confronting England. This exclusion is particularly ironic in that Smith is explicitly sensitive to the way in which the Borders region "is doubly marginalised: first by the invisibility of Scotland within England's Britain, and then lost within a Scotland marked out by its central belt, and signified by its Highlands and Islands" (1996:24). In this respect, the hill farming people of the Borders are triply marginalized by their invisibility in the portrayal of the Border region.

Neither Littlejohn nor I have found high levels of participation by farming people in these town-based Common Riding festivals. If, from the perspective of its towns, the Battle of Flodden symbolized Borders identity in opposition to England, reiving seemed to play the same role for hill sheep people in the countryside. Both histories provide romantic images of bravery and valor in glorifying Borderers' resistance to English rule, historical themes that find contemporary parallels in the region's continual appropriation by national and supranational institutions (see Nadel-Klein 1991). For hill sheep farmers, particularly, the European Union's agricultural policies have defined the Borders countryside as economically marginal in yet a further – quadruple – way in its classification as a Less Favoured Area for agricultural production (see Gray 1996b). It is perhaps not surprising that early in my fieldwork, when the effects of the new European Community Sheep Meat Regime were first being felt, a farmer gave me a copy of Fraser's book *The Steel Bonnets: The Story of the Anglo-Scottish Border Reivers*, saying that if I wanted to understand people of the Borders, I needed to know about reiving.[18] Reivers plundered on both sides of the Borders (Fraser 1971:9), but in the historical imagination of contemporary people in Teviothead, reiving was the foremost act of resistance at a time when Scotland was struggling for its independence from England. For people of the Borders, reiving remains the key symbol of that resistance as well as the distinctiveness of the region itself. This is the significance of those places in the hills that shepherds associated with reiving – Wrang Way Burn, Bloody Cleuch – and of other places in Teviothead, such as Caerlanrigg Farm where Johnnie Armstrong was betrayed and the Teviothead churchyard where he is buried.

As farmers relive their image of Borders identity everyday in their treks through the hills, reiving also links the hill sheep farming people of Teviothead into wider regional processes of identification in two ways. Town and country people evoke the same historical period in constructing the Borders as a separate place, thereby providing a common place and time to build a regional identity even if through different events. The Battle of Flodden and reiving are now synecdoches of the particular way town people and country people of the Borders were part of these historical events. On a recent visit to the Borders for fieldwork, I was struck by two tangible indications that reivers were gaining prominence in the image of a distinctive Border regional identity. The Borders Regional Council had erected signposts on all the main roads leading into the region announcing to travelers that they were entering "The Borders." These signposts contained a logo portraying the reivers' distinctive steel bonnets. And in Teviothead, on the main road between Edinburgh and Carlisle, a small commercial museum recently opened. Its name is The Johnnie Armstrong Museum and it portrays the exploits of this most (in)famous Border reiver, who was betrayed, captured and – "tradition has it" (Watson 1974:94) – hung at Caerlanrigg Farm in Teviothead.

NOTES

1 While referring to the point that de Certeau (1984) makes, I have not used the terms *space* and *place* as he does. See note 2 for explanation.

2 As will be discussed below, the terminology used by de Certeau to distinguish between "place," that is, localities as positions on maps and plans, and "space," that is, meaningful localities constituted through practice is the reverse of the terminology used by Heidegger (1971), the contemporary ethnographers cited in the text, and many phenomenological geographers (see, for example, Pickles 1985; Relph 1985). I follow de Certeau's terminology only at this point in the article because it is useful to me in framing the main problem. Throughout the remainder of the article, I revert to the terminology of Heidegger, contemporary ethnographers, and the phenomenological geographers.

3 By the mid 1990s, just over half of the hill shepherds in Teviothead were using four-wheel motorbikes to go around the hill. No one expressed any nostalgia or complained about lack of authenticity in this context. I asked shepherds who used bikes if they were less sensually conscious of the contours, soils, and vegetation of the hills than when they walked. All of the men said that they were just as aware of the topographical features and the nature of the ground on bike as on foot, and that surprisingly, they could approach the sheep more closely on a bike than on foot. They assessed the change to using bikes in terms of efficiency and labor costs. On farms with more than two shepherds, using a bike increased the number of sheep for which a hill shepherd was responsible and, thus, decreased the number of shepherds needed. Since most hired laborers on hill sheep farms are shepherds, using bikes decreases labor costs and enables farms to move toward a situation in which family labor predominates (see Gray 1996a).

4 The terms *place* and *space* are in quotation marks in this discussion of de Certeau because I am substituting the terminology used by Heidegger 1971, Pickles 1985, and Relph 1985 in which place ("space" for de Certeau) denotes meaningful localities constituted through human practice and space ("place" for de Certeau) denotes localities as positions on maps and plans.

5 A striking example of how "landscape denotes the external world mediated through subjective human experience" (Cosgrove 1984:13) is Karen Leonard's (1997) account of how Japanese and Punjabi migrants to California construed their new geographical surroundings in terms of landscapes in Japan and India as a means of creating collective identities for themselves.

6 Even when Hirsch defines landscape as a dynamic "cultural process," rather than a static cultural image, in which the foreground actualities of social life are brought into juxtaposition to the background ideal potentialities of social life, landscape still involves distancing:

> There is a relationship here between an ordinary, workaday life and an *ideal*, imagined existence, vaguely connected to, but still *separate* from, that of the everyday....Foreground actuality and background potentiality exist in a process of mutual implication, and as such everyday life can never attain the *idealized* features of a representation. [1995:4, 23, emphasis added]

Note that while Hirsch privileges the relation between foreground actuality and background potentiality, the existence of the relationships and the landscape's availability to portray another representation of social life depend upon a moral *distance* between foreground actuality and background potentiality.

7   There seems to be a tendency by those who adopt a landscape perspective for the ethnography of place making to privilege verbal practice generally and place naming in particular (Basso 1996; Dominy 1995; Feld 1996; Weiner 1991).

8   Most farms also raise suckler cows, but this accounts for less than 20 percent of the total grazing livestock (Anderson 1986:14).

9   Two breeds of hill sheep predominate in the Borders: South Country Cheviot and Blackface.

10 See Relph (1985:24–25) for a discussion of the distinction between geometric and geographical space, the former referring to the abstract conceptualization of the surface of the earth, the latter referring to the human experience of the earth's spatiality.

11 From the end of lambing in late April until they are clipped in late June or early July, ewes have a tendency to coup. Coup means a ewe that has rolled on her back and is unable to right herself, causing an accumulation of gas in her stomach. A couped ewe's stomach swells putting pressure on her lungs and diaphragm. This pressure would eventually suffocate the animal unless she is righted by a shepherd.

12 On other types of sheep farms, on more productive land, shepherds may be responsible for as many as 2,000 sheep. One man, who had been a shepherd in New Zealand, said that he had been responsible for over 5,000 sheep there; he had limited contact with them, mostly from the cab of a jeep.

13 In the past, hill shepherds' cottages were located in the hirsel itself – very isolated but indicative of the association between a shepherd and his sheep. Contemporary shepherds' cottages are located near their hirsels but also on roads, giving easy access to town.

14 I derive my concept of path from Relph, who describes paths as "routes which reflect the direction and intensities of intentions and experiences and which serve as the structural axis of existential space. They radiate from and lead toward nodes or centers of special importance and meaning" (1976:20–21). (See also Weiner 1991:32–34.)

15 This practice also maintains the cut in a land management sense, since the movement of sheep over the land ensures even grazing and clean ground, that is, without excessive build-up of dung where fluke might breed.

16 Johnnie Armstrong was one of the most famous of the Border reivers residing in the Debatable Land. He was captured and hanged at Caerlanrigg Farm in Teviothead.

17 For example, from the 17th to the mid-20th century, Hawick's growth and prosperity was as a mill town where wool from surrounding sheep farms was sold, distributed, and processed (see Neville 1994:6).

18 Unlike the situation encountered by Nadel-Klein, there was not a class division in the representational practices adopted by farmers and shepherds in Teviothead. Both adopted what Nadel-Klein described as the "romantic-resisting" combination of the representational "faces" of marginality (1991:503).

REFERENCES

Anderson, John L.
    1986 Profitability of Farming in South East Scotland 1984/85. Edinburgh: East of Scotland College of Agriculture, Agricultural Resource Management Department.
Basso, Keith H.
    1996 Wisdom Sits in Places: Landscape and Language among the Western Apache. Albuquerque: University of New Mexico Press.

Bender, Barbara, ed.
    1993   Landscape: Politics and Perspectives. Oxford: Berg.
Berdoulay, Vincent
    1989   Place, Meaning and Discourse in French Language Geography. *In* The Power of
        Place: Bringing Together Geographical and Sociological Imaginations. John A. Agnew
        and James S. Duncan, eds. Pp. 124–139. London: Unwin Hyman.
Bloch, Maurice
    1995   People into Places: Zafimaniry Concepts of Clarity. *In* The Anthropology of Land-
        scape: Perspectives on Place and Space. Eric Hirsch and Michael O'Hanlon, eds. Pp. 63–
        77. Oxford: Clarendon Press.
Casey, Edward S.
    1996   How to Get from Space to Place in a Fairly Short Stretch of Time: Phenomenological
        Prolegomena. *In* Senses of Place. Steven Feld and Keith H. Basso, eds. Pp. 13–52. Santa
        Fe, NM: School of American Research Press.
De Certeau, Michel
    1984   The Practice of Everyday Life. Berkeley: University of California Press.
Cohen, Anthony P.
    1982   Belonging: The Experience of Culture. *In* Belonging: Identity and Social Organiza-
        tion in British Rural Cultures. Anthony P. Cohen, ed. Pp. 1–18. Manchester: Manchester
        University Press.
Combe, Iris
    1983   Shepherds, Sheep and Sheepdogs. Lancaster: Dalesman Books.
Cosgrove, Dennis
    1984   Social Formation and Symbolic Landscape. London: Croom Helm.
Daniel, E. Valentine
    1984   Fluid Signs: Being a Person the Tamil Way. Berkeley: University of California Press.
Dominy, Michèle
    1995   Toponymy: Positionality and Containment of New Zealand High Country Stations.
        Landscape Review 2:16–41.
Duncan, James S.
    1990   The City as Text: The Politics of Landscape Interpretation in the Kandyan Kingdom.
        Cambridge: Cambridge University Press.
Feld, Steven
    1996   Waterfalls of Song: An Acoustemology of Place Resounding in Basavi, Papua New
        Guinea. *In* Senses of Place. Steven Feld and Keith H. Basso, eds. Pp. 91–136. Santa Fe,
        NM: School of American Research Press.
Feld, Steven, and Keith H. Basso
    1996   Introduction. *In* Senses of Place. Steven Feld and Keith H. Basso, eds. Pp. 3–12.
        Santa Fe, NM: School of American Research Press.
Fernandez, James W.
    1974   The Mission of the Metaphor in Expressive Culture. Current Anthropology
        15(2):119–145.
    1986   Edification by Puzzlement. *In* Persuasions and Performances: The Play of Tropes in
        Culture. Pp. 172–188. Bloomington: Indiana University Press.
Fraser, George Macdonald
    1971   The Steel Bonnets: The Story of the Anglo-Scottish Border Reivers. London: Pan
        Books.
Gray, John
    1984   Lamb Auctions on the Borders. European Journal of Sociology 24:54–82.
    1996a   Cultivating Farm Life on the Borders: Scottish Hill Sheep Farms and the European
        Community. Sociologia Ruralis 19(1):27–50.

1996b   Irony and Paradox in the Scottish Borderlands: Hill Sheep Farms and Their Rela-
tions with the European Union and United Kingdom. The Australian Journal of Anthro-
pology 7(3):191–217.
Gupta, Akhil, and James Ferguson
1997   Culture, Power, Place: Ethnography at the End of an Era. *In* Culture, Power, Place:
Explorations in Critical Anthropology. Akhil Gupta and James Ferguson, eds. Pp. 1–32.
Durham, NC: Duke University Press.
Gupta, Akhil, and James Ferguson, eds.
1997   Culture, Power, Place: Explorations in Critical Anthropology. Durham, NC: Duke
University Press.
Heidegger, Martin
1971   Building, Dwelling, Thinking. *In* Poetry, Language, Thought. New York: Harper
and Row.
Hirsch, Eric
1995   Landscape: Between Place and Space. *In* The Anthropology of Landscape: Perspec-
tives on Place and Space. Eric Hirsch and Michael O'Hanlon, eds. Pp. 1–30. Oxford:
Clarendon Press.
Hirsch, Eric, and Michael O'Hanlon, eds.
1995   The Anthropology of Landscape: Perspectives on Place and Space. Oxford: Clar-
endon Press.
Jackson, Michael
1996   Introduction: Phenomenology, Radical Empiricism, and Anthropological Critique.
In Things as They Are: New Directions in Phenomenological Anthropology. Michael
Jackson, ed. Pp. 1–50. Bloomington: Indiana University Press.
Layton, Robert
1995   Relating to the Country in the Western Desert. *In* The Anthropology of Landscape:
Perspectives on Place and Space. Eric Hirsch and Michael O'Hanlon, eds. Pp. 210–231.
Oxford: Clarendon Press.
Leonard, Karen
1997   Finding One's Own Place: Asian Landscapes Re-visioned in Rural California. *In*
Culture, Power, Place: Explorations in Critical Anthropology. Akhil Gupta and James
Ferguson, eds. Pp. 118–136. Durham, NC: Duke University Press.
Littlejohn, James
1963   Westrigg: The Sociology of a Cheviot Parish. London: Routledge and Kegan Paul.
Macdonald, J. S. M.
1991   The Place-Names of Roxburghshire. Hawick: The Hawick Archaeological
Society.
Mewett, Peter G.
1982   Exiles, Nicknames, Social Identities and the Production of Local Consciousness in a
Lewis Crofting Community. *In* Belonging: Identity and Social Organization in British
Rural Cultures. Anthony P. Cohen, ed. Pp. 1–18. Manchester: Manchester University
Press.
Myers, Fred
1986   Pintupi Country, Pintupi Self: Sentiment, Place, and Politics among Western Desert
Aborigines. Berkeley: University of California Press.
Nadel-Klein, Jane
1991   Reweaving the Fringe: Localism, Tradition, and Representation in British Ethnog-
raphy. American Ethnologist 18(3):500–517.
Neville, Gwen Kennedy
1979   Community Form and Ceremonial Life in Three Regions of Scotland. American
Ethnologist 6(1):93–109.

1989   The Sacred and the Civic: Representations of Death in the Town Ceremony of Border Scotland. Anthropological Quarterly 62(4):163–174.
1994   The Mother Town: Civic Ritual, Symbol, and Experience in the Borders of Scotland. Oxford: Oxford University Press.
Nicolaisen, Wilhelm Fritz Herman
1976   Scottish Place-Names: Their Study and Significance. London: B. T. Batsford.
Oliver, J. Rutherford
1887   Upper Teviotdale and the Scotts of Buccleuch: A Local and Family History. Hawick: W. and J. Kennedy.
Pickles, John
1985   Phenomenology, Science, and Geography: Spatiality and the Human Sciences. Cambridge: Cambridge University Press.
Porteous, J. Douglas
1990   Landscapes of The Mind: Worlds of Sense and Metaphor. Toronto: University of Toronto Press.
Relph, Edward
1976   Place and Placelessness. London: Pion Limited.
1981   Rational Landscapes and Humanistic Geography. London: Croom Helm.
1985   Geographical Experiences and Being-in-the-World: The Phenomenological Origins of Geography. In Dwelling, Place and Environment: Towards a Phenomenology of Person and World. David Seamon and Rubert Mugerauer, eds. Pp. 15–32. Dordrecht, the Netherlands: Marinus Nijhoff.
Robinson, Mairi
1985   The Concise Scots Dictionary. Aberdeen: Aberdeen University Press.
Rodman, Margaret C.
1992   Empowering Place: Multilocality and Multivocality. American Anthropologist 94(3):640–656.
Smith, Susan J.
1993   Bounding the Borders: Claiming Space and Making Place in Rural Scotland. Transactions, Institute of British Geographers (n.s.) 18:291–308.
1995   Where to Draw the Line: A Geography of Popular Festivity. In The Urban Context. A. Rogers and S. Vertovec, eds. Pp. 141–164. Oxford: Berg Publishers.
1996   Bordering on Identity. Scotlands 3(1):18–31.
Stuart-Murray, John
1995   Unnamable Landscapes. Landscape Review 2(2):30–41.
Thomas, Julian
1993   The Politics of Vision and the Archaeologies of Landscape. In Landscape: Politics and Perspectives. Barbara Bender, ed. Pp. 19–48. Oxford: Berg.
Tilley, Christopher
1994   A Phenomenology of Landscape: Places, Paths and Monuments. Oxford: Berg.
Watson, Godfrey
1974   The Border Reivers. Warkworth, Northumberland: Sandhill Press.
Weiner, James
1991   The Empty Place: Poetry, Space and Being among the Foi of Papua New Guinea. Bloomington: Indiana University Press.
Williams, Raymond
1975   The Country and the City. Frogmore, St. Albans, Herts: Paladin.

Part IV

Contested Spaces

The following collection of articles focuses attention on the variety of geographic sites associated with social conflicts that engage actors whose social positions are defined by differential control of resources and access to power in contests of confrontation, opposition, subversion, and/or resistance. While these conflicts principally center on the meanings invested in sites, or derived from their interpretation, they reveal broader social struggles over deeply held collective myths. In this way, contested spaces give material expression to and act as loci for creating and promulgating, countering and negotiating dominant cultural themes that find expression in myriad aspects of social life. Spaces are contested precisely because they concretize the fundamental and recurring, but otherwise unexamined, ideological and social frameworks that structure practice. We have included an article by Hilda Kuper describing some key Swazi sites that play a role in defining Swazi identity and their struggles over control with colonial administrators. Gary McDonogh describes the history of how bourgeois elites and residents diverge in their characterization of the *barrio chino* in Barcelona which makes it an appropriate target for urban development schemes. We have also included an excerpt from Steven Gregory's larger work, *Black Corona: Race and the Politics of Place in an Urban Community* (1998), to highlight how an urban American discourse conflating race, poverty, and place is countered and subverted through place-based activism in an urban community.

Further Reading

Bender, Barbara (1998) *Stonehenge: Making Space*. Oxford: Berg.

Lawrence, Denise (1992) Transcendence of Place: The Role of *La Placeta* In Valencia's *Las Fallas*. In I. Altman and S. Low (eds.) *Place Attachment* (pp. 211–230). New York: Plenum.

Low, Setha M. (2000) *On the Plaza: The Politics of Public Space and Culture*. Austin: University of Texas Press.

Moore, Donald (1998) Subaltern Struggles and the Politics of Place: Remapping Resistance in Zimbabwe's Eastern Highlands. *Cultural Anthropology* 13(3), 344–381.

Rotenberg, Robert (1995) *Landscape and Power in Vienna*. Baltimore: Johns Hopkins Press.

11

The Language of Sites in the Politics of Space[1]

Hilda Kuper

This paper emerged as the result of examining several events in my field data relating to political change in Swaziland, Southeast Africa. In each event I became aware of the significance attached to particular sites, special pieces of space. I recognized that these events had their parallels in other countries, and at local, national, and international levels.

I begin this paper with an outline of anthropological approaches to the concept of space, approaches that it seemed might be most relevant to an interpretation of sites; I then present very briefly three field events focused on sites; and I conclude with a discussion of what I call the language of sites in the context of the politics of space.

I

Space is one of those complex concepts that has been approached from different angles and at different levels – philosophical, scientific, and social – and it is obvious from dictionary definitions that the word "space" has a whole range of meanings related to these different approaches. Here it is necessary to point out that the concept of space as defined and developed by philosophers and scientists must not be confused with the experience of space, that is, the values attached through facts of social and personal existence, and that epistemologically we must be wary not to equate space as a feature of the physical (tangible) world, with "social space."

People everywhere face the reality of space and time, but how they cope with them is a cultural variable, evident in language classification, technology, and ideology; and because members of different cultures structure the same physical phenomena through different perspectives and techniques, we cannot assume that they have a concept of space equivalent to our own. It is our task as social scientists to try to analyze these differences as distinct conceptual models of reality; and I suggest that we might perhaps see sites as points of orientation in furthering our understanding of the meaning of space.

As far as I know, Durkheim, together with Mauss, was the first deliberately to bring the concept of "social space" into sociological theory, although the significance of the general concept of space was part of a continuing intellectual discourse and the significance of locality as a principle in the structuring of social relations had been emphasized (Maine 1861; Spencer 1873; Morgan 1877).

Durkheim's writings dealt with social relations at both the empirical and the cognitive level. At the empirical level he described how the pattern of local organization in simple societies was influenced by nature's seasonal supply of food, but his deeper concern was to develop, through examining native classifications of their universe, a general theory of knowledge (Durkheim 1965 [1915]; Durkheim and Mauss 1963 [1903]). To him, classification was a universal phenomenon of social origin, derived from the collective representations of a society and "even ideas so abstract as those of time and space are, at each point in their history, closely connected with the corresponding social organization" (1963 [1903]:88).

The different levels of Durkheimian analysis were extended and modified, but it is possible to distinguish the two levels, the one most clearly represented in the writings of Radcliffe-Brown, the other explored by Evans-Pritchard. Radcliffe-Brown focused empirical analysis on arbitrarily delineated localities:

> Every human society has some sort of territorial structure. We can find clearly-defined local communities, the smallest of which are linked together in a larger society, of which they are segments. This territorial structure provides the framework, not only for political organization, whatever it may be, but for other forms of social organization also, such as the economic. [Radcliffe-Brown in Fortes and Evans-Pritchard 1940:xiv]

The limitations and essentially static quality inherent in structural-functional models drove several social anthropologists, heralded by Gluckman (1958) to develop "situational" analyses which became elaborated in terms of "networks" and "extended case method" (Barnes 1954; Epstein 1961; Van Velson 1964, 1967; Colson 1958). A recent attempt to include the concept of "process" in a more flexible approach to social boundaries, i.e., the "spatial aspect of social structure" (Radcliffe-Brown 1952:193), led to the formulation of "social field" and "phase developments" (Swartz, Turner, and Tuden 1966). All these studies, irrespective of differences in emphasis, deal essentially with "systems on the ground," and the thrust of the field is on observable conflict as well as cooperation at different political levels.

The cognitive level of Durkheimian structuralism in terms of spatial analysis was developed and refined by Evans-Pritchard whose study of the Nuer (1940) serves both as a classic of formal structural analysis of the interaction of territorial units, and as a model for considering the ideational elements of "social space." He distinguished between physical, ecological and structural space – the physical being the most concrete and the measurable, the ecological being "a relation between communities defined in terms of density and distribution," and with reference to natural resources, and the structural "as the relations between groups of persons in a social system expressed in terms of values" (1940:190–210).

Since the publication of *The Nuer*, distinctions between spatial arrangements "on the ground," native classification of such arrangements, and the analyst's interpretation thereof, have been formulated with different degrees of precision in much ethnographic presentation (Leach 1954; Lévi-Strauss 1963). Leach in particular illuminated differences in spatial relations in social structure considered as an abstract model of an ideal society and the social structure of any actual empirical society (1954:15).

The relativity of the notion of space was vividly illustrated by Bohannan, who, with his flair for reversing the social mirror, argued that Westerners have a mechanistic "folk notion" of space, correlated with the development of the sextant and other "scientific" surveying equipment, while people who do not have "the same gadgetry" see it in terms of social relations, kinsmen, time, and effort (Bohannan 1963:44–45).

A more universalistic, and at the same time phenomenological, interpretation was pursued by Lévi-Strauss, who suggested that the study of such specific "spatial phenomena" as the distribution of particular camps, the layout of towns, the network of roads, "permits us to grasp the natives' own conception of their social structure; and, through our examination of the gaps and contradictions, the real structure, which is often very different from the natives' conception, becomes accessible" (1967 [1963]:328). Lévi-Strauss recognized that the correlation between "spatial configuration" and "social structure" may in some cases be obvious, in others evident but not clear, and in others "extremely difficult to discover." His controversial analysis of the Bororo was essentially an attempt to demonstrate that "their spatial configurations reflect not the true, unconscious social organization but a model existing consciously in the native mind, though its nature is entirely illusory and even contradictory to reality" (1967 [1963]:285). His assumption was that any manifestation of social phenomena – a mode of marriage, the arrangement of a village – constitutes a language in the sense that it can be reduced to a set of abstract rules and expressed in different models.

Despite the very real differences in the approaches ranging from that of Radcliffe-Brown to Lévi-Strauss, there is a fundamental shared intellectual orientation stemming from the Durkheimian stress on society and social relationships. Social space is analyzed as part of the total system which can be expressed at different levels and through different models of organization. Clearly so-called structuralists have examined the concept of space by different methods and at different levels of interpretation. Some have been concerned specifically with symbols and values evident in spatial arrangements, others with the manipulation of social relationships in territorially defined areas over a period of time, and others with model building. All can be included in the rubric of "structuralist" only because of their orientation towards social relationships and ideologies.

A somewhat different orientation to "space" was pioneered in the cultural approach of Malinowski, who considered space and time essential components of the "context of culture." His theoretical problem was how to get from the basic "biological needs" of individuals – needs shared with other animals – to the observable facts of culturally organized behavior. But he also considered territoriality, locality, propinquity, and contiguity as principles of grouping (1960[1944]:56) and demonstrated in brilliant ethnographic detail how people interpreted as well as utilized space, whether in gardening, building or trade exchange. Sites, specified by functional activities, were analyzed as part of every institution, and every institution had its diverse aspects – legal, economic, religious, political, social. His imprint is evident not only in the careful documentations of observed interaction made by students trained in the "Malinowski field methods" (e.g., Richards 1939;

Firth 1936; Evans-Pritchard 1937; Schapera 1938; Nadel 1942; Fortes 1945), but in the extensive literature on the symbolic significance of space (e.g., Griaule and Dieterlen 1954; Cunnison 1959; Gluckman 1963;[2] Middleton 1965; Turner 1969; Beidelman 1971; et al.).

A more extreme cultural behavioral approach to space is evident in recent studies by cultural anthropologists for whom Hediger, pioneer in animal psychology, not Durkheim, nor Heidigger, is a reference figure (Hall 1959, 1969; Watson 1970). The leading exponent, Hall, whose perceptive writings underline the importance of nonverbal behavior in interpersonal and cross-cultural communication, has gone so far as to coin a special term "proxemics" for the "interrelated observations and theories of man's use of space as a specialized elaboration of culture" (1969:103). Drawing from experimental work among all animals, he emphasizes the programming of messages to different individuals within each animal species (Hall 1959, ch. 10) and organizes models of classification of "proxemic behavior" at three levels – the infracultural based in man's phylogenetic past, the precultural based on perception through the senses, the structuring of space as modified by culture (Hall 1969). In dealing with cultural modifications, he distinguishes between fixed feature, semi-fixed feature, and informal space (1969:103ff.), and suggests a system for the notation of proxemic behavior in cross-cultural analysis based on quantifiable variables (Hall 1963, 1969; Watson 1970).

The approach of sociologically oriented anthropologists and behaviorally oriented proxemists appears conceptually antithetical. At its most extreme, the former assumes that society is a system *sui generis* with its own unique symbols and constituent elements (persons and groups) capable of deliberately changing as well as transmitting culture through organized modes of interaction. The cultural behaviorists assume the existence of cultural systems deeply rooted in biology and physiology. Even when the same terms are used they appear to receive different interpretations. Thus when Radcliffe-Brown wrote of territorial structure, he referred to arrangements of definable rights (political, legal, economic, religious) exercised by persons or groups within a local framework and validated by social means (Radcliffe-Brown 1940:xiv; Fortes and Evans-Pritchard 1940:10–11). Cultural proxemists list functions of territoriality and consider that "it is in the nature of animals, including man, to exhibit behavior which we call territoriality. In so doing they use the senses to distinguish between one space or distance and another" (Hall 1969:128).

Important as these differences are, they should not be exaggerated: the various approaches are not necessarily mutually exclusive and, instead of being treated as antithetical, may more constructively be considered as complementary and at times overlapping. At the extremes there are two distinctly different levels of approach to "man" – the individual and his behavior; the person and his relationships. But this particular dichotomy has almost disappeared from recent anthropology, and most studies use both levels in different degrees. Nor is it fruitful to emphasize the distinction between culture and society since both meet at the same point – the individual as a person, the person as individual. The contribution of studies of animal behavior was perhaps most explicitly recognized by Malinowski whose "theory of needs" emphasized the biological roots at all levels of cultural activities or institutions (1922, 1935, 1944); the criticism that this "theory" of biological similarities cannot account for cultural differences is equally applicable to the extreme cultural behaviorists.

The stress on symbolic behavior as a generative element is built into schemes of structural relationships as well as of cultural development, although social anthropologists would be more prone to analyze observable social distances in terms of enduring social relationships, general principles of stratification, and social values than by analogies of animal behavior. How can one "prove" Hall's suggestion that human groups (all of whose members surely belong to the same species) can be classified into "contact and non-contact types" in the way Hediger divided different species of animals? (Hall 1963, 1969). But the vocabulary of perception of space that Hall neatly sums up as the "silent language" is also recognized by social anthropologists as relevant ethnographic data, and it was taken for granted that Firth could begin his short book, *Human Types, An Introduction to Social Anthropology* (1956), with contrasts in "codes of manners."[3]

Different indices of social distance may be devised to measure dimensions of spatial relationships. Evans-Pritchard used the terms "distance" and "space" as though they were identical in meaning; analytically it would be more useful to retain "distance" for the specifics of scale, whether measurable by physical, ecological, or structural criteria, and retain the term "social space" for a more general notion, incorporating physical, ecological, and structural distance. The concern for greater methodological rigor is increasing (Mitchell 1967; Watson and Graves 1966); but it is necessary to remember that we should follow the advice that we try to make the important quantifiable rather than the quantifiable important.

Of special relevance at the more qualitative and conceptual level is the work of Mircea Eliade, leading historian of religion, who frequently refers to ethnographic data though his approach is from a level somewhat remote from empirical field situations as commonly understood by anthropologists.[4]

In his numerous writings, he has developed a model of cosmic space, combining ideas from French sociologists (more especially Durkheim and Lévi-Bruhl) with Jung's concept of archetypes – archaic symbols which recur unconsciously among all humans. Central to this model is the distinction between two types of society – archaic (sacred) and modern (technological and profane) – existentially represented by two different types of individual, religious and secular. The sacred is emotionally experienced as unity and order; outside is the profane, the world of chaos.

> For religious man, nothing can begin, nothing can be done, without a previous orientation and any orientation implies acquiring a fixed point. It is for this reason that religious man has always sought to fix his abode at "the centre of the world." If the world is to be lived in, *it must be founded* – and no world can come to birth in the chaos of the homogeneity and relativity of profane space [Eliade 1959:22].

Like Durkheim, Leach, and Lévi-Strauss, Eliade is concerned with models and underlying structures, but according to Eliade every society provides its own model of the cosmos characterized by its own sacred "centre" – the *axis mundi*, the cosmic pillar connecting earth and heaven (Eliade 1961). The importance of this concept will be evident in the events to be described.

Reference will also be made to the immensely perceptive writings of Kenneth Burke, who in *A Grammar of Motives* and *A Rhetoric of Motives* (1962 [1945]) focuses on five ingredients of drama – scene, act, agent, agency, and purpose – interrelated elements of drama corresponding to key questions in anthropology: where and when? what and how? who and why? He argues that the scene:agent ratio is governed by a principle of dramatic consistency to the point that the scene itself can become a force in the motivation of the action. His analysis of drama can, I think, be applied to any *event*, for when an anthropologist talks of an event he is not in fact presenting the event but an account thereof, and the theoretical and technical problem of anthropology is to construct accounts so as to render them comprehensible and comparable with other events in other times and places.

It is clear that there is a good deal of imprecision and confusion in the anthropological use of the concept of "space," and in the assumptions underlying various models involving spatial arrangements both in group and interpersonal interaction. While none of the anthropological approaches that I mentioned deal specifically with the problem which initiated my interest – the meaning of sites in political events – I suggest that by drawing somewhat eclectically but with discrimination on different approaches including that of Eliade and Burke, an examination of sites might provide an additional perspective to the relationship between space and political events.

II

An event can be interpreted as a series of interactions between people interested and involved in a particular issue. Their interests may be similar or divergent, with divergencies of different degrees ranging from almost compatibility to total and irreconcilable opposition. Considering politics as a struggle for power and its rewards in the field of public affairs, political events are by definition a series of more or less competitive divisive interactions. The three events to be described were selected fairly arbitrarily, and many other events from the same period would have served my purpose equally well; they would all illustrate the way key sites are interpreted, and manipulated in political situations by different sets of people at the same times, and by the same people at different times.

In November 1966, the last phase of colonial rule, a meeting was called by representatives of the Swazi people on behalf of the *Ngwenyama*, the hereditary ruler, to inform them of the contents of the new constitution which would recognize the *Ngwenyama* as King and Head of the independent state of Swaziland, a position which from the Swazi point of view he had retained throughout the colonial period. A representative gathering of roughly one thousand subjects gathered at Lobamba, traditional capital (*umphakatsi*) of the Swazi nation and residence of the *Ndlovukati*, mother of the *Ngwenyama*. The people anticipated that the meeting would be held in the *sibaya*, a large open-air arena crudely glossed in English as "cattle byre," but which is also the site of important national gatherings and royal rituals. Shortly before the time of the meeting, a message came from the secretariat at Mbabane, the colonial administrative capital some fifteen miles away, to say that the Queen's Commissioner, i.e., the highest local representative of the British government, would attend the meeting. After some indecision, the crowd moved from the village of Lobamba to the "Office" of the Swazi National Council, a Western public-works style building about half a mile away and out of sight of Lobamba village. Since the crowd was so large, most of the people squatted outside facing notables who sat on chairs on the veranda of the office. The Secretary of the Nation then informed the crowd that Her Majesty's Commissioner had come to present the *Ngwenyama* with a medal from the Red Cross. Having done this with full formality, the Queen's Commissioner left, explaining that he had a "very important" duty ahead – the Annual General Meeting of the Red Cross. As soon as he had driven off, the *Ngwenyama* announced in *siSwati* to the crowd, "Everyone speaks of matters of importance in the place of his own ancestral spirits (*emadloti*). We shall move from the site of foreign spirits (*emandzawe*) to the *sibaya*." This was greeted with great applause, and we all went back again to the village and into the *sibaya*, where everyone sat on the ground according to status. The real meeting took place according to customary procedure, and in an atmosphere palpably distinct from that of the "Office."

The political significance of the movement between *sibaya* and "Office" can be examined in a sociological, historical, and ideological perspective, with the two sites symbolizing contrasted and opposed values expressed in distinctive architectural plans and styles. In the pre-colonial era, i.e., before the Boer or British assumed control, the Swazi developed a complex dual monarchy represented by the *Ngwe-nyama* and the *Ndlovukati*. The network of government radiated from the *umpha-katsi*, the largest and most important royal village. Each *Ngwenyama* also established his own separate village but his first two queens, associated with him by special ritual, always remained at the *umphakatsi* with the *Ndlovukati*. A new *umphakatsi* was founded in each reign on a selected and sanctified site and to it were brought the most ancient and sacred objects, and into the new structures were built tangible symbols – ropes, poles, woven mats – from the previous *umphakatsi*. Swazi conceptualize each *umphakatsi* as a continuation and extension of their past; and old sites are remembered together with their founders, and a new *umphakatsi* is given the name of a historical landmark.

In the period of autonomous rulers, boundaries were flexible and reflected polit-ical loyalties; the measure was people rather than land *per se*. In the colonial regime boundaries were rigidly defined on the ground, irrespective of the people's loyalties.

In southern Africa where boundaries were delimited by the Boer, British, and Portuguese, Swaziland was delimited, without the consent of the Swazi, as a small country (6704 square miles), and approximately half of the Swazi population found themselves outside its borders. Moreover, in 1907, as a result of the Concessions Partition Proclamation, Swazi inside Swaziland were deprived of two-thirds of their land; and many of the powers formerly exercised by Swazi were explicitly taken over by the new rulers. But, partly because the Swazi were not defeated in open warfare and partly because of the relatively limited attempts at development or even active interference by the few colonial officials, many of the structures and beliefs of traditional Swazi culture persisted with "kingship" (*bukhosi*) as the central symbol of Swazi identity. The present Lobamba perpetuates the *umphakatsi* of Sobhuza I, also known as Somhlolo (The Wonder) great-grandfather of the present *Ngwe-nyama*, Sobhuza II.

Behind the *umphakatsi* lies a mental blueprint of the hierarchical scheme of Swazi kingship, a kingship in which the sacred and secular were subtly merged. The whole village is laid out in the form of a crescent moon (*umkhumbi*), or, as "horns of cattle," curving round the *sibaya*. People and things of greatest national value are protected by an outer semicircle of huts occupied by ordinary citizens and by the regiments whose barracks (*emalawu*) are built at the entrance to the village.

The *sibaya* is always the first structure, and it must be emphasized that cattle have a deeply religious as well as economic and legal significance in Swazi culture (Kuper 1947, 1963). Separated from the outer huts by a narrow lane is an inner semicircle of huts which include the *indlunkhulu*, *sigodlo*, and *tindlu talabakhulu*. The *indlunkhulu* (literally, hut great) contains the living, cooking, and store huts of the *Ndlovukati* and also *indlunkhulu* proper, the shrine hut dedicated to the spirits of past rulers. The *sigodlo* (from *kugodla* to keep, to protect) *is* the enclosure of wives of *Ngwenyama*. *Tindlu talabakhulu* (literally, huts of the great) occupy special sites on either side of the *indlunkhulu–sigodlo* complex. In the original plan two sites were reserved for *tinsila* (literally, filth, body sweat – the ritual blood brothers) of the *Ngwenyama* (Kuper 1947). Other national officials have their status and identity ritually "pegged" into the ground.[5] The ignorant outsider may see no difference between the huts of a queen and that of her lowliest attendant, but to a Swazi the symbolism of siting is obvious and meaningful.

Though major and conspicuous changes have taken place in Swaziland in recent years, the *umphakatsi* remains fundamentally the same since I first lived there in 1934. There are obvious changes including the use of some new building materials, more square houses, two public water points, an electric spotlight, a couple of police guard boxes – and also inevitable changes in the demographic composition, but the underlying structure persists; and as long as Swazi kingship (*bukhosi*) continues, it can be predicted that there will be an *umphakatsi*, an *axis mundi*, sacred center of the Swazi cosmos.

Lihovisi (the "Office"), on the other hand, is a relatively new establishment. It had been built after 1950 by the Public Works Department for the Swazi National Council (SNC) when the British succeeded in introducing three Acts, considered by them necessary for the model of "Indirect Rule" – the Native Authority Act, Native Courts Act, and Native Treasury Act. Swazi saw the SNC office not only as architecturally contrasted but ideologically opposed to the *sibaya*. It was a brick building with an iron roof, and contained only three small offices and a large hall with entrance and exit onto verandas that ran along the back and the front. One office used by two typists and a clerk led from the veranda into the office of the Swazi official who held the responsible position of Secretary of the Nation; the office on the other side of the hall served the two Swazi officials who ran the "Swazi National Treasury" which was less than one-tenth of the total revenue.

To the Swazi, the "Office" symbolized their position as a subordinated nation dominated by foreigners. It did not matter that the building was described by a British civil servant as "functional and adequate"! And it did not occur to him that it was insulting to them when he argued that it was of more durable material than "even the *indlunkhulu*," or pointed out that it was "equipped with typewriters and a telephone." To my Swazi friends it expressed the "colonial mentality," and they did not compare it to the buildings of the *umphakatsi* but to the offices and homes occupied by White civil servants. On several occasions the Secretary and different members of the National Council publicly enumerated obvious facts of racial discrimination (*lubandlululo*) – ranging from the absence of amenities such as lighting and water supplies to the differential rates of pay of Swazi traditional officials and White civil servants.

Discussing the meaning of the move from *umphakatsi* to *lihovisi* and back to the *sibaya*, informants expressed clearly the general theme that it was an assertion of their Swazi identity. This was summed up in a statement by one of the councillors: "We are Swazi and we meet in the *sibaya* for affairs of our nation." *Ngwenyama*'s reference to *emandzawe* was understood by all. *Emandzawe* were the spirits of Sotho killed in a battle with the Swazi; in revenge the spirits "entered" the bodies of Swazi warriors. This epidemic of "possession" killed some and made others temporarily mad. One informant gave an interesting semantic commentary: "When we meet in the *sibaya* to discuss, we must sit down (*hlala pansi*). We are close to *labaphansi* (those who are down below), that is the ancestors (*emadloti*). We remember them in the *sibaya*. In the office we sit on chairs (*hlala etitulweni*) like Europeans (*Belumbi*) who do not connect with our ancestors."

The message of the sites in this particular situation was obvious – *sibaya* and *lihovisi* though physically close were culturally incompatible; and in terms of social structure the distance between the group represented by the Queen's Commissioner and that represented by the "Office" was greater than the distance between residents of Lobamba and residents of the most remote of Swazi villages.

My second example relates to a long-drawn-out dispute about a site for a building in which the first parliament, consisting of a House of Assembly and a Senate, could hold sessions. The existing Legislative Council established by Order in Council, December 1963, had been using the office of the High Court at Mbabane. It was made up of twelve persons elected on a National Roll of whom four were Europeans (Whites), four persons elected on a European Roll, eight persons elected in accordance with Swazi traditional methods, four officials (all Europeans), and one nominated member. It was generally an unpopular imposed constitution, and at the first meeting, in September 1964, Prince Makhosini, leader of the Imbokodvo, the royalist party in power, formally requested that it be changed. This was eventually agreed to, and provisions were made for a new constitution, with a duly elected parliament, and a stage of internal self-government prior to independence.

The history of the dispute is very briefly as follows: the Queen's Commissioner had appointed a committee chaired by the Government Secretary, a British civil servant, to select a site. Swazi members included Prince Makhosini, who informed the committee that the Swazi wanted the building to be on land which would be allocated by the *Ngwenyama* in the Lobamba district, but the British officials insisted that it be at Mbabane. The Swazi members went along with this reluctantly until the matter came before the full Legislative Council in its final session (February, 1969). Then, to the "amazement" of the Government Secretary (a British civil servant) several leading Swazi members stood up and refused to accept the decision. Antagonism and criticims were openly voiced, and it was only when Prince Makhosini gave an obviously factual and totally convincing account of the negotiations which completely discredited the presentation by the Government Secretary, and drew support from some European Council members, that the British officials recognized defeat. Soon after Independence (September 6, 1968), Parliament was built on a piece of Swazi nation land, near the "Office," allocated by the *Ngwenyama* in the Lobamba district.

While in the first event the *sibaya* of the *umphakatsi* was contrasted with the "Office" built by the British, in the second event Lobamba was contrasted with Mbabane and Swazi nation land with White-owned land. The name Lobamba referred in this situation not only to the *umphakatsi* but to the surrounding area, which included the *lihovisi* that was the symbol of colonialism in the first event. The variation in the meaning of the term Lobamba indicates the relativity of group identifications. Depending on the context, Lobamba refers to the *sibaya* of the *umphakatsi*, to the *umphakatsi* as a total village and to the district in which it is situated. The folk model of Swazi identification can be described in Evans-Pritchard's terms: "A man sees himself as a member of a group only in opposition to other groups, and he sees a member of another group as a member of a social unity however much it may split into opposed segments" (1940:137).

Throughout the debate on the choice of site, Swazi members of the Legislative Council emphasized the emotional and historical significance of Lobamba, and the contrast in conceptualization between it and Mbabane was particularly well put by Councillor Prince Masitsela who said:

> If you are in possession of something you treasure most, it is our custom to take it to one's grandmother and enjoy it there. It is a known fact that if you are going to enjoy something delicious, you always enjoy it at home in the protection of your parents and ancestors. If this were enjoyed elsewhere fights might ensue ... All of us Swazi regard Lobamba as the home of our grandparents. Possibly Government regards Mbabane and not Lobamba as our ancestral headquarters [Swaziland Legislative Council, Official Report. February 16–March 7, 1967:43].

Suggestive perhaps of the difference in cultural orientation is the difference in derivation of the Swazi word *umphakatsi* and the English word "capital." To translate *umphakatsi* as "capital" is a distortion culturally analogous to glossing *sibaya* as "cattle byre." *Umphakatsi* is derived from *phakatsi*, within, the inner, the heart; "capital" of course is derived from the Latin word *caput*, the head, the seat of intellect. *Umphakatsi* carries a vital (visceral?) imagery; "capital" conveys the idea of administration and bureaucracy.

My third example of the language of sites focuses on the reactions of different political factions to a rebellious prince returning to the ancestral fold. In Swaziland as elsewhere the nationalist struggle gave rise to political factions, some of which crystallized into political parties. The great majority of the people support the Imbokodvo, created in 1963 as a national movement by the *Ngwenyama*; the main opposition, drawn largely from workers in urban areas and company towns, support the Ngwane National Liberatory Congress (N.N.L.C.), a party which was critical *inter alia* of hereditary chieftainship. In 1964 Dumisa, classificatory son of the *Ngwenyama*, was elected organizing secretary of the N.N.L.C., and became a popular hero by voicing many of the grievances of African workers. He was a leading figure in (peaceful) strikes which ended with the British flying in troops from Kenya. Dumisa was charged by the Swaziland government with committing various offenses, not all directly political, and his case was taken to the High Court at Mbabane. Pending trial he estreated bail and fled the country, visiting contracts in newly independent Africa and elsewhere, including Peking and Moscow. But he returned after a few months, gave himself up, and at the end of serving a relatively short sentence, announced in December 1966 through the *Times of Swaziland* – the only local newspaper – that he was resigning from the N.N.L.C. to join the Imbo-kodvo and "serve his King and country."

This news, which came as a surprise to many, although obviously not to those in positions of highest authority, set in motion a whole chain of meetings, some taking place simultaneously, in discrete places considered appropriate for action by separate interested groups. Members of the Imbokodvo, wishing to establish his bona fides before accepting him, held meetings at the "Office"; close kinsmen, whose privileges and authority he had indirectly challenged, met in the private enclosure of the *Ndlovukati*, at Lobamba the *umphakatsi*; and Congress supporters who considered he had betrayed them held a stormy rally in a public hall in the African township of Msunduza in Mbabane. Dumisa was re-admitted to the Imbokodvo and in a moving ceremony reconciled with the royal kin, but his life was considered to be in danger from some of his erstwhile followers and he was sent out of the country, "for further education."

The Swazi were not concerned with the legal aspects, which had been dealt with by Western-run courts; had they wished to hold a separate trial, they could have used a different procedure and their own hierarchy of courts. Cases brought on appeal to the capital are tried *enkhundleni* (locative of *inkhundla* – a specified area *outside* the *sibaya*).

The issues raised by Dumisa's particular political action were dealt with not in terms associated with the *inkhundla* or the *sibaya*, but with the *indlunkhulu*, the "Office," and Msunduza Hall. In every homestead, the *indlunkhulu* is the locus of important kinship decisions; and this applies to the *indlunkhulu* of the *umphakatsi* though the private life of members of the royal lineage is of public concern. Dumisa, as every Swazi knew, had the right by birth to go in and out of the *indlunkhulu* as freely as children sired by the *Ngwenyama* himself; the *umphakatsi* was his "home," the *Ndlovukati* was his loving *gogo* (grandmother). It was partly his position in the royal genealogy and partly his political activities that made him a dangerously controversial figure, a source of incipient friction among the princes; it was therefore their right to criticize and question him on his kinship loyalties within the privacy of the *indlunkhulu* of the *umphakatsi* and in the presence of the *Ngwenyama*, the *Ndlovukati*, and others of the inner circle.

The "Office" drew a somewhat overlapping but much wider audience. The Imbokodvo was nationally recognized as the political arm of the Swazi National Council (S.N.C.); the "Office" was thus the correct place for investigating Dumisa's application for admission to the Imbokodvo and his previous actions in the N.N.L.C. Here he was questioned not as a "prince" of the royal lineage, but as a politician, and neither the *Ngwenyama* nor the *Ndlovukati* was present.

Msunduza Hall, a large multi-functional room, was named after a progressive Resident Commissioner, Ainsworth Dickson, nicknamed *Msunduza* – One-who-pushes-forward; he inaugurated the Progressive Association in 1929 from which the first Swazi political party (the Swaziland Progressive Party) developed in 1959.

Many chiefs did not allow public meetings of the N.N.L.C. in their areas and the Msunduza Hall was one of the few places available for any functions, social as well as political. N.N.L.C. leaders had planned a great party to welcome Dumisa on his release from prison; many could not believe he had defected. Among them were those who had made it possible for him to get out of Swaziland and establish contacts with countries whose policies he was publicly rejecting.

In each of the events I have described, individuals played a series of political roles indicated in part by the scenes (sites) in which they appeared. It remains to expound a few general ideas on this approach.

III

A site can be defined as a particular piece of social space, a place socially and ideologically demarcated and separated from other places. As such it becomes a symbol within the total and complex system of communication in the total social universe. Social relations are articulated through particular sites, associated with different messages and ranges of communication. Thus a site can be a cattle byre, a house, a village, a building, a town, a country, and each conveys and evokes a range of responses. The importance of these sites is not only their manifest and distinctive appearance, but their qualifying and latent meaning. This can be derived only after studying both the social relations and the ideational system of ordering places within the universe of the particular society or group with which one is concerned. Relationships which we label political may replicate, reinforce, or contradict relationships expressed by economic, religious, or other social actions.

In discussing any event, it is necessary to understand why particular actions took place on a particular site or sites and not elsewhere; and although the same site may be used for different purposes (as in the examples where the *sibaya* was used for national meetings, stalling cattle, or royal rituals, and the courthouse was used for meetings of the Legislative Council as well as legal trials), each site conveys a limited range of messages, and can be used only for culturally related activities. In fact it might not be too far-fetched to consider a site as a scene in the sense used by Kenneth Burke who, in his analysis of drama, stated: "From the motivational point of view there is implicity in the quality of a scene, the quality of the action that is to take place within ... thus when the curtain rises to disclose a given stage-set, this stage-set contains, simultaneously, implicitly, all that the narrative is to draw out, as a sequence, explicitly" (1962 [1945]:6–7).

In describing "political events," sites such as a courtroom, a Red Square, Whitehall, the White House can be interpreted as giving an emotional effect, comparable to the power of rhetoric, to the voice of authority; similarly in describing "rituals," temples, shrines, or graveyards may be seen as generating an appropriate quality of sacredness; or in discussing economics, the market-place, the stock exchange, a bank, provide the impression of substance. In short, there is a condensation of values in particular sites, and transactions that constitute the totality of social life may be spatially mapped with specific sites expressing relatively durable structured interests and related values. Each site may be perceived in terms of social space – physical, ecological, and structural distance – so that there is a relativity of reference points for the groups involved in interaction. The same site may be differently manipulated according to specific group interests, but the total spatial arrangements form a general network of communication.

The process of political interaction may be expressed empirically through disputes over or manipulations of sites, and symbolically in the language of sites. It does not matter whether the site be a cattle byre, a house of parliament, a public hall, or even rooms in a university! Though the process is similar, the range of people and groups affected may vary from a few individuals to an entire nation.

Social space as Durkheim recognized and Eliade reemphasized is never neutral, never homogeneous. Some sites have more power and significance than others, and these qualities need have no *fixed* relationship to a physical, empirical dimension. Yet since they are often symbolized in tangible forms, including sites on the ground, political influence may manifest itself in bestowing these qualities through the manipulating of forms. Externally the *umphakatsi* is a sacred center where the cosmic forces converge with the political, economic, and military dimensions into the concept of Swazi kingship and national identity. Internally the *umphakatsi* is divided into its own sacred and secular sites, interpreted and manipulated for specific purposes by different, but not necessarily opposing, interest groups.

A "cosmic centre" can incorporate physical structures which *appear* to be contradictory, but the actual structures are less important than the permanent and enduring mental blueprint, an idealized conscious model which guides their layout. A traditional model can, therefore, incorporate into its timelessness, structures from different times. There is no anachronism in a model. The *indlunkhulu*, focus of past values, has been illuminated, since 1968, by a vast electric spotlight. There is no incompatibility between the traditional barracks and police guard boxes installed on the model of the shelters for the guards outside Buckingham Palace. The barracks represent the old modes of protection. The guard boxes were introduced in 1964 after a period of mysterious fires during the period of turmoil prior to the "first constitution."

Sites are verbally as well as spatially identified. Implicit in my description of events is the theme that values are embodied in words through which they influence behavior and, as Evans-Pritchard also argued, variations in the meaning of a particular word are not due to inconsistencies of the language, but to the relativity of group values to which the word refers (1940:135–138). The boundaries of sites may be said to fluctuate with oral articulation, and to overlap to the extent that words themselves shift their meaning.

Verbal imagery shapes and is shaped by empirical conditions and it is not surprising that in another culture the *axis mundi*, labeled *umphakatsi*, has its key structures shaped in circles, elemental cosmic forms.

Social interactions which take place within and between the inner circle and the outer world do not necessarily involve Lévi-Strauss's concept of opposition. Opposition only becomes acute when people holding different sets of imagery and valuing different sites are in a single politically defined territory. When one group is dominant it may express its domination by ignoring, neglecting, and even obliterating the established sites of the subordinated people.

The maximum effect of the politics of space is probably evident in countries where colonial powers assumed control and allocated to White settlers the more fertile and healthy areas. The most blatant and deliberate example of this at the present time is the Republic of South Africa where the master plan of *apartheid* is supported by racially discriminatory Land Acts and a Group Areas Act which restrict rights of domicile, residence, and work by race and ethnic zones.

Analysis of Swaziland events indicated that full desegregation of a colonial society was perceived by the colonized as more than the removal of discriminatory legislation; it requires the reallocation of social as well as physical space; that is, it is not only a redistribution of land and other resources but the creation of new spatial foci (new sites) of national identity.

Conclusion

I have attempted in this paper to interpret a number of field situations in which the question "where?" appeared to be a central issue: where a particular meeting should be held, an official building be erected, an investigation take place. In answering the question where, I had perforce to examine what was involved and how the issues were dealt with. And behind the where, what, and how, lay the question why – why those special sites? And built into the where, the what, the how, and why, was the question that relates to the essence of anthropology – the who – who were the participants in these events, those social dramas taking place in the shifting scenes of history?

I stated earlier that the events were rather arbitrarily selected but the presentation in terms of content and sequence indicated that there may have been an awareness of basic structural similarities and generalized processual stages that intuitively guided my selection. Each event revealed a wide range of social facts (common things and concepts) expressed in the language of sites. Ultimately the classification was a replication of the complex social classification embodied both in an enduring system and in historical change. It included rank by pedigree (a dominant classification within the traditional system), stratification by race (characteristic of the colonial situation), and opposition between political parties (in the period approaching national independence). The system of classification was not itself spatial but expressed in the language of space.

I deliberately excluded discussion of the complex interaction of space and time but some remarks are appropriate because of the nature of the events which are set in temporal as well as spatial contexts, and the extension of this type of analysis applies also to concepts of time. Thus, at least two levels of time appear parallel to this approach to space – the one could be described as the condensation of events into enduring structures across time and the other as sequential time in terms of historical interaction. The first is evident in the cycle of Swazi capitals and the network of native villages while the second is seen in the shifting, and conflicting, positions of Swazi and Europeans in the development of governmental institutions.

Though I had no preconceived theory into which I wanted to force my facts, and no specific propositions I was seeking to test, I found that a selective use of writings by structural and cultural anthropologists brought an intellectual order into the events, and that by focusing on the sites (Burke's "scenes") at which the action took place it was possible to "make sense" of the events in a particular perspective. The concept of "the politics of space" emerged in manipulating the language of sites – pieces of "social space."

NOTES

1   I wish to thank the National Science Foundation for a grant (1966–68) and the Guggenheim Foundation for a Fellowship (1969-70). The first version of this paper was presented to a graduate seminar at UCLA and subsequently delivered at the Southwestern Anthropology Association, Tucson, 1971. Comments were appreciated more particularly from Thoko Ginindza, David Kuby, William Lakeland, Jan Minnick, Beth Prinz, William Rittenberg, Professors Leo Kuper, Max Gluckman and Sally Moore.
2   Since completing this article, Max Gluckman drew my attention to his discussion of space in *The Ideas in Barotse Jurisprudence* (1963:129–141). His approach is somewhat similar to my own but his interest is different and he deals specifically with the symbolic significance of space in the legal relationship of man to land as immovable property. My focus is more directly on various meanings of sites in the context of complex and conflicting political interactions, and at a general level I would argue that the past is written into sites not because land is fixed and permanent and distinct from movable property, but because new sites can be established both to replicate and to develop relationships and because a range of concepts – political, economic, and religious, etc., – are carried through and over land in sets of symbols, including sites.
3   While the label "proxemics" is new, the field contents are not; there would be as much, or as little, justification for putting a circle round all the behavior of man in regard to the structuring of space as there would be to make an anthropological package of time – for which one could coin the appropriate term "tempotics": and provide equivalent opportunity for such cross-cultural measurement as punctuality, diurnal and nocturnal routine, long/short, sundowner/moonlighter!
4   Eliade is a Romanian who, after attending the University of Bucharest, spent three years studying Indian philosophy at the University of Calcutta and the techniques of yoga at the ashram of Rishikesh. During World War II he served as cultural attache in London and Lisbon, and after the war lectured in the department of the History of Religions at the Ecole des Hautes Etudes, Sorbonne (the same institute as Lévi-Strauss). Since 1956, Eliade has been in the U.S.A. Between the concepts of Eliade (Homo Religioso) and Lévi-Strauss, (Homo sic!) I perceive both "oppositions" and "transformations," although Lévi-Strauss does not refer to the writings of Eliade, and Eliade refers more frequently to Durkheim and Lévi-Bruhl, and both Eliade and Lévi-Strauss might resent the comparison!
5   In the ritual of building and securing a homestead against harm (*kubetsela*) a specialist (*inyanga*) stakes pegs (*tikhonknane*) of special wood into the site.

REFERENCES

Barnes, J. A.
   1954   Class and Committees in a Norwegian Island Parish. Human Relations 7:39-58.
Beidelman, T. O.
   1971   The Kaguru. New York: Holt, Rinehart & Winston.

Bohannan, Paul
   1963   Social Anthropology. New York: Holt, Rinehart & Winston.
Burke, Kenneth
   1962   A Grammar of Motives and A Rhetoric of Motives. New York: World Publishing,
      Meridian Books. (First published in 1945.)
Colson, E.
   1958   Marriage and the Family among the Plateau Tonga of Northern Rhodesia. Man-
      chester: Manchester University Press.
Cunnison, I.
   1959   The Luapula Peoples of Northern Rhodesia: Custom and History in Tribal Politics.
      New York: Humanities Press.
Durkheim, Emile
   1965   The Elementary Forms of Religious Life. New York: Macmillan. (First published in
      1915.)
Durkheim, Emile, and Marcel Manss
   1963   Primitive Classification. Chicago: University of Chicago Press. (First published in
      1903.)
Eliade, M.
   1959   The Sacred and the Profane. New York: Harcourt, Brace. (First published in 1957.)
   1961   Images and Symbols. London: Sheed and Ward. (First published in 1952.)
Epstein, A. L.
   1961   The Network and Urban Social Organization. Rhodes Livingstone Journal 29:29-
      62.
Evans-Pritchard, E. E.
   1937   Witchcraft, Oracles and Magic among the Azande. Oxford: Clarendon Press.
   1940   The Nuer. Oxford: Clarendon Press.
Firth, R.
   1936   We, the Tikopia. London: Allen and Unwin.
   1956   Human Types, revised edition. London: Nelson.
Fortes, M.
   1945   The Dynamics of Clanship among the Tallensi. London: Oxford University Press for
      the International African Institute.
   1949   The Web of Kinship among the Tallensi. London: Oxford University Press for the
      International African Institute.
Fortes, M., and E. E. Evans-Pritchard, Eds.
   1940   African Political Systems. London: Oxford University Press.
Gluckman, M.
   1958   Analysis of a Social Situation in Modern Zululand. Rhodes Livingstone Paper No.
      28. (Reprinted from Bantu Studies, 1940, and African Studies, 1942.)
   1965   The Ideas in Barotse Jurisprudence. New Haven: Yale University Press.
Griaule, M., and G. Dieterlen
   1963   The Dogon. In African Worlds. D. Forde, Ed. London: Oxford University Press.
      (First published in 1954.)
Hall, E. T.
   1959   The Silent Language. Greenwich, Connecticut: Fawcett.
   1963   A System for the Notation of Proxemic Behavior. American Anthropologist
      65:1003-1026.
   1969   The Hidden Dimension. New York: Doubleday. (First published in 1966.)
Kuper, H.
   1947   An African Aristocracy: Rank among the Swazi. London: Oxford University Press
      for the International African Institute.

   1963   The Swazi: A South African Kingdom. New York: Holt, Rinehart & Winston.
Leach, E.
   1954   Political Systems of Highland Burma. Boston: Beacon Press.
Lévi-Strauss, Claude
   1967   Structural Anthropology. New York: Basic Books. (First published in 1963.)
Maine, H.
   1861   Ancient Law. London: Murray, Everyman Ed. (Republished 1917, New York:
      Dutton & Co.)
Malinowski, B.
   1922   Argonauts of the Western Pacific. London: Routledge and Kegan Paul.
   1926   Myth in Primitive Psychology. London: Kegan Paul.
   1935   Coral Gardens and Their Magic. London: Allen & Unwin.
   1960   A Scientific Theory of Culture and Other Essays. Chapel Hill, North Carolina:
      University of North Carolina Press. (First published in 1944.)
Mitchell, J. C.
   1967   On Quantification in Social Anthropology. In The Craft of Social Anthropology. A.
      L. Epstein, Ed. London: Tavistock.
Morgan, L. H.
   1877   Ancient Society. New York: World Publishing.
Nadel, S. F.
   1942   A Black Byzantium. London: Oxford University Press for the International African
      Institute.
Radcliffe-Brown, A. R.
   1940   Preface. In African Political Systems. M. Fortes and E. E. Evans-Pritchard, Eds.
      London: Oxford University Press for the International African Institute.
   1952   Structure and Function in Primitive Society. London: Cohen and West.
Richards, A. I.
   1939   Land, Labour and Diet in Northern Rhodesia. London: Oxford University Press for
      the International African Institute.
Schapera, I.
   1938   A Handbook of Tswana Law. London: Oxford University Press for the International
      African Institute.
Spencer, H.
   1873   The Study of Sociology. New York: Appleton.
Swartz, M. J., V. W. Turner, and A. Tuden, Eds.
   1966   Political Anthropology. Chicago: Aldine.
Turner, V. W.
   1969   The Ritual Process. London: Routledge & Kegan Paul.
Van Velsen, J.
   1964   The Politics of Kinship. Manchester: Manchester University Press for Rhodes-Liv-
      ingstone Institute.
   1967   The Extended-case Method and Situational Analysis. In The Craft of Social Anthro-
      pology. A. L. Epstein, Ed. London: Tavistock.
Watson, O. M.
   1970   Proxemic Behavior: A Cross-Cultural Study. The Hague: Mouton.
Watson, O. M., and E. D. Graves
   1966   Quantitative Research in Proxemic Behavior. American Anthropologist 68:971-985.
Wilson, Monica
   1950   Communal Ritual of the Nyakusa. London: Oxford University Press.

12

Myth, Space, and Virtue: Bars, Gender, and Change in Barcelona's *Barrio Chino*

Gary Wray McDonogh

> When you see boards guarding a facade and workers busy on the bottom floor of a house, you need not bother them to ask what is going on. It means they are establishing a cafe. Or a bar. There is no doubt. Each day the number of cafes and bars grows extraordinarily. There are streets in which every other building has a bar. There are streets where even this accounting is unfair: every building has a bar.
>
> (Andrés Hurtado, *El Escándalo*, 1926:3)

The culture of cities is characterized by continual tensions among symbolic processes that imbue social spaces with meaning and social divisions that include and exclude social groups with regard to place and presence. Cities as social and conceptual spaces thus not only embody densities of peoples and activities and layers of history and function, but also incorporate continual cultural struggles over basic meanings of urban life. Urban places take shape within these constant conflicts over ideology as well as political economic power, even as the mappings of dominant groups appear to transcend their social production to constitute the "common sense" of "average" citizens. Thus, the cultural analysis of place demands both the delineation of salient features of the city and the dissection of the social formation of difference.

This article analyzes this conflictive formation of place in modern Barcelona through the intersection of cultural categories and power relations in an ambiguous social space – bars. Bars, here taken as a loose category including establishments for liquor, cabarets and related centers, long have been ubiquitous in the city, as the prefatory citation suggests. Yet, bars also may become defining characteristics of a single neighborhood, social group, or values, especially in discussions of the limits of citizenship and morality. Nor has this process been unique to Barcelona; in New York's Harlem and Greenwich Village, Paris's Montmartre or Hong Kong's Wan Chai, bars often become public markers in the description and control of zones of vice. Furthermore, this identification can be generalized to the neighborhood and, more importantly, to its inhabitants (Siegel 1986). Reformers (and voyeurs) may see bars as reproducing social problems – robbing the earnings of the working-class family – or threatening moral decay in the virtuous city (Rorabaugh 1979). Hence, bars as cultural signifiers, especially in reference to the *barrio chino*, the portside lower-class neighborhood of Barcelona where I have worked since 1975, intersect with geographies of power and constructions of gender as urban signifying systems. Space, power, and gender "meet in the bar" to define the hegemonically proper or "virtuous." Yet, such bars also permit alternative social values and cultural interpretations to be created and reproduced.

Of course, others also portray bars as intrinsic loci of urban civilization, relaxed and literate conversation and interactions that define civic refinement (see Berlanstein 2001). When the middle-class Barcelona barrio of Gràcia, for example, celebrated its 1989 patronal feast, the inaugural speaker proclaimed that "civilization begins where there are streets with bars." Yet, a newspaper commentator noted the next day that, "perhaps it would be better to say that civilization in Gràcia begins where there are streets with bars, because it would be difficult to qualify as civilized that which happens in some streets with bars in Lloret, Sitges[1], or in some areas of the misnamed barrio chino of Barcelona" (Navarro Arisa 1989:15). The evaluation of bars, therefore, reflects the position and agenda of the reader and concomitant evaluations of space and society.

Nonetheless, urban culture incorporates such interpretations, propagated by rumor, media and social critics, into wider "public" knowledge, myths of the city.[2] Power becomes embedded not only in evaluations and control but also in unexamined links among gender, virtue, space, class, and rights. As Liz Bondi has shown in her work on English gentrification, women and men in "marginal" areas become marked by the landmarks of vice that play a role in the romanticized historical imagery of their changing neighborhood (1998). "Spatializing" immorality allows others to differentiate themselves as virtuous by location and behavior as space and virtue reinforce each other while intimately dividing social worlds. Good Barcelona men relax in good bars in good neighborhoods, possibly with good women (who might also stay at home). Historically, men also confirmed their goodness (and that of their homebound women) in male expeditions to the *barrio chino*, where men and women were bad, as the depraved spectacle of bars proved.

In contrast to these widespread myths, my fieldwork in Barcelona's *barrio chino* revealed more complex and fluid social patterns of bars amid a multi-faceted range of establishments articulating varied local needs and links to the wider city. Shaped by yet sometimes opposed to urban myth and practice, these bars are not simple loci of resistance. Local customs and beliefs nuance, mirror, or invert wider urban interpretations of place, gender, and virtue including contradictions. Understanding the multiple meanings of bars in the *barrio chino*, however, fosters a more critical geography of social and symbolic spaces and their implications for a changing city.

From this research, I argue that Barcelona's cultural "localization" of "vicious" women in portside bars, which implies evil environs, lascivious temptations and sometimes urban reform, relies on and conceals complex repressive processes. Indeed, in the decade since this article appeared, this historical image of "a bad place" has fostered extensive transformations of the *barrio chino* through gentrification and aestheticization in conjunction with removal of problematic populations.

This essay first situates bars within historically constructed myths of the *barrio chino*. It then provides ethnographic analysis of such bars, primarily based on observations between 1976 and 1995,[3] to disentangle categories of gender, social function and urban interaction within them. The depiction of a single neighborhood bar over two decades also illustrates how social and cultural patterns in the barrio and city change over time. An epilogue on the 21st-century city underscores the ongoing impact of ideologies of space and virtue on this barrio, its peoples and places.

The *Barrio Chino* Myth: Bars, Gender, and Disorder

Multiple media have widely disseminated vivid images of the *barrio chino* for more than a century: literature, newspapers, theater, films, television, and anthropological and sociological texts (Paquer 1962; Fabre and Huertas 1977; Boatwright and Da Cal 1984; McDonogh 1987; Artigues Vidal et al. 1980, etc.). Anecdotes and rumors about the area and famous landmarks also enliven conversations with many Barcelonins, creating an oral tradition of urban moral geography. Yet, even the term 'barrio chino' (Chinatown), applied to the crowded streets of this central neighborhood, represents literary embellishment on more typical urban construction of zones of behavioral license. Historically, the Raval (merely designating an extramural area) began with urban overflow outside Barcelona's medieval core, although within the city's final set of early modern walls. The Raval's initial agricultural and monastic character gave way in the 19th century to industrialization and worker housing. Day labor, petty commerce, informal/illicit economic strategies, and amusement facilities also expanded in a densely urbanized triangle of streets near the harbor. Before the 1920s, this zone was occasionally labeled Drassanes\Atarazazanas, after a contiguous naval complex. "Chinatown," evoking the "mysterious" image of San Francisco's Chinese quarter rather than any Barcelona Asian population, was imposed by Barcelona authors in the 1920s to romanticize crime, immigration, prostitution and nightclubs, equating Barcelona to other global cosmopolitan cities (Madrid 1929; Marsà 1928?; Boatwright and Da Cal 1984; McDonogh 1987). These streets nonetheless shared many social and demographic characteristics with the more "proper" contiguous working-class and petty-bourgeois areas of the Raval (McDonogh 1991, 1999).

The "Chinatown" label became well established in the press and everyday conversation as a geographical designation with moral implications. Meanwhile, neutral other terms like Distrito V, a political designation for the Raval, took on similar implications of disorder and danger. While media images shifted from tales of a seductive demimonde at the turn of the century to leftist outcries against pitiable exploitation during the Spanish Republic (1931–1939), the elements of difference and danger remained strong.

The Raval remained a center for immigration and marginal activities after the Spanish Civil War, but by the 1960s and 1970s, many established immigrant worker families followed factories to suburban centers while problems diffused through the older urban core. The Franco regime closed "official" brothels, but neglect and nostalgia characterized post-war decades as much as any real reform until the

Socialists took power in the late 1970s. For the newly global city of the 1992 Olympics, however, the *barrio chino* became a visible problem with its central location and negative reputation. The older Catalan designation Raval thus has been revived in urban political discourse, evoking both a middle-class heritage of shopkeepers and established Catalan residents and a participation in Catalanist urban revitalization. Official publications also incorporate this district into the wider Ciutat Vella (old city) area, underscoring the shared history and culture of the city's medieval and renaissance core, while eliding problems of the present. Meanwhile, the area has faced intensive urban prophylaxis including widespread demolition, intensive social service activity (Maza 1999) and ideological reconstruction that relegates the *barrio chino* to a shameful past (McDonogh 1999).

Changing labels, like new names for Raval plazas and buildings, have been imposed upon both longterm residents and new immigrants – often from outside of Europe – who fill the remaining housing, businesses, and streets of the area. Meanwhile, many local inhabitants simply talk of their neighborhood as the "barrio," scarcely crediting the flows of political and cultural meaning that envelop them.

The use of bars as signifiers of the barrio and its mystery/problems already took on vivid meanings in 19th-century Barcelona (McDonogh 1987). Josep Maria Carandell, for example, in his *Nueva Guia Secreta de Barcelona* (1982), cites popular verses about the Raval's Café de La Alegría, a flourishing musical bar of the era: "The Cafe of Happiness/ is a place of perdition/where flamenco/is danced to perfection/ The worker's smock is not permitted/ whatever the excuse/ every gentleman who enters/ wears a hat" (1982:186). These stanzas identified this bar as a locus of both vice and non-Catalan (Andalusian) entertainment. Moreover, they associated these pleasures with the male bourgeoisie, symbolized by a hat, rather than the smock-clad proletariat of the neighborhood who provided a vital, flexible pool of labor for Barcelona expansion.

By the 1920s, both general motifs and references to specific bars pervaded newspapers, novels, theater and other media. In his acid novel *Vida Privada* (1932), for example, the Catalan novelist Josep Maria de Sagarra depicted well-known bars, disease-ridden prostitutes and sad entertainers to equate the depravity of the barrio with that of the 1920s Barcelona elite who visited it. Elsewhere, he described how the Eden Concert, heir to the Café de La Alegría had become a moral signifier for the bourgeoisie: "when one wanted to indicate (*significar*) that a person of the world was a ne'er-do-well, one said that he had been seen in the Eden, or that he frequented the Eden, and nothing else was necessary" (cited in Carandell 1982:156). The Eden, like other famous *barrio chino* establishments, became a mythic shorthand for the downfall of the good bourgeois male who spent too much time there among female artistes. Meanwhile, images of such *barrio chino* bars – and their environs – spread beyond Barcelona as novels from France would testify for decades, from Pierre MacOrlan and Jean Genet (whose 1949 *Journal du Voleur* chronicles hustling and drugs in the barrio) to Pieyre de Mandiargue, whose 1967 *La Marge* made the barrio a protagonist in his hero's decline.

While those on the left might speak for and to different groups, they nonetheless often concurred with the conservative/voyeuristic bourgeoisie about the depravity of the barrio even as they called for systematic reform. A 1936 report from the communist *Solidaridad Obrera*, for example, complains: "The detritus expelled from capitalist society is enclosed in a dark, unhealthy space. The lives of these unfortunates are characterized by complete abandon. They live in decaying houses without air or life... They live in the midst of promiscuity... these low neighborhoods must disappear" (Balius 1936:4). Even the medicalization of the area echoes Sagarra's emphasis on syphilis and tuberculosis to characterize moral and physical decay. Whether reformers sought to improve housing, education, employment opportunity, or social organization, the barrio and its places, including bars, constituted an immediate, compelling problem.

After the Spanish Civil War (1936–1939), the area suffered ongoing neglect, but remained a literary metaphor for the complex past of the city. Antonio Paquer's *Historia del barrio chino de Barcelona* (1962), for example, a nostalgic text from a publisher specialized in scandalous titles, distilled the myth through a mixture of literature, memoir, history, and alarmist reporting. While Paquer began his narrative with the ambience of the barrio in the past, before the 1950s closure of its black market and other "typical" sites (a nostalgia pervading many modern oral and literary representations of the neighborhood), he combined vivid images with insistent judgment:

> How much ignominy, how much shameful and shaming humanity, how many vital defects had their natural seat in that labyrinth of dark, narrow streets! Gamblers and free and undaunted women, pimps and thieves, sodomites and criminals of every class, exploiters and exploited, made that zone of the city its authentic warren. That neighborhood became, within Barcelona, an authentic, almost irremovable citadel of vice and degeneracy, the spiritual obscurity of whose caverns irresistibly attracted the vulgar sentimentalism of certain persons as chic as they were limited in mentality. (1962:6–7)

Paquer explicitly linked people and morality to bars: "Those little cafes and taverns, those brothels and those sophisticated 'nests of Art' constituted the vital alpha and omega of an entire humanity morally underdeveloped. Not only was vice embraced with the unanimous complicity of the barrio, but it was born there in the innocent flesh itself, in that ambience of infected human accumulation" (1962:7).

Paquer's book provided detailed information about individually famous establishments that he linked to crime and sex, including a savage chapter critiquing transvestite males: "*la última escala de la degradación*" (the last stage of degradation). Thus he merged gender, deviance, alcohol, and vulgarity to characterize places, to explain their spatial context and to establish a culturally complicit knowledge with his reader. Meanwhile, he scarcely mentions any families or other economic activities. Most men of his barrio are thieves and drunkards, homosexuals and transvestites; women are almost invariably shown in slatternly decay unless entertainers or temporarily successful prostitutes. The few urban women who appear as victims of seduction and abandonment affirm their fall by their new social space. Hence, the barrio becomes self-reproducing: a malign womb within the city rather than the result of urban forces long concealed by the perdurance of its myth representation.

In his epilogic discussion of plans to reform the neighborhood through Francoist urban hygiene, Paquer counterposed the barrio to the normal city with which it would be reunited when "the redoubt of corruption... came to be incorporated into the daily tasks of a population that had always remained faithful to its guilded, artisanal, sensible and traditional life" (1962:148). Some three decades after Paquer's comments, in fact, the Socialist regime of a new Barcelona tackled reform more systematically through demolition of inferior housing, construction of new global cultural facilities, and the creation of new open spaces. As older residents and businesses have disappeared, despite the continuing entrance of new third world populations, a new Raval yet still distinct has been grafted into urban moral geography. A 2001 "review" in Madrid's *El Pais* juxtaposes these old and new meanings:

> Traditionally an urban industrial enclave, it was in the early 20th century a center for the first workers' movements. It is a curious barrio, mixed (mestizo) and very lively, with as many varied faces as its geometric form promises. Seen from the Rambles, its face is impeccable: museums, the mythical central market (La Boqueria) and the theater of the Liceu guard the entry to tortuous streets and a multitude of bars and locales for spectacles. Since the 1980s, the Raval has been caught up in continuous and necessary reforms. (De la Torrente 2001:7)

One notes, however, that reforms are *necessary*, relegating workers' movements (and infamous reputations) to a safely distanced past.

Both media depictions and political opinions have resonated with other urban conversations about the Raval, its bars and its citizens. Over the last few decades, outsiders have shared many stories of the barrio with me while differentiating themselves from it in terms of gender and class. In the 1970s/1980s, older middle- and upper-class women, for example, generally insisted that they had never set foot in the notorious *barrio chino*. Only those in their 20s or 30s considered a visit there an "adventure" – this usually meant a quick absinthe in the Bar Marsella or an after-graduation party at the Bodega Bohemia. Some others talked about the barrio across charitable distances that echoed proper female roles of the Catholic Francoist state. Barrio residents, meanwhile, suggested that more women of the bourgeoisie had visited there. Thus, barrio women affirmed their own worth as working housewives as opposed to idle, dishonest elites.

Males of almost all ages, areas and backgrounds, however, have shared stories of barrio adventures with real relish (especially when conversing apart from their wives). The *barrio chino* became a right of passage for many men growing up under the sexual repression of the Franco regime and an escape from bourgeois norms for others. This, too, is a viewpoint barrio residents tended to recognize, ridicule, and exploit.

This difference between barrio and outside readings does not mean that two discrete systems of gender or place existed in the city. Most Barcelonins' models of gender in the 1970s and 1980s – and perhaps to this day – reflect a "modern," primarily middle-class interpretation of Mediterranean models in which women have maintained domestic life and culture while males are more active in public arenas. Practice and discussion, however, also have incorporated distinctions and changes based on class, ethnicity, and virtue. One of the clear hegemonic antinomies of the respectable woman, for example, remains the prostitute who publicly serves the private needs of men. Yet, this is an opposition maintained by men and women of the barrio as much as outsiders. Less apparent, but equally real, were oppositions through the middle 20th century between domestic respectability and everyday demands on the working woman/wife/mother (Kaplan 1982; Boatwright and Da Cal 1984; McDonogh 1989). Here, shared ideals might not be realized by some segments of the urban population. Still other contrasts emerge with immigrants, whether Andalusian in the 1920s or Filipina and Moroccan in the 1980s, who have brought languages and cultures to the Raval that distinguished them from middle-class Catalans (McDonogh 1991).

In all these areas, we must constantly scrutinize the interplay of mass media, metropolitan myths, and everyday spaces, actions, and interpretations. Even though most Raval women have distinguished their lives and reputations from local prostitutes, for example, they have shopped in the same streets and sometimes visited the same bars. Thus, they can become associated with prostitutes because of the intersection of everyday routes and cultural geography. Hence, one Raval woman complained to me about a newspaper photograph of "prostitutes in the barrio" by exclaiming, "And if I am walking down the street, to the store when they take the picture, what happens?"

Shared middle-class male ideals over the these decades also have contrasted the proper, productive man with the male who cannot provide because of poverty or depravity and the male who does not act as a sexual male. Both alternatives have reinforced the image of the barrio as a place of gendered as well as economic and political deviation. For many males in the barrio, in fact, an ability to manipulate images, visitors, and trying economic circumstances – *ser espabilado* – has also been a strategy of survival although scarcely one of longterm opportunity. Nor are the transvestite hustlers who beckoned passersby from doorways near the port taken as exemplars for male behavior or sociability. Yet, as in the case of Raval women, the myth of the *barrio chino* has made it easier to see all underemployed men in the post-industrial neighborhood as problems or failures.

Both myths and conversations can change, as the revitalization of the Raval as an area for students, arts, culture, and cosmopolitan migration in the 1990s suggests. Yet, new actions that have sanitized the barrio often rely themselves on "established" myths as justifications rather than emerging from the social lives and beliefs that barrio residents created and sustained in their own use of bars, to which I now turn.

Bars and Social Space: An Alternative Geography

In fieldwork, Gaspar Maza and I examined scores of bars in the Raval to understand both their social functions and their cultural implications. One obvious category comprised the spectacle bars that figured so prominently in metropolitan imagery. Yet, three other types proved more numerically and socially significant among the hundreds that have lined barrio streets for decades: business bars (*bares de negocios*) associated with prostitution; special interest bars/clubs and neighborhood bars. All were distinguishable in their physical setting/ambience, hours, origins, clientele, and interactions with the neighborhood and the city. Nonetheless, only the prostitution bars appeared regularly in mass media depictions of the barrio, although special interest bars occasionally cropped up in discussions of activists or immigrants.

Neighborhood bars are not even known by name outside the barrio. Yet to under-stand the barrio bar as a place, we must situate all four within a network of social choices and cultural meanings.

Spectacle bars

The barrio bars Paquer and others insistently depict have appeared in novels, plays, and anecdotes for generations. The Criolla, Cal Sagristà, Eden Concert, Marsella, and Villa Rosa in the 1920s, like Barcelona de Noche, Bar London, Bodega Bohe-mia, Marsella, Villa Rosa, and Pastís in the 1970s and 1980s, shared metropolitan reputations forged by place, clientele, and legend. They also shared characteristics that oriented them to an audience outside the barrio even if permitting occasional local contacts, including occasional employment. Hence, they constituted distinct-ive, even foreign places within the life of the barrio.

Such bars often have opened in late afternoon and stayed open after most other establishments closed. They also have tended to serve cocktails rather than beer, wine, and food, while their prices reflect fame and a wealthier, non-barrio clientele. Their ambience also transcended even barrio mythologies. The Bar London (founded 1909), for example, gained fame as a center for urban circus performers. El Pastís, by contrast, evokes French decadence with its artistic décor, absinthe and the music of Edith Piaf.

While some of these bars had lengthy pedigrees, many older bars disappeared during the Civil War or closed thereafter (Paquer 1962; Carandell 1982). Barcelona de Noche and its female impersonators, the ragged cabaret of Bodega Bohemia and the shows of the Villa Rosa survived into the 1980s, sometimes experiencing temporary resurgences of fashionable interest, but all have disappeared subse-quently. By the 1980s, new nightclubs were more likely to open in areas perceived as fashionable and modern, like Port Olimpic or the nearby MareMagnum complex in the refurbished post-industrial port. The image – and memory – of spectacle bars, however, remains a primary symbolic presence within the Raval/*barrio chino*, high-lighted even in contemporary guidebooks and newspapers.

My 1980s observations in the Bar Marsella illuminated the potential spatial ambiguity of spectacle bars vis-à-vis the barrio. In the 1920s, French novelists had associated Marsella's sweeping bar and mirrored walls with cabaret prostitution. Decades later, older, poor residents of nearby rooming houses huddled around its rickety wooden tables for much of the day, passing the time with beer, conversations, and card games. In the early evening, however, college-age students invaded, revel-ling in its "atmosphere," before disappearing when night made the barrio *seem* less safe. Some older barrio women developed regular interactions with these visitors, selling tissues and trinkets or regularly cadging drinks and telling stories. Later, until closing, television, cards, and neighborhood gossip again took over.

Within this symbiotic construction of spatial meaning, locals who used Marsella as a place to live also became part of the attraction for outsiders. Carandell's guide emphasized the "strongest atmosphere *(mas cargada)* in Barcelona, where the most unexpected beings play, drink, talk, smoke, shut up" (1982:184). Similarly, a novel by a university-educated woman used the lives of the women of the bar and nearby hotels as metaphors of individual transformation (Pottocher 1985). While most of the regulars I knew there were former workers surviving on meager pensions, the bar's faded grandeur evoked narratives of vice and glory that spectators could imagine for these inhabitants. The people as much as the décor became the spectacle, although regulars also commented on and profited from outsiders; some even saved me news clippings on the barrio in which they had appeared.

By the 1990s, however, the Marsella was caught between an appeal to more tourists and the needs of its declining local clientele. Ultimately, the owners chose to focus on live entertainment for an evening clientele, dropping neighborhood ties and daytime hours for an aesthetic but historical identification as "the ultimate bohemian bar. Now frequented by youths with much less intellectual pretension who enjoy its live events" (De la Torrente 2001:7).

Other spectacle bars rarely offered the complex accommodations of Bar Marsella. When I talked to neighborhood residents about these establishments, they consistently recalled them from the outside unless they had actually worked in one (for example, as waiters). The entertainers who frequented musical bars were known from their daytime activities, whether buying bread or looking for perfume and make-up in local shops. Yet, many adults recalled being warned as children to keep respectful distance from these women and to avoid their example. Neighborhood residents seemed to view these bars as foreign spaces, even if sometimes recognized as successful businesses whose clientele might spill over into neighboring venues. Still, even in the 1980s, owners and regulars in the Bar Gallart (below) claimed uncertainty about the location of the Bar Pastís, only a few blocks away, and derided the once-famous Villa Rosa as a "worthless tourist trap."

Spectacle bars, then, have created ambiguous intersections of behavior, gender, and meaning within Barcelona metropolitan culture. To outsiders – including tourists from the rest of Europe – they have typified the entire neighborhood and its inhabitants as colorfully sinful. To local residents, they were at least partially external, an exclusion that validated the integrity of barrio life. At complex points, however, like the Marsella of the 1980s, they became "normal" for residents but reinforced the myth of the barrio for those prepared to view its bars and people as spectacles. Through these bars in particular, the myth of the *barrio chino* mingled space, class, virtue, and gender, reinforcing narratives like Sagarra and Paquer by juxtaposition to "real" experience. As Clifford Geertz has said of common sense, with a striking relevance to urban cultural knowledge, it must "affirm that its tenets are immediate deliverances of experience, not deliberate reflections upon it" (1983:75). Other bars, however, challenged such simple convergences of gender, class, and virtue.

Bars, prostitution, and drugs

Legal prostitution existed in the Raval from the 14th century until the 1950s. Many brothels were located in the *barrio chino*, whether elegant houses for the elite or cramped establishments for sailors. When brothels closed, prostitution moved to the street and to the semi-public space of bars. In the 1960s, for example, *barras americanas* (American bars, an alternate identification of space and vice) offered dimly lit tunnels with bare formica counters where scantily clad women perched while others waited outside the door. Prostitutes generally made financial agreements with bar owners, who also profited from male clients. Unlike spectacle bars, in which sex might be evoked in a show and suggest other activities, these bars offered no other attractions to explain a client's presence. Nonetheless, these diverse working bars attracted their own literary/journalistic gaze which distinguished spaces and meanings among bars and prostitutes. Nobel Prize winner Camilo José Cela, for example, lyrically described these sad, weary urban prostitutes in his *Izas, Rabizas y Colipoterras* (1964). The older (mid-fifties) prostitutes along the Carrer de les Tapies took the spotlight in a 1980s dramatic monologue, *Dolça de les Tapies* (Valls 1984; see Draper Miralles 1982). Journalists, meanwhile, repeatedly "discovered" the younger, often immigrant prostitutes clustered near the Plaça Salvador Segui or decried male transvestites who appeared on the Rambles, the major downtown boulevard that marked one boundary of the barrio. Urban "knowledge" of such prostitutes was also highly gendered, belonging primarily (not unexpectedly) to males.[4] In the barrio, by contrast, males and females know prostitutes as neighbors, albeit within social limits.

Until the 1980s, most prostitution bars concentrated on three or four streets in the central Raval and in clubs having access to the Rambles. The narrow passage of Carrer d'En Robador, especially, teemed with bars, hotels, and clinics. As prostitutes moved outside on warmer days and men slowly passed and gazed at bar after bar, dense crowds coalesced, deindividualizing sites and people into an intense space of sexuality and desire.

Hours of these bars resembled those of the spectacle bars, built around night-time activities, although some opened from early morning onwards. All specialized in overpriced liquor; these were never places of conversation or group sociability. Outside working hours, when prostitutes would relax, they themselves would go to neighborhood bars instead.

I could not ascertain whether most prostitutes actually lived in the barrio. The clientele, however, generally came from outside the barrio. Despite legends of bourgeois patrons, most clients on the street seemed working-class men and immigrants (Draper Miralles 1982). Again, there were differences among sites: Robadors became famous for its *mirones* (men who walked and stared), while Tapies was associated with retired men on limited pensions (an association confirmed by the owner of the "hotel" there).

In the 1980s, prostitution and these bars became strongly attached in mass media to another publicly decried vice: drugs. Older sources (1910–1930s), in fact, had mentioned cocaine trafficking (Paquer 1962:85–89; Boatwright and Da Cal 1984); the image of cocaine reinforced horrors of the enticement of respectable women into depravity. When such drugs reappeared in Barcelona in the 1980s, traffic again erupted in the barrio, within a more widespread urban and Mediterranean circuit. Newspapers, television, and police nevertheless singled out bars in the barrio as dangerous points of sale, while the impact of drugs on the city became epitomized in the image of the wasted hooker-junkie there.

In newspaper reports and political rhetoric, moreover, the attack on drugs also converged with new discussions of race and immigration. Drug trafficking was associated with Arab and African immigrants, almost all male and many illegal, who concentrated in the Raval as an historic haven of immigration. Even bars that remained "clean" were heavily policed if frequented by Africans and Arabs.

Associations of race and drugs also meant that some residents rejected these immigrants as harbingers of problems, while criticizing the "young middle-class women" who used them as companions and dealers.

As noted, not all prostitution in the barrio involved heterosexual relations, a theme already raised in pre-Civil War coverage (Marsà 1928?) as well as Paquer. The public identification of the barrio and decadent male transvestites further converged with fear of AIDS in the 1980s and its identification with "illicit" sex and drugs. This added new medicalized visions of gender and space to an area already pathologized by epidemic disease, venereal disease, or socially conditioned disabilities like tuberculosis.

Of course, once again, gender roles were divided by class in ways that the isolated image of the *barrio chino* concealed. The most elegant transvestite prostitution in Barcelona in the 1970s (as even middle-class Barcelonins could observe it on weekend evenings) concentrated in the bourgeois Rambla Catalunya/Diagonal area. This activity later moved near the Pedralbes campus of the University of Barcelona, a space evoked by Pedro Almodovar in his 1999 film *All About My Mother*. In fact, art critic Robert Hughes suggested the transvestite as an appropriate symbol for the design consciousness of the Olympic city, leaving the barrio far behind (1992:111).

Prostitution, drugs, and sexuality, then, while features of bar and barrio life have never been uncomplicated. Their imagery justified interpretation and treatment of the entire barrio as a problem, especially in periods of urban reform like the 1930s or the 1980s. After the 1980s, the city systematically closed and/or demolished these bars in the barrio, although off-street prostitution elsewhere was tolerated and even advertised in major newspapers. Robadors, meanwhile, was bulldozed into the vast new open space of the Rambla del Raval.

For many living in the neighborhood, these bars also were problematic. Nonetheless, prostitution had been part of the dominant informal economy of the neighborhood for decades and transvestites frequented some neighborhood bars. *Bares de negócios* were integrated into barrio society, but this did not mean that they were perceived as central to the life or meaning of the neighborhood, or reflective of its range of social and cultural values. Moreover, there were also limits: drugs, by the 1980s, were perceived as a threat to the entire neighborhood and clashes emerged between earlier Spanish immigrants and those perceived as outsiders, whether Arab, African, or gypsy. These immigrants, nonetheless, could still create places – bars – for their own groups.

Special interest bars

A third category of bars, with a long historical presence in the neighborhood, encompasses establishments built around voluntary groups or social categories. At the turn of the century these bars were particularly associated with political and workers' groups that gave the barrio a reputation for radicalism as well as vice (Fabre and Huertas 1977). Today, some bars are still associated with strong working-class roots including those based on choral societies as well as political projects. Their identity is reinforced through memorabilia of place, organization, or political causes; they also are typically closed to outsiders, whether or not this is explicit.

Other bars are more open but structured around voluntary neighborhood groups, such as soccer teams. Here, relationships of insider and outsider are more fluid, although regulars are clearly participants in multiple interests reinforced by memorabilia, announcements, and conversations among tightly knit groups. Still other bars cater to ethnic interests based on ties of homeland and migration. In early immigration to the industrializing city, these were often Murcianos, Aragonese, and especially Andalusians (hence references to flamenco as a barrio spectacle). Ethnic bars tend to look like other neighborhood bars and are open to anyone throughout the day; they may convey their identity in name, décor (especially soccer fan materials), music, foodstuffs, or even specialized wines and liquors. Yet, even more than the examples above, their identity is defined by the social construction of their clientele.

As immigrants assimilated and moved on, few of these older bars endured into the 1980s, except in décor. Newer group bars, however, catered to Arabs and Blacks who arrived with newly globalized immigration (McDonogh 1991). An African center on Robadors in the 1980s, for example, played African and Caribbean music as well as serving occasional ethnic food items. Here, the African owner wanted the bar to be a social center despite police hostility and the negative associations of the street.

Most of these bars are dominated by men, although women may join them for social occasions. Again, this varies: the anarchist bar in the Raval has a younger, mixed clientele while immigrant bars reflect the male predominance among those who come to the city seeking work. Similarly, these bars vary in temporal and spatial patterns. Choral societies, club bars, and even political centers remain open after working hours and may provide a pool table or an office as well as storage. Generally, they seemed to close earlier than commercial bars, and much earlier than those associated with prostitution or spectacles.

These bars have not been clearly demarcated or numerous, although perhaps as common as bars specializing in prostitution; they certainly have been more prevalent than the spectacle bars. Yet, they rarely figure in metropolitan barrio mythology, unless evoked in times of political crisis because of their apparently closed or foreign character. After urban riots in the early 20th century, as in more recent periods of changing attitudes towards sub-Saharan immigrants, these bars became targets of urban media and police.

Similarly, such bars are more likely integrated into the barrio as a whole even if associated with visibly different core groups. Bar Gallart, discussed at length below, alternated over time between a general neighborhood clientele and ethnic specialization without changing menu, décor, or owners. In this sense, special interest bars also reveal processes of change and adaptation in the neighborhood not shared with spectacle or prostitution bars. This continuity includes an affirmation of local gender roles (with clear public male dominance) and the recognition of bars as nuclei of social solidarity. These bars underscore the potential of the most common barrio institution – the neighborhood bar – even as they remind us how little these last have figured in vivid urban myths.

Neighborhood bars

Over time, most bars in the *barrio chino* actually have been multi-service centers familiar from the ethnographic literature on rural and urban Spain (Almerich 1945; Hansen 1977; Brandes 1980; Collier 1986; Corbin and Corbin 1987; Gilmore 1987, etc). These originated centuries ago in pre-industrial taverns; a few remaining *barrio bodegas* that sell wine from casks and may offer drinks in a limited space still evoke this heritage. More modern local bars specialize in wine, beer, coffee, and conversation, although many offer food as a couple or family take responsibility for multiple services.

Such bars vary widely in size, hours, offerings, and the clientele who constitute *their* neighborhood via regular use of their semi-public space. The largest bars develop multiple rhythms to serve the widest possible range of clients, from cleaning women and night workers returning home at dawn to those who arrive after late-night jobs. Others are more specialized: in a street specialized in wholesale distribution, bars opened before the workday but closed by 9 p.m., when regular workers left. Still others focus on the lunch and after-lunch trade, although almost all open beforehand and remain active until midnight. In both functions and variations, they are scarcely distinguishable from bars found on any other streets of Barcelona.

In neighborhood bars, clients also vary through the day. Working women and men congregate for coffee (and occasional *copa*) in early mornings, while work breaks punctuate later mornings. Activities pick up before the main mid-day meal. Here, the clients are primarily male, although women and children also wander by before lunch while on other errands. Coffee, cigarettes, and liqueurs follow the mid-day meal, again inviting both males and females. Late afternoon usage again follows breaks among those working in the area, with regulars assembling as work winds down (8–10 p.m.).

While many evening clients are male, women and children also become involved in neighborhood bar social life, often in relationship to members of the proprietorial family. For families trapped in cheap rooms or cramped and crowded apartments, bars and nearby streetfronts have provided/provide welcome recreational spaces. After midnight, though, the clientele becomes predominantly male, even though prostitutes or passersby may drop in. Most women would be expected to deal with children and perhaps to avoid more raucous public spaces.

The regular presence of women and children, like the visits of apparently socially stigmatized clients such as prostitutes, transvestites, the homeless, or serious alcoholics, makes sense in a neighborhood with a history of minimal open space or community resources. In fact, the active construction of a diverse and regular social network was a key to commercial success for neighborhood bars which, in turn, reproduced values of respect and tolerance in the neighborhood itself. As Maza and I repeatedly have observed, the most marked category of persons for such bars is the outsider unknown to owners – including anthropologists as well as tourists. For regulars, meanwhile, bars become living-rooms, mailboxes, playgrounds, and social clubs.

The ambiguity of such bars as urban cultural signifiers can be seen in Paquer's description of the barrio's only "famous" pre-Civil War working-class tavern, La Mina:

Entering on the right, against the windows was the counter for drinks, where two lads, shirtsleeves rolled up, served endless glasses of wine and spirits in thick glasses. On the left was a window closing a small doorway, in which a woman sold cod fritters, sardines and pickled fish.

At the tables, men gave themselves over to various pasttimes. While some played cards, others in a corner planned some good gambit, taking drinks from their flagon, mute witness to the scene.

At another table, some took apart cigar butts that they had picked up in the streets. Reconverted into cigarettes, this dirty bespittled tobacco was used to make packets sold to the official tobacco dealers.

Scarcely would a dispute arise over a game or simply provoked by an "outsider" (*forastero*) and knives – with which the clientele was generally quite dexterous – would be stained with the rage of criminal minds that alcohol had made more violent. (1962:24)

Most of these activities typify neighborhood eating and drinking houses, which is how older barrio residents recalled this bar. Indeed, informal/illicit economic activities (food sales, tobacco gathering) clearly overshadow leisure or scandal; even knives served multiple functions to dockworkers and laborers. Paquer recognized, moreover, "that there was a code, tacitly established, that they always respected" (1962:25). Nonetheless, he caters to urban myth expectations with interpretations of a criminal atmosphere and his reading of a localized social organization as xenophobic or dangerous.

The construction of the social life in all Spanish bars, however, entails strategies to stabilize a consistent clientele. The particular intersections of local meanings and wider cultural significance, however, that set apart the *barrio chino* can be illuminated by a single neighborhood bar that I have known since 1975. This bar, which I call Bar Gallart, was founded by a couple who had immigrated separately from the South of Spain in the 1920s. They met and married in Barcelona, where they worked in hostelry. After the war (and the husband's imprisonment), they invested in a small bar as a stepping-stone to the larger Gallart, which they ran as a family after the 1960s.

In the mid-1970s, this bar with its long wood counter and four tables operated from 6:00 a.m. until 2:30 a.m. without breaks or vacations. This rigorous schedule, designed to attract as many customers as possible from nearby *pensiones* (rooming houses), businesses, and streets, demanded the labor of both parents, their four children, and the children's spouses. The father opened the bar each morning and the mother closed it at night – roles they maintained for decades, strictly controlling all finances. In the 1980s, the father handled mornings alone or with the help of an otherwise unoccupied child. Both daughters and one son-in-law worked in the kitchen at mid-day, when clients packed in. Later, they prepared appetizers and meals at almost any hour. Cigarettes were also sold outside legal channels. At night, the sons and another son-in-law tended the bar. All lived in a nearby apartment, increasingly crowded by grandchildren.

The bar thus provided a living for fifteen people and a center in which workers and residents of the neighborhood mingled for hours each day. It maintained a soccer team and frequent lotteries and hosted parties for seasonal and family events. Its clientele in the 1970s included both males and females, although the former predominated as regulars. Working women appeared in the early morning before or after work, and at night, generally with male partners and sometimes with children running amid the crowded tables and counters, cacophonous noise, and constant smoke. Single women, like foreigners, were unusual, although prostitutes, male and female, came in for food and breaks; several major *barras americanas* thrived nearby.

In the mid-1980s, this bar became increasingly popular with Arab immigrants, legal and illegal, who had moved into nearby rooming-houses. After the departure of morning workers, Arab males became more numerous throughout the day and night. Most ran up tabs to be settled by closing, including drinks, cigarettes, and food. In the evenings, some wives and families joined them, as did a few older regulars playing slot machines and drinking. Drugs (heroin and hashish) were sold, but the owners vehemently insisted that transactions and use remain outside the bar. They publicly and perhaps legally defended their virtue by forcing evil into the street, even locking the bathroom to prevent drug use, a policy they defended with anecdotes of overdosed corpses found in nearby bars. Young males and females with drug problems bought sandwiches and even received charity, but they were watched carefully for potential problems. Nevertheless, the street was only vaguely separated from inside sociability, and dealers who used the bar dominated a small nearby plaza. Increased police control around the neighborhood was also evident: after ten years without questions, I was stopped three times by the police within the first days of my return to the field in 1987.

The bar became less secured by neighborhood and family anchors. Many customers I had known in the 1970s shifted to other bars where I also would go with family members on days off. Both sons-in-law left: one divorced and the other took an outside job and moved out with his wife, who occasionally returned to help. A distant female relative also came to assist cooking. While older neighbors disapproved, family members were ambivalent about changes, living from the bar while trying to avoid associations with the drug trade.

By 1989, Arabs gave way to African immigrants who constituted a second wave of non-European immigration. Yet changing attitudes toward immigration as the EU drew tighter boundaries and national and city-wide confrontations erupted among ethnic groups put pressure on special interest locales. Thus, by my return to Barcelona in summer 1989, the owners had joined with police to reconvert the bar and street to neighborhood locales. Police put a mobile station at the entrance to the street. Rather than complaining as he once would have, the son lauded the effort: "*Pues, Gary, has visto como se ha puesto esto. Es mejor. Así no viene el hampa*" ("Well, Gary, you have seen what has happened. This is better. The trash won't come"). Everyday usage reverted to a more working-class pattern, with hours and some clientele familiar from a decade before. The core family staff diminished, though, as the next generation looked elsewhere for opportunities.

The bar still claimed the space of the neighborhood as its own. In 1989, for example, on the feast of Saint Joan, regulars tossed fireworks from the door, controlling the street. Core clients/neighbors, males and females, stayed on for closing and cleaning before adjourning to a *verbena* (party) at another nearby bar. This bar, whose clientele depended on neighborhood social ties, sponsored the street party to benefit its soccer team – an occasion where Bar Gallart's dispersed family was accidentally reunited.

By the late 1990s, though, Bar Gallart's economic survival became questionable. Urban renewal closed many rooming-houses that once had provided a core clientele, but the bar offered little to attract newcomers from the nearby Rambles or increasing student populations. Food disappeared and hours were shortened. This decline also converged with family changes as the founders died and older grandchildren moved away into marriage and new families. Even in the earlier 1990s, the remaining son and the grandchildren had talked longingly about leaving the neighborhood. By 2002, the family had become dissociated from the bar entirely, renting out their establishment to others.

Bar Gallart as a "community" has been shaped through time by continuing processes of external social categorization – including the active ignoring of racial or criminal categories – in a constant creative relation to the space and residents around it. For decades, family members publicly portrayed themselves as virtuous and orderly, despite the imagery of the barrio and the changes of the bar and provided a social center in which family and neighborhood lives took shape. Yet, they were aware that their claims would be dismissed outside the barrio, knowledge that guided the grandchildren away from the bar. Ultimately, the image of the barrio as a problem forced difficult choices on the family, which by 2002, could no longer sustain the bar as a neighborhood center. Thus, the Bar Gallart over time embodies the contradictory meanings of bars in the barrio, formed by daily contact and personal ties, but subject to external evaluation, change, and control.

Conclusions: Re-Reading Bars, Space, and Virtue

Bars exist as both spaces and symbols throughout Spanish and Catalan life. These arenas of drinking, eating, and social interaction reflect and participate in the reproduction of social structure, economic life, and cultural values. In urban centers such as Barcelona, complex networks of bars serve and create diversities of neighborhood, class, ethnicity, gender, interest, race, profession, and style and their intersections. Bars are also arenas in which social and cultural change is enacted, whether protests in Carnival or the less flamboyant endurance of neighborhood sociability and support in the *barrio chino*.

Yet, as Barcelonins talk about bars, these also may become loaded signifiers through which other urban values are discussed or concealed. Quite apart from the social or economic structure of any bar, interpretations subsume other categories and make wider connections that underpin a mythic construction of place and meaning. Hence, the *barrio chino* has been characterized by a dominant urban cultural portrayal of its bars as spectacular centers of vice to be eliminated. This attack has not targeted alcohol or recreation nor criticized the urban presence of bars per se. Nor has it explored the social formation of the neighborhood or those who inhabit it. Rather, the "myth" of the bars of the *barrio chino* became part of the interplay of cultural stereotypes that confirm the political, economic, and social marginalization of the area and its inhabitants. Indeed, as landmarks in the human symbolic geography of Barcelona, *barrio chino* bars appear to have become causes rather than attributes of marginality.

These images, moreover, show how production and employment intersect with gender, power, and virtue. As the *barrio chino* becomes reduced to bars of vice, working women there risk identification with women of vice, while women of other classes can confirm their virtue by their avoidance of this space (and the burdens of living there). Men frequent bars throughout Barcelona; but the mythic bars of the *barrio chino* reinforce middle-class urban males as daring visitors or sensible reformers against the failure of those in the barrio who might offer other visions of the world.

Within the barrio, the social structuring of bars has been more complex. Bars that typify the neighborhood for outsiders generally are perceived as external within the barrio: locals can affirm their virtue by their avoidance of these places or imposing their own negotiated boundaries – like pushing drugs into the street. Women and men, however, also found social contacts and values within neighborhood bars that allowed alternative models of virtue and community to survive in the shadow of a mythologized landscape.

Epilogue

In editing my 1992 publication, I have maintained its historical record of intense urban ethnography on marginality in Barcelona in the 1970s and 1980s, within a longer-term construction of categories, space and action in the city. Certainly any anthropologist, revisiting his or her own words and analyses, faces disjunctions from changes in both the observer and the object of study. Yet, today's *barrio chino*, the focus of widespread interventions since the 1980s, will be unrecognizable to readers. These changes, in fact, affirm the impact of ideology and the disparities of reading and power that this article explored.

The post-Franco governments of Barcelona have endeavored to change Barcelona from a provincial capital to a model for European and global cities (McDonogh 1999). Hence, dramatic planning projects and media events like the 1992 Olympics have mirrored dramatic social reform. Both physical and social planning have targeted the Raval as a zone of problems and neglect. As I noted, massive infusions of social services, law enforcement, and the reconstruction of spaces and centers became fundamental features of barrio life. By the mid 1990s, a new Raval was anchored in cultural facilities and metropolitan access, especially in the less infamous area further from port. Meanwhile, in the most notorious zones of the *barrio chino*, elimination of hundreds of homes in decaying buildings permitted a new central plaza and other facilities.

These planned changes have had devastating impact on lifeways in the *barrio chino*, whether in neighborhood bars, special interest areas, or places of prostitution which, even in the 1980s, were seen as incompatible with a new city. While bars that offered haven to dubious immigrants or criminal activities were actually targeted, bars as neighborhood social centers became threatened as their clientele disappeared. Where once multiple bars structured a street, now perhaps one survives – if the street itself does. In many new buildings, other commercial establishments are clearly favored over any proliferation of small, cheap bars.

Amid these changes, spectacle bars, ironically, have flourished and have been joined by trendy locales like Benidorm, Kasparo, Moog, and Muebles Navarro (in a former furniture store) that recast the aura of the old barrio for a young, hip clientele. Still, this renovation confirms devalorization of the past, especially of the complex fabric of social and cultural meanings which barrio residents created in bars, streets, markets, and other institutions. Whether in improving lives of citizens through social intervention or changing physical spaces as a whole, the city has fostered a replacement of an area "known" for vice by a moral city. The widespread urban ideology of space and virtue made it hard, moreover, for residents and transients to protest effectively; many merely have left. This is not to say that immigrants, prostitution, illicit activities, or bars do not continue to survive, even amid new squares named for Genet and Mandiargue. Yet neither these places nor their neighbors are seen as bearers of identity or a future for the area, so much as lingering problems pending future solutions.

NOTES

Acknowledgements. Initial funding came from the American Council of Learned Societies and the New College Anthropology Fund. Presentations and earlier versions have profited from comments by Stanley Brandes, Deborah Heath, Cindy Hing-Yuk Wong, Carles Carreras Verdaguer, Gaspar Maza, and Gerald Felz as well as friends in the barrio. I also recognize the inspiration of Dorsey Boatwright and Enric Da Cal (1984). For republication, I have revised the paper completely to eliminate infelicities and to follow these conflicts of ideological and social space through the convulsions of post-Olympic Barcelona. Subsequent research has been supported by Bryn Mawr College.

I did not update the collateral sources beyond ethnography and history in Barcelona, however, and have dropped some with changes in the text. One faces the difficulty of context here on several levels. Anthropologists have discussed issues of bars in Spain for decades, generally with reference to smaller settlements outside major metropoles. Gender also remains an exciting topic, for which I cite only a few people and writings from which to begin reading (Buxo 1978; Brandes 1981; Murphy 1983; Gilmore 1987, 1990; Del Valle 1985; etc). While I have drawn on many colleagues and sources to understand these issues, I have "reconnected" this piece to these continuing discussions by colleagues in the U.S. and Spain.

Similarly, as those whom I engaged on a theoretical level, from Foucault and Barthes to Sahlins and Bourdieu, have continued to spark debate and discussion I have not tried to resituate this piece in a new theoretical context. Instead, I rely on its evidence and arguments to be read and discussed in the new contexts of this anthology.

1 Both are mass tourist centers, the latter with gay associations.
2 My use of myth here synthesizes anthropological readings (Sahlins 1981) with interpretations of constructed knowledge from thinkers including Bourdieu (1972, 1979), Foucault (1972) and Barthes (1972).
3 After 1986, these observations were made in conjunction with Gaspar Maza Gutierrez of the Centre de Serveis Socials Erasme de Janer and the Universitat de Tarragona, who has been my constant interlocutor on this project. See Maza 1999 for his additional and illuminating readings of this area.
4 Nonetheless, in 1990, I was startled by an elite woman in her sixties who volunteered that "En Robadors had prostitutes that were not available anywhere else in Spain." This remark, she explained, was not based on first-hand knowledge, but on conversations and reading, and conveyed a peculiar pride in Barcelona life based on its depravity.

REFERENCES

Almerich, Luis 1945 *El hostal, la fonda, la taberna y el cafe en la vida barcelonesa*. Barcelona: Millà.
Ajuntament de Barcelona. 1971 *Informe Sociologico del Distrito V*. Barcelona: Colecció Serveis Socials.
Artigues Vidal, Jaume, Francesc Mas Palahi and Xavier Sunol Ferrer. 1980 *El Raval*. Barcelona: Colecció el Raval.
Balius 1936 "La ciudad de Barcelona: Los barrios bajos. El distrito V". *Solidaridad Obrera 16 august: 4f*.
Berlanstein, Leonard 2001 *Daughters of Eve*. Cambridge: Harvard University.
Barthes, Roland 1972 *Mythologies*. New York: Hill & Wang.
Boatwright, Dorsey and Enric Ucelav Da Cal. 1984. La dona del barrio chino: L'imatge dels baixos fons i la revista "El Escándalo". *L'Avenç* 76 CXI): 26–34.
Bondi, Liz 1998 "Sexing the City." In Fincher, Ruth and Jane M. Jacobs, eds. *Cities of Difference*. New York: Guilford: 177–200.
Bourdieu, Pierre 1977 *Outline of a Theory of Practice*. Cambridge: Cambridge University Press.
—— 1979 *La distinction*. Paris: Minuit.
Brandes, Stanley 1980 *Metaphors of Masculinity*. Philadelphia: University of Pennsylvania Press.
Buxó, Maria Jesús 1978 *Antropologia de Ia mujer*. Barcelona: Promoción cultural.
Carandell, José Maria 1982 *Nueva guía secreta de Barcelona*. Barcelona: Martínez Roca.
Cela, Camilo José 1964 *Izas rabizas y colipoterras*. Barcelona: Lumen.
Collier, Jane 1986 From Mary to modern woman. *American Ethnologist* 13(1): 100–107.
Corbin, J. and M. Corbin 1987 *Urbane Thought: Culture and Class in an Andalusian City*. Aldershot: Gowen.
Del Valle, Teresa 1985 *Mujer Vasca: imagen y realidad*. Barcelona: Anthropos.
De la Torrente, Eugenia 2001 "El Raval, un barrio en movimiento". *El País* 3 XI 2001, Viajero:7.
Draper Miralles, Ramón 1982. *La prostitución feminina en Barcelona*. Barcelona: Martínez Roca.
Fabre, Jaume and Josep Maria Huertas Claveria 1977 El Districte V. *Tots els barris de Barcelona*. VII: 277–368. Barcelona: 62.
Foucault, Michel 1972 *The Archeology of Knowledge*. New York: Pantheon.
Geertz, Clifford 1983 *Local Knowledge*. New York: Basic Books.
Genet, Jean 1949 *Journal du voleur*. Paris: Gallimard.
Gilmore, David 1987 *Aggression and Community*. New Haven: Yale.
—— 1990 *Manhood in the Making*. New Haven: Yale.
Hansen Edward 1977 *Rural Catalonia under the Franco Regime*. Cambridge: Cambridge University Press.
Harvey, David 1977 *The Urban Experience*. Baltimore: Johns Hopkins University Press.
Hurtado, Andrés 1926 Cosas de la Vida, *El Escándalo*, October 26.
Hughes, Robert 1992 *Barcelona*. New York: Knopf.
Johnson, Robert 1987 What is Cultural Studies anyway? *Social Text* 17 (Fall): 38–80.
Kaplan, Temma 1992 *Red City, Blue Period*. Berkeley: University of California Press.
Madrid, Francisco 1929 *Sangre en Atarazanas*. Barcelona: La Flecha.
Marsà, Angels 1928? *Los bajos fondos de Barcelona* (pseud. Mistral) n.p.
McDonogh, Gary 1986 *Good Families of Barcelona*. Princeton: Princeton University Press.

—— 1987 The geography of evil: Barcelona's *Barrio Chino*. *Anthropological Quarterly* 60: 174–84.

—— 1991 Terra de pas. In *Contemporary Catalonia in Spain and Europe*, ed. Milton Azevedo. Berkeley: International Studies Center: 70–97.

—— 1999 Discourses of the City: Post-transitional Planning in Barcelona. In Low, Setha ed. *Theorizing the City*. New Brunswick: Rutgers: 34–54.

Mandiargues, Andre Pieyre 1967 *La marge*. Paris: Gallimard.

Maza, Gaspar 1999 *Produccion, reproduccion y cambios en la marginación urbana*. Unpublished Ph.D Dissertation, Universitat Rovira Virgili, Tarragona.

Murphy, Michael 1983. Emotional confrontations between Sevillano fathers and sons. *American Ethnologist* 10:650–664.

Navarro Arisa, J. J. 1989 La crónica, *El País*. 15 agosto:13.

Paquer, Antonio 1962 *Historia del Barrio Chino de Barcelona*. Barcelona: Rodegar.

Pottocher, Beatriz 1985 *Ciertos tonos de negro*. Barcelona: Lumen.

Romani, Oriol. 1982. *Droga i subcultura*. Unpublished Ph.D. Dissertation, Universitat de Barcelona.

Rorabaugh, W. J. 1979 *The Alcoholic Republic*. New York: Oxford University Press.

Sagarra, Josep Maria 1932 *Vida Privada*. Reprinted 1977. Barcelona: Ayma.

Sahlins, Marshall 1981 *Historical Metaphors and Mythical Realities*. Ann Arbor: University of Michigan Press.

Siegel, Jerrold 1986 *Bohemian Paris*. London: Penguin Books.

Valls, Carles 1984 *Dolça de les Tapies*. Barcelona: Dalmau.

13

Black Corona: Race and the Politics of Place in an Urban Community

Steven Gregory

ON A February evening in 1987 Community Board 4's Neighborhood Stabilization Committee met in the basement of a co-op apartment building on the southern border of Corona, one block from the massive and predominantly black Lefrak City housing development. Helma Goldmark, chair of the all-white committee and a resident of the well-kept Sherwood Village co-ops, took her place alongside three other committee members at a folding table that had been set up in the back of the brightly lit community room. A handful of white and black residents, two uniformed police officers, and other invited guests chatted among themselves as they waited for the meeting to begin.

Goldmark invited Judith Shapiro, a Sherwood Village resident, to open the meeting and address the first item on the agenda: the problem of security at the Lefrak City library, a public library located next to the black housing development. Shapiro complained that the library was being used as an after-school "baby-sitting service" by Lefrak City parents. These "latchkey kids," she claimed, were disruptive and making it difficult for others to use the library appropriately. She called for increased library security so that "the problem kids can be identified and removed by force if necessary."

Joseph Sardegna, chief of investigation and security for the Queens Bonough Public Library, interrupted. Sardegna, invited by the committee to attend the meeting, argued that Shapiro was exaggerating the threat posed by the Lefrak City kids, remarking cryptically: "The mind conceives and the eyes perceive. Lefrak isn't so bad."

The official's comments provoked an outburst of protests. Rose Rothschild, Community Board 4's manager, retorted, "Lefrak security *is* bad. These kids are ten going on forty. They have no respect for authority." She went on to argue that people in Corona were afraid to use the Lefrak City library and for that reason wanted a library of their own. Goldmark agreed. She asked Sardegna to station a security guard in the library from 3:30 in the afternoon until closing.

"We don't want to have a library under siege," Sardegna responded, insisting that the security problem was not serious enough to justify stationing a uniformed guard.

He reached into the pocket of his powder blue blazer and pulled out a pager. "We are only a beep away," Sardegna declared, holding up the device. "We already have plainclothes guards a beep away."

Rothschild stood, pressing her palms against the table: "You know, you've already repeated the same thing in a million different ways. Lefrak City is an entity in itself – a city in a city. I don't care what you say, security is bad in Lefrak." When Sardegna reiterated his point that more security would not solve the Lefrak library problem, Rothschild threatened to call his supervisor. Indignant, the library official, trailed by his assistant and two librarians, walked out.

The Neighborhood Stabilization Committee turned to the next issue on its agenda: drug dealing on Fifty-seventh Avenue, a commercial strip bordering Lefrak City. New York City Police Officer Sharpner, assigned to the 110th Precinct in Elmhurst, reported on his department's efforts to arrest drug dealers. Ken Daniels, a white Lefrak City resident and member of the committee, testified that he could see drug dealers flagging down cars from the window of his apartment.

"You know, when I moved to this neighborhood," Rothschild remarked, "there was no crime. I met with [District Attorney] Santucci and for some reason they don't want to face the fact that we need more policemen."

Phil Clark, chief of Lefrak City's private security force, responded. "Lefrak City has a lower-than-average crime rate," he said, adding that there had been a decrease in violent crime in the housing complex in the past few years. What crime there was, the Lefrak official opined, was owing to a lack of "parental guidance." Rose Rothschild agreed. "No father around, single mothers. Isn't it a shame that people have to live in fear?"

Edna Baskin and two other black residents of Lefrak City remained relatively silent as committee members and security officials discussed the problem of the latchkey kids, drug dealing, and the lack of "parental guidance" in Lefrak City, offering only their confirmation that there were real security problems in the library and housing complex. As African-American tenants of the complex, they were excluded from this discourse of neighborhood stabilization that linked crime to family disorder in a racialized topography of urban space. It was their children and neighbors who were being described as "disruptive," as drug dealers, and as objects of surveillance and law enforcement.

Although race was never explicitly referred to, the issues of crime, drugs, and parental discipline bore racial connotations that remained precariously close to the surface of discourse. For example, when Officer Sharpner reported an incident involving two "white girls from Forest Hills" who were mugged after a drug buy in Lefrak City, Rothschild quickly interjected, "We're not talking about race." Later, when the committee's chair described a mugger who was robbing people in her co-op building, she avoided explicit reference to his race: "He is about thirty-five, has bushy hair, and is Jamaican." Ethnicity served in this latter case both to signal and to deflect race within a discourse of "stabilization" that was overdetermined by an ideology of black crime.

This chapter examines the struggle of black Lefrak City residents to disrupt this conflation of race, crime, and space in the discourse and practice of everyday politics. In public forums ranging from the monthly meetings of the Neighborhood Stabilization Committee and Community Board 4 to the mass-mediated reports of journalists, Lefrak City was viewed as a threat to the quality of life of surrounding neighborhoods; a potent symbol linking anxieties about urban decline and crime to ideologies of black welfare dependency and family pathology.

At stake in this politics of representation was more than the perpetuation of racial stereotypes: the all too familiar tropes of the deviant welfare mother and her "fatherless," crime-prone progeny. More important, by constructing Lefrak City and its residents as objects of surveillance and law enforcement, this discourse of black crime and family pathology hindered, if not precluded, their participation as subjects in the process of neighborhood stabilization. In presenting this case study I emphasize the close interplay between struggles over the representation of identity and the meaning of place, and those over the distribution of political power and resources.

In mobilizing to address the needs of the latchkey kids, Lefrak City activists would contest and subvert the discourse of black crime and family disorder underpinning the "stabilization" strategies of local governing institutions such as the community board. Moreover, they would create new political networks and spaces from which to construct alternative interpretations of the identities, needs, and interests of black youth.

Lefrak City: "Crucible of Racial Change"

Lefrak City's twenty high-rise apartment buildings occupy an entire census tract, roughly nine blocks in size, adjacent to the eight-lane Long Island Expressway that forms Corona's southern border with Rego Park, a predominantly white middle-class neighborhood across the expressway. The rental and co-op apartment buildings, office buildings, and bustling commercial strips in the Lefrak City area contrast sharply with the lower density single-family homes and storefront businesses typically found in Corona Heights and North Corona to the northeast.

In 1990 Lefrak City's population of nearly twelve thousand was 73 percent black and formed a population of African-Americans and people of diverse Caribbean and African origin in northern Queens second only in size to Corona–East Elmhurst to the north. Hispanics of equally diverse origins accounted for 19 percent of the complex's population in 1990, and whites and Asians, 5 and 2 percent, respectively.

Lefrak City was constructed on a forty-acre tract of swampy land that had served throughout much of Corona's history as a dump.[1] In 1960 Samuel J. Lefrak, one of New York City's most prolific developers of middle-income housing, purchased "Mary's Dump" from Lord William Waldorf Astor. Between 1945 and 1960 Lefrak's development company built nearly 20 percent of the new housing in Queens County (*New York Daily News*, 14 February 1982). In 1973 Samuel Lefrak was reported to be landlord to a quarter of a million, largely middle-income New Yorkers (Tobias 1973).

Completed in 1964 the six-thousand-unit Lefrak City apartment complex was envisioned by its planners to be a self-contained "city within a city" for the middle classes: a "magic world of total living" that would offer shopping, recreation, security, and other services and amenities within easy walking distance (*New York Times*, 24 October 1971).

Until the early 1970s Lefrak City's tenants were predominantly white and middle-class, reflecting the racial, if not socioeconomic, composition of the nearby and largely working-class neighborhood of Corona Heights (Cuomo 1983). [...]

But in 1972 the U.S. Justice Department filed a housing discrimination suit against the Lefrak organization charging that it had discriminated against blacks in the renting of apartments owned by the company in Brooklyn and Queens. [...]

Although the suit was not directed specifically at Lefrak City, the Lefrak organization by some accounts relaxed tenant screening procedures and income criteria and began aggressively recruiting black tenants for the twenty-building complex. A former Lefrak City tenant leader reported to me that the Lefrak organization had concentrated black tenants in Lefrak City so as to comply with the terms of the consent decree without affecting the racial composition of other Lefrak-owned properties.

As a result, the black population of Lefrak City increased dramatically from 25 percent in 1972 to nearly 80 percent in 1976. Many tenants and other area residents complained that the new arrivals were disruptive and were threatening the community with crime, drugs, and "urban blight." [...] The rapid increase in black tenants, coinciding with a precipitous decline in building maintenance and security services, fueled perceptions that Lefrak City had become a "welfare haven," a black ghetto enclave which, like the Northern Boulevard "strip" in Corona, menaced nearby white neighborhoods with poverty, crime, and drugs. [...]

Despite the findings of a 1976 city-sponsored report that only 3 percent of Lefrak City tenants were receiving public assistance, blacks, crime, and "welfare" were conflated in the political discourse of white community activists.[2] These images and anxieties were enlivened by two political conflicts that had been brewing in Corona and nearby Forest Hills since the mid-1960s involving the construction of low-income, "scatter-site" housing for minorities. White civic groups in both communities had opposed the New York City Housing Department's housing integration plan, and in 1972 (the year of the Lefrak City suit) the controversy in Forest Hills was coming to a head and receiving nationwide media coverage.[3] [...]

Mario Cuomo, appointed by Mayor John Lindsay in 1972 to mediate the Forest Hills dispute, described the attitudes he encountered while working with white anti-integration activists in Forest Hills.

> I'm inclined to think that no matter what statistics and evidence we're able to marshal, this community's fear will not be totally dissipated. One story of a mugging at a project – whether or not true – will overcome in their minds any array of statistics. The syllogism is simple: Welfare and Blacks are generally responsible for a great deal of crime; there are Welfare and Blacks in projects; there will be a great deal of crime in and around the project. And then, too, there is a quick projection from the problem of crime – however real, fancied, or exaggerated – to all other middle-class complaints: taxes, education, etc. All of these may be legitimate, but this coupling of them with the crime problem results eventually in an indictment of the project for all the sins against the middle class (1983:49).

This conflation of race, poverty, and social pathology was also encoded in media coverage of the Lefrak City "crisis." A 1976 *New York Times* article noted that the "principal issue within Lefrak City is not one of race but of standards of behavior," yet carried the headline, "Lefrak City Crucible of Racial Change" (1 February 1976). Complaints of poor building maintenance, inadequate security, and "undesirable tenants" were often reported as problems of *racial balance* as in "Lefrak Moves to Correct Racial Makeup at Project" in the *Long Island Press* (31 March 1976). In an effort to "stabilize" the complex and to allay neighborhood fears, the Lefrak organization pressured city officials for federal Section 8 rent subsidies which local community leaders were assured would make it possible to rent vacant apartments to low-income, elderly whites. An infusion of elderly white tenants was presented as a strategy for restoring the "racial balance," offsetting the threat symbolized by the welfare mother and her offspring.

A white member of Community Board 4 recalled the visit of a Lefrak organization official to one of its meetings to win the board's support for the rent subsidy plan. His account provides a good example of the complex and shifting entanglements of race and class in white activist ideology.

> [The Lefrak official] came to the Community Board and he wanted *us* to fill his vacant apartments. So we got Section 8 approved. And he claimed – well in Section 8, that he would put 90 percent senior citizens in. You know, in order to . . . uh . . . stabilize the area. And also he claimed that the . . . the Section 8 would be used mostly for elderly *white* people. You know, because they were the ones being displaced and whatever. So we went along and he got the approval. And then of course it turned out that – you know, he gave all the Section 8 to the *big* minority families and *not* to the senior citizens he promised to. And even the senior citizens he promised – the security was so *bad* that they . . . they were . . . that they would run for their *lives*, 'cause they couldn't survive with the kind of people he was letting in. But *again*, it was nothing to do with the color of the black people. We had Indians, we had Chinese, we had *all* kinds of people here. But they was – it was a different *class* of people.

The counterposed images of "big minority families" and "senior [white] citizens" fused race, class, and age differences in a symbolic shorthand that encoded complex and at times conflicting ideologies and social forces. White opposition to black welfare families converged symbolically and in practice with local resistance to the exercise of power by big government and big business. On the one hand, white residents felt that their neighborhood was being victimized by city officials because of its political weakness as a "middle-class" community: low-income housing and other undesirable projects were "dumped" on Corona because, as one resident put it, "we were a soft touch." On the other hand, many residents attributed the decline of Lefrak City to the greed and opportunism of the Lefrak organization which some held was resolving its lawsuit at their expense while failing to provide proper maintenance services.

For example, in response to the *New York Times* article, "Lefrak City Crucible of Racial Change," a Queens reader wrote to the editor: "It was sad to read about what is happening at Lefrak City. Yet an unhappy thought keeps nagging at my mind. Those young hoodlums, the modern-day Visigoths who are ripping doors off their moorings may not be bringing any new techniques to that high rise mausoleum. Perhaps they are merely continuing the ripoff policies of the management" (21 March 1976). Opposition to black "undesirables" in Lefrak City was entangled in white activist ideology with resistance to the power of big government and corporate greed.

[. . .] Within the span of a few years the "city within a city" for the middle class had been transformed in the minds of many residents into a predatory beachhead within a rapidly shrinking white enclave.

By the early 1980s the worst of the Lefrak City crisis appeared to be over. Community activists, supported by local politicians, city officials, and the local press, succeeded in their effort to pressure the Lefrak organization to evict "undesirable" tenants and embark on an extensive renovation program. Strict tenant screening procedures were enacted and minimum-income criteria were reinstated to reduce the number of low-income tenants. In "Troubled Lefrak City Turning the Corner," a *New York Times* article pronouncing the recovery, Samuel J. Lefrak praised his rehabilitated tenantry: "They're decent, hard-working, middle-class people who pay their rent and pay their full share of taxes. What's happened is the best kind of gentrification" (11 March 1984).

Despite such assertions, many white residents continued to regard Lefrak City as a site of black crime and poverty symbolizing the vulnerability of the community to violence, decay, and the arbitrary exercise of elite power. These perceptions were institutionalized in part with the founding of Community Board 4's Neighborhood Stabilization Committee. Created in 1973 under the auspices of the city's Commission on Human Rights, Corona's Neighborhood Stabilization Committee defined its purpose as the promotion of "understanding and cooperation between different ethnic groups."[4]

Although the committee's initial efforts focused on integrating Corona's rapidly growing Spanish-speaking population into neighborhood affairs, by 1976 the committee had turned its attention to Lefrak City where its on-site office coordinated the stabilization efforts of city officials, community groups, and the Lefrak organization. By 1987, when the Neighborhood Stabilization Committee met to address the problem of the Lefrak library's "latchkey kids," it was functioning as a subcommittee of Community Board 4. Unlike the board's other committees (e.g., Traffic, Public Safety, and Youth Services), the purview of the Neighborhood Stabilization Committee was limited to Lefrak City and its environs, thereby institutionalizing the perception that the black housing complex represented a peculiar threat to the stability of the community. Before the formation of Concerned Community Adults to which I now turn, black participation in neighborhood politics within Community Board 4 had been limited to, if not contained by, this committee.

"Rubbing Against the Grain"

Concerned Community Adults (CCA) was organized largely through the efforts of Edna Baskin, an African-American woman who moved to Lefrak City with her husband and two children in 1979. Raised in Buffalo, New York, Baskin had been active in community politics and Buffalo's antipoverty program as well as in a local Baptist church founded by her grandfather.

Although Baskin had been employed earlier as a medical lab technician, on her arrival in Queens she began working in her home as a "sitter" or child care provider for women living in her four-building section. Since the few licensed child care centers in the Lefrak City area were expensive, many parents used unlicensed sitters located within the apartment complex.[5] Baskin estimated that twelve of the eighteen floors in her building had sitters caring for preschool children.

Through her child care work, Baskin developed a network of relationships with Lefrak City women. Each evening, when these women, whom Edna referred to as her "mothers," came to pick up their children they would gather in her apartment to socialize and exchange information about community services and issues. Baskin also endeavored to welcome and orient new tenants to the apartment complex and the surrounding community, a consideration she found lacking when she arrived in Lefrak City.

> When I moved here, I had to try to learn about the community by myself, because there was nobody to help me or to tell me where things were. And when people move in now, I tell them where the best places are to shop and, if they have children, which schools I think are the best. Even people on my floor – like when new people move on this floor, I immediately go and introduce myself, tell them who I am, and give them a voter registration form – because the first couple of weeks we were here, I was like, "Well, will somebody come and tell us where we go to vote?"

These everyday networks of child care, communication, and exchange among women, linking households, floors, and buildings within the complex, would provide the social base for the mobilization of Lefrak City tenants as a political force within the community. Not long after Baskin arrived, her "mothers" and other neighbors elected her to be a representative to the Tenants Association.

The Lefrak City Tenants Association was organized during the 1970s crisis and was instrumental in pressuring the Lefrak organization to renovate the complex and tighten security. However, by the 1980s some tenants had come to feel that the association had sold out to management and become little more than a "social club." Moreover, though community leaders regarded the Tenants Association as the institutional voice of Lefrak City, its leadership played a relatively minor role in neighborhood affairs. The Tenants Association's lack of involvement in local politics, coupled with the perception of many that it was working in concert with Lefrak management, contributed to the political isolation of Lefrak City's black tenants. In 1987, for example, few if any Tenants Association members attended meetings of Community Board 4, the most important governing body in the community. [...]

In 1986 Baskin was encouraged by Rose Rothschild, Community Board 4's district manager, to participate in the Neighborhood Stabilization Committee. Rothschild and the board's chairperson, also a white woman, had made significant efforts to increase the involvement of people of color on the board. Under their leadership Korean, Chinese, and Latino persons had been seated on the predominantly white-American board, reflecting the changing demography of the community. However, despite Lefrak City's large black population, only one African-American sat on the thirty-four member Community Board in 1987. [...]

Meetings of the Stabilization Committee generally focused on crime, drug sales, and other "quality-of-life" issues in the Lefrak City vicinity, such as traffic congestion and price gouging by merchants. Agenda items frequently targeted threats posed by Lefrak City residents (primarily black youth) to the surrounding area rather than

Top down
Paternalistic to
Solutions to
Problems

to the problems faced by residents within the complex. Similarly, problem-solving strategies emphasized law enforcement rather than the mobilization of Lefrak City tenants around shared concerns.

After attending a number of Stabilization Committee meetings, Baskin came to feel that the committee was not addressing the needs of Lefrak City residents and, in particular, those of its youth. Her participation on the committee waned as she began to form her own group, organizing her "mothers" to that purpose. In June 1987, in her apartment, Baskin convened the first meeting of Concerned Community Adults.

[...]

Baskin and her "mothers" had drafted a statement of purpose for the new group and adopted the bylaws of a not-for-profit agency in Harlem. "The purpose of Concerned Community Adults," read the statement of purpose, "is to provide a wide range of youth advocacy, education, and development services to young people and their parents residing in Lefrak City and the surrounding area." [...]

CCA's first meeting began at 7:00 in the evening with a discussion of the bylaws. [...]

The group turned next to defining the needs of young people within Lefrak City. A problem underscored by all was the lack of a community center and, more generally, the lack of recreational public spaces for youths and adults alike to congregate. Despite its population of twelve thousand, Lefrak City had scant indoor or outdoor public facilities. An empty, apartment-size space located in the basement of one building served as an all-purpose meeting room for the entire development. Little playground space was located on the complex's grounds, and its two outdoor swimming pools were no longer in use. Much of the open space between buildings was taken up by parking lots.

[...]

This lack of public space, Baskin and others pointed out, also limited interaction among adults and made organizing tenants particularly difficult. [...]

For an hour, the board members discussed strategies for creating this "mutual meeting ground" at Lefrak City and for mobilizing its tenants. Baskin suggested pressuring the Lefrak organization to build a community center at the site of one of the abandoned pools. [...]

In the midst of this discussion Jonathan Bates arrived. A student in communications at Long Island University, Bates had attempted to form a youth organization in Lefrak City the year before. When he approached the Tenants Association with the idea, they invited him to head a youth committee within the association but provided little support. Moreover, the Tenants Association would not give the youth committee control over its budget, which Bates felt set limits on its effectiveness as well as its autonomy. When Jonathan heard that Baskin was forming a new organization, he telephoned her.

Dressed in a dark gray suit and red silk tie, Bates told the group about his organizing experiences in Lefrak City and stressed the importance of involving youth in decision making. Baskin and the others agreed and resolved that the goals and activities of the new organization should be defined by the young people themselves. To ensure this "youth viewpoint," the board decided that the first activity of Concerned Community Adults would be a public forum where Lefrak

Lack of
identity
space
↓
Need shared
space/place
to foster
organizing

Give the
youth a
voice

City youth could voice their concerns and set the group's agenda. Jonathan volunteered to make flyers for the event and said he would spread the word among youth in the complex. In the meantime Firdasha Jami would develop a "needs assessment survey" that would be passed out to parents in the complex before the meeting.

The first Lefrak City Youth Forum was held two weeks later in the Continental Room, Lefrak City's all-purpose community room in the basement of the Rome Building facing troubled Fifty-seventh Avenue. About fifty Lefrak City youth, a dozen parents, Boy Scout and Girl Scout troop leaders, and three members of Community Board 4 gathered in the dimly lit, narrow room. The Community Board representatives included its chairperson, Miriam Levenson, and Daok Lee Pak, a Korean-born woman who worked closely with business groups that represented Korean merchants in the Lefrak area. Baskin and her board had chosen Jonathan Bates to chair the meeting as a means of stressing youth involvement in the group and countering, as she put it, "negative images of black males."

A long, folding table had been set up at one end of the room for the members of CCA and the Community Board. Behind the table a large American flag had been tacked to the wood-paneled wall. Flanked by Baskin and three women members of her board, the youthful chair of the forum described CCA's purpose and then invited the young people present to speak about their needs and problems. The teenagers remained silent, but a few adults stood and made statements concerning the need for tutoring and recreational programs.

For some thirty minutes the forum dragged on, alternating between parents' appeals for more youth services and Jonathan's inspired lectures on career planning, positive thinking, and the "new world of computers." After an adult Scout leader asked about the possibility of getting funding for bus trips, a young man sitting in the back of the room stood to speak. He was the first teenager to do so that night.

> Um . . . all this time people been talkin' about "let's go on this trip and let's go on that trip." Why get away from the community? We should concentrate on having more fun *in* the community. They run us out – you know, like from the park or whatever. I . . . I mean they say it's late at night, but *think* about it. I recall last week Thursday, they ran us out of the park at 2:30 in the afternoon. You see, now there was only five of us. I mean sittin' on a *bench* – [they] said we couldn't sit on the bench. They run us out of Lefrak altogether. I don't understand that. Now you talkin' about "oh, let's go out, do this trip here, and have fun there." Why can't we have fun where we live?

The young audience erupted in wild applause. Baskin, who had not yet spoken, stood, nodding her head and motioning with her hand to the back of the room. The audience settled down.

> The young man who just made that comment – thank you very much. I did not *realize* there was a problem with Lefrak security running the youth *out*. See, that's another reason for us getting together – so that we, the *other* adults here who *don't* know what's going on, can be made aware.

In fact Baskin *did* know of this problem with Lefrak security, and she often complained about the harassment that her teenage son received from Lefrak security guards, as well as from city police officers. Her comments were directed to "the *other* adults" present, particularly to the members of Community Board 4 who, unlike those who were living in Lefrak City, had not yet heard this side of the story. This intervention, like many of CCA's activities to follow, served to contest and rework the discursive field within which Lefrak City was constructed as a racialized and pathological place.

The discussion, now animated and dominated by the young people, moved to the topic of the security services. A young man in his late twenties linked the harassment by Lefrak security to media representations of black teenagers as drug dealers. His comments are interesting because they mark the reduction of black teenagers to drug dealers and then expand the category at issue to include a broader "us" – an adult and employed "us": "They done blamed these young people as all drug pushers. That's what they doing. And they want to clear us *all* out. Every teenager is bad in their eyes. And the guys – you be comin' home from work and go to the park, and they push us out 'cause they suspect you to be a drug pusher."

This eruption of frustration and criticism over how black youth were stereotyped and harassed by Lefrak City's security services and the police challenged a central theme in white activist ideology and practice. By inverting the familiar relation between black teenagers and security, so central to the ideology of black crime, the testimony (and Edna's marking of its significance) raised the possibility that black teenagers who were often the targets of police action could play a constructive role in neighborhood stabilization. This novel prospect was given further support, ironically, when the forum's chair, intent on being a source of useful information, suggested that the teenagers voice their grievances about Lefrak security at the next meeting of the Neighborhood Stabilization Committee.

The Youth Forum, which ended with the planning of a youth and adult "march against crack," established CCA as a grass-roots force in the eyes of Lefrak City residents and representatives of Community Board 4 from its "outer perimeter." The importance of this event can be judged in part by the reaction of the Lefrak City Tenants Association. A few days after the Youth Forum, the president of the Tenants Association approached Baskin and asked her to place her organization under his "umbrella." When Baskin refused, the association's president warned that CCA would never get off the ground without his support. Nonetheless, the forum had legitimated Concerned Community Adults and encouraged the leadership of the Community Board to deal directly with Baskin on youth issues without the mediation of the Tenants Association.

Equally important, the mobilizing efforts of Baskin and CCA created new political spaces and ways of envisioning neighborhood stabilization that not only invited the involvement of residents who had been marginalized in local political institutions and discourses but also created public forums where alternative interpretations of the identities, interests, and needs of black residents could be publicly formulated.

Contesting the Politics of "Urban Blight"

A few weeks after the Youth Forum, CCA became involved in a neighborhood "cleanup" competition that further increased the organization's visibility and influence in neighborhood politics. Community boards in Queens were invited by the office of the Queens Borough president to organize teams of youth to clean sidewalks and educate merchants about sanitation codes. The winning team would go to Disneyland.

Again mobilizing her network of women, Baskin organized a team of twelve youth, many of whom she had "sat" for at one time or another. Since no other organization in the community had been able to organize a group, CCA's cleanup team, composed entirely of black Lefrak City youth, became the official representative of Community Board 4. CCA also gained the support of the area's Korean merchants through Daok Lee Pak, the Korean-born woman who had attended the Youth Forum representing the Community Board and the Mid-Queens Korean Association, an organization of Korean businesspersons. Because relations between Korean merchants and African-Americans in New York City had often been strained, this linkage was politically important.

The cleanup team's activities received considerable attention from community leaders and the press. Community Board members visited the cleanup team at work in the Lefrak City area. Merchants donated refreshments, free haircuts, and school supplies, and posed with team members during picture-taking sessions. The Korean owner of a local grocery store offered to hire two cleanup team members when business picked up. Lefrak City management informed Baskin that Samuel J. Lefrak himself had noticed that the neighborhood looked cleaner. Viewed within the context of Lefrak City's history as a political issue and object of discourse, the cleanup campaign was extremely significant.

The image of black Lefrak City youth removing rubbish from the streets surrounding the housing complex undermined the construction of Lefrak City as a site of danger and urban blight – images tied symbolically to pollution and disorder (Douglas 1966) as well as to "blackness" and poverty (Gilman 1985; cf. Conquergood 1992).[6]

The potency of garbage as a polysemous symbol of disorder and threat to community was intensified during the summer of 1987 by a highly publicized political brawl concerning the disposition of a garbage barge. A seagoing barge containing more than three thousand tons of New York area garbage had been turned away by officials in Louisiana where it was to be dumped. After wandering around the Gulf of Mexico for a few days, the barge returned to New York City where it triggered a crisis of sorts. City officials refused to allow the barge to dock until it could be tested for environmentally hazardous materials. A supreme court judge in Queens ordered the barge to be put under "24-hour surveillance" while city officials and politicians debated the origin and content of the garbage (*New York Newsday*, 21 May 1987).

"It's nothing but 100 percent, all-American garbage," a New York State inspector assured the public, responding to fears raised by some politicians that it might contain "vermin," carrying diseases from Mexico or Belize (*New York Newsday*, 19 May 1987). When the town of Islip, Long Island, agreed to accept the garbage for its landfill, the borough president of Queens refused to allow it to be transported across her borough until more testing was done. The town supervisor of Islip accused the Queens official of using the garbage as an issue to mask her "image problems," alluding to a political corruption scandal that had rocked Queens the year before. "I heard her say Islip's garbage will never travel the streets of Queens," he declared. "And she presides over the corruption capital of the universe" (*New York Newsday*, 20 May 1987).

The complex meanings associated with garbage, manipulated by Queens politicians to represent corruption and violations of turf, resonated with local symbolic deployments of such notions as "vermin" and "garbage" to signify the threat posed by Lefrak City. For example, a Community Board 4 member once reported to the board after a Lefrak "tour" sponsored by the Stabilization Committee that the inspection team had encountered the "smell of rats," a claim that was duly recorded in the minutes.

Baskin was well aware of the potency of the "garbage barge" as a mass-mediated symbol framing the activities of her cleanup crew.[7] I asked, "Do you think the fact that it was a cleanup campaign, as opposed to something else, had something to do with its success?"

> Of course. Because, all during the summer – you know – the garbage barge sitting out there – okay? – only emphasized the problem the whole country is having with *garbage*. You understand? And that *our children* could *see* that this is really a problem. See, we have to make our children aware that there's a problem today. So that when *they* become adults, *they* have some...some knowledge to draw on, as to how to *deal* with problems like this. You have to *learn* this. This is nothing that somebody...that you could read in a book and do. It's something you have to get out here and do.

Of interest here is less the symbolic investments of garbage per se than the manner in which Baskin and her organization deliberately engaged in a politics of representation that drew on and reworked deeply historical and mass-mediated discourses about the interrelation of race, place, and urban blight. The practice of constructing black identity was an integral component of CCA's strategy and tactics of community mobilization.

Although the CCA's team did not win the boroughwide cleanup competition, Baskin was able to strengthen support for her group among politicians, Community Board members, local merchants, and representatives of a major new immigrant community in Queens. The Mid-Queens Korean Association, noted above, invited Baskin, her team members, and representatives of Community Board 4 to a dinner party at a Korean restaurant to "honor" the young people. Although black-Korean relations were not the explicit focus of the event the topic surfaced repeatedly, suggesting that race and ethnic relations were being negotiated through activities surrounding the cleanup competition.

[...]

The cleanup competition, like the Youth Forum, undermined key ideological themes that had been articulated in activist and mass-mediated discourses since the desegregation of Lefrak City. Through cultural practices ranging from the cleaning up of streets and public spaces to everyday interactions with merchants, city officials, and neighborhood residents, CCA and its cleanup team challenged and reworked the racialized economy of space and its underlying power relations that had constructed Lefrak City as a threat to middle-class stability.

By summer's end CCA activities had attracted the attention of local politicians. An awards dinner held to honor members of the cleanup team was attended by Helen Marshall, the area's state assemblywoman, and by an aid to the local city councilman. Both officials had begun to explore ways to provide CCA with public funding in order to support a tutorial program the the group had begun in the Lefrak library. CCA awarded certificates of merit to merchants, supporters on Community Board 4, and to cleanup team members. Rose Rothschild, district manager of the board, described CCA's activities (and her certificate) at the Community Boards's next meeting and redoubled her efforts to have Baskin seated on the board.

[...]

For Edna Baskin and Concerned Community Adults, the "hard work" of community organizing rested less in mobilizing ready-made subjects in response to fixed grievances and ideologies than in constructing an alternative political space or public sphere in which the needs, interests, and identities of Lefrak City residents could be collectively contested, negotiated, and recast in empowering ways.[8]

CCA's Youth Forum, cleanup campaign, and other youth-oriented activities challenged and reworked politically disabling discourses about Lefrak City that had obscured and depoliticized the needs of black youth by constructing them as threats to neighborhood stability and by locating the origins of this criminal deviance in the disorder of the black family. As in the case of the "latchkey kids" and the teenage drug dealers, this ideology of black crime and family pathology interpellated black youth as subjects in need of discipline and policing rather than community services. By subverting this racialized ideology of space and identity, CCA established the educational and empowerment needs of black youth as legitimate subjects of political discourse and action within a more inclusive construction of community.

Subsequent activities, such as the Area Policy Board campaign, the creation of the Joint Youth Services Committee, and the publication of the *Clarion*, expanded and deepened this public sphere of neighborhood activism creating alternative and more inclusive arenas of political participation and deliberation. In mobilizing black "families" and households, Baskin and CCA not only contested ideologies of black family pathology but also disrupted and manipulated gendered constructions of political space and agency that privileged formal, officially recognized modes of political activism over the more fluid, "submerged," and sometimes household-based networks of everyday politics.

If an important legacy of the state's response to civil-rights-era activism has been a harnessing of the black public sphere and a depoliticizing of racial inequalities, the case of Edna Baskin and Concerned Community Adults demonstrates that these processes of subjugation are recognized and challenged through the everyday practices of neighborhood activists. CCA's success in mobilizing Lefrak City residents and in mustering the support of neighborhood institutions and political elites rested on the constitution of a heterogeneous and relatively autonomous public sphere through which the needs of residents could be publicly articulated in ways that yielded new and sometimes oppositional forms of collective action and identity.

NOTES

1   In the late 1940s the dump was cleaned up and Quonset huts were constructed to provide temporary housing for World War II veterans and their families (*New York Daily News*, 14 February 1982).

2   See Hall et al. (1978) for an analysis of the development of an ideology of black crime in Britain during the 1970s, and see Rieder (1985) for a discussion of how blacks, welfare, and "mugging" were conflated in the activist ideology of whites in Canarsie, Brooklyn.

3   "Scatter-site" housing was a federal housing initiative designed to integrate the black poor into white middle-income neighborhoods by requiring cities to devote a portion of their federal housing funds to the construction of low-income housing projects in white communities. In 1966 the New York City Housing Department designated a site in Corona for low-income housing. Subsequent protests led to the replacement of the Corona site with one in nearby Forest Hills. For a discussion of both controversies, see Cuomo (1983:3–23).

4   See the minutes of 8 January District Service Cabinet meeting, Office of Neighborhood Government, New York City Mayor's Office, page 3. The Neighborhood Stabilization Committee was formed within the structure of the Corona East Elmhurst District Cabinet, which operated under the authority of the Office of Neighborhood Government.

5   The only day care center located within Lefrak City in 1987 charged $85 per week and fined parents for picking up children late.

6   For example, a white resident of a middle-income housing complex in Brooklyn, responding to a 1987 court order requiring its owner to end discrimination against blacks, declared: "We're being dumped on. We worked so hard to keep this place the way it is. Why bring in the garbage?" (*New York Newsday*, 7 May 1987).

7   In fact Claire Shulman, the borough president of Queens, had spoken about the garbage barge and the political crisis it instigated at the "kick-off" ceremony for the cleanup competition, which Baskin and her crew attended.

8   Nancy Fraser, in her analysis of the politics of needs interpretation, highlights three axes, or "moments," of political struggle that prove helpful in conceptualizing the activist work and accomplishments of CCA:

> I take the politics of needs to comprise three moments that are analytically distinct but interrelated in practice. The first is the struggle to establish or deny the political status of a given need, the struggle to validate the need as a matter of legitimate political concern or to enclave it as a nonpolitical matter. The second is the struggle over the interpretation of the need, the struggle for the power to define it and, so, to determine what would satisfy it. The third moment is the struggle over the satisfaction of the need, the struggle to secure or withhold provision. (1989:164)

REFERENCES

Conquergood, Dwight. 1992. "Life in Big Red: Struggles and Accommodations in a Chicago Polyethnic Tenement." In *Structuring Diversity*, ed. Louise Lamphere, 95–144. Chicago: University of Chicago Press.

Cuomo, Mario. 1983. *Forest Hills Diary: The Crisis of Low-Income Housing*. New York: Vintage.

Douglas, Mary. 1966. *Purity and Danger*. New York: Praeger.

Fraser, Nancy. 1989. *Unruly Practices: Power, Discourse and Gender in Contemporary Social Theory*. Minneapolis: University of Minnesota Press.

Gilman, Sander. 1985. *Difference and Pathology*. Ithaca, N.Y.: Cornell University Press.

Hall, Stuart, Chas Critcher, Tony Jefferson, John Clarke, and Brian Roberts. 1978. *Policing the Crisis: Mugging, the State and Law and Order*. New York: Holmes and Meier.

Rieder, Jonathan. 1985. *Canarsie: The Jews and Italians of Brooklyn against Liberalism*. Cambridge: Harvard University Press.

Tobias, Andrew. 1973. "Someday We May All Live in Lefrak City." *New York* (May 12):36–42.

Part V

Transnational Spaces

This selection of articles on transnational spaces focuses on global, transnational, and translocal spatial transformations produced by the economy of late capitalism, emphasizing in particular the movement of people. Global spaces are created by the global economy and flows of capital and labor which produce homogenized, deterritorialized spaces. While capital and political economy has long been recognized to produce space and place, new spatial forms emphasize the global and informational city, uneven development, and flexible capital and labor in the social production of space. Ted Bestor uses a multisited ethnographic approach to link the global flows of sushi-quality tuna through commodity chains, trade centers, and markets that result in spatially discontinuous urban hierarchies. Akhil Gupta focuses on the effects of global flows of people for the formation of national identities based on affective commitments to territory. He argues that the Third World Nonaligned Movement has more problems in creating a supranational identity than the European Community, which uses its common history and contiguous national borders to project an imagined transnational sense of community. Cultural globalization, spread through electronic media and migration, challenges the territorial definition of the nation-state and creates translocal spaces based on imagined identities embedded in public culture. Arjun Appadurai suggests the emergence of a "postnational geography" that reformulates the concept of citizenship that recognizes heterogeneous units engaged in translocal cultural practices.

Further Reading

Kearney, Michael (1991) Borders and Boundaries of State and Self at the End of Empire. *Journal of Historical Sociology*, 4(1), 52–74.

Liechty, Mark (1996) Kathmandu as Translocality: Multiple Places in a Nepali Space. In P. Yaeger (ed.) *The Geography of Identity* (pp. 98–130). Ann Arbor: University of Michigan.

Malkki, Liisa (1992) National Geographic: The Rooting of Peoples and the Territorialization of National Identity Among Scholars and Refugees. *Cultural Anthropology*, 7(1), 24–44.

Mountz, Alison and Richard A. Wright (1996) Daily Life in the Transnational Migrant Community of San Augustín, Oaxaca, and Poughkeepsie, New York. *Diaspora*, 5(3), 403–428.

Rouse, Roger (1991) Mexican Migration and the Social Space of Postmodernism. *Diaspora*, 1(1), 8–23.

14

Markets and Places: Tokyo and the Global Tuna Trade

Theodore C. Bestor

Historically, of course, market and place are tightly interwoven. At its origins, a market was both a literal place and a symbolic threshold, a "socially constructed space" and "a culturally inscribed limit" that nonetheless involved a crossing of boundaries by long-distance trade and socially marginal traders. But markets were also inextricably bound up with local communities. In feudal times and beyond, local markets occupied a specific place and time... The denseness of interactions and the goods that were exchanged offered local communities the material and cultural means for their social reproduction – that is, their survival as communities.... [T]he social institutions of markets and places supported each other.

Sharon Zukin, *Landscapes of Power* (1991, p. 9)

The past tense in this paraphrase of Karl Polanyi is no doubt deliberate. Markets and places no longer support each other, we think. If Wall Street and the globalization literature are both to be believed, markets are now literally utopian – nowhere in particular and everywhere all at once.

Globalization is a much-discussed but as yet poorly defined concept. The presumed conditions of globalization include, to my way of thinking, the increasing velocity of capital (both economic and cultural), and the corresponding acceleration of transportation and telecommunications, all stitching together ever larger, ever more fluid, ever more encapsulating markets and other arenas for exchanges across multiple dimensions. Facilitating the velocity and frequency of such exchanges is the dispersal (and relative density) of people living outside the cultures or societies of their origins, and the increased potential that exists for these bi-, cross-, or multi-societal/cultural agents and brokers to effect linkages. Accompanying these changes (perhaps another way of saying the same thing) is the rapid cross-fertilization and "arbitrage" of cultural capital (in Bourdieu's terms) across many seemingly disparate domains of media, belief, political action, and economic organization, often in unintended or unanticipated ways. These phenomena increasingly occur within arenas that are global or *trans*national rather than *inter*national, precisely because these trends together diminish the nation-state as the sole or primary or uncontested organizing principle, mediator, or framing institution for transactions and interactions across societal or cultural boundaries.

Technicians of Globalization

A critical question, therefore, is the extent to which forces of globalization have altered or will alter the organization of regional, national, and inter- or transnational flows of people, material, ideas, power, and the like (Appadurai 1990, Hannerz 1996). I examine shifting relationships among globalization, markets, and places through a study of the transnational tuna trade and the commodity chains – the integrated social systems that connect production and consumption, through loosely coupled linkages across great social and geographical distance (Gereffi and Korzeniewicz 1994) – that constitute this trade. The trade and its commodity chains center on Japanese markets, especially Tokyo's Tsukiji wholesale market, the world's largest market for fresh and frozen seafood, and I focus in particular on the trade in Atlantic bluefin tuna.

My research focuses on middlemen (and they are almost all men, in my experience) in this trade, on the Japanese, Korean, American, Canadian, and Spanish buyers, dealers, agents, and other intermediaries who articulate the connections between producers and markets (and through markets, eventually to distant consumers). Viewed from a perspective that keeps these traders in the foreground, one can observe an enormous amount of institutional structure in constant play, swept along by flows of capital, both financial and symbolic, in multiple directions. I should underline the point that this is not a study of consumption or production *per se*. It is about distribution – what Hannerz refers to as "provisioning relationships" (1980) – enabled by the guys in the middle who make the system what it is, not as producers of the system but as technicians of globalization.

Through these traders, the commodities they trade, and the connections they make, I focus on the articulation of markets and urban places in a globalized environment. On one level, I am interested in how transnational networks of trade create institutions or social structures that complexly link previously unarticulated segments of local economies, societies, and polities. On another level, I am particularly interested in the ways in which such networks or commodity chains – and the markets they flow through – are inherently cultural in their processes and effects.

In many distribution channels or commodity chains that anthropologists have examined, the particular cultural idioms and linkages have been within an ethnic group that recognizes itself as possessing common identity. Robert Alvarez, for example, demonstrates the deployment of cultural identities and patterns of relationship as a means of integrating long-distance trade in chiles across the Mexican–U.S. border (1994, 1999, forthcoming), just as Abner Cohen illustrated the salience of ethnicity among Hausa producers and traders in agricultural trade in Nigeria (1969). Both of these examples involve commodity chains that are built around or which sustain cultural affinities or similarities, but the Atlantic bluefin tuna trade relies on cultural flows that cross national, societal, and cultural borders. That is, in this instance of globalization, the commodity chain itself shapes the framework for cultural interaction and influence against a broader background of cultural dissimilarity and the imaginative possibilities that creates.

I argue that market and place are not disconnected through the globalization of economic activity, but that they are re-connected in different ways. The process creates spatially discontinuous urban hierarchies in which Halifax, Boston, Pusan, and Cartagena are close neighbors in the hinterland of Tokyo, distant – on this marketscape – from Toronto or New York or Seoul or Madrid.

At the same time, however, these re-connections and juxtapositions create continuous economic and informational flows, as well as cultural images and orientations. The cultural processes involved include the imagination of commodities in trade, as items of exchange and consumption, as well as the imagination of the trade partner and the social contexts through which relationships are created, modified, or abandoned. Markets and urban places continue as the central nodes in the coordination of complex multiple flows of commodities, culture, capital, and people.

The Political Economy of Bluefin Tuna

To start, I must explain something about Atlantic bluefin tuna themselves.

Atlantic bluefin tuna ("ABT" in the trade notation; *Thunnus thynnus* in biological terms) are a pelagic species that ranges from roughly the equator to Newfoundland, from Turkey to the Gulf of Mexico. Atlantic bluefin tuna yield a firm red meat, lightly marbled with veins of fat, highly prized (and priced) in Japanese food culture. Atlantic bluefin tuna are almost identical to the bluefin tuna (*honmaguro* or *kuromaguro* in Japanese) which migrate through the waters around Japan. Both Atlantic and Northern Pacific bluefin are genetically very similar to another species found in the Pacific, known as Southern bluefin (*Thunnus maccoyi*; *minami maguro* or *indo maguro*) which are common in waters around Japan, as well as near Australia, New Zealand, and many other parts of the Pacific, Indian, and Southern Atlantic oceans. I should note that all these bluefin tuna are quite distinct from albacore tuna (*Thunnus albacares*) – often found in little cans – in terms of size, taste, methods of fishing, customary fishing grounds, affinities for dolphins, environmental regulations, and markets (National Research Council 1994).

Regardless of subspecies, bluefin tuna are huge fish; the record for an Atlantic bluefin is around 1,200 pounds (roughly 540 kilograms). In more normal ranges, 600 pound tuna eight-to-ten feet in length are not extraordinary, and a 250-to-300 pound fish, five or six feet in length is the commercial standard.

Bluefin tuna are fast fish. They have been clocked at speeds of 50 to 60 miles per hour. In a single season, they migrate thousands of miles. Along the coast of North America, bluefin tuna spawn in the Gulf of Mexico, migrate up the coast to Newfoundland, and then return in an annual cycle. Some may cross the Atlantic instead (taking two months), but how many make the grand tour, no one knows.

In New England, the tuna season runs from roughly July to September, corresponding to the bluefin's southward migration from Canadian waters, where they have fattened up for wintering in southern waters. Fishers off the Canadian Maritimes, in the Gulf of Maine, and off Cape Cod intercept bluefin at their peak of fatness, and thus what Japanese buyers call "Boston bluefin" command the highest prices. Because of the enormous Japanese demand for this species (a demand that persists despite Japan's economic downturns of the past decade) and the concentration of this demand – through Canadian and New England fishers operating in a narrow ecological and temporal window to harvest from a small (probably diminishing) population of bluefin in the Northwest Atlantic – many environmentalists argue that bluefin tuna populations have been vastly over-exploited and that the species may not survive much longer as a commercial one (e.g. Safina 1995).

The Atlantic bluefin tuna fishery has been almost exclusively focused on Japanese consumption, and indeed, until the 1970s when Japanese markets first became accessible to North American producers, there was no commercial fishery for Atlantic bluefin in North American waters; bluefin were trophy fish or by-catches. The advent of the jumbo jet, capable of flying non-stop from the North American Atlantic coast to Japan carrying heavy cargo, created the possibility of shipping fresh fish from one ocean to another. Today, Japan is the world's primary market for fresh tuna for *sushi* and *sashimi*; demand in other countries is largely a byproduct of Japanese influence and the creation of new markets by domestic producers looking to expand their sales at home.

In addition to jet cargo service, several other factors prompted the globalization of tuna supply. In Japan during the 1960s, the development of highly efficient commercial refrigeration and the expansion of high-speed trucking throughout Japan brought almost the entire country within one day's driving time from Tokyo which enabled major urban markets like Tsukiji to command the best-quality domestic seafood. The impact on consumer tastes was profound. Old-fashioned specialities of pre-refrigeration days, such as tuna pickled in soy sauce or heavily salted, gave way to preferences for simple, unadorned, but absolutely fresh fish. The massive pollution and overfishing of Japanese waters during the high-speed growth decades of the 1950s and 1960s had depleted local production, and just as demand for fresh fish began to rise, jumbo jets brought New England tuna into reach.

The extension, in the 1970s, of fishing limits around the world to 200 nautical miles excluded foreign fleets from the coastal fishing grounds of many nations. Japanese distant-water fleets, including many that pursued tuna, were forced out of prime fishing waters. International environmental campaigns brought fishing to the forefront of global attention, and the fishing industries in many countries, Japan among them, began to scale back their distant-water fleets, seeing reliance on local fishing industries as a perhaps lower-profile, less economically risky means of harvesting seafood. With Japanese fishing operations beginning to be downsized and the country's yen for sushi still growing, the Japanese seafood industry turned more and more to foreign suppliers in the 1970s and 1980s.

During the 1980s, Japan's consumer economy – a byproduct of the now disparaged "bubble" years – went into hyperdrive. The tuna business boomed. Japanese imports of fresh bluefin tuna worldwide increased from 957 metric tons (531 from the United States) in 1984 to 5,235 metric tons (857 from the United States) in 1993 (Sonu 1994). The average wholesale price peaked in 1990 at 4,900 yen per kilogram, bones and all, which trimmed out to approximately US$34 wholesale per edible pound.

Not surprisingly, Japanese demand for prime bluefin tuna created a gold-rush mentality on fishing grounds across the globe wherever bluefin tuna could be found. During the booming 1980s, a single prime fish might sell for $30,000, $50,000, even occasionally $90,000. Rising yen prices were magnified by fluctuating exchange rates which created added bonanzas for foreign producers. For example, between

1975 and the peak in 1990, the wholesale price in yen rose 327 per cent, but with foreign exchange rate shifts, the price in dollars rose a staggering 671 per cent, and even though the yen price plunged by 43 per cent between 1990 and 1995, the dollar price declined only eight per cent (Japan, *Japan Statistical Yearbook*, 1988: 196; 1991: 198; 1995: 270; 2000: 262 and 422).

Even during Japan's economic slump after the early 1990s, spectacular auction prices would electrify the market occasionally. On January 5th, 2001, the first day of auctions of the new millennium, a Tsukiji trader made global news for his purchase of a 202 kilogram bluefin tuna (caught in Northern Japan) for 100,000 yen per kilogram, roughly doubling the previous auction record. Although widely regarded as a publicity stunt, the purchase nonetheless was for some Japanese a comforting, for others a disturbing, reminder of free-wheeling consumption during Japan's boom times.

In the 1990s, as the U.S. bluefin industry was taking off and was riding a favorable combination of prices and exchange rates, the Japanese economy went into a stall, then a slump, then a dive. U.S. producers were vulnerable as their sole market collapsed. Fortunately for them, alternate domestic markets were growing, fueled by, and in turn further fueling, the North American sushi craze. A North American fishing industry built around Japanese tastes survived with American customers when Japanese buyers retreated in economic disarray.

Visible Hands

A 40-minute drive from Bath, Maine, down a winding two lane highway, the last mile on dirt road, the ramshackle wooden fish pier at West Point stands beside an empty parking lot. At 6:00 p.m. on a clear August day nothing much is happening. In a huge tub of ice on the loading dock, three bluefin tuna caught earlier in the day also wait. Between 6:45 and 7:00, the parking lot suddenly fills up with cars and trucks with license plates from New Jersey, New York, Massachusetts, New Hampshire, and Maine. Twenty tuna buyers clamber out – half of them Japanese. The three bluefin tuna – ranging from 270 to 610 pounds – are winched out of the tub, and the buyers swarm around them, extracting tiny core samples to examine the color, fingering the flesh to assess the fat content, sizing up the curve of the body to guess what the inside of each fish would look like when cut open, and checking carefully the condition of the bodies for damage from harpoons or careless handling. They pay little attention to the fishing crews, except to ask a few pointed questions about where, when, and how each fish was caught and handled.

Dozens of onlookers – many of them "summer folk" – watch the whole scene, some of them with video cameras.

After about 20 minutes of contemplative milling, many of the buyers return to their trucks to call Tokyo by cellular telephone to get the morning's prices – the Tsukiji market has just concluded its tuna auctions for the day. The buyers look over the tuna one last time and give written bids to the dock manager, who then passes the top bid on to the crews of the three boats that landed them. Each bid is anxiously examined by a cluster of young men, some with a father or uncle looking on to give advice, others with a young woman and a couple of toddlers trying to see Daddy's fish. Fragments of concern float above the parking lot: "That's *all*?" "We'd do better if we shipped it ourselves!" "Yeah, but my pickup needs a new transmission *now*!"

No one knows what prices are offered because the auction bids are secret; only the dock manager knows the spread. After a few minutes, the crews all come to terms with the deals offered them. Someone poses a crew member for one last snapshot next to the fish that made the mortgage payments. The buyers shake hands. The fish are quickly loaded onto the backs of trucks in crates of crushed ice, known in the trade as "tuna coffins." As rapidly as they arrived, the flotilla of buyers sails out of the parking lot – three bound for JFK where the tuna will be airfreighted to Tokyo for sale the next day, the others looking for another tuna to buy – leaving behind three Maine fishing crews maybe $14,000 richer.

Tuna Ranchers of Trafalgar

Two miles off the beach at Barbate, a huge maze of nets snakes several miles out into Spanish waters on the Atlantic approaches to the Straits of Gibraltar. A high-speed workboat (imported from Japan) heads out to the nets. On board are five Spanish hands, a Japanese supervisor, 2,500 kilograms of frozen herring and mackerel from Norway and Holland, and two American researchers. The headlands of Morocco are a hazy purple in the distance and just off Barbate's white cliffs to the northwest the light at the Cape of Trafalgar blinks on and off. For 20 minutes, the men toss herring and mackerel over the gunwales of the workboat while tuna the size (and speed) of motorcycles dash under the boat, barely visible until with a flash of silver and blue they wheel around to snatch a drifting morsel.

The nets, lines, and buoys are part of an *almadraba*, a huge fish trap or weir. The *almadraba* consists of miles of set nets anchored to the channel floor suspended from thousands of buoys, all laid out to cut across the migration routes of bluefin tuna into and out of the Straits. This *almadraba* is put in place for about 6 weeks in June and July to intercept tuna leaving the Mediterranean, after the spawning season is over. Those tuna who lose themselves in the maze end up in a huge pen, with a surface area roughly the size of a football field. By the end of the tuna run through the Straits, about 200 tuna are in the pen. For the next six months, they are fed twice a day, their nets tended by teams of scuba divers and watched over by guard boats sent out by the owner of the *almadraba*, the venerable *patron* of Barbate harbor, who has entered into a joint venture with a small Japanese fishing company. In November and December – after the season in New England and Canada is well over – the tuna are harvested, and shipped by air to Tokyo in time for the end-of-the-year spike in seafood consumption.

Two hundred fish may not sound like a lot, but if the fish survive, if the fish hit their target weights, if the fish hit the market at the target price, these two hundred tuna are worth $1.6 million dollars. Cold, wet cash. Liquid assets.

The pens – feed lots for tuna – are relatively new, but *almadraba* are not, and these waters have been transnational since time immemorial, since before there was nation. A couple of miles down the coast from Barbate is the evocatively named settlement of Zahara de la Atunes – Zahara of the Tuna – where Cervantes lived for two years in the late 16th century. The centerpiece of the village is a huge stone compound that housed the men and nets of Zahara's *almadraba* in Cervantes' day, when the port was only a seasonally occupied tuna outpost. Today, the crumbling remains enclose a parking lot, an outdoor cinema, and several ramshackle cafes that cater to Zahara's contemporary seasonal visitors: Euro-kids in dreadlocks who come to Zahara for the windsurfing and the Moroccan hashish. Up the coast beyond Cadiz, reputed to be Europe's oldest city, archaeological remains of a 2,000-year-old Phoenician site near the NATO base at Rota reveal tuna traps similar to those Cervantes observed and which the *patron* of Barbate still deploys when the tuna run.

In Barbate and the two other towns along the Costa de Luz that still have *almadraba*, small-scale Japanese fishing firms work with local fishing bosses who supply the customary fishing rights, the nets, the workers, the boats, and the locally embedded cultural capital to make the *almadraba* work.

Inside the Straits of Gibraltar, off the coast of Cartagena, another series of tuna farms operates under entirely different auspices, utilizing neither local skills nor traditional technology. The Cartagena farms rely on French purse-seiners to tow captured tuna to their pens, where highly capitalized joint ventures between major Japanese trading firms and large-scale Spanish fishing companies have set up farms using the latest in Japanese net technology.

Elsewhere in the Mediterranean, other competitors also rely on the high-tech, high-capital route to farming. In the Adriatic, for example, Croatia is emerging as a formidable tuna producer. In Croatia's case, the technology and the capital were transplanted to the Adriatic by émigré Croatians who returned to the country from Australia after Croatia achieved independence from Yugoslavia. Australia, for its part, has developed a major aquacultural industry for Southern bluefin, a species closely related to the Atlantic bluefin of the North Atlantic and Mediterranean, and almost equally desired in Japanese markets.

Tuna from Trafalgar, therefore, are brought into competition with fish from the Spanish Mediterranean, New England, the Canadian Maritimes, the Adriatic, and the Australian coast, as well as from waters off Turkey, Sardinia, Indonesia, New Zealand, Japan, and the Federated States of Micronesia. The competition takes place at Tokyo's Tsukiji market, where shipments from around the world meet in a single commodity stream that the market pieces together through its elaborate coordination of production that takes place on different seasonal schedules, in far-flung places, against the backdrops of many disparate local social systems for which the market is the sole – but exceedingly powerful – common place of reference.

The Market at the Center of the World

Commodity and cultural capital intersect at a central node in the global trade in seafood: Tsukiji, Tokyo's massive wholesale market for fresh, frozen, and processed seafood. This is a marketplace where 60,000 traders come each day to buy and sell seafood for Tokyo's 22 million mouths, where every day over 2.4 million kilograms of seafood changes hands, where individual tuna from Massachusetts or Murcia may sell for over $30,000 apiece and where octopus from Senegal, eel from Guangzhou, crab from Sakhalin, salmon from British Columbia and

Hokkaido, snapper from Kyushu, and abalone from California are all in a day's trade.

Along Tsukiji's wharf, tuna are auctioned fish by fish. The long rows of fresh tuna stretch meter after meter. They are sold at "moving auction" – the auctioneer, flanked by assistants who record prices and fill out invoice slips at lightning speed, strides across the floor just above the rows of tuna, moving quickly from one footstool to the next without missing a beat, or a bid. The cluster of buyers moves alongside. They know a lot about fish, of course, and they know a lot about the techniques, the fishing communities, and the places where tuna are caught. They are alert to fish from particular harbors or particular producers. They are equally alert to the desires of their customers: sushi chefs, restaurateurs, and up-scale fishmongers. In half an hour, tuna from around the globe – several hundred of them, some days, two thousand of them – are sold; faxes of prices realized are speeding to distant ports, and buyers are on their cell phones calling up chefs to tell them what they've got!

Boosters encourage the homey view that Tsukiji is *Tōkyō no daidokoro* – Tokyo's pantry – but it is a pantry where in 1995 almost $6 billion worth of fish changed hands. (By way of comparison, in the same year New York's Fulton Fish Market, the largest market in North America, handled only about $1 billion worth, and only about 13% of the tonnage of Tsukiji's seafood (*New York Times*, November 11, 1996, p. B4).)

Tsukiji stands at the center of a technologically sophisticated, multibillion-dollar international fishing industry, and every day the market's auctions match international supply with the traditional demands of Japanese cuisine, made ever more elaborate by Japan's prosperity and the gentrification of culinary tastes.

Today, the stale joke among Tsukiji traders is that Japan's leading fishing port is Tokyo's Narita International Airport; indeed in terms of the value of seafood landed, Narita does far surpass all of Japan's more conventionally watery fishing ports. Much of Narita's catch goes directly to Tsukiji. In many senses, Tsukiji is a command post for the global seafood trade. To explain the inner workings of Tsukiji would require another paper – indeed an entire book (Bestor, in press) – so I skip lightly over the market here, making only four main points. (1) First, and most obviously, Tsukiji sets prices. In a half-hour of bidding, the auctions unmistakably establish values that are instantaneously global standards. (2) The auction system and the "commodity chains" that flow into and out of the market are elaborate institutions that socially construct integration across levels within the market, and between the market and producers worldwide. (3) The flow of information that goes through the marketplace is a vital resource in structuring these forms of integration. Markets may make prices, but they run on information. Tsukiji is no exception. (4) Finally, Tsukiji creates and deploys enormous amounts of cultural capital, evident in its control of information, its enormous role in orchestrating and responding to the formation of Japanese culinary taste (and all the aspects of cultural legitimacy and authenticity that implies), and its almost hegemonic definitions of supply and demand and unassailable privileges to impose its own criteria of *distinction*, its own elaborate hierarchies of taste, which producers worldwide cannot ignore.

Stateless Fish

From a spartan suite of offices in an apartment complex in Madrid's suburbs, the headquarters staff of the International Commission for the Conservation of Atlantic Tuna (ICCAT, or "eye-cat" in the trade) administer an international regulatory regime that controls fishing for "tuna and tuna-like species" (which include sword-fish) throughout the Atlantic north of the equator and in the Mediterranean. Established by treaty in the late 1960s, ICCAT imposes fishing quotas and other regulations on its member nations and territories, based on the scientific recommendations of fisheries population biologists, filtered through the political lenses of the sovereign states that form ICCAT.

ICCAT currently has 28 members including Atlantic and Mediterranean fishing countries (ranging from the U.S., Canada, and the European Commission, to Croatia, Sao Tome e Principe, and St. Pierre et Miquelon) as well as three global fishing powers: Korea (ROK), China (PRC), and Japan. ICCAT assigns quotas, directs catch reporting, trade monitoring, and population assessments. Allocations of quotas within a nation's fishing industry, licensing, and enforcement of regulations are in the hands of the states and territories that belong to ICCAT. In the United States, the bluefin quotas are administered and the fishery is regulated by the National Marine Fisheries Service (NMFS, "nymphs").

Fisheries specialists classify bluefin tuna as a "highly migratory species" a label which is a statement not only about behavioral biology, but also about politics. That is, these are fish that swim across multiple national boundaries, which therefore requires states to enter into elaborate international agreements to regulate the fishery. Thus, ICCAT's ultimate task is to impose political order on stateless fish.

Science, politics, regulation, and potential profit make for troubled waters. As the tuna business grows ever more lucrative, the threat of overfishing looms larger (or has come to pass) and the question of who profits from the roaring global tuna market centered on Tokyo makes for nasty battles among fishers, regulators, and conservationists. During the past decade and a half, conservation groups have criticized ICCAT for not acting more aggressively to prevent or reverse an apparent bluefin population decline in the Western Atlantic in the early 1980s. Some activists have campaigned to have bluefin tuna protected under the umbrella of the Convention on International Trade in Endangered Species (CITES), a powerful global treaty. Japan is the major commercial destination for bluefin tuna and it fiercely resists CITES listing for bluefin tuna. In the past several years, Japan and ICCAT have put in place new systems to track (and regulate) trade; "undocumented fish" from flag-of-convenience fishing fleets and countries that are non-compliant with ICCAT regulations are now legally banned from Japanese markets. So every Atlantic bluefin arriving in Japan must be tagged and its papers must be in order.

The fact these fish travel far and fast poses other problems, too; no one can say for certain whether there is one population, or two, or more. A huge controversy revolves around the question of how many of these migrating fish cross the ocean and how many stay on one side or the other. ICCAT, the U.S. National Academy of Sciences (National Research Council 1994), the National Audubon Society, and industry groups pose somewhat different answers to this seemingly straightforward question. ICCAT, some biologists, and many conservationists take the position that the Western and Eastern Atlantic stocks of bluefin tuna are distinct breeding populations. Some biologists, the National Academy of Sciences, and almost all North American fishers take the position that they are not distinct breeding populations.

Why does this matter? If Atlantic bluefin tuna comprise two (or more) breeding stocks, then conservation regulations can be applied differently on either side of the Atlantic. If they form a single stock, all tuna fishers should be subject to similar regulations. Since the mid-1970s, ICCAT has held to the "two stock hypothesis," and has imposed stringent controls on North American catches. ICCAT reacted to the apparently dramatic decline in bluefin catches off North America in the 1980s by imposing stringent quotas (administered by NMFS) on the largely artisanal fishing efforts of small-scale North American fishers. On the European side of the Atlantic, however, industrial-strength fishing efforts continued or expanded under much less stringent quotas.

North American fishers, not surprisingly, point to the evidence of cross-Atlantic migration and genetic studies of intermingling to argue that if Western Atlantic stocks are dwindling or crashing, then Europeans also have a responsibility to make more strenuous efforts to conserve the Eastern Atlantic and Mediterranean stocks as well. And, they gripe that stiff U.S. regulations simply protect bluefin at Americans' expense, and ultimately fishers from other countries pocket Japanese yen.

Particularly galling from the North American point of view are aspects of Mediterranean food culture. For example in Spain and Italy – sitting near the Mediterranean spawning grounds – dried tuna roe is an expensive delicacy, produced in large quantities. Each slab of tuna roe drying in a Spanish processor's warehouse represents hundreds of thousands of potential fingerlings. Equally annoying to North Americans is the French purse-seiner effort targeted on the Mediterranean spawning grounds which, among other things, harvests the fish for the Cartagena tuna farms.

Discriminating Tastes

Disputes over tuna stocks, however, are more than just rivalries among producers: artisanal fishers who hunt wild tuna fish by fish versus industrial aquaculturalists who operate watery feed lots. The conflicts are also fueled by Japanese tastes and preferences which pit different regions of the producing world against one another. In the Japanese seafood trade, tuna is evaluated along several different but interrelated dimensions. On a conceptual level these include themes of seasonality, locale, purity, and nature. On the practical level, these abstract properties take shape through judgments about methods of catching, types of fishing gear used, the locations of catches, whether seafood is fresh or frozen, distances from markets, and the kinds of packaging in which fish is shipped. And all these considerations, both conceptual and pragmatic, place tuna against a complex backdrop of locality, cuisine, and national identity.

Fish cultivation or aquaculture has been practiced for centuries in Japan, and in recent decades Japanese developments in aquacultural technology have been enormously successful, not only in Spain and not only for tuna. As food produced on an industrial scale, cultivated fish have been particularly popular in the supermarket and mass-market restaurant industries, where demand for large quantities of highly standardized seafood available year-round is great. Tsukiji traders and their professional customers, like *sushi* chefs, draw an important conceptual distinction, however, between "wild" or "natural" fish (that is, those hunted and caught by fishers operating in open waters) and cultivated fish. Tsukiji traders usually regard cultivated fish as inferior to their "wild" cousins, and all other things being equal, a wild fish (whether live, fresh, or frozen) will command a premium over its comparable cultivated cousin.

Generally, cultivated fish are thought to suffer by comparison in terms of such things as fat content, firmness and tone of flesh, and flavor; all these are regarded as consequences of raising fish in captivity where they eat an unvarying diet of prepared feed and cannot range freely. Their image in the marketplace is also colored by fears of the potential hazards posed by contaminated feeds; or the fact that much aquaculture takes place in coastal waters that may be tainted by various forms of perhaps as yet undiscovered industrial pollution.

Advances in Japanese freezing technology have also had enormous impact on the global seafood trade. Japanese and other Asian fishing fleets go for voyages of several months in search of bluefin and other tuna species in the North and South Pacific, the Indian Ocean, and parts of the Atlantic. Tuna flash-frozen to minus 60 degrees Celsius on board factory ships can be maintained in deep-freeze storage for up to two years. Whole frozen tuna can be released on the market as conditions warrant, and so, like the products of aquaculture, these fish represent a triumph of industrial technology over season and place in a quest for stable production and price targets. But as with aquaculture, Tsukiji traders regard frozen fish as a product for the mass market, acceptable but necessarily inferior to the fresh, wild varieties. And like cultivated tuna, frozen tuna command a lower price and end up in supermarket cases and chain restaurants.

The typical shopper or restaurant customer, however, is unlikely to know much about aquaculture or be able to actually distinguish a cultivated from a wild fish, or a fresh from a carefully handled frozen one. Under such conditions, the snob appeal of connoisseurship flourishes. Premier *sushi* bars and elite restaurants (*ryōtei*) that specialize in Japanese haute cuisine make a point of *not* serving cultivated or frozen seafood, and some will avoid serving even the "wild" versions of seafood that are widely available in cultivated form simply to underscore their elite menus. Thus, they emphasize seafood that is at the height of local seasonality. Only the micro-local and the micro-seasonal can avoid the possible stigma of association with industrial production. Cultivated and frozen seafood thus ends up in processing plants, supermarkets, and the kitchens of large restaurant chains.

Other things being equal, Tsukiji traders also prefer domestically harvested or produced food items over imports. The preference for domestically produced foodstuffs mirrors the strong cultural meaning attached to locality and cuisine, and a suspicion that foreign foodstuffs may be simply inferior. It certainly reflects pragmatic concerns over the practices of production and shipping, and these are often couched in terms of *kata*, idealized form, and the inability of foreign producers to live up to Japanese standards.

This ideal of perfect external form – *kata* – adds an extra dimension to assessing foodstuffs. The slightest blemish, the smallest imperfection, or the most trivial deviation from a foodstuff's idealized form can make a product – or entire shipment – languish unsold. That is, the outward form – the *kata* – of the product must be perfect, since imperfection outside may signal imperfection within, just as the Japanese etiquette of wrapping symbolically ensures both ritual and hygienic purity (Hendry 1990). The shape of the tuna, the patterns of striation in the flesh, the color of the meat: these are among the elements of the ideal *kata* for tuna.

To achieve these ideals, of course, requires attention to seasonality and location, another strike for wild over cultivated fish. But other questions about the methods of catching fish come into play as well. There is a general hierarchy of fishing techniques, or gear types, ranked by the quality of the fish they yield. Harpooned fish rank highest; in the hands of a skilled harpooner a tuna can be killed quickly and cleanly. Fish caught by rod-and-reel come next; also favored because the fisher must pay attention to each fish individually, but also less highly regarded because in a protracted struggle against the rod – sometimes several hours long – the fish may overheat itself, resulting in "burn." Fish caught by purse seine (a tightening circular net surrounding a school of fish) do not receive individual handling and may thrash wildly in the net, seriously scarring themselves and others. And finally, fish caught in a weir – at least a traditional Mediterranean weir – suffer from the problems of purse-seining compounded by the often brutal harvesting of fish as they are speared from a thrashing school trapped in the giant traps. And so, the types of fishing utilized in different segments of the global mosaic impute very different values to the fish they produce, and to the people and places involved in seafood production.

Almost every Tsukiji dealer in imported fish has his favorite horror story about the improper handling of fish by foreign producers and brokers; in re-telling these tales traders return again and again to issues of Japanese food preferences as they are made manifest through "Tsukiji specs," the demanding specifications that the Tsukiji auction houses expect suppliers to adhere to (and which foreign exporters often seem to ignore or dismiss, according to Tsukiji traders). Japanese buyers laboriously instruct foreign fishers on the proper techniques for catching, handling, and packing tuna for export. Just as a fish must live up to its ideal *kata*, so too processing requires attention to the proper form. Special rice paper is sent from Japan for wrapping the fish before covering them in crushed ice. Despite the high shipping costs and the fact that 50 percent of the gross weight of a tuna is unusable, tuna is sent to Japan whole, not already sliced down into salable portions. Spoilage is one reason for this, but *kata* is another. Everyone in the trade agrees that Japanese workers are much more highly skilled in cutting and trimming tuna than Americans, and no one would want to risk sending botched cuts to Japan.

And in another way, the standard insistence on dealing in whole fish – with all the attendant difficulties and costs of shipping them – creates a higher threshold for foreign fish. A domestically caught fresh tuna, shipped to Tsukiji by truck from a Japanese port, will arrive for sale in good condition more easily and at much lower cost to the shipper than a foreign fish. Place matters and the preferences of the market continue to reinforce this message in myriad ways. Reassurances of safety and predictability are encoded in preferences for domestic products and by extension in the reliance on *kata* – ideal form – as an index of both purity and culinary authenticity against which foreign imports are judged.

Giant Fish for Japan

It's a slow August day on the pier of the Cape Anne Fisheries Cooperative in Yankee City, Massachusetts. Only a few boats tie up to try to sell their day's catch – a single bluefin tuna per boat per day, all that the law allows. The Cape Anne team consists of three men: Jack, the pier manager, Jimmy, his young assistant and negotiator, and Mitsu, a 21-year-old Japanese tuna technician sent by Cape Anne's Japanese partners to spend the season grading and buying tuna for shipment to Tokyo. When a boat ties up, Mitsu goes aboard to check out the condition of the fish. The best fishers have slit the belly, run cold water through it, and stored the fish in an insulated "tuna bag" to try to lower the temperature to avoid spoilage. The amateurs ignore all these standard techniques for properly handling a potentially valuable fish. Pro or amateur, many fishers arrive at the dock convinced *this* tuna, *their* tuna, is the prize of the day.

Mitsu's job puts him in direct confrontation with their expectations, their dreams. He takes the temperature of the fish, takes a core sample of flesh the width of a pencil from the midsection of the fish and examines it for discoloration, and cuts an inch-thick wedge from the base of the tuna's torso, just above the tail. The wedge looks rather like a half-round from a tree stump, and Mitsu checks it for the lines and whorls that tell him – like tree rings – the tuna's characteristics. It takes him about five minutes of silent concentration, before he clambers back up the deck and shows his findings to Jimmy and Jack. Together they consult in almost silent whispers, in a trade pidgin of Japanese fishing terms and English expletives, before they agree on a grade and an offering price.

Jimmy tells the anxiously waiting fisher the news. It's a case of good cop, bad cop. Mitsu never talks to the fishers himself. He's the youngest, most inexperienced guy on the dock, and his English is terrible, but even if it were fluent, he wouldn't talk to the fishers. They deal through Jimmy (who speaks less Japanese than Mitsu speaks English). Jimmy can play helpful ("I wish I could offer you a better price, man,") while nodding toward the silent and presumably hard-fisted Japanese buyer with the unspoken implication ("but, what the hell ya goin' do with these Japanese?"). The gambit usually works. Everyone on the dock "knows" that you can't understand the Japanese, and Jimmy and Mitsu's routine plays directly into those assumptions.

A guy arrives with a lousy fish. Small boat, poor equipment, clearly not experienced. The fish itself is long, skinny, poor color, poor handling on board. Jimmy tells him it is only a "domestic" fish, i.e., it won't be sent to Japan but will be sold for the American tuna market. $3 a pound. The guy is dumbstruck. Anguish shows on his face, in his body language. He begs for a re-examination. He demands that he be shown other, better fish. Jack demonstrates again how to read a tuna wedge. He explains all the signs that *his* really *is* a *lousy* fish. Jack explains the significance of color, the importance of a slippery but not rubbery feel, the signs of *yake* (scorching, caused by improper chilling of an overheated tuna) and *yamai* (cloudy discoloration, apparently caused by some illness in the fish) in the meat: the importance of visual appeal.

The guy doesn't give up. This is his first tuna of the year, and the season is fast coming to an end. "You guys are all against me," he yells, "working with that damned Japanese trying to screw us." Finally, he turns to me, in desperation:

"You've been in Japan, you know what a good fish looks like, look at this core, and tell these guys!"

The kings of this dock are harpooners – the guys who run so-called "stick boats." They never deign to haggle with Japanese tuna techs. Harpooners catch the best fish, take the most risks, and pioneered the use of spotter pilots to guide them to schools of tuna. Harpooners need a good eye and a strong arm to spear a tuna from a narrow bow sprit mounted on a turbo-charged fishing vessel. They are generally young, strong, articulate, and fiercely independent. Their territory runs from the Canadian line through the Gulf of Maine to roughly the BB buoy off Chatham on Cape Cod. The Stellwagen Bank across the mouth of Cape Cod Bay is a favorite and usually productive hunting ground.

They also have been the most aggressive in trying to shift the terms of trade out of the hands of Japanese and more into their own. Most of them are knowledgeable and experienced in consigning their fish directly to auction in Tokyo, bypassing the Japanese and American buyers on the docks. At Cape Anne, they definitely bypass Mitsu and Jimmy, and watch with amused contempt as lesser fishers try to negotiate their ways into better deals. As the consignment segment of the trade has grown, the nature of information exchanges between Japanese auction houses and American fishers has improved, much more of the economic decision making is in American hands, as are the potential profits and the clear and present risks. It is the harpooners who largely have wrought these changes and reaped the benefits. Their successes reflect the constantly shifting balance of power – of cultural "channel domination" – within the tuna trade; producers on the periphery who have mastered enough of the workings of the distant market to generate their own understandings, removed from yet enmeshed in its social and cultural systems.

Commodity, Cultural Imagination, and Strategic Essentialism

Culture and language are strategic tools in this business, not always deployed to convey information or understanding but sometime to obstruct its flow.

Tuna doesn't require much promotion among Japanese consumers, since it is consistently the most popular seafood and demand is high throughout the year. When the Japanese Federation of Tuna Producers (known as Nikkatsuren) runs ad campaigns for tuna, they tend to be low-key and whimsical, rather like the "Got Milk?" advertising in the U.S. Recently, the federation launched "Tuna Day" (*Maguro no hi*), providing retailers with posters and card for recipes more complicated than "slice and serve chilled." Tuna Day's mascot is Goro-kun, a colorful cartoon tuna swimming the Australian crawl. Despite the whimsical contemporary tone of the mascot, the date selected for Tuna Day carries much heavier freight. October 10, it turns out, commemorates the date that tuna first appears in Japanese literature, in the *Man'yoshu*, the 8th-century collection of court poetry – one of the towering classics of Japanese literature – in a poem dated the tenth day of the tenth month. An added twist is that October 10th is a national holiday, Sports Day (itself a commemoration of the 1964 Tokyo Olympics, Japan's postwar triumphal return to international goodwill), observed across the country with family sports contests sponsored by companies, communities, and schools. Goro-kun, the sporty tuna, scores a promotional hat-trick, suggesting intimate connections among national culture, healthy food for active lives, and happy family meals.

The fact that tuna did not become a common part of the Japanese diet until a couple of hundred years ago, and that the present modes of consuming tuna are essentially 20th-century developments, matters not a whit. Reference to the *Man'yoshu* establishes an impressive pedigree at the very core of Japanese civilization. Unassailable hierarchies of taste and distinction are erected through this device. If tuna = Japanese tradition, what then is the extra significance of *Japanese* tuna?

Emiko Ohnuki-Tierney has written about Japanese and foreign attitudes toward raw seafood as one of the pillars of "authentic" Japanese cuisine. Inverting Lévi-Strauss's famous dichotomy, Ohnuki-Tierney (1990:206) observes:

> For the Japanese raw or uncooked food is *food*, while in other cultures food usually means *cooked food*. The raw in Japanese culture thus represents culturalized nature; like a rock garden in which traces of [the] human hands that transformed nature into culturalized nature have been carefully erased, the raw food of the Japanese represents a highly crafted cultural artifact presented as natural food. [emphasis added]

None of the guys on the Cape Anne pier would say it so elegantly, but all would agree that cuisine is national essence and that *Japanese* cuisine is *natural* essence as well. All of them want to understand why fish that they regarded not so long ago as a sports fish with no commercial value – bluefin tuna used to go for a penny a pound for cat food, when any buyer could be found at all – has turned into treasure. As one guy on the dock put it, a tuna has become "my blue Toyota." They seek to explain the transformation from trash to treasure.

Sometimes they construct elaborate cultural rationales.

For some Americans the quick answer is simply national identity. The deep red of tuna served as sushi contrasts with the stark white rice, evoking the red-and-white of the Japanese national flag. Other fishers, a bit more sophisticated in cultural symbolism, also know that red-and-white is an auspicious color combination in Japanese ritual life (and they know that lobster tails are popular at Japanese weddings for just this reason).

Still other Americans favor a historical answer. For them the cultural prize is fighting spirit, pure machismo, both their own and the tuna's. The tuna they catch sometimes fight and fight and fight some more. Taken by rod and reel, a tuna may battle the fisher for four or five hours. Some tuna never give up. They literally fight to the death. So for some fishers, the meaning of tuna – the equation of tuna with Japanese identity – is simple.

Tuna is nothing less than the samurai fish!

Such local mystifications of the motivations of distant markets for local commodities are not unique. They have been the core of cargo cults and commodity fetishism throughout the anthropological literature, from New Guinea to Bolivia. In this instance, the ability of fishers to imagine a Japanese culture and imagine the place of tuna within its demanding culinary culture is not just the product of a one-sided commodity exchange; it also reflects the re-wired circuitry of global cultural affairs in which Japan is core and the Atlantic seaboard a distant periphery, acutely aware of but not terribly knowledgeable about the core that commands its markets.

Whether or not Japanese buyers and their knowing American colleagues actively encourage cultural and linguistic mystification – this strategic essentialism – is not the issue. They don't really have to. Japan is wired into the North American imagination as the inscrutable superpower, precise and delicate in its culinary tastes, feudal in its cultural symbolism, and insatiable in its appetites – whether buying tuna or buying Rockefeller Center. The mediascapes and ideoscapes of contemporary North American life already provide the cultural material out of which fishers can construct their own Japan. Were Japan not a prominent player in so much of the daily life of North Americans, the fishers would have less to think *with* in constructing their Japan. As it is, they struggle with unfamiliar exchange rates for cultural capital that compounds in a foreign currency.

Viewing distant markets through a glass darkly serves the interests of Japanese buyers, who in very pragmatic terms recognize that markets are formed around flows of information; to the extent that market information is couched in the terms of cultural particularism, foreign producers who are willing to accept essentialist discourse as the way to understand others will be perpetually at a disadvantage. The essentialist monologue generated in the fishers' imaginary, sustained in part by the linguistic screen of non-communication between buyer and seller, serves nicely to obscure both the productive and the cultural processes involved in the trade.

This is precisely what the more successful American fishers resist. The harpooners in particular want no part of this mystified ideoscape; they avoid it through their active exploration and expansion of trade channels to Japanese markets that leave them in control of economic decision making, even at the potential cost of greater market risk. It is through their efforts to establish direct sales to Japanese markets that new trade channels have opened up, even as the economic downturns of Japan during the 1990s lowered the value of the tuna being exported.

End of the Season

The tuna action at the Hampshire Co-op dock is about to begin on the second-to-the-last day of the 1999 season. The National Marine Fisheries Service has sent out faxes to all license holders and dealers, closing the quota the following day. NMFS calculates from daily catch reports that the season's catch is only a ton or two shy of the entire annual quota. Fishing will therefore stop.

The weather is stormy. Few boats are out. Only three fish, none of them terribly good, are up for sale today, and the half-dozen buyers at the auction, three Americans and three Japanese, gloomily discuss the impending end of a lousy season.

In July, the bluefin market collapsed just as the American fishing season was starting. In a stunning miscalculation, Japanese purse-seiners operating out of Kessennuma in Northern Japan managed to land the entire year's quota from that fishery in only three days. The oversupply sent tuna prices at Tsukiji through the floor, and they never really recovered during the rest of the American season.

Today, the news from Spain is not good. The day before, faxes and e-mails from Tokyo to the fish pier brought word that a Spanish fish farm had suffered a disaster. Odd tidal conditions near Cartagena led to a sudden and unexpected depletion of oxygen in the inlet where one of the great tuna nets is anchored, this one being part of a highly capitalized, high-tech joint venture between a major Japanese trading firm and a large-scale Spanish fishing company. Overnight, 800 fish suffocated in the oxygen-depleted water. Divers hauled the tuna out. The fish were quickly processed, several months before their expected prime, and were being shipped off to Tokyo, to salvage what could be saved from calamity. For the Japanese corporation and its Spanish partners, a harvest potentially worth $6.5 million would yield only a tiny fraction of that.

The buyers at the morning's auctions did not rejoice in the misfortunes of their Spanish competitors, recognizing instead that they would suffer as well. Whatever the fish today and tomorrow might turn out to be, they would arrive at Tsukiji in the wake of an enormous glut of hastily exported Spanish tuna.

Thinking Global, Acting Urban

Ulf Hannerz makes the point that globalization, or "world culture . . . is not a replication of uniformity but an organization of diversity, an increasing interconnectedness of varied local cultures" (1996:102).

The organization of diversity in this instance weaves together different modes of production in a complex temporal scheme. Here I have only briefly hinted at the varying modes of integration that this trade depends upon. Large multinational corporations with global cash flows and local fishing *patrons* whose capital is locally embedded cultural capital work hand in glove. Marine foraging coexists with heavily capitalized aquaculture. These industrial fishing operations coordinate their production schedules not only with the Tokyo market's demand cycles but also with the seasonality of the fishing efforts of artisanal fishers in North America and elsewhere. Production for local consumption is interwoven into production for export (exports sometimes to replace fish elsewhere that are *themselves* destined for export) – so Spanish tuna ends up in U.S. supermarkets in place of American tuna which was exported to Japan, and some of the best American tuna comes back to the U.S. from Japan, "certified" by its quick circulation through the Tsukiji marketplace.

The complex temporal structure of the trade requires coordination of producers and markets, supply and demand among many irreconcilable clocks. Timescapes, perhaps. There is natural time, somewhat beyond the ken of humans to accurately predict: the seasonal flows of fish, migrating, spawning, feeding, or just schooling. There is fishing time, as locals attempt to read natural time and code conditions that indicate this is the right time to fish. There is regulatory time, the managerial impulse to re-define natural time into fishing seasons so that fishing time corresponds to a bureaucratic rather than a natural cycle. And, there is market time, the temporal logic that coordinates far-flung activities carried out by disparate groups, using wildly different technologies, and engaging in seemingly incompatible modes of production, into a seemingly coherent and seamless master narrative of supply and demand.

Globalization links these timescapes together, not by forcing a uniform logic on each place but rather by filling in the gaps, coordinating activities at disparate locations, twisting perspectives on mosaic chips to make them appear to fit – not only organizing diversity, to echo Hannerz's phrase, but also acting as an arbitrageur, exploiting the minute differences in time and place in order to profit from the diversity it has exposed and then juxtaposed.

Just as Georg Simmel pointed out that the velocity of money and credit transform social relationships and the relationships attached to commodities, so, too, conditions of globalization transform relations among various parts of the globe and rewire the circuits of capital flow in all its varied manifestations. Time and money – the velocity of capital – is not the only issue at stake. As I have tried to suggest, the transformations of meanings attached to relationships and to commodities are equally important for understanding the global role of markets, the cultural processes of markets and commodity chains, and ever-shifting relationship between local actors and global stages.

All these phenomena take place through the interaction of market and place. It is through these interactions, perhaps re-arranged in time and space ("compressed" in David Harvey's terms) but not fundamentally altered, that communities – places – continue to encounter "the material and cultural means for their social reproduction," material and cultural means that in this example as in so many others may be new, alien, or transformed, but no less important for creating local meanings and local social conditions. It is in these interactions that one can find the local in the global.

The interactions of cultural meanings, economic process, and social structural forms, along multiple dimensions, in diverse juxtapositions of local places, in accelerating time, accomplish the "organization of diversity" of globalization, but they do so through substantially urban means: market, place, hierarchy, trade, and linkage. As Hannerz puts it, "cities . . . are good to think with, as we try to grasp the networks of relationships which organize the global ecumene of today. They are places with especially intricate internal goings-on, and at the same time reach out widely into the world, and toward one another" (1996:13).

ACKNOWLEDGEMENTS

This is a much-condensed version of an article originally published as " "Supply-Side Sushi: Commodity, Market, and The Global City," *American Anthropologist*, 2001, 102 (1): 76–95. A full list of fieldwork sites appears in the *American Anthropologist* article, as does a more extended bibliography. I am grateful to Setha Low for her encouragement with the original paper, as well as its revised version. Thanks also to Harumi Befu, Dorothy Bestor, Victoria Lyon Bestor, and Doug McGray. Fieldwork in Japan was supported in part by the National Science Foundation (Grants BNS 90-08696 and SBR 94-96163); the Abe Fellowship Program of the Japan Foundation's Center for Global Partnership; and the New York Sea Grant Institute (Grants R/SPD-3 and R/SPD-4). Research in Spain was made possible through a project on *Models of Global Japan and Globalization*, organized by Harumi Befu, supported by the Japanese Ministry of Education (Project Number 10041094).

REFERENCES

Alvarez, Robert R., Jr. 1994. "Changing Ideology in a Transnational Market: Chile and Chileros in Mexico and the U.S.," *Human Organization*. 53 (3): 255–262.

——. 1999. "La Maroma, or Chile, Credit, and Chance: An Ethnographic Case of Global Finance and Middlemen Entrepreneurs," *Human Organization*. 57 (1): 63–73.

——. Forthcoming. "Beyond the Border: Nation-State Encroachment, NAFTA, and Offshore Control in the U.S.-Mexican Mango Industry." *Human Organization*.

Appadurai, Arjun. 1990. "Disjuncture and Difference in the Global Cultural Economy," *Public Culture*. 2 (2): 1–24. reprinted in Appadurai, 1996, *Modernity at Large: Cultural Dimensions of Globalization*. Minneapolis: University of Minnesota Press.

Bestor, Theodore C. 1998. "Making Things Clique: Cartels, Coalitions, and Institutional Structure in the Tsukiji Wholesale Seafood Market," in Mark Fruin (ed.), *Networks, Markets, and the Pacific Rim: Studies in Strategy*. Oxford University Press.

——. 1999. "Wholesale Sushi: Culture and Commodity in Tokyo's Tsukiji Market," in Setha M. Low (ed.), *Theorizing the City: The New Urban Anthropology Reader*. Rutgers University Press.

——. 2000. "How Sushi Went Global," *Foreign Policy*. November–December. Pp. 53–64.

——. 2002. "Markets: Anthropological Perspectives," in *International Encyclopedia of the Social and Behavioral Sciences*. London: Elsevier Science.

——. In press. *Tokyo's Marketplace: Culture and Trade in the Tsukiji Wholesale Market*. University of California Press; publication expected Fall 2002.

Bourdieu, Pierre. 1984. *Distinction: A Social Critique of the Judgement of Taste*. Cambridge: Harvard University Press.

Cohen, Abner. 1969. *Custom and Politics in Urban Africa*. Berkeley: University of California Press.

Cronon, William. 1991. *Nature's Metropolis: Chicago and the Great West*. New York: Norton.

Dannhaeuser, Norbert. 1989. "Marketing in Developing Urban Areas," in S. Plattner (ed.), *Economic Anthropology*. Stanford: Stanford University Press. Pp. 222–252.

Gereffi, Gary, and Miguel Korzeniewicz (eds.). 1994. *Commodity Chains and Global Capitalism*. Westport CT: Praeger.

Hannerz, Ulf. 1980. *Exploring the City*. New York: Columbia University Press.

——. 1996. *Transnational Connections*. London and New York: Routledge.

Hendry, Joy. 1990. "Humidity, Hygiene, or Ritual Care: Some Thoughts on Wrapping as a Social Phenomenon," in Eyal Ben-Ari, Brian Moeran, and James Valentine (eds.), *Unwrapping Japan*. Manchester: Manchester University Press. Pp. 18–35.

Japan. 1988–2000. *Japan Statistical Yearbook*. Tokyo: Office of the Prime Minister.

Mintz, Sidney. 1985. *Sweetness and Power: The Place of Sugar in Modern History*. New York: Viking Penguin.

Mintz, Sidney. 1997. "Swallowing Modernity," in J. L. Watson (ed.), *Golden Arches East: McDonald's in East Asia*. Stanford: Stanford University Press. Pp. 183–200.

National Research Council. 1994. *An Assessment of Atlantic Bluefin Tuna*. Washington DC: National Academy Press.

Ohnuki-Tierney, Emiko. 1990. "The Ambivalent Self of the Contemporary Japanese," *Cultural Anthropology*. 5 (2): 197–216.

Omae, Kinjiro, and Yuzuru Tachibana. 1981. *The Book of Sushi*. Tokyo and New York: Kodansha International.

Plattner, Stuart (ed.). 1985. *Markets and Marketing*. Monographs in Economic Anthropology, no. 4. Lanham MD: Society for Economic Anthropology.

Plattner, Stuart (ed.). 1989. *Economic Anthropology*. Stanford: Stanford University Press.

Roseberry, William. 1996. "The Rise of Yuppie Coffees and the Reimagination of Class in the United States," *American Anthropologist*. 98(4):762–775.

Safina, Carl. 1995. "The World's Imperiled Fish," *Scientific American*. 273 (5): 30–37.

Sonu, Sunee C. 1994. *The Japanese Market for U.S. Tuna Products*. US Department of Commerce, National Oceanic and Atmospheric Administration, National Marine Fisheries

Service, Southwest Region: Technical Memorandum NOAA-TM-NMFS-SWR-029, September 1994.

Watanabe, Fumio (ed.). 1991. *Maguro o Marugoto Ajiwau Hon* [The Complete Book of Tuna Tasting]. Tokyo: Kobunsha.

Yoshino, Masuo. 1986. *Sushi*. Tokyo: Gakken.

Zukin, Sharon. 1991. *Landscapes of Power*. Berkeley: University of California Press.

15

The Song of the Nonaligned World: Transnational Identities and the Reinscription of Space in Late Capitalism

Akhil Gupta

Introduction

The nation is so deeply implicated in the texture of everyday life and so thoroughly presupposed in academic discourses on "culture" and "society" that it becomes difficult to remember that it is only one, relatively recent, historically contingent form of organizing space in the world. National identity appears to be firmly spatialized and seemingly immutable, becoming almost a "natural" marker of cultural and social difference. This article problematizes nationalism by juxtaposing it and other forms of spatial commitment and identity, particularly transnational ones. In so doing, it seeks to illuminate the specificity of nationalism in the post-colonial world. Beginning with the premise that the structures of feeling (R. Williams 1961:48–71) that produce a location called "the nation" are not identical in differently situated places, I wish to conceptualize the vastly dissimilar structural positions occupied by First and Third World[1] nationalisms by locating them with respect to late capitalism and to the postcolonial world order. Connecting such global phenomena with questions of place and identity is consonant with recent moves in anthropological theory that urge us to go beyond "the field" to see how transnationalism refracts and shapes "the local."[2]

The changing global configuration of postcoloniality and late capitalism have resulted in the repartitioning and reinscription of space. These developments have had profound implications for the imagining of national homelands and for the discursive construction of nationalism. To grasp the nature of these changes, we need to be bifocal in our analytical vision. On the one side, we need to investigate processes of place making, of how feelings of belonging to an imagined community bind identity to spatial location such that differences between communities and places are created. At the same time, we also need to situate these processes within systemic developments that reinscribe and reterritorialize space in the global political economy.

To spell out the argument, I make extensive use of two examples of non-national collectivities: the Nonaligned Movement (NAM) and the European Community (EC). The examination of imagined communities that transgress the spatial order of nation-states offers some important insights into nationalism. The section of this article that immediately follows offers an historical narrative of the Nonaligned Movement. After that, in a more comparative vein, I look at the differences between NAM, the EC, and nationalism. The third section pursues the question of nationalism in greater depth. Finally, the concluding section draws out some of the theoretical connections between space, place, identity, and the problematic of nationalism.

"Song of the Non-Aligned World"

In 1987, a little-noticed long-playing album was released in Belgrade. The cover has a photograph of the leaders of 25 nations in full national regalia at the first Nonaligned Summit held in Belgrade in 1961. Above and below the borders of the photograph is the album's title, "Song of the Non-Aligned World," repeated in Slavic, Hindi, Arabic, Spanish, and French. The back sleeve has a more recent color photograph of smiling children from what appears to be a veritable United Nations. Inside are photographs of the meeting sites of various Nonaligned Conferences and the words of the (only) song on the album, repeated in all the languages mentioned above. The lyrics of the song are as follows (Višekruna 1987):

Song of the Non-Aligned World

From Brioni[3] hope has come to mankind
Hope and justice for all men as one kind
Tito, Nehru, Nasser gave us peace of mind
When they built the movement of the Non-Aligned

In making us believe in the right things
They gave us a song which the world sings
Wisdom listens, violence is blind
The only promise is that of the Non-Aligned

The creators of the Non-Aligned world
Will be hailed forever by the whole world
In the world of justice all men will be free
Everyone will live in peace and harmony.

In its form, this song resembles those other songs that we call national anthems. Yet the type of community that is being invoked here is clearly not a national one. In this article, I propose that it is only by examining such non-national spatial configurations that the "naturalness" of the nation can be radically called into question. Therefore, the study of nationalism must necessarily refer to phenomena that transgress "the national order of things."[4] In other words, we need to pay attention to the structures of feeling that bind people to geographical units larger or smaller than nations or that crosscut national boundaries.

The Nonaligned Movement serves as a good example of such a transnational imagined community. Whereas an analysis that centers on late capitalism alone fails to explain the *political* impetus for a transnational organization of third world nations,[5] an analysis that centers exclusively on the political changes resulting from decolonization cannot explain why the Nonaligned Movement has been less successful than expected in forging third world unity, and why the European Community has already made impressive, albeit incipient, moves in that direction.[6] The powerful structural forces acting differently in these two cases can only be grasped by paying attention to their differential locations within a postcolonial world and to the reinscription of space in late capitalism (Harvey 1989; Jameson 1984). Spatial identities have been powerfully shaped by the accompanying processes of deterritorialization and displacement (Kaplan 1987; Martin and Mohanty 1986). Yet, as the Nonaligned Movement demonstrates, parallel to this are equally important, although less noted, processes that are involved in the repartitioning and *re*territorialization of space. It is in this changing relationship of space and identity that the problematic of nationalism needs to be situated.

The genesis of the Nonaligned Movement is usually traced to a meeting of 29 countries in the Indonesian resort city of Bandung in 1955. The conference was the first, groping expression of the idea of Afro-Asian unity, bringing together the leaders of independent states in the two continents. Many who were to become the most important statesmen on the world stage attended this meeting, including Nehru, Chou En-Lai, Nasser, and Sukarno. Although Bandung resulted in no concrete institutional changes, the presence of almost half the member states of the United Nations laid the framework for third world unity in the interstate system. The "spirit of Bandung" was to be evoked in all subsequent efforts to create a new "third bloc" in the postcolonial world.[7]

The pace of efforts to forge unity among third world countries accelerated after Bandung, particularly following a meeting between Nehru, Tito, and Nasser in Brioni, Yugoslavia, in 1956, culminating in the summit that formally launched the Nonaligned Movement in September 1961 in Belgrade. To understand the particular conjuncture that led the 25 participant states and the three "observers" to come together, one has to look at those eventful six years that separate Bandung from Belgrade. This period witnessed the Suez Canal crisis and the Soviet invasion of Hungary in 1956, the admission of 16 newly independent African countries to the United Nations in 1960, the escalation of Cold War tensions following the downing of an American U2 spy plane over Soviet air space in 1959, and growing U.S. military involvement in places as diverse as Cuba, Vietnam, the Congo, and Laos. For third world nation-states, especially newly independent ones, these actions only highlighted the fragility of their sovereignty. Superpower conflict and direct military intervention were grave external threats to the nationalistic goal of preserving and consolidating their independence.

The principles of nonalignment enunciated at the Belgrade Summit emphasized a commitment to nuclear disarmament, a reduction of Great Power tensions, and noninvolvement in the Cold War. Nonalignment was differentiated from "neutrality," which implies a passive, isolationist policy of noninvolvement in all conflicts.

Indeed, it was an assertion of *agency* on the part of third world nation-states that defined what it meant to be "sovereign" and "independent." For this reason, nations whose sovereignty was sullied by their participation in multilateral or bilateral military agreements with the superpowers were barred from membership. Hence, it would be a mistake to see the Nonaligned Movement entirely in the context of political conflicts among the superpowers. From the beginning, some of its most important themes have been the opposition to colonialism, neo-colonialism, imperialism, and racism.[8] Nonalignment was thus based upon nationalism at the same time that it helped consolidate it.

A particularly controversial position maintained by the nonaligned states has been their consistent criticism of the "cultural imperialism" of the West.[9] Here the United States' control of communication systems, news and information services, and mass-media-based cultural production has received particular condemnation. In calling for a New World Information and Communications Order, the nonaligned world has earned the undying hostility of the corporations that control these services in the West. Dissatisfaction with the present information order led to the innovation of a Nonaligned News Agency Pool that takes reports from various third world countries and distributes them horizontally instead of going through the Western-controlled wire services (Mankekar 1978a, 1978b, 1978c, 1981). Asserting the power to control the distribution of news flow and cultural products in this way, the Nonaligned Movement is attempting to "bind" space in a new manner.

The News Agency Pool is one of a small body of formal institutions run by the Nonaligned Movement. Other organizations include a permanent executive committee that plans the summits held every three years, a United Nations caucus group, and a series of economic working groups such as the International Centre for Public Enterprises in Yugoslavia, a Centre for Science and Technology in Peru, and an International Centre on Transnational Corporations in Cuba. Nevertheless, the Nonaligned Movement, true to its self-designated status as a movement, has maintained a diffuse and decentered profile. Its strength lies as much in its *interstitial* location between the superpowers as in its ability to resist the metanarratives that they attempt to impose on it. This proves annoying even to sympathetic first world scholars.

> The itinerant nature of intra-Third World diplomatic process has been an obstacle to a well-informed understanding of the role of the developing countries in international politics. The process appears to lack continuity in the absence of a central vantage point from which to view it. [Mortimer 1984:4]

Conventional explanations of the formation of the Nonaligned Movement emphasize the pressure of contingent events in world politics. Although such events were undoubtedly important, they have to be contextualized with respect to the structural shifts accompanying decolonization. Among the most important of such shifts was that which occurred with the end of direct rule: the new global political economy moved to exploitation through division of labor and unequal exchange. This significantly altered the spatial and political contours of resistance by colonized groups. The postcolonial context of sovereign, independent nation-states created a space for lateral political connections between formerly colonized nations, where previously such relations had been mediated by the colonial powers. In the Non-aligned Movement, we therefore have a recognition of the political significance of the formation of independent nations in the third world and at the same time an acknowledgement of the heavily overdetermined and tenuous nature of that independence. The next section explores this contradictory position by comparing the Nonaligned Movement both with nationalism and with the European Community.

Nonalignment, the European Community, and Transnationalism

As a form of imagined community, the Nonaligned Movement shares a great deal with nationalism. However, it is instructive to examine the ways in which it is different. Much of the impetus for the movement came from the *nationalist* desire on the part of weak third world nation-states to preserve some measure of independence for themselves. There is something paradoxical about the fact that nationalism should need *trans*nationalism to protect itself. This paradox cannot be explored by staying within the problematic of nationalism – the ideological claims it makes both about historic possibilities and the practical forms in which they can be realized (Chatterjee 1986:36–53). Why nations come to be such potent forms of imagining community can only be understood by contrasting them with other forms of im-agined community, both supranational and subnational. Although one can debate the efficacy of the Nonaligned Movement in creating a supranational imagined community, far more important for the purposes of my argument are the challenges that such an organization poses for the analysis of nationalism. How does the Nonaligned Movement (as an organization that includes most nations of the world) contrast with other forms of imagined community such as nations or ethnic groups? How are these differences to be characterized? What is it that distinguishes and privileges nations as a form of imagined community, that makes them so compelling to the hearts and minds of their citizens?

Like nationalism with respect to regionalism or ethnic movements, nonalignment is itself a metanarrative that incorporates the particular struggles of its member states within the "general" struggle of the third world. "The Song of the Non-Aligned World" is a variant of the national anthem, one that seeks (quite literally) to create a poetics of a new kind of transnational, "third world" identity. The effort to create a nonaligned identity and to give the notion of "third world" a positive valence can be interpreted, analogously to nationalism, as a move to create new, homogenizing narratives of resistance to domination by the core countries. But the Nonaligned Movement, too, has to be located within yet another overarch-ing narrative of world community, that provided by the United Nations. The understanding of themselves as a "third bloc" constitutes an important unifying strategy for these nations and enables a degree of resistance to the UN's master narrative of the world as a body of equal but different nation-states. In this context, nonalignment plays a role analogous to that played by the subnational vis-à-vis nationalism. In seeking an alternative identity, it rejects as fact the homogenizing premises of the UN – separate but equal. At the same time, it uses those premises as an ideal to assert another kind of identity, pointing to the discrepancy between the formal recognition of equality and actual practice. We can think of the Nonaligned

Movement as representing a "rainbow coalition" of dispossessed nations: united by their common exploitation vis-à-vis the superpowers, and demanding their constitutional rights as citizens of the world of nation-states. The Nonaligned Movement's efforts at imagining collectivity are thus caught between multiple levels of spatial commitment and organization.

It is for this reason quite revealing to compare attempts at building transnational imagined communities like the Nonaligned Movement and the European Community with the system of practices that constitute nationalism. In addition to practices oriented externally, that is, toward other states, some of the most important features that enable the nation to be realized are flags, anthems, constitutions and courts, a system of political representation, a state bureaucracy, schools, public works, a military and police force, and newspapers, television, and other mass media. The Nonaligned Movement possesses some of these features, such as an anthem, a founding charter, a bureaucracy, a spokesperson who represents the movement to the "world" media, and so on. Similarly, if one considers Europe 1992, the line between a "national" and some kind of larger unit becomes even more fuzzy. Internal travel without visas, a European parliament, a European bureaucracy, common schools, the relaxation of trade barriers, tariffs, and taxation, the free movement of labor, perhaps a common currency – these features resemble the practices of nationalism so much that it could be argued that what is being proposed is the dissolution of old national boundaries and the creation of a new, united nation of Europe. Yet, it is unlikely that the nations that constitute Europe today will just disappear. What may be happening is the creation of a hybrid form that lies somewhere between federal nations like India and the United States and a singular European nation. Europe 1992 will result not just in the redivision and repartition of space but in its reinscription – something new that shares many, but not all, of the practices that constitute a nation.[10]

Some of the problems arising in the integration of Europe bear a striking resemblance to dilemmas of nation building that continue to be experienced in a multiethnic, multilingual, religiously pluralistic, administratively divided federal political system such as India's. (Let me immediately add that I do not want to equate the integration of Europe with nation building, but merely to point to their similarities.) Take, for example, the schools that have been set up for the 15,000 children of the employees of the European Community to "create a whole new layer of identity in these kids" (Mapes 1990:A1). "Graduates emerge [from these schools] superbly educated, usually trilingual, with their *nationalism muted – and very, very European*" (1990:A1, emphasis added). The schools strive to educate students "not as products of a motherland or fatherland but as Europeans" (1990:A1). However, administrators find that the education ministries of the 12 EC countries are not "fighting for the European view in education...maybe they *think European* in the finance and trade ministries, but not in education. It will be the last thing to be harmonized" (1990:A16). History textbooks, usually published for students in one nation, pose further problems. "They tend to be blinkered histories of the great powers" (Mapes 1990:A16). Schools are one of the crucial sites where the nation comes to be imagined in the minds of generations of future citizens. It is for this reason that so much attention is given to the curricula in newly independent nation-states, especially the constructed "national" traditions embodied in history texts.

The European Community schools are creating new sets of relationships between peoples and spaces, forging a different type of identity in their students. The relationship they find between space, time, and historical memory in existing textbooks may be "blinkered," but what will be the blinkers on the new sense of community produced? Will this alternative production of Europe as "home" be one that, although not national, is still built on violence and the exclusion of others (Martin and Mohanty 1986)? Who will now be classified as the "other" of a "European" student? What the schools are attempting to do is to redescribe cultural differences, embedded so naturally in national traditions, so that the new kinds of cultural differences they produce no longer coincide with old boundaries. The European Community schools are thus actively involved in producing the reterritorialization of space.

According to Anderson (1983), one of the most important mechanisms for imagining the "deep horizontal comradeship" that a citizen feels for a fellow national is the mass media. In his view, the ability to imagine the nation is closely tied to print capitalism. Newspapers enable the nation to be represented by the juxtaposition under one date of stories from different "parts"; similarly, the nation is differentiated from others by the presentation of "international" and "foreign" news. In this regard, transnational organizations such as the Nonaligned Movement and the European Community contrast with nation-states in that they have no widely circulating newspapers or widely watched televisual programs that enable them to be represented to "their" citizens.[11] This is perhaps one of the reasons why such transnational communities have been less successfully imagined than have nations.

Although less successful overall, there are nevertheless clear differences in the degree to which distinct non-national communities have been realized. What makes the Nonaligned Movement and the European Community so different as federations is their respective locations in the postcolonial world system of late capitalism. Despite its longer history, the Nonaligned Movement has not managed to create the same bonds of solidarity linking peoples, locations, and spaces that the European Community has managed to do in a relatively short time span. This is in part because of the long historical project in which many European nations were, if not united, at least in cohort: colonialism. European unity in the postcolonial world, therefore, is based upon an entirely different structural position than unity among nonaligned nations.

A convincing argument could also be made linking the reinscription of space in Europe and the third world with the nature of late capitalism (Harvey 1989; Mandel 1975). Mandel predicted almost 20 years ago that the growing centralization and concentration of capital was likely to lead to the reterritorialization of space as ever-larger capitalist conglomerates ran up against the limits of specially protected but spatially segmented national markets (see also Harvey 1985). He visualized several scenarios, the most likely of which foresaw the creation of three regionally based capitals, one centered in Japan, the second in the United States, and the third in a united Europe. His uncanny foresight is borne out by the statement (quoted in full earlier) that administrators in the European Community already "think European" in the finance and trade ministries. This is not to argue that the move toward a united Europe follows in some direct fashion from the changing "requirements" of late capitalism, or even that it depends on it "in the last instance," but to emphasize that transformations in the global political economy are a central component in any explanation of the reterritorialization of space.

In contrast to the European Community, the Nonaligned Movement has had a much more difficult time in forging a common identity for its member nations, because building unity from the fragmenting experience of subjugation and displacement under colonialism is an inherently more difficult task. It is also because the rapid geographical expansion of the largest capitalist combines of the world system have put third world countries, who are producers of raw material and sellers of inexpensive labor power, under greater and greater competitive pressure vis-à-vis each other. Where third world countries have attempted to band together and promote regional economic cooperation to preserve their sovereignty, multilateral "development" aid has seduced them into a pattern of debt and dependence that has pried open their economies to multinational capital (see Ferguson 1990). The debt crisis that currently afflicts most of the developing world, leaving it completely vulnerable to control by the most powerful capitalist nation-states (and their proxies, the IMF and the World Bank), reinforces the vertical links characteristic of colonialism rather than horizontal cooperation and unity. Powerful structural forces such as these work against intra-third world unity; hence, building an identity based on nonalignment is more challenging than building one based on European-ness. The contrast between the Nonaligned Movement and the European Community illustrates the different ways in which postcoloniality articulates with late capitalism in the production of transnational imagined communities.

Nationalism in a Transnational World

If we examine the nature of the "independence" won by formerly colonized peoples and places (in most cases, it would be anachronistic to call them nations), three features stand out: the modernist form taken by the nation; the formal equality enjoyed by newly independent countries in a postcolonial global discourse about the "family of nations"; and the ambiguity of sovereignty in an unequal world.

What emerged from decolonization was a distinctively modernist institutional and ideological formation: the nation-state. One of the first things that new nation-states do is to write the history of the "nation" (itself an entity consolidated during or after colonial rule) stretching into the distant past (Dirks 1990). Such modernist practices have led two of the most influential recent theorists of nationalism, Partha Chatterjee (1986) and Benedict Anderson (1983), to emphasize the "secondary" character of 20th-century nationalist discourse. Whereas Chatterjee sees third world nationalism as a derivative discourse that inevitably, perhaps reluctantly, participates in the "thematic" of the Enlightenment, Anderson sees it as a modular form that draws on "more than a century and a half of human experience and three earlier models of nationalism" (1983:123). It is possible to attain a somewhat different understanding of anticolonial national struggles by placing them within a more macro perspective. One could fight the colonial power to "liberate" the nation only because the nation was already recognized as something that was waiting to be born. In other words, the discursive availability of the imagined geography of the nation allowed it to exist as a potential entity and made it a form of organizing space that had political legitimacy. The significance of this fact can be judged by comparing the relative success of nationalist movements with the relative failure of international working-class movements; as generations of Marxists after Marx found out, it is one thing to liberate a nation, quite another to liberate the workers of the world.

Second, just as the formal equality of citizens in the nation-state is often constitutionally enshrined (Anderson's "deep horizontal comradeship"), so the equality of nation-states in the world system is given concrete expression in the charter and functioning of international organizations such as the United Nations. The independence of third world countries, dependent as it is on the international order of the United Nations, thus redirects spatial identity from the nation at the same time that it produces it.

Last, independence from colonial rule made it imperative for postcolonial third world nation-states to examine the nature and meaning of sovereignty. They soon realized that the independence they had fought so hard to obtain could not be sustained under the pressure exerted by the superpowers to incorporate them into clientistic relationships. The only way to resist this pressure was to band together and form a common front and to use this union strategically to prevent absorption into either bloc. Sovereignty not only depends on the protection of spatial borders, but it is above all the ability of state elites to regulate activities that flow across those borders, such as the crossing of commodities and surpluses, the passage of people in the form of labor, tourists, et cetera, and the movement of cultural products and ideas. It is significant that the agenda of successive meetings of nonaligned nations moved from an initial emphasis on the Cold War and colonialism to questions of imperialism, unequal trading relationships, and the new information order. It was realized that economic dependence, indebtedness, and cultural imperialism were as great, if not greater, dangers to sovereignty as was military invasion. The Nonaligned Movement thus represented an effort on the part of economically and militarily weaker nations to use the interstate system to consolidate the nation-state.

The other way in which newly independent states attempted to protect their fragile sovereignty was by aggressively employing nationalist discourses and practices *within* the country. Nationalism as a distinctively modern cultural form attempts to create a new kind of spatial and mythopoetic metanarrative, one that simultaneously homogenizes the varying narratives of community while, paradoxically, accentuating their difference (B. Williams 1990). Taking an implicitly omniscient perspective, "a national narrative seeks to define the nation, to construct its (typically continuous and uninterrupted) narrative past in an assertion of legitimacy and precedent for the practices of the narrative present – its own relation of the national 'story' most especially" (Layoun 1990:7). The national narrative incorporates the local as one element in the "larger" spatial and temporal story of nationalism. In the Indian case, for example, rulers of small kingdoms who fought the British to preserve their own power are now considered nationalist heroes whose struggle contributed to the demise of colonialism. It is in this way that local struggles waged for local reasons are "written into" the nationalist narrative, either as a geographically limited instance of the whole or as a moment (perhaps an originary moment) in the gradual unfolding of the master narrative. Nationalism, therefore, gathers into its fold the dispersed historical narratives of diverse, and often unrelated, communities.

On the other hand, nationalist narratives also acknowledge, and sometimes celebrate, difference. It needs to be emphasized that shaping union through difference is also a mode of creating subject positions for subordinated narratives. As a reinscription of narratives of community, nationalism does not so much erase existing narratives as *recast* their difference. The recognition that different ethnic groups, different locales, different communities and religions each have their own role to play in the national project underlines their difference at the same time that it homogenizes and incorporates them. The Indian national anthem, for example, sequentially names the different regions (hence languages, cultures, religions, histories) that are all distinctive parts of the united Indian nation. Such an incorporation of difference hierarchically organizes subject positions for diverse groups of citizens. Pratt (1990) notes the fundamentally androcentric bias of nationalist longings: "Women inhabitants of nations were neither imagined as, nor invited to imagine themselves as part of the horizontal brotherhood." Women are generally recognized only in their roles as the producers of citizens and are thus precariously positioned as subjects of the nation.

To the extent that nationalism attempts to rewrite already existing narratives of community (mistakenly analyzed as "primordial"), resistance to it takes the form of a renewed emphasis on oppositional ethnic, subnational, or religious identities. Any emancipatory movement that tries to fashion a new, coherent identity (as nationalism attempts to do) carries with it its own repressive agenda (Radhakrishnan 1987:208). The containment that nationalist narratives seek to impose on their constituent elements – actors, actions, histories, and, most pertinent to this article, spaces – is predictably, but with varying degrees of success, resisted by those so confined. However, to the extent that it is successful in incorporating the recognition of difference, nationalism serves to negate in advance, to anticipate and thereby to diffuse, reshape, and contain particular forms of resistance.

Whether a hegemonic master narrative of the nation succeeds in establishing itself or not depends a great deal on the *practices* of the state. The nation is continually represented in state institutions such as courts, schools, bureaucracies, and museums, which employ the icons and symbols of the nation – flags, currency, seals, et cetera.[12] But, very important, the nation is also constituted by a state's external dealings with other states who recognize these practices as belonging to an entity of the same kind as themselves, thereby validating the ideology of nationalism. Such "externally oriented" practices, which constitute what it is to be a nation, include such things as marking borders (by erecting fences, maintaining troops to guard it, checking and stamping passports, issuing visas, levying duties, et cetera [Mitchell 1989]), maintaining embassies in each others' countries, keeping or breaking off diplomatic relations, signing treaties, declaring war, recognizing regimes, gaining admission to the United Nations, participating in the Olympics, the World Cup, and other international sport events, and so on. Those are some of the practices through which the "nation" is represented to *other* nation-states.

A consideration of these practices makes it clear that the potential forms that states can take in the modern world are severely circumscribed. It is for this reason that movements *against* the nation-states themselves aspire to the status of autonomous nationhood. The pervasiveness of nationalism as a system of practices and as a form of ideology cannot therefore be adequately explained simply by referring to the appeal that it has for those nationalist elites who clearly stand to gain the most from it. Instead, to understand why the nation comes to be such a privileged form of statehood, we need to locate the question of nationalism *centrally* within the context of the postcolonial interstate system. It is difficult to imagine what a state that is not a nation would look like and how it would operate in the contemporary world. By reflecting on the larger historical context, it is possible to mark the circumstances that have led to the emergence of the nation-state as a dominant organizational form. This also enables us to speculate about the conditions that may lead to its demise and the eventual development of an alternative hegemonic spatial formation. The reinscription of space in the context of late capitalism, by destabilizing the complacent equilibrium of the contemporary world system of nation-states, may very well be tending in that direction.

One conclusion that follows directly from this is that the processes that position people as citizens of nations *and* as members of larger, smaller, or dispersed units of agglomeration need to be conceptualized together. Citizenship ought to be theorized as one of the multiple subject positions occupied by people as members of diversely spatialized, partially overlapping or non-overlapping collectivities. The structures of feeling that constitute nationalism need to be set in the context of other forms of imagining community, other means of endowing significance to space in the production of location and "home."

A powerful mechanism for imagining the national community in most nations has traditionally been the mass media. However, efforts to employ the mass media to that end are persistently undercut by the transnational character of those media. In fact, representing the nation in an age where the public sphere is thoroughly transnational is a major challenge facing state elites. The control exerted by multinational corporations in particular sets severe limits on both the extent and form of nationalism practiced in different parts of the world today. The dominant social blocs of third world nations find that the power of nationalism as a unifying metanarrative is thus inherently compromised. In the transnational public sphere, people's identities as citizens of a nation are multiply refracted by their inventive appropriation of goods, images, and ideas distributed by multinational corporations.[13] There are thus processes at work that bind space and construct communities of people in a manner that dilutes the power of the nationalist project.

Such a challenge is not only being raised by transnational cultural and commodity flows. It also arises because loyalty to oppositional identities, especially subnational ones, dominates feelings of nationalism. Three examples could be given here: subnationalism, identities that crosscut the boundaries of contiguous nations, and transnationalism. Considering subnationalism first, in South Asia alone, one could point to the examples of Bengalis in the former East Pakistan (Bangladesh), Sikhs in India, and Tamils in Sri Lanka. Then there are ethnic loyalties that cut across national boundaries without, however, being transnational in the same sense as the Nonaligned Movement. Here, one could point to Kashmiris in India and Pakistan, Tamils in India and Sri Lanka, Gorkhas in Nepal and India, and Kurds in Turkey, Iran, Iraq, and the Soviet Union. Finally, one could point to a few genuinely transnational identities like that forged on the lines of the Islamic community. Hence, any effort to understand how identity and location become tied through nationalism must examine those situations where the imagined community does *not* map out a national terrain. The displacement of identity and culture from "the nation" not only forces us to reevaluate our ideas about culture and identity but also enables us to denaturalize the nation as the hegemonic form of organizing space. To place nationalism within a transnational context therefore enables one to pose new questions about spatial identities and commitments.

Structures of Feeling and the Reinscription of Space

Efforts to create identities based on transnational imagined communities, epitomized by the NAM and the EC, throw into sharp relief the structures of feeling that go under the name of nationalism. It becomes clear that any attempt to understand nationalism must set it in the context of other forms of imagining community, other mechanisms for positioning subjects, other bases of identity. Some of these loyalties refer to units of space larger than the nation, some smaller, and yet others to spaces that intersect nations or are dispersed. The analytical challenge is to explain why certain forms of organizing space, specific boundaries, particular places, attain the singular importance that they do in a given historical context. Why the hegemonic representation of spatial identity in the world has become that of the naturalized borders of nation-states cannot be understood by just studying the processes within a nation that enable it to be imagined. One of the ways of stepping "outside" the nation (and the problematic of nationalism) is to see how nations are created and reproduced as a consequence of the global interstate system. By doing this, we can fathom what effects specific patterns of the reinscription of space in the postcolonial, late-capitalist world have on the nation-state. Will nations as we know them today continue to be the hegemonic form of spatial organization in an increasingly postmodern world? And if not, in what ways will the structures of feeling that characterize nationalism be transformed? It seems to me that any answer to these questions of identity, location, and nationalism must begin with the redefinition of space in the context of postcoloniality and late capitalism.

In addition to the theoretical limitations of studies that ignore these transnational factors, the burgeoning scholarship on the "national" question in recent years runs into a problem similar to that faced by those attempting to understand the state. Just as analyzing "the state" may involve the scholar in an unwitting collusion with state elites in their efforts to represent a naturalized, unified entity called "the state," so may the studies of nationalism unknowingly contribute to its privileging as *the* most important form of imagining community and shaping identity.

Another direction from which the discourse of nationalism receives unexpected, if dubious, support is what may be termed "third worldism." Jameson (1986:69), for example, argues that all third world texts are necessarily *national* allegories. His reasoning is that what is particular to literary production in the third world is that it is always shaped by the experience of colonialism and imperialism. The binary opposition between a first and a third world embedded in the Three Worlds Theory leads to the over-valorization of nationalist ideology; indeed, since the third world is constituted through the singular experience of colonialism and imperialism, there is nothing else to narrate but the "national" experience (Ahmad 1987:5–8). The problem with employing a monologic ideology such as "third worldism" is that it encapsulates all narratives of identity within the master narratives of imperialism and nationalism. It thus serves to foreclose a richer understanding of location and identity that would account for the relationships of subjects to multiple collectivities.

In this article, I have argued that nationalism, as a model of imagining community, articulates with, rewrites, and often displaces other narratives of community. The production of a location called "nation" thus involves the creation of a new order of difference, a new alignment of "self" in relation to "other." Yet, the positioning of subjects as citizens of nation-states is multiply refracted by their identities as members of other collectivities. It then becomes pertinent to inquire why the hegemonic representation of spatial identity in the world continues to be that of the naturalized border of nation-states. For to call the nation a hegemonic spatial form is to foreground the fact that the identity it gathers in and encloses is often contested and unstable (Hall 1986).

This becomes especially evident when one examines the character of contemporary third world nationalism. The unitary nature of analyses and critiques of nationalism make it impossible for one to appreciate the depth of the differences in the construction of the nation between, say, Canada and Sri Lanka (both countries with "ethnic" minority problems). A more contextualized understanding of third world nationalism would begin by accounting for its specific location within two macrologies. On the one hand, it has to be located within the postcolonial world order, since everything from territorial boundaries, administrative and judicial systems, and international alliances is tied to the political changes surrounding decolonization. On the other hand, it cannot be understood without paying attention to the global system of production and distribution within late capitalism.

But what is the relationship between these two contexts? The central objective of this article has been to discuss attempts to forge transnational forms of community such as the NAM and the EC with the aim of demonstrating the manner in which late capitalism and postcoloniality converge to simultaneously produce and problematize the nation. Hence, I argue that the multiple spatial grids through which identity is mapped need to be conceptualized in such a way as to de-essentialize and denaturalize nationalist discourses of authenticity. Processes of migration, displacement, and deterritorialization are, increasingly, sundering the fixed association between identity, culture, and place. In this context, nationalist narratives are being brought under increasing critical scrutiny by those marginalized or excluded from them. It is perhaps not surprising, therefore, that there is a renewed scholarly interest in nationalism.

To understand these phenomena, we need to pay bifocalized attention to two processes. On the one hand, we need to study structures of feeling that bind space, time, and memory in the production of location. By this I mean processes by which certain spaces become enshrined as "homelands," by which ideas of "us" and "them" come to be deeply felt and mapped onto places such as nations. On the other hand, we need to pay attention to those processes that redivide, reterritorialize, and reinscribe space in the global political economy. Only then can we understand why the naturalized divisions and spaces that we have always taken for granted become problematic in certain circumstances, and only then can the "problem" of nationalism be posed adequately.

NOTES

Acknowledgments. I would like to thank Purnima Mankekar, Lisa Rofel, Roger Rouse, and C. Rajamohan for their critical comments and Arun Kumar for bringing some important material to my attention. I would also like to thank participants of the Faculty Seminar on Cultural Nationalism at Stanford where an earlier version was presented on 2 May 1990.

1   Although I am aware that the notion "Third World" is often employed in "the West" to homogenize what are in fact quite distinctive histories and places (to construct in effect a space of "otherness") (Mohanty 1988), it has become a positive tool of solidarity in the postcolonial world system. Self-identification as "third world" has served a central constructive purpose in movements such as the NAM. For this reason, I have chosen not to put the phrase in capital letters, quotes, or italics in the rest of this article.
2   I have been especially influenced by the work of Arjun Appadurai in this regard. See Appadurai (1986), Appadurai and Breckenridge (1988), their journal, *Public Culture*, Marcus (1986), and Hannerz (1987).
3   Brioni, Yugoslavia, was the site of the first tripartite summit between Nehru, Tito, and Nasser, which first led to speculation in the world press that a new third world bloc was in the process of formation.
4   The phrase is Liisa Malkki's.
5   It also fails to appreciate the genuinely *popular* aspects of an admittedly largely elite-based, postcolonial nationalism.
6   I want to emphasize here that in what follows I do not mean to imply that the European Community is already an accomplished fact rather than a contested, conflictual entity in the process of formation.
    Roger Rouse (private communication) has suggested that a distinction be made between these three terms such that "transnational" refer to phenomena that crosscut or intersect national boundaries, "international" be used to denote that which occurs between and among nations, and "supranational" denote spatial configurations that stand above and incorporate nations. The Nonaligned Movement displays all three of these features.
7   Not all scholars of the Nonaligned Movement accept that Bandung marked the beginning. For example, Peter Willetts (1978:3) says: "In the states that attended, in the tone of the debates and in the resulting decisions, Bandung was not a forerunner of the Non-Aligned conferences."
8   The last theme was particularly prominent in the third summit at Lusaka, Zambia, in 1970, where the issue of continuing first world support of South Africa occupied center stage. The increasing importance of concerns dealing with problems of economic development and structural dependence on the superpowers is reflected in the call for a New International Economic Order (NIEO) at the fourth summit in Algiers in 1973.
9   Despite ritual invocations acknowledging the power of the ethnographer, the full implications of this fact for anthropological theory have not been realized (for an exception, see Talal Asad's essay [1986] on the inequality of languages).
10 It should be clear that I am by no means implying that Europe 1992 be seen as some kind of forerunner to developments in the rest of the world.
11 However, it must be noted that one of the more successful programs of the Nonaligned Movement has been its wire service, which feeds stories horizontally to other nonaligned nations. This has the advantage of creating stronger links among the third world, but it does not necessarily create a new form of identity analogous to national identity.
12 In some cases, institutions like Britain's National Theatre serve as a medium of national representation (Kruger 1987).

13 See Appadurai (1990) for an effort to map theoretically these different transnational flows.

REFERENCES

Ahmad, Aijaz
   1987 Jameson's Rhetoric of Otherness and the "National Allegory." Social Text 17:3–25.
Anderson, Benedict
   1983 Imagined Communities: Reflections on the Origin and Spread of Nationalism. London: Verso.
Appadurai, Arjun
   1986 Theory in Anthropology: Center and Periphery. Comparative Studies in Society and History 28(1):356–361.
   1990 Disjuncture and Difference in the Global Political Economy. Public Culture 2(2):1–24.
Appadurai, Arjun, and Carol A. Breckenridge
   1988 Why Public Culture? Public Culture 1(1):5–9.
Asad, Talal
   1986 The Concept of Cultural Translation in British Social Anthropology. *In* Writing Culture: The Poetics and Politics of Ethnography. James Clifford and George E. Marcus, eds. Pp. 141–164. Berkeley: University of California Press.
Chatterjee, Partha
   1986 Nationalist Thought and the Colonial World: A Derivative Discourse? London: Zed Press.
Dirks, Nicholas
   1990 History as a Sign of the Modern. Public Culture 2(2):25–32.
Ferguson, James
   1990 The Anti-Politics Machine: "Development," Depoliticization, and Bureaucratic Power in Lesotho. Cambridge: Cambridge University Press.
Hall, Stuart
   1986 Gramsci's Relevance for the Study of Race and Ethnicity. Journal of Communication Inquiry 10(2):5–27.
Hannerz, Ulf
   1987 The World in Creolization. Africa 57(4):546–559.
Harvey, David
   1985 The Geopolitics of Capitalism. *In* Social Relations and Spatial Structures. Derek Gregory and John Urry, eds. Pp. 128–163. New York: St. Martin's Press.
   1989 The Condition of Postmodernity: An Enquiry Into the Origins of Cultural Change. New York: Blackwell.
Jameson, Frederic
   1984 Postmodernism, or the Cultural Logic of Late Capitalism. New Left Review 146:53–92.
   1986 Third-World Literature in the Era of Multinational Capitalism. Social Text 15:65–88.
Kaplan, Caren
   1987 Deterritorializations: The Rewriting of Home and Exile in Western Feminist Discourse. Cultural Critique 6:187–198.
Kruger, Loren
   1987 Our National House: The Ideology of the National Theatre of Great Britain. Theatre Journal 39(1):35–50.

Layoun, Mary
  1990   Narrating Nationalism: Who Speaks and How? Who Listens and How? Or, Whose
    Story is this Anyway? Unpublished MS.
Mandel, Ernest
  1975   Late Capitalism. Joris De Bres, trans. New York: Verso.
Mankekar, D. R.
  1978a Three Kinds of Gaps. *In* Proceedings of the Seminar on Non-Aligned News Pool.
    Jag Parvesh Chandra, ed. Pp. 12–21. New Delhi: All-India Newspaper Editors' Confer-
    ence.
  1978b Why News Pool. *In* Proceedings of the Seminar on Non-Aligned News Pool. Jag
    Parvesh Chandra, ed. Pp. 85–93. New Delhi: All-India Newspaper Editors' Conference.
  1978c One-Way Free Flow: Neo-Colonialism via News Media. New Delhi: Clarion Books.
  1981   Whose Freedom? Whose Order? New Delhi: Clarion Books.
Mapes, Glynn
  1990   Polyglot Students Are Weaned Early Off Mother Tongue. Wall Street Journal,
    March 6:A1, A16.
Marcus, George E.
  1986   Contemporary Problems of Ethnography in the Modern World System. *In* Writing
    Culture: The Poetics and Politics of Ethnography. James Clifford and George E. Marcus,
    eds. Pp. 165–193. Berkeley: University of California Press.
Martin, Biddy, and Chandra Talpade Mohanty
  1986   Feminist Politics: What's Home Got to Do With It? *In* Feminist Studies/Critical
    Studies. Teresa de Lauretis, ed. Pp. 191–212. Bloomington: Indiana University Press.
Mitchell, Timothy
  1989   The Effect of the State. Department of Politics, New York University, unpublished MS.
Mohanty, Chandra
  1988   Under Western Eyes: Feminist Scholarship and Colonial Discourses. Feminist
    Review 30:61–88.
Mortimer, Robert A.
  1984   The Third World Coalition in International Politics. 2d edition. Boulder, Colo.:
    Westview.
Pratt, Mary Louise
  1990   Women, Literature, and National Brotherhood. *In* Women Culture and Politics in
    Latin America. Emile Bergmann, ed. Pp. 48–73. Berkeley: University of California Press.
Radhakrishnan, R.
  1987   Ethnic Identity and Post-Structuralist Diffarence. Cultural Critique 6:199–220.
Višekruana, Dušan
  1987   Song of the Non-Aligned World. Belgrade: Radio-Television Belgrade (RTB).
Willetts, Peter
  1978   The Non-Aligned Movement: The Origins of Third World Alliance. New York:
    Nichols.
Williams, Brackette F.
  1990   Nationalism, Traditionalism, and the Problem of Cultural Inauthenticity. *In* Na-
    tionalist Ideologies and the Production of National Cultures. American Ethnological
    Society Monograph Series, 2. Richard G. Fox, ed. Pp. 112–129. Washington, D.C.:
    American Anthropological Association.
Williams, Raymond
  1961   The Long Revolution. New York: Columbia University Press.

16

Sovereignty without Territoriality: Notes for a Postnational Geography

Arjun Appadurai

Introduction

I have elsewhere argued that we need to think ourselves beyond the nation.[1] In this essay, I seek to deepen that argument by paying close attention to one dimension of the modern nation form – territoriality. Recognizing with Anderson[2] that the nation is an imagined thing, I also recognize the critical reciprocal of his insight, that it is the imagination that will have to carry us beyond the nation. Thus what follows is a critical work of the imagination, which recognizes the difficulty, sharply articulated by Shapiro, of constructing "post-sovereign" moral geographies.[3]

After the agreements associated with the Westphalian peace settlements of 1648, the embryonic principle of territorial sovereignty becomes the foundational concept of the nation-state,[4] though many other ideas affect its subsequent cultural self-imaging and self-narrativizing. These include ideas about language, common origin, blood, and various other conceptions of ethnos. Still, the fundamental political and juridical rationale and basis of the system of nation-states is territorial sovereignty, however complexly understood and delicately managed in particular postimperial settings.[5]

Nationality and Locality

While nationalism (whatever that might exactly mean) is showing many signs of recrudescence, the modern nation-state as a compact and isomorphic organization of territory, ethnos, and governmental apparatus is in a serious crisis. I have elsewhere laid out the argument for the transnational conditions for this crisis,[6] my evidence for the emergence of major non-national and indeed postnational social formations,[7] and a perspective on the globalized production of locality in the contemporary world.[8] I shall not review these prior observations but shall paraphrase them in the following paragraphs, since they constitute the background for the arguments put forward here.

The production of locality,[9] as a dimension of social life, as a structure of feeling, and in its material expression in lived "copresence,"[10] faces two challenges in a postnational order. On the one hand, the production of locality challenges the order and orderliness of the nation-state. On the other hand, human motion in the context of the crisis of the nation-state encourages the emergence of *translocalities*. This double challenge is addressed below.

The work of producing localities, in the sense that localities are life-worlds constituted by relatively stable associations, relatively known and shared histories, and collectively traversed and legible spaces and places, is often at odds with the projects of the nation-state. This is partly because the commitments and attachments that characterize local subjectivities (sometimes mislabeled "primordial") are more pressing, more continuous, and sometimes more distracting than the nation-state can afford. It is also because the memories and attachments that local subjects have to their neighborhoods and street names, to their favorite walkways and street-scapes, to their times and places for congregating and escaping are often at odds with the needs of the nation-state for regulated public life. Further, it is the nature of local life to develop partly by contrast to other localities by producing its own contexts of alterity (spatial, social, and technical), contexts that may not meet the needs for spatial and social standardization prerequisite for the modern subject-citizen.

Paradoxically, the human movements characteristic of the contemporary world are as much a threat to the nation-state as are the attachments of local subjects to local life. The isomorphism of people, territory, and legitimate sovereignty that constitutes the normative charter of the modern nation-state is under threat from the forms of circulation of people characteristic of the contemporary world. It is now widely conceded that the world we live in is one in which human motion is more often definitive of social life than it is exceptional. Work, both of the most sophisticated intellectual sort and the most humble proletarian sort, drives people to migrate, often more than once. The policies of nation-states, particularly toward populations regarded as potentially subversive, create a perpetual motion machine, where refugees from one nation move to another, creating new instabilities there, which cause further social unrest and thus more social exits.[11] Hence the "people" production[12] needs of one nation-state can mean ethnic and social unrest for its neighbors, creating open-ended cycles of ethnic cleansing, forced migration, xeno-phobia, state paranoia, and thus further ethnic cleansing. Eastern Europe in general, and Bosnia-Herzegovina in particular, are perhaps the most tragic and complex examples of such state/refugee domino processes. In many such cases, people and whole communities are turned into ghettos, refugee camps, concentration camps, or reservations, sometimes without anyone moving at all.

Other forms of human movement are created by the reality or lure of economic opportunity (this is true of much Asian migration to the oil-rich parts of the Middle East). Yet other forms of movement are created by permanently mobile groups of specialized workers (United Nations soldiers, oil technologists, development specialists, agricultural laborers, etc.) Still other forms of movement, particularly in sub-Saharan Africa, involve major droughts and famines, often tied to disastrous alliances between corrupt states and opportunistic international and global agencies. In yet other communities, the logic of movement is provided by the leisure industries, which create tourist sites and locations around the world. The ethnography of these tourist locations is just beginning to be written in detail,[13] but what little we do know suggests that many such locations create complex conditions for the production and reproduction of locality, in which ties of marriage, work, business, and leisure weave together various circulating populations with various kinds of "locals" to create localities that belong in one sense to particular nation-states but are, from another point of view, what we might call *translocalities*.

Translocalities come in many forms and, as an emergent category of human organization, require serious attention. Border zones are now becoming spaces of complex quasi-legal circulation of persons and goods. The border between the United States and Mexico is an excellent example of one kind of translocality. Similarly, many tourist zones may be described as translocalities, even where they may lie nominally within the jurisdiction of particular nation-states. All Free Trade Zones (FTZs) are to some extent translocalities. Finally, every major refugee camp, migrant hostel, or neighborhood of exiles and guest workers is a translocality.

Many cities are becoming translocalities, substantially divorced from their national contexts. These cities fall into two types: those major economic centers that are so deeply involved in foreign trade, finance, diplomacy, and media that they have become cultural islands with very weak national referents: Hongkong, Vancouver, and Brussels are examples of this type of city. Whether because of global economic processes that tie these cities together more than they tie them to their hinterlands or because of implosive, transnationally driven civil wars, other cities are becoming translocalities, weakly tied to their national hinterlands: Sarajevo, Beirut, Belfast, and Mogadishu are examples of this second type. I shall return to the relevance of translocalities at a subsequent point in the argument.

In this paper, I propose some ways to examine how the foundational principle of the modern nation-state – the principle of territorial sovereignty – is faring in the sort of world I have described, not as a narrow legal or jurisdictional issue but as a broader cultural and affiliational one.

Mobile Sovereignties

Throughout the world, the problem of immigrants, cultural rights, and state protection of refugees is growing, since very few states have effective ways of defining the relationship of citizenship, birth, ethnic affiliation, and national identity. The crisis is nowhere clearer than in France today, where the struggle to distinguish the Algerian population within France is threatening to unravel the very foundation of French ideas of full citizenship and to expose the deeply racialized foundation of French thinking about cultural markers of national belonging. But in many countries race, birth, and residence are becoming problems of one or other kind.

One source of this problem is that modern conceptions of citizenship, tied up with various forms of democratic universalism, tend to demand a homogenous people with standardized packages of rights. Yet the realities of ethnoterritorial thinking in the cultural ideologies of the nation-state demand discrimination among different categories of citizens even when they all occupy the same territory. The civil status (or nonstatus) of Palestinians in respect to the Israeli state is only the extreme example of this contradiction. Resolving these conflicting principles is increasingly a violent and uncivil process.

With economic liberalization in many parts of the world, there is also a cultural form of liberalization that invites citizens who have moved abroad to reinvest in their nations of origin, especially if they have not switched passports. India, for example, has the category Non-Resident Indian (NRI). At the present moment, in the continued euphoria over the end of communism and the command economy, as well as the wave of enthusiasm over marketization and free trade, NRIs have special rights, driven by national and regional forces seeking expatriate money and expertise in India. Thus Indian banks, states, and private enterpreneurs, in their desire for this expertise and wealth, are committed to special deals for NRIs, especially in regard to taxation, property rights, and freedom of movement in and out of India. At the same time, in their lives in the United States, many diasporic Indian communities are deeply involved in reproducing "Hindu" identity for themselves and their children and have thus become active supporters of Hindu right-wing movements and organizations in India. This is a complex story, which needs detailed engagement elsewhere, but it is worth noting the link between the cultural politics of NRIs, which draws them into communal politics in India, and the willingness of state and capitalist interests in India to extend them extraterritorial economic rights.

This sort of territorial paradox (special rights for citizens who are outside the national territory) is part of a broader set of postnational geographic processes. There is growing tension between issues of territorial sovereignty and issues of military security and defense, as with the current campaigns through the United Nations to demand on-site inspections in Iraq and North Korea. Likewise, as with Haiti, Somalia, and Bosnia, the distinction between "civil" and international war is becoming increasingly blurred. Finally, debates in North America, Japan, and Europe about NAFTA and GATT indicate that "commodity conquests" are increasingly viewed as threats to national sovereignty and integrity: an excellent example is the French panic about Americanization through Hollywood products. Dangers to sovereignty are thus not always tied up with warfare, conquest, and defense of borders. Territorial integrity and national integrity are themselves not always consistent or coeval issues.

National space can come to be differently valorized for the state and for its citizen-subjects. The state is typically concerned with taxation, order, general stability and fixity, whereas from the point of view of subjects, territory typically involves rights to movement, rights to shelter, and rights to subsist. Thus "soil" needs to be distinguished from territory ("sons of the soil"). While soil is a matter of a spatialized and originary discourse of belonging, territory is concerned with integrity, surveyability, policing, and subsistence.

As fissures emerge among local, translocal, and national space, territory as the ground of loyalty and national affect (what we should mean when we speak of national "soil") is increasingly divorced from territory as the site of sovereignty and state control of civil society. The problem of jurisdiction and the problem of loyalty are increasingly disjunct. This does not bode well for the future of the nation-state in its classic form, in which the two are imaged as coextensive and mutually supportive.

Not all state apparatuses are concerned about territorial integrity in the same way and for the same reasons. In some cases, state panic has to do with major, and restive, populations of refugees: the presence of large numbers of Afghans is this sort of concern for the government of Pakistan. Other states are worried about borders, which they may see as imperfect membranes, letting in undesirable aliens and commodities, while deterring legitimate tourists and workers. The U.S.–Mexico border is clearly of this kind, with osmotic capabilities (to filter out the wrong kinds of goods and services) now seen as highly imperfect. Yet other states, for example in Africa, care less about policing borders but focus their energies on policing and sanctifying important cities, monuments, and resources at the urban centers of the regime. Some states worry about commodity violations of territory; others worry more about people or diseases or political pollution. In the new South Africa, concerns about territory are tied up with the question of the reclamation of valuable agricultural lands previously monopolized by the white minority and with the rehabilitation of the vast squatter communities previously meant to be minimal containers for blacks and now seen as the living space of the enfranchised majority. These variations in state anxiety about territory have much to do with other aspects of state security and viability and varying resources for civil society, which cannot be discussed here.

For many national citizens, the practicalities of residence and the ideologies of home, soil, and roots are often disjunct, so that the territorial referents of civic loyalty are increasingly divided for many persons among different spatial horizons: work loyalties, residential loyalties, and religious loyalties may create disjunct registers of affiliation. This is true whether migration of populations is across small or large distances and whether or not these movements traverse international boundaries.

From the point of view of the nation, there is a rapidly growing distance between the promiscuous spaces of free trade and tourism, where national disciplines are often relaxed, and the spaces of national security and ideological reproduction, which may be increasingly nativized, authenticated, and culturally marked. Thus the Sri Lankan state encourages a remarkable cultural promiscuity and "inauthenticity" in its beach resorts (which are now explicitly pushed into a translocal Caribbean-style aesthetic) while intensively nationalizing other spaces, which are carefully marked for enacting "Sinhala" national development and "Buddhist" national memory.[14]

These disjunctures in the links among space, place, citizenship, and nationhood have several far-reaching implications. One of these is that territory and territoriality are increasingly the critical rationale of state legitimacy and state power, while ideas of nation seem increasingly driven by other discourses of loyalty and affiliation – sometimes linguistic, sometimes racial, sometimes religious, but *very rarely territorial*.

The question of why state and nation seem to be developing different relationships to territory is critical to the main argument of this essay and requires some elaboration, especially because not all nation-states are equally wealthy, ethnically coherent, internally contested, or globally recognized. Given that all state apparatuses are faced, in one or other way, with the reality of moving populations, legal and illegal commodity flows, and massive movements of arms across state borders, there is very little that they can realistically monopolize except the idea of territory as the crucial diacritic of sovereignty. Yet what Monroe Price has called the global "market for loyalties"[15] is not one in which states are set up to compete very well: the global competition for allegiances now involves all sorts of nonstate actors and organizations and various forms of diasporic or multilocal allegiance. The result is a historically peculiar development. Where states could once be seen as legitimate guarantors of the territorial organization of markets, livelihoods, identities, and histories, they are now to a very large extent arbiters (among other arbiters) of various forms of global flow. So territorial integrity becomes crucial to state-sponsored ideas of sovereignty, which, on close inspection, may be in the interest of no other organization than the state apparatus itself. In short, states are the only major players in the global scene that really need the idea of territorially based sovereignty. All sorts of other global competitors for popular allegiance (artists and writers, refugees and guest workers, scientists and scholars, health workers and development specialists, feminists and fundamentalists, transnational corporations and United Nations bureaucracies) are already evolving nonstate forms of macro-political organization: interest groups, social movements, and actually existing transnational loyalties. Transnational religious formations (often associated with Islam but equally salient with respect to Christianity, Hinduism, and Judaism) are the richest examples of such loyalties.[16]

Postnational Cartographies

Where does this perspective leave the hyphen between the nation and the state, a hyphen that I have elsewhere argued is the true site of crisis?[17] There is no doubting that the national imaginary has not given in readily to the emergence of non-national, transnational, or postnational markets for loyalty. Indeed, many observers have noted that new nationalisms, often tied up with ethnic separatism and state-level turbulence, are on the rise. Can we make sense of these emergent nationalisms in relation to the problematic of territory and sovereignty? Let us consider some concrete examples of the extent to which discourses of nationalism remain vessels for the ideology of territorial nationalism.

The search for homelands and autonomous states by groups as different as the Palestinians, the Kurds, the Sikhs, and others seems to suggest that territory is still vital to the national imaginary of diasporic populations and stateless peoples of many sorts. It is this impulse that was cynically manipulated by the white South African government in earlier times to create the idea of "homelands" for various South African populations. In fact, in all these cases, territory is not so much the driving force behind these movements as a response to the pressure of already sovereign states, which couch their opposition to these groups in territorial terms. The case of Khalistan is particularly interesting. Khalistan is the name of the imagined nation that some Sikhs in India (and throughout the world) have given to the place that they would like to think of as their own national space, outside of the territorial control of the Indian state. Khalistan is not simply a separatist, diasporic nationalism in the classic post-Westphalian mode of the modern nation-state. Rather, Sikhs who imagine Khalistan are using spatial discourses and practices to construct a new, postnational cartography in which ethnos and demos are unevenly spread across the world and the map of nationalities cross-cuts existing national boundaries and intersects with other translocal formations.[18] This topos of

Sikh "national" identity is in fact a topos of "community" (*qom*), which contests many national maps (including those of India, Pakistan, England, and Canada) and contains one model of a post-Westphalian cartography.

This emergent postnational cartography will probably issue from a variety of translocal affiliations; some global or globalizing, as in the case of Islamic, Christian, and Hindu fundamentalisms; some continental, such as the emerging European Union; and some racial and diasporic, for example the discourses of "Afro-diasporic" consciousness in Latin America, the Caribbean, Britain, and Africa,[19] and others involving counterhegemonic conceptions of race and space.[20] None of these relies on the idea of separate and bounded territorial entities on which our current nation-state cartography relies. Rather, in these new cartographies, counterhistories and counteridentities are used to organize maps of allegiance and affiliation that are built around historical labor flows, emergent racial solidarities, and counternational cartographies. In several cases, such as those of the Sikhs and the Kurds, counternational movements are sedimenting into permanent trans-national forms. This process is one example of the general challenge of identifying the emergent morphologies (and cartographies) of a postnational order. The most important feature of these emergent cartographies is that they do not appear to require horizontally arranged, contiguous, and mutually exclusive claims to terri-tory. They frequently involve transecting maps of allegiance and a politics of non-exclusive, territorial copresence. Kurds, Sri Lankan Tamils, and Sikhs may have their various problems as citizens in the new Germany, but they appear to have no difficulty with the territorial overlapping, in Frankfurt, Berlin, or Hamburg, of their diasporic maps. When violence does occur in these diasporic contexts, it usually involves factional issues within exile communities or extraterritorial warfare between diasporic communities and their states of origin,[21] as in the recent episodes of violence between Kurds and Turks in contemporary Germany.

The "capitals" of this emergent postnational cartography, as I have already suggested, are likely to be found in a variety of spatial formations that may not have much to do with the self-representation of sovereign states. Some of these postnational capitals will be found in the different sorts of translocalities to which I alluded earlier. These translocalities might be formed by refugee dynamics, by permanent efforts to organize social life around tourism, or by the structural effects of the emergent global networks of labor and capital.[22] Such places, usually cities, tend to be weakly associated with their national environments and are, rather, integrally involved with transnational allegiances and interests. Of course, nation-states often try to exercise strong control over these cities and their civic life (as with China in respect to the anticipated acquisition of Hongkong). But such efforts will no longer be able to rely on the commonsense that there is a national territory to which these cities and their inhabitants naturally belong. The relationship of such "translocal" places to the quotidian production of locality as a feature of human life[23] and to the changing cartographies of diasporic groups will require serious rethinking of our existing images of cities, space, and territorial affiliation.

The United Nations, which continues to operate as a powerful validator of the territorial nation-state, might also seem to contradict my suggestion that the terri-torial basis of the nation-state is rapidly eroding. Yet, if we look at the moral and material role of the United Nations in peacekeeping and humanitarian operations throughout the world, it seems clear that it is itself emerging as a major trans-national force in Africa, the Middle East, Cambodia, Eastern Europe, and elsewhere. Of course, its troops are few, its funds are limited, and it often seems incapable of decisive action. But until we have more careful studies of the composition, commitment, and politics of United Nations forces, their national sources and their ideological practices, it would not be wise to dismiss the possibility that the U.N. is helping to erode the idea of the territorial integrity of existing nation-states. In this sense, whether in Korea or Cambodia, Somalia or Palestine, the United Nations is in the process of exemplifying the transmutation of national resources into transnational interests of a new and puzzling sort. What is puzzling about this example is that national resources given over to an organization intended to be a vehicle of international wishes are subsidizing activities that might actually reduce national control over a growing number of "trouble spots." Thus the United Nations, particularly after the Cold War, looms as a serious player in its own right in the global market for loyalty.

Territorial Habits

Territorial tropes for the idea of the nation persist in part because our very ideas of cultural coherence have become imbricated with the commonsense of the nation. In the history of culture theory, of course, territory and territoriality have played an important role: in a general way the idea that cultures are coherent, bounded, contiguous, and persistent has always been underwritten by a sense that human sociality is naturally localized and even locality-bound. The concern of anthropologists with rules of residence and their relation to descent groups and other social formations, for example, is based on a continuing sense that territorial realities of one or other sort both bound and determine social arrangements. Despite some vigorous efforts to counter such varieties of territorial determinism,[24] the image of spatial resources and practices as both constituting and determining forms of sociality is remarkably resilient. This idea is utterly explicit in those branches of ecology, archaeology, and material culture studies that take spatial practices as their main source of evidence and analysis. Though books like Robert Ardrey's *The Territorial Imperative* are no longer in vogue, there is still a widespread sense that human beings are conditioned to demand spaces of allegiance that are extensions of their bodies. Variations of this assumption not only characterize anthropology but are also deeply entwined with the discipline of geography as a component of various national and imperial projects.[25]

The tenacity of the primordialist thesis reminds us that such thinking is very much with us, and in one or other form the primordialist hypothesis underwrites otherwise different theories of nationalism. In spite of the heavy inroads of historical and historicizing critiques of the primordialist thesis,[26] it frequently reappears in both popular and academic thinking about nationalism. It is nowhere more apparent than in recent popular and media opinion about Eastern Europe, in which it is assumed that the ethnocide and terror of Bosnia-Herzegovina is part of a long history of primordial ethnic conflict only briefly interrupted by communist rule. Weak and unscholarly as this thesis is, it is particularly weak on the issue of territory as part of what nationalism is about.

In contemporary Europe, in fact, the divorce of ethnonationalism from territory takes the form of a disturbing reversal that increasingly informs the neo-fascist movements of Germany, Hungary, and elsewhere; the argument simply is: wherever there are Germans, there is Germany. Here – far from the classical Romanticist argument that blood, soil, language, and perhaps race are the isomorphic foundations of the sentiments of nationhood – is the peculiar inverse argument that ethnic affiliation generates territory. Thus Germanness creates German soil rather than being produced by it. This inversion is a possible, though not necessary, pathology of diaspora, because it involves a process of reterritorialization, antecedent to processes of deterritorialization. It is, more exactly, a pathology of territorial nationalism, provoked by the historical specificities of German national socialist ideology, the particular history of state formation in Europe after the Hapsburg Empire, and the tempting contiguity of "ethnic" Germans, separated by relatively recently created state borders.

In general, though the world we live in has been referred to by me and others as "deterritorialized,"[27] it needs to be pointed out that "deterritorialization" generates various forms of "reterritorialization." Not all reterritorialization is counternationalist or nativist. Reterritorialization can involve the effort to create new localized residential communities (slums, refugee camps, hostels) that rest not on a national imaginary but only on an imaginary of local autonomy or of resource sovereignty. In such "transit communities," there is frequently an effort to create and defend various forms of rights (formal and informal; legal and illegal) that allow the displaced community to continue its reproduction under unstable conditions by assuring reliable access to the material needs of reproduction: water, electricity, public safety, bank loans. Such resources are frequently siphoned off from "legitimate" civic structures by large communities of "slum" dwellers, refugee camps, and other quasi-legitimate built communities. It is often under these conditions that discourses of exile and homeland emerge, and only rarely (as in Germany) do these reterritorializing efforts involve direct attempts to extend national maps outward to follow diasporic communities. Most often, as in the case of the "civics" of the new South Africa, these efforts are exercises in the creation of new local imaginaries, relatively free of the discourses of patriotism and nationality but rich in the discourses of citizenship, democracy, and local rights.

There is a vital difference between such imagined cartographies as those of the Sikhs in respect to Khalistan and those of the German neo-fascists about Sudetenland. In the first case there is an effort to create a diasporic ethnos by carving out a homeland from existing national territories (in the Sikh case with respect to India). In the German neo-fascist case, there is an effort to extend and expand a majority ethnos already in command of a territorial nation-state into the territories of other, existing nation-states. This extension of official nationalism through linkage with emigrants needs to be sharply distinguished from the construction of a breakaway nationalism on the basis of a global diaspora.

Yet these different efforts to extend the territorial imaginary to situations of political change and diaspora do have something in common, which is a tendency to use the territorial imaginary of the nation-state to grasp and mobilize the large-scale and dispersed populations of the contemporary world into transnational ethnic formations. This effort often creates tension with one or more nation-states, since the logics of deterritorialization and reterritorialization often generate various sorts of local, regional, and global domino relations. As I suggested earlier, the ethnic cleansing exercises of many nation-states (especially those committed to some sort of "son of the soil" ideology) inevitably create refugee problems for neighboring or distant societies, thus exacerbating local problems in the always delicate relationship among residence, race, and rights in modern societies.

Territory thus can be seen as the crucial problem in the contemporary crisis of the nation-state, or, more precisely, the crisis in the relationship between nation and state. Insofar as actually existing nation-states rest on some implicit idea of ethnic coherence as the basis of state sovereignty, they are bound to minoritize, degrade, penalize, murder, or expel those seen to be ethnically minor. Insofar as these minorities (as guest workers, refugees, or illegal aliens) enter into new polities, they require reterritorialization within a new civic order, whose ideology of ethnic coherence and citizenship rights they are bound to disturb, since all modern ideologies of rights depend, ultimately, on the *closed* (enumerated, stable, and immobile) group of appropriate recipients of state protection and patronage. Thus second-classness and third-classness are conditions of citizenship that are inevitable entailments of migration, however plural the ethnic ideology of the host state and however flexible its accommodation of refugees and other weakly documented visitors.

None of this would be a problem except that the conditions of global economic, labor, and technological organization create dramatic new pushes and pulls in favor of uprooting individuals and groups and moving them into new national settings. Since these individuals and groups have to be cognized within some sort of vocabulary of rights and entitlements, however limited and harsh, they pose a threat to the ethnic and moral coherence of all host nation-states, which is at bottom predicated on both a singular and an immobile ethnos. In these conditions, the state as a push factor in ethnic diasporas is constantly obliged to pump out the sources of ethnic noise that threaten or violate its integrity as an ethnically singular territorial entity. But, in its other guise, virtually every modern nation-state is either forced or seduced to accept into its territory a whole array of non-nationals, who demand and create a wide variety of territorially ambiguous claims on civic and national rights and resources.

Here we are at the heart of the crisis of the contemporary nation-state. It looks at first glance as if the crisis is the mere fact of ethnic plurality, which is the inevitable result of the flow of populations in the contemporary world. But on closer inspection, the problem is not ethnic or cultural pluralism as such but the tension between diasporic pluralism and territorial stability in the project of the modern nation-state. What ethnic plurality does (especially when it is the product of population movements within recent memory) is to violate the sense of isomorphism between territory and national identity on which the modern nation-state relies. What diasporic pluralisms particularly expose and intensify is the gap between the powers of the state to regulate borders, monitor dissent, distribute entitlements within a finite territory *and* the fiction of ethnic singularity on which most nations ultimately rely. In other words, the territorial integrity that justifies states and the ethnic singularity that validates nations are increasingly hard to see as seamless aspects of each other. Put another way, since states, territories, and ideas of national ethnic singularity are always complicated historical coproductions, diasporic pluralism tends to embarrass all narratives that attempt to naturalize such histories.

Conclusion

I suggested that a series of paired ideas that we have taken to be closely connected are gradually coming apart. In my title, I implied that sovereignty and territoriality, once twin ideas, live increasingly separate lives. This split is related to other disjunctures that are becoming apparent. Territorial integrity is increasingly not a simple expression of national integrity, as the privileges of overseas Indians make clear. Discourses of the soil tend to flourish in all sorts of populist movements, both local and transnational, while discourses of territory tend to characterize border conflicts and international law. Loyalty often leads individuals to identify with transnational cartographies, while the appeals of citizenship attach them to territorial states. These disjunctures indicate that territory, once a commonsense justification for the legitimacy of the nation-state, has become the key site of the crisis of sovereignty in a transnational world.

Yet a postnational geography will not emerge from our researches in the academy, even from the newest of our geographies and the most technically inventive of our cartographic technologies. It will emerge – indeed, it is emerging – from the actual spatializing contests between diasporic groups and the efforts of various states to accommodate them without giving up on the principle of territorial integrity. That principle is hardly likely to survive, in the long run, but it would be foolhardy to look to some simple new organizational principle for the large-scale political organization of human societies. It may well be that the greatest peculiarity of the modern nation-state was the idea that territorial boundaries could indefinitely sustain fictions of national ethnic singularity. This utopian idea might be our most lasting memory of the modern nation-state.

NOTES

This paper was first presented as a forum lecture at the Institute for the Humanities, University of Michigan, in April 1994. It was subsequently revised for presentations at the Universities of Oslo, Stockholm, and Copenhagen during September 1994, and at Northwestern University (Chicago) in February 1995. It was the basis for the Ecumene Lecture delivered at the annual meetings of the Association of American Geographers in Chicago in April 1995. I am grateful for criticisms and queries raised on all these occasions. An earlier version of this paper was delivered (on my behalf) at a conference sponsored by the Wenner-Gren Foundation in Mijas, Spain on 14–22 June 1994. I am especially grateful for the feedback I received from the organizers of that conference. I would like to make special mention of the critical contributions, in various of these contexts, of Fredrik Barth, Fred Cooper, Gudrun Dahl, Micaela di Leonardo, Ulf Hannerz, and Jane Jacobs. Special thanks to Patricia Yaeger, for her patience, her probing questions, and her enthusiasm.

This text reflects a moment of transition between two extended research projects, one focused on the cultural dynamics of global cultural flow and another, just beginning, on the relationship between liberal social theory and the modern idea of the nation-state. It is in many ways preliminary and does not take up many important and related problems. Two large areas that are relevant to this argument are not taken up in the current essay. The first is the relation between the crisis of territorial sovereignty that I have described and the workings of colonial capitalism in the ex-colonies of Africa, the Middle East, and Asia. There is also the wider historical issue of the extent to which the crisis I have described has always been part of the history of the nation-state in the West, both in the domain of political theory and in the actual material workings of national formations on the ground. These are matters that I consider to be very important and will be taking up in future work on this subject.

1   Arjun Appadurai, "Patriotism and Its Futures," *Public Culture* 5, 3 (1993): 411–29.
2   Benedict Anderson, *Imagined Communities: Reflections on the Origin and Spread of Nationalism* (London: Verso 1983).
3   Michael J. Shapiro, "Moral Geographies and the Ethics of Post-Sovereignty," *Public Culture* 6, 3 (1994): 479–502.
4   The importance of this moment is discussed in many sources. One interesting discussion is to be found in Hans Gross, *Empire and Sovereignty: A History of the Public Law Literature in the Holy Roman Empire, 1599–1804* (Chicago: University of Chicago Press, 1973), who places the Westphalian treaties in the context of a wider discussion of the evolution of public law in the Holy Roman Empire in the seventeenth and eighteenth centuries.
5   For an interesting discussion of the principle of territorial sovereignty in the framework of international law, and its vagaries during and after colonial rule in Africa, see Malcolm Shaw, *Title to Territory in Africa: International Legal Issues* (Oxford: Clarendon Press, 1986).
6   Arjun Appadurai, "Disjuncture and Difference in the Global Cultural Economy," *Public Culture* 2, 2 (1990): 1–24.
7   Appadurai, "Patriotism and Its Futures."
8   Arjun Appadurai, *Modernity at Large: Cultural Dimensions of Globalization* (Minneapolis: University of Minnesota Press, forthcoming 1996).
9   Appadurai, *Modernity at Large*.
10 Deidre Boden and Harvey L. Molotch, "The Compulsion of Proximity," in *NowHere: Space, Time and Modernity*, ed. R. Friedland and D. Boden (Berkeley: University of California Press, 1994).
11 A. Zolberg, A. Sahrke, and S. Aguayo, *Escape from Violence: Conflict and the Refugee Crisis in the Developing World* (Oxford: Oxford University Press, 1989).
12 Etienne Balibar, "The Nation Form: History and Ideology," in *Race, Nation, Class: Ambiguous Identities*, ed. E. Balibar and I. Wallerstein (London: Verso, 1991).
13 I have been stimulated to think about the complexities of cultural reproduction in tourist translocalities by the work-in-progress of Jacqueline McGibbon, of the Department of Anthropology at the University of Chicago, who is engaged in a study of the village of St. Anton in the Tirolean Alps.
14 Valentine Daniel, oral communication.
15 Monroe Price, "The Market for Loyalties: Electronic Media and the Global Competition for Allegiances," *The Yale Law Journal* 104, 3 (1994): 667–705.
16 Suzanne H. Rudolph, "Religion, the State and Transnational Civil Society," unpublished paper prepared for Program in International Peace and Security (SSRC).
17 Appadurai, "Disjuncture and Difference."
18 I owe my awareness of emergent Sikh cartographies to the important ongoing research of Brian Axel of the Department of Anthropology at the University of Chicago.
19 Michael Hanchard, "Black Cinderella?: Race and Public Sphere in Brazil," *Public Culture* 7, 1 (1994): 165–85.
20 Paul Gilroy, *The Black Atlantic: Modernity and Double Consciousness* (Cambridge, MA: Harvard University Press, 1993).

21 Yossi Shain, *The Frontier of Loyalty: Political Exiles in the Age of the Nation-State* (Middletown, CT: Wesleyan University Press, 1989).

22 Saskia Sassen, *Global City: New York, London, Tokyo* (Princeton: Princeton University Press, 1991), and *Cities in a World Economy* (Thousand Oaks, CA: Pine Forge Press, 1994).

23 Appadurai, *Modernity at Large*.

24 Marshall Sahlins, *Stone Age Economics* (Chicago: Aldine-Atherton, 1972), and *Culture and Practical Reason* (Chicago: University of Chicago Press, 1976).

25 Anne Godlewska and Neil Smith, eds., *Geography and Empire* (Oxford: Blackwell Publishers, 1994).

26 Appadurai, *Modernity at Large*; J. Comaroff and J. L. Comaroff, "Of Totemism and Ethnicity," in *Ethnography and the Historical Imagination* (Boulder, CO: Westview Press, 1992).

27 G. Deleuze and F. Guattari, *A Thousand Plateaus: Capitalism and Schizophrenia*, trans. B. Massumi (Minneapolis: University of Minnesota Press, 1987); Appadurai, "Disjuncture and Difference."

Part VI
Spatial Tactics

Our final section focuses on the use of space as a strategy and/or technique of power and social control, but also as a way to obscure these relationships. The illusory transparency of space conceals the contradictions of its social production. The consideration of architectural forms reveals the often ephemeral or detached relationship between material and representational space. Paul Rabinow draws on Michel Foucault to demonstrate the connection between spatial forms of political power and the development of aesthetic theories in the creation of modern urbanism. By the end of the 19th century, the French employed science to underpin architectural and urban forms as a means to exercise political control by one group over another. Michael Herzfeld examines the disjunction between architectural materiality and representation in historic preservation practices in Crete. He illuminates how citizens resist and subvert the power of the state to defend their residences, but also participate in negotiations with the state over how history is to be materially represented. Eric Gable and Richard Handler incorporate these insights in their study of how the materiality of collective forgetting and remembering is accomplished at the colonial site of Williamsburg, Virginia. The spatial tactic of gating residential communities, and employing anti-crime rhetoric, is increasingly used by North Americans to disguise what Setha Low describes as class-based strategies of exclusion.

Further Reading

Dorst, John D. (1989) *The Written Suburb: An American Site, An Ethnographic Dilemma.* Philadelphia: University of Pennsylvania Press.

Fjellman, Stephen M. (1992) *Vinyl Leaves: Walt Disney World and America.* Boulder: Westview.

Holston, James (1989) *The Modernist City.* Chicago: University of Chicago Press.

Rabinow, Paul (1989) *French Modern: Norms and Forms of Missionary and Didactic Pathos.* Cambridge: MIT Press.

17

Ordonnance, Discipline, Regulation: Some Reflections on Urbanism

Paul Rabinow

Modern urban planning emerged under the aegis of French colonialism between 1900 and 1930. Colonial urban policies were jointly conceived by self-declared professional planners and powerful colonial officials. Both viewed the cities where they worked as social and aesthetic laboratories. The colonies, in particular Morocco, Vietnam, and Madagascar, offered both groups the opportunity to try out new, large-scale urban planning concepts. They could then test the political effectiveness of these plans, both in the colonies and eventually, they each hoped, at home. The colonialists sought to use architecture and city planning to demonstrate the cultural superiority of the French, both to the indigenous populations and to the French themselves. Urban design was an integral part of colonial domination, especially after the end of the nineteenth century. It provided one of the means to establish military control, regulate activities, separate populations, and establish a comprehensive order, on both an aesthetic and political level.

My recent work has involved exploring the evolution of modern European urbanism as a self-consciously scientific discipline – armed with sanitation, statistics and sociology. It then places this discipline, which sought to be universal and reformist, within a distinct sociological and political context. As the work has progressed, it has become clear that to understand why the emergence of modern urbanism was an important turning point in the evolution of aesthetic theories – and also the evolution of the social sciences, the growth of modern forms of political power, and the elaboration of specific techniques for relating the three – one had to understand the historically variable links between spatial relations, aesthetics, social science, economics, and politics. Why, after all, should it be held that the ordering of space, here the necessity for urban planning, was (1) important, even essential, and (2) new?

In order to answer these questions, or even to pose them, it has been necessary to retrace the steps by which a particular group of French Beaux-Arts students came to pose such questions in these very terms. This has entailed a comprehensive interpretation of space, power, and social science. Although this challenge is clearly beyond my capacities and my intentions, some extremely useful and brilliant elements of a response can be found in the work of Michel Foucault.

Foucault is one of a very few thinkers in modern times who has given concerted attention to space as a problem. In fact, the more I began to look to Foucault's work for aid, the more the centrality of spatial considerations in his work became apparent. One only has to think of the famous analysis of Velasquez's *Las Meninas* 'in which the examination of three hundred years of intellectual history is brilliantly summed up by showing how such a painting was organized, or the discussions of *enfermement* in the *History of Madness*, or the discussion of Bentham's Panopticon, to be assured that Foucault has given a lot of considered attention to space.

The strong emphasis on space that one finds in Foucault's work arose in part from a larger philosophic combat he was waging against the philosophy of the subject. This stance has, of course, historical parameters. The destruction of the philosophy of the subject and of consciousness (of phenomenology and existentialism) was carried out by several diverse French thinkers in the 1960s under the banner of structuralism. During this period Foucault sought to elaborate a spatial analysis of discourse as a means of undermining and replacing the philosophies of language, science, and knowledge which remained in the Cartesian tradition. But it was not only the individual subject of Descartes or the Husserlian or Sartrian phenomenologies that were his targets, but also the universal and historical subject of the Hegelian and Marxist tradition. Each of these philosophies of the subject had given questions of temporality a central place. This, in Foucault's reading, was the problem. As he says, "Anyone envisaging the analysis of discourse solely in terms of temporal continuity would inevitably be led to approach and analyse it like the internal transformation of an individual consciousness. Which would lead to his erecting a great collective consciousness as the scene of events. Metaphorising the transformation of discourse in a vocabulary of time necessarily leads to the utilisation of the model of individual consciousness with its intrinsic temporality."[1]

The deconstruction of the subject (either individual or historical) of consciousness and of discourse led Foucault, in *The Order of Things* and especially in *The Archaeology of Knowledge*, to attempt a unified analysis of discourse treated as if it were autonomous, rule-governed, discontinuous, and self-produced. The aim was a kind of topology of discursive space viewed as a distribution of mute discourse objects. These mute monuments could be viewed from afar by the archaeologist and their spatial distribution could be plotted.

The attempt to construct such an autonomous archaeology failed and has been duly abandoned. This is not the place to analyze why. In our recent book,[2] Burt Dreyfus and I show at length why this project of an autonomization of discourse as a strategy for destroying the philosophy of the subject won't and can't work. Foucault himself agrees and has moved on to another more powerful approach, that of genealogy (although it should be remembered and underlined that he has not jettisoned archaeology, only its most imperialistic claims of autonomy).

The second reason for this attention to space is historical and analytic. On the analytic level, space could be used as one of several tools to locate and identify the relations of knowledge and power. Space therefore provided the genealogist with a level of analysis "that enables one to grasp precisely the points at which discourses are transformed in, through and on the basis of relations of power."[3]

The object was not to construct a theory of space. Just as Foucault was not and is not attempting to construct a general theory of power, he is not, I think, trying to construct a general theory of space which has somehow been suppressed from the corpus of philosophy. In both instances, he is, I think, looking to develop what he calls an analytics. That is to say, to isolate a group of historical characteristics which permit us to see how in a particular situation these components have provided a grid of intelligibility which enabled those engaged in action to proceed in a way that seemed intelligible to them; to make sense of how these practices and intentions have gone beyond the conscious intentions of the historical actors, but nonetheless still have a signification, the famous "intentionality without a subject" to which Foucault alludes in *The History of Sexuality;* and finally to enable us today to pick out these historically given but alterable elements which have made us what we are, without positing any laws of history or of consciousness, an inherent logic, a determinism, an essentiality, or a conscious design to those combinations.

Just as Foucault has dramatically increased our awareness of bodies and of the importance of the relations of knowledge and power in Western civilization, he has also raised the problem of the centrality of space – not as an ontological issue, but as a political and an analytic one.

If one regards the scholarly and intellectual treatment of the history of urban planning in the nineteenth and twentieth centuries, it is strangely apparent that when questions of power are treated at all, it is almost entirely in one of two ways: either in terms of capital cities and their monuments, that is, the organization of space as essentially an aesthetic issue; or – and on the left this is the dominant mode – the analysis of space and power as ownership of property and control of institutions in a disciplinary mode. How segregation of populations, classes, or races evolved is read as a plot of this or that group. There is a fixation on a stale alternative between architecture and urbanism as purely aesthetic creation and hence benign, and as motivated appropriation and hence malignant.

Without denying the importance of formal traditions of architecture or the obvious centrality of speculation in any way, Foucault's approach opens up a much more fertile and complex ground which enables us to take more fully into account the disciplinary components in, say, Haussman's urbanism or the Beaux Arts' glorification and symbolization of state power, to understand them not as preformed and static elements, but as themselves part of a shifting field of power and knowledge in which we can see the gradual self-formation of a class, a nation or a civilization which is crossed in innumerable ways by power but which, to a surprisingly large extent, remains to be analyzed.

There are two specifications to be made here. First, Foucault is absolutely not maintaining, as has sometimes been alleged, that architectural form by itself carries with it an inherent political significance or function. Rather, he maintains only that spatial localizations, and particularly certain architectural projects, have been part of political strategies at certain historical moments: "Architecture begins at the end of the eighteenth century to become involved in problems of population, health, and the urban question.... [It] becomes a question of using the disposition of space for economico-political ends."[4] (More of this in a moment.)

Second, Foucault is not trying to discover or construct ideal types of spatial deployments of power. Weber's ideal type is a device which retrospectively brings together a variety of historical considerations, so as to highlight the "essence" of the historical object being studied, for example, Calvinism, capitalism, or worldly asceticism. It is the ideal type which brings disparate phenomena into a meaningful model from which the historian can explain them. Foucault maintains that his approach differs in that he is interested in isolating "explicit programs," like the Panopticon, which functioned as actual programs of action and reform. There is nothing hidden about them; they are not invented by the historian to bring together an interpretation. Hence, as he told a group of French historians: "Discipline is not the expression of an ideal type (that of the disciplined man); it is the generalization and the connection of different techniques which are themselves responses to local objectives (apprenticeship in school, the formation of troops capable of handling rifles)."[5] At the same time these explicit programs were never directly and completely realized in institutions. This is not because reality never totally imitates an ideal, but rather because there were counter-programs, local conflicts, and other strategies which were perfectly analyzable, even if they were finally distinct from the initial program. Foucault's effort as genealogist is to stay as much as possible on the surface of things, to avoid recourse to ideal significations, ideal types or essences.

So, if philosophically the emphasis on space was used as a device for combating the centrality of the subject and of temporality, historicopolitically this analysis led to the conclusion that at a certain period of our history, read genealogically, space and architecture became central components in the localization and operation, the micro-politics, of a specific form of power in the West.

* * *

I now want to shift to a brief outline of the main components of this schema for relating space, power, knowledge and history.

In a lecture given at the Collège de France in 1978, Foucault presented an analysis of three urban plans as a means of schematizing the interrelations of space and power during the Classical Age. The separation of these three schemes of space and power is not, of course, absolute, either temporally or conceptually. Although all three regimes can be isolated historically, they are important because they still function in modified ways today. In fact, from the Classical Age forward, a complex interplay has been established between them. But, because the story is being told genealogically from the present, it is the most recent scheme, the bio-power – that regime of power in which political intervention takes place at the level of the species as a natural and historical population to be known and controlled – which provides the grid of interpretation for the other two, the disciplinary and the sovereign. For it is the growth and spread of bio-power which has become Foucault's subject matter, while spatial plans are a means for analyzing the tactics employed in that spread. Consequently, the investment of the other regimes and technologies of power into a larger, more complex, and differentiated apparatus of power is read within the grid of intelligibility provided by bio-power.

Let us therefore look briefly at the relations of space and power in these three schemes. In the *sovereign* regime of power, the basic spatial unit is the *territory*, which must be supervised and given a harmonious order such that all relations of science, the arts, the law, industry, and commerce, as well as agriculture, fall under the benevolent government of the sovereign and serve to increase his glory. In the *disciplinary* technology of power, the problem is the control and distribution of *bodies* and *individuals* in a spatial ordering whereby they can be made to function in such a manner that efficiency, docility, and hierarchy are simultaneously achieved. Finally, under the technologies of *bio-power*, power is exercised on a *population* existing in a specific *milieu* which is both natural and historical. The components of both the population and the milieu must be known empirically so that the specific historical, demographic, ecological, and social forces which compose the population and the milieu can be systematically regulated and made to flourish.

Three urban projects demonstrate the relative simultaneity of these different spatial–political concerns in the Classical Age. The example of a treatise entitled *La Métropolitee*,[6] written in 1682 by Alexandre Le Maitre, a French Protestant engineer working for the Prussians, presents the spatial dimensions of power under the regime of a sovereign. Le Maitre's topic was the capital. In the capital, the sovereign, his administration, and the necessary artisans must be given a space which perfectly represents and aids the workings of power. This demanded not only a perfect ordering of the capital city itself but also a correct placement of the capital within the territory over which the sovereign ruled. Hence, in good Classical terms (which Foucault has analyzed at length archaeologically in *Les Mots et les choses*) the most adequate representation of that which is being represented, here sovereign power, should have the form of that which it is seeking to represent. Consequently and logically, Le Maitre proposed a symmetrical geometrical plan for the spatial ordering of the entire territory. It follows that the capital should be located at the geographical center. And, for the capital to be most perfectly placed at the center, the ideal kingdom should have the form of a circle. In this scheme, the symbolic joins the aesthetic and they are both representations of the political.

By placing the capital at the geometric center of his territory, the sovereign would be in a perfect position to oversee and regulate the correct relations of science, the arts, and trade throughout the realm. All that moved in the kingdom must pass through this center. Thus there is a perfect superposition of commerce, politics, and space in Le Maitre's utopian plan.

* * *

Richelieu, one of a number of planned cities undertaken in France during the Classical Age, provides an example of a disciplinary ordering of space.[7] We are all familiar with disciplinary space, although we usually associate it with the spatial ordering found in factories, workshops, schools, prisons, and hospitals. A more complex and total ordering of groups, but a highly functionally specific one, can be found in the army camp and its Roman predecessors. It is therefore both interesting and somewhat unexpected to uncover an even more functionally complex disciplinary order of space in a less obviously controlled and disciplined setting. But Foucault's point was, after all, precisely the way in which disciplinary technologies invested numerous institutions and could expand without being too highly visible.

The organization of Richelieu was based on a preconceived plan for an entire city, one that flowed from well-articulated interests. We find in this project not a representation of an ideal situation, but a concrete project meant to function in a historically and geographically specific context. Discipline involved an ongoing control, a response to a particular set of needs, not a timeless or utopian representation. Its space was not envisioned as the capital or a larger territory, nor as a pre-existent town which had to be reordered. Rather, Richelieu was conceived as a self-enclosed space within which a hierarchical, visible and functional order could be established. It was also planned as a geometric figure – this time not a circle but a double rectangle. The whole town was plotted onto a graphic space composed of larger and smaller rectangles. The largest streets, appropriately where the most prestigious, powerful, and wealthy people lived, were located at the center of the city along its main axis. The smaller and more peripheral streets were to be inhabited by those occupied with commerce and artisanal trades.

Architecture also had a precise role in the laying out of distinctions and functions. Two major categories of houses were constructed in such a manner as to make differences in power perfectly recognizable. On the main axis stood the largest and most imposing houses (a sort of linear Place des Vosges), whose size and decoration were strictly controlled to create a harmonious visual and social order. On the smaller streets, perpendicular to the main axis, were proportionally smaller and less luxurious houses. A church and a market were erected on two grand places at each end of the main avenue.

This artificial, closed, and orderly space visibly articulates a type of power which both made a hierarchy operational and ensured an efficient circulation of goods and power. A series of individuals were fixed in a larger order. By their very location, they contributed to a larger set of Richelieu's own aims – for the town itself, as well as for his personal ambitions.

Richelieu was indeed built, a planned town for several thousand inhabitants, as Foucault indicates; moreover, the Cardinal's real aim in having this town constructed alongside his new grandiose chateau was to use it as a means of keeping his closest counselors and courtiers under a strict surveillance. Each courtier, arrived or aspiring, was informed that he had the privilege of paying for one of the large and expensive houses on the main avenue where Richelieu's architect was designing residences under the Cardinal's orders. Hence, it was the upper classes for whom this disciplinary space was primarily designed.

In *Discipline and Punish*, Foucault had given us an interpretation of disciplinary technology as a strategic implantation of a set of devices for the implementation and expansion of a normalizing power essentially applied to the working classes and sub-proletariat. Richelieu offers a somewhat different reading of disciplinary technology as one of the elements in the self-construction and auto-regulation of the middle and upper classes. It provides a good example of how a technology of power operates not simply as a device of domination and exploitation, but as a formative process whereby all those enmeshed in its space are involved in its operation. A hierarchical ordering of classes was certainly intended in the way the town was planned. But, in this instance, disciplinary ordering of space was applied primarily to the fixing and surveillance of the rulers, under conditions of luxury and privilege.

Yet, although all of the expensive residences were constructed and sold, almost no one moved into them. The town of Richelieu was, in fact, too far from the court and the capital. Instead, in the following years, the artisans who had built the town, small-scale shopkeepers and servants eventually appropriated the houses in a kind of carnivalesque reversal of power, and the town became a modest success, although clearly not the kind of success Richelieu had originally envisioned.

* * *

Nantes in the eighteenth century illustrates the role of space within a framework of bio-power.[8] Nantes was not a royal city, nor can it be read as an example of disciplinary space, although there were attempts to introduce both types of spatial/political organization. There was a certain amount of Baroque glorification of the state in a few monuments and their surrounding squares, but this never amounted to much. There was also a proposal for a grid-like development of the main island in the Loire adjoining the old city, but this never passed beyond the architect's drawings. Rather, the city of Nantes went its own way. A wave of prosperity brought on by the growth of trade with America, particularly the traffic in cloth and slaves, stimulated commerce in the first part of the eighteenth century. Growth, circulation, and trade rather than glory, harmony, or hierarchical order became the central planning concerns of the architects and burghers of Nantes.

These goals too generated particular urban plans. One of the first attempts to reanimate the central city was drawn up by an architect named Rousseau. This Rousseau designed a new quarter in the shape of a heart: clearly, in this age of correct representations, the most appropriate form to stimulate health and a vigorous circulation of goods, people, and air through the congested valves of the medieval city. *Hélas*, Rousseau's plan also never got farther than the drawing board, although it did receive some praise and the principles it embodied were incorporated by other city designers.

A series of rather less elegant plans were to guide the actual development of Nantes. First, a series of *percées*, or widened streets for heavier traffic, were cut through the older medieval lanes. The interior street network and the main commercial activities of the town could thereby be connected for a more extended network of circulation, both within the city and to outlying areas. For the growth of the city was clearly tied to a wider commercial world than that of Nantes itself. The city was not conceived as a self-enclosed, geometrically representable unit. Rather, its future prosperity depended on the vital, regulated flow of goods, people, and air, within the city itself and far beyond its boundaries. While this system of circulation increased activity, it also provided a means for the effective surveillance and control of such activity. Taxes could be collected, health measures enforced, movements of population controlled, all in such a manner as to maximize the beneficial effects and minimize the nefarious ones.

The problem for the architects of Nantes was thus how to make operational a space that would promote a regular and vigorous circulation. This was not simply a question of extending or perfecting an administrative *cadréage* of equal units following a fixed plan, but rather a differentiation of space according to its specific functions and particularities. In this scheme, space was not taken as a neutral medium to be ordered *ex nihilo*, as was the case in Richelieu. Rather – and here the specific components of bio-power enter in – space was continually analyzed and manipulated as something to be known and used. It had to be considered in its empirical relation to a specific site; to the demographic, commercial, and social characteristics of the already existing population; and, most importantly, to the potential future development of those diverse human and geographical particularities, now understood as resources to be known, regulated, and maximized. Hence, while the solution to the problem of how to increase the health and prosperity of Nantes might well draw on general principles applicable elsewhere, the solution itself had to be resolutely particular.

For it follows that if the aim was to increase, make prosper, encourage, and maximize the current functioning and future growth of Nantes, starting with what was already there, then the need for a precise knowledge of the state of such matters as the geology, geography, demography, the market, the dispositions and possibilities of the inhabitants' trades, the conditions of hygiene, dangers of infection from abroad, and so on, was evident. All of these constantly changing conditions had to be known in precise detail in order to plan for the population of the city. Moreover this knowledge was not static, for it had to be projected in time in order to plan for development.

The combination of empirical social studies and calculated efforts to plan for future needs became the task of a particular spatial inscription of power and knowledge. Indeed, the "knowledge" side was so highly developed by the early nineteenth century that a local doctor named Ange Guépin could produce a historical sociology of Nantes which ran to fifteen hundred pages, detailing every aspect of the city's social life and its historical development, and then in innumerable other publications the good doctor could outline what he saw as the healthiest and most efficient manner for Nantes to evolve, guided by the principles of social hygiene.[9] Empirical, statistical, and historical sociology thus began in France long before Durkheim.

The "power" aspect was also surprisingly clear: a shift in focus from the state itself and well established institutions of power toward the industrial and commercial classes themselves, with their particular conceptions of growth and effectiveness. While certain steps in Nantes's urban transformation, such as the grand *percées* through and around the medieval fabric, were easily agreed upon, the local merchants debated among themselves where the port facilities on the Loire should be expanded and who should pay for this development. The thorniest issue for them was how to combine speculative development of housing with a centralized control of the city's services and projected needs. These issues, of course, raised the question of who was responsible for these complex spatial decisions, their financing and their implementation. The sources indicate that, instead of the state or even a single powerful administrative official directing the planning, the most successful aspects of the urban development of Nantes were carried out by individual capitalists, who were given quarters to develop, or by groups of investors, whose common interest was the most efficient and profitable development of particular activities such as the port facilities.

We can point to an important dislocation here. There is no longer a direct relationship between the operation of political power and its spatial representation. In fact, as the example of Nantes indicates, it was no longer the state which was directly responsible for the planning of space. This is not to say that spatial organization and its planning and control lost their importance; in fact, one could argue that, if anything, the centrality of the manipulation, remodeling, and control of spatial decisions in the nineteenth and twentieth centuries have taken on a degree of importance and, indeed, a visibility previously unparalleled. Everything from genetic engineering to the coordination of world-wide economic relations, to the reworking of the entire ecosphere involves critical spatial dimensions. However, space has lost its privileged role as a medium through which these changes can be *represented*. The organization of territory, of routes of communication, of whole cities, and so on, now follows another set of considerations in which the economy and society provide the guidelines and imperatives. The problem has shifted from the correct ordering of space to the regulation of a milieu: how, given a series of elements in a multivalent and transformable *cadre*, to bring them together such that, in all likelihood, they will prosper in an orderly, efficient, and coherent way.

* * *

This brings me back to the spatial, political, and social problems posed by my group of early-twentieth-century French urbanists. Given more time, it could be argued that throughout the course of the nineteenth century, spatial considerations per se (that is, the teaching at the Ecole des Beaux-Arts or the Ecole Nationale des Ponts et Chaussées), political considerations (the dramatic changes of regime in nineteenth-century France as well as the steady consolidation of the Napoleonic administrative system), and social science considerations (the emergence of detailed studies about working conditions, health, marginal and dangerous groups, economic science, geographical studies, anthropology, and so on), although crossing each other in innumerable ways, did not have, nor did they seem to feel the need for, a common practical or conceptual linkage. The examples of the railroads or campaigns for electrification, the construction of the road network, or the Haussmanization of the cities all indicate the fact that power, social science knowledge, and spatial planning were hardly dissociated. But it was only towards the end of the century that a need was felt to articulate them into a common framework. Partially under the spur of the defeat of 1870 and the Commune, Frenchmen concerned with such issues began to look abroad, and they found in Germany and England the beginnings of a new discipline, urbanism, which sought to combine the planning of space with political control based on a scientific understanding of society. It was to be a long time indeed before any comprehensive urban planning was done in France – really not until after the Second World War. But in the interim a good deal of discourse about the need for it was generated, and an impressive amount of experimentation in urban design, which combined political, social, and cultural factors, was carried out in the colonies. In that spatial/political experimentation is to be found, I believe, the emergence of a new attempt to articulate space, power, and knowledge.

NOTES

1 "Questions on Geography" in *Power/Knowledge: Selected Interviews and Other Writings by Michel Foucault, 1972–1977*, ed. Colin Gordon (New York: Pantheon, 1980), pp. 69–70.

2 Hubert Dreyfus and Paul Rabinow, *Michel Foucault: Beyond Structuralism and Hermeneutics* (Chicago: University of Chicago Press, 1982).
3 "Questions on Geography," pp. 69–70.
4 "The Eye of Power" in *Power/Knowledge*, p. 148.
5 *L'Impossible Prison*, ed. Michelle Perrot (Paris: Editions du Seuil, 1980), p. 49.
6 Alexandre Le Maitre, *La Métropolitee* (Amsterdam: B. Boekhilt, 1682).
7 The essential historical material, a bibliography, and photos can be found in *Richelieu, ville nouvelle*, by Philippe Boudon (Paris: Dunod, 1978).
8 A good architectural and urban history of Nantes is Pierre Lelièvre's *L'Urbanisme et l'architecture à Nantes au XVIII siècle* (Nantes: Durance, 1972).
9 Dr. Ange Guépin, *Histoire de Nantes* (Nantes: Editions Sebire, 1839). See also Dr. Ange Guépin and E. Benamy, *Nantes au XIX Siècle, Statistique, Topographie Industrielle et Morale* (Nantes: Editions Sebire, 1835).

18

A Place in History:
Social and Monumental
Time in a Cretan Town
Histories in Their Places

Michael Herzfeld

Antiquity as Pollution: Contesting the Value of the Past

This account of Rethemnos has been about conflicting visions of the past and their realization in the present. History is experienced both as an immanent property and as an external threat. The same question returns time and again: whose is the history, and whose the discourse about it? Who decides what constitutes the history of this place? What are the common places of its warring histories? The development of the Old Town gives shape, smell, and sound to a contested cultural topography.

The very name of antiquity provokes resentment. Some feel that it is arbitrarily applied, that it should be confined to monumental architecture. Certainly the perception that some of the antiquities are of "Turkish" date does not increase people's respect for them. Official historiography falls victim to decades of its own derision of anything Turkish and is hard put to defend its position, given the absence of a uniformly clear break in domestic architecture between the Venetian and Turkish periods. Conversely, an elderly refugee from Asia Minor described his house as *katharo*, "pure" or "clean," because it contained virtually nothing of antiquarian interest.[1]

In a town where house-proud women and fiercely independent men resent the intervention of bureaucratic archaeologists, this devaluation of antiquity symbolically reinforces the general distress that residents express at the physical dirt which crumbling, damp-ridden walls impose upon them. At the same time, most residents recognize that *some* buildings deserve to be preserved as monuments. These are not their houses but certain landmark constructions. Not all of them have survived into the present day, and poorer residents bitterly condemn the wealthy merchants who demolished them and thus deprived the town of major tourist attractions.

Thus, for example, it was a merchant who in 1945 demolished the Venetian sun-clock and tower, having first, in 1936–1938, removed a group of buildings serving as shops. The demolition was carried out secretly and in great haste in order to provide a better access route to the harbor storage area. In this way, the high and mighty struck at the collective interest of the town (see also Youmbakis 1970:29), depriving it of what might, in the long term, have drawn many visitors. The poor use this as an example of the selfishness of the rich. The old fabric of the town thus suffered on both sides of the main class division, for the poor, in turn, were not above reusing hewn Venetian masonry, as the Venetians themselves and then the Turks had done in earlier times.

By lending their rhetoric to the preservation of monumental architecture, the poor can thereby deploy the official ideology in support of their own goals. In so doing, they make a clear distinction between monumental and domestic architecture. Many also agree that the preservation of the monumental remains brings tourism and therefore also money. An elderly man mourned the old slaughterhouses, torn down in 1955. The state should not have done that even to beautify the area with a park, he complained, as these old slaughterhouses were *dhiatiritea* ("scheduled for conservation"). These, like the antics of the OTHOA leadership (if its critics are correct), are merely episodes in the shameful history of collusion between bureaucrats and wealthy citizens. Why should the state persecute the poor for doing with their own houses what the rich have already done, with impunity, with the entire monumental heritage of Rethemnos? Like the charge that the domestic architecture consists of *tourkospita*, these tactics turn official reasoning against itself. Once the rhetoric of national heritage has entered the protesters' vocabulary, it can be turned to their advantage. It may also reflect changes in attitude that themselves index changes in an individual's economic fortunes. Suddenly envisaging the benefits that might accrue to him from the tourist boom, for example, a suitably remorseful hotelier permits himself the cautious self-criticism that he has "perhaps committed a crime" against his own building by making illegal alterations to it. Now, instead, he takes care to conduct the remaining conversion work strictly within the rules, matching the antiquarian design of the house with a sanitized folk heritage of neatly organized wooden chairs and patterned hangings. While, to get his hotel started, he had first sought to demolish most of its distinguishing traces of antiquity, it now pays him to find new ways of endowing it with picturesque antiquity – a strategy into which bureaucrats and fellow entrepreneurs lost little time in initiating him.

Although increasing numbers of Rethemniots have similarly been drawn into the new economic nexus, resistance to the historic conservation office is certainly far from dead. The embittered logic of that resistance today may be summarized in a few sentences. The task of the office is to preserve the monuments of a glorious, European past. Instead of rescuing the last few true monuments from the rapacious rich, however, its detractors maintain that it foists "Turkish" misery upon a poor and victimized populace. To them, domestic quarters are not "archaeology," a term that most Greeks associate with such monuments as the Acropolis in Athens. Even some of those who are comparatively well-to-do and moderate in their opinions voice such objections. One lawyer, for example, echoed Nianias's position in arguing that, while the people of Rethemnos do not deny their history or their culture, the state should make sure that the burden of the expenses should not fall on private citizens. Others are less temperate. Money forces its will on the state, they say, and the state – which in turn is a "bandit" (*listriko*)[2] institution – forces the poor to become lawbreakers in a game whose rules are defined by the rich and bureaucratic: "The bonds that cannot be undone [i.e., regulations] are [simply] broken." In the multiply refracted contest over the meaning of the past and its relics, situated actors adopt attitudes that will serve their interests best. As they variously succeed or fail, their position in the nexus of power also shifts, and their engagement with the past alters with it. These changes are often reflected in tactical alterations of course, as we shall now see.

Negotiating Tactics and Contingent Facts

Conflicts among the various official agencies have complicated the search for a solution. No less vexing are the power struggles of private interests. When some neighbors began agitating to have the space next to the Hüseyin Paşa mosque cleared of the rubble and weeds that presently litter it, the bank that owned the space refused to cooperate. The bank itself had wanted to build there, but the historic conservation office had succeeded in blocking its proposal. The only change on which neighbors, owners, and officialdom could agree was to close a short-lived "nightclub" that turned out to be a brothel and was promptly and decisively shut down. The Fortezza was the place for such establishments, not a neighborhood in the heart of town that had maintained its respectability since Turkish times. As a result, the open space has become a parking lot for the neighborhood, which suggests that in the end the residents were the sole beneficiaries of this impasse between the big power brokers.

This incident shows how each new disposition of space embodies the consequences of a particular negotiation of the relevant facts. As citizens and bureaucrats alike – and sometimes individuals trying to reconcile both these roles – pursue a variety of evanescent but intensely focused interests, they recast the history of the built environment, the classification of the buildings, and the relative pertinence of a set of often mutually incompatible regulations. Because these all appear to be matters of fact, they are paradoxically more liable to the grandstanding style of social debate that Rethemniots favor than are matters more openly labeled as opinions. To the extent that a building can be classified as Venetian or Turkish, or that a law can be cited in defense of inaction rather than intervention, "self-evidence" (Douglas 1975) is not only a matter of cultural assumptions but an object of intense strategic manipulation. This is how bureaucracy actually works: official classification provides an uncompromisingly fixed point of reference around which swirl the eddies of intense, volatile negotiation over meaning and interpretation.

Residents can capitalize for short-term purposes on the state's sometimes crippling legalism. Cynics, proceeding from a personal rather than an institutional view of the state apparatus, even argue that the state cannot afford to suppress illegality. One went so far as to suggest that the state would never suppress drugs because then it would have no need of police or judiciary: "What is it [the state] going to do? Is it going to play church [a popular anticlerical metaphor for 'busy work']?" He went on: "The state saves (*ikonoma*), makes money, from illegality." The aggrieved citizen can thus claim to be the victim of state oppression and, as such, can justify the cunning and lawlessness to which the state leaves no alternative. This self-vindicating rhetoric deploys the morality of the state against itself and provides the framework for most of the tactics with which citizens pursue their interests against the law.

Citizens have a thoroughly practical view of the ways in which the state apparatus works. Thus, for example, they play adroitly on officials' fear of their superiors' possible wrath. A coffee shop in one of the best-preserved Venetian segments of the Old Town was connected with the opposite side of the street by a small buttress arch, which prevented the owner from putting up a modern glass frontage to make his establishment more attractive to potential customers. One rainy January night in 1974, he demolished the whole thing. Inside the building, he also constructed a lavatory and shower stall. He had proposed to perform this operation jointly with his neighbor, who backed off in fear at the very last moment. When the police eventually came to investigate at the request of the historic conservation office, he told them that the work had cost him 500,000 drachmas, and that if they wanted him to remove the glass frontage, they would have to finance the change. This aggressive stance protected him from further prosecution, since the authorities found themselves facing a fait accompli, which gave them a moral alibi for inaction.

Violence, too, may be effective against state functionaries, especially when conjoined with the rhetoric of citizens' rights. A knife-wielding butcher chased a historic conservation agent away from his brother-in-law's property and so gained the latter a short respite. Another resident, at a very early stage in the conservation effort (1972), having been thwarted for some twelve months in his desire to build a new house on an empty plot in the Old Town, went to Iraklio and burst in on the then *ephor* (superintendent), who at that stage still directed the entire Rethemnos operation from the larger city. When the Rethemniot refused to budge, and threatened to return and kill the ephor if he tried calling the police, the ephor checked his files and, as the client later claimed, discovering that the file had been sitting there all along, feigned anger at his subordinates' inefficiency. Sometimes one has to go higher still. One resident demanded an interview with the Prefect, then refused to leave until she agreed to telephone the historic conservation office and have matters sorted out to his satisfaction. In all such cases, violence served as an extreme means of making some change in the supposedly immutable dictates of existing paperwork; ultimately, the citizen must reckon with due process, but this does not preclude preemptive strikes. Violence and legal-mindedness actually do go hand-in-hand in Rethemnos. Like the urbanity and wildness that Prevelakis describes, they inform the practical dialectic of everyday life.

The state prosecutes offenders easily and wins many of its cases. Even this, however, does not necessarily represent a defeat for unruly citizens. Since the sanctions are weak – jail terms can be officially substituted by fines – many calculate that the fines cost less than waiting interminably for a permit that may never be granted and losing business because of the delay. This was the budgetary tactic of the man who altered his house six times and claims he was reported for this to the authorities by hostile neighbors. Venetian houses had stone kitchen fireplaces, the form of which was stable well into Turkish times (see Dimakopoulos 1977:147). Local taste, uninterested in such historical niceties, held that fireplaces were too Turkish or too rustic. The householder feared that "[someone might] say,

'Are you in the village now, putting fireplaces in?'" He therefore destroyed the old fireplace, which he now admits was a fine feature of his house. Fashions change, and the meaning accorded to such features changes with them (see also Pavlides 1983). Accordingly, he later replaced the fireplace with a modern fireplace, at the substantial cost of 125,000 drachmas. This time, however, the fireplace went into the *saloni*, the public display area of the house, rather than into the intimacy of the kitchen. The social capital of modernity was worth more to him than avoiding a few cash fines.

This calls for some further comment about the significance of fireplaces in Rethemnos. For residents who move away to the New Town, keeping the old house as a place of work, the fireplace serves as an affective focus of memory. An elderly retiree, recently returned from Athens, whose well-preserved old house contains a fine stone *tzaki*, covered the whole fireplace with a tacked-up piece of oilcloth. He explained that the fireplace needed cleaning before it could be displayed, thereby showing that the functionally small value of these old *tzakia* has been displaced by their display value and by their objectification as the loci of nostalgia. Another resident, whose small house displayed all the signs of a carefully achieved respectability (matching upholstered furniture and a well-displayed multi-volume encyclopedia), pointed with deep pride to the modern brick fireplace his brother had built for his living room. On all sides, the status of the fireplace remains instructively ambiguous. Once the symbolic and practical center of domesticity, it has now become the carrier of conflicting ideologies. On the one hand, fireplaces are antiquities; on the other, the repositories of familiar but private memories. People do not adhere to the principles of conservation merely because the state tells them to. Rather, while increasingly using cultural criteria that the state has taught them to represent the European essence of Greekness, they try to memorialize their own old life-style in terms that would give it value in a modern world hungry for nostalgia. Those who no longer own an old fireplace now turn instead to a more collective sense of "tradition," one that is more aggressively bourgeois and "European."

Different types of fireplace mark different accommodations to the objectification of tradition. The process whereby people negotiate these embodiments of nostalgia, however, are all effectively drawn from the practical calculus of the *pazari* rather than from the bureaucratic formalism of the official marketplace. Decisions that should ostensibly be proof against the subversion of precision and order are affected by a subtle drawing of the bureaucrats into the pazari idiom. As we have seen, the Tax Office provides another striking example of this process, with its former practice of basing assessments on the assumption that most citizens will automatically halve the value of any property being sold. Within the range of fiscal ambiguity thus established, a wide range of social negotiations balances personal relations against legal requirements.

In much the same way, historic conservation and town-planning officials alike must weigh social consequences against legal sanctions. The more they incline toward negotiation, the less convincing becomes their pose of disinterested public service – a pose that Greeks conventionally find hard to credit since they know that bureaucrats are always vulnerable to pressure from kin, neighbors, and business associates. By that same token, however, the more bureaucrats attempt to withdraw behind their official facade, with its ideological pretensions rooted in "European" ideals of civic probity, the more they become outsiders in a community where only insiders can function to full effect. Their skill as public officials may largely be measured in terms of how successfully they maintain this improbable balance.

It also turns on the ability to negotiate facts. Questions of precision and consistency, or whether a house is Venetian or Turkish, are surprisingly labile. While the historic conservation office strikes its more unwilling clients as merely capricious, it prides itself on the clarity of its guidelines and their application. Residents perceive its task as the preservation of "Venetian" monuments and object to its intervention on behalf of "Turkish" domestic quarters, as we have noted. They find it hard to understand why it forbids the destruction of definitively Turkish architectural elements such as the *kioskia* (wooden window extensions) that used to grace virtually all the old houses, for example. Or why it allegedly opposes the construction of modern buildings opposite kioskia, even when open space is available, yet through its dilatory management encourages the destruction of many old stone structures. On the one hand, again, it turned down a request to place concrete underneath some so-called "Byzantine" tiles; its rationale was that this might have entailed unnecessary structural strain. In a different project, on the other hand, the office director took great pride in a small guest house with an arched ground-floor room and heavy stone paving above, where precisely this technique held the older masonry in place – "because some weight was really needed to counteract the tendency to slip sideways" – and also put an end to water leakage. Such eminently practical decisions may, from an adversarial perspective, appear merely capricious.

Some residents ridicule what they see as the historic conservation office's dominant obsessions: arched doors and windows (which "also" – though in very different style – exist in some modern buildings!), and walls of Sandorini earth. Of the latter, an irritated comment, that it doesn't "write" (*ghrafi*) what it is, expresses all the bafflement of citizens required to preserve apparently quite undistinguished and indistinguishable broken-down masonry. An inscription, by contrast, is something people can understand. Yet inscriptions are a form of writing, and, as such, they are the visible reminder and the most potent symbol of bureaucratic repression past and present. Those who are willing to concede that the control of interior construction has been lifted are more willing to praise the conservation of buttresses and arched entrances, since these do not materially affect living conditions. (But we should also remember that the term *kamara*, "arch," is a synonym for the traditional "Turkish" house type that residents find so appallingly dark and damp.) A nonlocal woman who wants to convert her proud mansion on one of the main commercial streets into a hotel fumes that none of the small houses currently receiving attention is "like mine." She would welcome the benison of antiquarian interest for sound commercial reasons and so claims to envy the poorer residents the attention that the conservation office lavishes on their houses as much as they themselves resent it. Here, as in virtually every encounter with the bureaucracy, the citizen seeks to effect advantageous change by playing with the rhetoric of an idealized impartiality with which none actually credit the bureaucracy in practice.

[...]

NOTES

1　This man once complained that a child's name, Nektarios, was not "Greek" (*elliniko*) but "ancient" (*arkheo*) – a reversal of the official equation of Greekness with Classical antiquity. To compound the irony still further, Nektarios was in fact a modern saint, canonized in 1961!

2　This is a nice example of the use of official rhetoric against the official state. The term *kleftes* (thieves), noted above, recalls the guerrillas who fought against Turkish domination before national independence. After independence, those who continued to fight against the state were branded "brigands" (*liste*[s]) and outlawed by the Greek authorities. Through a process of linguistic engineering, the distinction between listes and the erstwhile freedom fighters became increasingly unambiguous (see Herzfeld 1982:60–69; Koliopoulos 1987). Today, describing the state as *listriko* is a strategic representation by citizens who recognize that they can only achieve limited goals, and those only by working within the dominant discourse.

REFERENCES

Dimakopoulos, Iordanis
　　1977 The houses of Rethemnos: Contribution to the study of the Renaissance architecture of Crete in the 16th and 17th centuries. Athens: Ministry of Culture and Sciences.
Douglas, Mary
　　1975 Implicit Meanings: Essayes in Anthropology. London: Routledge and Kegan Paul.
Herzfeld, Michael
　　1982 Ours Once More: Folklore, Ideology, and the Making of Modern Greece. Austin: University of Texas Press.
Koliopoulos, John S.
　　1987 Brigands with a Cause: Brigandage and Irredentism in Modern Greece, 1921–1912. Oxford: Clarendon Press.
Pavlides, Eleftherios
　　1983 Modernization and the fireplace in Eressos, a Greek rural town. Oz 5:20–23.
Youmbakis, Markos G.
　　1970 Fortezzo: The history of the Venetian citadel of Rethimno. Rethemnos: n.p.

19

After Authenticity at an American Heritage Site

Eric Gable and Richard Handler

An enduring image of modernist anxiety is that the world we inhabit is no longer authentic – that it has become fake, plastic, a kitschy imitation. Anxiety, so the common wisdom has it, goes hand in hand with desire. We may have lost authenticity, but we want to find it again, and will pay what it costs (within reason) to get it. This image of "authenticity lost" has also been at the center of much "countermodern" cultural critique, and it has given anthropology a kind of romantic aura – a longing for a lost authenticity. Thus it often seems that the scholarly study of late modern or postmodern culture is a study of a reverse alchemy. What was once golden is now plastic.

Lately cultural critics claim to have shed their romanticism. Countermodern romanticism is no longer an unacknowledged scholarly motive, but an object of study, even an object of derision.[1] However, as several scholars have noted, most recently Edward Bruner in an article appearing in this journal (1994), it often seems that cultural critics do not go beyond the assertion that the world is empty, that outward appearances are facades, that everything is somehow constructed. In part, this is because one standard assumption among such critics is that those in power benefit from the prevailing definition of the authentic. They need the authority of authenticity to legitimate their power. Moreover, many of the critics assume that the public at large, the more or less disenfranchised masses of consumers, are co-opted into buying, say, a pedigree or an experience to make up for what they have been taught is the emptiness of their daily lives. The critic's dream is that once already anxious natives are exposed to the constructedness of authenticity, they will stop buying it. As a result, much of current cultural criticism involves exposing the authentic as construction. If the real past is revealed to be a present-day invention, if the natural fact is revealed to be a cultural convention, then the ruling order will topple and the masses will be freed from the yoke of anxious desire.

Museums – and especially heritage museums – play a peculiar role in all of this, for they are perfect topoi upon which to enact such critiques, even as they are also outgrowths of precisely the kind of countermodern anxiety that is the enduring basis for cultural critique.[2] Heritage is one form of cultural salvage. A "lost world" or a world about to be lost is in need of "preservation," and the museum or heritage site bills itself as the best institution to perform this function. Heritage museums become publicly recognized repositories of the physical remains and, in some senses, the "auras" of the really "real." As such, they are arbiters of a marketable authenticity. They are also objective manifestations of cultural, ethnic, or national identity, which outside the museum is often perceived as threatened by collapse and decay. Yet preservation entails artful fakery. Reconstruction, as it were, is the best evidence for the validity of a constructivist paradigm. Critics of this or that version of authenticity have before them in a heritage site ample evidence from which to build their deconstructive arguments.

In this essay, we would like to explore what happens to a heritage site "after authenticity" – where the pursuit of an elusive authenticity remains a goal even as it generates public statements intended to call into question the epistemology of authenticity.[3] Colonial Williamsburg – a place that fashions itself as one of the most ambitious and extensive reconstruction projects ever undertaken – intends to be experienced as an objective correlate of an American national "identity." Because Colonial Williamsburg makes such claims for itself, it has throughout its history also been subject to critiques of its authenticity by those who wish to undermine its authority to speak as the voice of an all-encompassing America. Moreover, in the past 20 years, the professional historians who ostensibly set the pedagogic agenda at Colonial Williamsburg have become increasingly articulate on-site critics of the epistemological underpinnings of authenticity as they promulgate, at this particular site, a historiography currently popular in history museums at large and in the academy.

The question that frames our essay is, What happens to authenticity when the public are both openly skeptical about the capacity of the powers that be at Colonial Williamsburg to make definitive judgments about authenticity and also openly skeptical about authenticity itself as a foundational value? We will argue that the vernacular concept of authenticity changes very little, that it shows a remarkable resilience, in a sense, because it is under threat. This is because one crucial way that Colonial Williamsburg maintains its authority is by selective or managed admissions of failure to discern what is fact, fancy, real, or fake. This attention to the management of impressions allows for the dream of authenticity to remain viable even in an environment in which all available empirical evidence could easily be perceived as supporting constructivist paradigms or alternatively as undermining authenticity-based claims to truth or value. When constructivist paradigms flourish, as they currently do at sites such as Colonial Williamsburg, they do so not in the service of a critique of the status quo but in defense (to borrow from Durkheim) of what come to be perceived as socially "necessary illusions." While we draw our examples from research we carried out at Colonial Williamsburg from 1990 to 1993, the arguments are applicable to heritage sites in general and ultimately to the way constructivist paradigms are deflected or domesticated in the American vernacular in the "post-authentic" age.[4]

Colonial Williamsburg: The Ethnographic Setting

Colonial Williamsburg's central district, the Historic Area, which covers 173 acres and includes over 500 buildings, is an inherently ambiguous object of authenticity.

Of this collection of buildings, 88 are said to be original and the rest are advertised as reconstructions. These buildings range in size from large public buildings, such as the Governor's Palace and the Capitol, to the dozens of outbuildings dotting the backyards of the stores and residences of the museum-city's streets. Outside the Historic Area are three major museums (devoted to folk art, decorative arts, and archaeology) and a James River plantation called Carter's Grove. The museum was founded in 1926 with the backing of John D. Rockefeller Jr. and is today owned and operated by the nonprofit Colonial Williamsburg Foundation. The foundation has a for-profit subsidiary, Colonial Williamsburg Hotel Properties, Inc., which operates several hotels and restaurants, with the profits used to support the museum. The foundation employs well over 3,000 people, and about a million people visit it each year. It had an annual budget of close to $130 million and an endowment of close to $200 million in 1989 (Colonial Williamsburg 1989:21–27).

The history that Colonial Williamsburg teaches has changed over the decades. In the past two decades, a crucial shift has occurred. The museum's patriotic, celebratory story of the American founding has been challenged by a new generation of historians hired at Colonial Williamsburg beginning in the late 1970s. These historians were profoundly influenced by the "new social history" that had developed in academic history departments in response to the social turmoil of the 1960s. When they came to Colonial Williamsburg, they wanted to revive what they saw as a moribund cultural institution by making it tell a new story, one that included the total colonial community. In other words, to the story of the colonial elites, which the museum had always told, the new historians wanted to add stories about the masses, the middle classes, the tradesmen, the lower classes, and, crucially, the African-American slaves. They wanted to depict the total social life of the community in order to emphasize inequality, oppression, and exploitation. The new story of the American Revolution was to be one of complicated social, political, and economic motivations and relationships, not simply a glorious triumph of democratic principles.

Moreover, the new historians at Colonial Williamsburg were explicitly constructivists. Not only did they wish to replace a patriotic history with one that was more critical, they wanted to teach the public that history making itself was not simply a matter of facts and truth. It was, instead, a process shot through with hidden cultural assumptions and ideological agendas. Indeed, when we began our research at Colonial Williamsburg, we were particularly interested in the ways that constructivist theory operated and how it fared in the face of an entrenched objectivist historiography that celebrated the authenticity of the site and the truth of the history it embodied. As we shall see, the relationship of authenticity to credibility speaks to a kind of compromise between constructivism and objectivism, a compromise that allows business to continue as usual at mainstream institutions such as Colonial Williamsburg – an institution on the cutting edge of the way heritage is packaged and produced and at the same time typical.

Authenticity, Credibility, and the Tourist Market

Despite the fact that Colonial Williamsburg's historians espouse a constructivist epistemology, the daily discourse that one hears on the site stresses the museum's commitment to total authenticity, that is, to historical truth in every detail.[5] To understand why the institution is willing to live with this contradiction, we need to examine how Colonial Williamsburg tries to position itself in the tourist market-place. Ironically, but perhaps not surprisingly, Disneyland is a dominant presence, both symbolically and literally, in that market (Kratz and Karp 1993). One of the first things that staff members told us when we began our field study is that Colonial Williamsburg "isn't some historical Disneyland." Instead, they asserted, it was a "serious educational institution." Colonial Williamsburg differs from Disneyland, in the view of the museum's staff, because it presents "the real past" rather than one that is made up. It strives for historical accuracy. In so doing, it is constrained by "documented facts" and by historiographical methods of interpretation and presentation. By contrast, theme parks like Disneyland can make up whatever imaginary past, present, or future they wish, since they purvey amusement and fantasy, not education and history. In sum, Colonial Williamsburg is real, while Disneyland is fake.

Interestingly, the Disney corporation accepts this division of the labor of cultural representation. Late in 1993, Disney announced plans to build an American history theme park in northern Virginia. Though Colonial Williamsburg's administrators must have been worried by the possibility of head-to-head competition with Disney, they put on a brave face, as the headlines in local newspapers announced, "Williamsburg hopes Disney park will draw interest to the real thing." Moreover, that Disney was clearly distinguished from "the real thing" was taken as a given throughout the "history-based tourism industry." As a spokesperson for Monticello, the "historic house" of Thomas Jefferson, put it, "It will be interesting for people to get the Disney experience and then...to come here and get the real thing." Disney executives, too, spoke the same language, at least to the press: "Colonial Williamsburg has the same thing the Smithsonian and the Manassas battlefield have: real history. We can do everything we want, but we can't create that."[6]

Despite the fact that the Disney corporation publicly accepts the "reality" of the historical presentations at Colonial Williamsburg, the museum's critics often do not. An example of their critique appeared recently in the *New York Review of Books*, in the form of an attack on contemporary architecture by critic Ada Louise Huxtable. Huxtable's essay opened with a tirade against Colonial Williamsburg, which she saw as "predating and preparing the way for the new world order of Disney Enterprises," an order that systematically fosters "the replacement of reality with selective fantasy." According to Huxtable, Colonial Williamsburg "has perverted the way we think," for it has taught Americans

> to prefer – and believe in – a sanitized and selective version of the past, to deny the diversity and eloquence of change and continuity, to ignore the actual deposits of history and humanity that make our cities vehicles of a special kind of art and experience, the gritty accumulations of the best and worst we have produced. This record has the wonder and distinction of being the real thing. [Huxtable 1992:24–25]

These remarks epitomize an enduring critique of Colonial Williamsburg. Many of the museum's critics have said that it is literally too clean – that it does not include the filth and stench that would have been commonplace in an 18th-century colonial town. Many of these critics also find that Colonial Williamsburg is metaphorically too clean; it avoids historical unpleasantness like slavery, disease, and class oppression in favor of a rosy picture of an elegant, harmonious past.[7] This, of course, is exactly what similarly positioned critics say of Disneyland. Indeed, from the perspective of the people who take this critical stance, Colonial Williamsburg is all too much like Disneyland. Both produce the kinds of tidy, oversanitized products they do because they are big, middle-of-the-road "corporate worlds" who sell entertainment rather than education.

Credibility Armor

Colonial Williamsburg has suffered the too-clean critique almost from the moment of its founding (Kopper 1986:165). That critique – which labels Colonial Williamsburg a fake like Disneyland instead of an authentic historic site – strikes at the museum's very conception of itself. Indeed, because authenticity is what Colonial Williamsburg sells to its public, the institution's claims to authenticity become a point of vulnerability. This is especially true for the foundation's professional intelligentsia – its historians, curators, and the like – for they are in many respects the peers of Huxtable and the others who snipe at them from the ivory tower. But the too-clean critique extends to the public at large, and so a defense against this critique becomes the business of the institution as a whole, especially on the "front line" where interpreters meet the public.

Every day hundreds of people visit Colonial Williamsburg, an institution whose mission is to show the public what colonial Virginia "was really like." Foundation staff know that in every crowd there are individuals casting a cold and critical eye on the museum's claim to present that reality. In these circumstances, Colonial Williamsburg staff work hard not only to present an authentic site but to maintain the institution's reputation for authenticity. Moreover, maintaining an image of authenticity means protecting Colonial Williamsburg's chosen institutional identity – that of a serious history museum, not a theme park. As one interpreter put it, "It is important to discuss facts because each facility wants to be accurate and to present to our customers and visitors the best historical interpretation possible and to retain its authentic reputation" (see Bruner 1994:401).[8]

"Reputation" is something that pertains to the self or to the institution as a corporate personality, yet it is made and maintained vis-à-vis others. As Colonial Williamsburg staff see it, the museum's reputation for authenticity is on the line every day, and every one of the myriad historical details it exhibits is both a witness to institutional authenticity and a window of vulnerability. When we asked a manager who was working on increasing the accuracy of the museum's costumes to explain the "educational payoff" of attention to historical detail, he responded by talking about reputation rather than pedagogy:

> The clothing is just as important as creating an accurate interior, creating any sort of accuracy. Any time you have a break in your credibility, then everything that is credible is lost, or it's called into question. If you have someone who comes in, and they happen to see plastic buttons, or someone wearing obvious knee socks, instead of proper

hosiery, then to me that's saying, well, that's not accurate. I wonder if the way that tea service is laid out is accurate? I wonder if the fact that that garden's laid out the way it is, I wonder if that's accurate? You start to lose it. That's why it's so important that our interpreters have the ability to take things that are less than accurate and get people to start thinking beyond them. And catching people, anticipating problems of credibility. Now if we can catch them up, by using better tools, better floor arrangements, better costumes, better gardens, then that's one less chink in our credibility armor that we have to worry about.

Colonial Williamsburg defends its credibility every day on the streets of the reconstructed capital, but its defenses are not perfect. Mistakes happen, visitors complain. In Colonial Williamsburg's corporate archives is a revealing record of how such complaints are resolved – files containing letters from disappointed visitors, along with the foundation's responses to them. These files record an ongoing effort to put the best spin it can on these criticisms by invoking Colonial Williamsburg's unwavering fidelity to authenticity.

For example, an elderly couple wrote that their most recent visit had turned into "a long disappointing day" because they "found many things that did not fit the Williamsburg we've known over the past 20 years." They complained that the "lovingly truly preserved past of our America" was being marred by the presence of employees with nail polish, plastic earrings, and tennis shoes. Charles Longsworth, president of the Colonial Williamsburg Foundation, replied:

> You brought a sharp eye with you on your recent visit to Colonial Williamsburg. You caught a few of our interpretive staff with their authenticity and courtesy down. You may be sure that each of the violations you cite of courtesy standards and 18th-century apparel and appearance is being addressed by the supervisors of the violators. Your standards are ours, and we strive to see them honored by all employees. Being human, we sometimes fail, but our efforts to achieve authenticity and friendliness have been and will continue to be unflagging.[9]

Phrases such as "reputation" and "credibility armor," and the image of being caught with one's authenticity (pants?) down, suggest the pervasive insecurity that, apparently, accompanies Colonial Williamsburg's claims to possess the really real. Even the foundation's professional historians, who espouse a relativistic or constructivist philosophy of history, experience this embattled concern for reputation.[10] An architectural historian, for example, told us what he characterized as a humorous story about an encounter he had with a visitor early in his career at Williamsburg. The visitor came up to him and said that Colonial Williamsburg did not have a single padlock on the reconstructed buildings that was genuinely 18th-century in design. In response to this criticism, the historian spent a day tracking down all the information he could find on the locks in the reconstruction. Then he went to a museum famous for its collection of early American artifacts "to study the 24 or so 18th-century padlocks they had." He made drawings of those. Next, he told us, he "developed a rough typology – I think there were four recognizable styles of padlock, and the visitor was right, none of ours were like these." As a result, the historian wrote the visitor thanking him and promising that while Colonial Williamsburg could not afford to change all the old locks, "on every subsequent project" they would make more faithful reproductions.

The historian prefaced his humorous story by explaining that he and his colleagues sweat the details so that "you aren't a joke" in the eyes of the public. His humorous portrayal of himself as an insecure ferret let loose on the problem of padlocks – because veracity in every detail is Colonial Williamsburg's hallmark and because he doesn't want to be a joke – reflects an abiding institutional concern, for the visitor who points out flaws in the mimetic portrait of the past Colonial Williamsburg professes to create is a stock character in many stories employees tell about their encounters with the visitors. He is, as one supervisor of frontline interpreters told us, like "a magpie" that weaves odd trinkets – tinfoil, some colored yarn – into its nest. A human magpie at places such as Colonial Williamsburg is someone who collects, indeed is obsessed with, a certain category of obscure historical facts.

Frontline employees are, if anything, more sensitive to the threat of the magpie than are backstage personnel like research historians. To these employees at Colonial Williamsburg, the magpie is an embarrassing nuisance who may be hiding among every flock of tourists, threatening to reveal the guide's ignorance (and knock the guide off his or her storyline) with a pointed query about some object or some theme about which the guide will have no clue.

Magpies threaten individual reputations during brief encounters at particular sites, and they also threaten institutional reputations. When the architectural historian says that it is a point of honor that Colonial Williamsburg get the details right, it is in part to protect his reputation, but also to protect the institution's reputation. Veracity, authenticity, or getting the facts right is a deep value at Colonial Williamsburg and it has a double quality. People like the architectural historian sweat the details, in part, because they too are like magpies. The architectural historian used to tell us how he loved the detective work involved in tracking down just such stray facts. But he and his colleagues also get the facts right so that they won't be exposed as a joke in public. The institution rewards employees for responding to the magpie's trivial or tangential queries because this keeps the credibility armor nicely burnished.

Constructivist Ploys in Defense of Objectivist Authenticity

Credibility armor is important because those who work at Colonial Williamsburg assume (and often have such assumptions confirmed) that the public is concerned with authenticity.[11] Every claim to possess or represent the "real" at least implies a claim to possess or represent the knowledge and authority to decide what's real and what isn't. Furthermore, Colonial Williamsburg employees expect that a significant number of their public are always somewhat skeptical of such claims to authority, especially those made on behalf of large corporate institutions like Colonial Williamsburg. As one of the foundation's historians put it, during a workshop we led concerning historical relativism and African American history,

> I think there are a lot of interpreters who share with many of our visitors this suspicion, that, in fact, there are official histories, and that this institution has been in the past, and may still be ... either consciously or unconsciously purveying an official history. Which is simply to say, a history that somebody knows to be wrong, but has good reasons for

wanting to promote anyway, either because if we tell the real story we'll turn off visitors, or we'll open up questions of racial antipathy which a well-behaved place – which Americans, good citizens – don't want to [hear]. . . . So there are lots of reasons why an institution like ours – particularly a slick institution like ours – is likely to have a hidden agenda. Which is only to say that there are probably lots and lots of people who don't know they're relativists, but fear that history is something that is concocted.[12]

People, in sum, are oftentimes predisposed to think (unkindly) of Colonial Williamsburg as a "slick institution" manufacturing facades and cover-ups rather than the authentic truth. Faced with such skepticism, and with the more sophisticated critiques of the intelligentsia, Colonial Williamsburg routinely deploys what might be called a proactive attitude, trying to defuse criticisms by anticipating them. Sometimes this takes the form of teaching visitors about "mistakes" the foundation has made in its depiction of the past. For example, on one tour that we took, the interpreter explained that in an earlier era in the museum's history all the clapboard outbuildings had been kept freshly painted and the woodwork had been of the highest quality. At that time, she explained, "We assumed that every building on the property would be as neat as every other." But now, she continued, researchers know better: "Only the front's important, that's your first impression, so buildings out back are going to be rougher." As a result, outbuildings were being painted less frequently and allowed to wear unevenly. Thus, as we looked at the crisp, white clapboard in front of us, we were asked to imagine more shabbily painted outbuildings elsewhere.

Another proactive ploy is to point out the purposeful artifice of the museum-city, a place meant to recreate an 18th-century reality but one that also, of necessity, must negotiate 20th-century realities. For example, many buildings in the Historic Area are used either as office space or as residences for foundation employees. In such cases, 20th-century elements must be "disguised." "The rules say you can't show anything 20th-century," one interpreter explained. "No anachronisms! That means no television antennas . . . no Christmas lights." Other interpreters told us that garages were made to look like stables, central air-conditioning was allowed because it did not have to be visible, and garbage cans could be hidden behind hedges. When we came across these artfully disguised elements, they were duly pointed out to us. As we paused, on one occasion, to marvel at 200-year-old boxwoods, we were reminded that "we also have wonderful things like fire hydrants, trash cans, and soda machines that we try to hide." As we continued our stroll beneath some tall trees, our guide added that "if you look up in trees this time of year you see things that look like an upside down bucket, and it's a light. You don't find them in the summer because of the leaves."

A third ploy for parrying criticisms entails blaming the visitors for inauthenticities. The best example of this ploy concerns trees (cf. Bruner 1994:402; Gable and Handler 1993a). The streets of the Historic Area are shaded by tall and stately oaks and other deciduous trees. Inevitably, interpreters would call our attention to these beautiful and obviously old trees and remark that they would not have been there in the colonial era. They would go on to explain that the foundation would never cut down those trees because, despite its commitment to authenticity, it had also to consider visitor comfort. Without the shady trees, the streets in summer ("when most of our visitors come") would be unbearable. In pointing to the trees, our guide on one occasion enjoined us to "keep in mind that many changes have been made to the town itself, things we have done to make it basically more comfortable for… 20th-century people." As on many tours, he advised us to look past or through these anachronisms in order to imagine the real past. It was as if the foundation was trying to shape the visitor's appreciation of the landscape in such a way as to confirm that, yes, the town is artificial, but Colonial Williamsburg could not be as accurate as it wished to be because the visitors' needs precluded it.

These rhetorical tactics might be seen as a kind of "impression management" – constructivism deployed in the defense of objectivism. Interpreters point out repeatedly (and indeed they are trained to do so) that history changes constantly, that what is believed to be true at one moment is discovered to be inauthentic later on, and that the business of history making involves all sorts of compromises. Yet these constructivist confessions, as it were, stem ultimately from a concern for maintaining Colonial Williamsburg's reputation as an arbiter of authenticity. Constructivist caveats shore up the assertion that the foundation aims for authenticity in every detail. As we discovered in interviews with visitors, its public by and large expects that, but some are also inclined to doubt the museum's honesty. Cognizant of that doubt, the museum repeatedly highlights not only the authenticity of its exhibits but the details that fall short of total authenticity. Employed to manage impressions, these admissions of small errors are expected to bolster the public's faith that the institution is diligently working toward its larger goal: to re-create the past in its totality, that is, with complete authenticity.

But Colonial Williamsburg recognizes that there are some elements of its public for whom authenticity – if authenticity is defined as fidelity to objective truth – is anathema. In interviewing them, we occasionally encountered such visitors. An elderly widow stands out, perhaps because she was among the first visitors we talked to. She had been coming to Colonial Williamsburg for over 30 years and always stayed in the Williamsburg Inn, a five-star hotel famous for its slightly rusticated elegance. Explaining to us that she was one of the foundation's regular donors (we never asked her how much she was accustomed to giving), she admitted that she was somewhat chagrined by the "recent," as she put it, preoccupation with refashioning the town as it "really was." Christmas, she told us, was her favorite time to visit, precisely because of the "festive decorations," although, she emphasized, they were not true to the 18th century. Would Williamsburg do away with these anachronisms? she worried aloud.

For the widow, the recent move toward greater truth was threatening to ruin what lay at the heart of Williamsburg's appeal. It was a place, she reminded us, where she, an old woman, could still stroll the streets at night. She explained Colonial Williamsburg's appeal by way of a vignette having to do with an early stay at the inn. She had been eating in the luxurious dining room and, desiring sugar for her coffee, was about to dip her spoon into a large pewter cup in front of her when a liveried black waiter quickly bent over, moved the cup, and spooned sugar from a smaller container into her coffee. The first container, she elaborated, was salt. Apparently, in colonial times, she added, they served salt in what today might look like a sugar bowl. But it wasn't the inn's attention to that little piece of authenticity that she wanted us to see through her eyes. Rather, it was the black waiter's silent skill. Ever attentive, waiting unobtrusively but alertly in the background, he'd anticipated her faux pas and resolved her problem without calling attention to her mistake. Skilled waiters like that, she emphasized, could not be reproduced, or faked, or trained. They embodied for her the essence of what Colonial Williamsburg used to stand for before "that new word, 'authenticity,'" had become such a concern.

Visitors such as the widow are not significant characters in the imaginary public Colonial Williamsburg employees created and re-created in daily conversations.[13] Nevertheless, it is entirely plausible that people such as the widow played a larger (if not explicitly recognized) role in the way Williamsburg's higher-ups imagined their *donating* public – a close to 50,000-strong subgroup that Colonial Williamsburg was increasingly relying on for the gifts and grants that would enable the museum to preserve itself.

To this public, the powers that be at Colonial Williamsburg employed what could be characterized as a constructivist historiography, but in the service of the status quo, as celebration, not critique. Consider President Longsworth's annual report for the years 1980 and 1981 – a report that introduces Colonial Williamsburg's donating public to the new social history and reassures them that old celebratory history will not be erased as a result.

Longsworth's report is in the form of a history of shifts in the major ideas – couched as consumer preferences – that guided the foundation. In short, it is a constructivist history. It begins with the aesthetic motives of the customers – "visitors came here . . . to see buildings and furnishings." Later, in "the days of the cold war . . . interpretation was fired by a sense of duty to inspire and encourage patriotism, to imbue visitors with a perception of the preciousness and fragility of personal freedom." In Longsworth's historical sketch, the new social history "reflected the dominant characteristics of the 1960s: suspicion and distrust of leaders and a concomitantly populist view of the world" (1982:6–7).

Longsworth notes that the new social history "inevitably caused a strong reaction from those whose commitment to the patriots as the source of inspiration was steadfast." And while he avers that it is "the tension of these differences of view that . . . creates a lively learning environment," the tenor of his report is to defend the patriots against the new social historians. He does so by embracing a constructivist historiography:

> It would be easy and perhaps popular to embrace social history with passionate abandon and forsake the patriots, retaining their memory as symbolic of an outworn and naive view of America's past. But I know of no one who advocates such a course. One needs to retain always a cautious view of any claim of exclusive access to the true history. I believe one must accept the puzzlement, confusion, ambiguity, and uncertainty that characterizes scholarship – the search for truth. [1982:8]

Longsworth recognizes that the "reasonable and dispassionate interpretation of evidence" is fogged by "some ideological base." But, given that history cannot escape ideology, Colonial Williamsburg should "maintain an ideological blend rather than develop a pure strain." Ultimately this ideological blend of the "dramatic, inspiring story that never loses its significance" and the new social history is good for Colonial Williamsburg as an institution. It is a strategy that guarantees survival, for it gives the public what it wants, or, at least, what Colonial Williamsburg has gotten them used to: "An organization such as this has by its longevity and its success created certain expectations. They may not be blunted summarily by a generation of scholars or administrators who have discovered the new historiography" (Longsworth 1982:8–9).

Because the foundation must cater to the desires of a market that it has, in a sense, created, Longsworth concludes that "we shall . . . continue to do what we do." As proof he cites the 60 percent increase in the collections budget and the construction of the De Witt Wallace Decorative Arts Gallery – meant to house a collection of colonial era "masterworks," which, according to the social historians' canons of authenticity, could no longer be displayed in the well-appointed homes of the reconstructed village because they were neither made nor used in Williamsburg itself (1982:9–10).

Longsworth (who left the presidency in 1992, remaining at Colonial Williamsburg as chairman of the board) has consistently used constructivist rhetoric to promote the preservation of a certain patriotism linked to a certain aesthetic. In a preface to Philip Kopper's sumptuous coffee-table history of the site, he argues that Colonial Williamsburg makes myths "because of America's need for myth." "It is easy," he writes, "to dismiss Williamsburg as a purveyor of patriotism," but, he argues, "the stimulus provided by patriotic feeling will be a vital tonic to the body politic." He goes on to assert that Colonial Williamsburg "is constantly changing, as it stands its iconographic ground" – that "the recreation of our usable past" is a necessary social process. In concluding, he notes how the old idea

> that Colonial Williamsburg would be "finished" rather than an ongoing enterprise of great vigor and complexity seems naive today. But, I suppose, it also seemed naive, or at least highly unlikely to many, that the dream of a new nation would ever be realized. So, out of our dreams we find reality and in myth our dreams are forged. [Longsworth 1986:6–7]

Here Longsworth invokes a "usable" past – a self-conscious, ongoing invention of history – in the twin service of national identity and corporate survival.

The Uses of Constructivism

In a challenging recent essay, Edward Bruner uses similar observations from his fieldwork at New Salem, Illinois – a site associated with Abraham Lincoln – to suggest that authenticity from the native point of view is evidence of a homegrown cultural constructivism. He shows that authenticity has several meanings for the staff and visitors at New Salem, one of which is "historical verisimilitude." As Bruner puts it, "*authentic* in this sense means credible and convincing, and this is the objective of most museum professionals, to produce a historic site believable to the public, to achieve mimetic credibility" (1994:399). "Some museum professionals go further," Bruner continues, and this entails a second native meaning of authenticity – to "speak as if the 1990s New Salem not only resembles the original but is a complete and immaculate simulation, one that is historically accurate and true to the 1830s" (1994:399). Bruner elaborates upon the distinction between the former and latter senses:

In the first meaning, based on verisimilitude, a *1990s* person would walk into the village and say, "This looks like the 1830s," as it would conform to what he or she expected the village to be. In the second meaning, based on genuineness, an 1830s person would say, "This looks like 1830s New Salem," as the village would appear true in substance, or real. I found that museum professionals use *authenticity* primarily in the first sense, but sometimes in the second. [1994:399]

The important point for Bruner is that insiders at the site are well aware that what they are producing is not a perfect copy, but something that is credible to an audience. The implication is that the natives (and here Bruner is referring especially to the professional staff at New Salem) do not confuse the reproduction with the real. Instead, they are aware that what they are creating is "verisimilitude" – something that will convince an audience or be congenial to an audience's sensibilities.

Bruner takes this a step further. Just as professionals are not preoccupied with recreating the real thing, so, too, are visitors to the site less concerned with this kind of absolute authenticity:

The tourists are seeking in New Salem a discourse that enables them to better reflect on their lives in the 1990s. New Salem and similar sites enact an ideology, recreate an origin myth, keep history alive, attach tourists to a mythical collective consciousness, and commodify the past. The particular pasts that tourists create/imagine at historic sites may never have existed. But historic sites like New Salem do provide visitors with the raw material ... to construct a sense of identity, meaning, attachment, and stability. [1994:411]

Bruner concludes his essay by noting that "New Salem can be read in two different ways" – from a pessimistic view or an optimistic one. The pessimists see such sites "as exploitative, as strengthening the ruling classes, as deceit, as false consciousness, as manipulation of the imagination of already alienated beings." Bruner counts himself among the optimists who focus on the ways the site offers "the utopian potential for transformation, offers hope for a better life, says people can take charge of their lives and change themselves and their culture."[14]

According to Bruner, visitors and employees alike "take charge" of the way they consume and produce culture. He emphasizes that visitors and guides "bring their own interests and concerns to the interaction" (1994:410). He describes these interactions as "playful," as "improvisation." The upshot, for Bruner, is that Americans "seeking ... a discourse that enables them to better reflect on their lives in the 1990s" (1994:411) can and do find such a discourse at New Salem.

Having made these ethnographic observations, Bruner wishes to link native notions of authenticity to anthropological theories of culture. Bruner is a constructivist. He asserts that the production of authenticity-as-verisimilitude is no more or less than a clear manifestation of what culture everywhere and always is – an invention (in many instances based on an attempt at replication). As such it is a benign fact. It is benign, too, because it allows natives to play with an invented past and revivify certain enduring ideals relevant to their present and future.

What Bruner observed at New Salem and what we observed at Colonial Williamsburg are essentially the same phenomena. Yet we interpret them in almost opposite ways. Let us examine the ways our interpretations differ, and what this implies for theories of cultural production at (what some natives at least like to claim are) "shrines" to an American identity.

Perhaps most significantly, we have different attitudes toward our respective sites. If Bruner celebrates the native preoccupation with authenticity-as-verisimilitude as a benign sign of a universal human tendency to construct culture (and, in the American case, to be aware that they are doing so), then we criticize authenticity-as-impression-management as a symptom of an ongoing preoccupation in American culture with a certain kind of past. For us, it is bad enough that this kind of authenticity allows an airbrushed past to become exactly the kind of mythological standard middle-class Americans aspire to. What disturbs us just as much is that authenticity-as-impression-management is one of an array of practices (both intentional and unintentional) that effectively enervate constructivist insights at a place whose built environment is living proof, as it were, of the power of constructivist theory as a model for what history, as narrated or embodied or objectified memory, really is.

We, like Bruner, are constructivists. Along with Bruner, we would even go so far as to say that constructivist theory has been the bread and butter of most cultural anthropologists for a long time. For us, the pervasiveness of constructivist theory raises some ethnographic questions when an anthropologist studies American culture, particularly at sites such as New Salem and Colonial Williamsburg. The first question is whether constructivism is also a native theory in the sense that it is part of the commonsense baggage of people who are not professional anthropologists.[15]

When we began our research at Colonial Williamsburg, we were interested in the ways constructivist theory operated on the ground. At first, it seemed to us that native discussions of authenticity-as-impression-management revealed commonsense understandings of constructivist theories of culture. But authenticity-as-impression-management turned out to have less to do with teaching about constructivist historiography than with protecting or shoring up a threatened reputation. To talk of verisimilitude as credibility armor, to sweat the details so you're not a joke in public in a reconstructed place that was "always changing because new facts are found," but that was nonetheless always being criticized by powerful outsiders for producing a bowdlerized past – this was, we decided, a tactic meant to protect the dream of authenticity as perfect copy.

As we have argued elsewhere (1994), Colonial Williamsburg is a shrine to a "naive objectivism." One of the ways that the priesthood of this shrine protects this cherished paradigm is by judicious legerdemain in the service of public relations. So, one way that we differ from Bruner is that we would argue that a Kuhnian paradigm shift has not occurred at Colonial Williamsburg. The site's authority – its reputation, if you will – depends on the public enactment of fidelity to an essentialist authenticity, not on constructivism.

This does not mean, however, that there are no spaces on Colonial Williamsburg's rhetorical terrain for native versions of constructivist notions as Bruner describes them. Ironically, just as the new social history began to make headway, advocates of the older, more celebratory history were able to use constructivist rhetoric against the new social history in order to repackage celebratory history and reassert its claims to ultimate authority. Longsworth's defense of the status quo reminds us of what philosophers have occasionally pointed out (cf. Hiley 1988), but what we, in the midst of the "culture wars," perhaps overlook. You can be a constructivist and a conservative. Longsworth does this in a speech we quoted above. If all is relative, then why not "continue to do what we do" – while, in effect, relabeling it?

This kind of constructivism has the added benefit of insulating the particular social actors (or institutions) from their own personal skepticism. Longsworth does not have to personally believe in the authenticity of the reconstructed Williamsburg. Instead, he simply has to be convinced that myths, if they contain morally uplifting messages, are salutary. In this way, a conservative constructivism protects an obviously empirically false image of the past, because it is a "necessary illusion" of the same kind Durkheim, personally an atheist, posited for religion. We might add that in America, conservative constructivism has usually been tinged with a willful optimism. If we all believe, or "think positive" as one euphemism has it, then it will come true. Or more cynically still, if we pretend to believe, or, in our role as leaders, if we ensure that "they," the herd, the mass, believe, then it will come true. It is this kind of constructivism that lends itself to conservatism in its political and cultural sense.

This, then, is a chief way that constructivist notions thrive at Colonial Williamsburg. Authorities such as President Longsworth use constructivist arguments to justify supporting good myths over bad facts, or authenticity as a model for, rather than a model of, a reality. They do so, as often as not, in the name of consumer preference. They do so in order to protect what they take to be universal ideals and values, and, nowadays, they do so against the implied background of a society under siege – a society threatened by postmodern plague. When they lay claim to being the enlightened arbiters of universal values – servants and guides to the public – they import what to us are self-serving visions about how the world should look.

This is the reason why we are more pessimistic than Bruner about the ways Americans construct identities for themselves at shrines such as Colonial Williamsburg and New Salem. It is not that we are essentialists – that we see such sites as unreal or inauthentic. Rather, we are ultimately less sanguine than Bruner that what goes on there is a universal form of cultural construction. Natives exhibit what to us is a kind of divided consciousness. On the one hand, they continue to be preoccupied with the past as the last refuge of the really real. On the other hand, some of them, at least, allow for the possibility that the really real is myth. Yet, according to them, it is "myth" that, if institutions such as Colonial Williamsburg and the American nation itself are to survive and prosper, people must believe.

NOTES

1   Walter Benjamin's seminal essay "The Work of Art in the Age of Mechanical Reproduction" is the starting point for much of this literature (1969:217–251). Among many others, see Handler 1986; Orvell 1989; Spooner 1986; and Trilling 1971.

2   This literature grows out of work in a number of areas. On museums, see Karp and Lavine 1991; Pearce 1990; and Vergo 1989. On consumerism, see McCracken 1988 and Miller 1987. On the ethnography of markets and trade goods in a transnational world, see Appadurai 1986; Schildkrout 1992; and Thomas 1991.

3   We borrow the aptly ambivalent framing quality of "after" from the philosopher Gary
     Shapiro (1995) and from Clifford Geertz (1995).
4   Assisted by Anna Lawson, we carried out fieldwork at Colonial Williamsburg between
     January 1990 and August 1991. Our research was supported by grants from the Spencer
     Foundation, the National Endowment for the Humanities, and the University of Virginia.
     Published results of this research include Gable and Handler 1993a, 1993b, and 1994,
     and Gable et al. 1992.
5   Carson 1981; Chappell 1989; and Colonial Williamsburg 1985.
6   *Daily Progress* 1993a, 1993b.
7   The critique of Colonial Williamsburg's sanitized history has been elaborated by Leone
     (1981), Van West and Hoffschwelle (1984), Wallace (1981), and Wells (1993), among
     others. For an analysis of dirt as a metaphor with respect to history museums, see Gable
     and Handler 1993b.
8   Quotations from Colonial Williamsburg staff are verbatim, taken from our field notes or,
     in most cases, from the transcriptions of tape-recorded interviews and tours.
9   Colonial Williamsburg Foundation Archives, file "Colonial Williamsburg Criticisms,
     1987," letter dated February 20, response of President Longsworth dated March 9.
10   On historical relativism and constructivism at Colonial Williamsburg and in American
     history museums in general, see Carson 1981, 1991; Chappell 1989; Gable et al. 1992;
     and Krugler 1991.
11   For a thoroughly researched study of the way Americans conceptualize authenticity and
     seek it out in tourism, see Cameron and Gatewood 1994.
12   The workshop in question was a preliminary presentation of material that was eventually
     published in Gable et al. 1992.
13   This public tended to be populated by history buffs (the magpies), by various versions of
     the rube from Toledo – the person who asks in all seriousness if the squirrels are
     mechanical – and by families with obnoxious children.
14   Bruner's optimism scans as a kind of faith in the consumer because, for Bruner, the very
     "popularity and frequency" of sites such as New Salem is a sign that they do something
     good for their publics (1994:411–412).
15   Given that we anthropologists have been spouting a constructivist line for so long, given
     that other disciplines also have made constructivist theories of culture central to what
     they teach about the human condition, given that people who work at or visit Colonial
     Williamsburg and New Salem are "educated," one would expect that such a theory has
     been incorporated into the commonsense views they bring to such sites. Moreover, given
     that we are natives, and that we don't manufacture our theories out of thin air but out of
     the cultural environment in which we live, we would hypothesize that constructivist
     theory has commonsense analogues.

REFERENCES

Appadurai, Arjun, ed.
    1986   The Social Life of Things: Commodities in Cultural Perspective. Cambridge: Cam-
           bridge University Press.
Benjamin, Walter
    1969   Illuminations: Essays and Reflections. New York: Schocken Books.
Bruner, Edward M.
    1994   Abraham Lincoln as Authentic Reproduction: A Critique of Postmodernism. Ameri-
           can Anthropologist 96:397–415.

Cameron, Catherine M., and John B. Gatewood
   1994   The Authentic Interior: Questing *Gemeinschaft* in Post-industrial Society. Human
      Organization 53(1):21–32.
Carson, Cary
   1981   Living Museums of Everyman's History. Harvard Magazine 83 (July–August):
      22–32.
   1991   Front and Center: Local History Comes of Age. *In* Local History, National Heri-
      tage: Reflections on the History of AASLH. Pp. 67–108. Nashville: American Association
      for State and Local History.
Chappell, Edward A.
   1989   Social Responsibility and the American History Museum. Winterthur Portfolio 24
      (Winter): 247–265.
Colonial Williamsburg
   1985   Teaching History at Colonial Williamsburg. Williamsburg: Colonial Williamsburg
      Foundation.
   1989   Annual Report. Williamsburg: Colonial Williamsburg Foundation.
Daily Progress (Charlottesville, VA)
   1993a   Disney Magic Will Draw Cash to Area, Officials Say. November 11: A1, A9.
   1993b   Williamsburg Hopes Disney Park Will Draw Interest to the Real Thing. November
      14: B1–B2.
Gable, Eric, and Richard Handler
   1993a   Colonialist Anthropology at Colonial Williamsburg. Museum Anthropology
      17(3):26–31.
   1993b   Deep Dirt: Messing Up the Past at Colonial Williamsburg. Social Analysis 34:3–16.
   1994   The Authority of Documents at Some American History Museums. Journal of
      American History 81(1):119–136.
Gable, Eric, Richard Handler, and Anna Lawson
   1992   On the Uses of Relativism: Fact, Conjecture, and Black and White Histories at
      Colonial Williamsburg. American Ethnologist 19:791–805.
Geertz, Clifford
   1995   After the Fact: Two Countries, Four Decades, One Anthropologist. Cambridge,
      MA: Harvard University Press.
Handler, Richard
   1986   Authenticity. Anthropology Today 2(1):2–4.
Hiley, David R.
   1988   Philosophy in Question: Essays on a Pyrrhonian Theme. Chicago: University of
      Chicago Press.
Huxtable, Ada Louise
   1992   Inventing American Reality. New York Review of Books 39(20):24–29.
Karp, Ivan, and Steven D. Lavine, eds.
   1991   Exhibiting Cultures: The Poetics and Politics of Museum Display. Washington, DC:
      Smithsonian Institution Press.
Kopper, Philip
   1986   Colonial Williamsburg. New York: Harry N. Abrams.
Kratz, Corinne A., and Ivan Karp
   1993   Wonder and Worth: Disney Museums in World Showcase. Museum Anthropology
      17(3):32–42.
Krugler, John D.
   1991   Behind the Public Presentations: Research and Scholarship at Living History
      Museums of Early America. William and Mary Quarterly 48 (July): 347–385.

Leone, Mark
    1981   Archaeology's Relationship to the Present and the Past. *In* Modern Material Culture. R. A. Gould and M. B. Schiffer, eds. Pp. 5–14. New York: Academic Press.
Longsworth, Charles R.
    1982   Communicating the Past to the Present. *In* Communicating the Past to the Present: Report on the Colonial Williamsburg Foundation with a Summary of the Years 1980 and 1981. Pp. 5–10. Williamsburg: Colonial Williamsburg Foundation.
    1986   Foreword to *Colonial Williamsburg*, by Philip Kopper. New York: Harry N. Abrams.
McCracken, Grant
    1988   Culture and Consumption: New Approaches to the Symbolic Character of Consumer Goods and Activities. Bloomington: Indiana University Press.
Miller, Daniel
    1987   Material Culture and Mass Consumption. Oxford: B. Blackwell.
Orvell, Miles
    1989   The Real Thing: Imitation and Authenticity in American Culture, 1880–1940. Chapel Hill: University of North Carolina Press.
Pearce, Susan, ed.
    1990   Objects of Knowledge. London: Athlone.
Schildkrout, Enid, ed.
    1992   Trade, Ethnicity, and Material Culture. Museum Anthropology 16(3), special issue.
Shapiro, Gary
    1995   Earthwards: Robert Smithson and Art after Babel. Berkeley: University of California Press.
Spooner, Brian
    1986   Weavers and Dealers: The Authenticity of an Oriental Carpet. *In* The Social Life of Things: Commodities in Cultural Perspective. Arjun Appadurai, ed. Pp. 195–235. Cambridge: Cambridge University Press.
Thomas, Nicholas
    1991   Entangled Objects: Exchange, Material Culture, and Colonialism in the Pacific. Cambridge, MA: Harvard University Press.
Trilling, Lionel
    1971   Sincerity and Authenticity. Cambridge, MA: Harvard University Press.
Van West, Carroll, and Mary Hoffschwelle
    1984   "Slumbering on Its Old Foundations": Interpretation at Colonial Williamsburg. South Atlantic Quarterly 83(2):157–175.
Vergo, Peter, ed.
    1989   The New Museology. London: Reaktion Books.
Wallace, Michael
    1981   Visiting the Past: History Museums in the United States. Radical History Review 25:63–96.
Wells, Camille
    1993   Interior Designs: Room Furnishings and Historical Interpretations at Colonial Williamsburg. Southern Quarterly 31:89–111.

20

The Edge and the Center: Gated Communities and the Discourse of Urban Fear

Setha M. Low

Contemporary anthropological studies of the city focus predominantly on the center, producing ethnographies of culturally significant places such as markets, housing projects, gardens, plazas, convention centers, waterfront developments, and homeless shelters that articulate macro- and micro-urban processes (Low 1999). These studies illuminate both the material and metaphorical power of spatial analysis for theorizing the city. One problem, however, is the perpetuation of an uneasy relationship between suburban and urban studies. The historical division between "rural" and "urban" exacerbates this tendency by sorting researchers into separate disciplinary and methodological camps.

The shift to a spatial analysis of the city requires reconsidering this separation in that contradictions and conflicts at the center are often drawn more vividly at the edge.[1] So we find that the suburban "malling of America" is a spatial counterpart of economic restructuring and the de-industrialization of central cities (Zukin 1991); and the cultural diversity and racial tensions of the center are reflected in the segregation and social homogeneity of the suburbs (Massey and Denton 1988). The gated residential development is particularly intriguing, mirroring changes in social values that accompany rapid globalization. Understanding this spatial form, its historical and cultural context, and why residents choose to live there provides an important perspective on the central city that is often overlooked.

For a majority of Americans the distance from suburb to city, or from work to home, is maintained through a complex social discourse. Anti-urban sentiment is often expressed as fear of violence and crime that is said to pervade the city. Within gated communities, though, the intensity of the discourse of urban fear suggests other underlying societal explanations. In this study, I explore the complex interconnections between this discourse, loss of a sense of place, and increasing class separation. I suggest that adding walls, gates, and guards produces a landscape that encodes class relations and residential (race/class/ethnic/gender) segregation more permanently in the built environment (Low 1997). Understanding how this landscape is legitimated by a discourse of fear of crime and violence helps to uncover how this design form is materially and rhetorically created.

I use thematic content analysis to document the existence of urban fear in its many forms and its influence on residents' residential narratives. Critical discourse analysis provides a complementary methodology for decoding talk about urban fear as an acceptable, socially constructed discourse about class exclusion and racial/ethnic/ cultural bias. The use of urban fear discourse reinforces residents' claims for their need to live behind gates and walls because of dangers or "others" that lurk outside.

Unlocking the Gated Community

Estimates of the number of people who live in gated communities within the United States vary from 4 million to 8 million (Architectural Record 1997). One-third of all new homes built in the United States in recent years are in gated residential developments (Blakely and Snyder 1997), and in areas such as Tampa, Florida, where crime is a high-profile problem, gated communities account for four out of five home sales of $300,000 or more (Fischler 1998).

Systems of walls and class division are deeply ingrained in historic Europe as a means of wealthy people protecting themselves from the local population (Blakely and Snyder 1997; Turner 1999). In the United States, the early settlements of Roanoke and Jamestown and Spanish fort towns were walled and defended to protect colonists from attack. But with the virtual elimination of the indigenous population, the need for defensive walls ceased to exist (King 1990).

At the turn of the twentieth century, secured and gated communities in the United States were built to protect family estates and wealthy citizens, exemplified by New York's Tuxedo Park or the private streets of St. Louis. By the late 1960s and 1970s, planned retirement communities were the first places where middle-class Americans could wall themselves off. Gates then spread to resorts and country club developments, and finally to middle-class suburban developments. In the 1980s, real estate speculation accelerated the building of gated communities around golf courses designed for exclusivity, prestige, and leisure. This emerging social phenomenon of white, middle-class people retreating to new, walled private communities was reported in magazine articles (Guterson 1992), radio talk shows on National Public Radio, television talk shows such as Phil Donahue (Donahue 1993), and feature articles in the *New York Times* (Fischler 1998).

The first centers of construction activity were the Sunbelt states focusing on retirees moving to California and Florida during the 1970s, followed by Texas and Arizona in the 1980s. Since the late 1980s, gates have become ubiquitous, and by the 1990s they have become common even in the Northeast (Blakely and Snyder 1997).

The literature on gated communities identifies a number of reasons for their increase in number and size. I argue elsewhere that gating is a response to late-twentieth-century changes in urban North America (Low 1997). Economic restructuring during the 1970s and 1980s produced a number of social and political changes as a consequence of uneven development resulting from rapid relocation of capital (Harvey 1990; Smith 1984). The shift to the political right during the Reagan years, and the mixture of conservatism and populism in U.S. politics, intensified an ideological focus on free market and capitalist values tilting power, wealth, and income toward the richest portions of the population (Phillips 1991). While the income share of the upper 20% of Americans rose from 41.6% to 44% from 1980 to 1988, the average after-tax income of the lowest ten percent dropped 10.5% from 1977 to 1987 (Phillips 1991), producing a two-class system of "haves" and "have-nots" based on these structural readjustments to late capitalism (Mollen-kopf and Castells 1991).

Mike Davis (1990, 1992) argues that the creation of gated communities, and the addition of guardhouses, walls, and entrance gates to established neighborhoods, is an integral part of the building of the "fortress city." He identifies the so-called militarization of Los Angeles as a strategy for controlling and patrolling the urban poor that is made up of predominantly ethnic – Latino and Black – minorities.[2] Susan Fainstein adds that large development projects in cities like New York and London produce this built environment by forming:

> contours which structure social relations, causing commonalities of gender, sexual orientation, race, ethnicity, and class to assume spatial identities. Social groups, in turn, imprint themselves physically on the urban structure through the formation of communities, competition for territory, and segregation – in other words, through clustering, the erection of boundaries, and establishing distance. [1994:1]

The political and economic democratic practices mediating some forms of class separation in the United States, however, are not found in Brazil (Caldeira 1996; Carvalho 1997), other parts of Latin America (Low 1996), or South Africa (Western 1981) where gated condominiums and fortified enclaves are omnipresent. Teresa Caldeira examines São Paulo's economic transformation from 1940 through the 1980s that resulted in increased violence, insecurity, and fear, such that São Paulo became a "city of walls" (1999:87). Through field visits, I have observed the use of walls, gates, locks, and guards by the upper and middle classes in Nairobi, Accra, Dakar, Mexico City, and Caracas to protect residents from assault and property crime and/or the consequences of political upheaval (Low n.d.). Although the cross-cultural examples of gating appear similar, their histories and attributed causation vary tremendously: from racism in South Africa, to property vandalism in Accra, kidnapping and robbery in Mexico City, and carjacking and homicide in Nairobi.[3]

The processes that produce urban and suburban separation in the United States also have a long history based on racism and racial segregation. Blacks in U.S. cities continue to experience a high level of residential segregation based on discrimin-atory real estate practices and mortgage structures designed to insulate Whites from Blacks (Bullard and Lee 1994; Massey and Denton 1988). Nancy Denton (1994) argues that since the 1980s there has been a pattern of hyper-segregation in the suburbs, reinforced by patterns of residential mobility by race in that Blacks are less likely to move to the suburbs in the first place, and then more likely to return to the city (South and Crowder 1997).

Sally Merry found that middle-class and upper-middle-class urban and suburban neighborhoods exhibit an increasing pattern of building fences, cutting off relation-ships with neighbors, and moving out in response to problems and conflicts. At the same time: "Government has expanded its regulatory role.... Zoning laws, local police departments, ordinances about dogs, quiet laws, laws against domestic and interpersonal violence, all provide new forms of regulation of family and neighbor-hood life" (1993:87). Merry argues that the regulation of space through architec-tural design and security devices such as gated communities is generally understood as a complement to disciplinary penalty, and that this new spatial governmentality is fundamentally different in its logic and techniques. Thus, residential segregation created by prejudice and socioeconomic disparities is reinforced by planning prac-tices and policing, implemented by zoning laws and regulations, and subsidized by businesses and banks.

The suburb as an exclusionary enclave where upper-class followed by middle-class residents search for sameness, status, and security in an ideal "new town" or "green oasis" reinforces these patterns (Langdon 1994; McKenzie 1994). Land speculation beginning with the street car suburbs of Philadelphia accelerated the growth of new middle-class enclaves (Jackson 1985). The expanding suburbs of the 1950s, 1960s, and 1970s generated "white flight" from densely populated, heterogeneous cities (Sibley 1995; Skogan 1995).

The development of common interest developments (CIDs) provides the legal framework for the consolidation of this form of residential segregation (Judd 1995). CID describes "a community in which the residents own or control common areas or shared amenities," and that "carries with it reciprocal rights and obligations enforced by a private governing body" (Louv 1985:85 as cited in Judd 1995:155). Specialized covenants, contracts, and deed restrictions (CC&Rs) create new forms of collective private land tenure and new forms of private government called "homeowner associations" (McKenzie 1994).

The "pod" and "enclave" suburban designs further refine the ability of land-use planners and designers to develop suburban environments where people of different income groups – even in the same development – would have little to no contact with one another (Langdon 1994). Resident behavior, house type, and "taste culture," however, are more subtle means of control (Bourdieu 1984). Nancy and James Duncan (1997) demonstrate how landscape aesthetics function as suburban politics of exclusion, and Evan McKenzie (1994) documents the growing number of legal proceedings in California courts as residents attempt to deregulate their rigidly controlled environments.

The psychological lure of defended space becomes more enticing with increased media coverage and national hysteria about urban crime (Flusty 1997; Judd 1995). News stories chronicle daily murders, rapes, drive-by shootings, drug busts, and kidnapping. An ever-growing proportion of people fear that they will be victimized, such that the fear of crime has increased since the mid-1960s even though there has been a decline in all violent crime since the 1980s (Colvard 1997; Judd 1995; Stone 1996). Violent crime (homicide, robbery, sexual assault, and aggravated assault) fell 12% nationally between 1994 and 1995, while property crime (burglary, theft, and auto theft) declined 9% (Brennan and Zelinka 1997).

Barry Glassner (1999) points out that we are inundated with media reports about the prevalence of crime and violence creating a "culture of fear." But when the actual crime statistics are consulted, the reality is never as grim or devastating as the newspaper and television portrayal. For example, parents are overwhelmed by the amount of media attention given to child abduction and cyberporn. A *Time* article estimating that more than 800,000 children are reported missing every year generated a national panic (Glassner 1999:61). According to Glassner, three out of four parents in a national survey said they fear their child will be kidnapped by a stranger. Criminal justice experts, however, estimate that only 200 to 300 children a year are abducted by non-family members and kept for long periods of time or murdered, while 4,600 (of 64 million children) are abducted and then returned. He makes the point that reporters overstate the actual threat to add drama, convince an editor, or justify more extensive media coverage. His answer to why Americans harbor so many fears is that "immense power and money await those who tap into our moral insecurities and supply us with symbolic substitutes" (Glassner 1999:xxviii).

There has been considerable research that links fear of crime to the physical environment. Although none of it focuses specifically on gated communities, it suggests how communities and individuals deal with fear within the context of a local neighborhood. Urban ethnographies suggest that familiarity, avoidance, and surveillance play important roles in allaying these fears. Sally Merry (1982) documents the interactions and perceptions of Black, White, and Chinese residents in a high-rise, low-income project in a large Northeastern city and concludes that lack of familiarity plays an important role in the perception of danger. Eli Anderson (1990) documents avoidance as a coping strategy in his study of "streetwise" behavior of Philadelphians in which residents cross the street when faced with oncoming young Black males. Philippe Bourgois (1995) dramatizes the fear and sense of vulnerability experienced by residents of El Barrio and depicts their strategies of avoidance and surveillance used to deal with street crime. These studies describe how fear is spatially managed in urban contexts, and how avoidance and streetwise behavior are used by low- to middle-income people to mitigate their fears.

Environmental design studies also connect crime with the built environment beginning with Jane Jacobs's (1961) recommendations for creating safer streets and neighborhoods. But it was Oscar Newman (1972) who brought the relationship of crime and the physical environment to the attention of the public. He argues that the reason high-rise buildings are considered dangerous is that the people who live in them cannot defend – see, own, or identify – their territory. Newman proposes that gating city streets can promote greater safety and higher house values as long as the percentage of minority residents is kept within strict limits (Newman 1980). Timothy Crowe (1991), a criminologist who coined the phrase "crime prevention through environmental design (CPTED)," has instituted a widespread CPTED program that involves all local agencies – police, fire, public works, traffic, and administration – as well as planners in the formulation and review of neighborhood plans and designs implementing Newman's defensive space concepts.

These diverse studies depict a social world with increasing reliance on urban fortification, policing, and segregation. A number of legal solutions have emerged, such as common interest developments and homeowners' associations, planning solutions such as pod and enclave development, design solutions such as crime prevention through environmental design, and behavioral solutions such as avoidance and surveillance of the street. Gated communities respond to middle-class and upper-middle-class individuals' desire for community and intimacy and facilitate avoidance, separation, and surveillance. They bring individual preferences, social forces, and the physical environment together in an architectural reality and cultural metaphor.

Upon completing a national survey of gated community residents, Edward Blakely and Mary Gail Snyder come to a similar conclusion:

> In this era of dramatic demographic, economic and social change, there is a growing fear about the future of America. Many feel vulnerable, unsure of their place and the stability of their neighborhoods. . . . This is reflected in an increasing fear of crime that is unrelated to actual crime trends or locations, and in the growing numbers of methods used to control the physical environment for physical and economic security. The phenomenon of walled cities and gated communities is a dramatic manifestation of a new fortress mentality growing in America. [1997:1–2]

Methodology

Research Setting

The study is based on two gated communities, each located at the edge of a culturally diverse city with publicized incidents of urban crime. San Antonio and New York City are known for their multiculturalism, cultural inclusiveness, as well as interethnic conflicts resulting from rapid changes in neighborhood composition. Both cities have increasing socioeconomic disparities, a history of residential segregation, and a documented movement of middle-class residents moving to an ever-widening outer ring of suburbs. They also provide excellent comparative cases because of differences between them in (1) population size and density, (2) history of gated community development, (3) scale and design of the gated communities, (4) legal and governmental structure, (5) crime rates for the region, and (6) cultural context and norms of behavior. Because of the complexity and size of New York City, I use Queens, the outer borough adjacent to the study site, to describe the cultural context, population size, and crime statistics relevant to this analysis. Many of the residents cited in this article moved from Queens to their gated community.

San Antonio is a medium-size city with an estimated population of 1,464,356 inhabitants in 1995. The city began in the eighteenth century as a cohesion of different Spanish missions and has retained much of its Mexican-Spanish heritage. Since 1990, Texas has accounted for 14% of all new jobs created in the United States, including rapid growth in high-tech manufacturing causing labor shortages of highly trained workers. Population growth in the Metropolitan Statistical Area (MSA)[4] grew 21.5% from 1980 to 1990 and an additional 10.1% from 1990 to 1994 (America's Top-Rated Cities 1997). This increase in skilled jobs and numbers of residents stimulated construction of new middle class suburbs and a downtown renovation project known as Riverwalk. It was in San Antonio that I first gained entrance to a number of homes located within a locked, gated, and walled community on the outskirts of the city and found young, white, middle-class teenagers discussing their fear of "Mexicans" who lived nearby.

San Antonio's high rates of crime – 7,993.9 crimes per 100,000 in the city compared to 3,906.3 per 100,000 in the suburbs in 1995 – occur in poorer, urban neighborhoods and not in the suburban areas (U.S. Department of Justice 1995). In 1995, murder occurred almost four times more frequently in the city than in the suburbs – 14.2 per 100,000 compared to 3.7 per 100,000; robberies occurred more than five times more frequently – 234.5 per 100,000 compared to 42.4 per 100,000. Nevertheless, suburban residents feel afraid. They read about kidnapping and drive-by shootings, or they hear stories from their friends of burglaries in the suburbs. One resident called it a "crime movement" at one point in the interview – an interesting commentary that captures the "waves of crime" reported in San Antonio's only newspaper, the *San Antonio Express-News*.

New York City, in comparison to San Antonio, is a global city of more than 7 million inhabitants. Located on the eastern seaboard, New York City has been a major entryway for immigrants from Europe, via Ellis Island, and more recently from Africa, parts of Asia, and the Middle East. Queens, the easternmost borough, is known for its cultural diversity and ethnic neighborhoods where over 138 languages are spoken (Sanjek 1998). Queens became incorporated into New York City in 1897, linked by both the Long Island Railroad and electric trolleys to Brooklyn, and to Manhattan-bound ferries from Long Island City (Gregory 1998). With a population of 1,966,685 in 1997, it provides a better comparison to San Antonio because of its scale and proximity to Long Island suburbs.

Even though Seagate in Brooklyn is an example of a gated community built more than one hundred years ago, and doorman buildings of Manhattan have guarded entrances, there are only a few gated residential developments in New York City. In Queens, there are only three gated condominium complexes comprising townhouses and apartments. The loss of manufacturing jobs – 10 million square feet of industrial space has been converted to retail, residential, or office space – as well as lower salaries and lack of available land for development may account for this slow growth. Although Queens is the most economically diverse of the New York City boroughs with manufacturing, transportation, trade, and service each accounting for at least ten percent of private sector jobs in 1998, it has not experienced the same accelerated growth in the service sector as the rest of New York City (McCall 2000). Further, in the early 1990s, higher-paying jobs were being replaced with lower-paying ones as growth occurred in areas offering lower average salaries (McCall 2000).

Nassau County, Long Island, on the other hand, experienced a resurgence of residential development, some of it gated, following the decline of the real estate market in the early 1990s. With a population of 1,298,842 in 1997, Nassau County abuts the eastern boundary of Queens and provides a suburban comparison for the analysis of crime statistics.

Crime rates have fallen much faster around New York City than in the nation. From 1990 to 1995, violent crime had dropped 44.4% in New York City compared to a 6.5% drop for the nation as a whole. But the rate of violent crime is still double the national average, with 1,324 violent crimes per 100,000 for New York City and 685 violent crimes per 100,000 for the United States reported in 1996 (*New York Times* 1997). Property crime has experienced a similar drop with a decline of 47% in New York City compared to 9.7% for the nation from 1990 to 1995 (*New York Times* 1997). Urban crime rates, though, are still higher than those in the suburbs. For example, in 1997 the total number of crimes of all types was 95,751 for Queens with a population of 1,966,685 compared to 29,770 for Nassau County with a population of 1,298,842 – about double[5] in the city compared to the suburb. For violent crimes, such as murder, the difference is even greater with 207 murders in

Queens and 26 murders in Nassau County reported in 1997 (National Archive of Criminal Justice Data 1997).

New suburban housing developments with surrounding walls and restrictive gates located approximately thirty minutes drive from their respective downtown city halls were selected at the edge of each city. Single-family house prices ranged from $650,000 to $880,000 in New York and $350,000 to $650,000 in San Antonio in 1995.[6] Each gated community has its own regional style and distinctive design features, but all are enclosed by a five- to six-foot masonry wall broken only by the entry gates and monitored in person by a guard (New York) or by video camera from a central guardhouse (San Antonio).

The New York development is situated on an old estate with the original manor house retained as a community center. The individual houses are large (approximately 3,500 to 4,500 square feet), mostly two-story structures, built in a variety of traditional styles: Hampton Cottage, Nantucket Village, Mid-Atlantic Colonial, and Western Ranch. Houses are organized along a winding thoroughfare with dead-end streets branching off, leading to groups of houses clustered quite close together on small lots of less than a third of an acre. The remaining property is landscaped to create a park-like atmosphere. Since the community was developed as a community interest development, all of the common grounds are maintained by the homeowners association. The final community will contain 141 houses, tennis courts, a swimming pool, and a clubhouse. Not all the lots have been purchased, and houses are still being built.

The San Antonio gated community is part of a much larger northern suburban development centered on a private golf and tennis club with swimming pools, restaurant, and clubhouse. The subdivision includes 120 lots, a few fronting one section of the golf course, surrounded by a six-foot masonry wall. The main entrance is controlled by a grid-design gate that swings open electronically by a hand transmitter or by a guard who is contacted by an intercom and video camera connection. The broad entrance road divides into two sections leading to a series of short streets ending in cul-de-sacs. The houses are mostly large (3,500–5,500 square feet), two-story brick Colonials or stucco Scottsdale designs, with a few one-story brick ranch-style houses. More than two-thirds of the houses have been built and occupied, while the remaining lots are currently under construction.

Research design and specific methods

Field methods included open-ended interviews with residents, participant-observation within and around the communities, interviews with key informants such as the developers and real estate agents, and the collection of marketing, sales, and advertising documents. An unstructured interview guide was developed to elicit residents' decision-making processes concerning their move to the gated community. The research team[7] collected field notes and interviews in the New York area, while I worked alone in San Antonio. The interviews lasted between one and two hours, depending on whether the interviewer was taken on a tour of the house. We did not ask to be taken on a tour, but many times interviewees offered, and we used the tour to learn more about the person's tastes, interests, and preferences.

It was difficult to obtain entry into these communities and to contact residents. A sales manager in the gated community outside of New York City helped by contacting two residents she thought would be willing to speak with us. We then used introductions either from the sales manager or from other interviewees to complete the first ten interviews. In San Antonio, a local resident provided entree by contacting two residents; those residents referred four others, and I met three interviewees strolling on the golf path on the weekends.

Opportunities for participant-observation were limited, but it was possible to talk with people while they were exercising or walking their dogs, attending homeowner and club meetings, and participating in neighborhood celebrations. Further, spending time in the local commercial areas – shopping, going to restaurants, and visiting real estate agents – provided other contexts for learning about everyday life.

Open-ended, unstructured interviews were conducted in the home with the wife, husband, or husband and wife together over a three-year period from 1995 to 1998. The majority of the interviewees were European Americans and native born, however, three interviews were in households where one spouse was born in Latin America, one interviewee's spouse was born in the South Pacific, and one interviewee's spouse was born in the Middle East. Interviewees were aged 27 through 75; all husbands were either professionals such as doctors or lawyers, businessmen, or retired from these same pursuits. In most cases the wives remained at home, while the husband commuted to his place of work. A few women worked part-time.

Analysis

Ethnographic analysis

The ethnographic analysis of participant-observation field notes focused on identifying empirical evidence of changes in the local environment. Further, it produced data on casual conversations and everyday observations that naturally occurred and provided a test of ecological validity for data collected through the interviews. Field notes were coded by the themes that emerged during the research process.

Content analysis

A thematic content analysis of the interviews and documents collected from the media, marketing, and sales materials provided both a qualitative and quantitative understanding of the range of discourse available. The interviews were coded based on themes identified in the interviews and in the ethnographic fieldwork. The list of themes provided a qualitative presentation of the data. Depending on the number and specificity of the themes, they were consolidated to allow for a quantitative presentation (ranking, numbering, calculation of percentages) of the expression of those themes.

Critical discourse analysis

A critical discourse analysis of the 20 interviews identified covert concerns with social order, social control, xenophobia, ethnocentrism, class consciousness and status anxiety, social mobility, and racism, as well as fear of crime and violence, and overt expressions of a desire for a new home, beautiful setting, and sense of community. Following Fairclough (1995), I assume that language is a form of social practice that is historically situated and dialectical to the social context, that is, language is both socially shaped and socially shaping. Since language is widely perceived as transparent, it is difficult to see how language produces, reproduces, and transforms social structures and social relations. Yet, it is through texts that social control and social domination are exercised – through the everyday social action of language. Thus, it is necessary to establish a "critical language awareness" (Fairclough 1995:209) to uncover the social and political goals of everyday discourse. Critical discourse analysis, through (1) the analysis of context, (2) the analysis of processes of text production and interpretation, and (3) the analysis of the text, reinterprets traditional models of interview analysis. For instance, in Fairclough's theory, urban fear of crime and violence could be a discursive practice used to "naturalize" social and physical exclusionary practices, as well as a statement of emotion and/or explanation for an action or decision. Charles Briggs's (1986) emphasis on reflexivity and the relationship of politics to methodology also informs my analysis.

Nineteen of the twenty interviews were transcribed in full.[8] Next, I read through the interview transcripts and systematically noted all instances in which the covert concerns (see above) were discussed or alluded to. This process produced the body of the data set. In the final stage, I identified different strategies used to talk about living in a gated community. The details of the linguistic constructions with their immediate functions produced an outline of the ideological structure of the conversation. The goal was not to quantify the occurrence of particular themes or rhetorical strategies, but, more importantly, to illustrate their situated effects (Dixon and Reicher 1997:368)

The Search for Safety and Security

A majority of interviewees perceive an increase of the crime in their urban neighborhoods before moving to a gated community. Eighteen of the twenty interviews include discussions of residents' search for a sense of safety and security in their choice of a gated community, and their relief upon settling in that they did feel safer and more secure with the addition of gates, walls, and guards. Many interviewees mention changes in social composition of the surrounding areas as a primary motivation for moving, and the loss of local amenities, particularly in the New York area. Interviewees also talk about the investment value of the house, the status implications of their move, and their need for more space and privacy, but these concerns are not examined in this analysis.

One noteworthy finding is that, once a person lives in a gated community, they say that they would always choose a gated community again, even if safety was not the basis of their initial decision. Three of the twenty interviewees had lived previously in gated developments: one family lived in Latin America where they enjoyed the security of a gated and guarded compound; one family retired first in Florida where most retirement communities are gated; and one newly married woman had lived in a gated condominium complex. These couples did not even consider a non-gated community when looking for a new home.

New York

Nine of the ten interviewees in New York mention urban crime as a major reason for selecting a gated community. The tenth interviewee, although she says that crime and safety had no bearing on why they moved, mentions that in her old neighborhood her car had been stolen from outside her door.

Nine of the ten interviewees are from the local area and moved from New York City or a nearby Long Island urban center. Many are quite vocal about the changes that they experienced in their original neighborhoods. For instance, Sharon is willing to "give up community convenience for safety." She says that increased local political corruption and neighborhood deterioration left her feeling uncomfortable in the house where she had lived for more than twenty-five years. Even though she knew everyone in her old neighborhood and enjoyed walking to the corner store,

> when Bloomingdale's moved out and Kmart moved in, it just brought in a different group of people ... and it wasn't the safe place that it was .... I think it's safer having a gated community.... They are not going to steal my car in the garage .... [In the old neighborhood] every time we heard an alarm we were looking out the window. My daughter and son-in-law lived next door and their car was stolen twice.

Barbara and her husband Alvin express it differently:

Alvin :	[Our old neighborhood was] a very, very educated community. You know so every one goes on to college, and it stressed the role of family, and you know, it's just a wonderful community. But it is changing, it's undergoing internal transformations.
Barbara :	It's ethnic changes.
Alvin :	Yeah, ethnic changes, that's a very good way of putting it.
Interviewer :	And is this something that started to happen more recently?
Barbara :	In the last, probably, seven to eight years.

Cynthia also is concerned about staying in her old neighborhood. At first she did not want to live in a house at all since she would feel afraid being alone. She had grown up in Queens and would never live in a house there, because they had been robbed. Her childhood home had been in a nice neighborhood where thieves knew they could find valuable things to steal:

Cynthia :	And then I have a lot of friends who live in a neighborhood in Queens, and there's been more than 48 robberies there in the last year and a half. And I said to myself, those are homes with security and dogs and this and that ...
Interviewer :	And are they gated?
Cynthia :	No, they're not gated. They had alarms, and they were getting robbed because they were cutting the alarms, the phone wires outside. So I'm saying to myself, all this is in my mind, and I'm saying ... I can get robbed. That's why I moved ...

Sally also feels that the neighborhood where she lived was changing: she was having problems finding a place to park, and people were going through her trash at night. Her bicycle was stolen off her terrace, and her friend's car was stolen. Her husband began to travel a lot, and she could not accompany her husband on his trips because she was worried about being robbed. They loved their old neighborhood, but it no longer offered safety and comfort. So they decided to move to a gated community that would provide the security that she felt they now needed. Once having made the decision and completed the move, she said that she loved her newly found freedom from house responsibilities and parking problems. As she put it:

> I got to feel like I was a prisoner in the house.... You didn't park on the street too long because you are afraid your car is going to be missing something when you get out, or the whole car is missing.... So there's a lot of things we have the freedom here to do that we didn't do before....

Helen comments that it was "very nice at night to come in...and to have a gate and there's only one entrance to the property, so I think that makes for possibly less robberies...." For her, safety is:

> not a main concern, but a concern. Otherwise, if I bought something...on two acres of land, I would have been very uncomfortable there...no children around...just being alone now in the dark...and my husband would get home later. I just didn't want to be surrounded by two acres of land.

She has friends (in the old neighborhood) who were burglarized and had become more distressed. She feels the guards at the entrance are not careful, but it is still difficult for thieves to escape. Her mother and her children also live in gated communities.

San Antonio

Nine of the interviewees in San Antonio mention crime and a fear of "others" as a reason for moving. Stay-at-home mothers like Felicia and Donna worry about threats to their children. Felicia states her feelings about her fear of crime and other people very clearly:

Setha :   ...has it changed how you feel about being in the gated community?
Felicia :   Yes. It allows a lot more freedom for my daughter to go outside and play. We're in San Antonio, and I believe the whole country knows how many child kidnappings we've had.... And I believe that my husband would not ever allow her outside to play without direct adult supervision unless we were gated. It allows us freedom to walk at night, if we choose to. It has, you know, it does have a flip side.
Setha :   What flip side?
Felicia :   Several things. First of all, it's a false sense of safety if you think about it, because our security people are not "Johnny-on-the-spot," so to speak, and anybody who wants to jump the gate could jump the gate.... There's a perception of safety that may not be real, that could potentially leave one more vulnerable if there was ever an attack.

* * *

Setha :	Who lives in your community?
Felicia :	People who are retired and don't want to maintain large yards.... People who want to raise families in a more protected environment [long pause].
Setha :	What do you mean by that?
Felicia :	There are a lot of families who have, in the last couple of years, after we built, as the crime rate, or the reporting of that crime rate, has become such a prominent part of the news of the community, there's been a lot of "fear flight." I've mentioned that people who were building or going to build based on wanting to get out of the very exclusive subdivisions without a gate, solely for the gate.
Setha :	Really. There has been?
Felicia :	Oh, yeah. I was telling you about a family that was shopping [for a house in Felicia's gated community] because they had been randomly robbed many times.

* * *

Felicia :	When I leave the area entirely and go downtown [little laugh], I feel quite threatened, just being out in normal urban areas, unrestricted urban areas.... Please let me explain. The north central part of this city, by and large, is middle-class to upper middle-class. Period. There are very few pockets of poverty. Very few. And therefore if you go to any store, you will look around and most of the clientele will be middle-class as you are yourself. So you are somewhat insulated. But if you go downtown, which is much more mixed, where everybody goes, I feel much more threatened.
Setha :	Okay.
Felicia :	My daughter feels very threatened when she sees poor people.
Setha :	How do you explain that?
Felicia :	She hasn't had enough exposure. We were driving next to a truck with some day laborers and equipment in the back, and we were stopped beside them at the light. She wanted to move because she was afraid those people were going to come and get her. They looked scary to her. I explained that they were workmen, they're the "backbone of our country," they're coming from work, you know, but...

Donna's concerns with safety also focus on her child and his reactions to the city. She, like Felicia, is aware that a false sense of security develops living inside the gates putting her and her children in greater danger:

Donna :	You know, he's always so scared.... It has made a world of difference in him since we've been out here.
Setha :	Really?
Donna :	A world of difference. And it is that sense of security that they don't think people are roaming the neighborhoods and the streets and that there's people out there that can hurt him.
Setha :	Ah... that's incredible.
Donna :	... That's what's been most important to my husband, to get the children out here where they can feel safe, and we feel safe if they could go out in the streets and not worry that someone is going to grab them.... We feel so secure and maybe that's wrong too.

Setha :   In what sense?

Donna :   You know, we've got workers out here, and we still think "oh, they're safe
            out here".... In the other neighborhood I never let him get out of my sight
            for a minute. Of course they were a little bit younger too, but I just, would
            never, you know, think of letting them go to the next street over. It would
            have scared me to death, because you didn't know. There was so much traffic
            coming in and out, you never knew who was cruising the street and how fast
            they can grab a child. And I don't feel that way in our area at all...ever.

Other San Antonio interviewees are less dramatic in expressing their concerns
with safety and concentrate more on taxation and the quality of the security system
and guards. Harry and his wife feel that the biggest difference with gating is "not just
anyone can come by." They are more upset about the way that the government treats
private gated communities in terms of taxation. Karen was not even looking for a
place in a secured area:

Karen :   It was just by accident that it was [gated].... But after living here, if we
            moved it would be different.

Setha :   And why is that?

Karen :   Because after seeing...this is a very nice neighborhood and after seeing that
            there are so many beautiful neighborhoods here and in other parts of the
            country that are not in a secure area, that's where burglary and murders take
            place, not here, because it's an open door [there]...come on [in]. Why should
            they try to do anything here when they can go somewhere else first? It's a
            strong deterrent, needless to say.

Other residents are not so sure that the gates are an adequate deterrent. Edith talks
about her problems with the security guards who supposedly patrol at night and
monitor the gates with security cameras. She feels the guards do not do their job.
Another interviewee points out that with any gate monitored by a security camera
and a guard in a remote station, two cars can enter at the same time creating an
unsafe situation.

There seems to be no end to residents' concern with safety and security. In both
New York and San Antonio, most residents have burglar alarms they keep armed
even when home during the day.

Critical discourse analysis findings

In order to get at underlying social values, I selected sections of the interviews that
refer to "others" (see Felicia and Barbara and Alvin excerpts presented above). I am
trying to get at what Michael Billig calls "the dialogic unconscious," a concept by
which the processes of repression can be studied discursively (1997:139). I assume
that some of the evidence I am looking for is "repressed," that it is hidden not
only from the interviewer, because it is socially unacceptable to talk about class
and race, but from the interviewee as well because these concerns are also
psychologically unacceptable. According to Billig (1997), conversational interaction

can have repressive functions as well as expressive ones, so what is said can be used to get at what is not said.

Using John Dixon and Steve Reicher's article "Intergroup Contact and Desegregation in the New South Africa" as a model, I focus on the rhetorical dimension of intergroup contact to elicit narratives about maintaining, justifying, or challenging racist (or elitist) practices (1997:368–369). For instance, Dixon and Reicher identify a number of "disclaiming statements" about their interviewees' racist attitudes they were able to elicit by asking their respondents about their new Black neighbors in a legalized squatter settlement. In the interviews, similar questions were asked, about "Mexican laborers" in San Antonio or "recent immigrants" in New York, to produce disclaiming statements and lead to a better understanding of the social categories used by gated community residents.

For instance, after a long discussion identifying middle-class spaces in the city, Felicia tells a story about her daughter feeling threatened by day laborers. She ends the story with a disclaiming statement, explaining to her daughter in the story (and indirectly to me) that they are "workmen," the "backbone of our country." Her disclaiming statement highlights her acute understanding of social categories and how she uses those categories to legitimate her discursive goals.

Another example of disclaiming occurs when the husband and wife in New York begin talking about the deterioration of their urban neighborhood. Barbara offers "it's ethnic changes" to Alvin who is trying to articulate what happened that made them leave. He then repeats her term, "ethnic changes," to characterize the more elusive transformations that he was trying to get at.

In a recent presentation, Collette Daiute (2000) suggests that there are five ways to interrogate a narrative: (1) as reporting an event, (2) as evaluating the event, (3) as constructing the meaning of the event, (4) as a critique of the event, and (5) as socially positioning the speaker. I have found her method helpful in identifying otherwise unarticulated discursive goals of the interviewees. For instance, Cynthia reports that there were more than 48 robberies in her neighborhood in Queens last year. She then evaluates those robberies by pointing out that they were of homes with security and dogs, but not with gates. She then uses the logic of these two statements to construct the meaning of her move to a gated community. Finally, she critiques her own understanding: "so I'm saying to myself, all this in my mind, and I'm saying.... I can get robbed," and positions herself with people inside the gated community (the smart ones) rather than with those living outside (those who are vulnerable to robberies).

Discussion

In New York, residents are fleeing deteriorating urban neighborhoods with increased ethnic diversity and petty crimes, concluding that the neighborhood is "just not what it used to be."[9] New Yorkers cite changes in the local stores, problems with parking and securing a car, and frequent robberies of bicycles and cars. In San Antonio there is a similar pattern, but here the emphasis is on a fear of kidnapping and illegal Mexican workers. Residents cite newspaper stories of children being kidnapped, drive-by shootings, neighbors being burglarized, and talk about the large number of "break-ins."

The intensity of the language and underlying social discourse seems more intense in San Antonio. As a younger, sprawling, Southern city it has much greater horizontal spatial segregation than the older boroughs and Long Island suburbs of New York City. As Felicia explains, residents of the northern outskirts of San Antonio are physically insulated from the poorer sections of the city. In New York City this kind of spatial and social insulation is much harder to achieve. Nonetheless, in both cities, residents move to gated communities based on what Felicia calls "fear flight," the desire to protect oneself, family, and property from dangers perceived as overwhelming them. Yet gating offers a kind of incomplete boundedness[10] in that workers from feared groups enter to work for residents, and residents themselves need to leave to shop.[11]

Whether it is kidnapping or bike snatching, Mexican laborers or "ethnic changes," the message is the same: residents are using the walls, entry gates, and guards in an effort to keep the perceived dangers outside of their homes, neighborhoods, and social world. The physical distance between them and the "others" is so close that contact incites fear and concern, and in response they are constructing exclusive, private, residential developments where they can keep other people out with guards and gates. The walls are making visible the systems of exclusion that are already there, now constructed in concrete.

Conclusions

From these interviews there appears to be a wealth of data about fear of crime, increased social diversity, and neighborhood change. Residents talk about their fear of the poor, the workers, the "Mexicans," and the "newcomers," as well as their retreat behind walls where they think they will be safe. But there is fear even behind the walls. As the two mothers from San Antonio point out, there are workers who enter the community every day, and they must go out in order to buy groceries, shop, or see a movie. The gates provide some protection, but they would still like more. I wonder what "more" would be? Even though the gates and guards exclude the feared "others" from living with them, "they" can slip by the gate, follow your car in, crawl over the wall, or worse, the guard can fall asleep or be a criminal himself. Informal conversations about the screening of guards and how they are hired, as well as discussions about increasing the height and length of the protective walls as new threats appear, are frequent in the locker room of the health club, on the tennis court, and during strolls in the community in the evening. What would be the next step in this progression?

In this paper, I have not considered why developers are building gated communities, yet even without an analysis of marketing strategies, the allure of the gated community is clear. Even residents who did not select the community for its gates now would only live behind protective walls. Further, during the day residents are primarily women who do not work. Is the gated community creating new patterns of gendering in these spaces? What about the men who go outside the community by day to work? Are they the ones who primarily find a refuge from diversity when coming home? And gates and walls also have an impact on children and their relationship to other people and environments. Will the children who grow up in these new communities depend on walls for their sense of security and safety? What does it mean that 17 teenage heroin overdoses occurred in the suburban gated communities of Plano, Texas, in 1998 (Durington 1999)? Will the walls and gates become standard for any middle-class home? And with what consequence for the future?

This paper suggests that the discourse of urban fear encodes other social concerns including class, race, and ethnic exclusivity as well as gender separation.[12] It provides a verbal component that complements, even reinforces, the visual landscape of fear created by the walls, gates, and guards. By matching the discourse of the inhabitants with the ideological thrust of the material setting, we enrich our understanding of the social construction and social production of places where the well-to-do live (Low 2000; Tuan 1979).[13]

Urban fear, and its relationship to new forms of social ordering, need to be better understood in the context of the entire metropolis. The spatial ordering of the edge responds to the social dialectic of the center, played out in an ever-changing suburban landscape.

NOTES

Acknowledgments. Funding from the Wenner-Gren Foundation for Anthropological Research and from the Research Foundation of the City University of New York made this research project possible. I would like to thank Joel Lefkowitz, Laurel Wilson, Stephane Tonnelat, Kristin Koptiuch, Kevin Birth, Carole Browner, Sally Merry, Ivelisse Rivera-Bonilla, and Gary McDonogh for their contributions to this project. I also would like to thank my co-researchers Elena Danaila, Suzanne Scheld, and Mariana Diaz-Wionczek. Elena Danaila and Mariana Diaz-Wionczek worked on the analysis of these interviews, adding their understanding to my formulation of the problem. Melissa Waitzman, Cindi Katz, and the members of the Social Theory seminar contributed insightful comments on the theoretical ideas presented here. I, however, am solely responsible for the conclusions. An earlier version of this paper was presented as the Class of 1905 lecture at Bryn Mawr College and at the American Anthropological Association annual meeting in Chicago.

1   Kristin Koptiuch contributed this idea during a discussion of this paper at the American Anthropological Association annual meeting in Chicago. I greatly appreciate her sharing her insight.

2   I would like to thank Ivelisse Rivera-Bonilla for linking Mike Davis's concept of militarization to the racial/ethnic segregation of Los Angeles.

3   These observations are based on visits to each of these cities and brief interviews with either experts or residents. They provide some cross-cultural perspective, but the empirical data must still be collected. I am currently analyzing ten interviews collected in a gated community in Mexico City.

4   Includes unincorporated suburbs.

5   When the crime rates are adjusted for population, they are 43/1000 for Queens vs. 22/1000 for Nassau County.

6   The disparity in prices reflects the considerable differences in the housing markets rather than any substantive differences in socioeconomic status and quality of life of the residents or the nature of the homes.

7   The research team was made up of Elena Danaila, a graduate student in Environmental Psychology, and Suzanne Scheld, a graduate student in Anthropology, and the PI.
8   One interview could not be fully transcribed because of problems with the tape recording. The transcribed portion was used whenever possible, otherwise we relied on the field notes of the interview. All interviews were recorded and field notes were taken as a precaution.
9   Ivelisse Rivera-Bonilla (1999) makes the distinction between "neighborhood" and "community" because one doesn't necessarily imply the other. She comments that in the gated residents' narratives about their former neighborhoods they talk about the corner store, yet when they talk about their present surroundings they seem to refer more to their immediate families rather than their neighbors and community. This could be because the gated communities are relatively new, and to answer this question they must be examined over time.
10 I would like to thank one of the reviewers of this article for suggesting that the boundedness is incomplete.
11 Kevin Birth suggests that looking at the ethnic backgrounds of the home health care workers, groundskeepers, and nannies in the gated communities might tell something more about how often residents encounter non-Whites in their everyday lives.
12 Kevin Birth also suggests that age may play a role in structuring these communities, especially the age of those who are feared.
13 I would like to thank one of the reviewers of this article for pointing out the strength of the verbal and visual components reinforcing one another in this setting.

REFERENCES

Altman, Irwin, and Setha Low
  1992   Place Attachment. New York: Plenum Publishing.
America's Top-Rated Cities
  1997   A Statistical Handbook. Volume: Southern Region. 5th edition. Boca Raton, FL: Universal References Publications.
Anderson, Eli
  1990   Streetwise: Race, Class and Change in an Urban Community. Chicago: Chicago University Press.
Architectural Record
  1997   To Gate or Not to Gate. Record News. Architectural Press Roundup, April 24:45.
Billig, Michael
  1997   The Dialogic Unconscious. British Journal of Social Psychology 36:139–159.
Blakely, Edward J., and Mary Gail Snyder
  1997   Fortress America. Washington, DC: Brookings Institute.
Brennan, D., and A. Zelinka
  1997   Safe and Sound. Planning, August:4–10.
Briggs, Charles L.
  1986   Learning How to Ask. Cambridge: Cambridge University Press.
Bourdieu, Pierre
  1984   Distinction. London: Routledge and Kegan Paul.
Bourgois, Philippe
  1995   In Search of Respect. New York: Cambridge University Press.

Bullard, R., and C. Lee
  1994   Racism and American Apartheid. *In* Residential Apartheid. R. D. Bullard, J. E. Grigsby III, and C. Lee, eds. Pp. 1–16. Los Angeles: Center of Afro-American Studies.
Caldeira, Teresa
  1996   Fortified Enclaves: The New Urban Segregation. Public Culture 8:303–328.
  1999   Fortified Enclaves: The New Urban Segregation. *In* Theorizing the City. S. Low, ed. Pp. 83–107. New Brunswick, NJ: Rutgers University Press.
Carvalho, M., R. V. George, and K. H. Anthony
  1997   Residential Satisfaction in Condominios Exclusivos in Brazil. Environment and Behavior 29(6):734–768.
Colvard, Karen
  1997   Crime Is Down? Don't Confuse Us with the Facts. The HFG Review 2(1):19–26.
Crowe, Timothy
  1991   Crime Prevention through Environmental Design. Stoneham, MA: Butterworth-Heinemann.
Daiute, Collette
  2000   Narrative Transformation of Institutions. Paper presented at the Second Biennial Conference on Qualitative Methods in Psychology. CUNY Graduate Center. March 2.
Davis, Mike
  1990   City of Quartz: Excavating the Future in Los Angeles. London: Verso.
  1992   Fortress Los Angeles: The Militarization of Urban Space. *In* Variations on a Theme Park. M. Sorkin, ed. Pp. 154–180. New York: Noonday Press.
Denton, Nancy
  1994   Are African-Americans Still Hypersegregated? *In* Residential Apartheid. R. D. Bullard, J. E. Grigsby III, and C. Lee, eds. Pp. 49–81. Los Angeles: Center for Afro-American Studies.
Devine, J.
  1996   Maximum Security. Chicago: University of Chicago Press.
Dixon, J. A., and S. Reicher
  1997   Intergroup Contact and Desegregation in the New South Africa. British Journal of Social Psychology 36:361–381.
Donahue, Phil
  1993   Town Builds Fence to Keep People Out. Transcript of television show aired December 2.
Duncan, Nancy, and James Duncan
  1997   Deep Suburban Irony. *In* Visions of Suburbia. R. Silverstone, ed. Pp. 161–179. London: Routledge.
Durington, Matthew
  1999   Unpredictable Spaces: The Discourses of Drugs in Suburban Dallas. Paper presented at the Annual Meeting of the American Anthropological Association.
Etzoni, A.
  1995   Rights and the Common Good. New York: St. Martin's Press.
Fainstein, Susan
  1994   City Builders. Oxford: Blackwell.
Fairclough, N.
  1995   Critical Discourse Analysis. London: Longman.
Fischler, M. S.
  1998   Security the Draw at Gated Communities. New York Times, August 16: section 14LI, p. 6.

Flusty, S.
  1997   Building Paranoia. *In* Architecture of Fear. N. Ellin, ed. Pp. 47–60. New York: Princeton Architectural Press.
Glassner, Barry
  1999   The Culture of Fear. New York: Basic Books.
Gregory, Steve
  1998   Black Corona. Princeton, NJ: Princeton University Press.
Guterson, D.
  1992   No Place Like Home. Harper's Magazine, November:35–64.
Harvey, David
  1990   The Condition of Postmodernity. New York: Blackwell.
Higley, S. R.
  1995   Privilege, Power, and Place. London: Rowman and Littlefield.
Jackson, Kenneth T.
  1985   Crabgrass Frontier. Oxford: Oxford University Press.
Jacobs, Jane
  1961   The Death and Life of Great American Cities. New York: Vintage Books.
Judd, D.
  1995   The Rise of New Walled Cities. *In* Spatial Practices. H. Ligget and D. C. Perry, eds. Pp. 144–165. Thousand Oaks: Sage Publications.
King, Anthony
  1990   Urbanism, Colonialism, and the World Economy. New York: Routledge.
Lang, R. E., and K. A. Danielson
  1997   Gated Communities in America. Housing Policy Debate 8(4):867–899.
Langdon, Philip
  1994   A Better Place to Live. Amherst: University of Massachusetts Press.
Lofland, Lynn
  1998   The Public Realm. New York: Aldine de Gruyter.
Low, Setha M.
  1996   A Response to Castells: An Anthropology of the City. Critique of Anthropology 16:57–62.
  1997   Urban Fear: Building Fortress America. City and Society. Annual Review:52–72.
  2000   On the Plaza: The Politics of Public Space and Culture. Austin: University of Texas Press.
  2003   Behind the Gates: The New American Dream. New York and London: Routledge.
Low, Setha M., ed.
  1999   Theorizing the City: The New Urban Anthropology Reader. New Brunswick, NJ: Rutgers University Press.
Marcuse, Peter
  1997   The Enclave, the Citadel, and the Ghetto. Urban Affairs Review 33(2):228–264.
Massey, D. S., and Nancy Denton
  1988   Suburbanization and Segregation. American Journal of Sociology 94(3):592–626.
McCall, C.
  2000   Queens: An Economic Review. New York: Office of the State Deputy Comptroller.
McKenzie, Evan
  1994   Privatopia. New Haven, CT: Yale University Press.
Merry, Sally
  1982   Urban Danger. Philadelphia: Temple University Press.
  1993   Mending Walls and Building Fences: Constructing the Private Neighborhood. Journal of Legal Pluralism 33:71–90.

2001   Spatial Governmentality and the New Urban Social Order. Controlling Gender
    Violence through Law. American Anthropologist 103(1):16–29.
Mollenkopf, John, and Manuel Castells
1991   The Dual City. New York: Russell Sage.
National Archive of Criminal Justice Data
1997   Ann Arbor: University of Michigan.
Newman, Oscar
1972   Defensible Space. New York: Macmillan.
1980   Community of Interest. Garden City, NY: Anchor Press.
New York Times
1997   Portrait of Crime. February 17:B4.
Phillips, Kevin
1991   The Politics of Rich and Poor. New York: HarperCollins Publishers.
Rivera-Bonilla, Ivelisse
1999   Building "Community" Through Gating: The Case of Gated Communities in San
    Juan. Paper presented at the Annual Meeting of the American Anthropological Associ-
    ation.
Sanjek, Roger
1998   The Future of Us All. Ithaca, NY: Cornell University Press.
Sibley, D.
1995   Geographies of Exclusion. London: Routledge.
Skogan, W. G.
1995   Crime and the Racial Fears of White Americans. Annals of the American Academy
    of Political and Social Science 539(1):59–72.
Smith, Neil
1984   Uneven Development. Oxford: Basil Blackwell.
South, S., and K. D. Crowder
1997   Residential Mobility Between Cities and Suburbs: Race, Suburbanization and Back-
    to-the-City Moves. Demography 34(4):525–538.
Stone, C.
1996   Crime and the City. In Breaking Away: The Future of Cities. C. Stone, ed. Pp. 98–103.
    New York: The Twentieth Century Fund Press.
Tuan, Y.
1979   Landscapes of Fear. New York: Pantheon Books.
Turner, E. S.
1999   Gilder Drainpipes. London Review of Books, June 10:31–32.
United States Department of Justice
1995   Uniform Crime Reports. Washington, DC.
Western, J.
1981   Outcast Cape Town. Minneapolis: University of Minnesota Press.
Zukin, Sharon
1991   Landscapes of Power. Berkeley: University of California Press.

Index

Note: page numbers in italics refer to illustrations or figures